A-Z BUCKINGH

CONTENTS

Key to Map Pages	2-5
Map Pages	6-131
Road M... (Referen...	...37
Index to...	...174
Index to Hospitals & Hospices	175-176

REFERENCE

Motorway M40

Primary Route A41

Proposed

A Road A40

B Road B4009

Dual Carriageway

One-way Street

Traffic flow on A Roads is indicated by a heavy line on the driver's left.

Road Identification Numbers (Milton Keynes)

Horizontal Roads H1

Vertical Roads V1

Junction Names SILBURY

Restricted Access

Pedestrianized Road

Track / Footpath

Residential Walkway

Railway — Level Crossing — Tunnel

Stations: National Rail Network; Heritage Station

Local Authority Boundary

Posttown Boundary

Postcode Boundary (within Posttown)

Built-up Area HIGH ST.

Map Continuation 54 — Road Map Pages 133

Airport

Car Park (Selected)

Church or Chapel

Cycleway (Selected)

Fire Station

Hospital

House Numbers (Selected Roads) 13 8

Information Centre

National Grid Reference 480

Park & Ride — Milton Keynes P+R

Police Station

Post Office

Toilet: without facilities for the Disabled

with facilities for the Disabled

Disabled facilities only

Viewpoint

Educational Establishment

Hospital or Hospice

Industrial Building

Leisure or Recreational Facility

Place of Interest

Public Building

Shopping Centre or Market

Other Selected Buildings

Scale

Map Pages 6-131 1:16,896

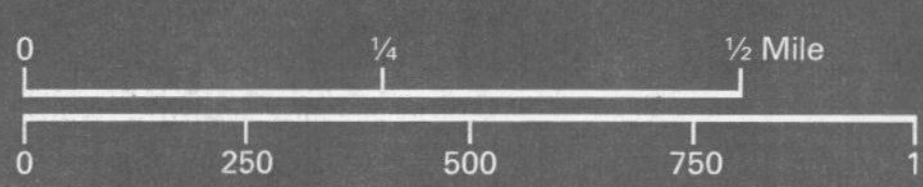

3¾ inches (9.52 cm) to 1 mile

5.9cm to 1km

Fairfield Road, Borough Green, Sevenoaks, Kent TN15 8PP

Telephone: 01732 781000 (Enquiries & Trade Sales)

01732 783422 (Retail Sales)

www.a-zmaps.co.uk

EDITION 1 2006

KEY TO MAP PAGES

North Section

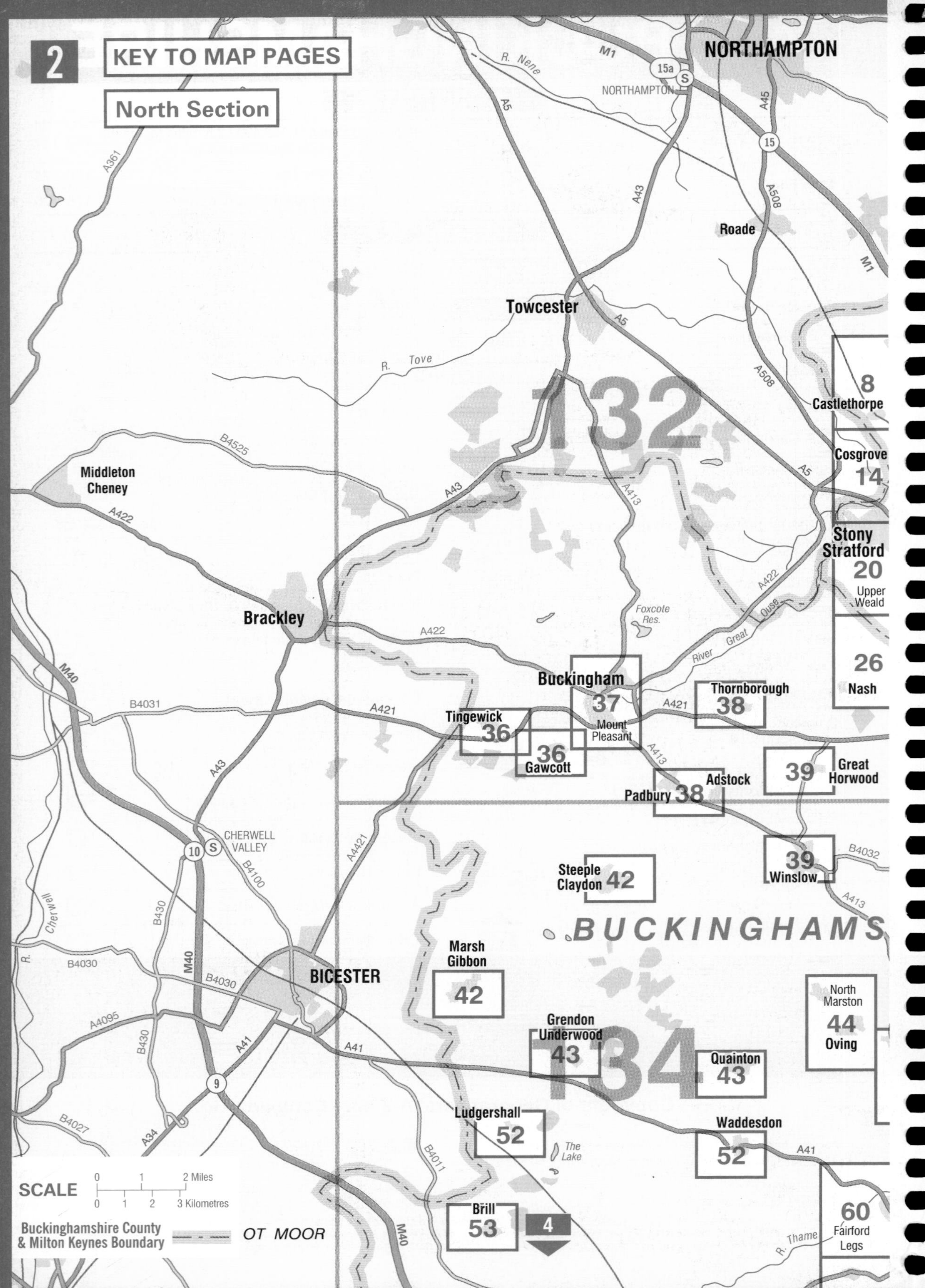

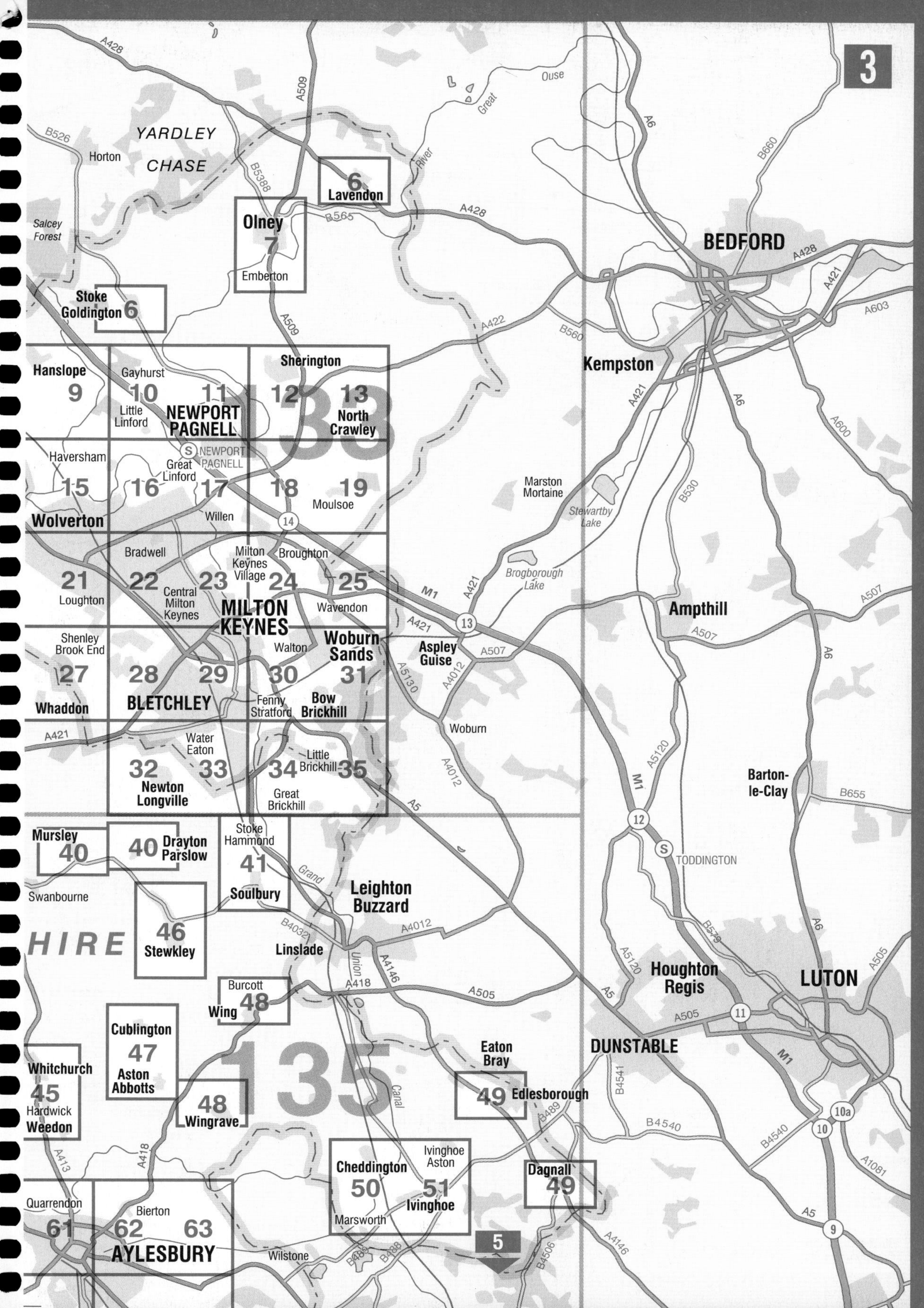

YARDLEY
CHASE
Horton
Salcey Forest
Lavendon 6
Olney 7
Emberton
Stoke Goldington 6
BEDFORD
Kempston
Hanslope 9
Gayhurst 10
Little Linford
NEWPORT PAGNELL 11
Sherington 12
13 North Crawley
133
Haversham
15 Wolverton
Great Linford 16
17 Willen
18
19 Moulsoe
Marston Mortaine
Stewartby Lake
Brogborough Lake
Bradwell 22
21 Loughton
Central Milton Keynes 23
Milton Keynes Village 24
Broughton
25 Wavendon
MILTON KEYNES
Ampthill
Aspley Guise
Woburn Sands
Shenley Brook End
27 Whaddon
28 BLETCHLEY
29
Walton 30
31
Fenny Stratford
Bow Brickhill
Woburn
Water Eaton 33
32 Newton Longville
34 Great Brickhill
Little Brickhill 35
Barton-le-Clay
Mursley 40
40 Drayton Parslow
Stoke Hammond 41 Soulbury
Swanbourne
TODDINGTON
Leighton Buzzard
HIRE
46 Stewkley
Linslade
Houghton Regis
LUTON
Burcott 48 Wing
Cublington 47 Aston Abbotts
DUNSTABLE
Eaton Bray
135
Whitchurch 45 Hardwick Weedon
48 Wingrave
49 Edlesborough
Cheddington 50 Marsworth
Ivinghoe Aston 51 Ivinghoe
Dagnall 49
Quarrendon 61
Bierton 62 63
AYLESBURY
Wilstone
5
Great Ouse
River
Grand Union Canal

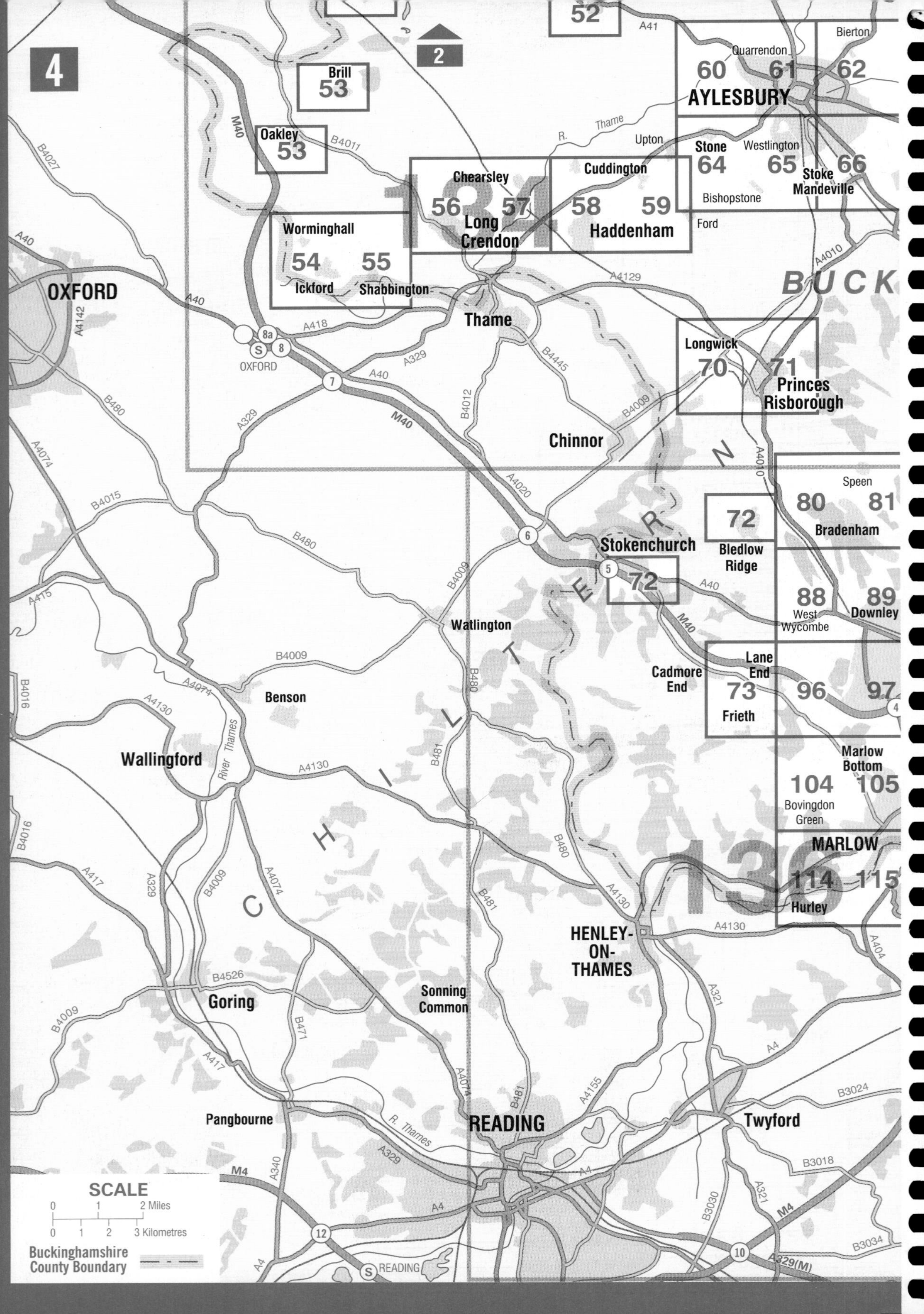

2
52
Brill
53
Oakley
53
Worminghall
54
55
Ickford
Shabbington
Chearsley
56
57
Long
Crendon
134
Cuddington
58
59
Haddenham
Quarrendon
60
61
62
Bierton
AYLESBURY
Stone
64
Westlington
65
Stoke
Mandeville
66
Bishopstone
Upton
Ford
R. Thame
OXFORD
Thame
Chinnor
Longwick
70
71
Princes
Risborough
BUCK
CHILTERN
72
Bledlow
Ridge
Stokenchurch
72
Speen
80
81
Bradenham
88
89
West
Wycombe
Downley
Watlington
Benson
Wallingford
River Thames
Cadmore
End
Lane
End
73
Frieth
96
97
Marlow
Bottom
104
105
Bovingdon
Green
MARLOW
114
115
Hurley
136
HENLEY-
ON-
THAMES
Goring
Sonning
Common
Pangbourne
READING
Twyford
R. Thames
M40
A40
A418
A329
A4129
B4011
B4027
B4445
B4012
B4009
A4010
A4142
B480
A4074
B4015
A415
A4020
B4016
A4130
A417
B4009
B481
B480
B4526
B471
A4155
A321
A4
A404
B3024
B3018
B3030
B3034
A340
M4
A329(M)
A41
8a
8
7
6
5
4
12
10
S
OXFORD
READING
SCALE
0 1 2 Miles
0 1 2 3 Kilometres
Buckinghamshire
County Boundary

South Section

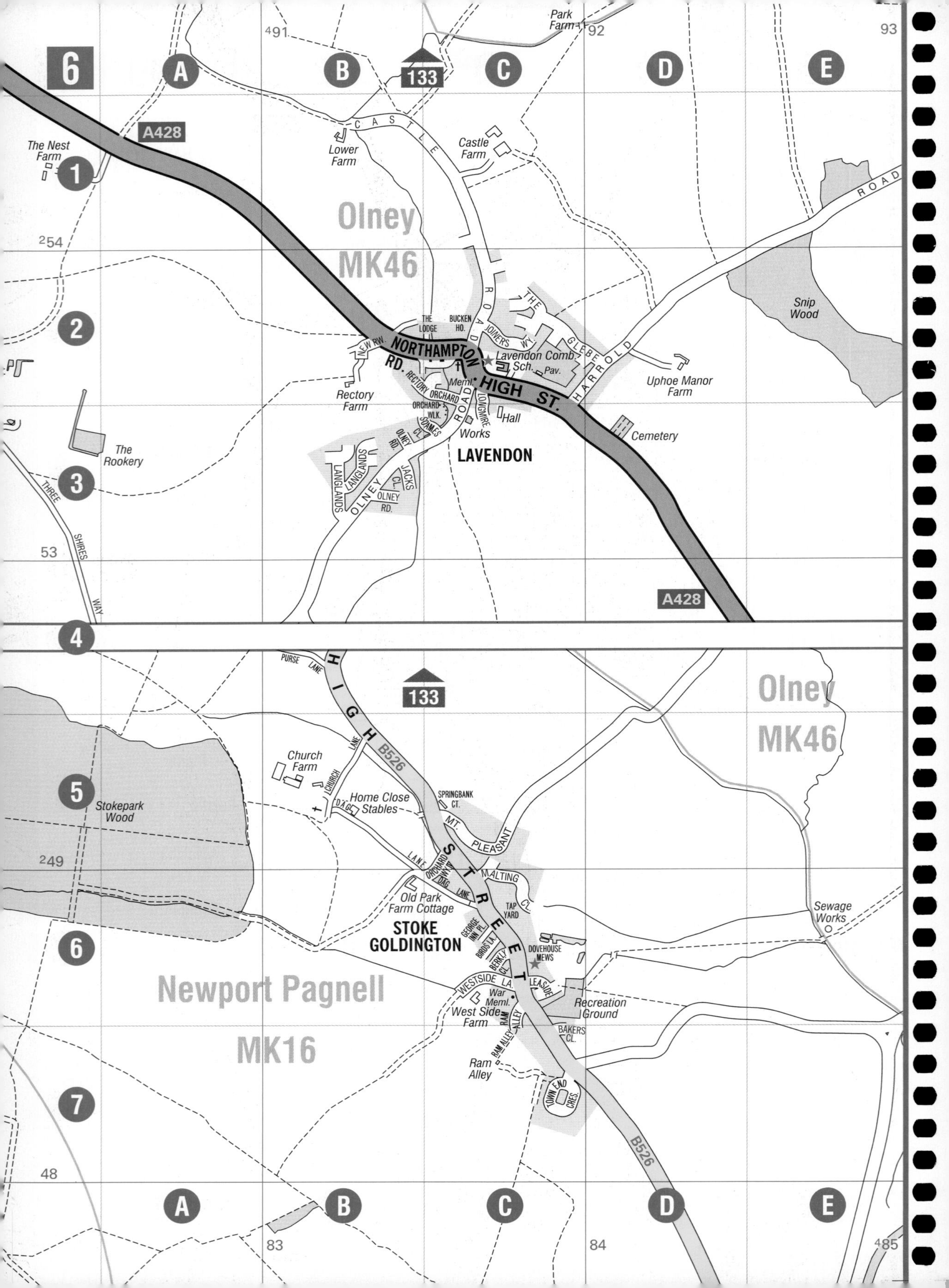

A
B
C
D
E
1
2
3
4
5
6
7
133
A428
The Nest Farm
Lower Farm
Castle Farm
CASTLE ROAD
Park Farm
Olney
MK46
THE GLEBE
JOINERS WY.
THE LODGE
BUCKEN HO.
NEW RW.
NORTHAMPTON RD.
HIGH ST.
Lavendon Comb. Sch.
Pav.
HARROLD ROAD
Snip Wood
Uphoe Manor Farm
Rectory Farm
RECTORY ORCHARD
ORCHARD WLK.
Meml.
LONGMIRE
Hall
Works
Cemetery
SOAMES CL.
OLNEY RD.
LANGLANDS
JACKS CL.
LAVENDON
The Rookery
THREE SHIRES WAY
PURSE LANE
HIGH STREET
B526
Church Farm
CHURCH LANE
Home Close Stables
SPRINGBANK CT.
MT. PLEASANT
DAG LANE
ORCHARD WAY
MALTING CL.
TAP YARD
Old Park Farm Cottage
STOKE GOLDINGTON
GEORGE INN PL.
BIRDS LA.
BERKLY CL.
DOVEHOUSE MEWS
LEASIDE
WESTSIDE LA.
War Meml.
West Side Farm
RAM ALLEY
Ram Alley
BAKERS CL.
Recreation Ground
TOWN END CRES.
Stokepark Wood
Newport Pagnell
MK16
Sewage Works
491
92
93
254
53
249
48
83
84
485

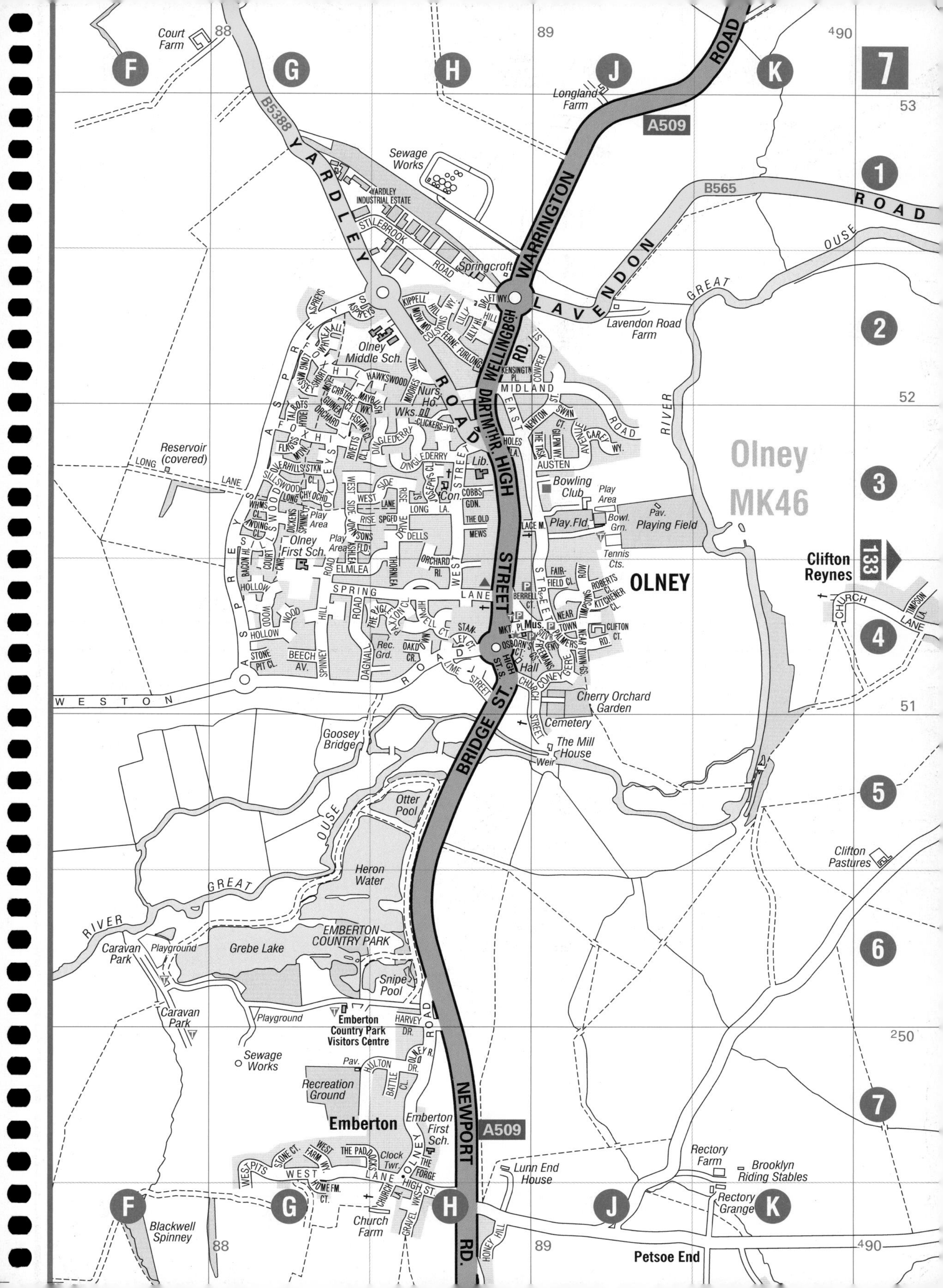

7
F
G
H
J
K
88
89
490
53
52
51
250
1
2
3
4
5
6
7
Court Farm
Longland Farm
A509
B5388
YARDLEY
Sewage Works
YARDLEY INDUSTRIAL ESTATE
STILEBROOK ROAD
Springcroft
WARRINGTON ROAD
B565
ROAD
OUSE
GREAT
LAVENDON
Lavendon Road Farm
ASPREYS
Olney Middle Sch.
WELLINGBGH RD.
KENSINGTN PL.
COWPER
MIDLAND
EAST ST.
NEWTON
SWAN CT.
AVENUE
CAREY WY.
ROAD
RIVER
Olney
MK46
HAWKSWOOD
Nurs. Ho.
Wks.
CLICKERS YD.
DINGLEDERRY
DARTMTHR. HIGH STREET
HOLES LA.
THE TASK
AUSTEN
Reservoir (covered)
LONG LANE
Lib.
Con
COBBS GDN.
Bowling Club
Play Area
Play. Fld.
Bowl. Grn.
Pav.
Playing Field
Tennis Cts.
Clifton Reynes
133
WEST SIDE
LONG LA.
THE OLD MEWS
Play Area
Olney First Sch.
DELLS
ORCHARD RI.
ELMLEA
SPRING LANE
FAIR-FIELD CL.
ROBERTS CL.
KITCHENER CL.
OLNEY
CHURCH LANE
TIMPSON LA.
HOLLOW
Mus.
NEAR TOWN
CLIFTON RD.
Rec. Grd.
OAKDOWN CR.
OSBORN'S CT.
Hall
BEECH AV.
STONE PIT CL.
SPINNEY
DAGNALL
LIME STREET
CHURCH STREET
CONEYGERE
WESTON ROAD
BRIDGE ST.
Cherry Orchard Garden
Cemetery
The Mill House
Weir
Goosey Bridge
Otter Pool
OUSE
Heron Water
Clifton Pastures
GREAT
RIVER
Caravan Park
Playground
Grebe Lake
EMBERTON COUNTRY PARK
Snipe Pool
Caravan Park
Playground
Emberton Country Park Visitors Centre
HARVEY DR.
Sewage Works
Pav.
HILTON DR.
OLNEY R.
Recreation Ground
BATTLE CL.
Emberton
Emberton First Sch.
NEWPORT RD.
A509
WEST FARM WY.
THE PADDOCKS
Clock Twr.
THE FORGE
WEST PITS
STONE CT.
WEST LANE
HOME FM. CT.
HIGH ST.
CHURCH LA.
WKS.
Church Farm
GRAVEL
Lunn End House
Rectory Farm
Brooklyn Riding Stables
Rectory Grange
Blackwell Spinney
HONEY HILL
Petsoe End

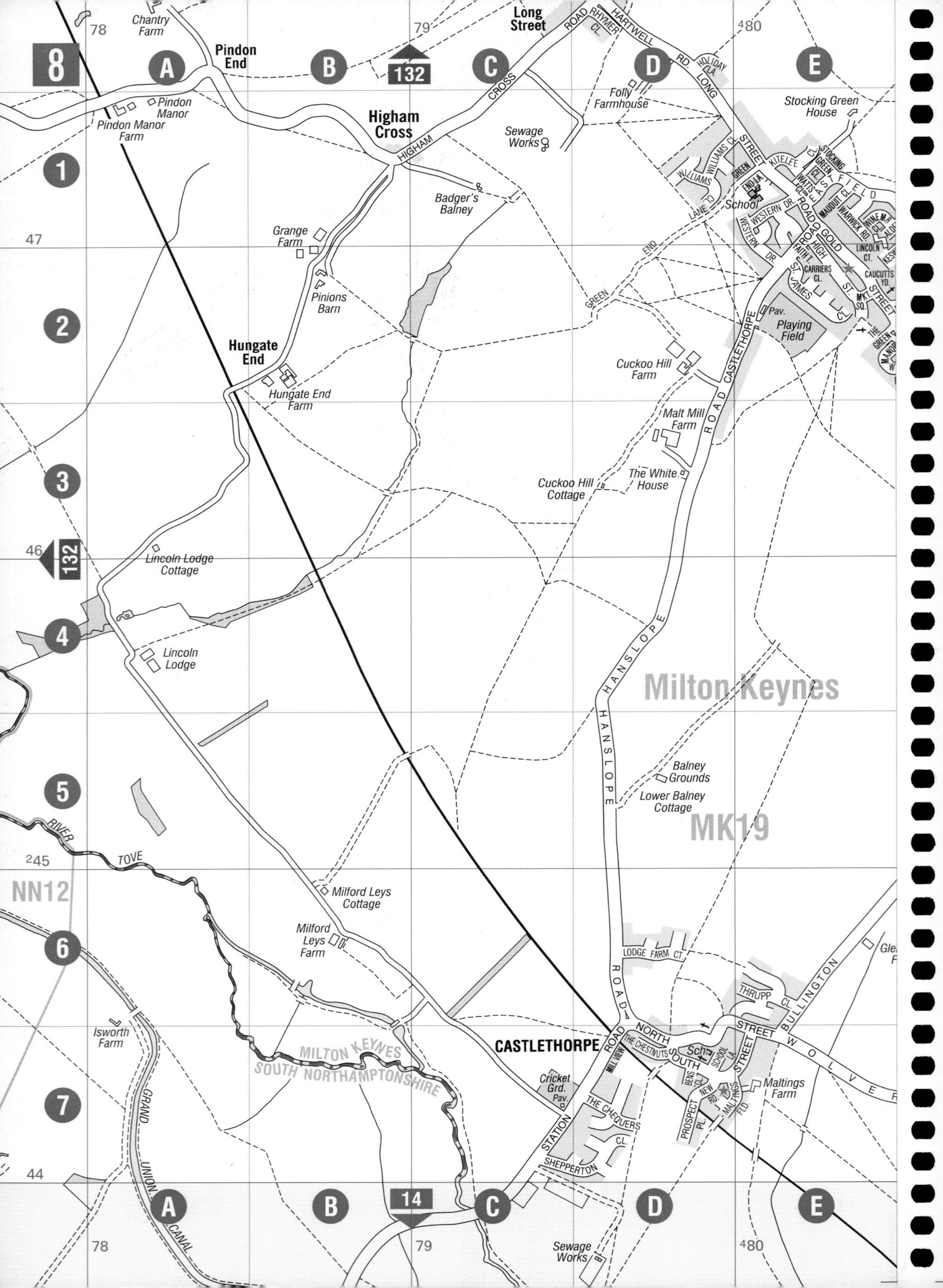

8
A
B
C
D
E
1
2
3
4
5
6
7
132
14
78
79
480
47
46
245
44
Chantry Farm
Pindon End
Long Street
Pindon Manor
Pindon Manor Farm
Higham Cross
Folly Farmhouse
Sewage Works
Stocking Green House
Badger's Balney
Grange Farm
Pinions Barn
Hungate End
Hungate End Farm
Cuckoo Hill Farm
Malt Mill Farm
The White House
Cuckoo Hill Cottage
Lincoln Lodge Cottage
Lincoln Lodge
Milton Keynes
Balney Grounds
Lower Balney Cottage
MK19
NN12
RIVER TOVE
Milford Leys Cottage
Milford Leys Farm
Isworth Farm
MILTON KEYNES
SOUTH NORTHAMPTONSHIRE
GRAND UNION CANAL
CASTLETHORPE
Cricket Grd. Pav.
Maltings Farm
Sewage Works
School
Playing Field
Pav.
HIGHAM CROSS ROAD
HARTWELL RD.
RHYMER CL.
HOLIDAY LA.
LONG STREET
WILLIAMS CL.
GREEN END LA.
GREEN END
WESTERN DR.
KITELEE CL.
STOCKING GREEN CL.
WATTS CL.
EASTFIELD
MAUDUIT CL.
WARWICK RD.
GOLD ROAD
HIGH ST.
FAITH T.
ST. JAMES CL.
CARRIERS CL.
LINCOLN CT.
CAUCUTTS YD.
MKT. SQ.
CASTLETHORPE ROAD
HANSLOPE ROAD
LODGE FARM CT.
THRUPP CL.
BULLINGTON
NORTH STREET
THE CHESTNUTS
MILL VIEW
SOUTH STREET
SCHOOL LA.
BENS CL.
NEW RD.
MALTINGS FLD.
PROSPECT PL.
THE CHEQUERS
STATION ROAD
SHEPPERTON CL.
WOLVERTON

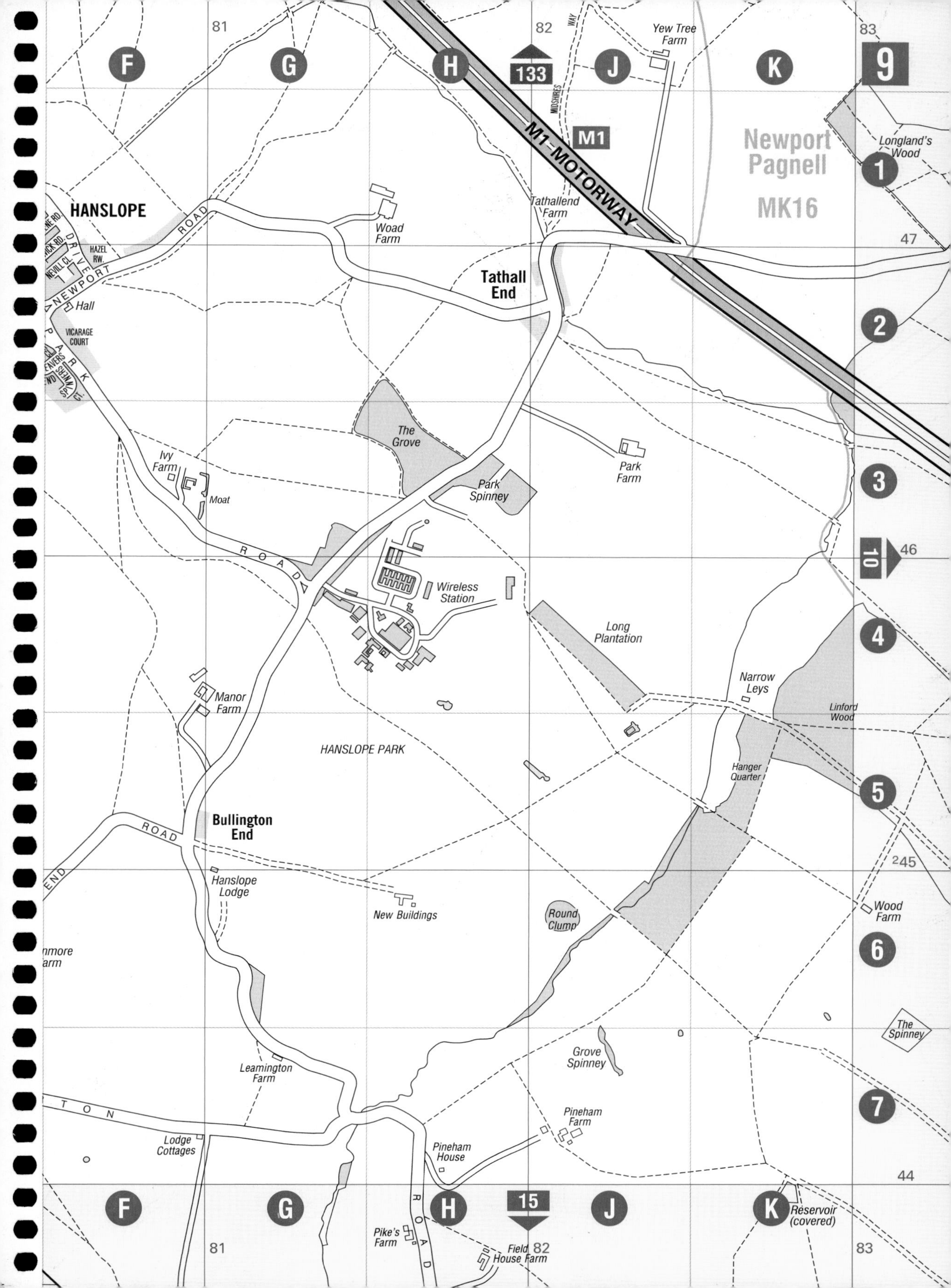

9
F
G
H
J
K
133
M1
M1 MOTORWAY
MIDSHIRES WAY
Yew Tree Farm
Newport Pagnell
MK16
Longland's Wood
1
2
3
4
5
6
7
HANSLOPE
NEWPORT ROAD
PARK DRIVE
HAZEL RW.
NEVILL CL.
Hall
VICARAGE COURT
Wood Farm
Tathallend Farm
Tathall End
47
The Grove
Park Spinney
Park Farm
Ivy Farm
Moat
ROAD
Wireless Station
10
46
Long Plantation
Manor Farm
Narrow Leys
Linford Wood
HANSLOPE PARK
Hanger Quarter
Bullington End
ROAD
245
Hanslope Lodge
New Buildings
Round Clump
Wood Farm
The Spinney
Grove Spinney
Leamington Farm
TON
Pineham Farm
Lodge Cottages
Pineham House
44
15
Reservoir (covered)
Pike's Farm
Field House Farm
ROAD
81
82
83

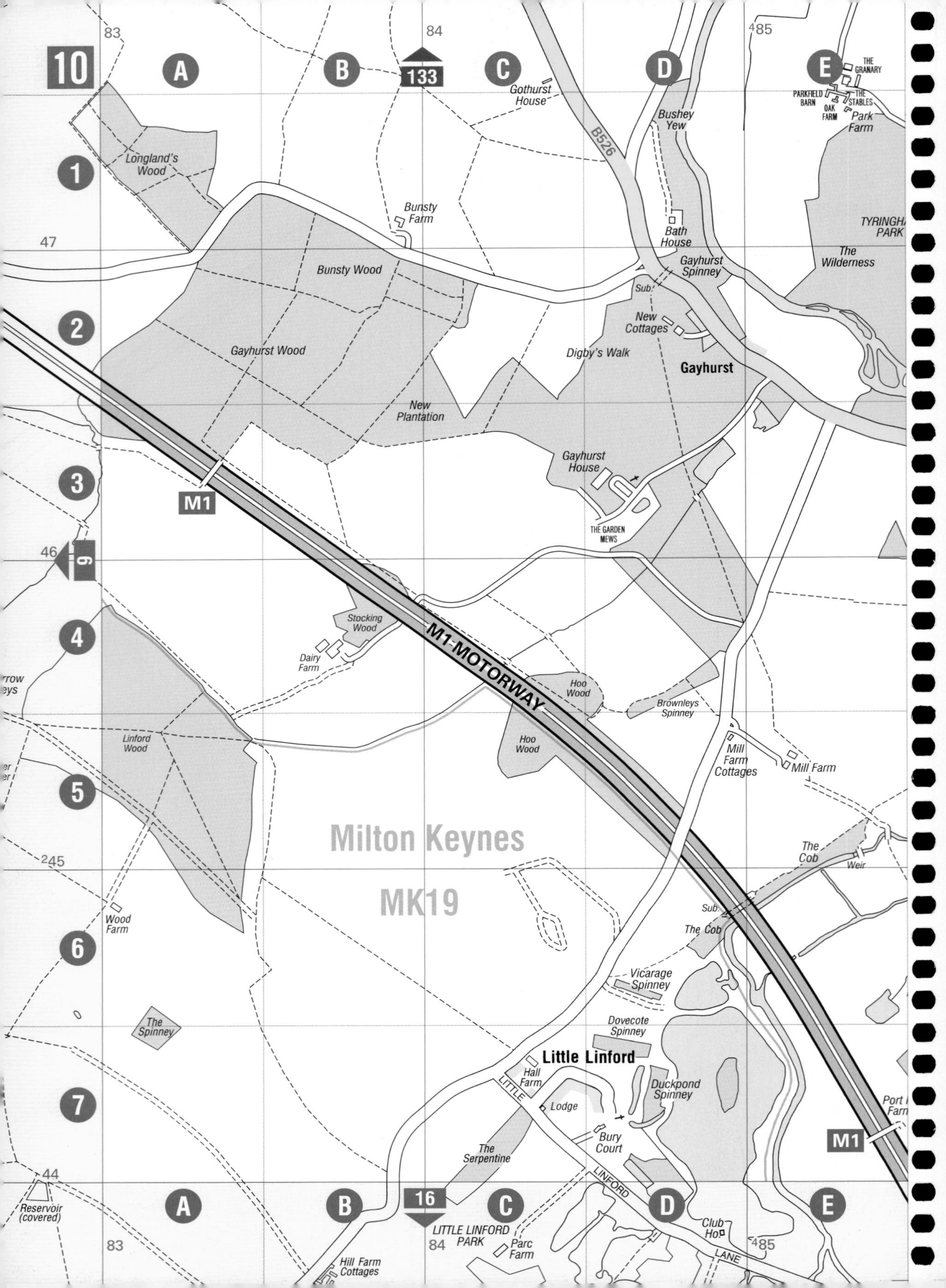

83
84
485
A
B
133
C
D
E
1
2
3
4
5
6
7
47
46
245
44
THE GRANARY
PARKFIELD BARN
THE STABLES
OAK FARM
Park Farm
Gothurst House
Bushey Yew
B526
Longland's Wood
Bunsty Farm
Bath House
TYRINGHAM PARK
The Wilderness
Gayhurst Spinney
Bunsty Wood
Sub.
New Cottages
Gayhurst
Gayhurst Wood
Digby's Walk
New Plantation
Gayhurst House
M1
THE GARDEN MEWS
9
Stocking Wood
Dairy Farm
M1-MOTORWAY
Hoo Wood
Brownleys Spinney
Linford Wood
Hoo Wood
Mill Farm Cottages
Mill Farm
Milton Keynes
MK19
The Cob
Weir
Sub.
The Cob
Wood Farm
Vicarage Spinney
The Spinney
Dovecote Spinney
Little Linford
Hall Farm
Duckpond Spinney
LITTLE
Lodge
Bury Court
The Serpentine
LINFORD
M1
Reservoir (covered)
16
LITTLE LINFORD PARK
Parc Farm
Club Ho
LANE
Hill Farm Cottages

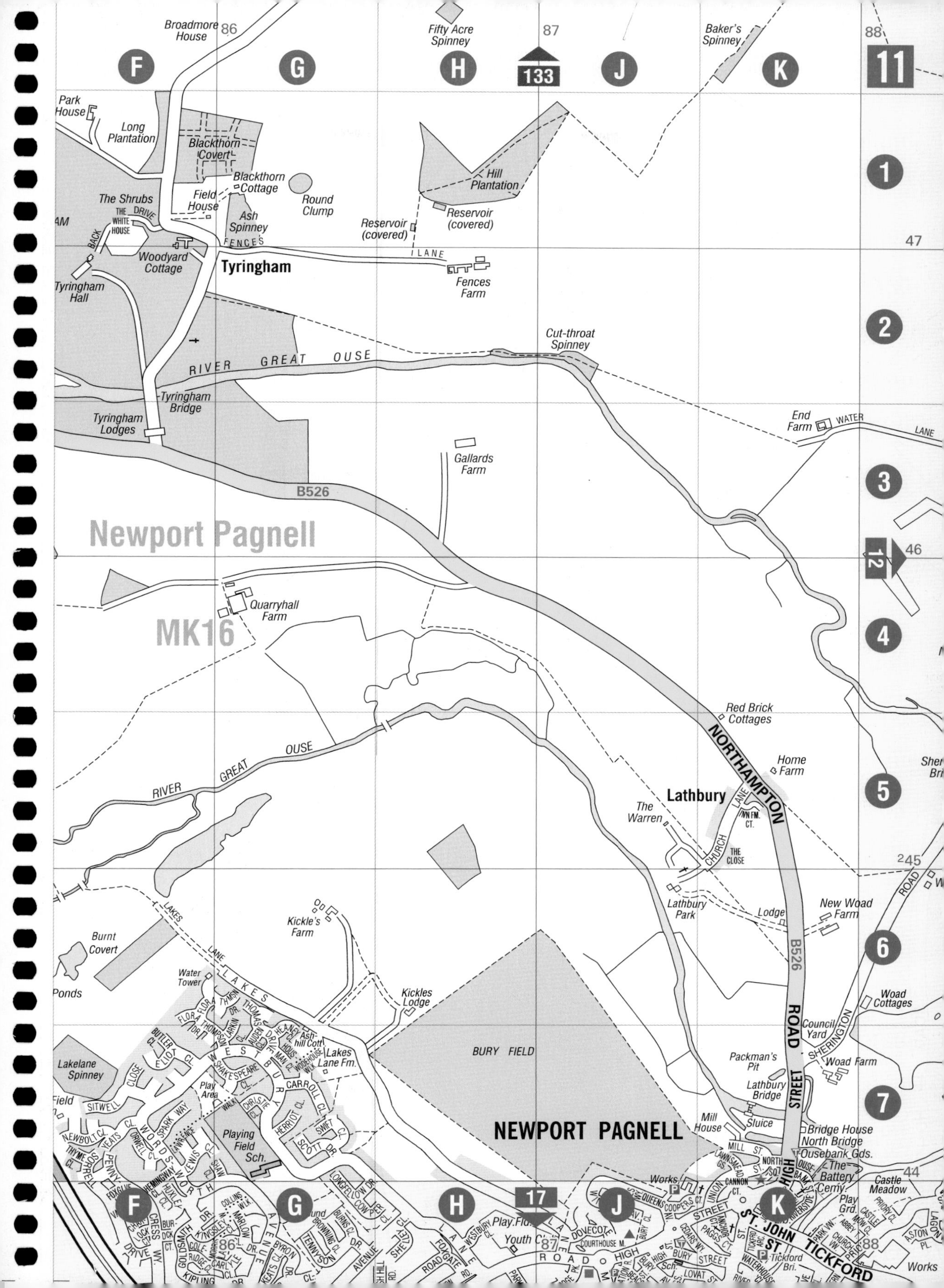

11
133
17
12
F
G
H
J
K
86
87
88
47
46
45
44
1
2
3
4
5
6
7
Broadmore House
Fifty Acre Spinney
Baker's Spinney
Park House
Long Plantation
Blackthorn Covert
Blackthorn Cottage
Hill Plantation
Field House
Round Clump
The Shrubs
Ash Spinney
Reservoir (covered)
The White House
Woodyard Cottage
Tyringham
Fences Lane
Fences Farm
Tyringham Hall
Cut-throat Spinney
River Great Ouse
Tyringham Bridge
Tyringham Lodges
End Farm
Water Lane
Gallards Farm
B526
Newport Pagnell
MK16
Quarryhall Farm
Red Brick Cottages
Northampton Road
Home Farm
Lathbury
The Warren
Church Lane
The Close
Lathbury Park
Lodge
New Wood Farm
Burnt Covert
Kickle's Farm
Lakes Lane
Water Tower
Ponds
Kickles Lodge
Wood Cottages
Council Yard
Sherington Road
Lakelane Spinney
Lakes Lane Fm.
Bury Field
Packman's Pit
Wood Farm
Lathbury Bridge
High Street
Play Area
Playing Field
Sch.
Mill House
Sluice
Bridge House
North Bridge
Ousebank Gds.
Newport Pagnell
The Battery
Cemy.
Castle Meadow
Westbury
Shakespeare Cl.
Carroll Cl.
Sitwell
Yeats Cl.
Newbolt Cl.
Wordsworth Avenue
Herriot Cl.
Swift Cl.
Scott Dr.
Longfellow Dr.
Cowper Cl.
Tennyson
Browning
Burns Cl.
Byron
Kingsley
Marlow
Collins Wk.
Goldsmith Dr.
Hemingway
Kipling
Play.Fld.
Youth C.
Dovecot
Courthouse M.
High Street
Queens Ct.
Coopers Ct.
Union Street
St. John Street
Tickford Bri.
Tickford Street
Lovat
Bury Street
Cedars Wy.
Paggs Ct.
Play Grd.
Priory Cl.
Castle Mdw.
Abbey
Church
Aston Pl.
Works
Mill St.
Cannon Ct.
Lawnsmead Gs.
Foxgate
Shelley Cl.
Avenue
Eliot Cl.
Butler Cl.
Close
Thompson Dr.
Lewis Cl.
Shaw
Huxley
Penny
Sorrel
Thyme Cl.
Foxglove
Cress Wy.
Drive
Riverside

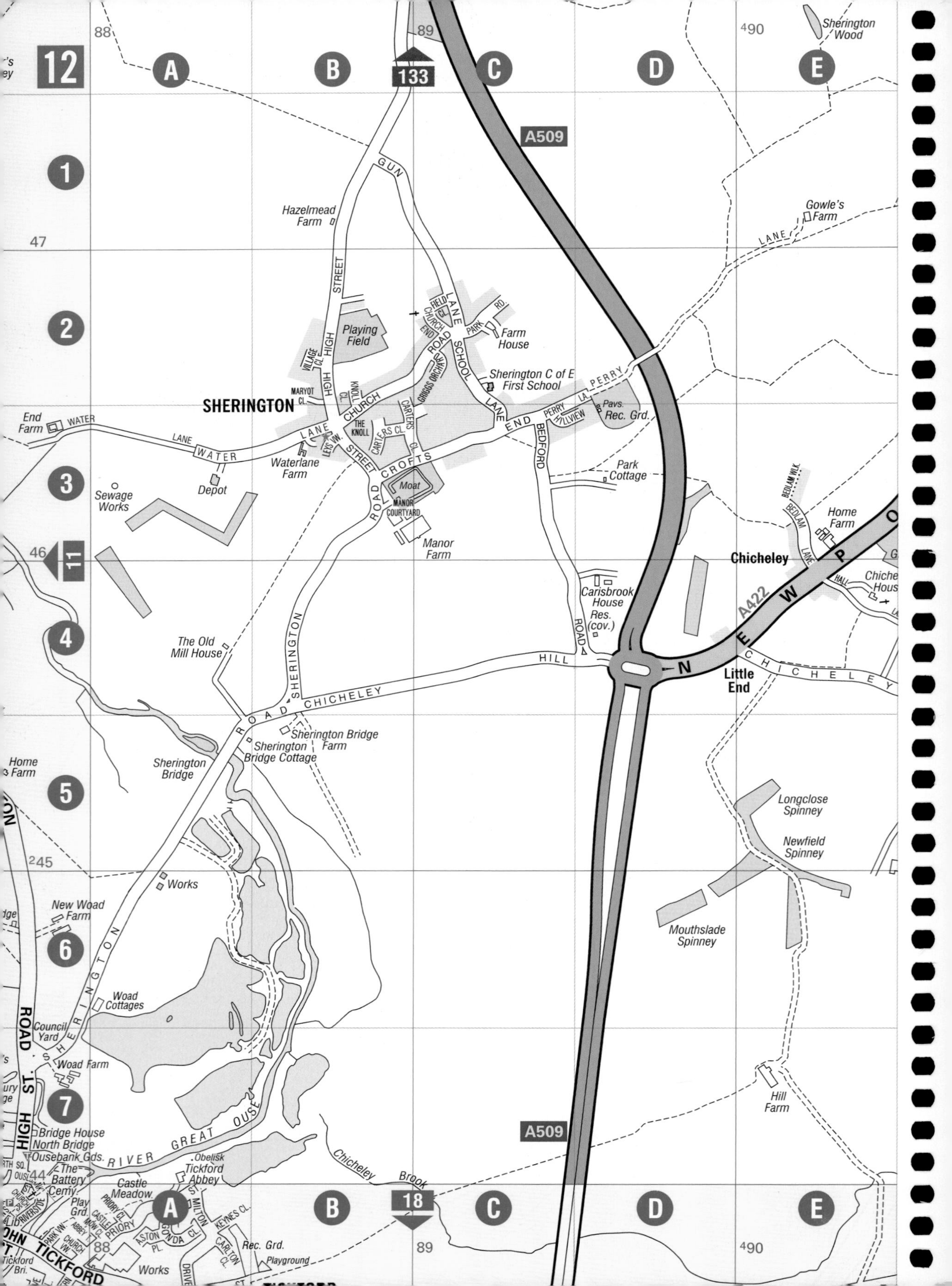

12
A
B
C
D
E
133
18
1
2
3
4
5
6
7
11
88
89
490
47
46
245
44
A509
A422
Sherington Wood
Gowle's Farm
Hazelmead Farm
GUN LANE
HIGH STREET
Playing Field
VILLAGE CL.
FIELD CL.
CHURCH END
PARK RD.
Farm House
SCHOOL LANE
Sherington C of E First School
PERRY LA.
PERRY END
HILLVIEW
Pavs.
Rec. Grd.
MARYOT CL.
KNOLL CL.
CHURCH ROAD
GRIGGS ORCHARD
CARTERS CL.
THE KNOLL
LEYS VW.
SHERINGTON
End Farm
WATER LANE
Waterlane Farm
Depot
Sewage Works
CROFTS END
Moat
MANOR COURTYARD
Manor Farm
BEDFORD ROAD
Park Cottage
Carisbrook House
Res. (cov.)
Home Farm
BEDLAM WLK.
BEDLAM LANE
Chicheley
NEWPORT
HALL
Little End
CHICHELEY
The Old Mill House
SHERINGTON ROAD
CHICHELEY HILL
Sherington Bridge Farm
Sherington Bridge Cottage
Sherington Bridge
Longclose Spinney
Newfield Spinney
Mouthslade Spinney
Works
New Woad Farm
Woad Cottages
Council Yard
Wood Farm
HIGH ST.
Bridge House
North Bridge
Ousebank Gds.
The Battery
Cemy.
RIVER GREAT OUSE
Obelisk
Tickford Abbey
Castle Meadow
Play Grd.
Chicheley Brook
Hill Farm
PRIORY CL.
CASTLE MDW. CL.
PRIORY
ASTON PL.
GONDA CL.
ST. MILTON
KEYNES CL.
CARLTON CL.
Rec. Grd.
Playground
Works
TICKFORD ST.
Tickford Bri.

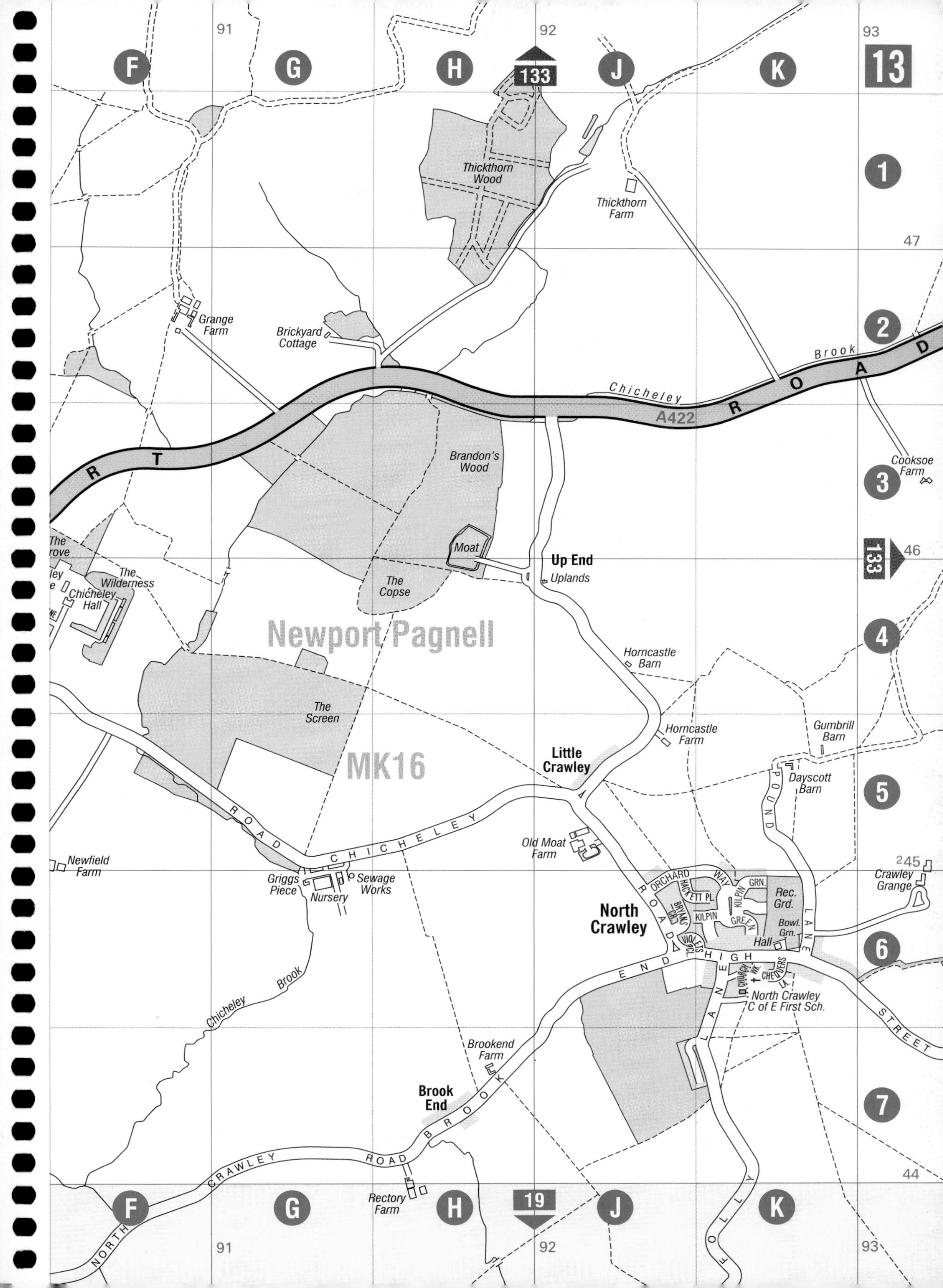
91
92
93
F
G
H
J
K
133
1
2
3
4
5
6
7
47
46
2 45
44
Thickthorn Wood
Thickthorn Farm
Grange Farm
Brickyard Cottage
Brook
Chicheley
A422
ROAD
RT
Cooksoe Farm
Brandon's Wood
Moat
Up End
Uplands
The Copse
The Grove
The Wilderness
Chicheley Hall
Newport Pagnell
Horncastle Barn
The Screen
Horncastle Farm
Gumbrill Barn
Little Crawley
MK16
Dayscott Barn
POUND
ROAD CHICHELEY
Old Moat Farm
Newfield Farm
Griggs Piece
Nursery
Sewage Works
ORCHARD WAY
HACKETT PL.
BRYANS CR.
KILPIN
KILPIN GREEN
GRN.
Rec. Grd.
Bowl. Grn.
Hall
North Crawley
VIOLETS CL.
HIGH
CHURCH WK.
CHEQUERS LA.
END
LANE
Crawley Grange
North Crawley C of E First Sch.
STREET
Chicheley Brook
Brookend Farm
Brook End
BROOK
ROAD
NORTH CRAWLEY
FOLLY
Rectory Farm
19

CASTLETHORPE
8
Sewage Works
Elm Tree Farm
GRAND UNION CANAL
Weirs
Cobbs Bush Farm
The Priory
RIVER TONE
YARDLEY ROAD
A508
NORTHAMPTON ROAD
Rectory Farm
Cosgrove Prim. Sch.
Elms Farm
Ivy Cottage
Pumping Station
St. Vincent's Well (Chalybeate)
Works
Cricket Grd.
The Little Manor
COSGROVE
Pipe Line
Lodge
Cosgrove Hall
Jetties
Boat House
COSGROVE LODGE PARK
132
STRATFORD ROAD
Brook Farm
Dogsmouth Bridge
Buckingham Branch (disused)
Old Stratford Cut. (disused)
Broad Water
Iron Trunk Aqueduct
Milton Keynes
SOUTH NORTHAMPTONSHIRE
MILTON KEYNES
A5
Old Wolverton
Depot
Weir
GREAT OUSE
OLD STRATFORD
STONY STRATFORD NATURE RESERVE
OUSE VALLEY PARK
Motte & Bailey
Vicarage
The Mill
Wolverton Mill
Wolverton House
Wolverton Park
QUEEN ELEANOR ST.
Football Field
Ancell Trust Sports Grd.
Pumping Station
St.Mary & St.Giles C.of E. Sch.
Play. Fld.
Stony Stratford
Russell First Sch.
Wolverton Mill South
Wolverton Mill East
STRATFORD OFFICE VILLAGE
Industrial Estate
Youth Club
20

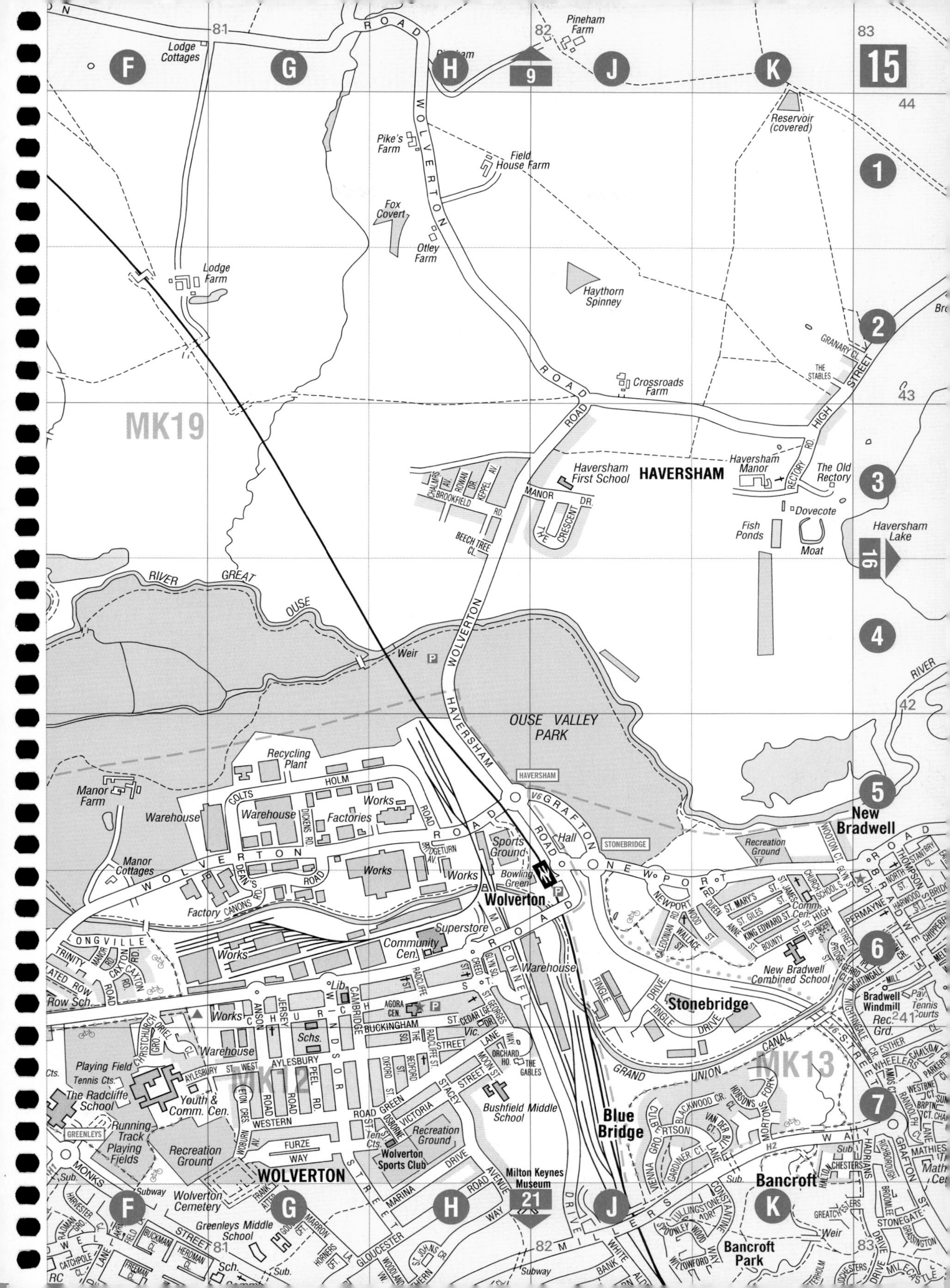

15
F
G
H
J
K
81
82
83
44
43
42
1
2
3
4
5
6
7
9
16
21
Lodge Cottages
Pineham Farm
Reservoir (covered)
Pike's Farm
Field House Farm
Fox Covert
Otley Farm
Lodge Farm
Haythorn Spinney
Crossroads Farm
MK19
Haversham First School
HAVERSHAM
Haversham Manor
The Old Rectory
Dovecote
Fish Ponds
Moat
Haversham Lake
RIVER GREAT OUSE
Weir
OUSE VALLEY PARK
Recycling Plant
Manor Farm
Warehouse
Works
Factories
Manor Cottages
Sports Ground
Hall
Bowling Green
Wolverton
Superstore
Community Cen.
Warehouse
Stonebridge
New Bradwell
Recreation Ground
New Bradwell Combined School
Bradwell Windmill
Rec. Grd.
MK13
GRAND UNION CANAL
Blue Bridge
MK12
Playing Field
Tennis Cts.
The Radcliffe School
Youth & Comm. Cen.
Running Track
Playing Fields
Recreation Ground
WOLVERTON
Wolverton Cemetery
Greenleys Middle School
Bushfield Middle School
Recreation Ground
Wolverton Sports Club
Milton Keynes Museum
Bancroft
Bancroft Park
Weir
WOLVERTON ROAD
HAVERSHAM ROAD
HIGH STREET
GRAFTON ROAD
NEWPORT ROAD
MCCONNELL DRIVE
STRATFORD ROAD
WINDSOR STREET
MONKS WAY
MILLERS WAY
GRAFTON STREET
HAVERSHAM
STONEBRIDGE
GREENLEYS

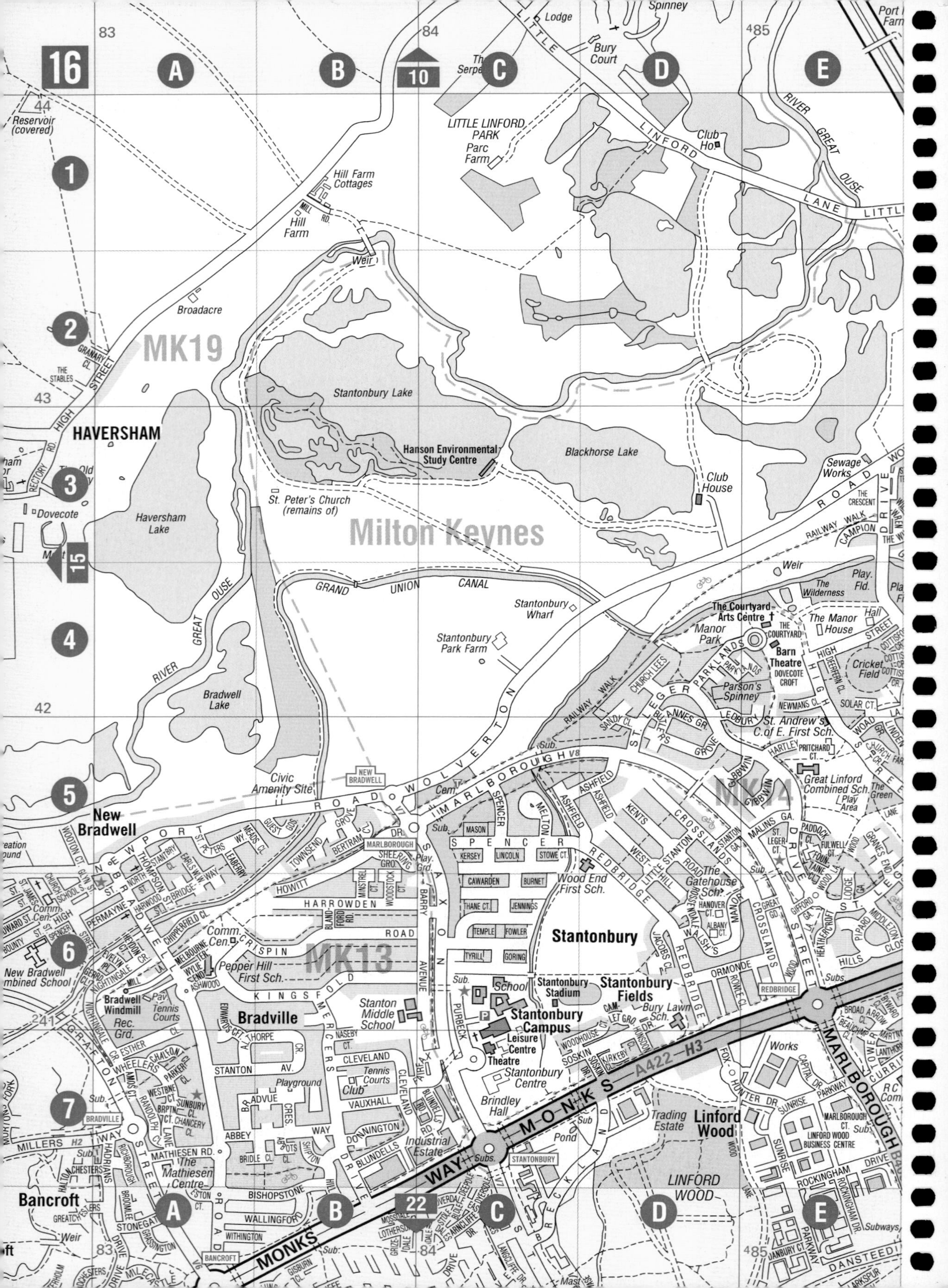

A
B
C
D
E
1
2
3
4
5
6
7
83
84
485
44
43
42
41
10
15
22
Reservoir (covered)
Lodge
Spinney
Bury Court
LITTLE LINFORD PARK
Parc Farm
Hill Farm Cottages
Hill Farm
Broadacre
Weir
LITTLE LINFORD LANE
Club Ho
RIVER GREAT OUSE
MK19
HAVERSHAM
Stantonbury Lake
Hanson Environmental Study Centre
Blackhorse Lake
Club House
Sewage Works
St. Peter's Church (remains of)
Haversham Lake
Dovecote
Milton Keynes
GRAND UNION CANAL
Stantonbury Wharf
Stantonbury Park Farm
Bradwell Lake
Civic Amenity Site
NEW BRADWELL
New Bradwell
WOLVERTON ROAD
MARLBOROUGH
The Courtyard Arts Centre
Manor Park
The Manor House
Barn Theatre
Cricket Field
Parson's Spinney
St. Andrew's C. of E. First Sch.
Great Linford Combined Sch.
MK14
Wood End First Sch.
Stantonbury
Stantonbury Stadium
Stantonbury Fields
Bury Lawn Sch.
The Gatehouse Sch.
MK13
Pepper Hill First Sch.
New Bradwell Combined School
Bradwell Windmill
Bradville
Stanton Middle School
Stantonbury Campus
Leisure Centre
Theatre
Stantonbury Centre
Brindley Hall
Industrial Estate
Trading Estate
Linford Wood
LINFORD WOOD
LINFORD WOOD BUSINESS CENTRE
MONKS WAY
A422 H3
MARLBOROUGH STREET
The Mathiesen Centre
Bancroft
BRADVILLE
STANTONBURY
BANCROFT
REDBRIDGE
Playground
Tennis Courts
Rec. Grd.

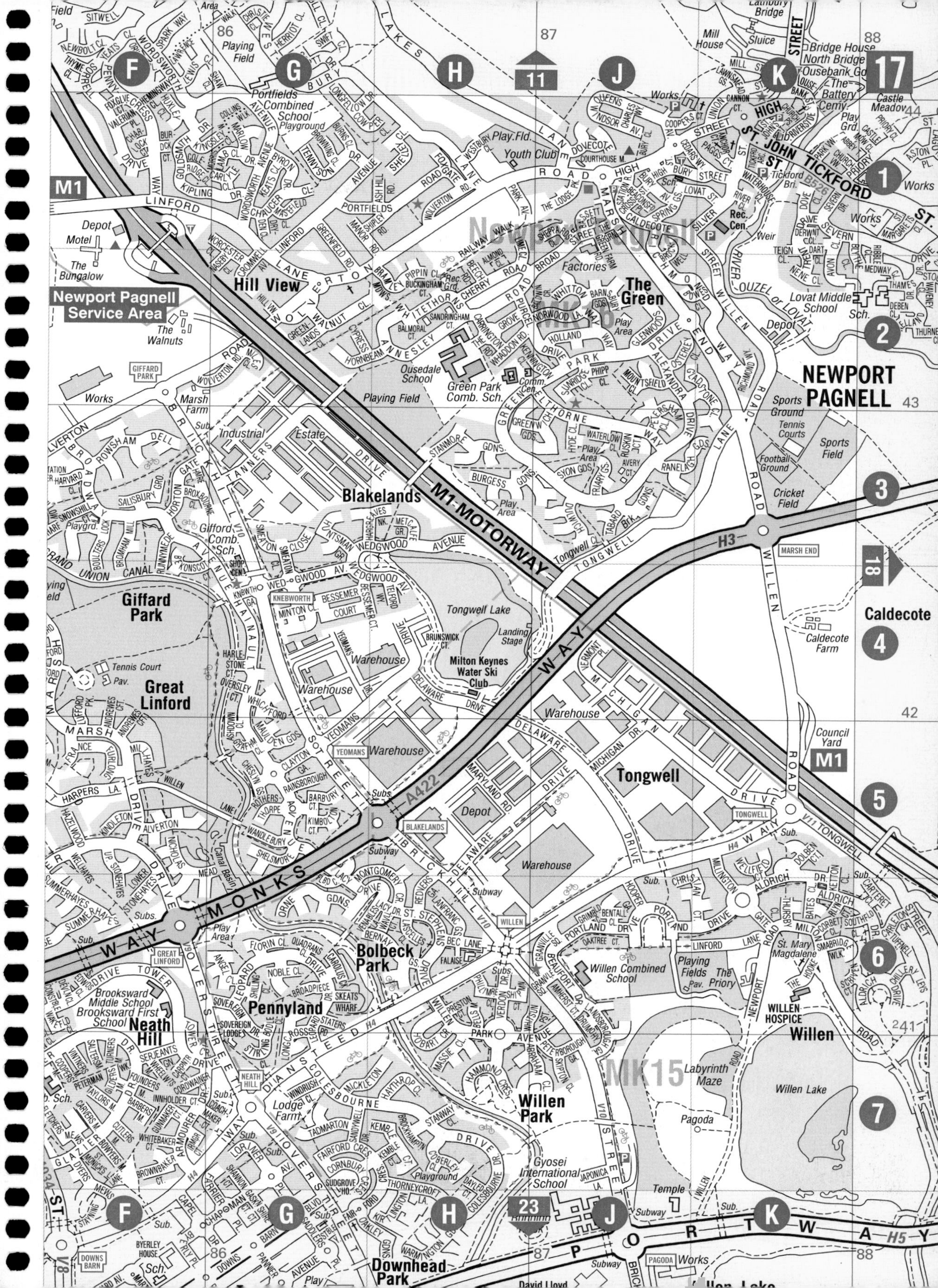

17
11
18
23
M1
M1-MOTORWAY
Newport Pagnell
NEWPORT PAGNELL
Newport Pagnell Service Area
MK16
MK15
Hill View
The Green
Blakelands
Giffard Park
Great Linford
Tongwell
Caldecote
Caldecote Farm
Bolbeck Park
Pennyland
Neath Hill
Willen
Willen Park
Downhead Park
Tongwell Lake
Milton Keynes Water Ski Club
Willen Lake
Labyrinth Maze
Pagoda
Temple
Gyosei International School
Willen Combined School
WILLEN HOSPICE
St. Mary Magdalene
The Priory
Playing Fields
Brooksward Middle School
Brooksward First School
Ousedale School
Green Park Comb. Sch.
Portfields Combined School
Lovat Middle School
Gifford Comb. Sch.
Youth Club
Industrial Estate
Warehouse
Depot
Works
Factories
Sports Ground
Sports Field
Tennis Courts
Football Ground
Cricket Field
Council Yard
Playing Field
Grand Union Canal
River Ouzel or Lovat
MONKS WAY
PORTWAY
TONGWELL STREET
WILLEN ROAD
MARSH END ROAD
WOLVERTON ROAD
LINFORD LANE
HIGH STREET
ST. JOHN STREET
TICKFORD ST.
A422
H3
H4
H5
V10
V11
B526
Mill House
Bridge House
North Bridge
Castle Meadow
Lathbury Bridge
Depot
Motel
The Bungalow
The Walnuts
Marsh Farm
Lodge Farm

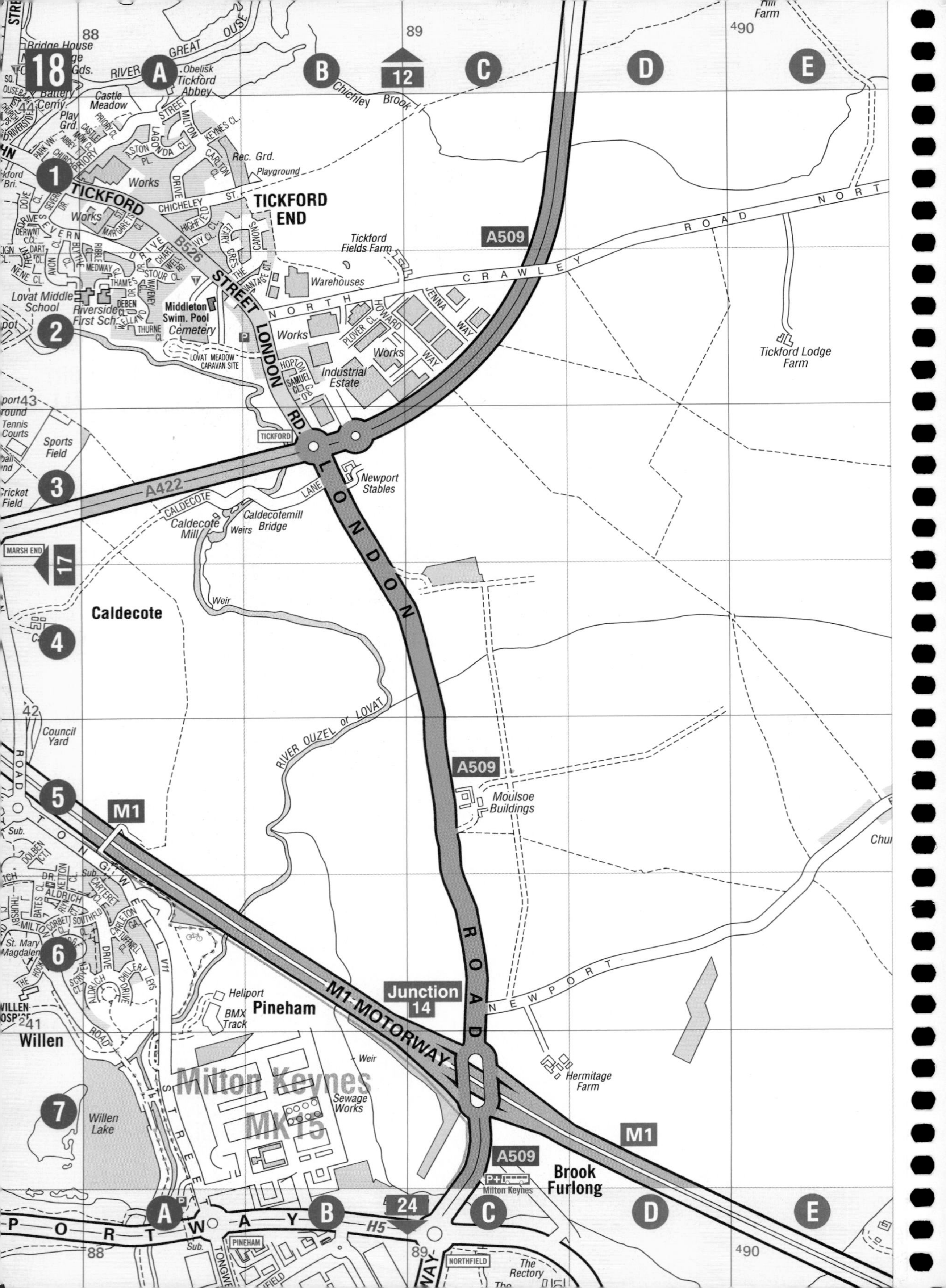

TICKFORD END
Tickford Abbey
Obelisk
Castle Meadow
RIVER GREAT OUSE
Chichley Brook
Rec. Grd.
Playground
Works
TICKFORD
CHICHELEY ST.
Tickford Fields Farm
Warehouses
NORTH CRAWLEY ROAD
A509
Lovat Middle School
Riverside First Sch.
Middleton Swim. Pool
Cemetery
LOVAT MEADOW CARAVAN SITE
Industrial Estate
B526
STREET
LONDON RD.
Tickford Lodge Farm
Sports Field
Tennis Courts
Cricket Field
A422
Newport Stables
CALDECOTE LANE
Caldecote Mill
Weirs
Caldecotemill Bridge
MARSH END
17
12
Caldecote
Weir
LONDON ROAD
RIVER OUZEL or LOVAT
Council Yard
M1
Moulsoe Buildings
St. Mary Magdalen
Heliport
BMX Track
Pineham
Willen
Willen Lake
M1 MOTORWAY
Junction 14
NEWPORT
Hermitage Farm
Milton Keynes
MK15
Sewage Works
Brook Furlong
P+L Milton Keynes
PORTWAY
H5
PINEHAM
NORTHFIELD
The Rectory
24
88
89
490

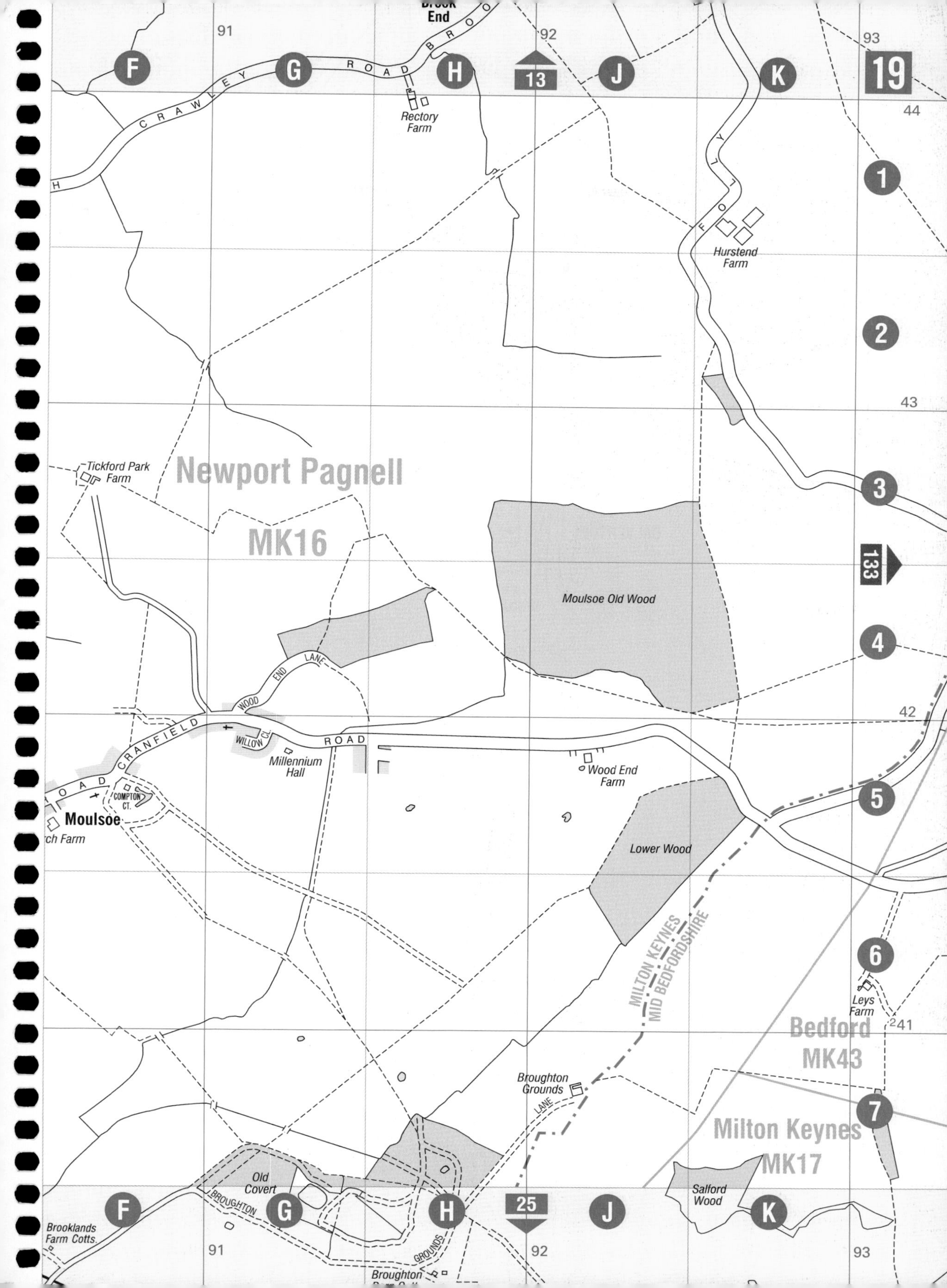

Brook End
91
92
93
F
G
H
J
K
13
19
CRAWLEY ROAD BROOK
Rectory Farm
44
1
FOLLY
Hurstend Farm
2
43
Tickford Park Farm
Newport Pagnell
MK16
3
133
Moulsoe Old Wood
4
WOOD END LANE
42
CRANFIELD ROAD
WILLOW CL.
Millennium Hall
Wood End Farm
COMPTON CT.
Moulsoe
rch Farm
5
Lower Wood
MILTON KEYNES
MID BEDFORDSHIRE
6
Leys Farm
41
Bedford
MK43
Broughton Grounds
LANE
7
Milton Keynes
MK17
Old Covert
Salford Wood
BROUGHTON
GROUNDS
25
Brooklands Farm Cotts.
Broughton

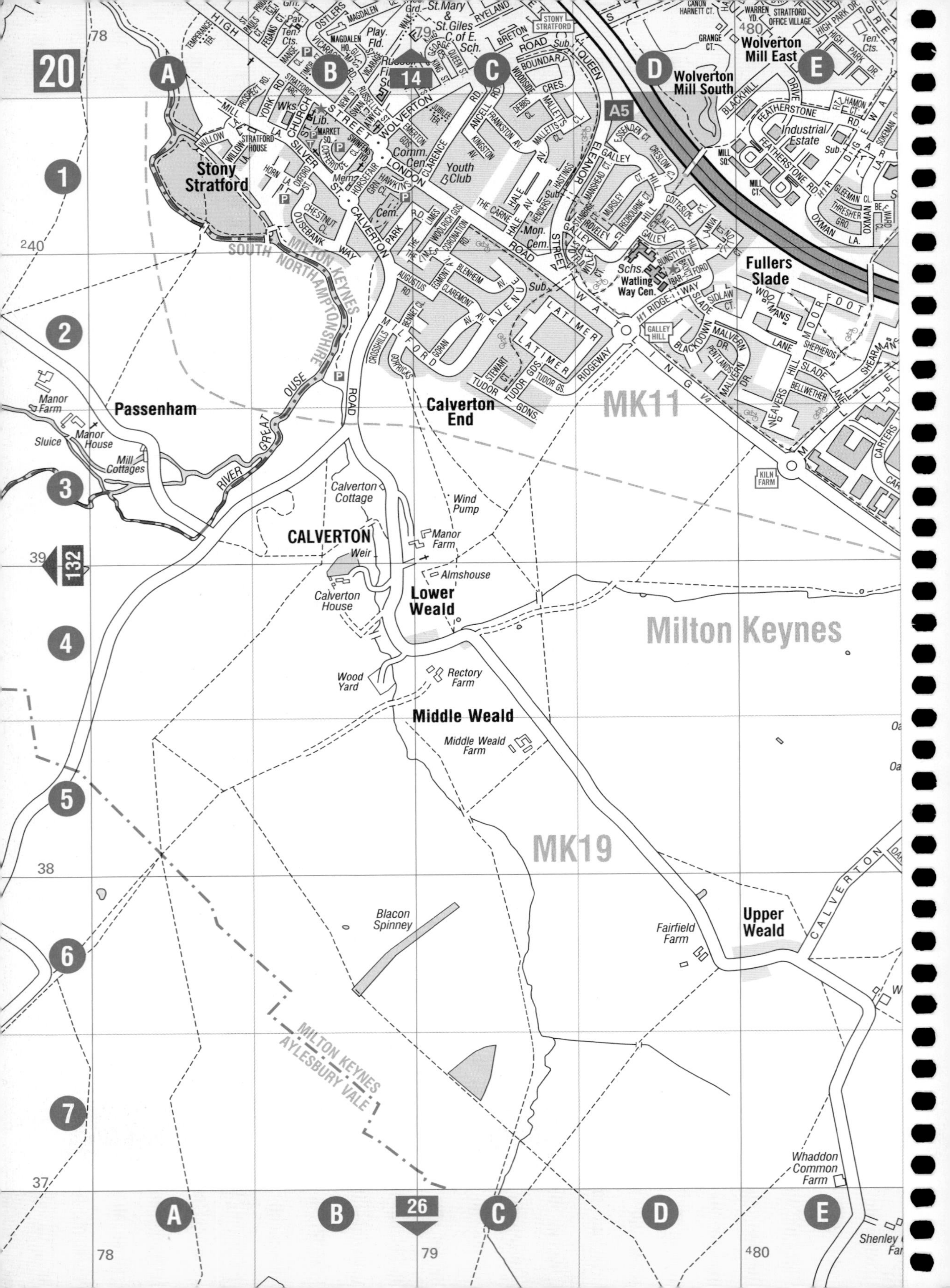

14
26
132
A
B
C
D
E
1
2
3
4
5
6
7
78
79
480
240
39
38
37
Stony Stratford
St.Mary & St.Giles C.of E. Sch.
Wolverton Mill South
Wolverton Mill East
Industrial Estate
Youth Club
Comm. Cen.
Mon. Cem.
Watling Way Cen.
Fullers Slade
Schs.
Lib.
Wks.
Cem.
Mem.
Play. Fld.
Passenham
Manor Farm
Manor House
Mill Cottages
Sluice
RIVER GREAT OUSE
SOUTH NORTHAMPTONSHIRE
MILTON KEYNES
Calverton End
Calverton Cottage
Wind Pump
CALVERTON
Weir
Manor Farm
Almshouse
Calverton House
Lower Weald
Wood Yard
Rectory Farm
Middle Weald
Middle Weald Farm
MK11
MK19
Milton Keynes
Blacon Spinney
Fairfield Farm
Upper Weald
Whaddon Common Farm
Shenley
MILTON KEYNES
AYLESBURY VALE
A5
H1 RIDGEWAY
V4
GALLEY HILL
KILN FARM
STONY STRATFORD
HIGH ST.
WOLVERTON RD.
LONDON RD.
CALVERTON RD.
CHURCH ST.
SILVER ST.
MILL LA.
WILLOW LA.
STRATFORD HOUSE
MARKET SQ.
HORSEFAIR GRN.
CHESTNUT CL.
OUSEBANK WAY
CALVERTON PARK
ANCELL RD.
KINGSTON AV.
CLARENCE RD.
JUBILEE TER.
BOUNDARY CRES.
BRETON
RYELAND
OSTLERS
MAGDALEN
WATLING STREET
ELEANOR
GALLEY HILL
LATIMER
AUGUSTUS RD.
EGMONT AV.
CLAREMONT AV.
BLENHEIM AV.
CORONATION RD.
AVENUE
MILFORD AV.
GORAN AV.
CROSSHILLS
TUDOR GDNS.
RIDGEWAY
STEWART CT.
MALVERN DR.
BLACKDOWN
PENTLANDS
SIDLAW CT.
WOOMANS LANE
FOOT
MOOR
SHEPHERDS
BELLWETHER
WEAVERS HILL
SLADE LANE
FEATHERSTONE RD.
BLACKHILL DRIVE
OXMAN LA.
GLEEMAN CL.
THRESHER GRO.
CALVERTON
ROAD
CARTERS
WARREN YD.
STRATFORD OFFICE VILLAGE
GRANGE CT.
HIGH PARK DR.
Ten. Cts.
MILL SQ.
Sub.

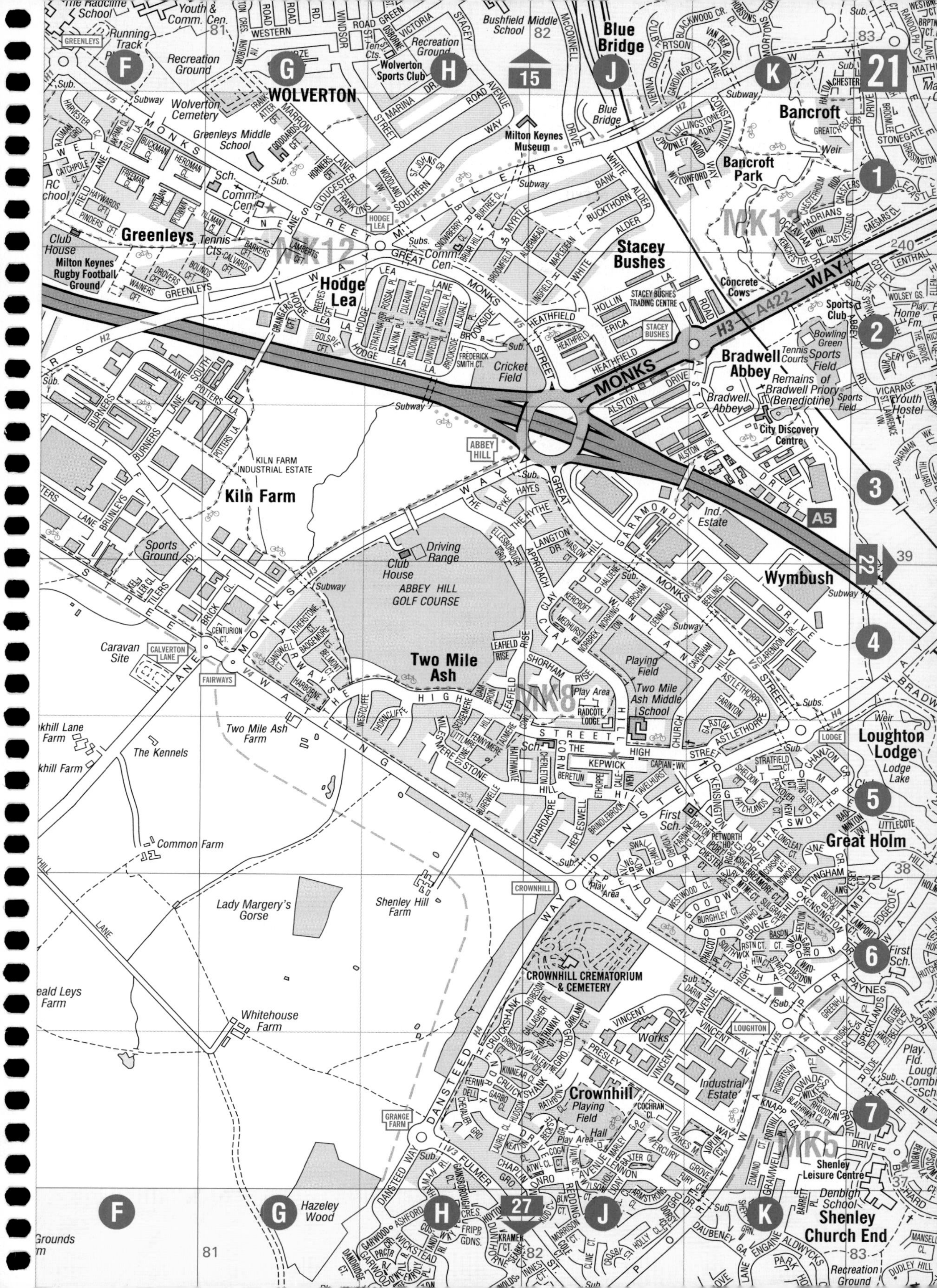

21
15
22
27
WOLVERTON
Greenleys
Hodge Lea
Blue Bridge
Bancroft
Bancroft Park
Stacey Bushes
Bradwell Abbey
Kiln Farm
Wymbush
Two Mile Ash
Loughton Lodge
Great Holm
Crownhill
Shenley Church End
MK12
MK13
MK8
MK5
MONKS WAY
A422
A5
ABBEY HILL GOLF COURSE
Milton Keynes Museum
CROWNHILL CREMATORIUM & CEMETERY
City Discovery Centre
Shenley Leisure Centre
Lady Margery's Gorse
Hazeley Wood
Two Mile Ash Farm
Shenley Hill Farm
Common Farm
Whitehouse Farm
The Kennels
F
G
H
J
K
1
2
3
4
5
6
7
81
82
83
37
38
39

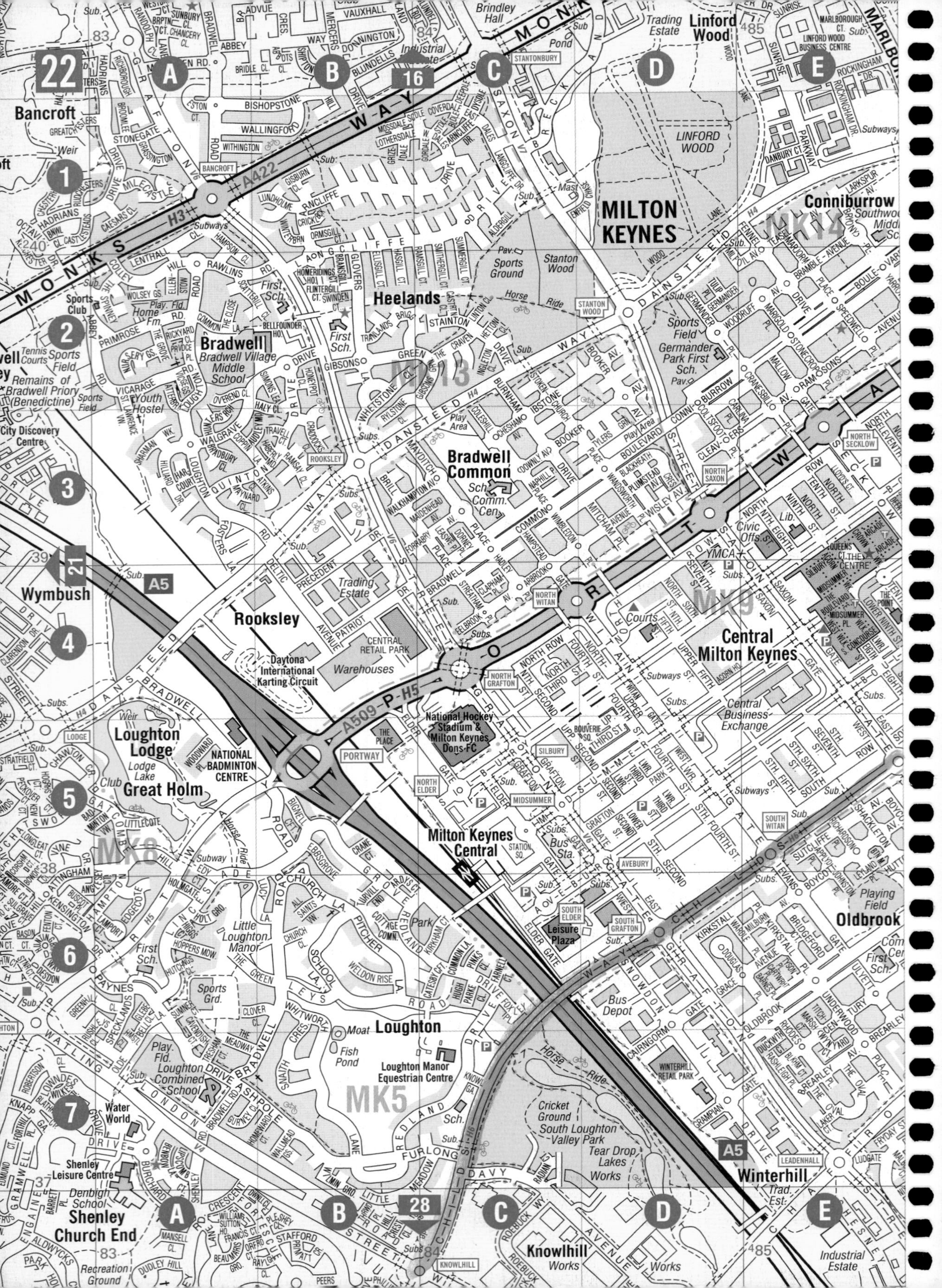
22
16
21
28
A
B
C
D
E
1
2
3
4
5
6
7
Bancroft
Linford Wood
Trading Estate
Brindley Hall
MILTON KEYNES
LINFORD WOOD
Conniburrow
MK14
Heelands
Bradwell
Bradwell Village Middle School
Remains of Bradwell Priory (Benedictine)
Youth Hostel
City Discovery Centre
MK13
Bradwell Common
Stanton Wood
Sports Ground
Germander Park First Sch.
Wymbush
Rooksley
Trading Estate
CENTRAL RETAIL PARK
Warehouses
Daytona International Karting Circuit
MK9
Central Milton Keynes
Central Business Exchange
Loughton Lodge
Lodge Lake
Great Holm
NATIONAL BADMINTON CENTRE
National Hockey Stadium & Milton Keynes Dons FC
THE PLACE
Milton Keynes Central
MK8
Little Loughton Manor
Loughton
Loughton Manor Equestrian Centre
MK5
Loughton Combined School
Water World
Shenley Leisure Centre
Denbigh School
Shenley Church End
Recreation Ground
Cricket Ground
South Loughton Valley Park
Tear Drop Lakes
Works
Knowlhill
Winterhill
Trad. Est.
Industrial Estate
Oldbrook
Playing Field
Leisure Plaza
Bus Depot
WINTERHILL RETAIL PARK
MONKS WAY
A422
A5
A509
DANSTEED WAY
PORTWAY
CHILDS WAY
WATLING STREET

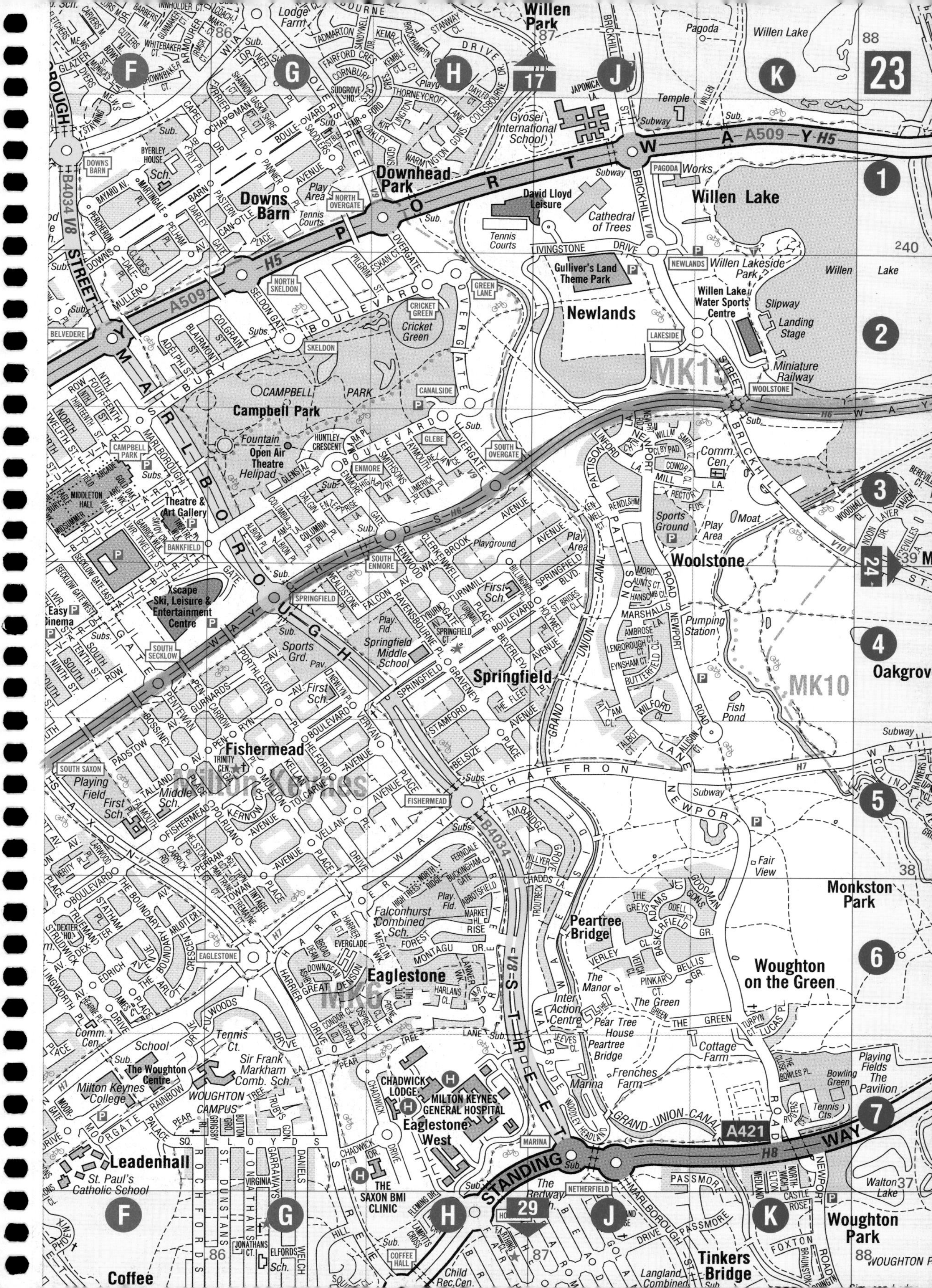

23
Willen Park
Willen Lake
Downhead Park
Downs Barn
Campbell Park
Newlands
Woolstone
Springfield
Fishermead
Milton Keynes
Eaglestone
Peartree Bridge
Woughton on the Green
Monkston Park
Oakgrove
Leadenhall
Tinkers Bridge
Woughton Park
Gyosei International School
David Lloyd Leisure
Cathedral of Trees
Gulliver's Land Theme Park
Willen Lakeside Park
Willen Lake Water Sports Centre
Theatre & Art Gallery
Xscape Ski, Leisure & Entertainment Centre
Springfield Middle School
Falconhurst Combined Sch.
Milton Keynes General Hospital
Chadwick Lodge
Eaglestone West
The Saxon BMI Clinic
The Woughton Centre
Milton Keynes College
Sir Frank Markham Comb. Sch.
St. Paul's Catholic School
Inter Action Centre
Pear Tree House
Grand Union Canal
MK13
MK10
MK6
A509
A421
H5
H6
H7
H8
V8
V9
V10
B4034
17
24
29

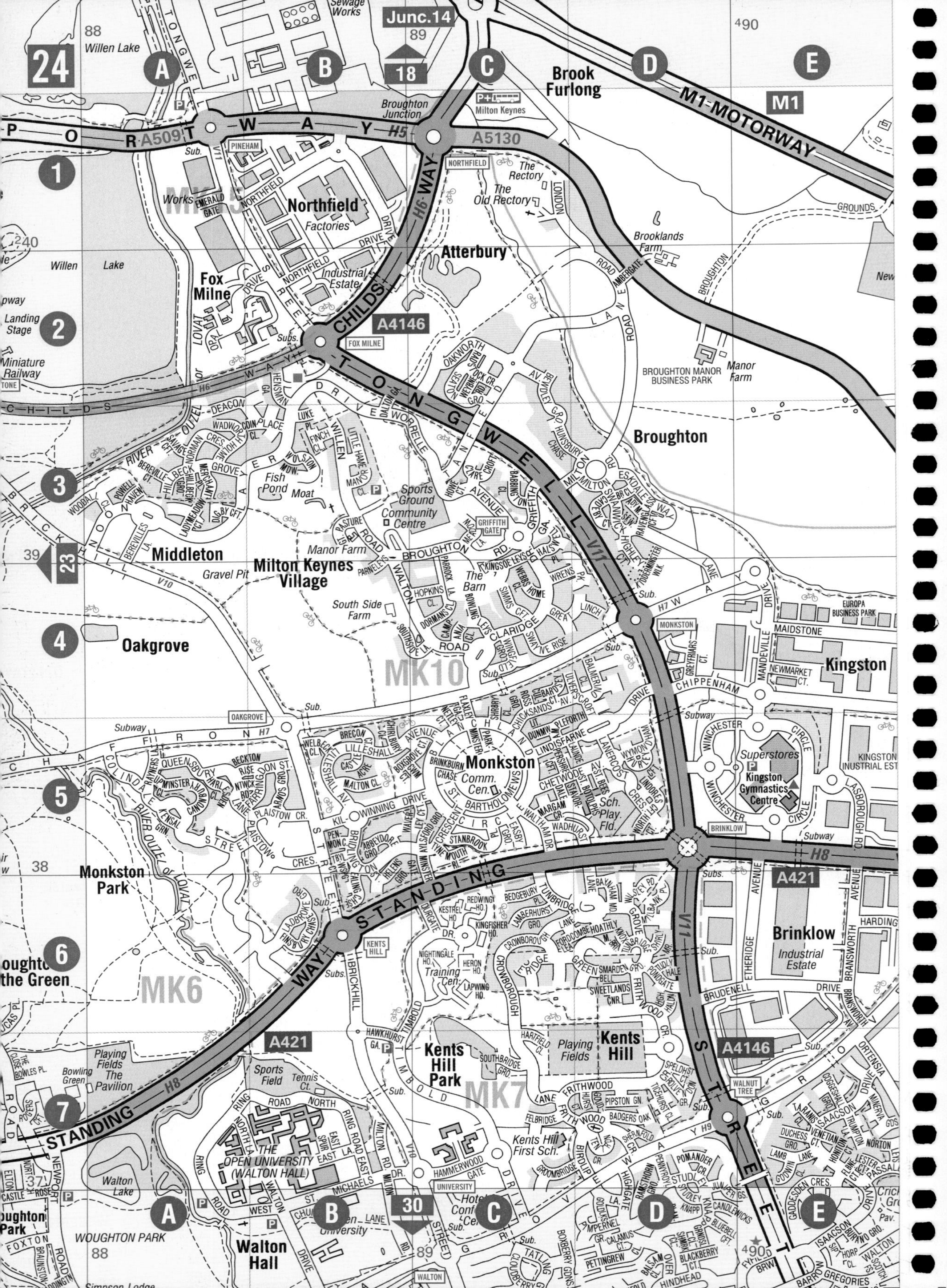

Junc.14
18
M1 MOTORWAY
Brook Furlong
Broughton Junction
Milton Keynes
A509
A5130
H5
Northfield
Factories
Atterbury
Willen Lake
Fox Milne
Industrial Estate
CHILDS WAY
A4146
TONGWELL
Broughton Manor Business Park
Manor Farm
Broughton
Middleton
Milton Keynes Village
Oakgrove
MK10
Monkston
Kingston
Superstores
Kingston Gymnastics Centre
Monkston Park
STANDING WAY
A421
Brinklow Industrial Estate
MK6
MK7
Kents Hill Park
Kents Hill
Playing Fields
The Open University (Walton Hall)
Walton Hall
Walton Lake
Woughton Park
30
23

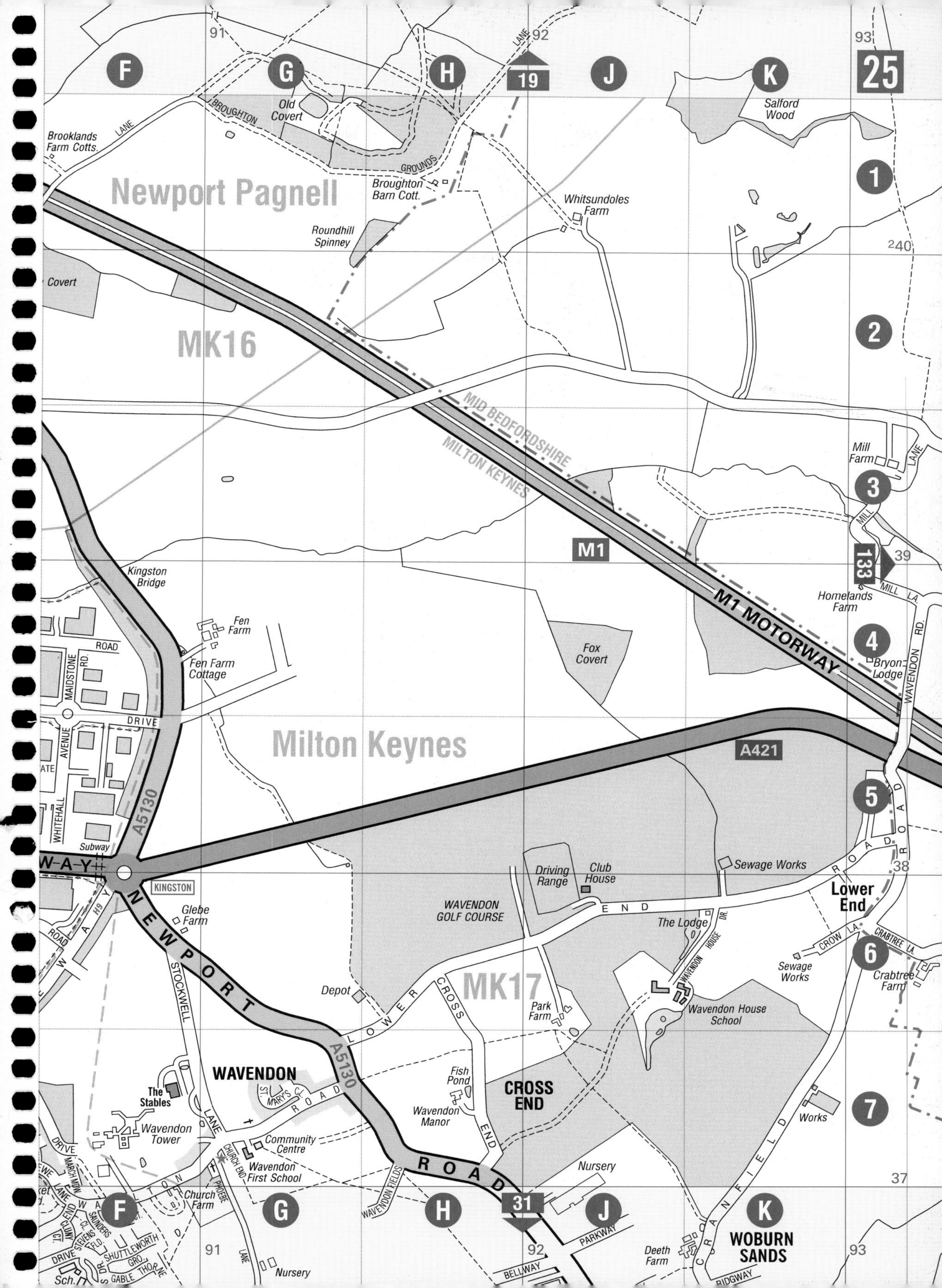

25
Newport Pagnell
MK16
Milton Keynes
MK17
Brooklands Farm Cotts.
Broughton Lane
Old Covert
Broughton Grounds Lane
Broughton Barn Cott.
Roundhill Spinney
Covert
Whitsundoles Farm
Salford Wood
Mid Bedfordshire
Milton Keynes
M1
M1 Motorway
Mill Farm
Mill Lane
Homelands Farm
Mill La.
Wavendon Rd.
Bryon Lodge
Fox Covert
Kingston Bridge
Fen Farm
Fen Farm Cottage
Road
Maidstone Rd.
Drive
Avenue
Whitehall
A5130
A421
Subway
Kingston
Newport Road
Glebe Farm
Stockwell Lane
Driving Range
Club House
Wavendon Golf Course
Sewage Works
Lower End Road
Lower End
The Lodge
Wavendon House Dr.
Crow La.
Crabtree La.
Sewage Works
Crabtree Farm
Depot
Lower Cross End
Park Farm
Wavendon House School
Wavendon
The Stables
St. Mary's Cl.
Fish Pond
Wavendon Manor
Cross End
Works
Cranfield Road
Wavendon Tower
Community Centre
Wavendon First School
Church End
Phoebe Lane
Nursery
Church Farm
Wavendon Fields
Parkway
Bellway
Deeth Farm
Woburn Sands
Ridgway
Shuttleworth Gro.
Gable Thorne
Stevens Fld.
Saunders Cl.
Sch.
Drive
19
31
133
91
92
93
240
39
38
37
F
G
H
J
K
1
2
3
4
5
6
7

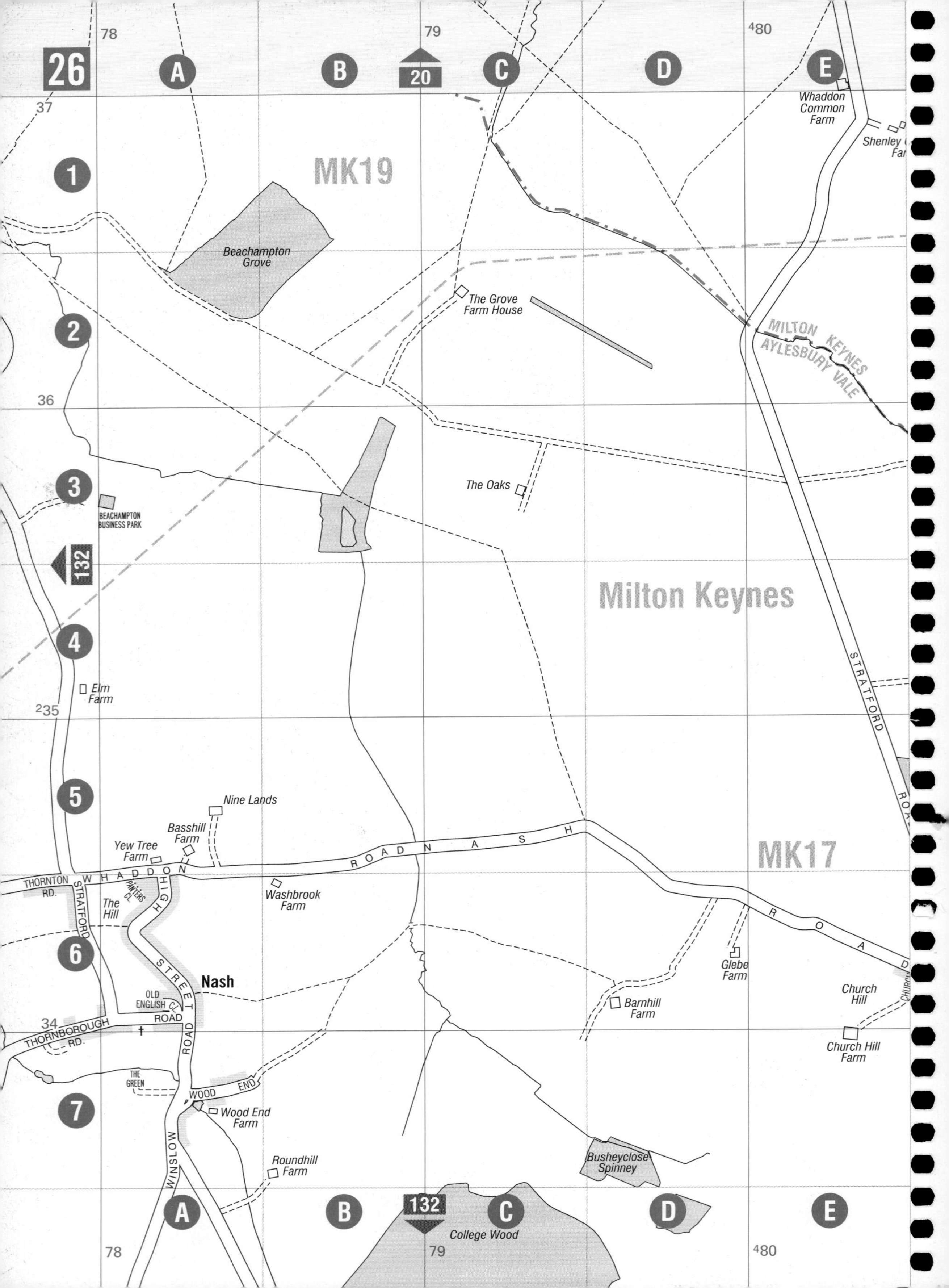

78
79
480
A
B
C
D
E
20
37
1
2
3
4
5
6
7
36
235
34
MK19
Beachampton Grove
The Grove Farm House
The Oaks
Whaddon Common Farm
Shenley
MILTON KEYNES
AYLESBURY VALE
BEACHAMPTON BUSINESS PARK
132
Milton Keynes
Elm Farm
STRATFORD
Nine Lands
Basshill Farm
Yew Tree Farm
WHADDON
NASH ROAD
THORNTON RD.
STRATFORD
PAINTERS CL.
HIGH STREET
The Hill
Washbrook Farm
MK17
ROAD
Glebe Farm
Church Hill
CHURCH
Barnhill Farm
Church Hill Farm
Nash
OLD ENGLISH CL.
THORNBOROUGH RD.
ROAD
THE GREEN
WOOD END
Wood End Farm
WINSLOW ROAD
Roundhill Farm
Busheyclose Spinney
College Wood

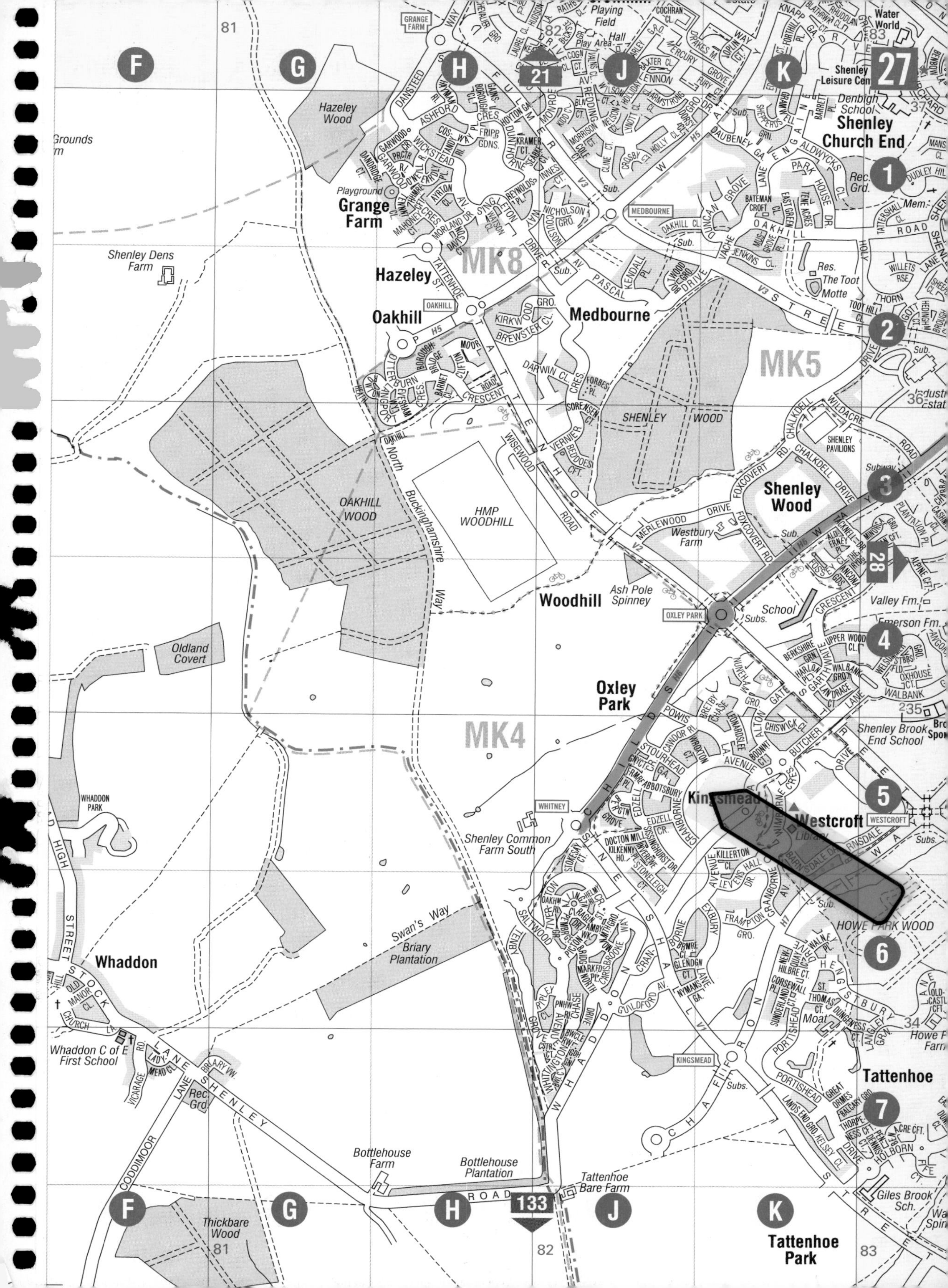
27
21
28
133
F
G
H
J
K
1
2
3
4
5
6
7
81
82
83
Shenley Church End
Shenley Leisure Centre
Denbigh School
Water World
Hazeley Wood
Grange Farm
Hazeley
Oakhill
Medbourne
MK8
MK5
MK4
Shenley Dens Farm
Shenley Wood
SHENLEY WOOD
OAKHILL WOOD
HMP WOODHILL
North Buckinghamshire Way
Woodhill
Ash Pole Spinney
Westbury Farm
Oxley Park
Oldland Covert
Kingsmead
Westcroft
Library
Shenley Common Farm South
Shenley Brook End School
HOWE PARK WOOD
Whaddon
WHADDON PARK
Whaddon C of E First School
Swan's Way
Briary Plantation
Bottlehouse Farm
Bottlehouse Plantation
Tattenhoe Bare Farm
Thickbare Wood
Tattenhoe
Tattenhoe Park
Giles Brook Sch.
Valley Fm.
Emerson Fm.
SHENLEY PAVILIONS
Playing Field
Play Area
Res.
The Toot Motte
Rec. Grd.
Playground
V2
V3
H5
H6
H7
V1

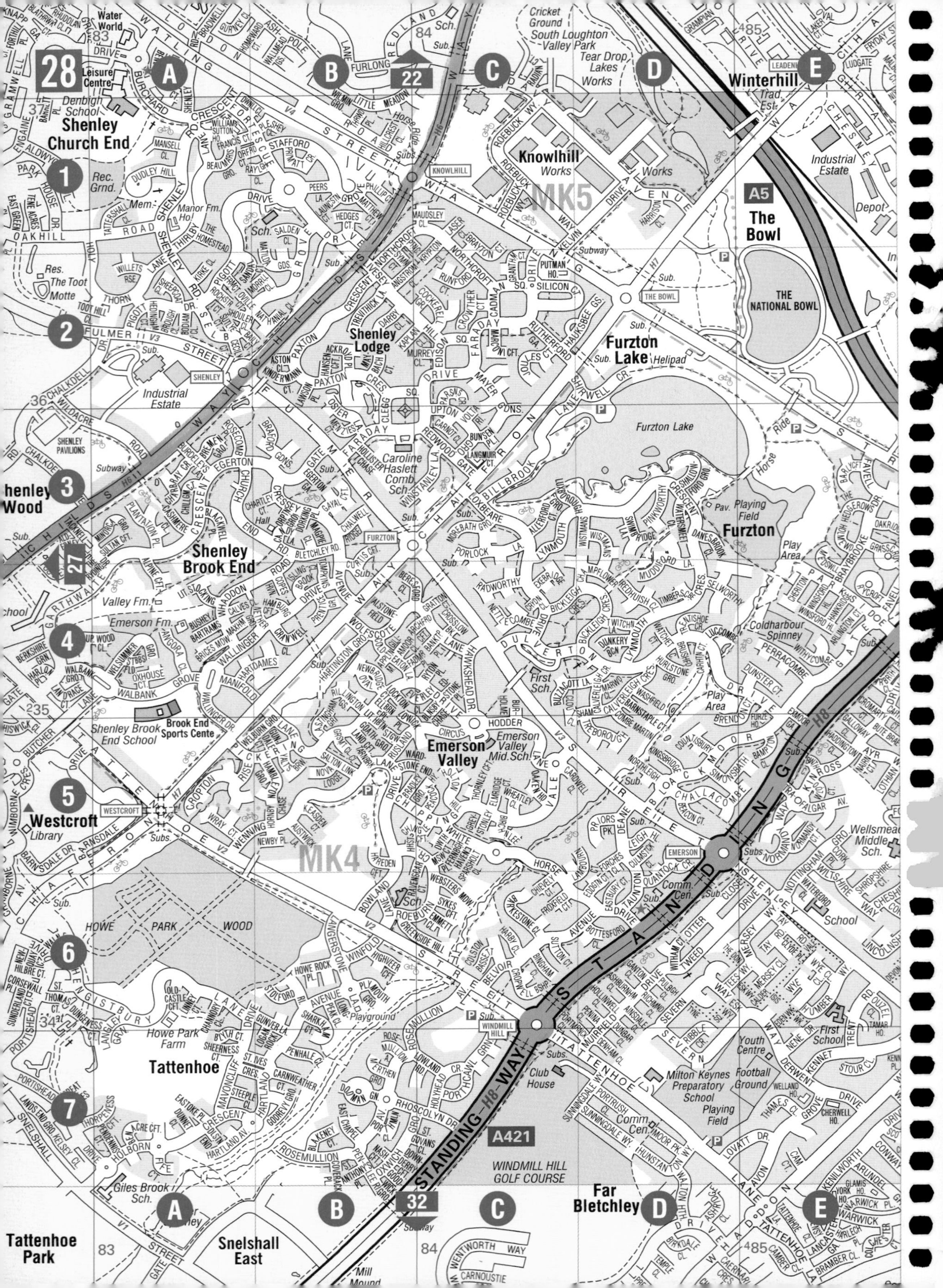
Shenley Church End
Water World
Leisure Centre
Denbigh School
Rec. Grnd.
Manor Fm. Ho.
Res. The Toot Motte
Industrial Estate
SHENLEY PAVILIONS
Shenley Wood
Shenley Lodge
Knowlhill Works
MK5
Cricket Ground
South Loughton Valley Park
Tear Drop Lakes Works
Winterhill Trad. Est.
Industrial Estate
A5
The Bowl
THE NATIONAL BOWL
Furzton Lake
Helipad
Caroline Haslett Comb. Sch.
Furzton
Playing Field
Play Area
Shenley Brook End
Valley Fm.
Emerson Fm.
Coldharbour Spinney
Shenley Brook End School
Brook End Sports Centre
Emerson Valley
Emerson Valley Mid.Sch.
First Sch.
Westcroft Library
MK4
HOWE PARK WOOD
Howe Park Farm
Tattenhoe
Giles Brook Sch.
Club House
WINDMILL HILL GOLF COURSE
Milton Keynes Preparatory School
Youth Centre
Football Ground
Playing Field
Wellsmead Middle Sch.
First School
A421
STANDING H8 WAY
Far Bletchley
Tattenhoe Park
Snelshall East
Mill Mound
22
27
32

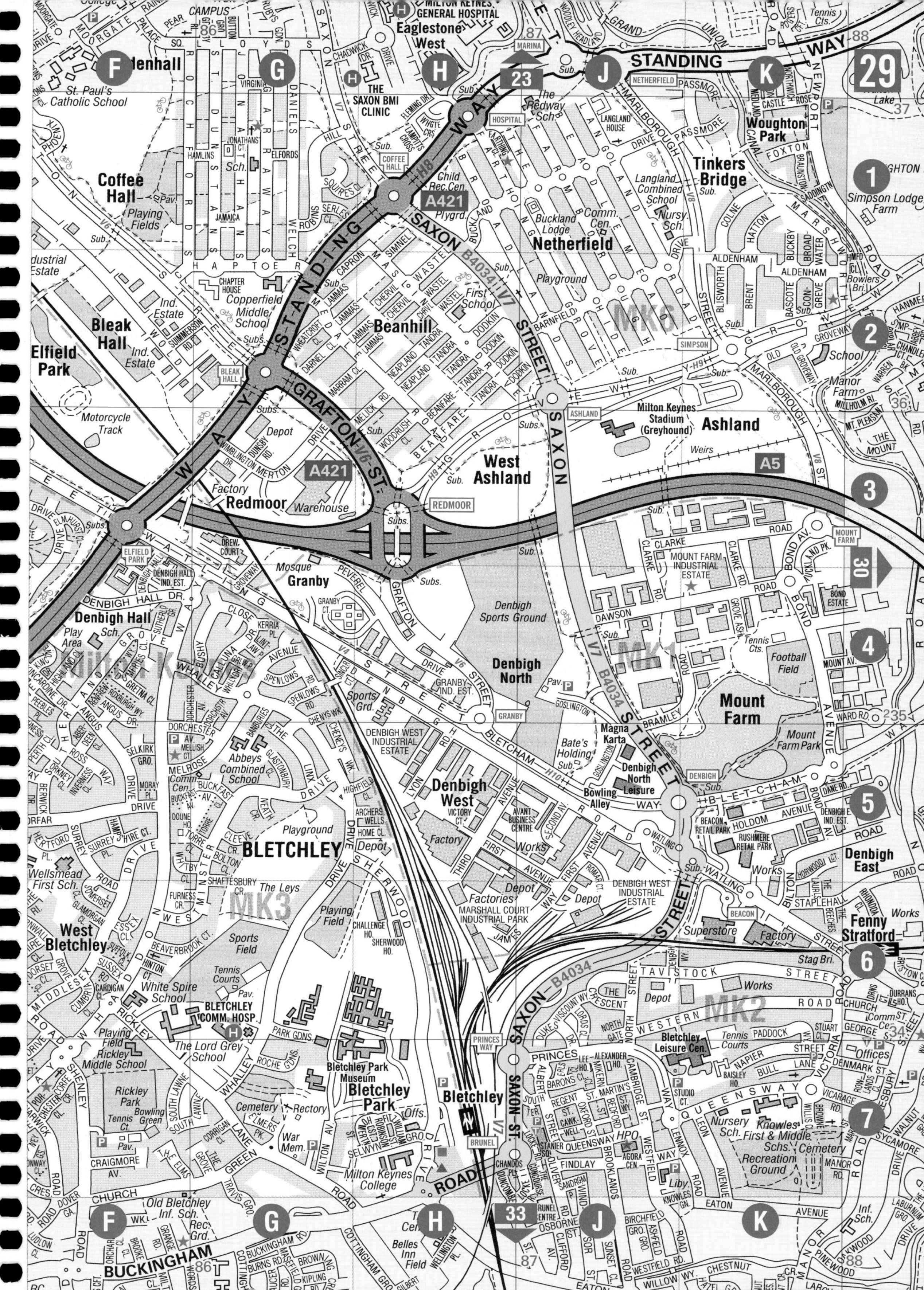
29
STANDING WAY
MILTON KEYNES GENERAL HOSPITAL
Eaglestone West
MARINA
23
THE SAXON BMI CLINIC
St. Paul's Catholic School
Coffee Hall
Playing Fields
Netherfield
Tinkers Bridge
Woughton Park
Simpson Lodge Farm
Langland Combined School
Buckland Lodge
Comm. Cen.
Playground
MK6
Industrial Estate
Bleak Hall
Ind. Estate
Elfield Park
Copperfield Middle School
CHAPTER HOUSE
Beanhill
First School
A421
SAXON STREET
B4034
V7
H8
H9
V6
GRAFTON ST.
Motorcycle Track
Depot
Warehouse
Factory
Redmoor
West Ashland
Ashland
Milton Keynes Stadium (Greyhound)
Weirs
A5
Manor Farm
School
REDMOOR
ELFIELD PARK
BLEAK HALL
ASHLAND
SIMPSON
MOUNT FARM
30
Mosque
Granby
Denbigh Sports Ground
MOUNT FARM INDUSTRIAL ESTATE
BOND ESTATE
MK1
Denbigh Hall
Play Area
Milton Keynes
Denbigh North
Football Field
Mount Farm
Mount Farm Park
Tennis Cts.
GRANBY IND. EST.
GRANBY
Magna Karta
Bate's Holding
Denbigh North Leisure
Bowling Alley
DENBIGH
BLETCHAM WAY
H10
Sports Grd.
DENBIGH WEST INDUSTRIAL ESTATE
Denbigh West
VICTORY CT.
AVANT BUSINESS CENTRE
Abbeys Combined School
BLETCHLEY
Playground
The Leys
Wellsmead First Sch.
MK3
West Bletchley
Playing Field
Sports Field
Tennis Courts
White Spire School
BLETCHLEY COMM. HOSP.
The Lord Grey School
Rickley Middle School
Rickley Park
Bowling Green
Tennis Ct.
Pav.
Factories
MARSHALL COURT INDUSTRIAL PARK
Depot
Works
BEACON RETAIL PARK
RUSHMERE RETAIL PARK
DENBIGH E. IND. EST.
Denbigh East
Fenny Stratford
Stag Bri.
Superstore
Factory
BEACON
MK2
Bletchley Leisure Cen.
Tennis Courts
Offices
Comm. Cen.
Bletchley Park Museum
Bletchley Park
Bletchley
PRINCES WAY
BRUNEL
Cemetery
Rectory
War Mem.
Milton Keynes College
Nursery Sch.
Knowles First & Middle Schs.
Cemetery
Recreation Ground
HPO
AGORA CEN.
Liby.
Old Bletchley Inf. Sch.
Rec. Grd.
Belles Inn Field
33
BUCKINGHAM
CHURCH
QUEENSWAY
WATLING ST.
VICTORIA ROAD
Inf. Sch.
F
G
H
J
K
1
2
3
4
5
6
7
86
87
88
34
36
37
235

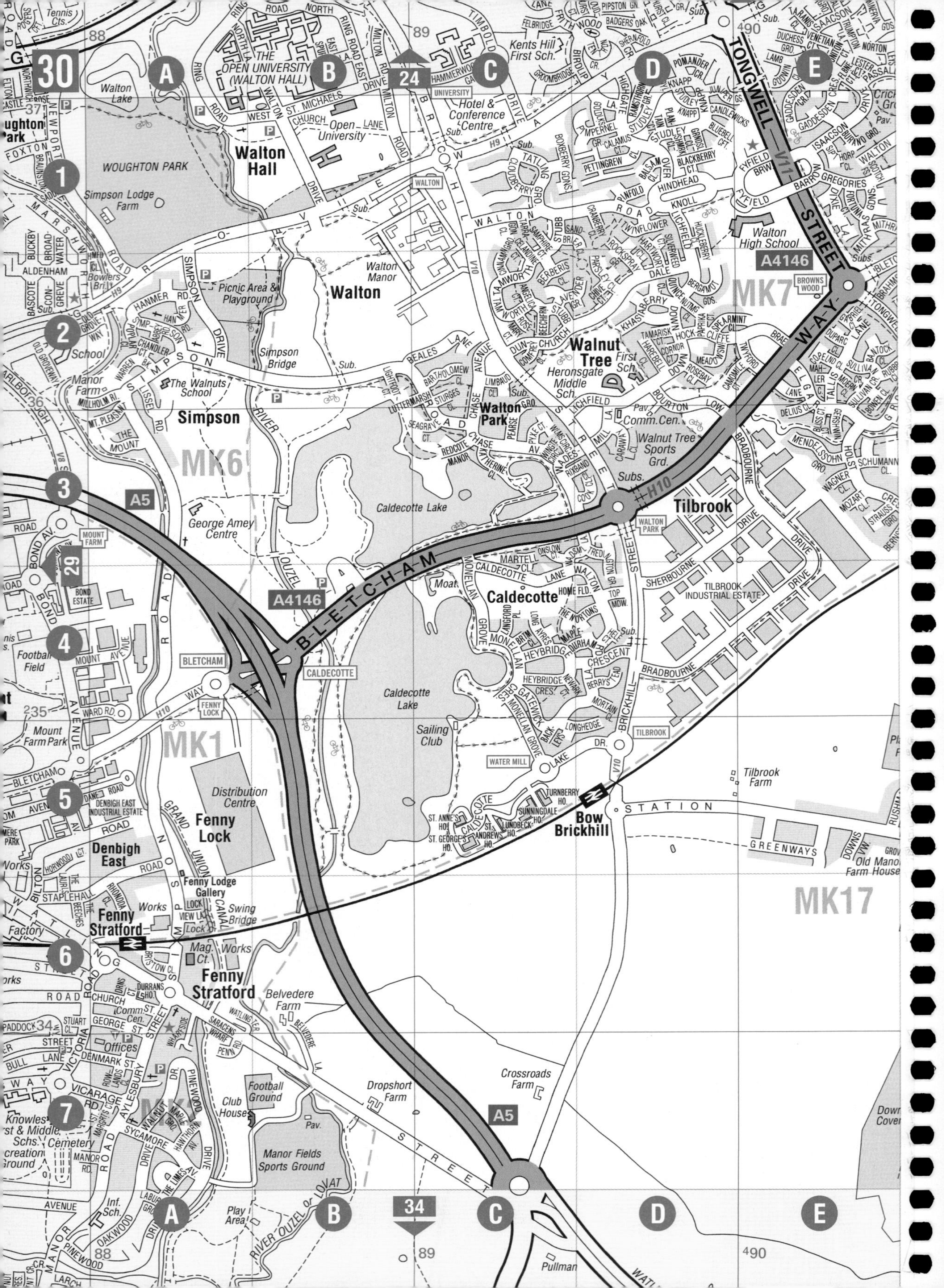
Walton Lake
WOUGHTON PARK
Simpson Lodge Farm
THE OPEN UNIVERSITY (WALTON HALL)
Walton Hall
Open University
Hotel & Conference Centre
Kents Hill First Sch.
Walton Manor
Walton
Picnic Area & Playground
Simpson Bridge
The Walnuts School
Simpson
MK6
Walnut Tree
Heronsgate Middle Sch.
Walton Park
Comm.Cen.
Walnut Tree Sports Grd.
Walton High School
MK7
A4146
Caldecotte Lake
George Amey Centre
A5
BLETCHAM
Tilbrook
TILBROOK INDUSTRIAL ESTATE
Caldecotte
Moat
Sailing Club
Caldecotte Lake
Distribution Centre
Fenny Lock
MK1
Denbigh East
DENBIGH EAST INDUSTRIAL ESTATE
Mount Farm Park
Football Field
Fenny Lodge Gallery
Swing Bridge
Fenny Stratford
Bow Brickhill
Tilbrook Farm
Old Manor Farm House
MK17
Belvedere Farm
Crossroads Farm
Dropshort Farm
Football Ground
Club House
Manor Fields Sports Ground
Play Area
RIVER OUZEL or LOVAT
Cemetery
Pullman
B-L-E-T-C-H-A-M W-A-Y
TONGWELL STREET
V11
H10
V10
H9
STATION
GREENWAYS
WATLING STREET
24
29
34
88
89
490
A B C D E
1 2 3 4 5 6 7

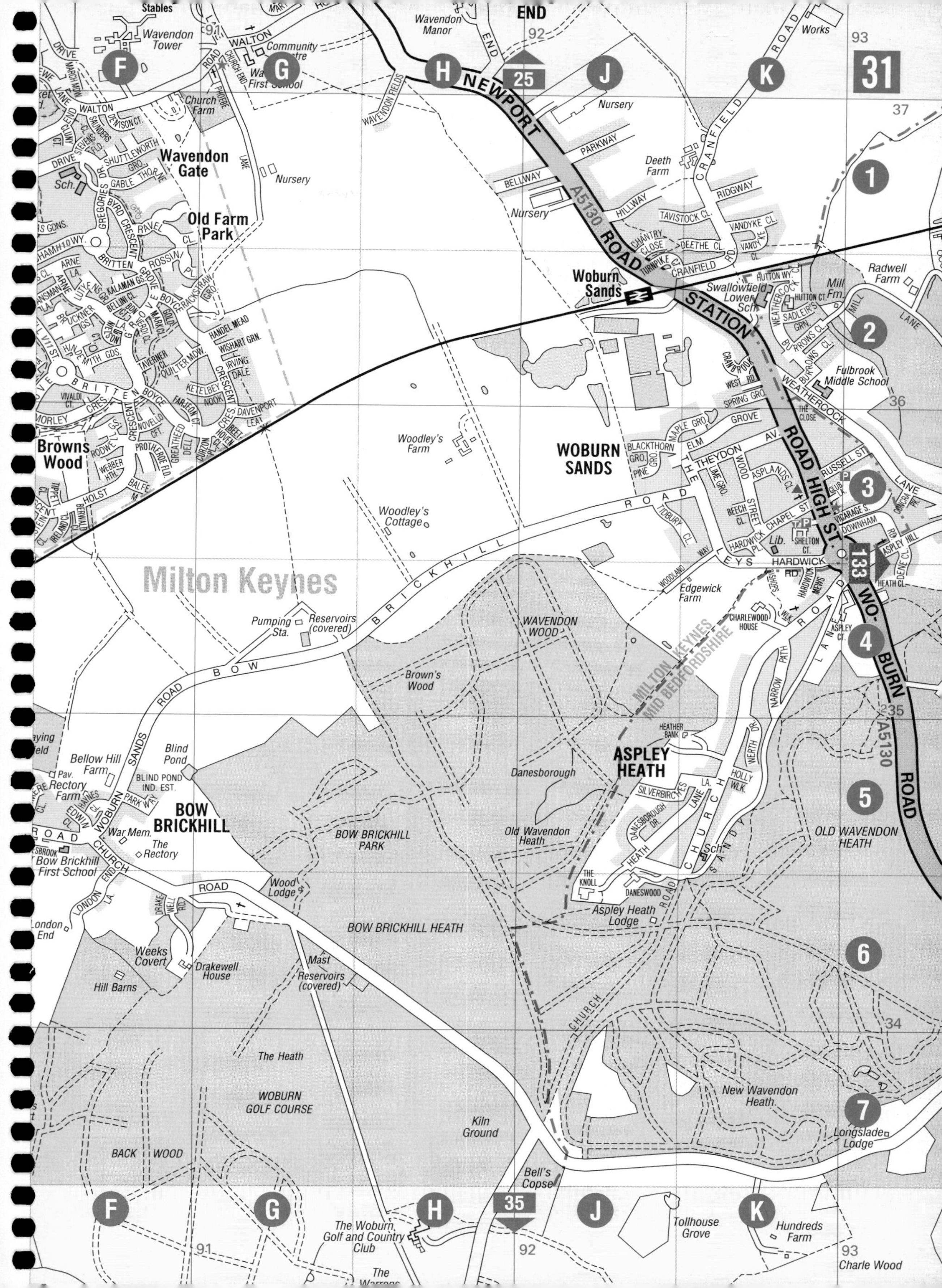
Wavendon Tower
Wavendon Manor
Community Centre
Walton First School
Church Farm
NEWPORT
ROAD
A5130
Nursery
PARKWAY
BELLWAY
Deeth Farm
CRANFIELD
RIDGWAY
HILLWAY
TAVISTOCK CL.
VANDYKE CL.
Wavendon Gate
Sch.
Old Farm Park
BRITTEN GROVE
Woburn Sands
STATION
Swallowfield Lower Sch.
Radwell Farm
Mill Fm.
Fulbrook Middle School
WEATHERCOCK
SPRING GRO.
MAPLE GRO.
GROVE
ELM
THEYDON AV.
Woodley's Farm
Woodley's Cottage
WOBURN SANDS
ROAD HIGH ST.
RUSSELL ST.
BLACKTHORN GRO.
PINE GRO.
LIME GRO.
ASPLANDS CL.
BEECH CL.
CHAPEL ST.
Lib.
HARDWICK RD.
LEYS
Browns Wood
HOLST
BRICKHILL ROAD
Milton Keynes
Pumping Sta.
Reservoirs (covered)
Edgewick Farm
CHARLEWOOD HOUSE
WAVENDON WOOD
Brown's Wood
BOW
MILTON KEYNES
MID BEDFORDSHIRE
WOBURN ROAD
A5130
Blind Pond
Bellow Hill Farm
Rectory Farm
BLIND POND IND. EST.
BOW BRICKHILL
Danesborough
ASPLEY HEATH
Old Wavendon Heath
OLD WAVENDON HEATH
BOW BRICKHILL PARK
War Mem.
The Rectory
Bow Brickhill First School
Wood Lodge
THE KNOLL
DANESWOOD
Aspley Heath Lodge
London End
Weeks Covert
Drakewell House
Hill Barns
BOW BRICKHILL HEATH
Mast
Reservoirs (covered)
The Heath
WOBURN GOLF COURSE
New Wavendon Heath
Longslade Lodge
Kiln Ground
BACK WOOD
Bell's Copse
The Woburn Golf and Country Club
Tollhouse Grove
Hundreds Farm
Charle Wood
F G H J K
1 2 3 4 5 6 7
25
35
133
91 92 93
37 36 35 34

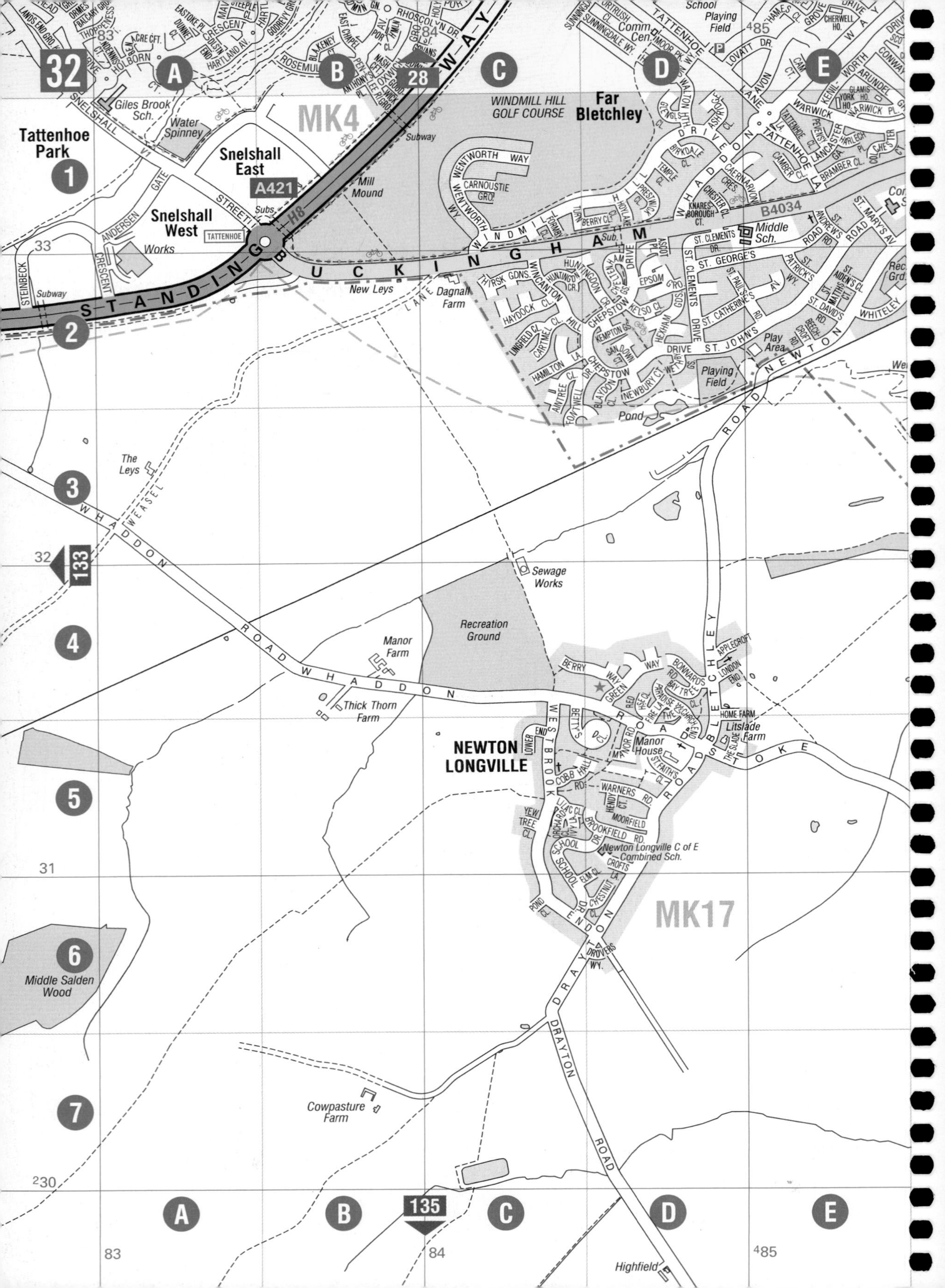

32
A
B
C
D
E
28
MK4
MK17
Tattenhoe Park
Giles Brook Sch.
Water Spinney
Snelshall East
Snelshall West
A421
Mill Mound
Subs.
Subway
TATTENHOE
Works
WINDMILL HILL GOLF COURSE
Far Bletchley
School Playing Field
Comm. Cen.
WENTWORTH WAY
CARNOUSTIE GRO.
B4034
BUCKINGHAM
STANDING
STREET
WHADDON WAY
WINDMILL HILL
Middle Sch.
St. CLEMENTS DR.
ST. GEORGE'S
ST. CLEMENTS DRIVE
ST. CATHERINE'S AV.
ST. JOHN'S DRIVE
Play Area
Playing Field
NEWTON ROAD
Pond
New Leys
Dagnall Farm
HAYDOCK CL.
CHEPSTOW
WINCANTON
HUNTINGDON
EPSOM GRO.
NEWBURY CL.
WHITELEY
The Leys
WHADDON ROAD
WEASEL
Sewage Works
Recreation Ground
Manor Farm
Thick Thorn Farm
NEWTON LONGVILLE
BERRY WAY
BONNARDS RD.
APPLECROFT
LONDON END
HOME FARM
Litslade Farm
Manor House
WESTBROOK END
COBB HALL RD.
WARNERS RD.
MOORFIELD
BROOKFIELD RD.
SCHOOL DR.
Newton Longville C of E Combined Sch.
CROFTS LA.
CHESTNUT
DROVERS WY.
DRAYTON ROAD
STOKE
BLETCHLEY ROAD
Middle Salden Wood
Cowpasture Farm
Highfield
133
135
1
2
3
4
5
6
7
83
84
485
33
32
31
230

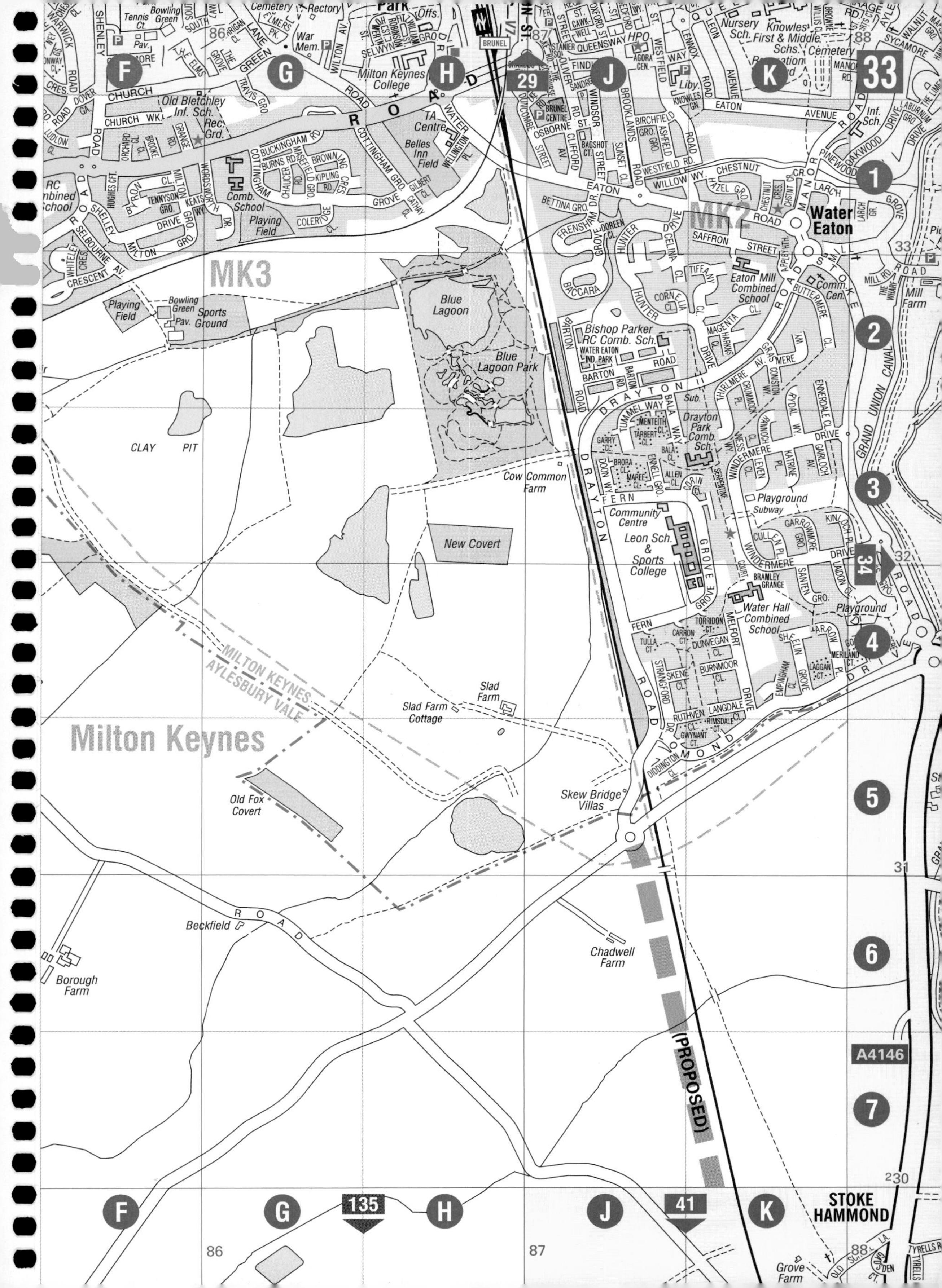
33
MK3
MK2
Milton Keynes
Water Eaton
Blue Lagoon
Blue Lagoon Park
CLAY PIT
New Covert
Cow Common Farm
Slad Farm
Slad Farm Cottage
Old Fox Covert
Skew Bridge Villas
Beckfield
Chadwell Farm
Borough Farm
STOKE HAMMOND
Grove Farm
MILTON KEYNES
AYLESBURY VALE
(PROPOSED)
GRAND UNION CANAL
A4146
Leon Sch. & Sports College
Community Centre
Drayton Park Comb. Sch.
Water Hall Combined School
Eaton Mill Combined School
Bishop Parker RC Comb. Sch.
Milton Keynes College
Old Bletchley Inf. Sch.
Comb. School
Playing Field
Sports Ground
Belles Inn Field
TA Centre
29
34
41
135
F
G
H
J
K
86
87
88

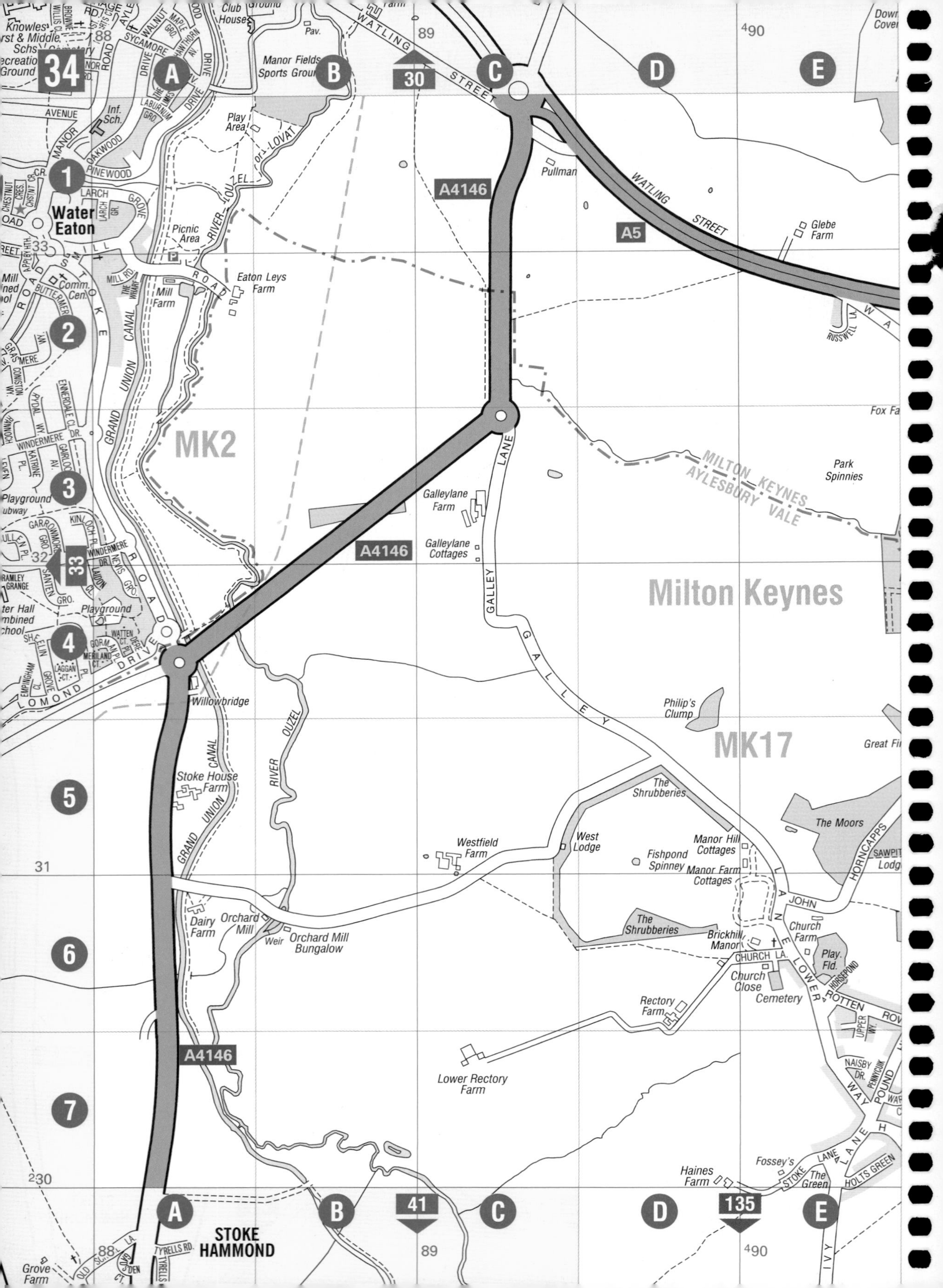

Water Eaton
MK2
MK17
Milton Keynes
MILTON KEYNES
AYLESBURY VALE
A4146
A5
WATLING STREET
GRAND UNION CANAL
RIVER OUZEL
GALLEY LANE
STOKE ROAD
LOMOND DRIVE
Manor Fields Sports Ground
Play Area
Picnic Area
Eaton Leys Farm
Mill Farm
Pullman
Glebe Farm
Galleylane Farm
Galleylane Cottages
Fox Farm
Park Spinnies
Philip's Clump
Willowbridge
Stoke House Farm
Westfield Farm
West Lodge
The Shrubberies
Manor Hill Cottages
Fishpond Spinney
Manor Farm Cottages
Dairy Farm
Orchard Mill
Weir
Orchard Mill Bungalow
Brickhill Manor
Church Farm
Church Close
Cemetery
Rectory Farm
Lower Rectory Farm
The Moors
Haines Farm
Fossey's
The Green
HOLTS GREEN
STOKE HAMMOND
Grove Farm
Playground
Comm. Cen.
Inf. Sch.
Pav.
Club House
Great Fi
RUSSWELL LA.
HORNCAPPS
CHURCH LA.
JOHN
LOWER
ROTTEN ROW
HORSEPOND
UPPER WY.
NAISBY DR.
POUND
IVY
TYRELLS RD.
30
33
41
135
88
89
490
31
230

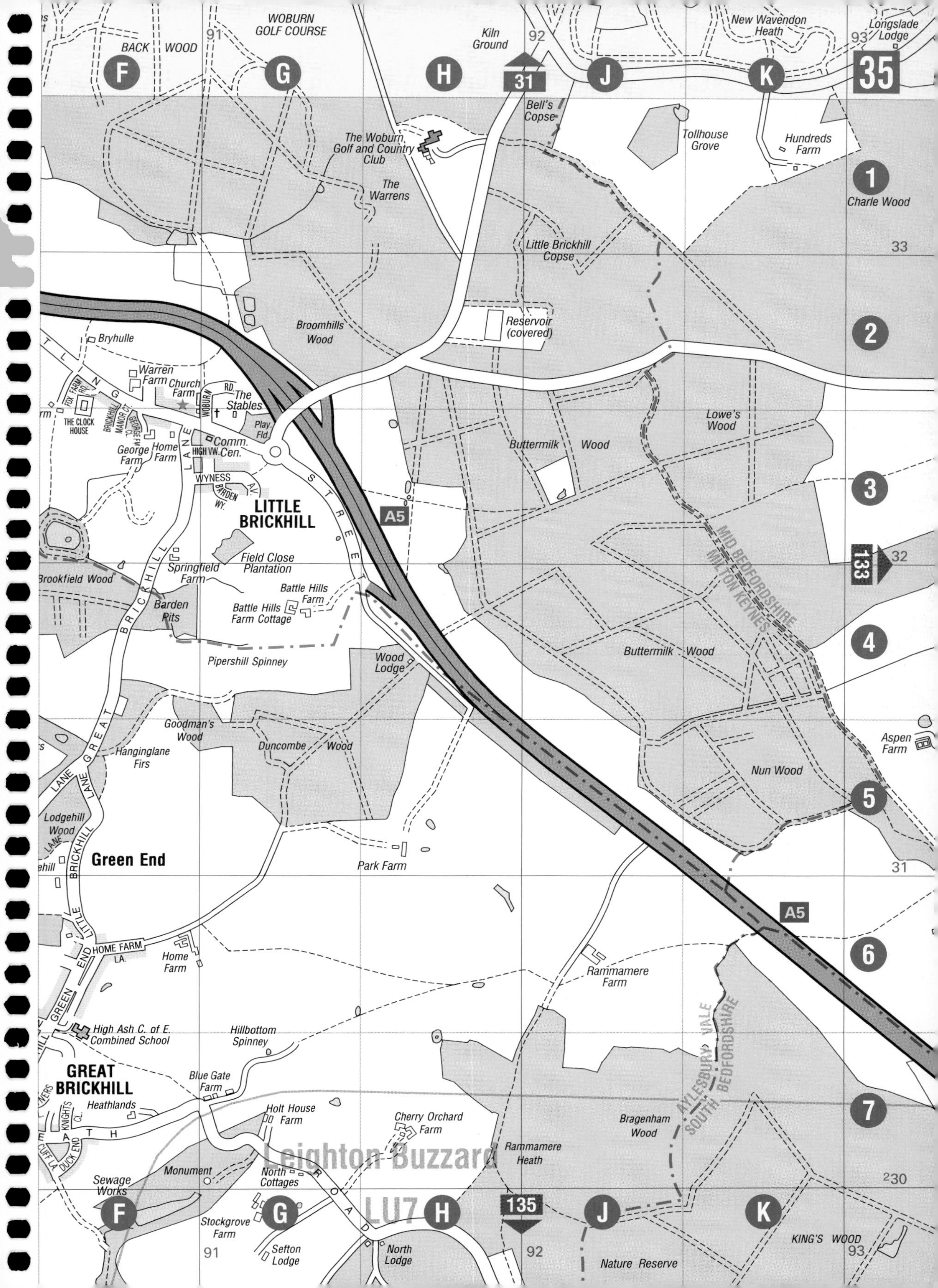

WOBURN GOLF COURSE
BACK WOOD
Kiln Ground
New Wavendon Heath
Longslade Lodge
F
G
H
31
J
K
Bell's Copse
The Woburn Golf and Country Club
Tollhouse Grove
Hundreds Farm
1
Charle Wood
The Warrens
Little Brickhill Copse
Reservoir (covered)
Broomhills Wood
2
Bryhulle
Warren Farm
Church Farm
The Stables
THE CLOCK HOUSE
Play. Fld.
Comm. Cen.
George Farm
Home Farm
WYNESS AV.
BARDEN WY.
Lowe's Wood
Buttermilk Wood
3
LITTLE BRICKHILL
A5
MID BEDFORDSHIRE
MILTON KEYNES
Field Close Plantation
Springfield Farm
Brookfield Wood
133
Battle Hills Farm
Battle Hills Farm Cottage
Barden Pits
4
Buttermilk Wood
Pipershill Spinney
Wood Lodge
Goodman's Wood
Duncombe Wood
Aspen Farm
Hanginglane Firs
Nun Wood
5
Lodgehill Wood
Green End
Park Farm
A5
6
Home Farm
Rammamere Farm
High Ash C. of E. Combined School
Hillbottom Spinney
AYLESBURY VALE
SOUTH BEDFORDSHIRE
GREAT BRICKHILL
Blue Gate Farm
Heathlands
Holt House Farm
Cherry Orchard Farm
Bragenham Wood
7
Leighton Buzzard
Rammamere Heath
Sewage Works
Monument
North Cottages
LU7
135
Stockgrove Farm
Sefton Lodge
North Lodge
KING'S WOOD
Nature Reserve
91
92
93
33
32
31
230

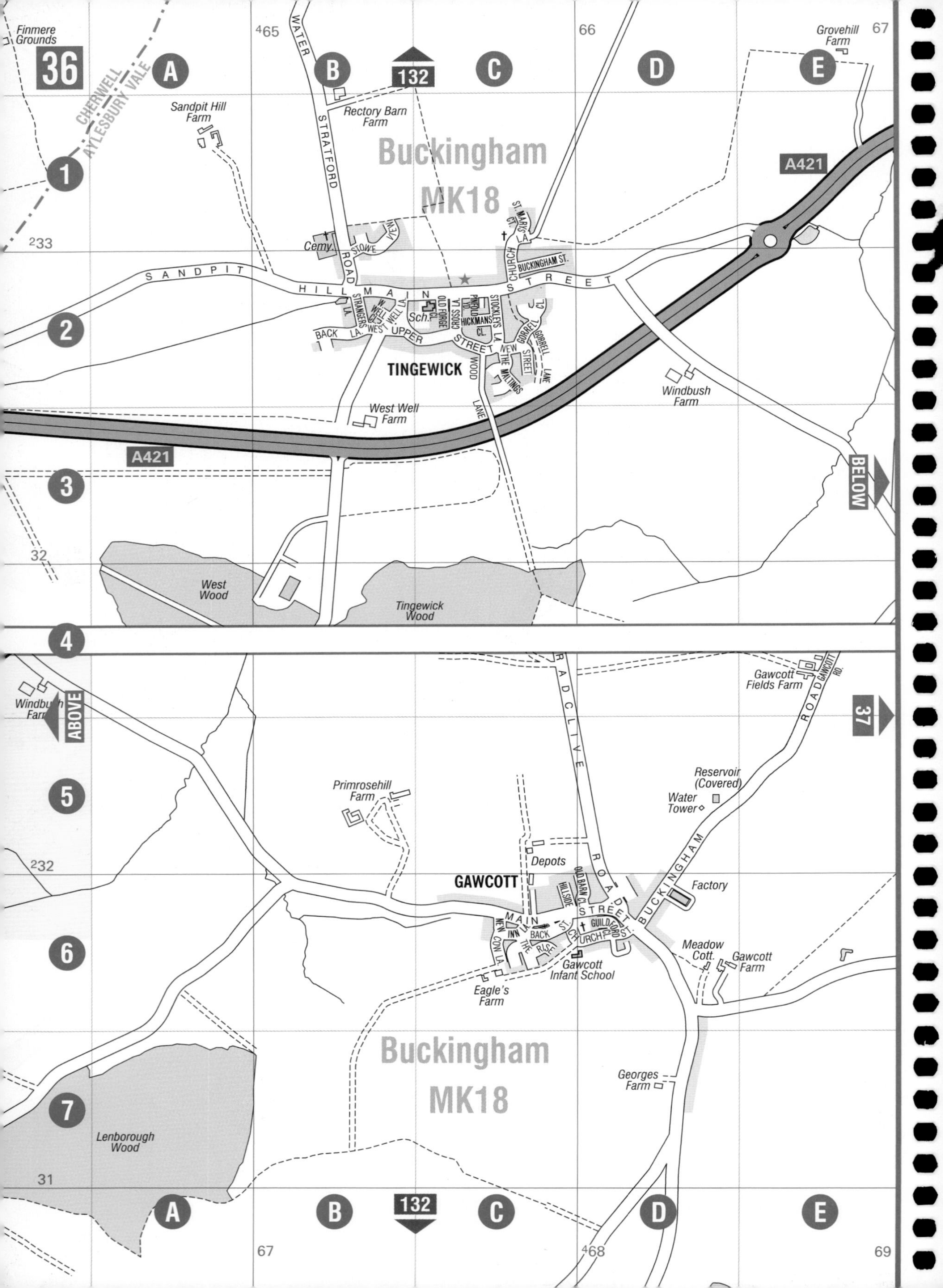
36
Finmere Grounds
CHERWELL
AYLESBURY VALE
Sandpit Hill Farm
Rectory Barn Farm
Buckingham
MK18
132
Cemy.
TINGEWICK
West Well Farm
Windbush Farm
A421
West Wood
Tingewick Wood
Grovehill Farm
BELOW
ABOVE
37
Gawcott Fields Farm
Primrosehill Farm
Reservoir (Covered)
Water Tower
Depots
GAWCOTT
Factory
Meadow Cott.
Gawcott Farm
Eagle's Farm
Gawcott Infant School
Georges Farm
Lenborough Wood
Buckingham
MK18
132

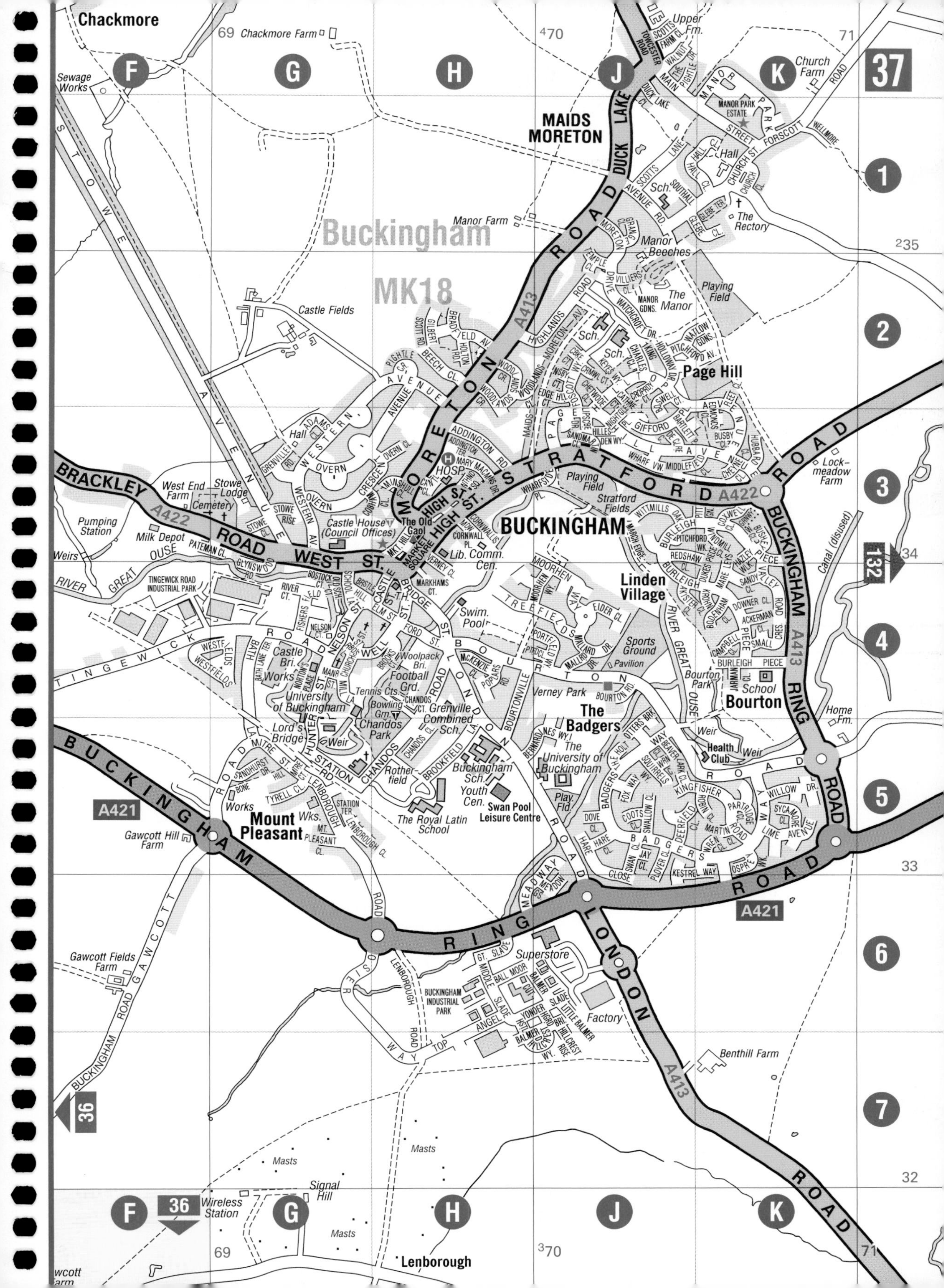
Chackmore
Chackmore Farm
Sewage Works
Upper Fm.
Church Farm
MANOR PARK ESTATE
MAIDS MORETON
Hall
Sch.
The Rectory
Manor Farm
Buckingham
MK18
Manor Beeches
Playing Field
The Manor
Castle Fields
Page Hill
Hall
West End Farm
Stowe Lodge
Cemetery
Pumping Station
Milk Depot
Weirs
RIVER GREAT OUSE
TINGEWICK ROAD INDUSTRIAL PARK
HOSP.
Castle House (Council Offices)
The Old Gaol
Lib. Comm. Cen.
BUCKINGHAM
Stratford Fields
Lock-meadow Farm
Linden Village
Swim. Pool
Sports Ground
Pavilion
Castle Bri.
Works
University of Buckingham
Woolpack Bri.
Football Grd.
Tennis Cts.
Bowling Grn.
Chandos Park
Grenville Combined Sch.
Verney Park
The Badgers
Bourton Park
School
Bourton
Home Fm.
Health Club
Weir
Lord's Bridge
Rotherfield
Buckingham Sch.
Youth Cen.
The University of Buckingham
Swan Pool Leisure Centre
The Royal Latin School
Play. Fld.
Mount Pleasant
Wks.
Works
Gawcott Hill Farm
Canal (disused)
Gawcott Fields Farm
Superstore
BUCKINGHAM INDUSTRIAL PARK
Factory
Benthill Farm
Masts
Signal Hill
Wireless Station
Lenborough
BRACKLEY ROAD
WEST ST.
STRATFORD ROAD
MORETON ROAD
DUCK LAKE
BUCKINGHAM RING
RING ROAD
LONDON ROAD
TINGEWICK ROAD
GAWCOTT ROAD
STOWE AVENUE
A413
A422
A421
F G H J K
1 2 3 4 5 6 7
69 470 71 235 34 33 32 370
132
36

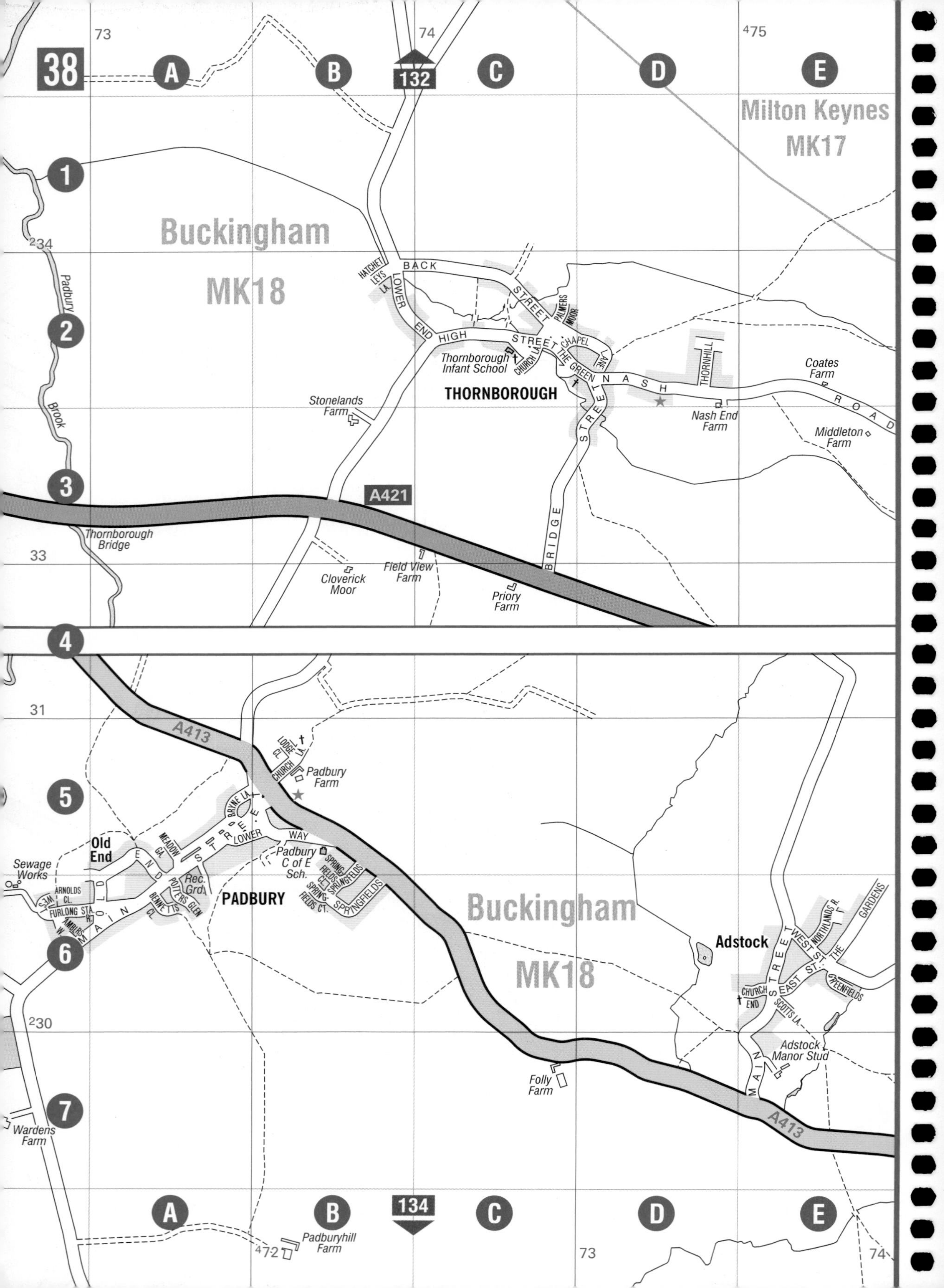

132
134
A
B
C
D
E
1
2
3
4
5
6
7
73
74
475
234
33
31
230
472
Milton Keynes
MK17
Buckingham
MK18
Padbury Brook
HATCHET LEYS LA.
LOWER END
BACK STREET
PALMERS MOOR
HIGH STREET
CHURCH LA.
CHAPEL LANE
THE GREEN
STREET
NASH ROAD
THORNHILL
Thornborough Infant School
THORNBOROUGH
Stonelands Farm
Coates Farm
Nash End Farm
Middleton Farm
A421
BRIDGE STREET
Thornborough Bridge
Cloverick Moor
Field View Farm
Priory Farm
A413
LODGE CL.
CHURCH LA.
Padbury Farm
BRYNE LA.
STREET
LOWER WAY
MEADOW GA.
Old End
END
Sewage Works
ARNOLDS CL.
WEST
FURLONG STA. R.
AMBURS
MAIN
OLD
BENNETTS CL.
POTTERS GLEN
Rec. Grd.
Padbury C of E Sch.
SPRINGFIELDS
SPRING-FIELDS CL.
SPRING-FIELDS CT.
PADBURY
Buckingham
MK18
Adstock
STREET
WEST ST.
NORTHLANDS R.
GARDENS
THE
CHURCH END
EAST ST.
GREENFIELDS
SCOTTS LA.
Adstock Manor Stud
MAIN ST.
Folly Farm
Wardens Farm
Padburyhill Farm
73
74

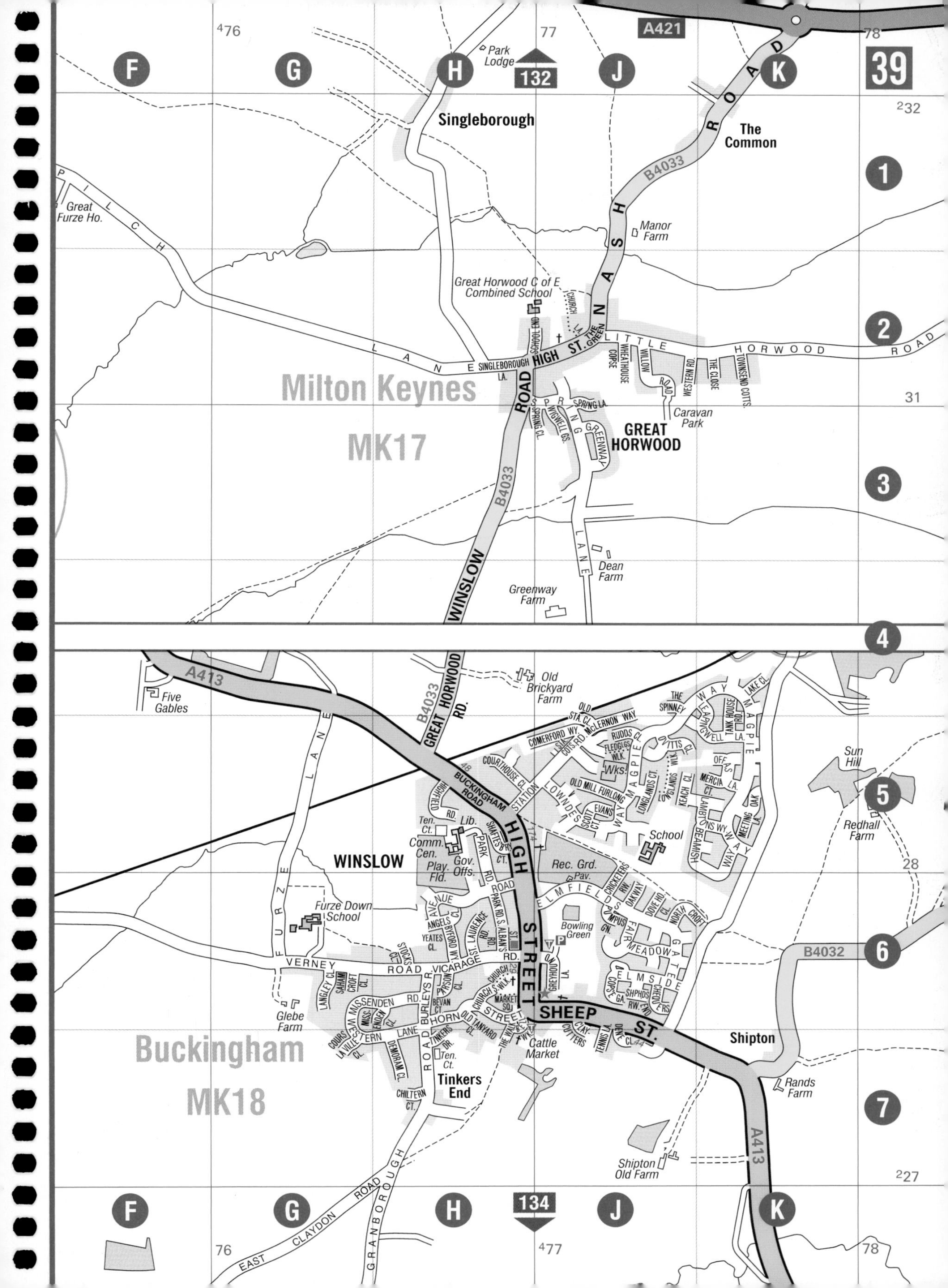
A421
Park Lodge
132
Singleborough
The Common
B4033
NASH ROAD
Great Furze Ho.
PILCH LANE
Manor Farm
Great Horwood C of E Combined School
SINGLEBOROUGH LA.
HIGH ST.
THE GREEN
CHURCH LA.
SCHOOL END
LITTLE HORWOOD ROAD
COPSE
WHEATHOUSE
WILLOW ROAD
WESTERN RD.
THE CLOSE
TOWNSEND COTTS.
Milton Keynes
MK17
SPRING LA.
SPRING CL.
WIGWELL GS.
GREENWAY
GREAT HORWOOD
Caravan Park
LANE
Dean Farm
Greenway Farm
WINSLOW ROAD
A413
Five Gables
GREAT HORWOOD RD.
Old Brickyard Farm
OLD STA. CL.
McLERNON WAY
COMERFORD WY.
THE SPINNEY
MAGPIE WAY
LAKE CL.
TANK HOUSE RD.
LEAPINGWELL LA.
RUDDS CL.
FLEDGLGS WLK.
COTSWOLD
Wks.
POTTS CL.
OFFAS LA.
MERCIA CT.
KEACH CL.
LAMBTONS WY.
MEETING OAK LA.
BEAMISH WAY
Sun Hill
Redhall Farm
COURTHOUSE CL.
STATION RD.
OLD MILL FURLONG
LONGLANDS CT.
LONGLANDS WLK.
LOWNDES WAY
SCOTT CT.
EVANS
School
BUCKINGHAM ROAD
HIGHFIELD RD.
Ten. Ct.
Lib.
Comm. Cen.
SHAFTESBURY CT.
PARK RD.
WINSLOW
Play. Fld.
Gov. Offs.
Rec. Grd.
Pav.
CRICKETERS RW.
OAKWAY
DOVE HO. CL.
NORTH CROFT
FURZE LANE
Furze Down School
AVENUE
ANGELS CL.
BYFORD WY.
YEATES CL.
ST. LAURENCE RD.
PARK RD. S.
ST. ALBAN'S
HIGH STREET
ELMFIELDS
Bowling Green
CAMPUS GN.
FAIR MEADOW
GATE
ELMSIDE
VERNEY ROAD
STOCKS CL.
VICARAGE RD.
LANGLEY CL.
SAHAM CROFT CL.
PARSONS CL.
GREYHOUND LA.
CHURCH WLK.
MARKET SQ.
SHEEP ST.
MISSENDEN RD.
BEVAN CT.
HORN ST.
BURLEYS RD.
OLD TANYARD CL.
CHURCH ST.
WESTERN LANE
LA VILLE CL.
TINKERS DR.
DEMORAM CL.
Ten. Ct.
Cattle Market
COTTERS
TENNIS LA.
DENE CL.
Shipton
B4032
Glebe Farm
Buckingham
MK18
Tinkers End
CHILTERN CT.
Rands Farm
EAST CLAYDON ROAD
GRANBOROUGH ROAD
Shipton Old Farm
134
F G H J K
1 2 3 4 5 6 7
476 77 78
232 31 28 227
76 477 78

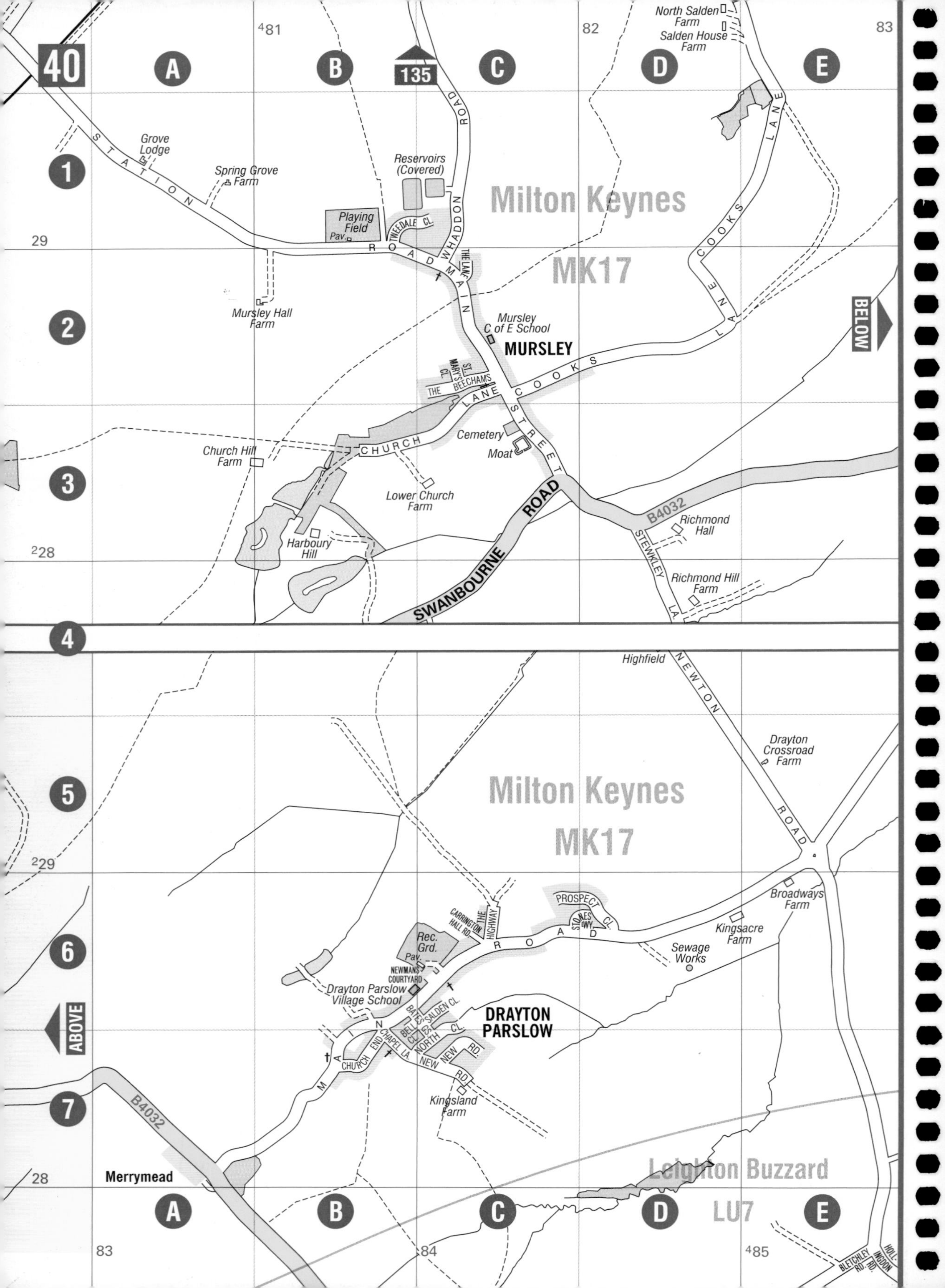

135
A
B
C
D
E
1
2
3
4
5
6
7
481
82
83
29
228
229
28
84
485
North Salden Farm
Salden House Farm
Grove Lodge
Spring Grove Farm
Reservoirs (Covered)
STATION
ROAD
WHADDON ROAD
Playing Field
Pav.
TWEEDALE CL.
Milton Keynes
MK17
MAIN
THE LANE
COOKS LANE
Mursley Hall Farm
Mursley C of E School
MURSLEY
ST. MARY'S CL.
THE BEECHAMS
CHURCH LANE
STREET
Cemetery
Moat
Church Hill Farm
Lower Church Farm
SWANBOURNE ROAD
B4032
Richmond Hall
STEWKLEY LA.
Richmond Hill Farm
Harboury Hill
BELOW
Highfield
NEWTON ROAD
Drayton Crossroad Farm
Milton Keynes
MK17
PROSPECT CL.
STONES WY.
CARRINGTON HALL RD.
THE HIGHWAY
ROAD
Broadways Farm
Kingsacre Farm
Sewage Works
Rec. Grd.
Pav.
NEWMANS COURTYARD
Drayton Parslow Village School
BATES CL.
SALDEN CL.
DRAYTON PARSLOW
BELLS CL.
NORTH CL.
MAIN
CHURCH END
CHAPEL LA.
NEW RD.
NEW RD.
Kingsland Farm
ABOVE
B4032
Merrymead
Leighton Buzzard
LU7
BLETCHLEY RD.
HOLLINGDON RD.

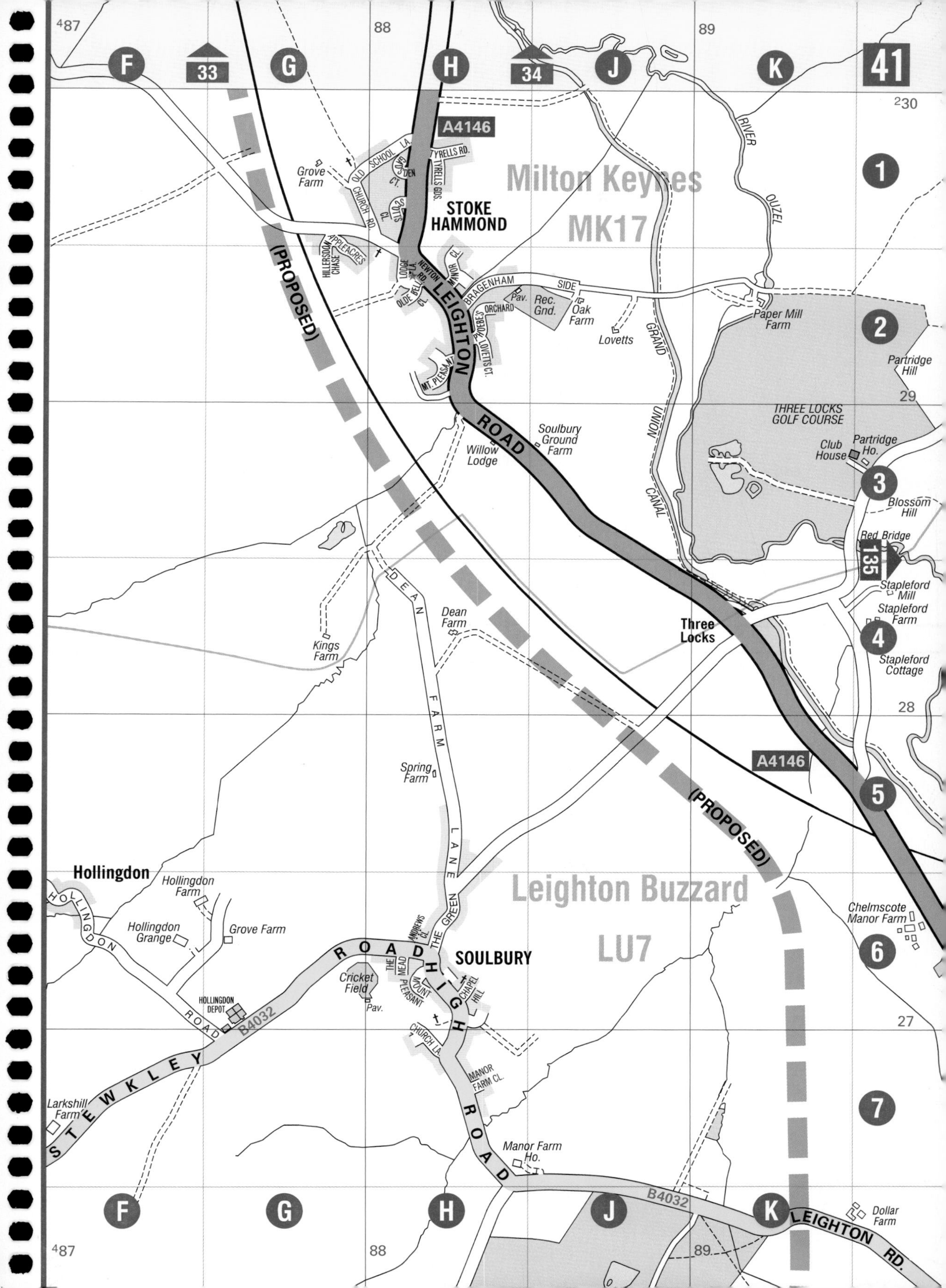

41
F
G
H
J
K
33
34
A4146
Milton Keynes
MK17
STOKE HAMMOND
Grove Farm
OLD SCHOOL LA.
TYRELLS RD.
TYRELLS GDS.
CHURCH RD.
HILLERSDON CHASE
APPLEACRES
LODGE LA.
NEWTON RD.
MANOR CL.
OLDE BELL CL.
BRAGENHAM SIDE
Pav.
Rec. Gnd.
Oak Farm
ORCHARD
PHOEBE'S
LOVETTS CT.
MT. PLEASANT
Lovetts
GRAND UNION CANAL
RIVER OUZEL
Paper Mill Farm
Partridge Hill
THREE LOCKS GOLF COURSE
Club House
Partridge Ho.
Blossom Hill
Red Bridge
135
Stapleford Mill
Stapleford Farm
Stapleford Cottage
LEIGHTON ROAD
(PROPOSED)
Soulbury Ground Farm
Willow Lodge
DEAN FARM LANE
Dean Farm
Kings Farm
Three Locks
Spring Farm
Leighton Buzzard
LU7
Hollingdon
Hollingdon Farm
HOLLINGDON ROAD
Hollingdon Grange
Grove Farm
HOLLINGDON DEPOT
B4032
STEWKLEY ROAD
Larkshill Farm
SOULBURY
THE GREEN
ANDREWS CL.
Cricket Field
Pav.
THE MEAD
MOUNT PLEASANT
HIGH ROAD
CHAPEL HILL
CHURCH LA.
MANOR FARM CL.
Manor Farm Ho.
Chelmscote Manor Farm
Dollar Farm
LEIGHTON RD.
1
2
3
4
5
6
7
230
29
28
27
487
88
89

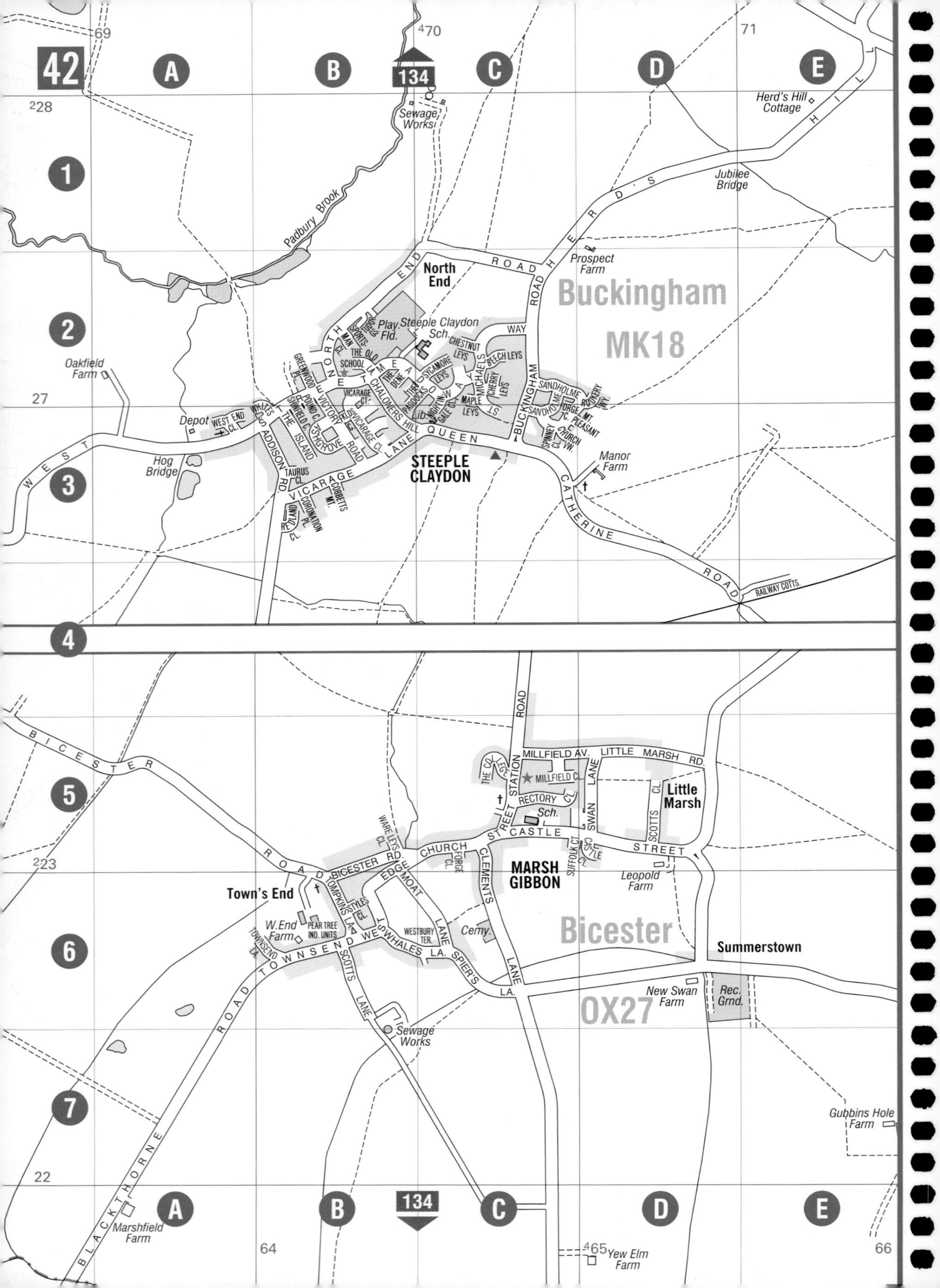

134
Sewage Works
Herd's Hill Cottage
Padbury Brook
Jubilee Bridge
North End
Prospect Farm
Buckingham
MK18
Play. Fld.
Steeple Claydon Sch.
Oakfield Farm
Depot
Hog Bridge
STEEPLE CLAYDON
Manor Farm
RAILWAY COTTS.
BICESTER ROAD
MILLFIELD AV.
LITTLE MARSH RD.
Little Marsh
MARSH GIBBON
Town's End
W.End Farm
PEAR TREE IND. UNITS
Leopold Farm
Bicester
Summerstown
New Swan Farm
Rec. Grnd.
OX27
Cemy.
Sewage Works
Gubbins Hole Farm
Marshfield Farm
Yew Elm Farm
BLACKTHORNE ROAD
TOWNSEND
WHALES LA.
SPIERS LA.

134

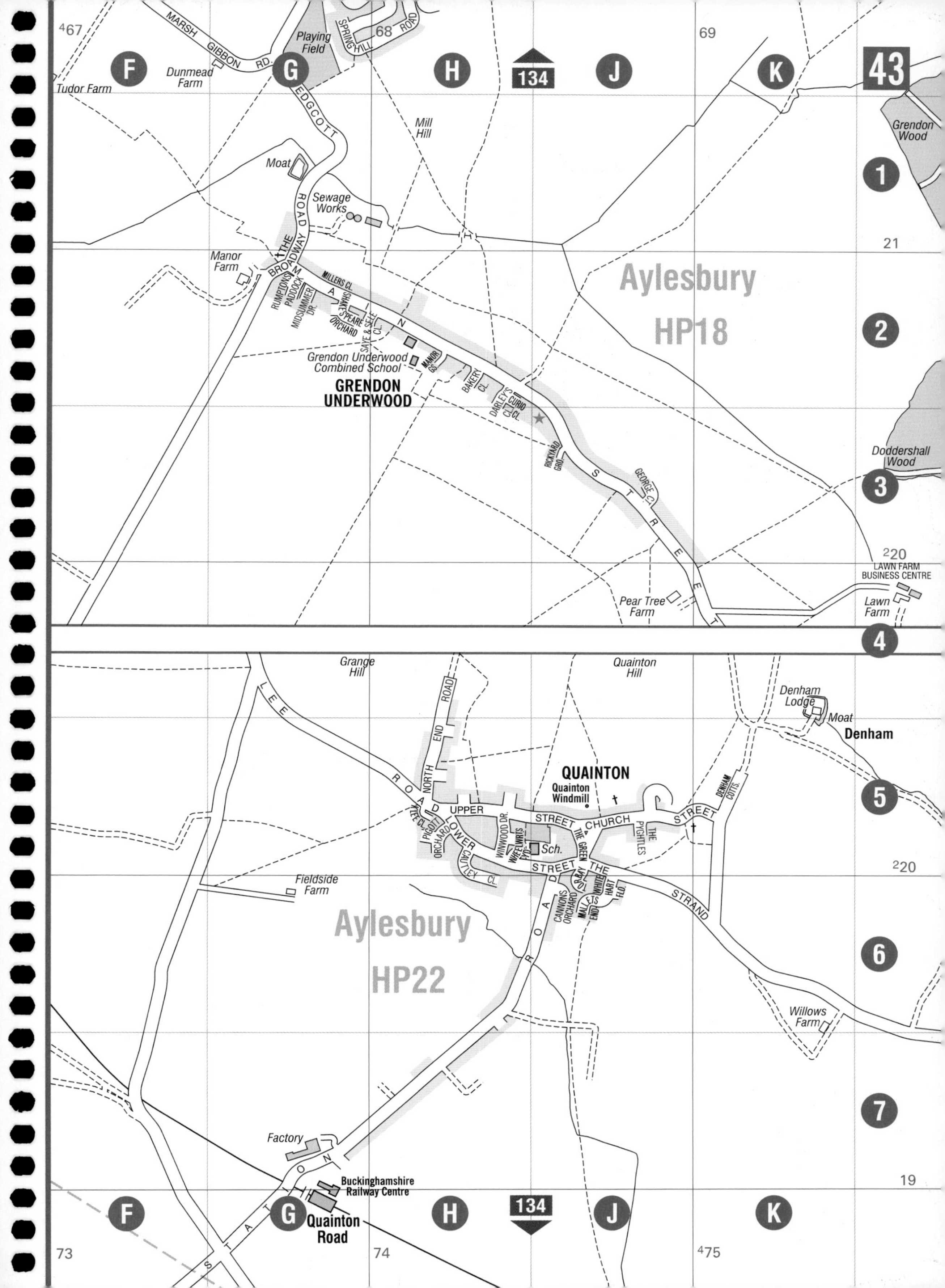

467
MARSH GIBBON RD.
Playing Field
SPRING HILL 68 ROAD
69
F
G
H
134
J
K
Dunmead Farm
Tudor Farm
EDGCOTT
Grendon Wood
Mill Hill
Moat
1
ROAD
Sewage Works
THE BROADWAY
21
Manor Farm
Aylesbury
HP18
MILLERS CL.
RUMPTONS PADDOCK
MIDSUMMER DR.
SHAKESPEARE ORCHARD
SAYE & SELE CL.
M A I N
2
Grendon Underwood Combined School
MANOR GS.
GRENDON UNDERWOOD
BAKERY CL.
DARLEY'S CL.
CURIO CL.
Doddershall Wood
RICKYARD GRO.
S T R E E T
GEORGE CL.
3
220
LAWN FARM BUSINESS CENTRE
Pear Tree Farm
Lawn Farm
4
Grange Hill
Quainton Hill
LEE ROAD
NORTH END ROAD
Denham Lodge
Moat
Denham
QUAINTON
Quainton Windmill
DENHAM COTTS.
5
UPPER STREET
CHURCH STREET
TREE CL.
PIGOTT ORCHARD
LOWER STREET
WINWOOD DR.
WHEELWRITS YD.
Sch.
THE GREEN
THE PYGHTLES
CAUTLEY CL.
Fieldside Farm
220
ROAD
CANNONS ORCHARD
DORMAY
MALLETS END
WHITE HART FLD.
THE STRAND
Aylesbury
HP22
6
Willows Farm
7
Factory
STATION
Buckinghamshire Railway Centre
Quainton Road
19
F
G
H
134
J
K
73
74
475

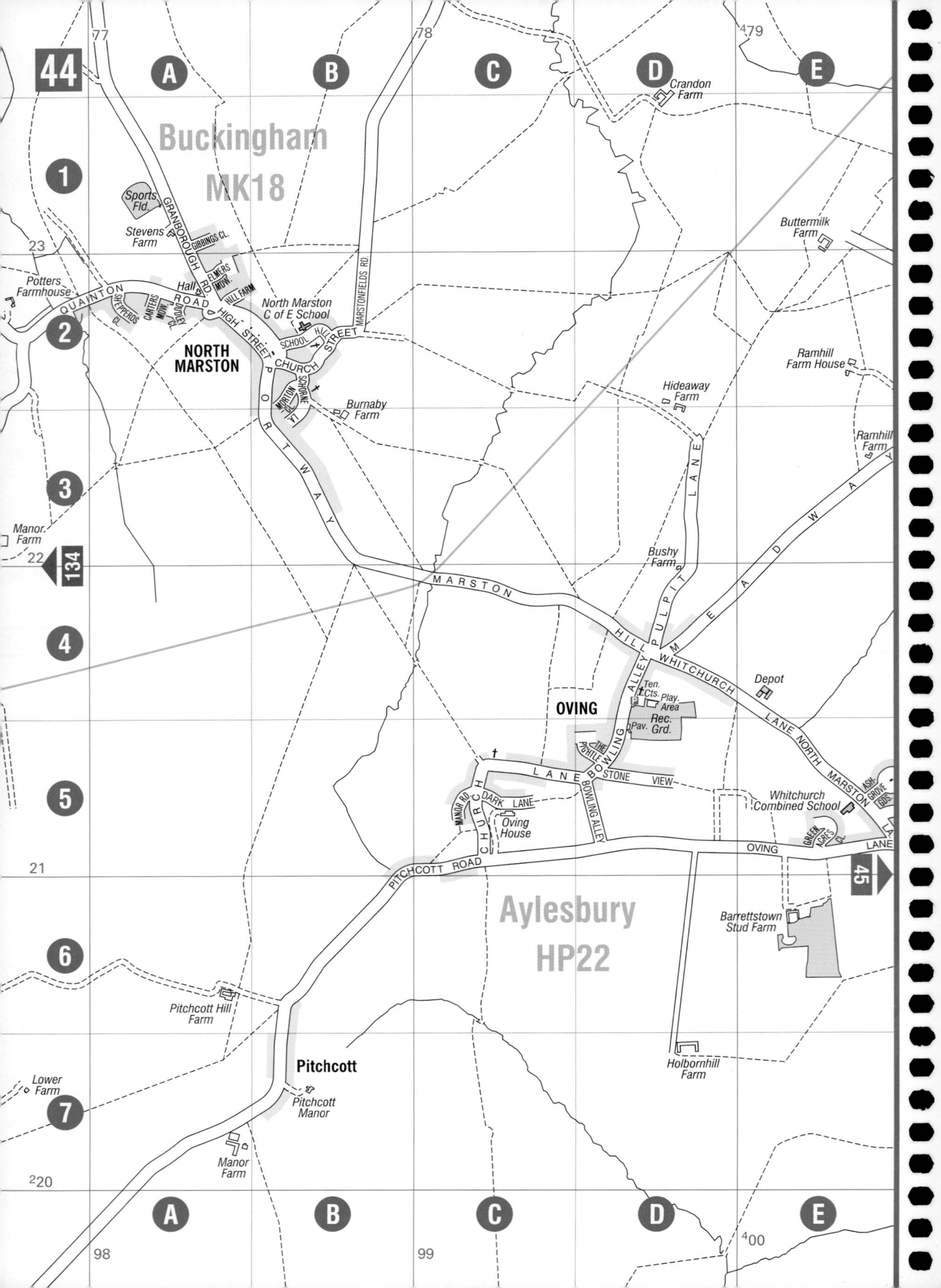
Buckingham
MK18
Aylesbury
HP22
NORTH MARSTON
OVING
Pitchcott
Sports Fld.
Stevens Farm
Potters Farmhouse
Hall
North Marston C of E School
Burnaby Farm
Crandon Farm
Buttermilk Farm
Ramhill Farm House
Hideaway Farm
Ramhill Farm
Bushy Farm
Depot
Ten. Cts.
Play. Area
Rec. Grd.
Pav.
Whitchurch Combined School
Oving House
Barrettstown Stud Farm
Holbornhill Farm
Pitchcott Hill Farm
Lower Farm
Pitchcott Manor
Manor Farm
GRANBOROUGH RD
GIBBINGS CL.
ELMERS MDW.
HILL FARM
QUAINTON ROAD
SHEPPERDS CL.
CARTERS MDW.
DUDLEY
HIGH STREET
SCHOOL HILL
STREET
CHURCH
MORTON CL.
SCHORNE LA.
MARSTONFIELDS RD.
PORTWAY
MARSTON HILL
PULPIT LANE
MEADWAY
ALLEY
WHITCHURCH LANE NORTH MARSTON LANE
ASH GROVE
GDS.
BOWLING ALLEY
THE PIGHTLE
LANE
STONE VIEW
DARK LANE
MANOR RD.
CHURCH
GREEN ACRES CL.
OVING LANE
PITCHCOTT ROAD
A
B
C
D
E
1
2
3
4
5
6
7
77
78
479
23
22
21
220
98
99
400
134
45

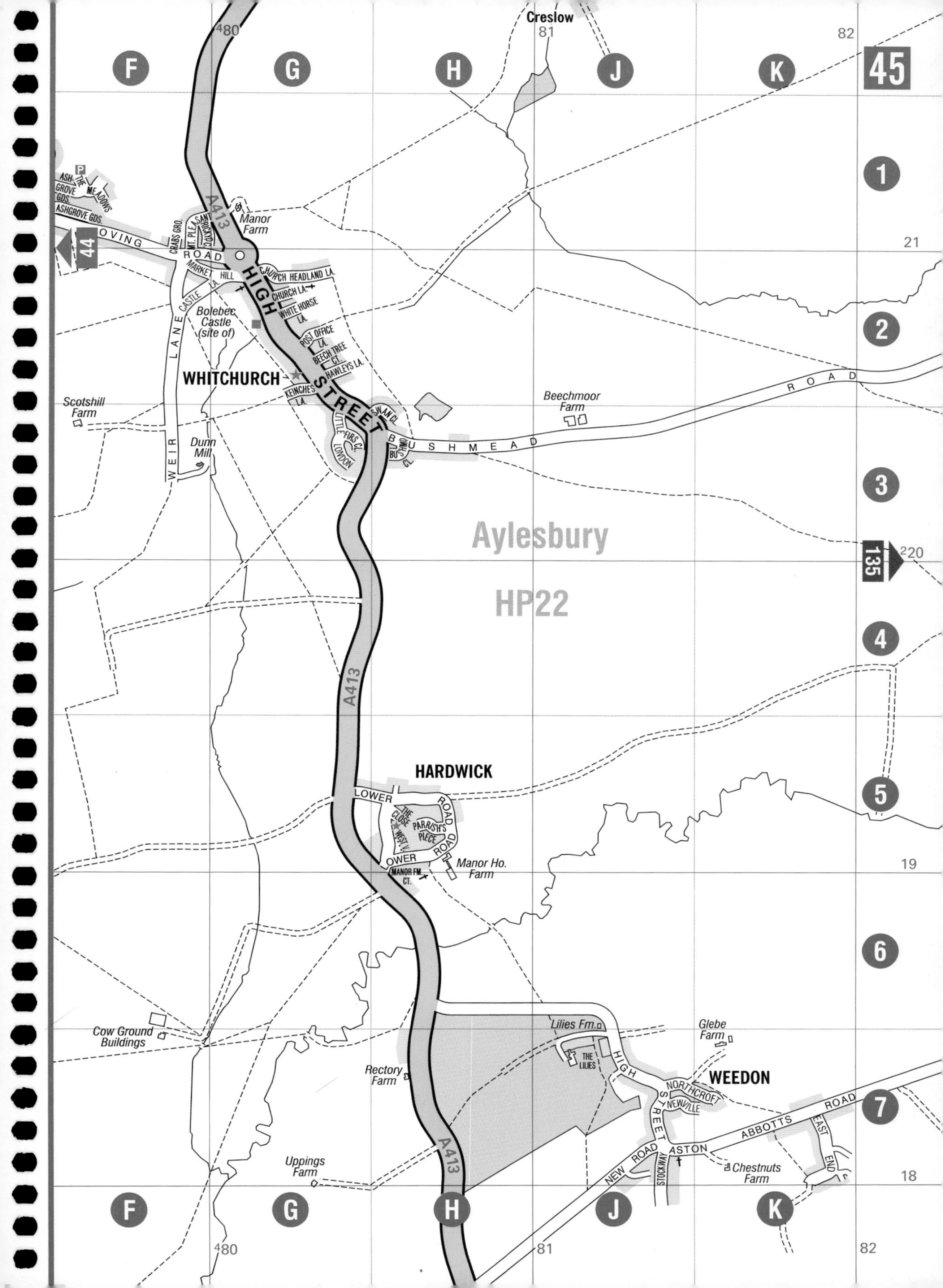

Creslow
F
G
H
J
K
1
2
3
4
5
6
7
44
135
480
81
82
21
220
19
18
A413
HIGH STREET
OVING ROAD
Manor Farm
ASHGROVE GDS.
THE MEADOWS
CRABS GRO.
MT. PLEASANT
MARKET HILL
CASTLE LA.
CHURCH HEADLAND LA.
CHURCH LA.
WHITE HORSE LA.
POST OFFICE LA.
BEECH TREE CT.
HAWLEYS LA.
KEINCHES LA.
SWAN CL.
LITTLE LONDON
FIRS CL.
BUSHMEAD ROAD
BUSHMEAD CL.
Bolebec Castle (site of)
WHITCHURCH
WEIR LANE
Scotshill Farm
Dunn Mill
Beechmoor Farm
Aylesbury
HP22
HARDWICK
LOWER ROAD
THE CLOSE
PARRISH'S PIECE
WEST V.
MANOR FM. CT.
Manor Ho. Farm
Cow Ground Buildings
Lilies Fm.
THE LILIES
Glebe Farm
Rectory Farm
WEEDON
HIGH STREET
NORTHCROFT
NEWVILLE
ABBOTTS ROAD
EAST END
ASTON
NEW ROAD
STOCKWAY
Chestnuts Farm
Uppings Farm

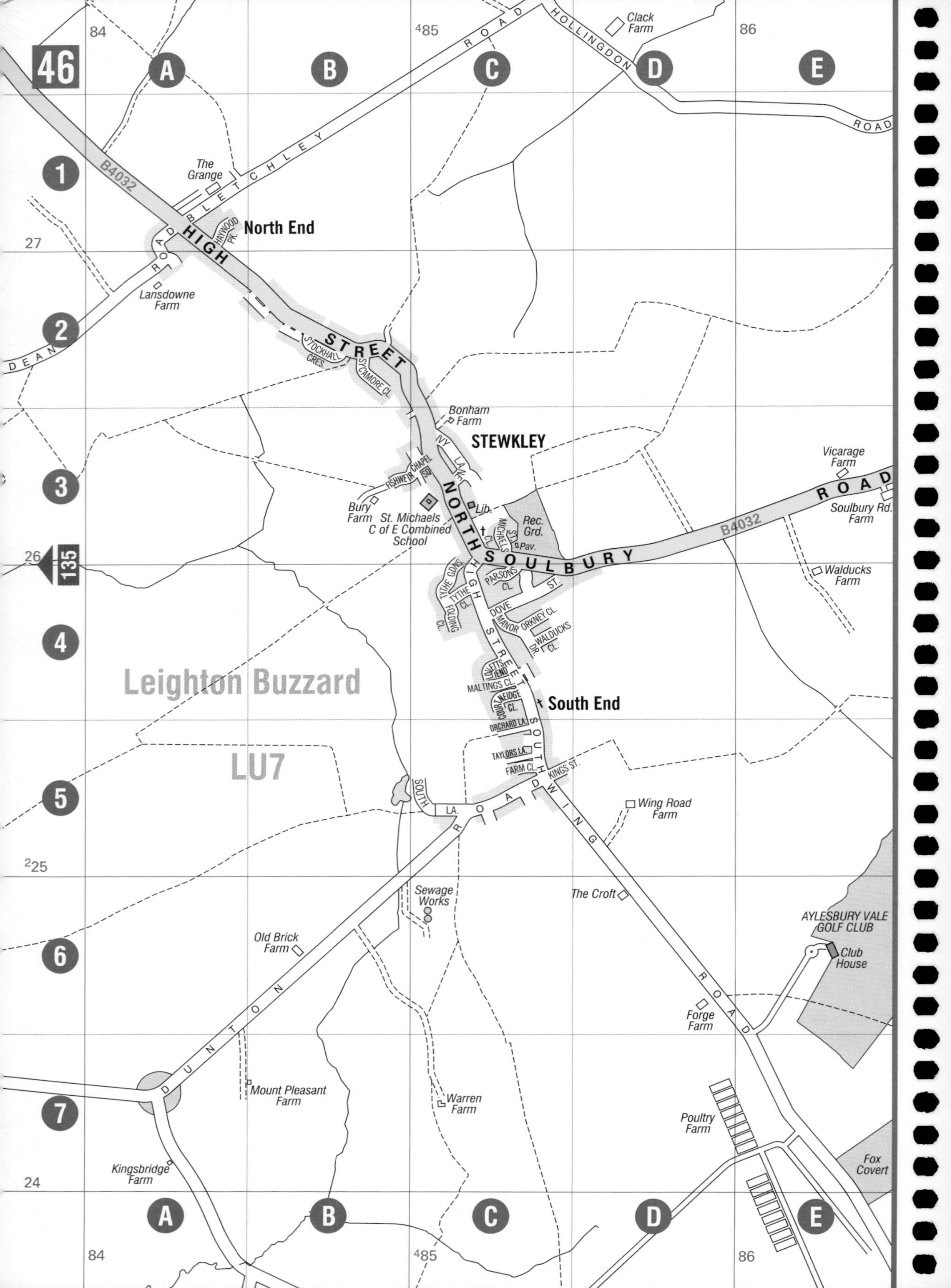

84
485
86
A
B
C
D
E
1
2
3
4
5
6
7
27
26
25
24
Clack Farm
HOLLINGDON
ROAD
BLETCHLEY ROAD
B4032
The Grange
North End
HIGH STREET
HAYWOOD PK.
Lansdowne Farm
DEAN
STOCKHALL CRES.
SYCAMORE CL.
Bonham Farm
STEWKLEY
IVY LANE
CHAPEL SQ.
FISHWEIR
NORTH
Lib.
Bury Farm
St. Michaels C of E Combined School
Rec. Grd.
Pav.
MICHAELS ST.
CL.
SOULBURY ROAD
B4032
Vicarage Farm
Soulbury Rd. Farm
Walducks Farm
135
TYTHE GDNS.
TYTHE CL.
FOLDING CL.
PARSONS CL.
ST.
DOVE
MANOR
ORKNEY CL.
WALDUCKS CL.
DR.
HIGH STREET
LOVETTS END
MALTINGS CL.
Leighton Buzzard
COURT
NEIDGE CL.
South End
ORCHARD LA.
SOUTH
TAYLORS LA.
FARM CL.
KINGS ST.
LU7
SOUTH LA.
ROAD
WING ROAD
Wing Road Farm
Sewage Works
The Croft
AYLESBURY VALE GOLF CLUB
Club House
Old Brick Farm
DUNTON ROAD
Forge Farm
Mount Pleasant Farm
Warren Farm
Poultry Farm
Fox Covert
Kingsbridge Farm

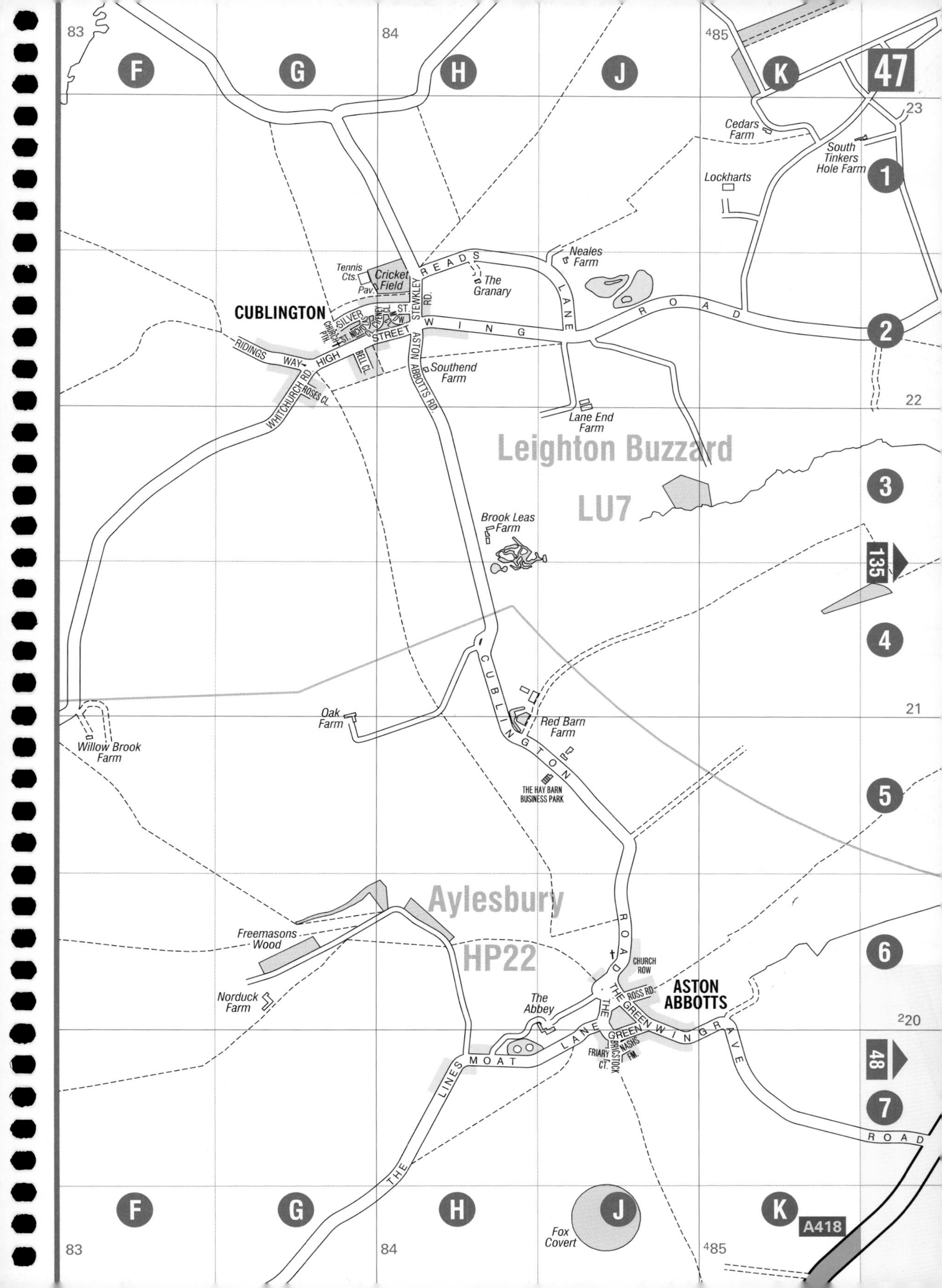
47
83
84
485
F
G
H
J
K
1
2
3
4
5
6
7
23
22
21
220
Cedars Farm
South Tinkers Hole Farm
Lockharts
Neales Farm
The Granary
Tennis Cts.
Cricket Field
Pav.
CUBLINGTON
READS LANE
WING ROAD
STEWKLEY RD.
HIGH STREET
RIDINGS WAY
WHITCHURCH RD.
ROSES CL.
BELL CL.
SILVER ST.
CHURCH PTH.
ASTON ABBOTTS RD.
Southend Farm
Lane End Farm
Leighton Buzzard
LU7
Brook Leas Farm
135
CUBLINGTON ROAD
Oak Farm
Red Barn Farm
Willow Brook Farm
THE HAY BARN BUSINESS PARK
Aylesbury
HP22
Freemasons Wood
Norduck Farm
CHURCH ROW
ASTON ABBOTTS
ROSS RD.
THE GREEN
The Abbey
MOAT LANE
FRIARY CT.
BRICSTOCK
NASHS FM.
WINGRAVE ROAD
THE LINES
48
Fox Covert
A418

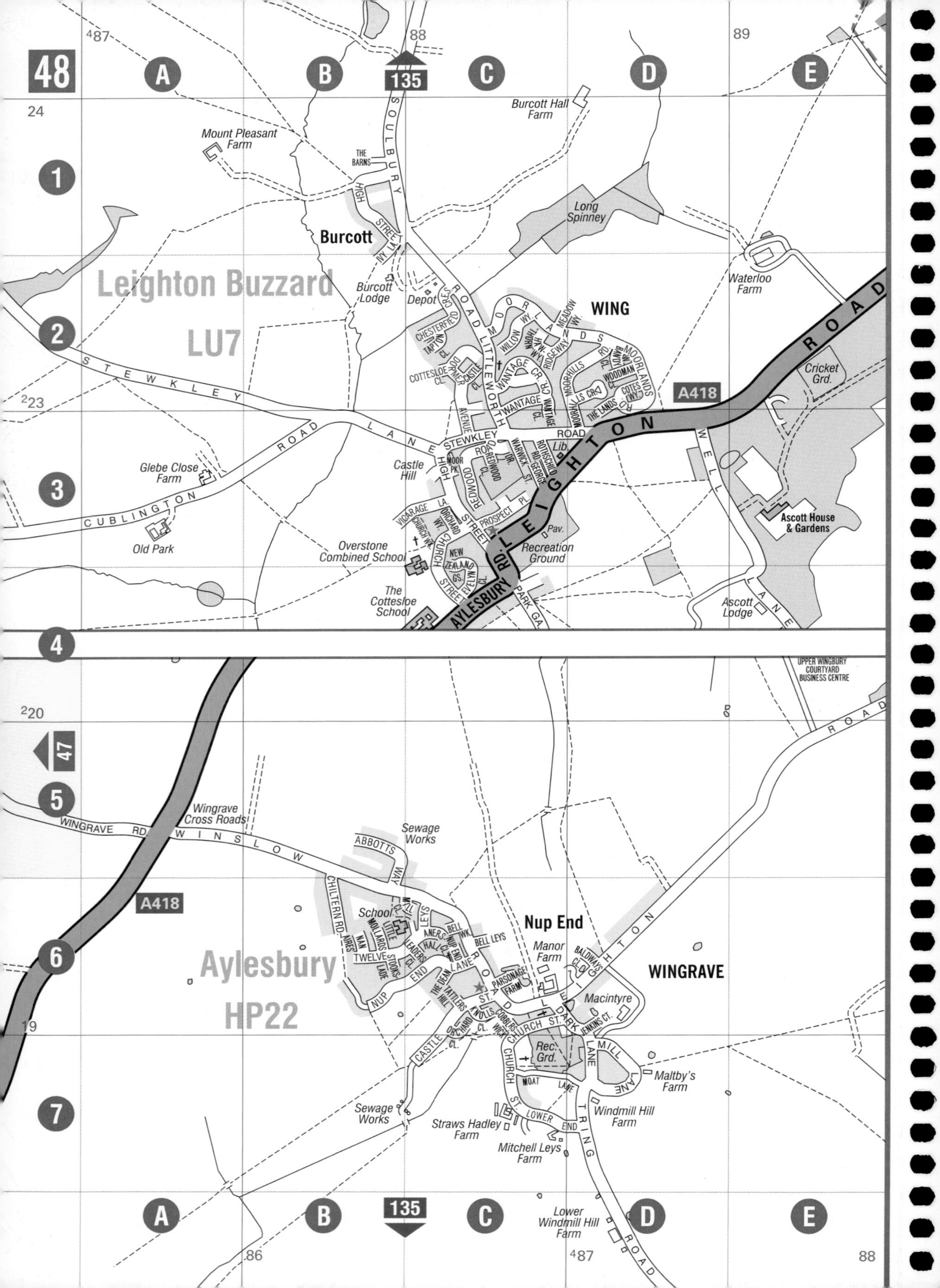
Leighton Buzzard
LU7
Burcott
WING
Mount Pleasant Farm
Burcott Hall Farm
Long Spinney
Waterloo Farm
Burcott Lodge
Depot
Cricket Grd.
Glebe Close Farm
Castle Hill
Old Park
Overstone Combined School
Recreation Ground
Ascott House & Gardens
The Cottesloe School
Ascott Lodge
STEWKLEY LANE
CUBLINGTON ROAD
SOULBURY ROAD
LEIGHTON ROAD
AYLESBURY RD.
A418
UPPER WINGBURY COURTYARD BUSINESS CENTRE
Aylesbury
HP22
Wingrave Cross Roads
WINGRAVE RD
WINSLOW ROAD
Sewage Works
Nup End
WINGRAVE
Manor Farm
Macintyre
Rec. Grd.
Maltby's Farm
Windmill Hill Farm
Straws Hadley Farm
Mitchell Leys Farm
Lower Windmill Hill Farm
TRING ROAD
LEIGHTON ROAD

135
47
135

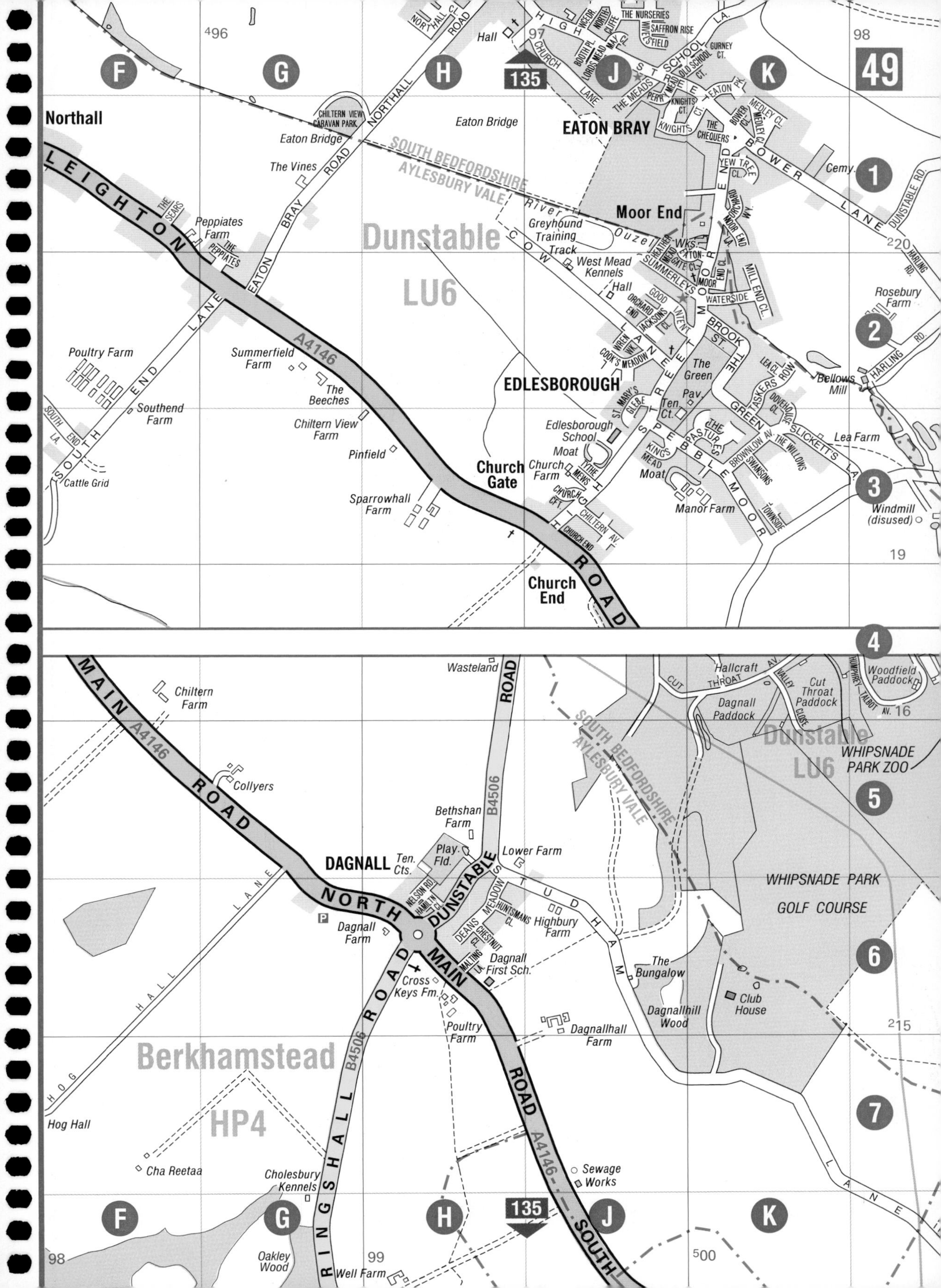

49
135
Northall
Eaton Bridge
EATON BRAY
Moor End
Dunstable
LU6
EDLESBOROUGH
Church Gate
Church End
SOUTH BEDFORDSHIRE
AYLESBURY VALE
LEIGHTON ROAD
A4146
EATON BRAY ROAD
NORTHALL ROAD
HIGH STREET
SCHOOL LANE
BOWER LANE
DUNSTABLE RD.
HARLING RD.
COW LANE
MOOR END
HIGH STREET
BROOK ST.
THE GREEN
SLICKETT'S LA.
BLEMOOR
SOUTH END LANE
River Ouzel
Chiltern View Caravan Park
The Vines
Peppiates Farm
The Peppiates
The Sears
Poultry Farm
Southend Farm
Cattle Grid
Summerfield Farm
The Beeches
Chiltern View Farm
Pinfield
Sparrowhall Farm
Greyhound Training Track
West Mead Kennels
Hall
Edlesborough School
Moat
Church Farm
The Green
Pav.
Ten. Ct.
Bellows Mill
Rosebury Farm
Lea Farm
Manor Farm
Windmill (disused)
Cemy.
Wks.
THE NURSERIES
SAFFRON RISE
WIVES FIELD
GURNEY CT.
EATON PL.
MEDLEY CL.
THE CHEQUERS
YEW TREE CL.
KNIGHTS CT.
THE MEADS
LORDS MEAD
BOOTH PL.
OLD SCHOOL CT.
MILL END CL.
WATERSIDE
SUMMERLEYS
ORCHARD END
JACKSONS CL.
GOOD INTENT
WREN WK.
COOK'S MEADOW
ST. MARY'S GLEBE
TITHE MEWS
CHURCH CFT.
CHURCH END
CHILTERN AV.
TASKERS ROW
DOVEHOUSE CL.
THE WILLOWS
BROWNLOW AV.
SWANSONS
KING'S MEAD
THE PASTURES
TOWNSIDE
LEA CL.
DAGNALL
MAIN ROAD
NORTH ROAD
DUNSTABLE ROAD
B4506
RINGSHALL ROAD
STUDHAM LANE
HOG HALL LANE
Wasteland
Chiltern Farm
Collyers
Bethshan Farm
Play. Fld.
Ten. Cts.
Lower Farm
Dagnall Farm
Highbury Farm
Dagnall First Sch.
Cross Keys Fm.
Poultry Farm
Dagnallhall Farm
The Bungalow
Dagnallhill Wood
Club House
WHIPSNADE PARK GOLF COURSE
WHIPSNADE PARK ZOO
Hallcraft
CUT THROAT AV.
Dagnall Paddock
Cut Throat Paddock
Woodfield Paddock
HUMPHREY TALBOT AV.
VALLEY CLOSE
NELSON RD.
HAMILTON CL.
DEANS MEADOW
HUNTSMANS CL.
CHESTNUT CL.
MALTING LA.
Berkhamstead
HP4
Hog Hall
Cha Reetaa
Cholesbury Kennels
Oakley Wood
Well Farm
Sewage Works
F G H J K
1 2 3 4 5 6 7
496 97 98 99 500
220 19 16 215

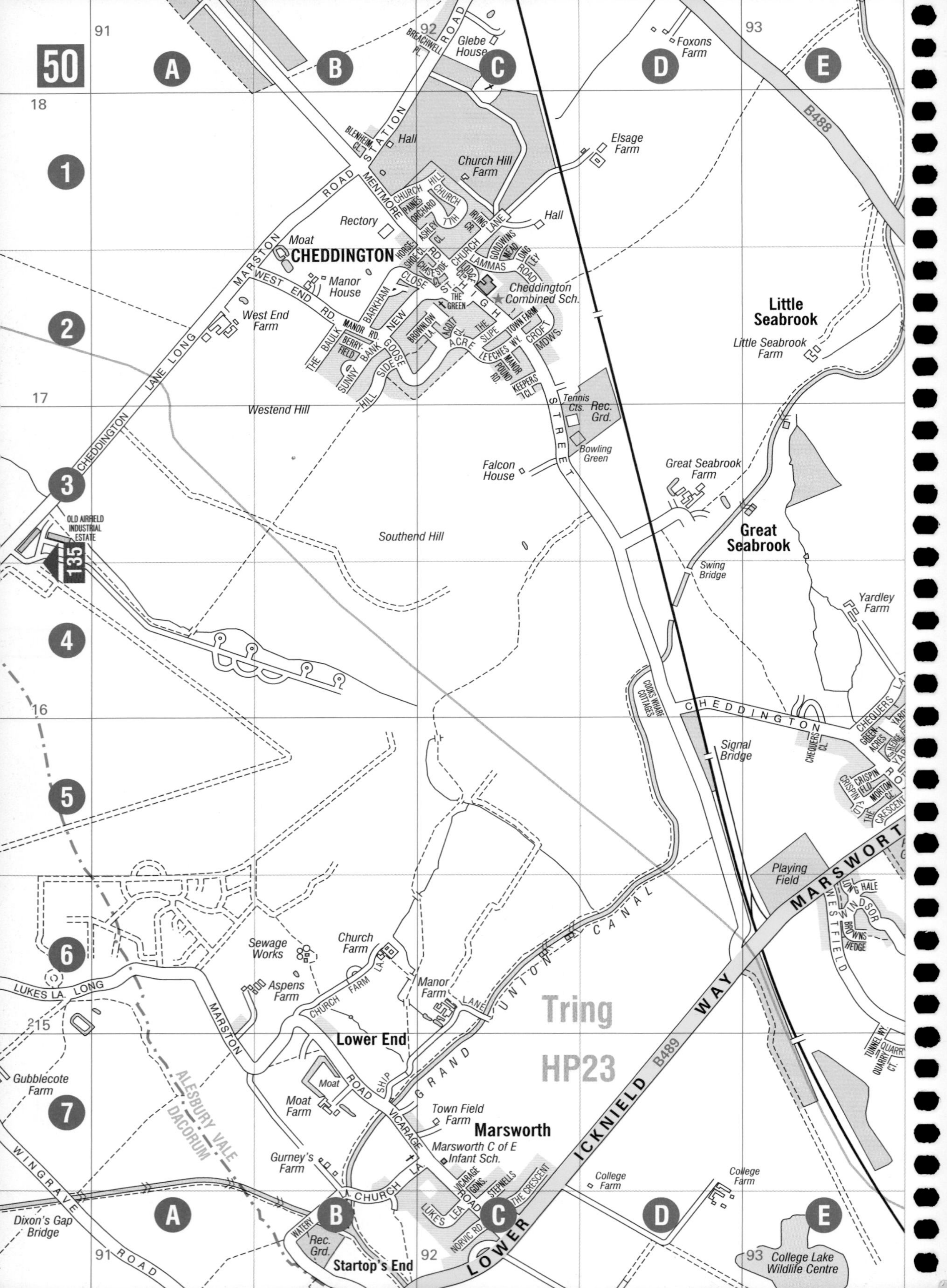
CHEDDINGTON
Little Seabrook
Great Seabrook
Lower End
Marsworth
Startop's End
Tring
HP23
Glebe House
Foxons Farm
Hall
Church Hill Farm
Elsage Farm
Rectory
Moat
Manor House
West End Farm
Cheddington Combined Sch.
Little Seabrook Farm
Westend Hill
Tennis Cts.
Rec. Grd.
Bowling Green
Falcon House
Great Seabrook Farm
OLD AIRFIELD INDUSTRIAL ESTATE
Southend Hill
Swing Bridge
Yardley Farm
Signal Bridge
Playing Field
Sewage Works
Church Farm
Aspens Farm
Manor Farm
Gubblecote Farm
Moat Farm
Town Field Farm
Marsworth C of E Infant Sch.
Gurney's Farm
College Farm
Dixon's Gap Bridge
College Lake Wildlife Centre
GRAND UNION CANAL
ALESBURY VALE
DACORUM
LOWER ICKNIELD WAY
B489
B488
MARSWORTH
CHEDDINGTON LANE
MARSTON ROAD
LONG MARSTON
WINGRAVE ROAD
STATION ROAD
MENTMORE ROAD
WEST END RD.
HIGH STREET
CHURCH LA.
VICARAGE ROAD
LUKES LA.
135

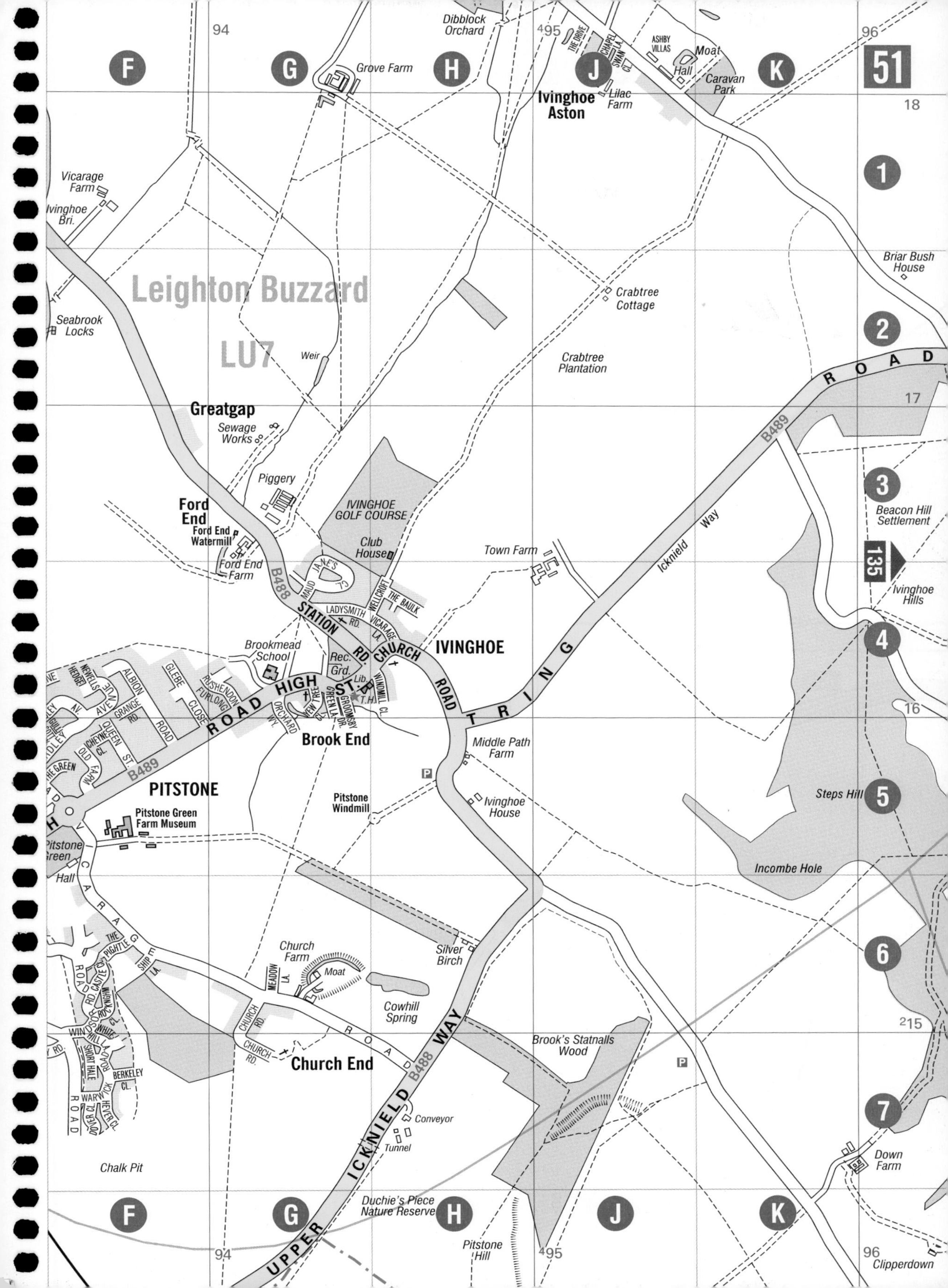
F
G
H
J
K
94
495
96
18
17
16
215
Dibblock Orchard
Grove Farm
THE DRIVE
CHAPEL LA.
SWAN CL.
ASHBY VILLAS
Moat
Hall
Caravan Park
Ivinghoe Aston
Lilac Farm
Vicarage Farm
Ivinghoe Bri.
Briar Bush House
Leighton Buzzard
LU7
Seabrook Locks
Crabtree Cottage
Weir
Crabtree Plantation
ROAD
Greatgap
Sewage Works
B489
Piggery
Ford End
Ford End Watermill
Ford End Farm
IVINGHOE GOLF COURSE
Club House
Town Farm
Icknield Way
Beacon Hill Settlement
135
Ivinghoe Hills
B488
MAUD JANE'S
THE BAULK
WELLCROFT
LADYSMITH RD.
VICARAGE LA.
STATION RD.
CHURCH RD.
IVINGHOE
TRING ROAD
Brookmead School
Rec. Grd.
Lib.
T.H.
WINDMILL CL.
HIGH ST.
ROAD
GLEBE CLOSE
RUSHENDON FURLONG
ORCHARD WY.
YEW TREE CL.
GREEN LA.
GROOMSBY DR.
NEWELLS HEDGE
ALBION
AVENUE
GRANGE RD.
ROAD
CHEYNE CL.
QUEEN ST.
OLD FARM
THE GREEN
Brook End
Middle Path Farm
PITSTONE
B489
Pitstone Windmill
Ivinghoe House
Steps Hill
Pitstone Green Farm Museum
Pitstone Green
Hall
VICARAGE
Incombe Hole
THE PIGHTLE
SHIP LA.
CASTLE
Church Farm
Moat
MEADOW LA.
Silver Birch
Cowhill Spring
CHURCH RD.
ROAD
WINDSOR HILL
SHORT HALE
BERKELEY CL.
WARWICK
HEVER CL.
DOVER CL.
Brook's Statnalls Wood
Church End
B488
UPPER ICKNIELD WAY
Conveyor
Tunnel
Chalk Pit
Down Farm
Duchie's Piece Nature Reserve
Pitstone Hill
Clipperdown
1
2
3
4
5
6
7

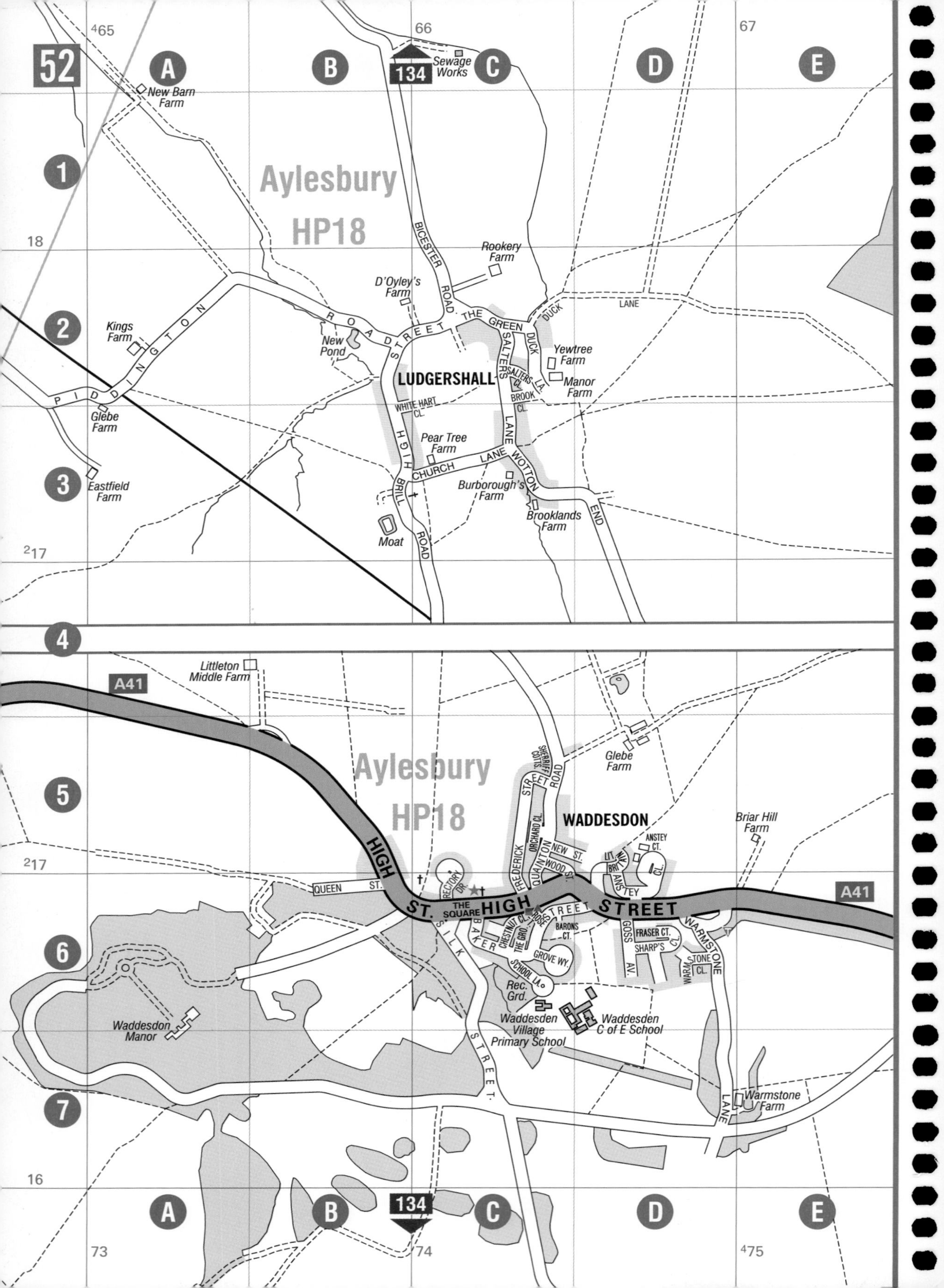

Aylesbury
HP18
LUDGERSHALL
New Barn Farm
Sewage Works
134
Kings Farm
Glebe Farm
Eastfield Farm
Rookery Farm
D'Oyley's Farm
New Pond
Yewtree Farm
Manor Farm
Pear Tree Farm
Burborough's Farm
Brooklands Farm
Moat
PIDDINGTON ROAD
BICESTER ROAD
STREET
THE GREEN
DUCK LANE
DUCK LA.
SALTERS LANE
SALTERS CL.
BROOK CL.
WHITE HART CL.
HIGH STREET
CHURCH LANE
WOTTON END
BRILL ROAD
LANE
Aylesbury
HP18
WADDESDON
A41
Littleton Middle Farm
Glebe Farm
Briar Hill Farm
SHERRIFF COTTS.
STREET
ROAD
ORCHARD CL.
FREDERICK
QUAINTON
NEW ST.
WOOD ST.
ANSTEY CT.
ANSTEY
QUEEN ST.
RECTORY DR.
HIGH ST.
THE SQUARE
HIGH STREET
STREET
BAKER
CHESTNUT CL.
THE GRO.
ROSE
BARONS CT.
GROVE WY.
SCHOOL LA.
SILK STREET
GOSS AV.
FRASER CT.
SHARP'S CL.
WARMSTONE LANE
WARMSTONE CL.
Rec. Grd.
Waddesden Village Primary School
Waddesden C of E School
Waddesdon Manor
Warmstone Farm

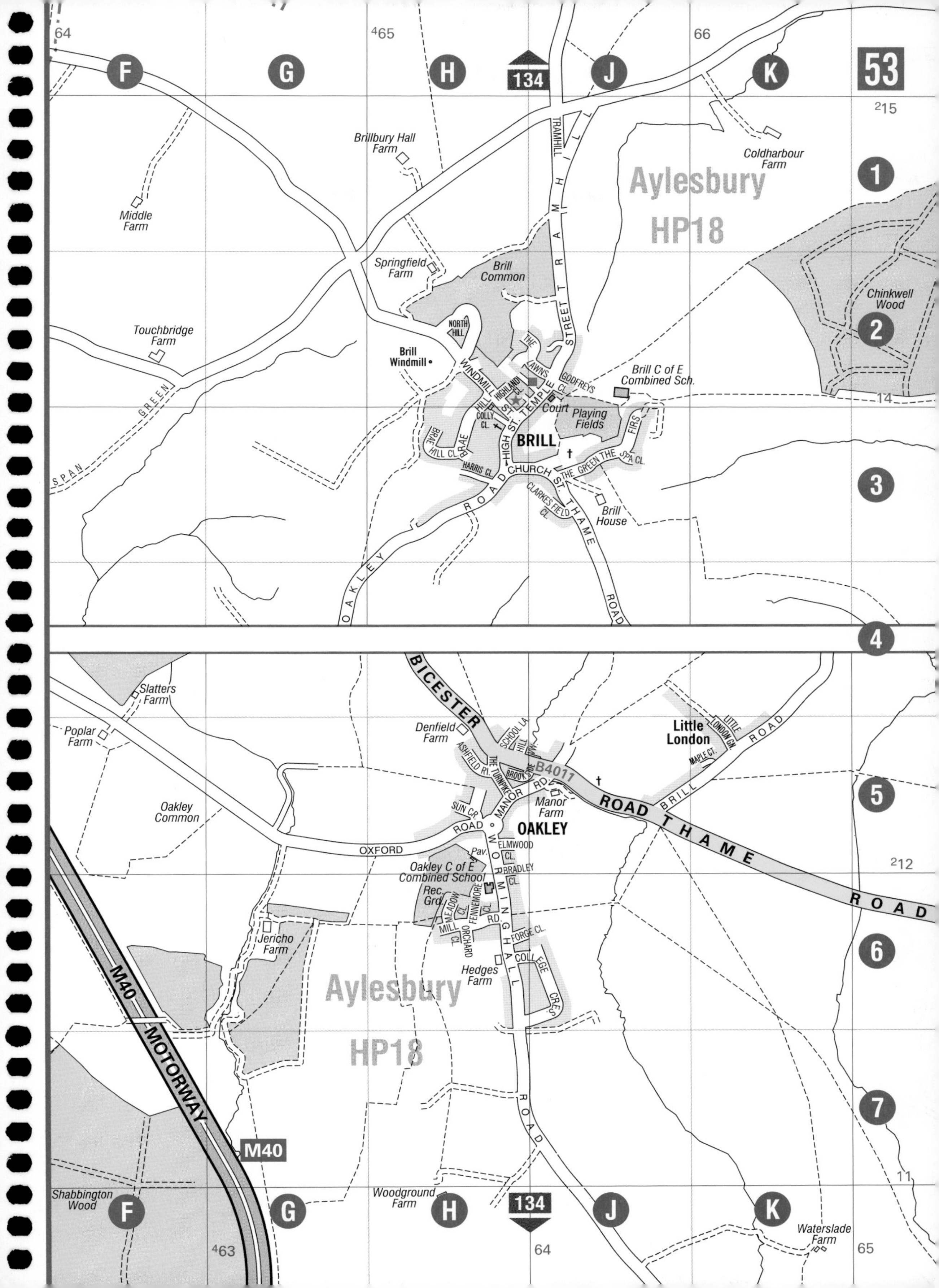

F
G
H
134
J
K
64
465
66
215
1
2
3
4
5
6
7
14
212
11
463
64
65
Brillbury Hall Farm
Coldharbour Farm
Aylesbury
HP18
Middle Farm
Springfield Farm
Brill Common
Chinkwell Wood
Touchbridge Farm
NORTH HILL
Brill Windmill
Brill C of E Combined Sch.
WINDMILL
HIGHLAND CL.
THE LAWNS
GODFREYS CL.
STREET
TRAMHILL
TEMPLE ST.
Court
Playing Fields
COLLY CL.
BRAE HILL CL.
BRAE
HILL
HIGH ST.
BRILL
HARRIS CL.
CHURCH ST.
THE GREEN
THE FIRS
SPA CL.
CLARKES FIELD CL.
THAME
ROAD
Brill House
SPAN GREEN
OAKLEY ROAD
BICESTER
Slatters Farm
Poplar Farm
Denfield Farm
SCHOOL LA
HILL
ASHFIELD RI.
THE TURNPIKE
BROOKSIDE
B4011
MANOR RD
Manor Farm
Little London
LITTLE LONDON GN.
MAPLE CT.
BRILL ROAD
ROAD THAME ROAD
Oakley Common
SUN CR.
ROAD
OAKLEY
OXFORD
Pav.
ELMWOOD CL.
BRADLEY CL.
WORMINGHALL ROAD
Oakley C of E Combined School
Rec. Grd.
MEADOW CL.
FENNEMORE CL.
MILL RD.
ORCHARD CL.
FORGE CL.
COLLEGE CRES.
Jericho Farm
Hedges Farm
M40
MOTORWAY
Shabbington Wood
Woodground Farm
Waterslade Farm

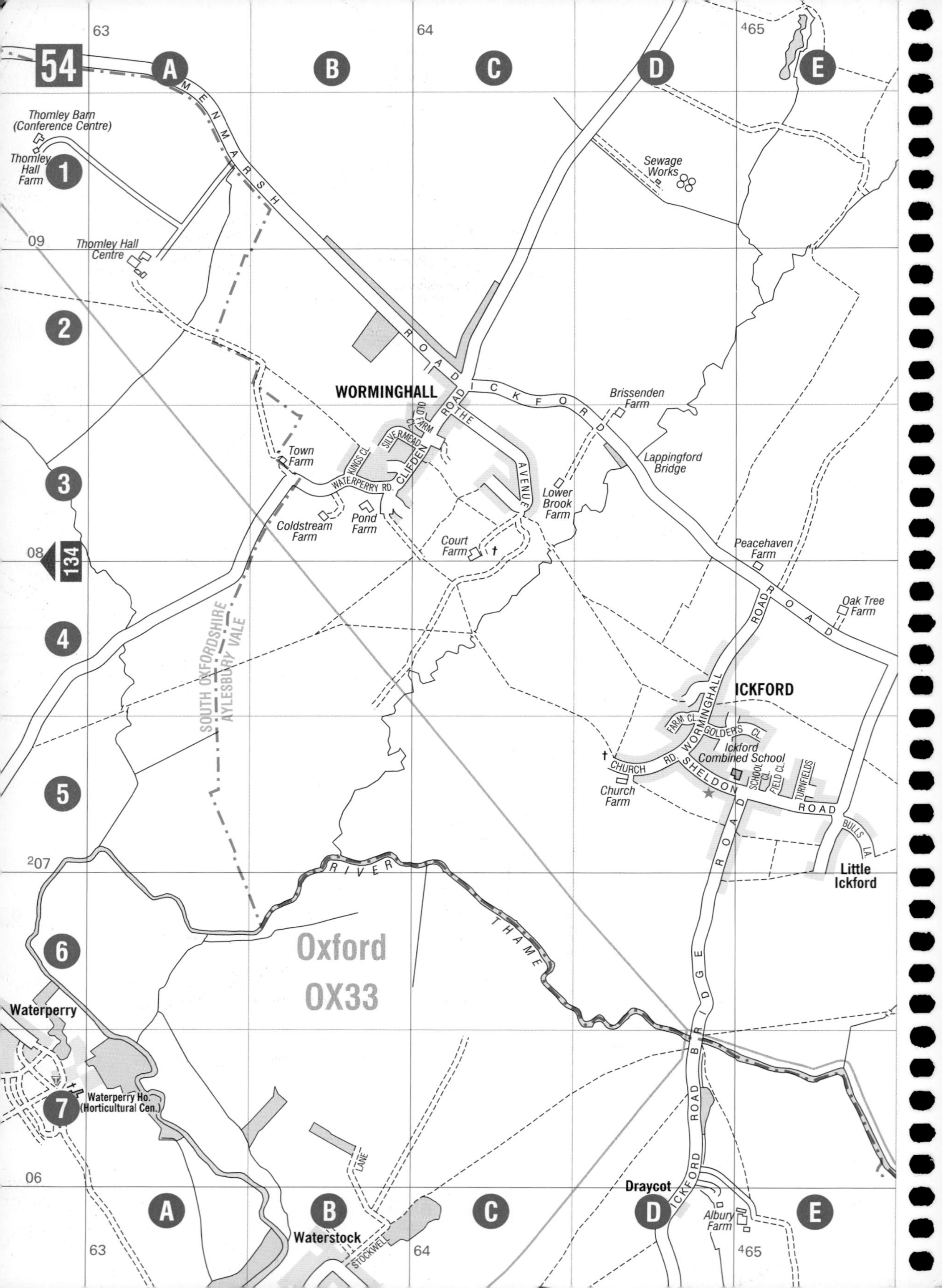
63
64
465
A
B
C
D
E
Thomley Barn (Conference Centre)
Thomley Hall Farm
Thomley Hall Centre
MENMARSH ROAD
09
08
207
06
1
2
3
4
5
6
7
134
Sewage Works
WORMINGHALL
Brissenden Farm
ICKFORD ROAD
OLD FARM CL.
SILVERMEAD
KINGS CL.
CLIFDEN ROAD
THE AVENUE
WATERPERRY RD.
Town Farm
Lappingford Bridge
Lower Brook Farm
Coldstream Farm
Pond Farm
Court Farm
Peacehaven Farm
Oak Tree Farm
SOUTH OXFORDSHIRE
AYLESBURY VALE
ICKFORD
WORMINGHALL ROAD
FARM CL.
GOLDERS CL.
Ickford Combined School
CHURCH RD.
SHELDON ROAD
SCHOOL CL.
FIELD CL.
TURNFIELDS
Church Farm
BULLS LA.
Little Ickford
RIVER THAME
Oxford OX33
BRIDGE ROAD
Waterperry
Waterperry Ho. (Horticultural Cen.)
LANE
ICKFORD ROAD
Draycot
Albury Farm
Waterstock
STOCKWELL

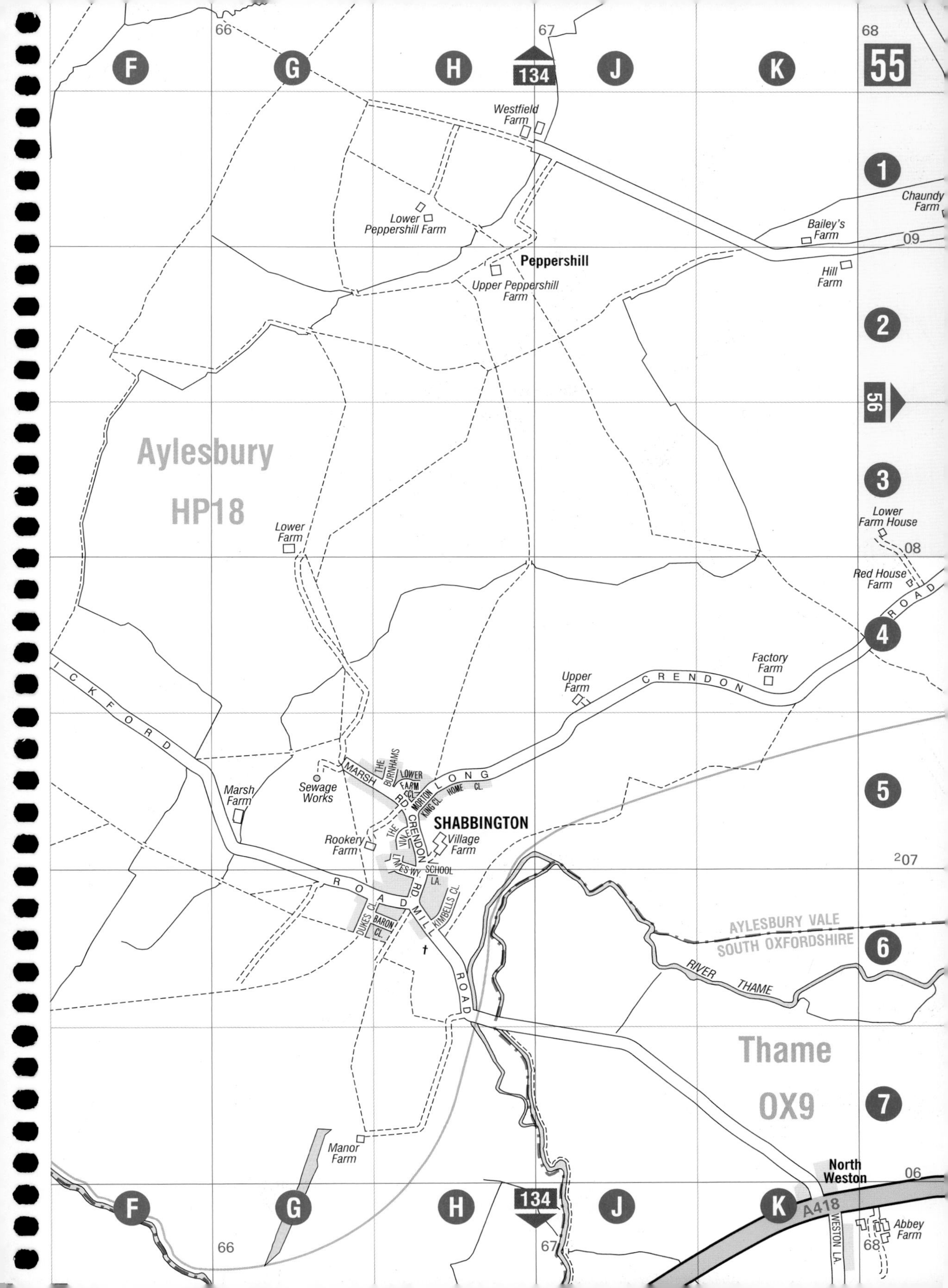

F
G
H
134
J
K
66
67
68
Westfield Farm
1
Chaundy Farm
Lower Peppershill Farm
Bailey's Farm
09
Peppershill
Upper Peppershill Farm
Hill Farm
2
56
Aylesbury
HP18
3
Lower Farm House
Lower Farm
08
Red House Farm
ROAD
4
Factory Farm
Upper Farm
CRENDON
ICKFORD ROAD
THE BURNHAMS
MARSH RD.
LOWER FARM CL.
LONG
MORTON
KING CL.
HOME CL.
Sewage Works
Marsh Farm
5
SHABBINGTON
THE VINE
CRENDON RD.
Rookery Farm
Village Farm
LIMES WY.
SCHOOL LA.
07
ROAD
DUKES CL.
BARON CL.
MILL
KIMBELLS CL.
ROAD
AYLESBURY VALE
SOUTH OXFORDSHIRE
6
RIVER THAME
Thame
OX9
7
Manor Farm
North Weston
06
A418
WESTON LA.
Abbey Farm

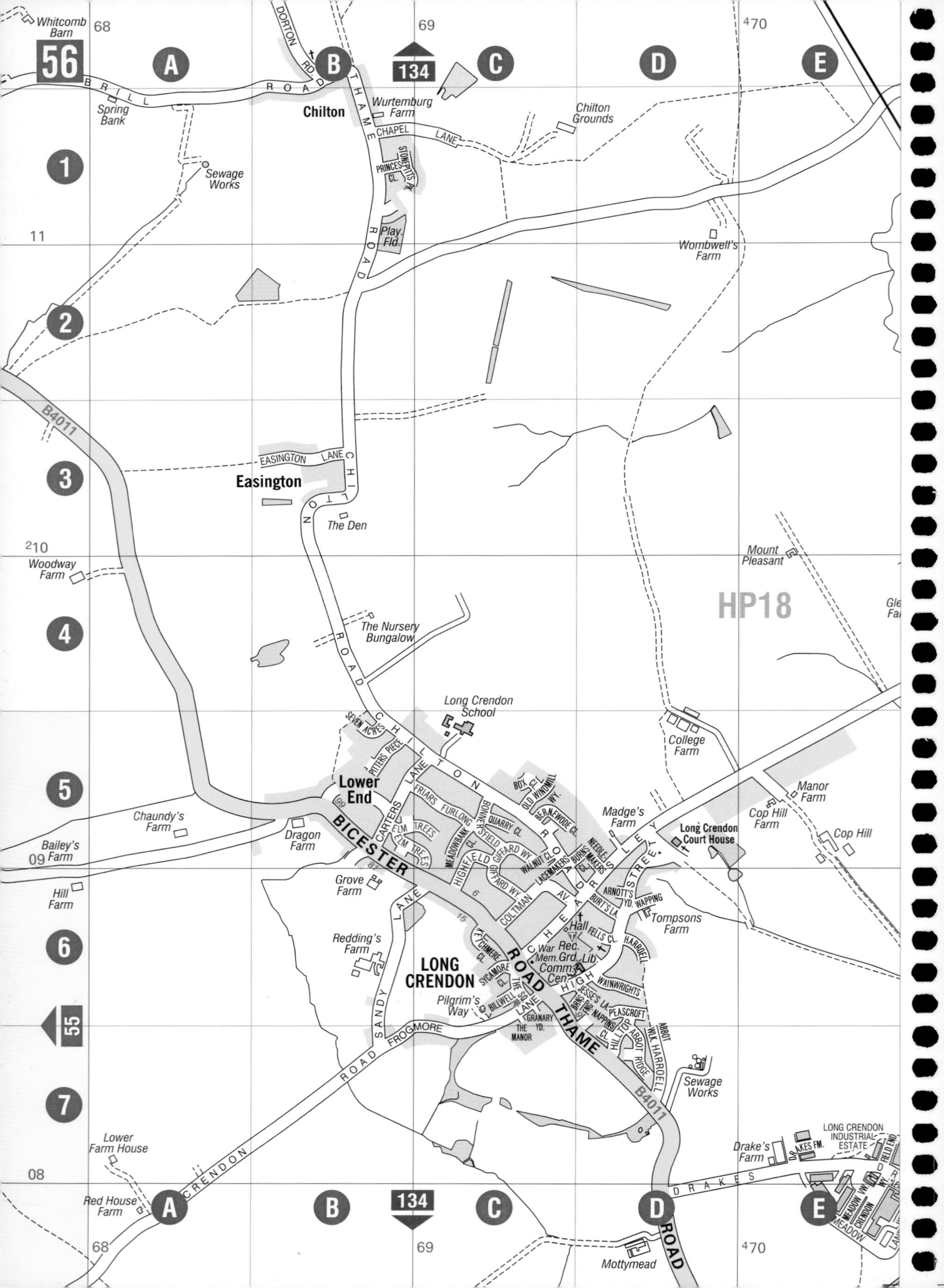
56
Whitcomb Barn
68
69
470
A
B
C
D
E
134
BRILL ROAD
DORTON RD.
Spring Bank
Chilton
Wurtemburg Farm
CHAPEL LANE
Chilton Grounds
1
Sewage Works
PRINCES CL.
STONEPITS PK.
Play. Fld.
THAME ROAD
11
Wombwell's Farm
2
B4011
3
EASINGTON LANE
Easington
CHILTON
The Den
210
Woodway Farm
Mount Pleasant
HP18
4
The Nursery Bungalow
ROAD
Long Crendon School
SEVEN ACRES
PITTERS PIECE
College Farm
5
Lower End
Manor Farm
Chaundy's Farm
Madge's Farm
Cop Hill Farm
Long Crendon Court House
Cop Hill
Dragon Farm
Bailey's Farm
09
BICESTER
Grove Farm
Hill Farm
Tompsons Farm
6
Redding's Farm
LONG CRENDON
ROAD
THAME
Pilgrim's Way
SANDY LANE
FROGMORE
55
7
Sewage Works
Lower Farm House
LONG CRENDON INDUSTRIAL ESTATE
Drake's Farm
08
CRENDON
DRAKES
Red House Farm
Mottymead

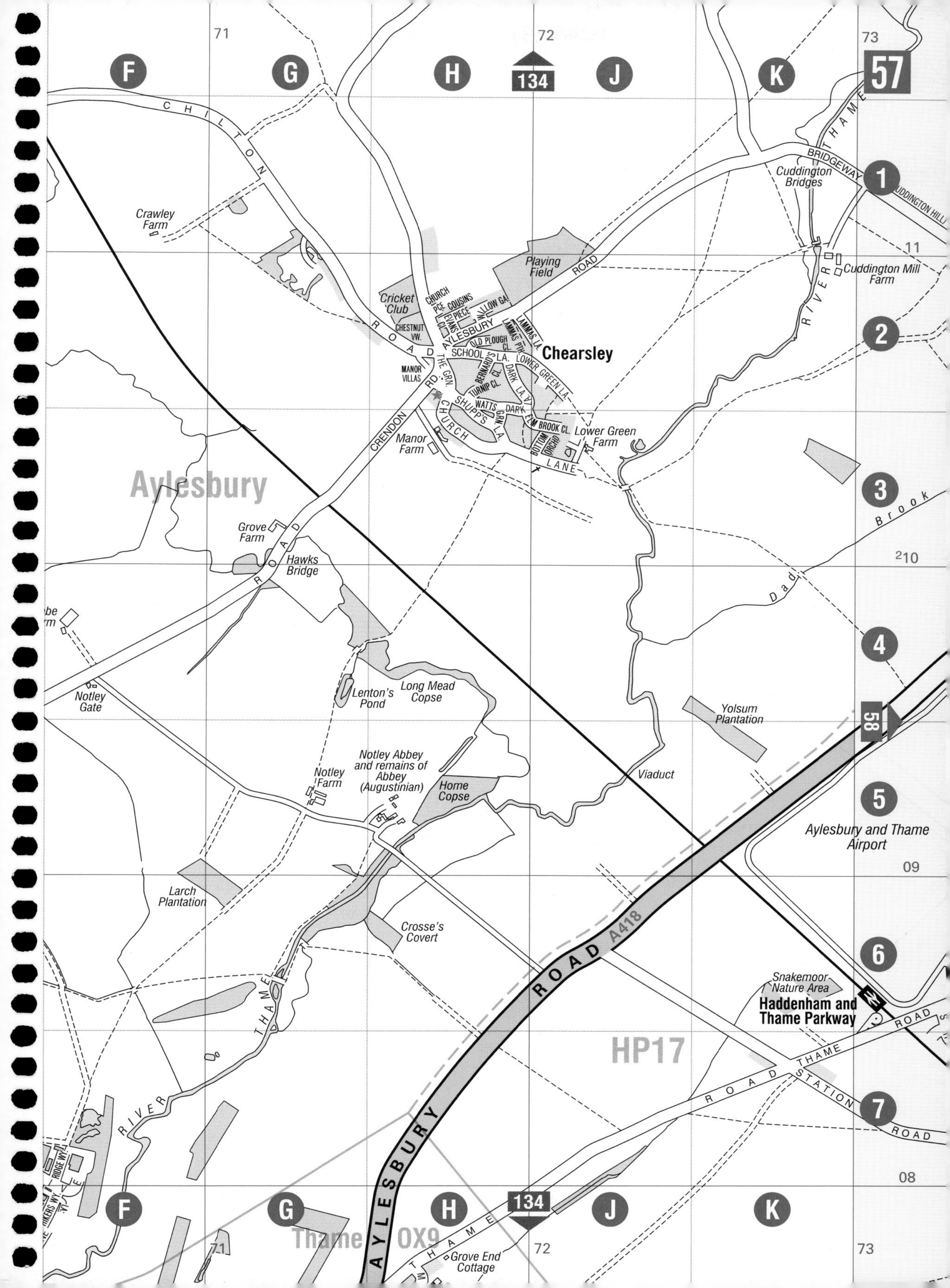

71
72
73
F
G
H
134
J
K
1
2
3
4
5
6
7
11
210
09
08
CHILTON
Crawley Farm
Playing Field
ROAD
Cricket Club
CHURCH PCE.
COUSINS PIECE
EVANS CL.
CHESTNUT VW.
AYLESBURY
WILLOW GA.
LAMMAS LA.
LAMMAS PTH.
OLD PLOUGH CL.
Chearsley
SCHOOL LA.
BERNARD'S CL.
LOWER GREEN LA.
MANOR VILLAS
THE GRN.
TURNIP CL.
DARK LA.
SHUPP'S
WATTS GRN. LA.
DARK
ELM BROOK CL.
BOTTOM ORCHD.
Lower Green Farm
CHURCH
LANE
Manor Farm
CRENDON RD.
ROAD
Cuddington Bridges
BRIDGEWAY
THAME
CUDDINGTON HILL
Cuddington Mill Farm
RIVER
Aylesbury
Grove Farm
Hawks Bridge
Brook
Dad
Notley Gate
Lenton's Pond
Long Mead Copse
Yolsum Plantation
58
Notley Abbey and remains of Abbey (Augustinian)
Notley Farm
Home Copse
Viaduct
Aylesbury and Thame Airport
Larch Plantation
Crosse's Covert
ROAD A418
Snakemoor Nature Area
Haddenham and Thame Parkway
THAME
HP17
ROAD
THAME ROAD
STATION
ROAD
RIVER
AYLESBURY
Thame
OX9
THAME
Grove End Cottage
134

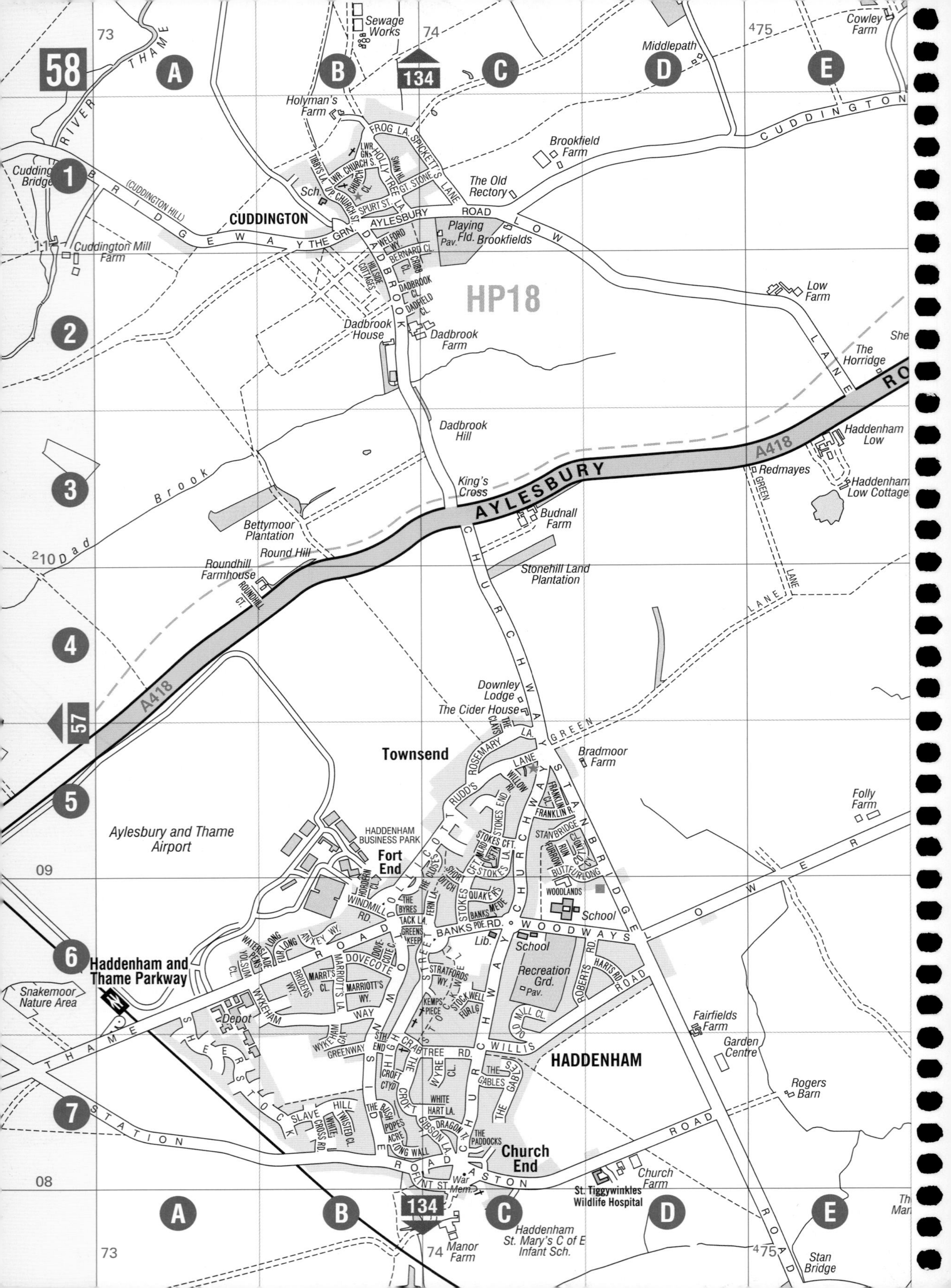
134
57
A
B
C
D
E
1
2
3
4
5
6
7
73
74
475
210
09
08
HP18
CUDDINGTON
Sewage Works
Holyman's Farm
Middlepath
Cowley Farm
Brookfield Farm
The Old Rectory
Cuddington Bridge
Cuddington Mill Farm
RIVER THAME
BRIDGEWAY
(CUDDINGTON HILL)
FROG LA.
SPICKETT'S LANE
AYLESBURY ROAD
LOW
CUDDINGTON
Playing Fld.
Pav.
Brookfields
DADBROOK
Dadbrook House
Dadbrook Farm
Low Farm
The Horridge
Dadbrook Hill
King's Cross
AYLESBURY
A418
Budnall Farm
Redmayes
Haddenham Low
Haddenham Low Cottage
Bettymoor Plantation
Round Hill
Roundhill Farmhouse
ROUNDHILL CT.
Stonehill Land Plantation
Dad Brook
CHURCHWAY
Downley Lodge
The Cider House
Townsend
Bradmoor Farm
Folly Farm
Aylesbury and Thame Airport
HADDENHAM BUSINESS PARK
Fort End
WINDMILL RD.
STANBRIDGE
Woodlands
School
Lib.
Recreation Grd.
Pav.
WOODWAYS
LOWER
Haddenham and Thame Parkway
Snakemoor Nature Area
Depot
THAME ROAD
STATION ROAD
HADDENHAM
Fairfields Farm
Garden Centre
Rogers Barn
Church End
ASTON ROAD
Church Farm
St. Tiggywinkles Wildlife Hospital
War Mem.
Haddenham St. Mary's C of E Infant Sch.
Manor Farm
Stan Bridge
GREEN
LANE

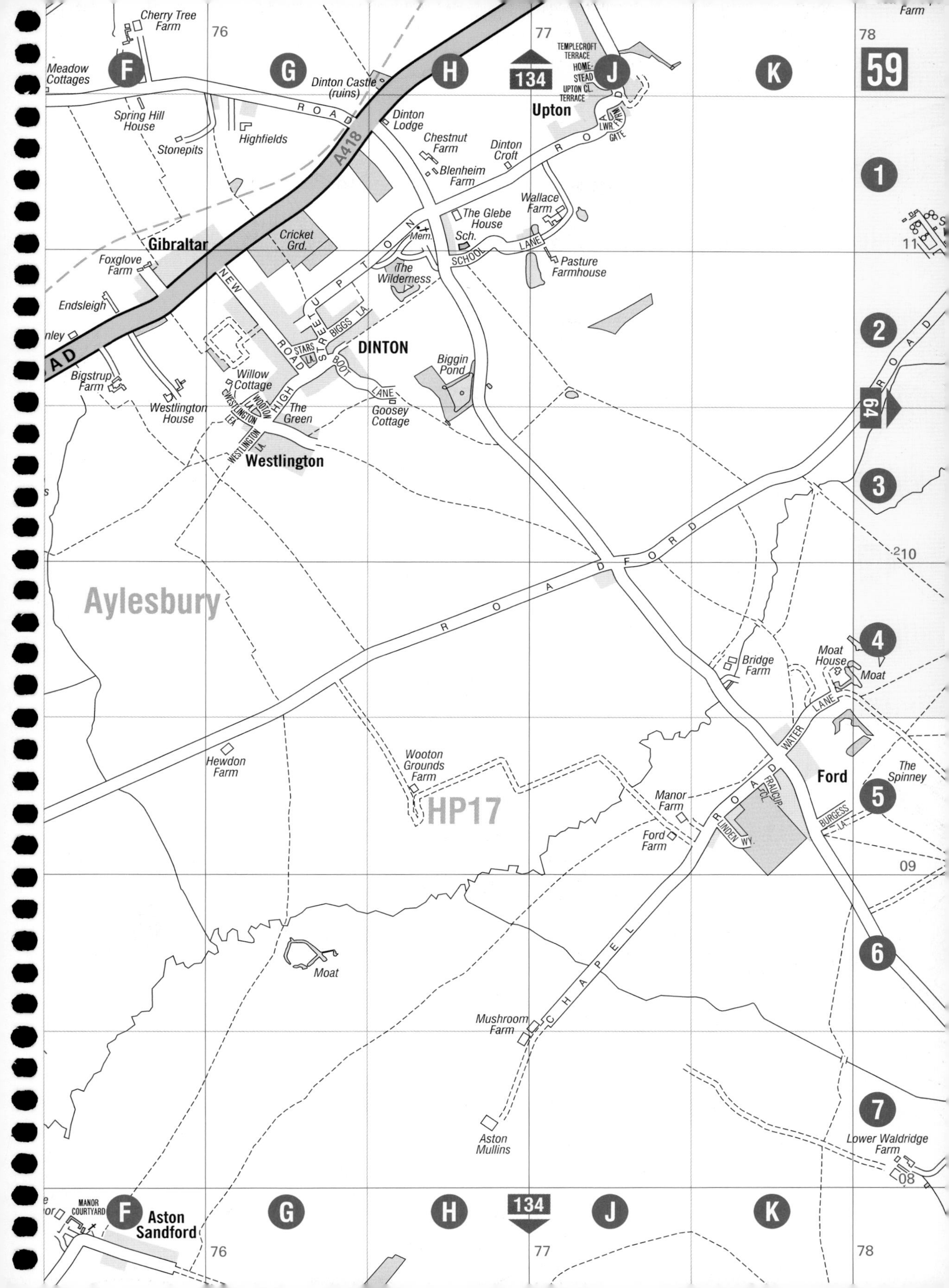
Cherry Tree Farm
Meadow Cottages
Dinton Castle (ruins)
ROAD
A418
Spring Hill House
Stonepits
Highfields
Dinton Lodge
Chestnut Farm
Blenheim Farm
Dinton Croft
TEMPLECROFT TERRACE
HOMESTEAD
UPTON CL.
TERRACE
Upton
LWR FARM GATE
Wallace Farm
The Glebe House
Sch.
Mem.
Gibraltar
Cricket Grd.
Foxglove Farm
UPTON
SCHOOL LANE
Pasture Farmhouse
The Wilderness
NEW ROAD
Endsleigh
BIGGS LA.
STREET
STARS LA.
DINTON
BOOT LANE
Biggin Pond
Bigstrup Farm
Willow Cottage
WOOTON LA.
WESTLINGTON LA.
HIGH
Westlington House
The Green
Goosey Cottage
Westlington
Aylesbury
ROAD
FORD
ROAD
Bridge Farm
Moat House
Moat
WATER LANE
Hewdon Farm
Wooton Grounds Farm
HP17
Ford
The Spinney
Manor Farm
FRAUCUP CL.
Ford Farm
LINDEN WY.
BURGESS LA.
CHAPEL
Moat
Mushroom Farm
Aston Mullins
Lower Waldridge Farm
MANOR COURTYARD
Aston Sandford
F G H J K
1 2 3 4 5 6 7
76 77 78
11 10 09 08
134
64
Farm

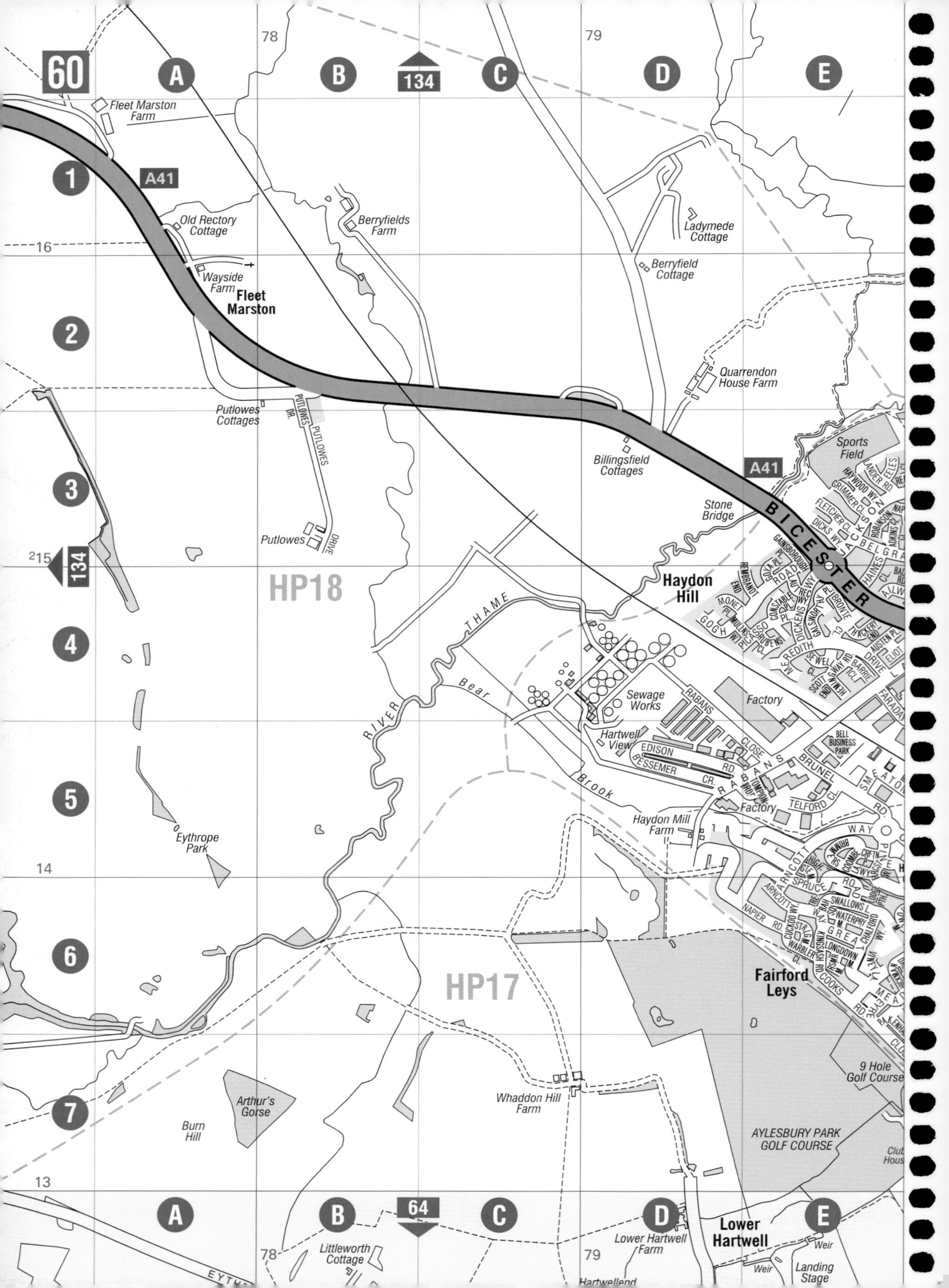
60
134
64
78
79
16
15
14
13
A41
Fleet Marston Farm
Old Rectory Cottage
Berryfields Farm
Wayside Farm
Fleet Marston
Ladymede Cottage
Berryfield Cottage
Quarrendon House Farm
Putlowes Cottages
PUTLOWES DR.
PUTLOWES DRIVE
Putlowes
Billingsfield Cottages
Sports Field
Stone Bridge
BICESTER
Haydon Hill
HP18
HP17
RIVER THAME
Bear Brook
Sewage Works
Factory
Hartwell View
EDISON RD.
BESSEMER CR.
RABANS CLOSE
RABANS
BRUNEL
TELFORD CL.
BELL BUSINESS PARK
Haydon Mill Farm
Eythrope Park
Fairford Leys
9 Hole Golf Course
AYLESBURY PARK GOLF COURSE
Whaddon Hill Farm
Arthur's Gorse
Burn Hill
Lower Hartwell
Lower Hartwell Farm
Littleworth Cottage
Weir
Landing Stage
Hartwellend

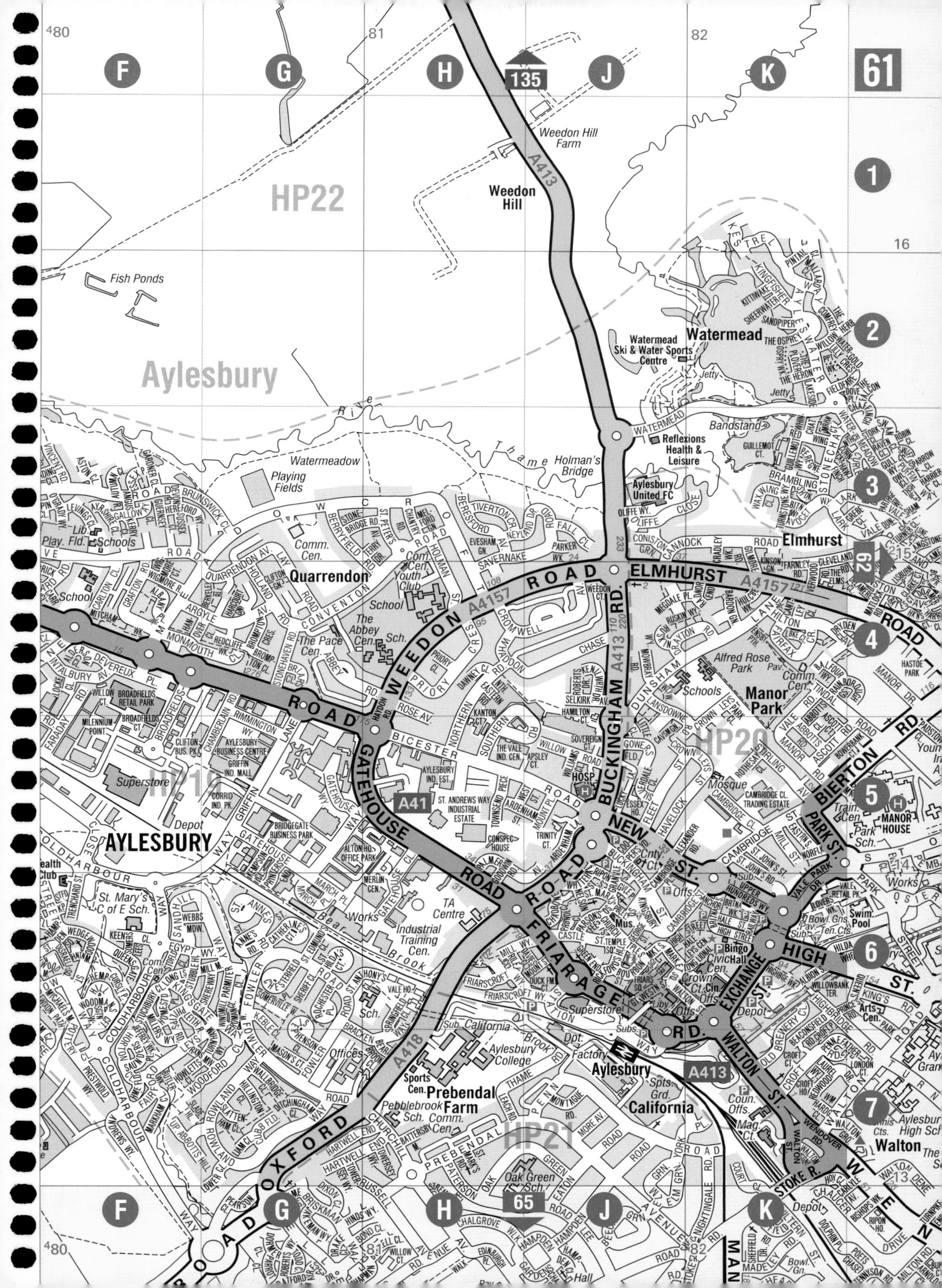
480
81
82
F
G
H
J
K
135
Weedon Hill Farm
A413
Weedon Hill
HP22
16
Fish Ponds
Watermead
Watermead Ski & Water Sports Centre
Aylesbury
Jetty
Bandstand
Reflexions Health & Leisure
Watermeadow
Playing Fields
Holman's Bridge
River Thame
Aylesbury United FC
Elmhurst
62
Quarrendon
Comm. Cen.
Com. Cen. Youth Club
School
The Abbey Cen.
The Pace Cen.
WEEDON ROAD
A4157
ELMHURST ROAD
Alfred Rose Park
Manor Park
Schools
BUCKINGHAM RD.
BICESTER ROAD
GATEHOUSE ROAD
BROADFIELDS RETAIL PARK
MILLENNIUM POINT
AYLESBURY BUSINESS CENTRE
GRIFFIN IND. MALL
Superstore
HP19
HP20
AYLESBURY
Depot
A41
ST. ANDREWS WAY INDUSTRIAL ESTATE
AYLESBURY IND. EST.
Mosque
CAMBRIDGE CL. TRADING ESTATE
BIERTON RD.
Manor House
Swim. Pool
Works
BRIDGEGATE BUSINESS PARK
ALTON HO. OFFICE PARK
TA Centre
Industrial Training Cen.
St. Mary's C of E Sch.
Bear Brook
FRIARAGE RD.
EXCHANGE ST.
HIGH ST.
Mus.
Bingo Hall
Civic Cen.
Crown Ct.
Cin.
Offs.
Superstore
Arts Cen.
Depot
California
Aylesbury College
Sports Cen.
Prebendal Farm
Pebblebrook Sch.
Comm. Cen.
A418
OXFORD ROAD
A413
Aylesbury
Spts. Grd.
California
Coun. Offs.
Mag. Ct.
WALTON ST.
Walton
HP21
Oak Green Sch.
65
WENDOVER RD.
Depot
1
2
3
4
5
6
7

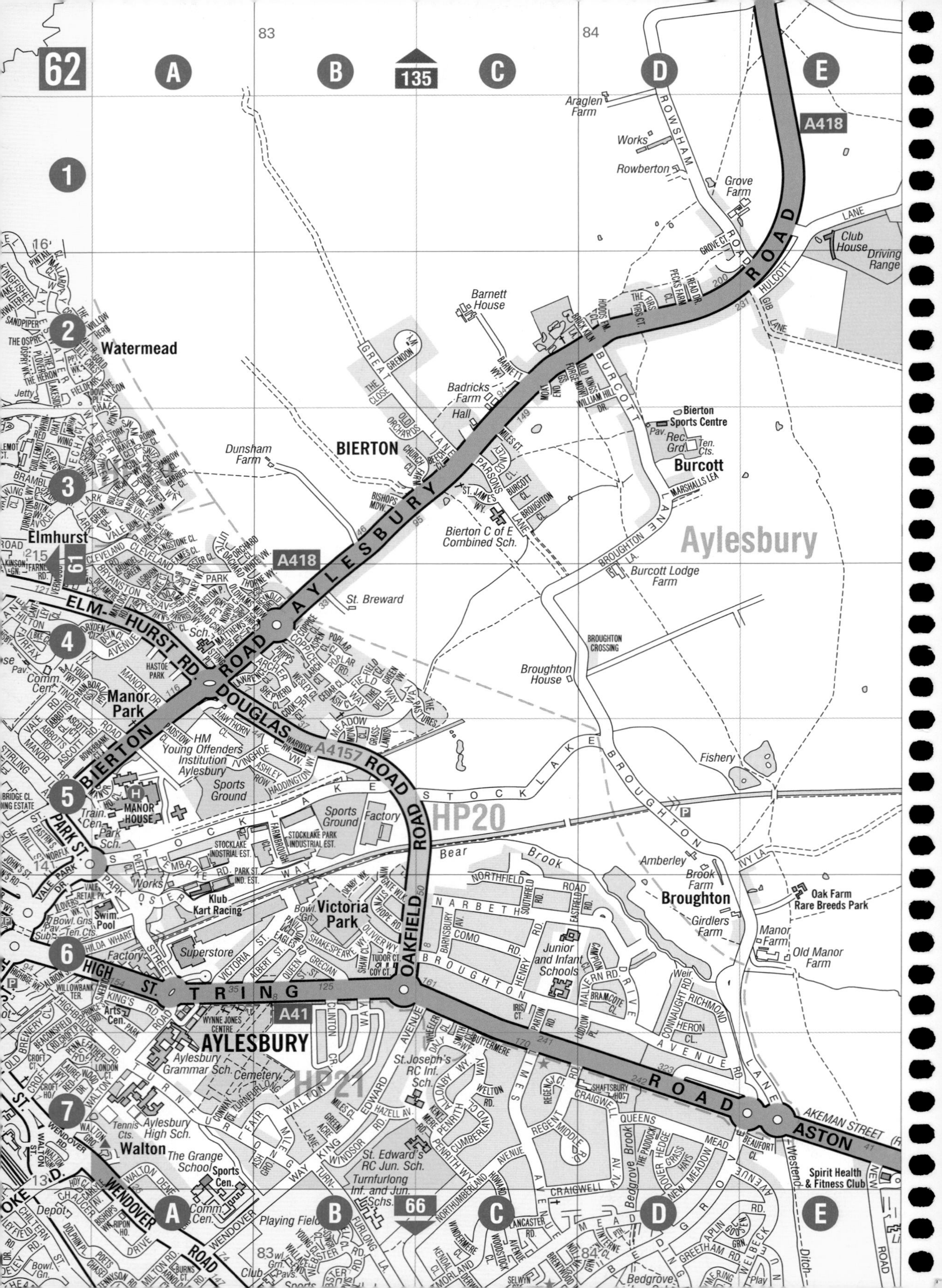

135
A418
Araglen Farm
Works
Rowberton
Grove Farm
Club House
Driving Range
Watermead
Barnett House
Badricks Farm
Hall
Bierton Sports Centre
Rec. Grd.
Burcott
Dunsham Farm
BIERTON
Bierton C of E Combined Sch.
Aylesbury
Elmhurst
61
Burcott Lodge Farm
St. Breward
BROUGHTON CROSSING
Broughton House
Manor Park
HM Young Offenders Institution Aylesbury
Sports Ground
Fishery
MANOR HOUSE
HP20
Factory
Amberley
Brook Farm
Broughton
Oak Farm Rare Breeds Park
Klub Kart Racing
Victoria Park
Girdlers Farm
Manor Farm
Old Manor Farm
Superstore
Junior and Infant Schools
A41
AYLESBURY
Aylesbury Grammar Sch.
Cemetery
HP21
St.Joseph's RC Inf. Sch.
Aylesbury High Sch.
Walton
The Grange School
Sports Cen.
St. Edward's RC Jun. Sch.
Turnfurlong Inf. and Jun. Schs.
Spirit Health & Fitness Club
66
Playing Field
Depot
Bedgrove

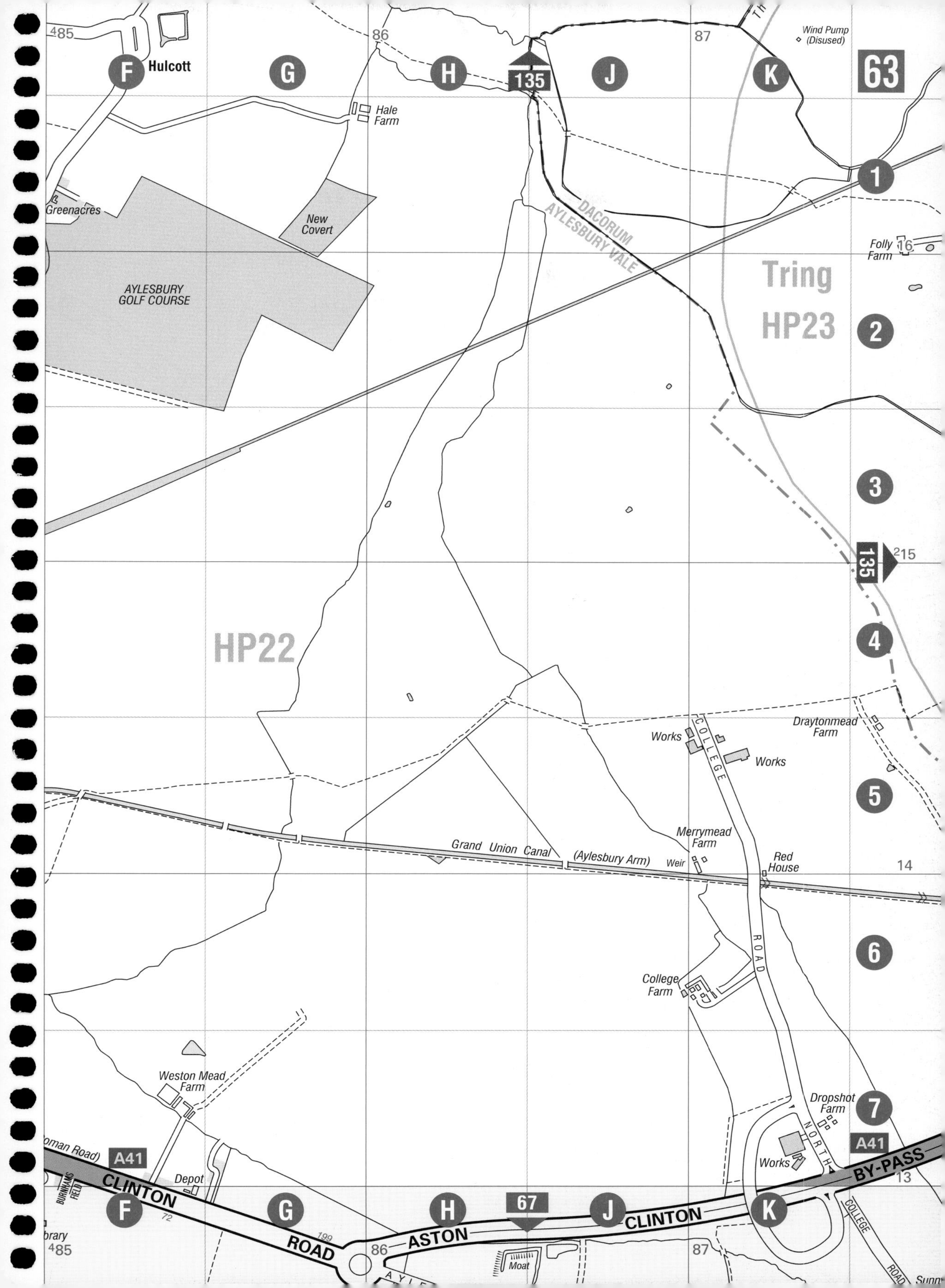

Hulcott
Hale Farm
Wind Pump (Disused)
135
Greenacres
New Covert
DACORUM
AYLESBURY VALE
AYLESBURY GOLF COURSE
Folly Farm
Tring
HP23
HP22
Draytonmead Farm
Works
COLLEGE
Works
Grand Union Canal (Aylesbury Arm)
Merrymead Farm
Weir
Red House
ROAD
College Farm
Weston Mead Farm
Dropshot Farm
NORTH
Works
A41
BY-PASS
oman Road)
A41
CLINTON
ROAD
Depot
BURNHAMS FIELD
brary
67
ASTON
CLINTON
Moat
COLLEGE ROAD
Sunn

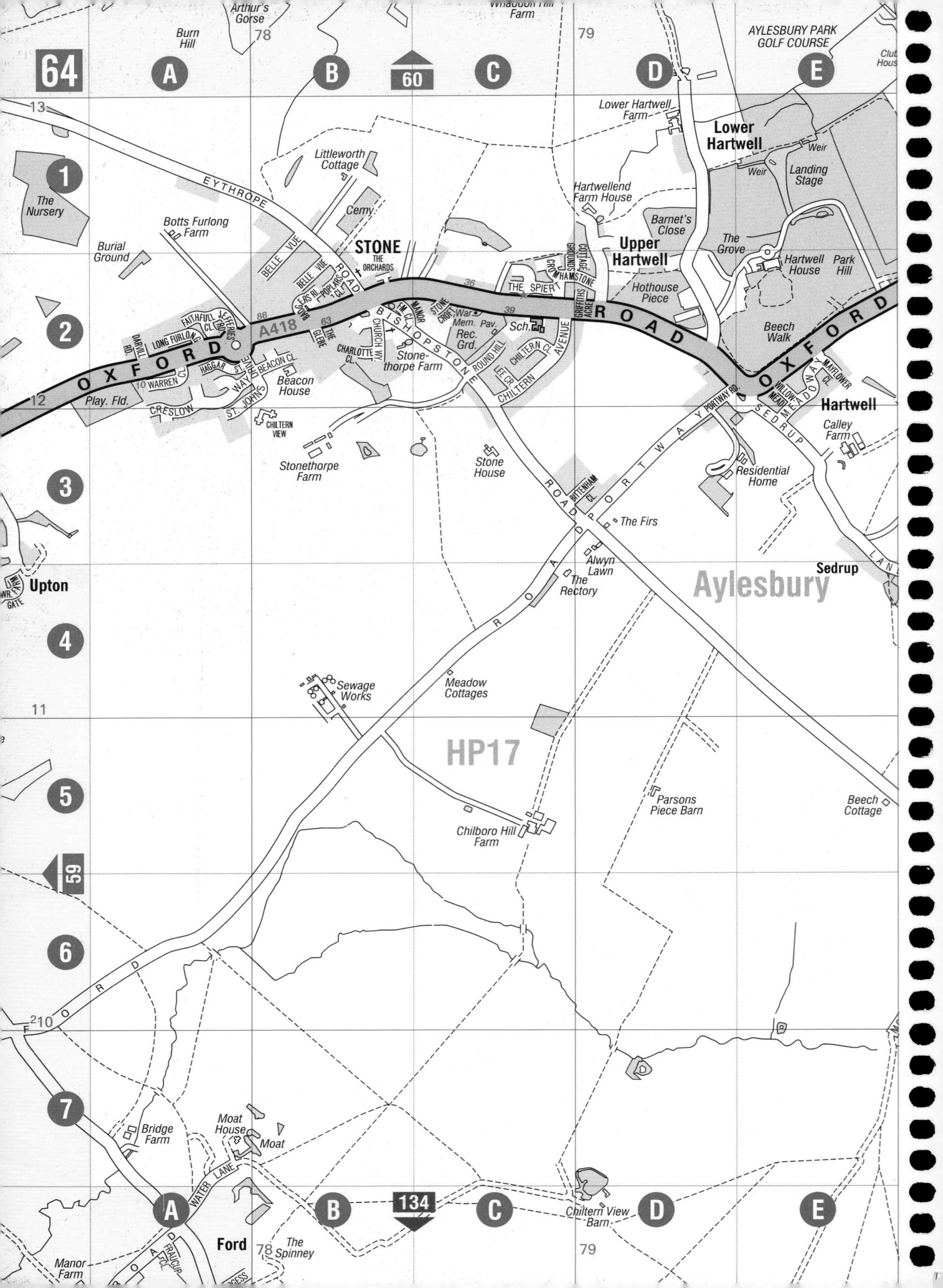

60
134
59
A
B
C
D
E
1
2
3
4
5
6
7
Arthur's Gorse
Burn Hill
Whaddon Hill Farm
AYLESBURY PARK GOLF COURSE
Club House
Lower Hartwell Farm
Lower Hartwell
Weir
Landing Stage
Littleworth Cottage
The Nursery
EYTHROPE
Botts Furlong Farm
Cemy.
Hartwellend Farm House
Barnet's Close
Upper Hartwell
The Grove
Hartwell House
Park Hill
Burial Ground
STONE
THE ORCHARDS
BELLE VUE
Hothouse Piece
OXFORD
ROAD
A418
THE SPIERT
War Mem.
Pav.
Rec. Grd.
Sch.
Beech Walk
Stonethorpe Farm
Beacon House
Play. Fld.
CRESLOW
ST. JOHN'S
CHILTERN VIEW
CHILTERN
AVENUE
BISHOPSTONE
PORTWAY
SEDRUP
Hartwell
Calley Farm
Residential Home
Stonethorpe Farm
Stone House
The Firs
Alwyn Lawn
The Rectory
Sedrup
Upton
Aylesbury
Sewage Works
Meadow Cottages
HP17
Parsons Piece Barn
Chilboro Hill Farm
Beech Cottage
Bridge Farm
Moat House
Moat
WATER LANE
Chiltern View Barn
Ford
The Spinney
Manor Farm
78
79
12
11
13
10

65
61
135
99
F
G
H
J
K
F
G
H
J
K
1
2
3
4
5
6
7
480
81
82
480
81
82
13
12
11
210
California
Pebblebrook Farm
Sch. Comm. Cen.
OXFORD RD.
PREBENDAL
Oak Green Sch.
Coun. Offs.
Mag. Ct.
WEND. OVER RD.
STOKE RD.
Aylesbury High Sch.
Tennis Cts.
Depot
Bowl. Gn.
HP19
HP21
HP22
A418
ROAD
The Oaks
Hartwell Cottage
Park Villa
Glebe House
COLDHARBOUR WAY
Edinburgh Sports Ground
Southcourt
Pav.
Hall
MANDEVILLE
B4443
Walton Court
WALTON CT. CEN.
Comm. Cen.
Ashmead Combined Sch.
Playing Field
STOKE MANDEVILLE HOSPITAL
Sports Centre
The Mandeville School
Playing Field
LOWER ROAD
Sports Grd.
Kynaston School
Stoke Leys Sch.
CHURCHILL AVENUE
CHURCHILL
TAYLOR
COTTESLOE
CARRINGTON
GRENVILLE
ELLEN ROAD
ORWELL
TYNE
RAVENSCROFT
ISIS CLOSE
Sedrup Farm
Hall End
Manor Farm
Bishopstone
Standal's Farm
Bishopstone Farm
Model Farm
BISHOPSTONE
AYLESBURY VALE
WYCOMBE
Marsh Crossing
MARSH LANE
NORTH LEE LANE
Marsh
Brook Farm
Marsh Mill Farm
Dodd's Farm

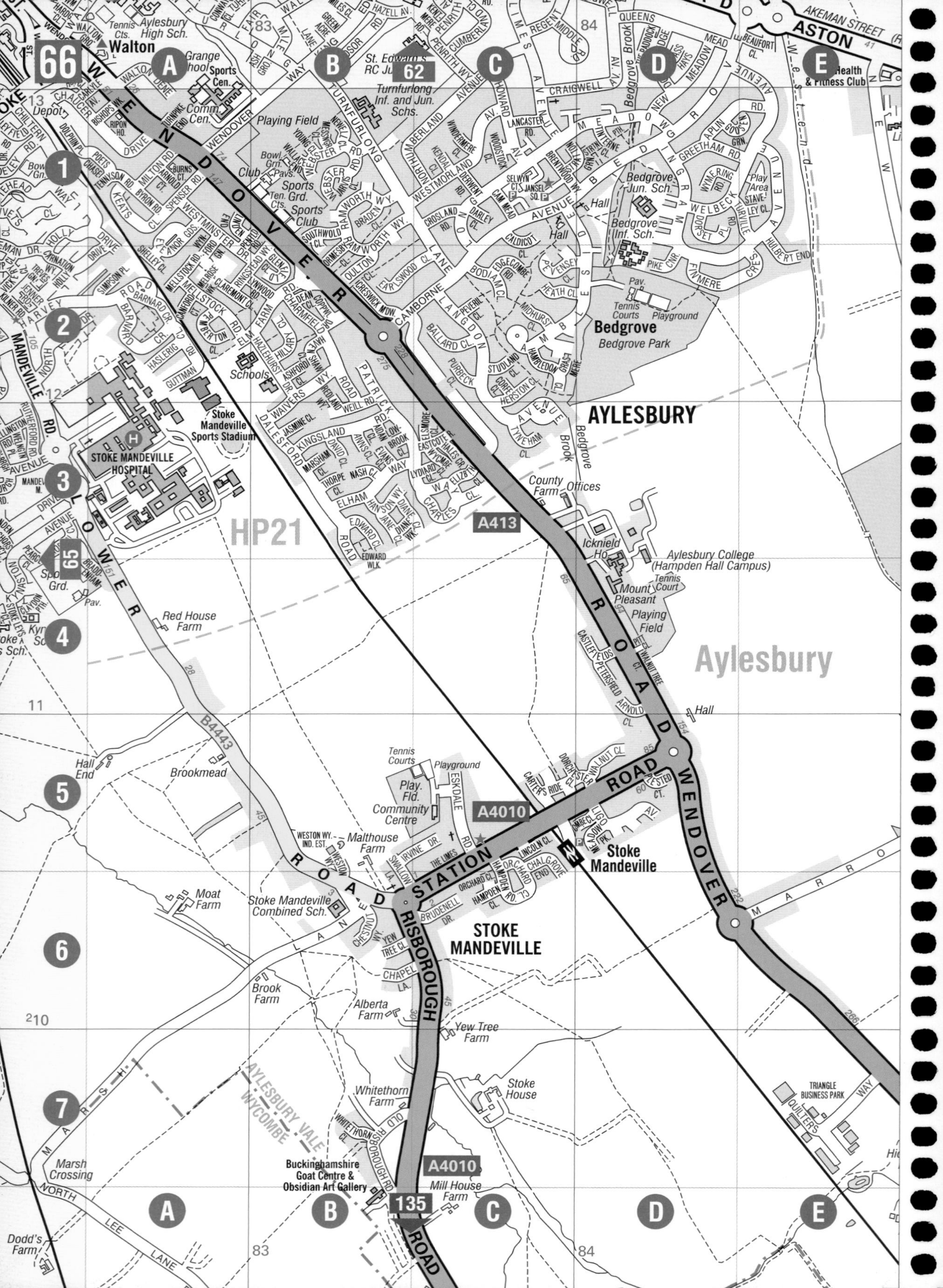

A
B
C
D
E
1
2
3
4
5
6
7
62
65
135
83
84
13
12
11
10
Walton
Tennis Cts.
Aylesbury High Sch.
Grange School
Sports Cen.
Comm. Cen.
St. Edward's RC Jun.
Turnfurlong Inf. and Jun. Schs.
Playing Field
AKEMAN STREET
ASTON
QUEENS
MEAD
BEAUFORT CL.
Health & Fitness Club
WENDOVER
ROAD
Club
Bowl Grn.
Sports Grd.
Ten. Cts.
Sports Club
Bedgrove Jun. Sch.
Bedgrove Inf. Sch.
Hall
Pav.
Tennis Courts
Playground
Bedgrove
Bedgrove Park
AYLESBURY
Bedgrove Brook
Schools
Stoke Mandeville Sports Stadium
STOKE MANDEVILLE HOSPITAL
MANDEVILLE RD.
LOWER
HP21
A413
County Farm
Offices
Icknield Ho.
Aylesbury College (Hampden Hall Campus)
Tennis Court
Mount Pleasant
Playing Field
Aylesbury
Red House Farm
Hall
B4443
Hall End
Brookmead
Tennis Courts
Playground
Play. Fld.
Community Centre
A4010
STATION
ROAD
Stoke Mandeville
Malthouse Farm
WESTON WY. IND. EST.
Moat Farm
Stoke Mandeville Combined Sch.
STOKE MANDEVILLE
RISBOROUGH
Brook Farm
Alberta Farm
Yew Tree Farm
Whitethorn Farm
Stoke House
MARROW
TRIANGLE BUSINESS PARK
QUILTERS WAY
AYLESBURY VALE
WYCOMBE
Marsh Crossing
NORTH LEE LANE
Dodd's Farm
Buckinghamshire Goat Centre & Obsidian Art Gallery
Mill House Farm
A4010
ROAD

67
63
68
69
F
G
H
J
K
485
86
87
CLINTON ROAD
ASTON CLINTON BY-PASS
A41
Roman Road
Depot
Moat
AYLESBURY ROAD
NORMILL TERRACE
TURNER'S MEADOW
AKEMAN STREET
(Roman Road)
Dropshot Farm
The Lawn
Brook Farm
Factory
LONDON RD
Rectory Farm
Weston Turville Golf & Squash Club
WESTON TURVILLE GOLF COURSE
Brookfield Farm
WESTON
Vale Farm
Rooke House
Home Farm
Rookery Farm House
Splash Covert
Rugby Ground
Bye Green
Brook End
Weston Turville C of E Sch.
Hall
AIRFIELD
Brook Farm
Mill Farm Bungalow
Mill Farm
HP22
West End
WESTON TURVILLE
Manor Farm
West End Farm
Motte & Baileys
The Manor House
Rosemead Covert
Tanks
Tree Tops
Lower Farm
Church Farm
Tennis Courts
HALTON
Engine House Belt
Clinkers Farm
Cricket Ground
Pav.
Halton Stadium (Sports Arena)
Boat House
Weston Turville Reservoir
Jetty
Sports Field
Clayfield Clump
Perch Cottage
Low Moors
Top Moors
A413
AYLESBURY RD.
Lower Meadow
Springfield Farm
Chilterns
Rifle Range
Rowborough

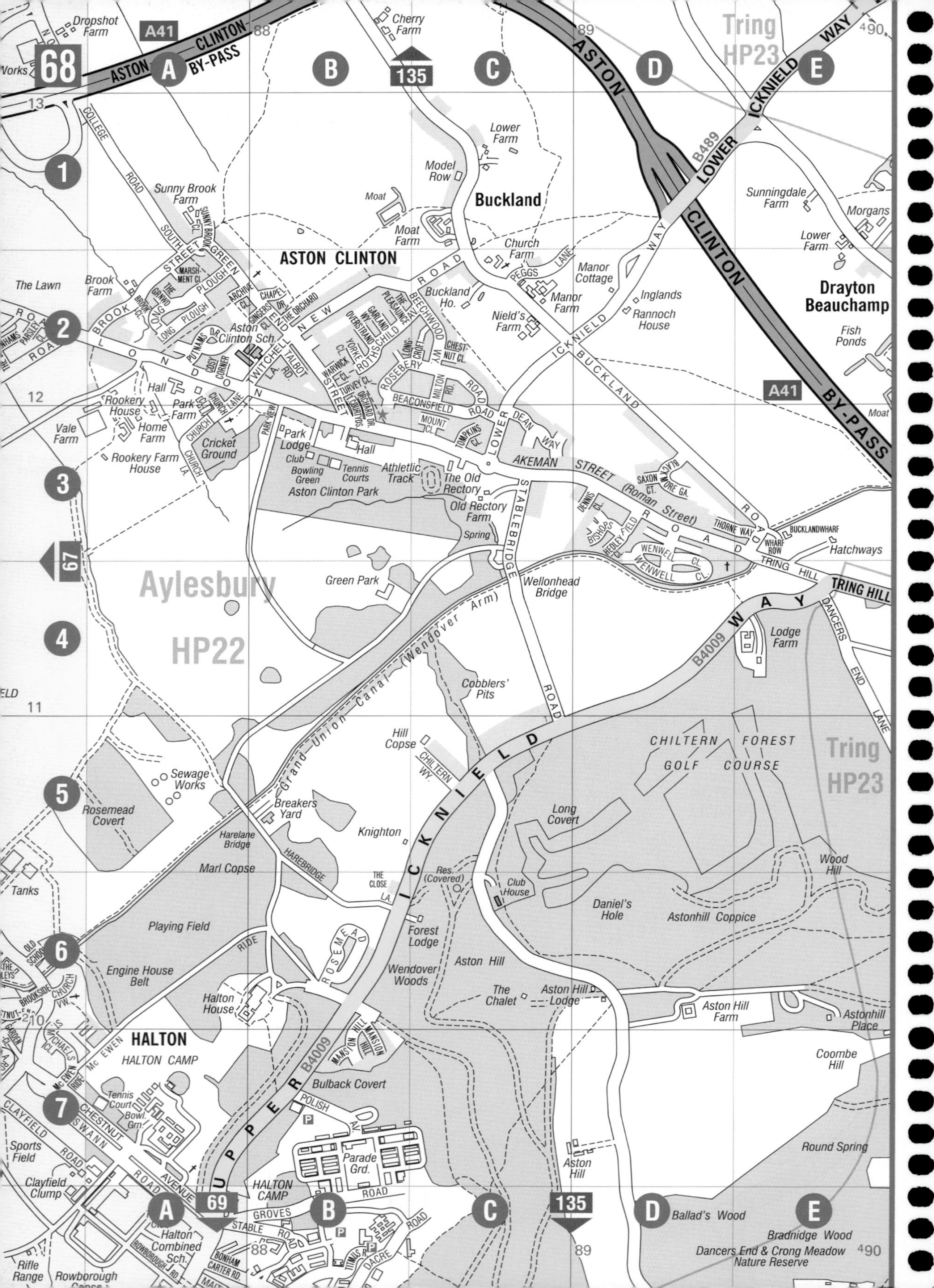

Dropshot Farm
A41
ASTON CLINTON BY-PASS
Works
Cherry Farm
135
Tring HP23
ICKNIELD WAY
A
B
C
D
E
88
89
490
13
1
COLLEGE ROAD
Sunny Brook Farm
SUNNY BROOK CL.
SOUTH STREET
GREEN END
Lower Farm
Model Row
Moat
Buckland
Moat Farm
ASTON CLINTON
Church Farm
PEGGS LANE
Manor Cottage
Manor Farm
Nield's Farm
Buckland Ho.
B489
LOWER ICKNIELD WAY
ASTON CLINTON
Sunningdale Farm
Morgans
Lower Farm
Drayton Beauchamp
Fish Ponds
Inglands
Rannoch House
The Lawn
Brook Farm
MARSH-MENT CL.
PLOUGH
THE GRAVINO
LONG PLOUGH
ARCHIVE CL.
CHAPEL DR.
GINGERS CL.
THE ORCHARD
BUCKLAND ROAD
NEW ROAD
2
BROOK CL.
BROOK ROAD
PASSLEY CL.
Aston Clinton Sch.
PUTNAMS DR.
COSY CORNER
LONDON ROAD
TWITCHELL LA.
TALBOT RD.
WARWICK CL.
YORKE CL.
ROTHSCHILD AV.
GARLAND WY.
OVERSTRAND
THE PLEASAUNCE
BEECHWOOD WAY
LONGCROFT
CHESTNUT CL.
ROSEBERY WY.
MILTON RD.
ROAD
TURVEY CL.
ORCHARD DR.
COURTYDS.
STREET
BEACONSFIELD ROAD
MOUNT CL.
TOMPKINS CL.
LOWER
DEAN WAY
A41
BY-PASS
Moat
12
Hall
Rookery House
Park Farm
CHURCH LANE
Vale Farm
Home Farm
CHURCH LA.
Cricket Ground
PARK VIEW
Park Lodge
Hall
Club
Bowling Green
Tennis Courts
Athletic Track
The Old Rectory
Aston Clinton Park
Rookery Farm House
3
AKEMAN STREET (Roman Street)
SAXON CT.
BLACKMORE GA.
DENNIS CL.
Old Rectory Farm
STABLEBRIDGE
BISHOPS CL.
HEDLEY FIELD
ROAD
THORNE WAY
WHARF ROW
BUCKLANDWHARF
Hatchways
Spring
WENWELL CL.
TRING HILL
67
Green Park
Wellonhead Bridge
Aylesbury
Grand Union Canal (Wendover Arm)
HP22
4
B4009 WAY
DANCERS END LANE
Lodge Farm
Cobblers' Pits
ROAD
11
ICKNIELD
Hill Copse
CHILTERN WY.
CHILTERN FOREST GOLF COURSE
Tring HP23
5
Sewage Works
Rosemead Covert
Breakers Yard
Long Covert
Knighton
Harelane Bridge
Marl Copse
HAREBRIDGE
THE CLOSE LA.
Res. (Covered)
Club House
Wood Hill
Daniel's Hole
Astonhill Coppice
Tanks
Playing Field
Forest Lodge
6
OLD SCHOOL
ROSEMEAD
RIDE
Engine House Belt
Wendover Woods
Aston Hill
BROOKSIDE
CHURCH VW.
The Chalet
Aston Hill Lodge
Aston Hill Farm
Astonhill Place
Halton House
MANSION HILL
HALTON
MICHAELS CL.
McEWEN RIDE
HALTON CAMP
Coombe Hill
B4009
Bulback Covert
Tennis Court
Bowl. Grn.
7
POLISH AV.
CLAYFIELD RD.
CHESTNUT
SWANN ROAD
Parade Grd.
Sports Field
Round Spring
Clayfield Clump
ROAD
AVENUE
UPPER
HALTON CAMP
ROAD
Aston Hill
69
GROVES
STABLE ROAD
135
Ballad's Wood
Halton Combined Sch.
ROAD
DACRE
TITMUS R.
BONHAM CARTER RD.
ROWBOROUGH RD.
Bradnidge Wood
Dancers End & Crong Meadow Nature Reserve
Rifle Range
Rowborough
88
89
490

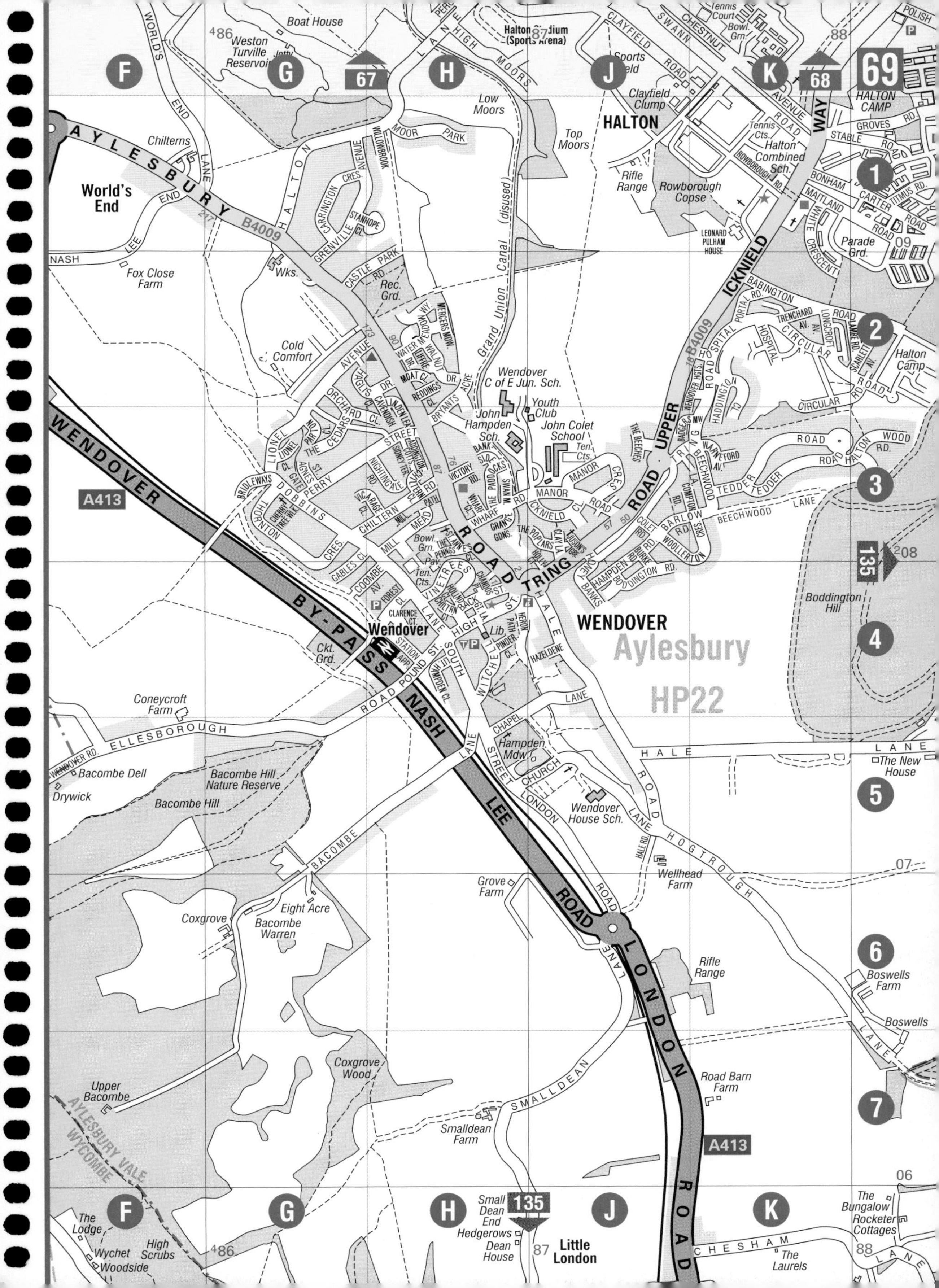

69
F
G
H
J
K
67
68
135
1
2
3
4
5
6
7
486
87
88
208
07
06
09
Boat House
Weston Turville Reservoir
Jetty
Halton Stadium (Sports Arena)
Sports Field
Tennis Court
Bowl. Grn.
POLISH
HALTON CAMP
Low Moors
Top Moors
HALTON
Clayfield Clump
CLAYFIELD ROAD
SWANN
CHESTNUT AVENUE
HIGH MOORS
MOOR PARK
WORLD'S END LANE
Chilterns
World's End
AYLESBURY ROAD
B4009
NASH LEE
Fox Close Farm
Wks.
HALTON LANE
CARRINGTON CRES.
GRENVILLE AVENUE
STANHOPE CL.
WILLOWBROOK
CASTLE PARK RD.
Rec. Grd.
MERCERS MDW.
WATER MEADOW WY.
Cold Comfort
Grand Union Canal (disused)
Rifle Range
Rowborough Copse
Tennis Cts.
Halton Combined Sch.
ROWBOROUGH RD.
LEONARD PULHAM HOUSE
UPPER ICKNIELD WAY
GROVES RD.
STABLE RD.
BONHAM
CARTER
TITMUS RD.
MAITLAND
WHITE CRESCENT
Parade Grd.
BABINGTON RD.
TRENCHARD AV.
LONGCROFT AV.
HOSPITAL ROAD
HOSPITAL CIRCULAR ROAD
PORTAL RD.
SCARLETT AV.
LAMBE RD.
Halton Camp
HADDINGTON CL.
CIRCULAR RD.
WOOD RD.
HALTON ROAD
TEDDER RD.
BEECHWOOD LANE
Wendover C of E Jun. Sch.
Youth Club
John Hampden Sch.
John Colet School
Ten. Cts.
MANOR CRES.
MANOR ROAD
ICKNIELD CL.
TRING ROAD
THE BEECHES
BADGERS MW
WENDOVER HGTS.
BEECHWOOD
WAVENEY AV.
COMPTON RD.
BARLOW RD.
COLET RD.
BURKE RD.
WOOLLERTON CRES.
HAMPDEN RD.
BODDINGTON RD.
HONEY BANKS
A413
WENDOVER BY-PASS
BRIDLEWAYS
THORNTON CRES.
DOBBINS LANE
CHERRY TREE WLK.
LIONEL CL.
AGNES GATE
PERRY ST.
THE CEDARS
ORCHARD CL.
NIGHTINGALE RD.
VICARAGE CL.
CHILTERN RD.
MILL END CL.
MILL MEAD
GABLES CL.
COOMBE AV.
FOREST CL.
CLARENCE CT.
VINETREES
BACK ST.
HIGH ST.
AYLESBURY ROAD
VICTORY RD.
WHARF CL.
THE PADDOCKS
SWAN MW.
GRANGE GDNS.
THE POPLARS
CLAY LA.
BOSWELLS FOLD
HERON PATH
PINDER CL.
HAZELDENE
HALE
Bowl. Grn.
Pav.
Ten. Cts.
Lib.
Wendover
Ckt. Grd.
STATION APP.
POUND ST.
SOUTH ST.
HAMPDEN CL.
WITCHELL
WENDOVER
Aylesbury
HP22
Boddington Hill
Coneycroft Farm
ELLESBOROUGH ROAD
WENDOVER RD.
Bacombe Dell
Drywick
Bacombe Hill Nature Reserve
Bacombe Hill
CHAPEL LANE
Hampden Mdw.
CHURCH LANE
LONDON ROAD
Wendover House Sch.
HALE LANE
The New House
HALE ROAD
HOGTROUGH LANE
HALE RD.
Wellhead Farm
NASH LEE ROAD
BACOMBE LANE
Grove Farm
Eight Acre
Coxgrove
Bacombe Warren
LONDON ROAD
Rifle Range
Boswells Farm
Boswells LANE
Coxgrove Wood
Road Barn Farm
Upper Bacombe
AYLESBURY VALE
WYCOMBE
SMALLDEAN LANE
Smalldean Farm
Small Dean End
Hedgerows
Dean House
Little London
The Lodge
Wychet
Woodside
High Scrubs
The Bungalow
Rocketer Cottages
CHESHAM LANE
The Laurels

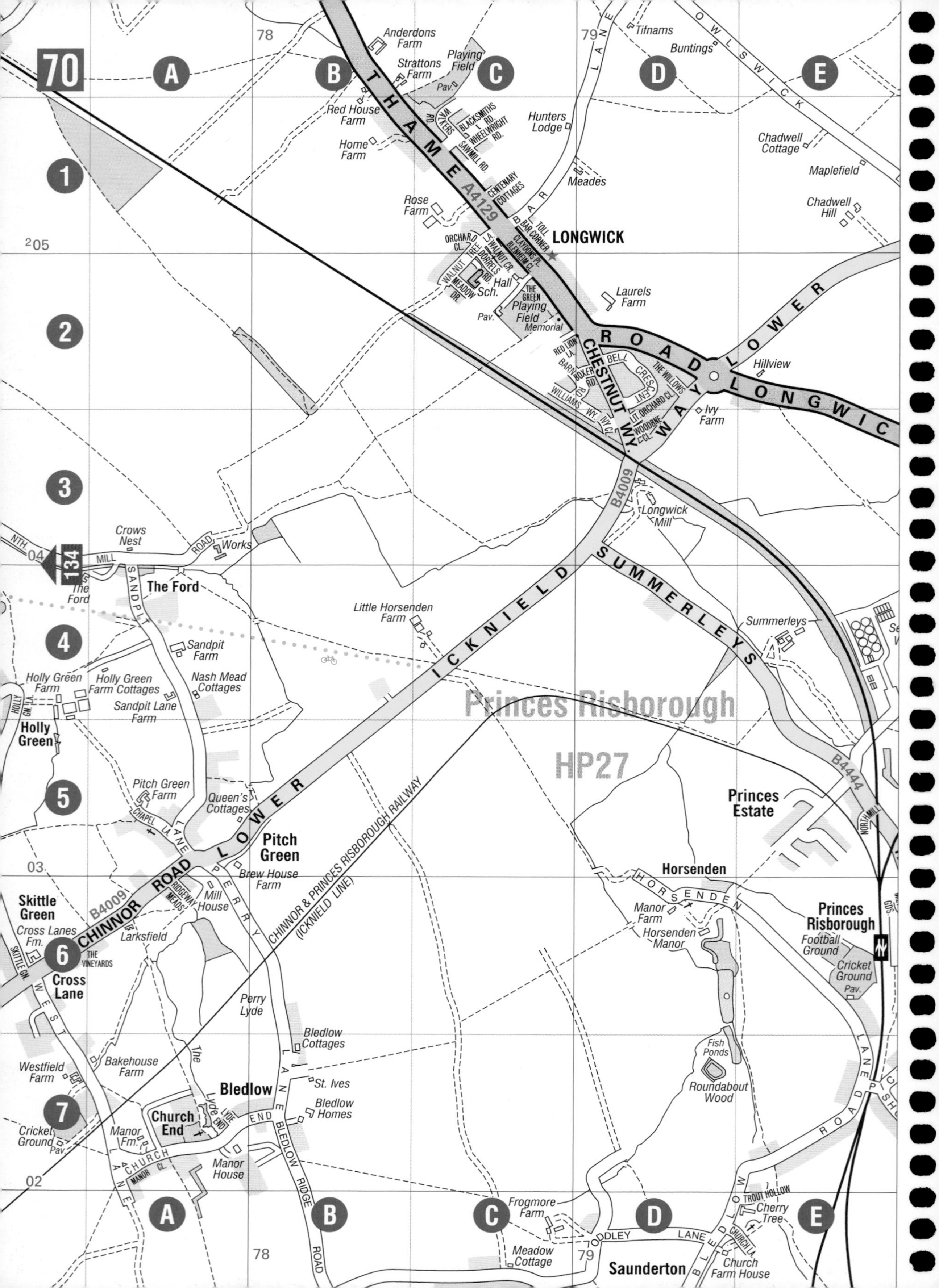

LONGWICK
Princes Risborough
HP27
Princes Estate
Horsenden
Princes Risborough
Pitch Green
Skittle Green
Cross Lane
Holly Green
The Ford
Bledlow
Church End
Saunderton
A4129
B4009
B4444
THAME
LOWER ROAD LONGWICK
ICKNIELD WAY
SUMMERLEYS
CHINNOR ROAD
LOWER
CHINNOR & PRINCES RISBOROUGH RAILWAY
(ICKNIELD LINE)
Anderdons Farm
Strattons Farm
Playing Field
Red House Farm
Home Farm
Rose Farm
Hunters Lodge
Meades
Tifnams
Buntings
Chadwell Cottage
Maplefield
Chadwell Hill
Laurels Farm
Hillview
Ivy Farm
Longwick Mill
Crows Nest
Works
Little Horsenden Farm
Summerleys
Sandpit Farm
Holly Green Farm
Holly Green Farm Cottages
Nash Mead Cottages
Sandpit Lane Farm
Pitch Green Farm
Queen's Cottages
Brew House Farm
Mill House
Larksfield
Cross Lanes Fm.
Perry Lyde
Bledlow Cottages
Bakehouse Farm
Westfield Farm
St. Ives
Bledlow Homes
Manor Fm.
Manor House
Cricket Ground
Manor Farm
Horsenden Manor
Football Ground
Cricket Ground
Fish Ponds
Roundabout Wood
Frogmore Farm
Meadow Cottage
Cherry Tree
Church Farm House
134
78
79
205
04
03
02

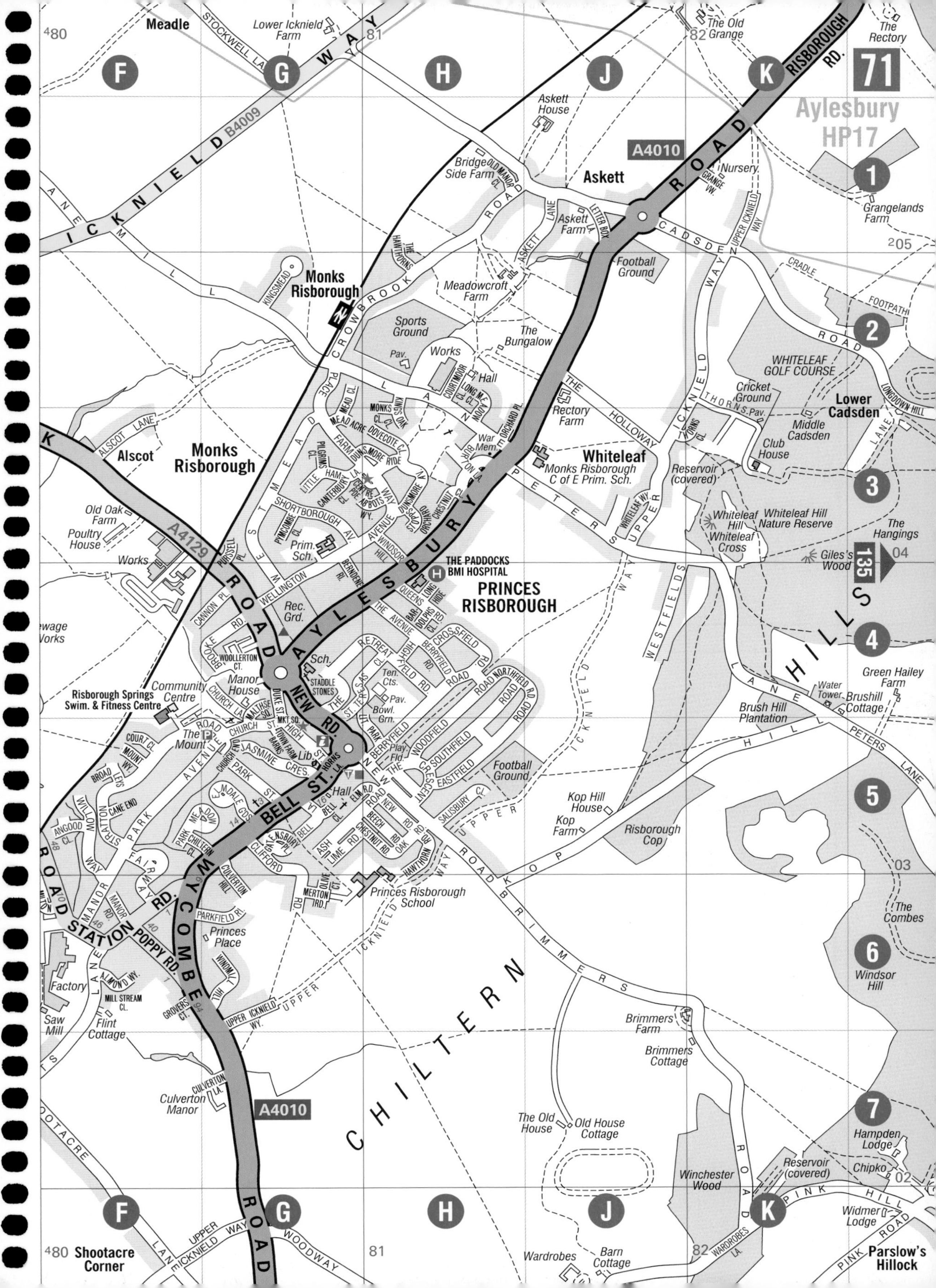
71
Aylesbury
HP17
A4010
A4129
A4010
B4009
ICKNIELD WAY
RISBOROUGH RD.
ROAD
Meadle
Lower Icknield Farm
The Old Grange
The Rectory
STOCKWELL LA.
Askett House
Bridge Side Farm
OLD MANOR CL.
Askett
Nursery
GRANGE VW.
Grangelands Farm
Askett Farm
ASKETT LANE
LETTER BOX LA.
UPPER ICKNIELD WAY
CADSDEN
Football Ground
CRADLE FOOTPATH
Monks Risborough
KINGSMEAD
MILL LANE
CROWBROOK ROAD
THE HAWTHORNS
Meadowcroft Farm
Sports Ground
Pav.
Works
The Bungalow
Hall
COURTMOOR CL.
LONG MEADOW CL.
ORCHARD PL.
THE HOLLOWAY
Rectory Farm
WHITELEAF GOLF COURSE
Cricket Ground
THORNS LA.
Lower Cadsden
LONGDOWN HILL
Middle Cadsden
Club House
Whiteleaf
Monks Risborough C of E Prim. Sch.
Reservoir (covered)
War Mem.
Alscot
ALSCOT LANE
Monks Risborough
Old Oak Farm
Poultry House
Works
PETERS LANE
WHITELEAF WY.
Whiteleaf Hill
Whiteleaf Hill Nature Reserve
Whiteleaf Cross
The Hangings
Giles's Wood
135
04
MEAD CL.
MONKS CL.
KINGS OAK
MEAD ACRE
DOVECOTE CL.
DUNSMORE RIDE
PILGRIMS CL.
FARM
LITTLE HAM LA.
CANTERBURY CL.
ABBOTS WY.
DUNSMORE AV.
CHESTNUT CL.
ORCHARD CL.
SHORTBOROUGH AV.
PYMCOMBE CL.
Prim. Sch.
WINDSOR HILL
AVENUE
THE PADDOCKS BMI HOSPITAL
PRINCES RISBOROUGH
WELLINGTON
BERNDENE RI.
QUEENS
LONG RIDE
CANNON PL.
PURSSELL PL.
Rec. Grd.
AYLESBURY
THE AVENUE
DOLPHIS CL.
CROSSFIELD RD.
WESTFIELDS
ICKNIELD WAY
Sewage Works
BROOKE RD.
WOOLLERTON CT.
Sch.
STADDLE STONES
RETREAT
HIGHFIELD RD.
BERRYFIELD RD.
NORTHFIELD RD.
Ten. Cts.
Pav.
Bowl. Grn.
Green Hailey Farm
Water Tower
Brushill Cottage
Brush Hill Plantation
HILLS
Risborough Springs Swim. & Fitness Centre
Community Centre
Manor House
CHURCH LA.
MALTHSE SQ.
DUKE ST.
NEW RD.
MKT. SQ.
HIGH ST.
TOWN FARM BARNS
CHURCH ST.
The Mount
COURT CL.
MOUNT WY.
JASMINE CRES.
Lib.
HORNS LA.
BERRYFIELD
Play. Fld.
WOODFIELD
SOUTHFIELD
EASTFIELD
CRESCENT
Football Ground
PETERS LANE
HILL
BROAD LEYS
CANE END
CHURCH END
PARK ST.
BELL ST.
Hall
ELM RD.
NEW ROAD
SALISBURY CL.
Kop Hill House
Kop Farm
KOP HILL
Risborough Cop
ANGOOD CL.
WILLOW
STRATTON
PARK WAY
MEADOW
CHILTERN
FAIRWAY
GATESBURY
CLIFFORD
ASH
LIME RD.
CHESTNUT RD.
BEECH RD.
OAK RD.
HAWTHORN RD.
WYCOMBE
CULVERTON HILL
OLIVE CL.
MERTON RD.
Princes Risborough School
BRIMMERS ROAD
03
The Combes
Windsor Hill
MANOR RD.
STATION RD.
POPPY RD.
PARKFIELD RI.
Princes Place
WINDMILL HILL
ALMOND WY.
MILL STREAM CL.
Factory
Saw Mill
Flint Cottage
GROVERS CT.
UPPER ICKNIELD WY.
CHILTERN
Brimmers Farm
Brimmers Cottage
Culverton Manor
CULVERTON LA.
The Old House
Old House Cottage
Hampden Lodge
Reservoir (covered)
Chipko
02
Winchester Wood
PINK HILL
Widmer Lodge
PINK ROAD
Parslow's Hillock
SHOOTACRE
Shootacre Corner
UPPER ICKNIELD WAY
WOODWAY
Wardrobes
Barn Cottage
WARDROBES LA.
F G H J K
1 2 3 4 5 6 7
480 81 82
205

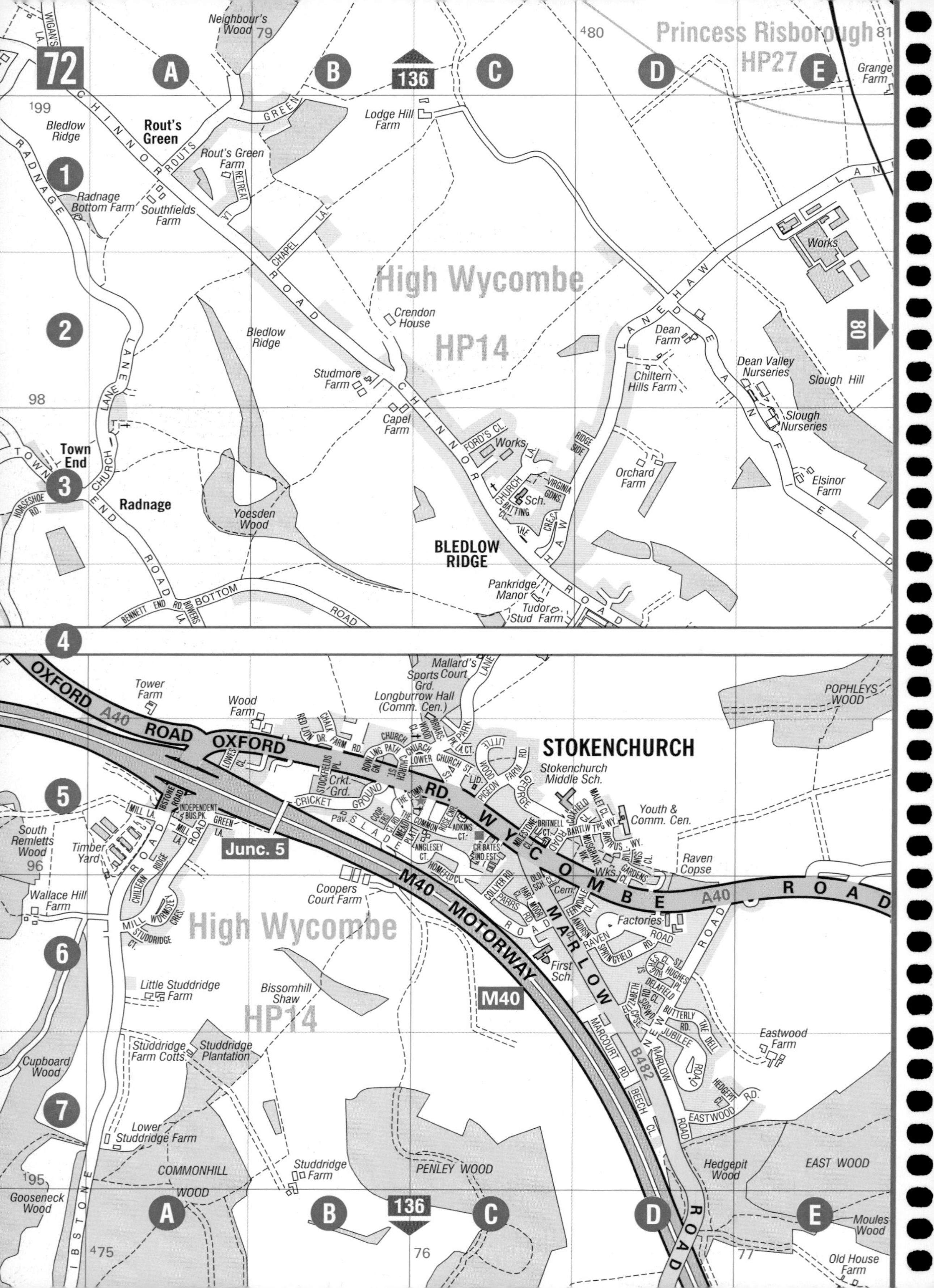
Princess Risborough
HP27
High Wycombe
HP14
Rout's Green
Bledlow Ridge
Radnage Bottom Farm
Southfields Farm
Rout's Green Farm
Lodge Hill Farm
Neighbour's Wood
Grange Farm
Works
Crendon House
Bledlow Ridge
Studmore Farm
Capel Farm
Dean Farm
Chiltern Hills Farm
Dean Valley Nurseries
Slough Hill
Slough Nurseries
Town End
Radnage
Yoesden Wood
Orchard Farm
Elsinor Farm
BLEDLOW RIDGE
Pankridge Manor
Tudor Stud Farm
CHINNOR ROAD
RADNAGE LANE
CHURCH LANE
BOTTOM ROAD
OXFORD ROAD
A40
Tower Farm
Wood Farm
Mallard's Court
Sports Grd.
Longburrow Hall (Comm. Cen.)
STOKENCHURCH
Stokenchurch Middle Sch.
POPHLEYS WOOD
Youth & Comm. Cen.
Crkt. Grd.
South Remletts Wood
Timber Yard
Junc. 5
Raven Copse
Wallace Hill Farm
Coopers Court Farm
Factories
WYCOMBE ROAD
M40 MOTORWAY
MARLOW ROAD
B482
High Wycombe
HP14
First Sch.
Little Studdridge Farm
Bissomhill Shaw
M40
Eastwood Farm
Cupboard Wood
Studdridge Farm Cotts
Studdridge Plantation
Lower Studdridge Farm
COMMONHILL WOOD
Studdridge Farm
PENLEY WOOD
Hedgepit Wood
EAST WOOD
Gooseneck Wood
Moules Wood
Old House Farm
IBSTONE ROAD
136
80

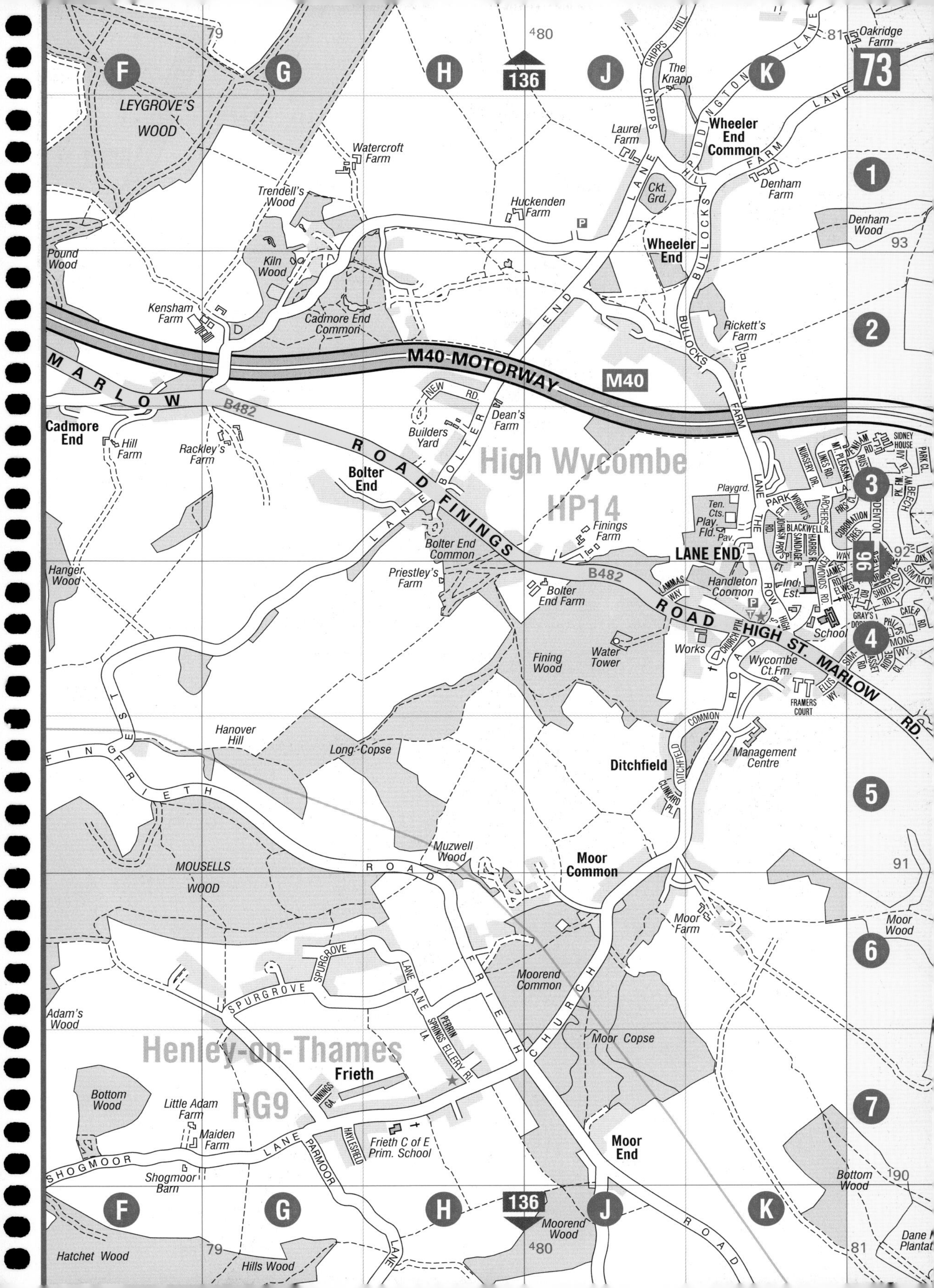

LEYGROVE'S WOOD
Watercroft Farm
Trendell's Wood
Huckenden Farm
Laurel Farm
The Knapp
Wheeler End Common
Denham Farm
Denham Wood
Pound Wood
Kiln Wood
Ckt. Grd.
Wheeler End
Kensham Farm
Cadmore End Common
Rickett's Farm
M40 MOTORWAY
M40
MARLOW
B482
Cadmore End
Hill Farm
Rackley's Farm
Builders Yard
Dean's Farm
High Wycombe
HP14
Bolter End
ROAD
FININGS
Finings Farm
Bolter End Common
Priestley's Farm
Bolter End Farm
LANE END
Handleton Coomon
Ind. Est.
Hanger Wood
Fining Wood
Water Tower
Works
Wycombe Ct.Fm.
School
HIGH ST.
MARLOW RD.
FRAMERS COURT
Hanover Hill
Long Copse
Ditchfield
Management Centre
FINGEST
FRIETH
MOUSELLS WOOD
Muzwell Wood
Moor Common
Moor Farm
Moor Wood
SPURGROVE
Moorend Common
Adam's Wood
Moor Copse
Henley-on-Thames
RG9
Frieth
Bottom Wood
Little Adam Farm
Maiden Farm
Frieth C of E Prim. School
SHOGMOOR LANE
Shogmoor Barn
PARMOOR
Moor End
Bottom Wood
Moorend Wood
Hatchet Wood
Hills Wood
Oakridge Farm

136
96
136

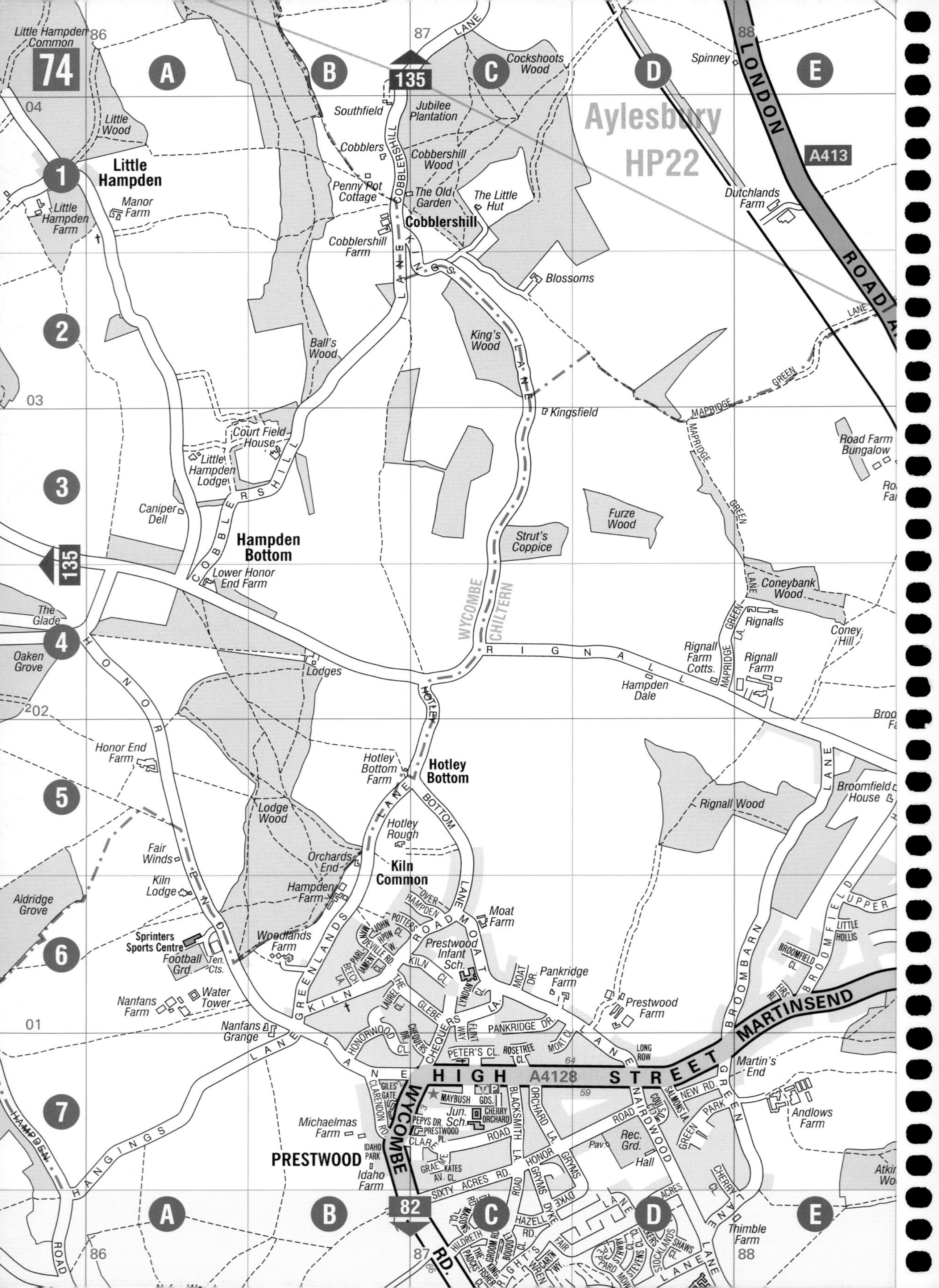

74
Little Hampden Common
Little Wood
Little Hampden
Manor Farm
Little Hampden Farm
Southfield
Cobblers
Jubilee Plantation
Cockshoots Wood
Cobbershill Wood
Penny Pot Cottage
The Old Garden
The Little Hut
Cobblershill
Cobblershill Farm
Blossoms
Aylesbury HP22
Spinney
LONDON ROAD
A413
Dutchlands Farm
Ball's Wood
King's Wood
Kingsfield
MAPRIDGE GREEN LANE
Court Field House
Little Hampden Lodge
Caniper Dell
Hampden Bottom
Lower Honor End Farm
Strut's Coppice
Furze Wood
Road Farm Bungalow
Coneybank Wood
Rignalls
Coney Hill
Rignall Farm Cotts.
Rignall Farm
Hampden Dale
RIGNALL ROAD
WYCOMBE CHILTERN
The Glade
Oaken Grove
Lodges
HOTLEY BOTTOM LANE
HONOR END LANE
Honor End Farm
Hotley Bottom Farm
Hotley Bottom
Broomfield House
Rignall Wood
Lodge Wood
Hotley Rough
Fair Winds
Orchards End
Kiln Common
Kiln Lodge
Hampden Farm
Aldridge Grove
Moat Farm
Sprinters Sports Centre
Football Grd.
Ten. Cts.
Woodlands Farm
Prestwood Infant Sch.
Pankridge Farm
Nanfans Farm
Water Tower
Prestwood Farm
Nanfans Grange
PANKRIDGE DR.
LONG ROW
MARTINSEND
Martin's End
HIGH STREET A4128
Andlows Farm
Michaelmas Farm
Jun. Sch.
Rec. Grd.
Hall
PRESTWOOD
Idaho Farm
SIXTY ACRES RD.
HANGINGS LANE
HAMPDEN ROAD
WYCOMBE RD.
Thimble Farm
135
82

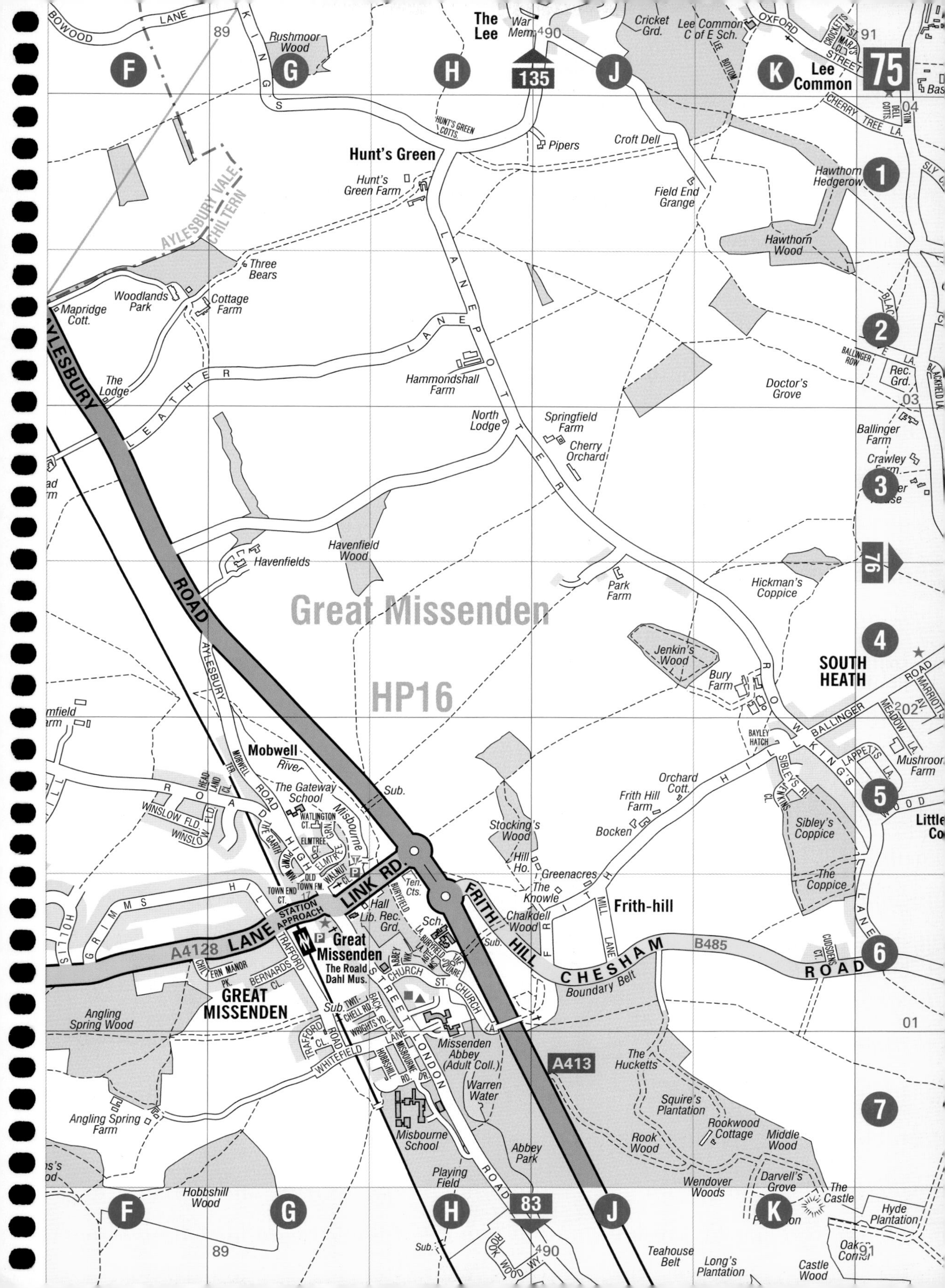
75
135
83
76
Great Missenden
HP16
GREAT MISSENDEN
The Lee
Lee Common
Hunt's Green
SOUTH HEATH
Frith-hill
Mobwell
Rushmoor Wood
Hunt's Green Farm
Pipers
Croft Dell
Field End Grange
Hawthorn Hedgerow
Hawthorn Wood
Three Bears
Woodlands Park
Cottage Farm
Mapridge Cott.
The Lodge
Hammondshall Farm
North Lodge
Springfield Farm
Cherry Orchard
Doctor's Grove
Ballinger Farm
Havenfield Wood
Havenfields
Park Farm
Hickman's Coppice
Jenkin's Wood
Bury Farm
Orchard Cott.
Frith Hill Farm
Bocken
Stocking's Wood
Greenacres
The Knowle
Chalkdell Wood
Sibley's Coppice
The Coppice
Mushroom Farm
The Gateway School
Angling Spring Wood
Angling Spring Farm
The Roald Dahl Mus.
Missenden Abbey (Adult Coll.)
Warren Water
Misbourne School
Abbey Park
Playing Field
The Hucketts
Squire's Plantation
Rookwood Cottage
Rook Wood
Middle Wood
Wendover Woods
Darvell's Grove
The Castle
Hyde Plantation
Hobbshill Wood
Teahouse Belt
Long's Plantation
Castle Wood
Boundary Belt
AYLESBURY ROAD
LEATHER LANE
POTTER ROW
FRITH HILL
CHESHAM ROAD
A4128
A413
B485
LINK RD.
STATION APPROACH
GRIMMS HILL
KINGS LANE
BOWOOD LANE
AYLESBURY VALE
CHILTERN

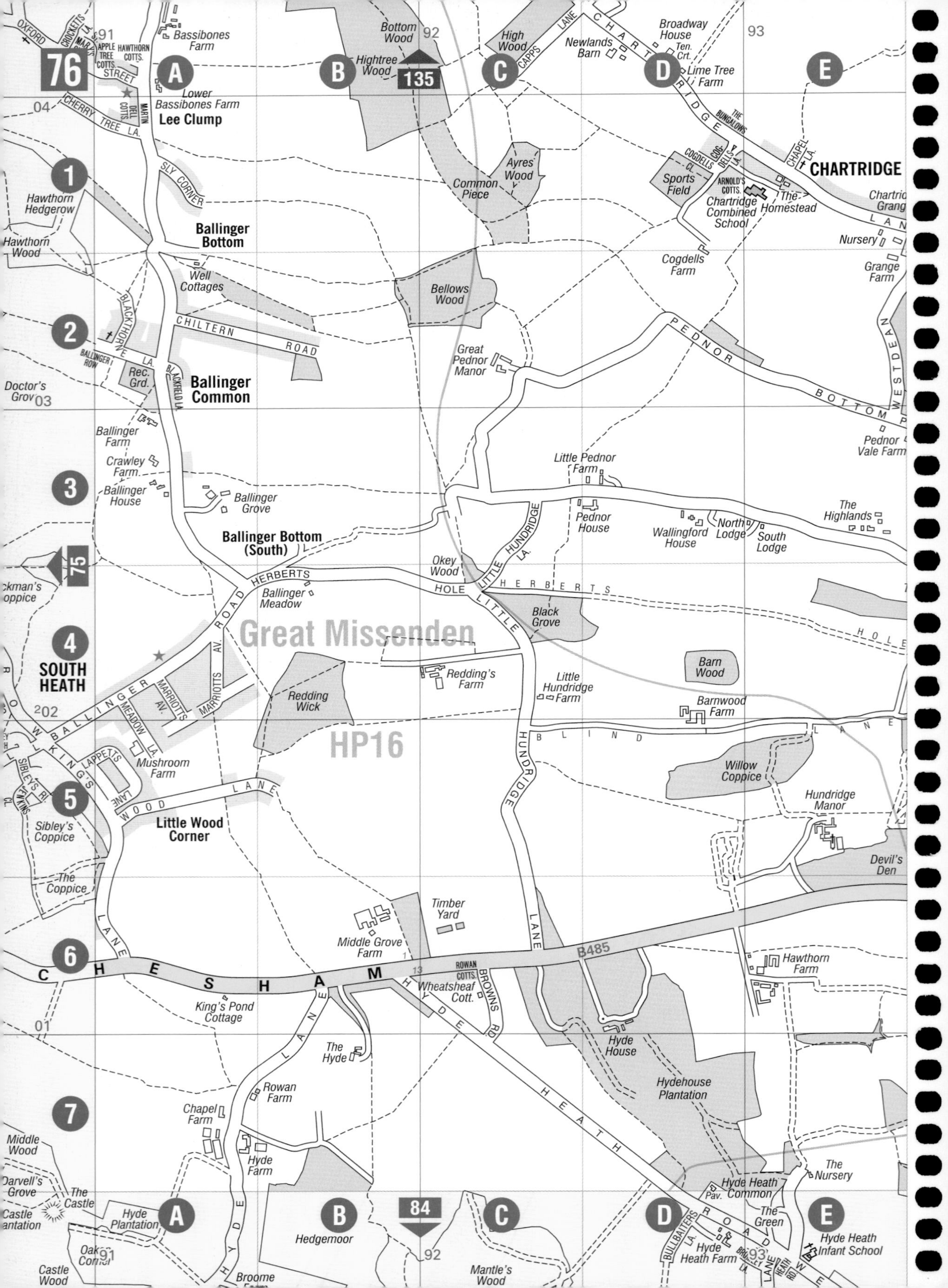

Bassibones Farm
Lower Bassibones Farm
Lee Clump
Bottom Wood
Hightree Wood
135
High Wood
Newlands Barn
Broadway House
Lime Tree Farm
CHARTRIDGE
Ayres Wood
Common Piece
Sports Field
Chartridge Combined School
The Homestead
Cogdells Farm
Hawthorn Hedgerow
Hawthorn Wood
Ballinger Bottom
Well Cottages
Bellows Wood
CHILTERN ROAD
PEDNOR BOTTOM
Great Pednor Manor
Ballinger Common
Rec. Grd.
Doctor's Grove
Ballinger Farm
Crawley Farm
Ballinger House
Ballinger Grove
Little Pednor Farm
Pednor House
Wallingford House
North Lodge
South Lodge
The Highlands
Pednor Vale Farm
Nursery
Grange Farm
Ballinger Bottom (South)
75
Okey Wood
HERBERTS HOLE
Ballinger Meadow
Black Grove
SOUTH HEATH
Great Missenden
Redding's Farm
Little Hundridge Farm
Barn Wood
Redding Wick
Barnwood Farm
BLIND LANE
HP16
Mushroom Farm
Willow Coppice
Hundridge Manor
Little Wood Corner
WOOD LANE
Sibley's Coppice
The Coppice
Devil's Den
Timber Yard
Middle Grove Farm
B485
CHESHAM
Wheatsheaf Cott.
Hawthorn Farm
King's Pond Cottage
The Hyde
Hyde House
Hydehouse Plantation
Rowan Farm
Chapel Farm
Hyde Farm
Middle Wood
Darvell's Grove
The Castle
Castle Plantation
Hyde Plantation
Hedgemoor
84
Mantle's Wood
Broome Farm
Hyde Heath Common
The Nursery
The Green
Hyde Heath Farm
Hyde Heath Infant School
Castle Wood
Oak Copse

77
Asheridge
Hardell Spring
Garrett's Wood
Stroutsfield Spring
135
Great Hivings
Broadview Farm
CHESHAM VALE
Captain's Wood
Mount Nugent Farm
Hazeldene Farm
Greenacres
Raymonds
Caravan Site
Tennis Court
Club House
CHARTRIDGE PARK GOLF COURSE
Smallholding
Pavilion
Playing Fields
(Nature Reserve)
Captain's Wood
Pond Park
Portobello Farm
Pednor Bottom
Short Grove
Pendor Stables
Wych Elm Farm
Long Grove
Great Friar's Hill
Depot
Works
Wks.
Elmtree Sch.
Newtown
Chesham
Cherry Tree Farm
The Old Sun House
Pednor Mead Farm
Rose Acre
Little Friar's Hill
Sears Barn
Poultry Farm
Chesham Park Community College
Playing Field
Lowndes Park
HP5
CHESHAM
Skottowe's Pond
The Elgiva
Superstore
Chesham
The Plantation
Spring Wood
Bury Pond
The Bury
Lower Hundridge Farm
The Bury Farm
Tennis Courts
Pednormead End
Halfway House Farm
Bishop's Hill
Snowdrop Belt
Wellington's Wood
Sports Grd.
Cricket Grd.
Chesham Utd. FC Ground
Topnotch Health Centre
Chesham Bois Manor
Gracelets
White's Wood
Amersham HP6
Monk's Wood
White House Farm
85
Beech Wood
Elvidge Wood
Pen Grove
Howlet's Wood
Fullers Hill Farm
Little Hodds Wood
MISSENDEN ROAD
B485
A416
HALFWAY HOUSE LANE
FULLER'S
AMERSHAM RD.
F G H J K
1 2 3 4 5 6 7

Little Pressmore Farm
Pressmore Farm
135
Woodside
Cassett's Spring
Dean's Wood
Kennels
Felmoor Wood
Little Grove Wood
Broadview Farm
CHESHAM VALE
Francis Wood
Ashley Hall Farm
Nashleigh Farm
Torrington Farm
Chesham Preparatory School
Orchard Leigh Villas
Amersham & Wycombe College (Chesham Campus)
Electricity Transformer Station
Pond Park
Whitethorn's Farm
Depot
Lye Green
Smallholding
Lyegreen Farm
Lycrome Wood
Warehouse
Brushwood Junior School
Brockhurst Farm
Chesham
Hilltop
Newtown
Heritage Ho. Sch.
HP5
Codmore
Rec. Grd.
Lee Farm
Botley
Hollybush Farm
Chesham High School
Playing Field
CHESHAM
The Elgiva
Chesham Leisure Centre
Mapletree Wood
Hollybush Wood
Tyler's Hill
Chesham
Dungrove Farm
Cowcroft Grange
Cowcroft Farm
Big Round Green
Cowcroft Wood
The Balks
CHESHAM HOSPITAL
Hill Farm Plantation
Waterside
Topnotch Health Centre
Hill Farm
Ladies Wood
Chessmount
Sports Centre
Hill Farm Spring
Waterside Combined School
Playing Fields
Chalk Dell
Beech Wood
Chesham Moor
86
Elvidge Wood
Aldridge's Dell
Lower Bois
River Chess
Little Hodds Wood
Trout Farm
Milk Hall Barns
Wychfield Spring
NASHLEIGH HILL
ASHLEY GREEN ROAD
LYE GREEN
RUSHMERE LANE
BOTLEY ROAD
ST. BERKHAMPSTEAD RD.
ESKDALE AVENUE
BROAD ST.
RED LION ST.
AMERSHAM ROAD
A416
B4505

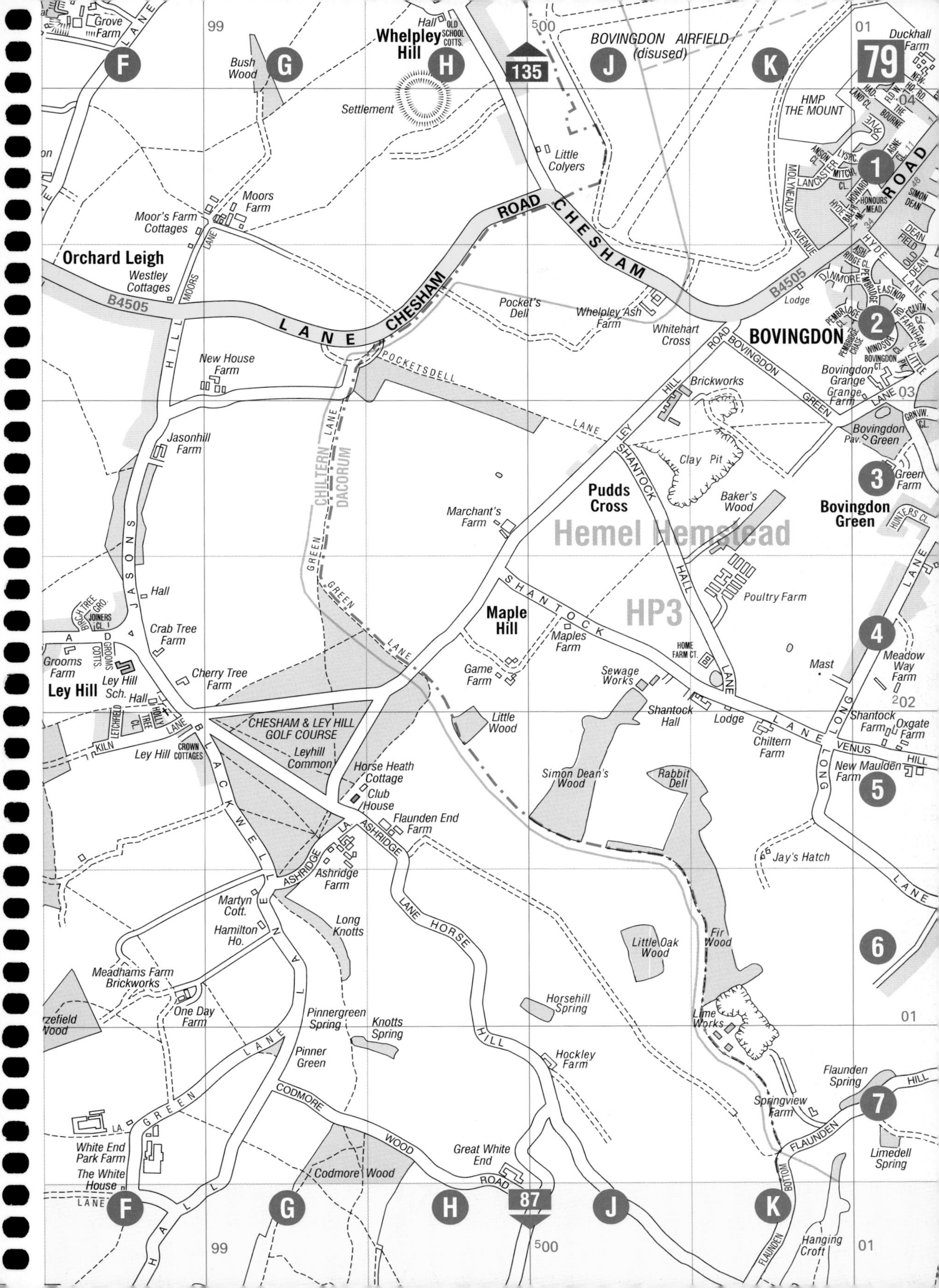

Whelpley Hill
BOVINGDON AIRFIELD (disused)
135
HMP THE MOUNT
Duckhall Farm
Bush Wood
Settlement
Little Colyers
Moors Farm
Moor's Farm Cottages
Orchard Leigh
Westley Cottages
B4505
CHESHAM ROAD
CHESHAM LANE
Pocket's Dell
Whelpley Ash Farm
Whitehart Cross
BOVINGDON
New House Farm
POCKETSDELL LANE
Brickworks
Bovingdon Grange
Grange Farm
Bovingdon Green
Jasonhill Farm
CHILTERN
DACORUM
Clay Pit
Pudds Cross
Baker's Wood
Marchant's Farm
Hemel Hempstead
HP3
Poultry Farm
Maple Hill
Maples Farm
JASONS HILL
Crab Tree Farm
Cherry Tree Farm
Grooms Farm
Ley Hill
Ley Hill Sch.
Game Farm
Sewage Works
Shantock Hall
Lodge
Mast
Meadow Way Farm
Little Wood
CHESHAM & LEY HILL GOLF COURSE
Leyhill Common
Horse Heath Cottage
Club House
Flaunden End Farm
Simon Dean's Wood
Rabbit Dell
Chiltern Farm
Shantock Farm
Oxgate Farm
VENUS HILL
New Maulden Farm
Jay's Hatch
Ashridge Farm
Martyn Cott.
Hamilton Ho.
Long Knotts
Little Oak Wood
Fir Wood
Meadhams Farm Brickworks
One Day Farm
Pinnergreen Spring
Knotts Spring
Horsehill Spring
Lime Works
Pinner Green
Hockley Farm
Flaunden Spring
Springview Farm
FLAUNDEN
White End Park Farm
The White House
CODMORE WOOD ROAD
Codmore Wood
Great White End
Limedell Spring
87
Hanging Croft

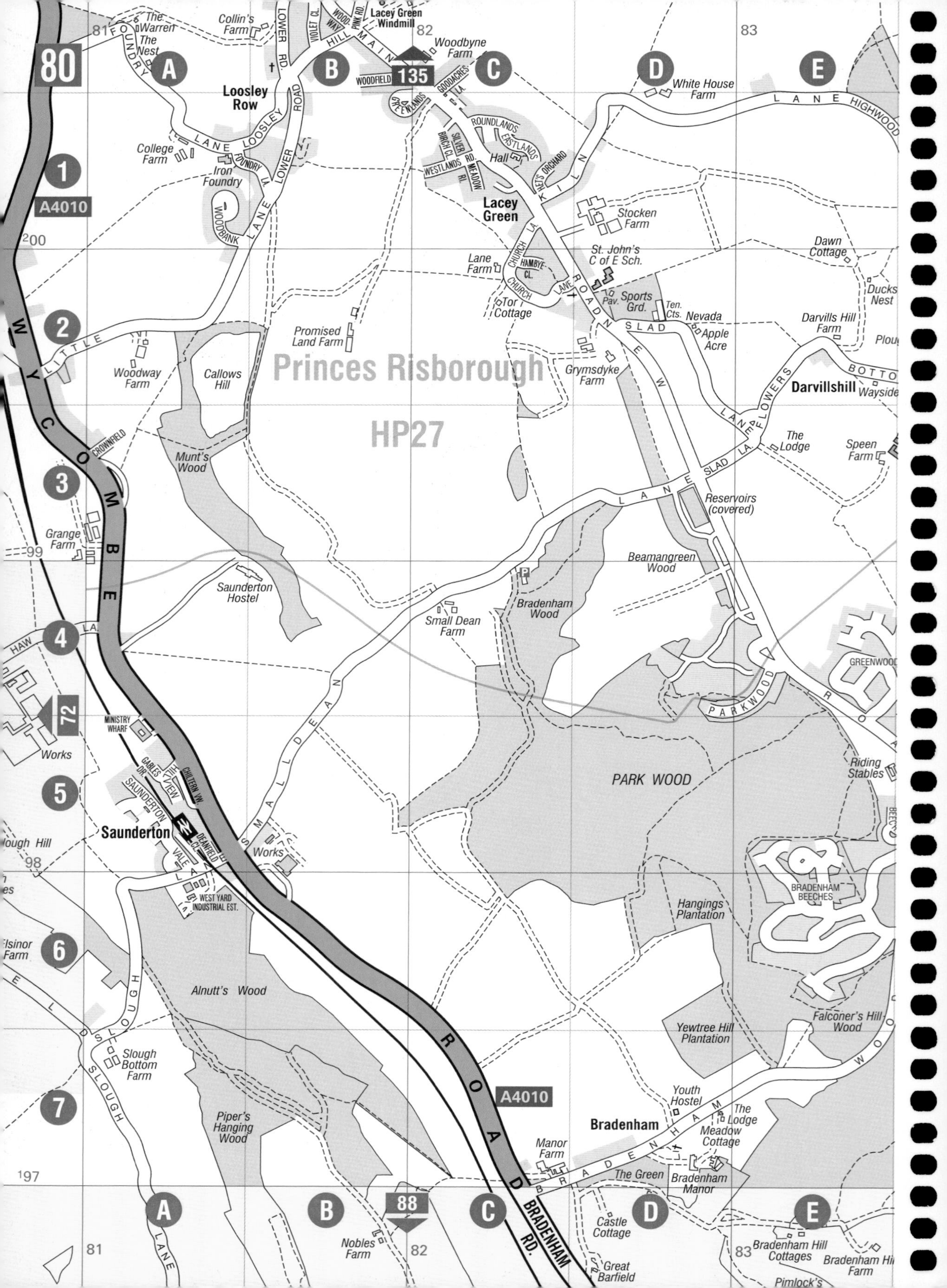
80
Princes Risborough
HP27
Loosley Row
Lacey Green
Lacey Green Windmill
Darvillshill
Saunderton
Bradenham
The Warren
The Nest
Collin's Farm
Woodbyne Farm
White House Farm
College Farm
Iron Foundry
Stocken Farm
St. John's C of E Sch.
Lane Farm
Tor Cottage
Sports Grd.
Pav.
Ten. Cts.
Nevada
Apple Acre
Dawn Cottage
Ducks Nest
Darvills Hill Farm
Wayside
Promised Land Farm
Woodway Farm
Callows Hill
Grymsdyke Farm
Munt's Wood
The Lodge
Speen Farm
Reservoirs (covered)
Grange Farm
Beamangreen Wood
Saunderton Hostel
Bradenham Wood
Small Dean Farm
Works
Ministry Wharf
PARK WOOD
Riding Stables
Bradenham Beeches
Hangings Plantation
West Yard Industrial Est.
Alnutt's Wood
Yewtree Hill Plantation
Falconer's Hill Wood
Slough Bottom Farm
Piper's Hanging Wood
Youth Hostel
The Lodge
Meadow Cottage
Manor Farm
The Green
Bradenham Manor
Castle Cottage
Great Barfield
Nobles Farm
Bradenham Hill Cottages
Pimlock's
A4010
WYCOMBE ROAD
ROAD
BRADENHAM RD.
LITTLE HAW LA.
LOOSLEY LANE
LOWER ROAD
LOWER RD.
WOODBANK
FOUNDRY LA.
FOUNDRY
MAIN
HILL
WOODFIELD
GREENLANDS
GOODACRES LA.
ROUNDLANDS
EASTLANDS
SILVER BIRCH CL.
WESTLANDS RD.
MEADOW RI.
KILN
HIGHWOOD LANE
CHURCH LA.
CHURCH LANE
HAMBYE CL.
NEW ROAD
SLAD LANE
SLAD LA.
FLOWERS LA.
BOTTOM
LANE
SMALLDEAN LANE
CROWNFIELD
PARKWOOD
GREENWOOD
GABLES DR.
HILL VIEW
CHILTERN VW.
SAUNDERTON VALE
DEANFIELD CL.
SLOUGH LANE
BRADENHAM WOODS
135
72
88
A B C D E
1 2 3 4 5 6 7
81 82 83
200 99 98 197

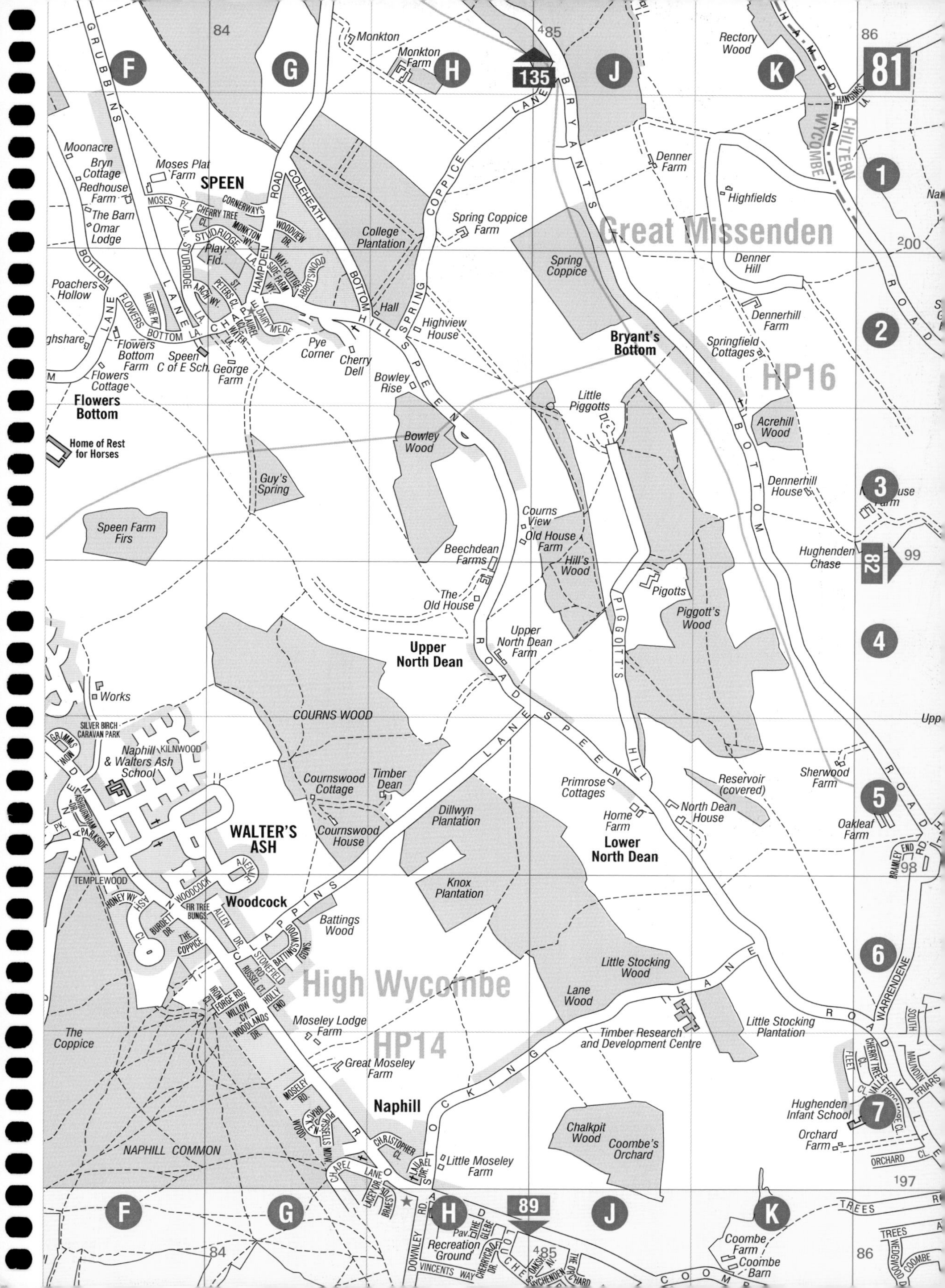
SPEEN
Moonacre
Bryn Cottage
Redhouse Farm
The Barn
Omar Lodge
Moses Plat Farm
Poachers Hollow
Flowers Bottom Farm
Flowers Cottage
Flowers Bottom
Speen C of E Sch.
George Farm
Pye Corner
Cherry Dell
Home of Rest for Horses
Guy's Spring
Speen Farm Firs
Monkton
Monkton Farm
College Plantation
Hall
Highview House
Bowley Rise
Bowley Wood
Spring Coppice Farm
Spring Coppice
Great Missenden
Rectory Wood
Denner Farm
Highfields
Denner Hill
Dennerhill Farm
Springfield Cottages
HP16
Acrehill Wood
Dennerhill House
Bryant's Bottom
Little Piggotts
Courns View
Old House Farm
Hill's Wood
Beechdean Farms
The Old House
Pigotts
Piggott's Wood
Hughenden Chase
Upper North Dean
Upper North Dean Farm
COURNS WOOD
Works
SILVER BIRCH CARAVAN PARK
Naphill & Walters Ash School
WALTER'S ASH
Woodcock
Cournswood Cottage
Timber Dean
Cournswood House
Dillwyn Plantation
Knox Plantation
Battings Wood
Primrose Cottages
Home Farm
North Dean House
Lower North Dean
Reservoir (covered)
Sherwood Farm
Oakleaf Farm
High Wycombe
Little Stocking Wood
Lane Wood
Little Stocking Plantation
Timber Research and Development Centre
Moseley Lodge Farm
HP14
Great Moseley Farm
Naphill
The Coppice
NAPHILL COMMON
Little Moseley Farm
Chalkpit Wood
Coombe's Orchard
Hughenden Infant School
Orchard Farm
Recreation Ground
Coombe Farm
Coombe Barn
GRUBBINS LANE
BOTTOM LANE
FLOWERS BOTTOM LA.
COLEHEATH BOTTOM
HAMPDEN ROAD
SPRING COPPICE LANE
BRYANT'S BOTTOM ROAD
SPEEN ROAD
PIGGOTT'S HILL
LAPPINS LANE
STOCKING LANE
WARRENDENE ROAD
HAMPDEN WYCOMBE CHILTERN
F G H J K
135
89
82
1 2 3 4 5 6 7
84
485
86
200
99
98
197

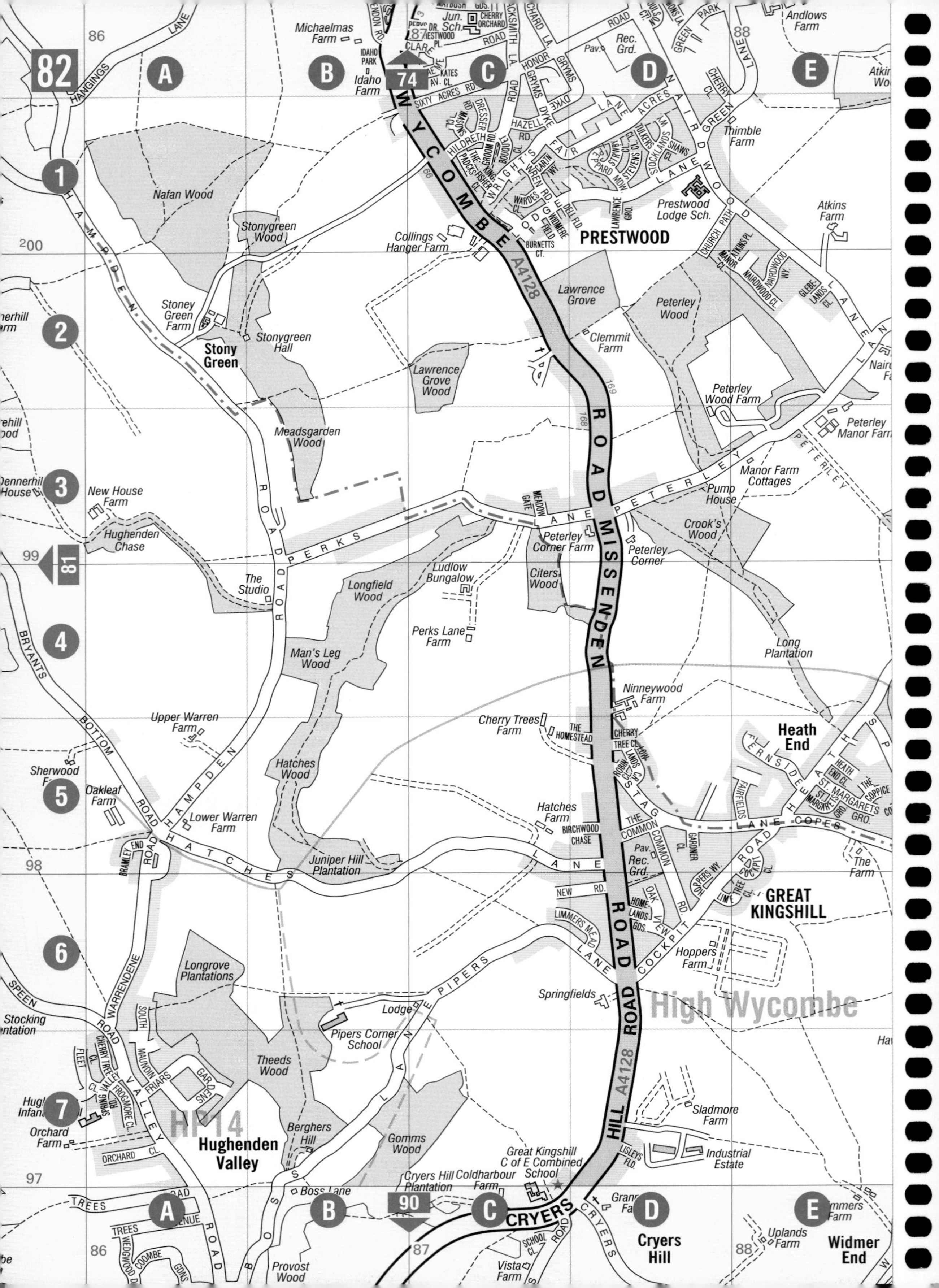
Michaelmas Farm
Idaho Farm
74
Nafan Wood
Stonygreen Wood
Collings Hanger Farm
PRESTWOOD
Prestwood Lodge Sch.
Atkins Farm
Andlows Farm
Thimble Farm
Rec. Grd.
Stoney Green Farm
Stony Green
Stonygreen Hall
Lawrence Grove
Peterley Wood
Clemmit Farm
Lawrence Grove Wood
Peterley Wood Farm
Peterley Manor Farm
Meadsgarden Wood
Manor Farm Cottages
Pump House
New House Farm
Hughenden Chase
Crook's Wood
Peterley Corner Farm
Peterley Corner
81
The Studio
Longfield Wood
Ludlow Bungalow
Citers Wood
Perks Lane Farm
Man's Leg Wood
Long Plantation
Ninneywood Farm
Upper Warren Farm
Cherry Trees Farm
Heath End
Sherwood
Hatches Wood
Oakleaf Farm
Lower Warren Farm
Hatches Farm
Juniper Hill Plantation
The Farm
GREAT KINGSHILL
Longrove Plantations
Hoppers Farm
Springfields
Lodge
High Wycombe
Pipers Corner School
Theeds Wood
HP14
Sladmore Farm
Orchard Farm
Berghers Hill
Gomms Wood
Industrial Estate
Hughenden Valley
Great Kingshill C of E Combined School
Cryers Hill Plantation
Coldharbour Farm
Boss Lane
90
Cryers Hill
Uplands Farm
Widmer End
Provost Wood
Vista Farm
WYCOMBE
A4128
MISSENDEN ROAD
HILL ROAD
PETERLEY LANE
PERKS
HAMPDEN ROAD
BRYANTS BOTTOM ROAD
HATCHES LANE
PIPERS LANE
COCKPIT ROAD
LIMMERS MEAD
SPEEN ROAD
WARRENDENE
VALLEY
CRYERS

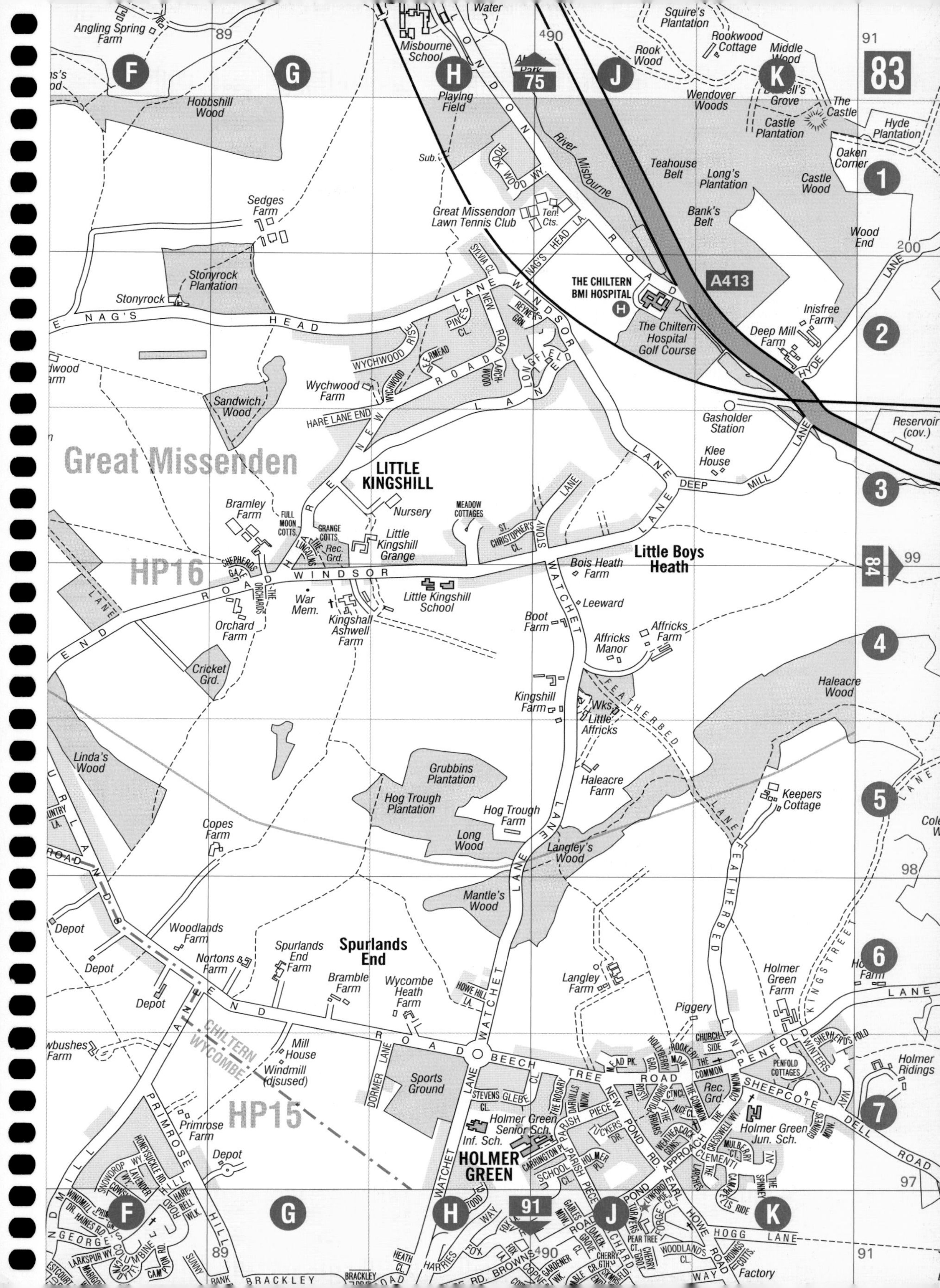
Great Missenden
LITTLE KINGSHILL
Little Boys Heath
Spurlands End
HOLMER GREEN
HP16
HP15
A413
THE CHILTERN BMI HOSPITAL
The Chiltern Hospital Golf Course
Great Missenden Lawn Tennis Club
Misbourne School
Playing Field
River Misbourne
LONDON ROAD
Hobbshill Wood
Sedges Farm
Stonyrock Plantation
Stonyrock
NAG'S HEAD LANE
Sandwich Wood
Wychwood Farm
HARE LANE END
WINDSOR ROAD
WINDSOR LANE
Bramley Farm
Nursery
Little Kingshill Grange
Little Kingshill School
War Mem.
Kingshall Ashwell Farm
Orchard Farm
Cricket Grd.
Linda's Wood
Copes Farm
Woodlands Farm
Nortons Farm
Spurlands End Farm
Bramble Farm
Wycombe Heath Farm
Mill House
Windmill (disused)
Primrose Farm
Depot
Sports Ground
Grubbins Plantation
Hog Trough Plantation
Hog Trough Farm
Long Wood
Langley's Wood
Mantle's Wood
Langley Farm
Bois Heath Farm
Leeward
Boot Farm
Affricks Manor
Affricks Farm
Kingshill Farm
Little Affricks
Haleacre Farm
Haleacre Wood
Keepers Cottage
Holmer Green Farm
Holmer Ridings
Holmer Green Senior Sch.
Holmer Green Jun. Sch.
Inf. Sch.
Rec. Grd.
Piggery
Gasholder Station
Klee House
Deep Mill Farm
Inisfree Farm
Teahouse Belt
Long's Plantation
Castle Wood
Bank's Belt
Wood End
Oaken Corner
Castle Plantation
The Castle
Hyde Plantation
Wendover Woods
Rookwood Cottage
Squire's Plantation
Rook Wood
Middle Wood
Reservoir (cov.)
WATCHET LANE
FEATHERBED LANE
DEEP MILL LANE
BEECH TREE ROAD
SHEEPCOTE DELL ROAD
HOGG LANE
Factory
CHILTERN WYCOMBE
75
91
84
89
90
91
97
98
99
200

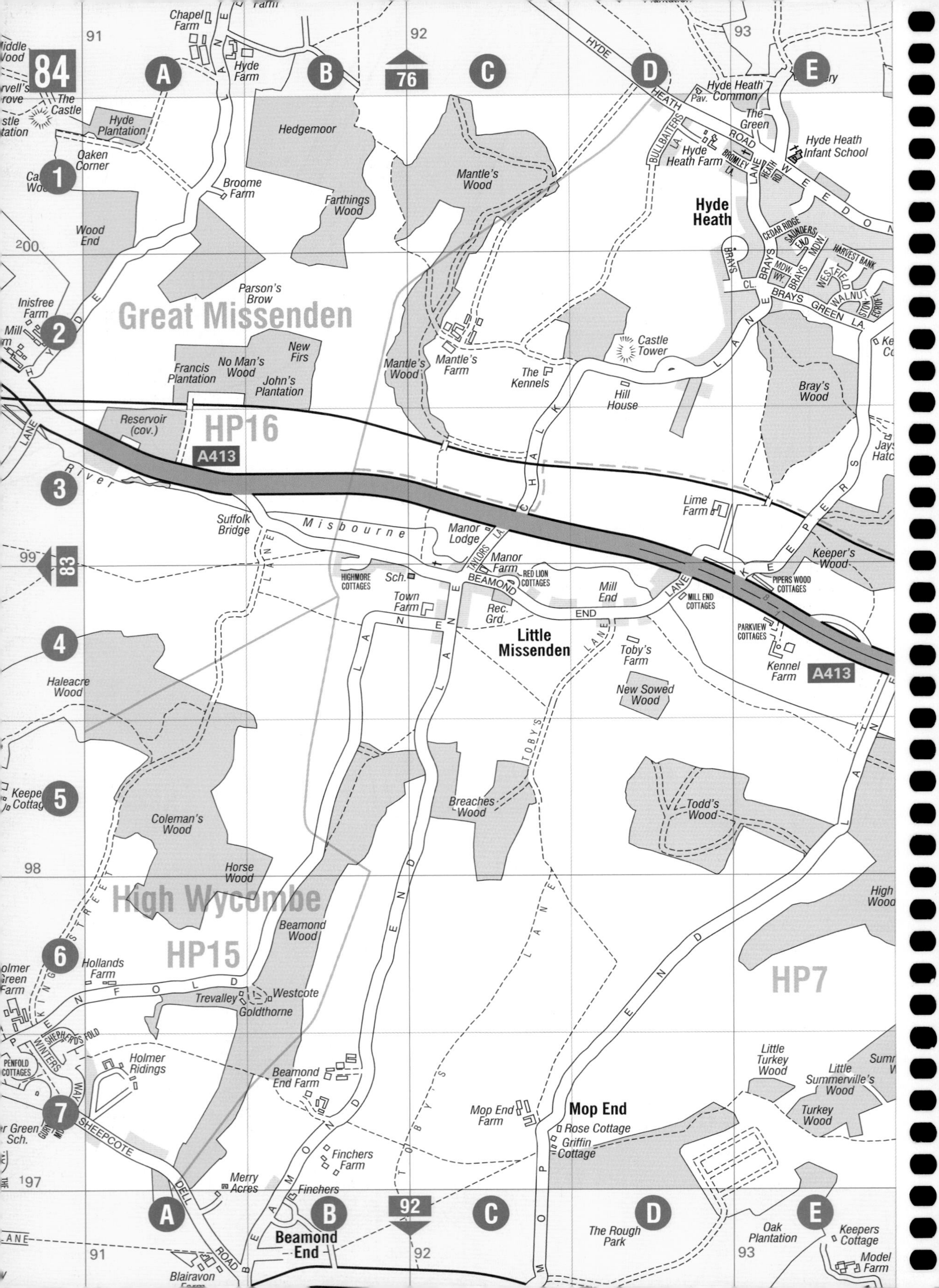

Chapel Farm
Hyde Farm
Hyde Plantation
The Castle
Oaken Corner
Hedgemoor
Broome Farm
Mantle's Wood
Farthings Wood
Wood End
Parson's Brow
Great Missenden
Inisfree Farm
New Firs
Francis Plantation
No Man's Wood
John's Plantation
Mantle's Wood
Mantle's Farm
The Kennels
Castle Tower
Hill House
Reservoir (cov.)
HP16
A413
River
Suffolk Bridge
Misbourne
Manor Lodge
Manor Farm
TAILORS LA.
RED LION COTTAGES
HIGHMORE COTTAGES
Sch.
Town Farm
BEAMOND
Rec. Grd.
END
Mill End
MILL END COTTAGES
Little Missenden
Toby's Farm
New Sowed Wood
PARKVIEW COTTAGES
Kennel Farm
PIPERS WOOD COTTAGES
Keeper's Wood
Lime Farm
HYDE HEATH ROAD
Hyde Heath Common
Pav.
The Green
Hyde Heath Infant School
BULLBAITERS LA.
Hyde Heath Farm
BROMLEY LA.
HEATH RD.
Hyde Heath
CEDAR RIDGE
SAUNDERS END
MDW.
HARVEST BANK
BRAYS
BRAYS CL.
MDW. WY.
WESTFIELD
WALNUT
BRAYS GREEN LA.
Bray's Wood
KEEPERS LANE
CHALK LANE
A413
Haleacre Wood
Coleman's Wood
Breaches Wood
Todd's Wood
Horse Wood
High Wycombe
HP15
Beamond Wood
TOBY'S LANE
HP7
Hollands Farm
PENFOLD
Trevalley
Westcote
Goldthorne
Holmer Ridings
KINGS STREET
SHEPHERDS FOLD
WINTERS WAY
PENFOLD COTTAGES
SHEEPCOTE DELL ROAD
Beamond End Farm
Mop End Farm
Mop End
Rose Cottage
Griffin Cottage
Finchers Farm
Merry Acres
Finchers
Beamond End
Blairavon
The Rough Park
Oak Plantation
Keepers Cottage
Model Farm
Little Turkey Wood
Little Summerville's Wood
Turkey Wood
High Wood
MOP END LANE
BEAMOND END LANE
A B C D E
1 2 3 4 5 6 7
91 92 93
200 99 98 197
76 83 92

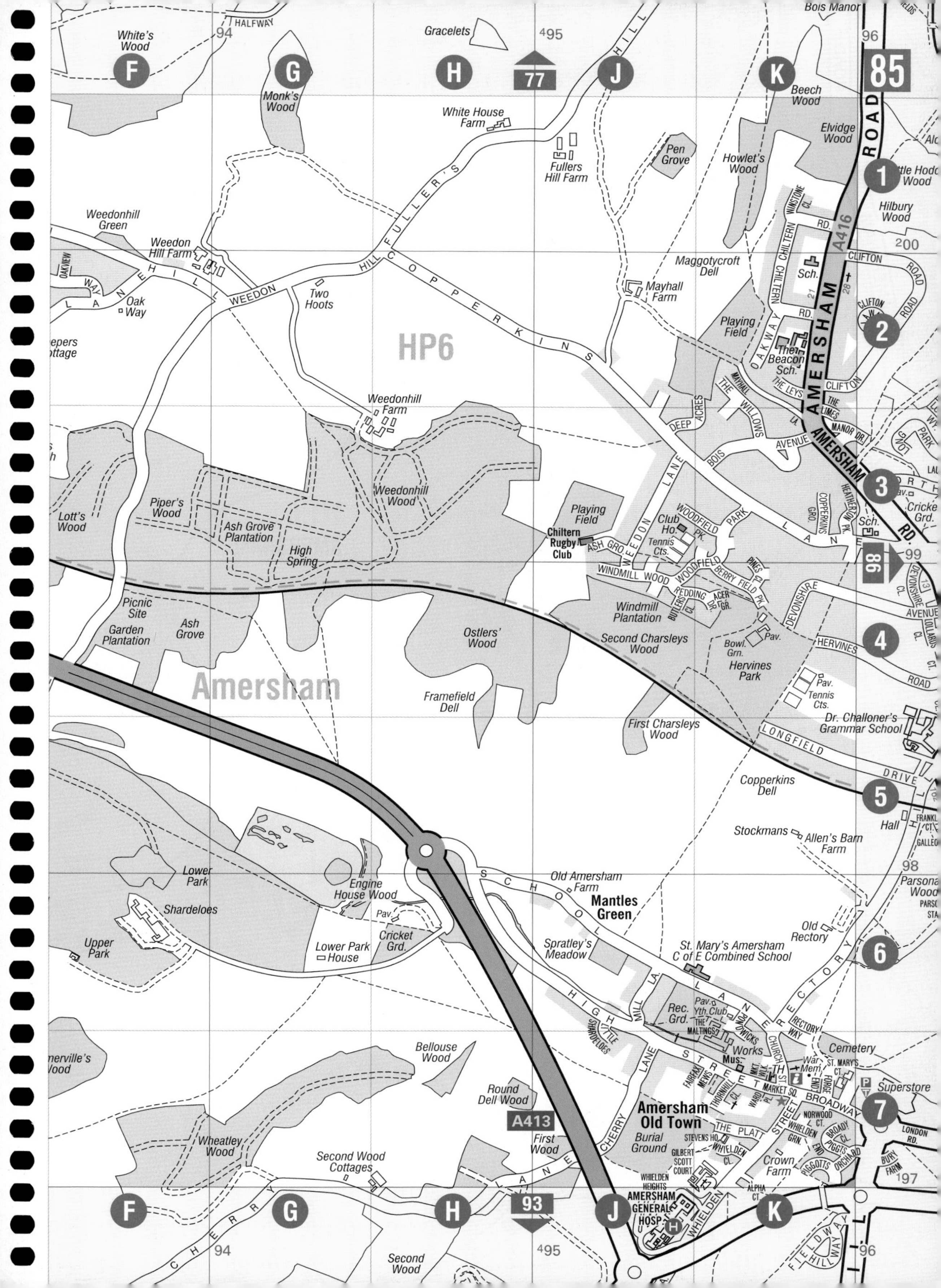

White's Wood
Monk's Wood
Gracelets
White House Farm
Fullers Hill Farm
Pen Grove
Howlet's Wood
Beech Wood
Elvidge Wood
Hilbury Wood
Weedonhill Green
Weedon Hill Farm
Oak Way
Two Hoots
Maggotycroft Dell
Mayhall Farm
Playing Field
The Beacon Sch.
HP6
Weedonhill Farm
Weedonhill Wood
Piper's Wood
Ash Grove Plantation
High Spring
Lott's Wood
Chiltern Rugby Club
Windmill Plantation
Second Charsleys Wood
Hervines Park
Picnic Site
Garden Plantation
Ash Grove
Ostlers' Wood
Amersham
Framefield Dell
First Charsleys Wood
Dr. Challoner's Grammar School
Copperkins Dell
Stockmans
Allen's Barn Farm
Lower Park
Engine House Wood
Shardeloes
Upper Park
Lower Park House
Cricket Grd.
Old Amersham Farm
Mantles Green
Spratley's Meadow
St. Mary's Amersham C of E Combined School
Old Rectory
Parsonage Wood
Bellouse Wood
Round Dell Wood
Cemetery
Superstore
Amersham Old Town
Burial Ground
Crown Farm
Wheatley Wood
First Wood
Second Wood Cottages
Amersham General Hosp.
Second Wood
A413
A416
77
93
98

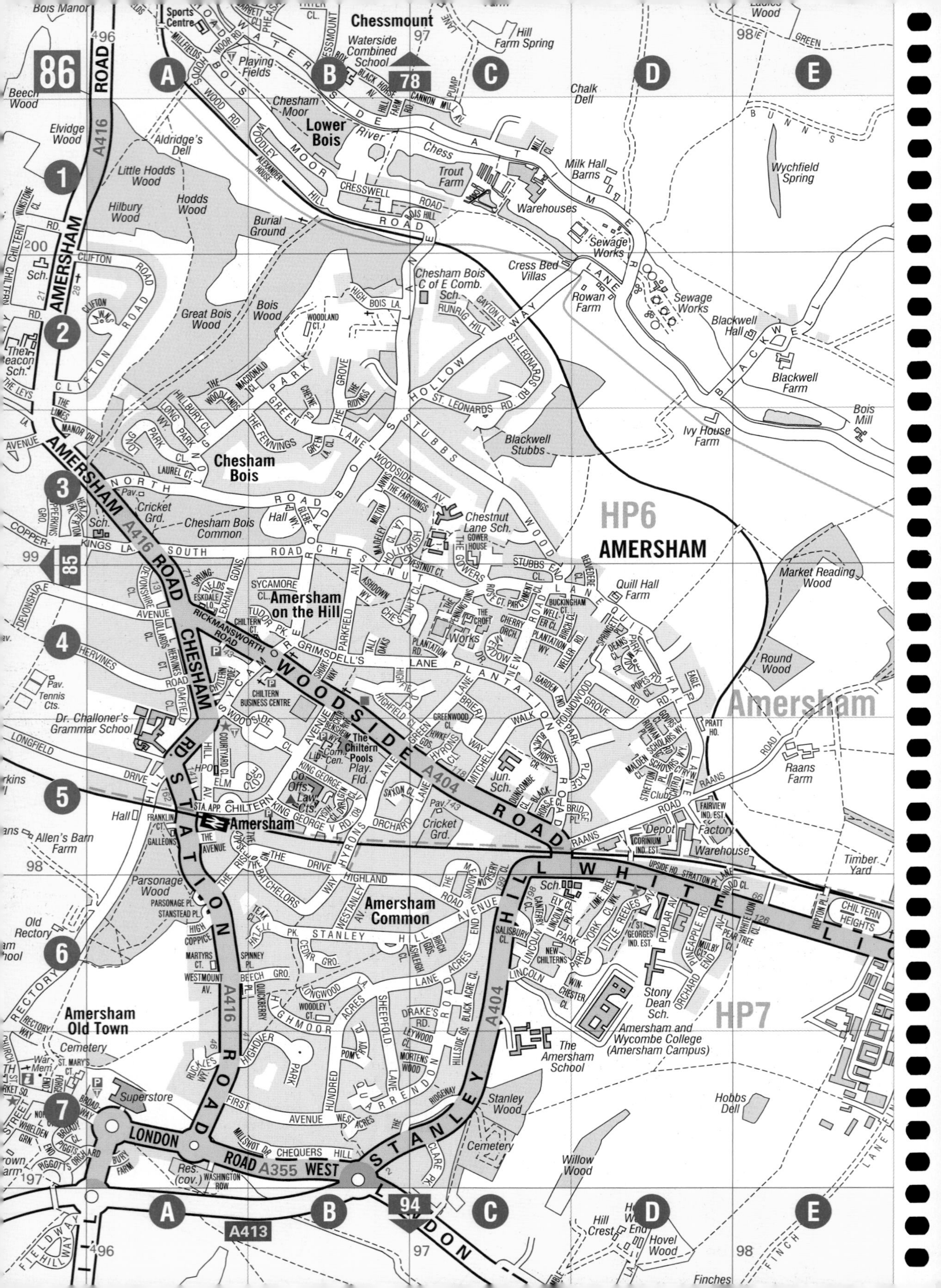
Chessmount
Waterside Combined School
Playing Fields
Sports Centre
Bois Manor
Beech Wood
Elvidge Wood
Aldridge's Dell
Little Hodds Wood
Hilbury Wood
Hodds Wood
Burial Ground
Chesham Moor
Lower Bois
River Chess
Trout Farm
Chalk Dell
Milk Hall Barns
Warehouses
Sewage Works
Cress Bed Villas
Rowan Farm
Wychfield Spring
Blackwell Hall
Blackwell Farm
Ivy House Farm
Bois Mill
Chesham Bois C of E Comb. Sch.
Bois Wood
Great Bois Wood
Blackwell Stubbs
Chesham Bois
Cricket Grd.
Chesham Bois Common
Chestnut Lane Sch.
HP6
AMERSHAM
Quill Hall Farm
Market Reading Wood
Round Wood
Amersham on the Hill
Works
Chiltern Business Centre
The Chiltern Pools
Play. Fld.
Dr. Challoner's Grammar School
Tennis Cts.
Jun. Sch.
Raans Farm
Fairview Ind. Est.
Factory
Warehouse
Depot
Corinium Ind. Est.
Amersham
Allen's Barn Farm
Cricket Grd.
Timber Yard
Parsonage Wood
Amersham Common
Old Rectory
Amersham Old Town
Cemetery
Superstore
Stony Dean Sch.
St. Georges Ind. Est.
HP7
The Amersham School
Amersham and Wycombe College (Amersham Campus)
Hobbs Dell
Stanley Wood
Cemetery
Willow Wood
Hill Crest
Hovel Wood
Finches
AMERSHAM ROAD
A416
CHESHAM ROAD
STATION ROAD
WOODSIDE ROAD
A404
WHITE LION ROAD
LONDON ROAD WEST
A355
STANLEY HILL
A413
LONDON ROAD
RAANS ROAD
BLACKWELL
A B C D E
1 2 3 4 5 6 7
96 97 98 99 200

78
85
94

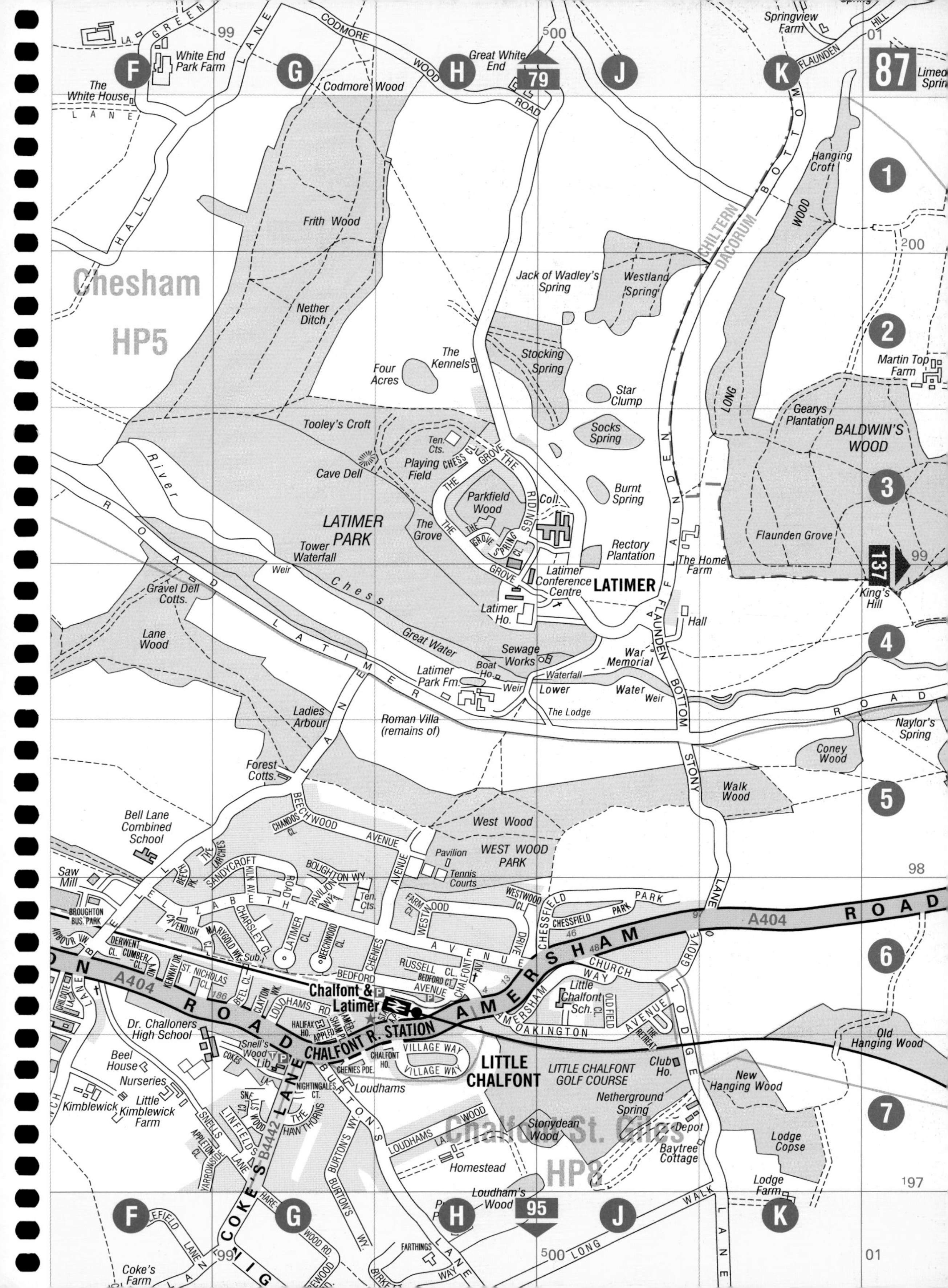
Chesham
HP5
White End Park Farm
The White House
Codmore Wood
Great White End
79
Springview Farm
Hanging Croft
Frith Wood
Nether Ditch
Jack of Wadley's Spring
Westland Spring
Stocking Spring
The Kennels
Four Acres
Star Clump
Socks Spring
Burnt Spring
Tooley's Croft
Cave Dell
Playing Field
Parkfield Wood
The Grove
LATIMER PARK
Tower Waterfall
Rectory Plantation
Latimer Conference Centre
LATIMER
Latimer Ho.
The Home Farm
Hall
Gearys Plantation
BALDWIN'S WOOD
Flaunden Grove
Martin Top Farm
King's Hill
137
Gravel Dell Cotts.
Lane Wood
River Chess
Great Water
Sewage Works
War Memorial
Latimer Park Fm.
Boat Ho.
Waterfall
Lower Water
The Lodge
Ladies Arbour
Roman Villa (remains of)
Naylor's Spring
Coney Wood
Forest Cotts.
Walk Wood
West Wood
WEST WOOD PARK
Bell Lane Combined School
Saw Mill
Pavilion
Tennis Courts
Chalfont & Latimer
CHALFONT R. STATION
LITTLE CHALFONT
LITTLE CHALFONT GOLF COURSE
Little Chalfont Sch.
Club Ho.
Old Hanging Wood
New Hanging Wood
Dr. Challoners High School
Beel House
Nurseries
Little Kimblewick Farm
Kimblewick
Snell's Wood
Lib.
Loudhams
Netherground Spring
Stonydean Wood
Chalfont St. Giles
HP8
Depot
Baytree Cottage
Lodge Copse
Homestead
Loudham's Wood
95
Lodge Farm
Coke's Farm
A404
AMERSHAM ROAD
LATIMER ROAD
FLAUNDEN BOTTOM
STONY LANE
LODGE LANE
COKE'S LANE
B4442
LONG WALK
CHILTERN
DACORUM
LONG WOOD
CODMORE WOOD ROAD
HALL LANE
GREEN LA.
BEECHWOOD AVENUE
ELIZABETH AVENUE
BEDFORD AVENUE
CHESSFIELD PARK
WESTWOOD PARK
OAKINGTON AVENUE
VILLAGE WAY
BURTON'S LANE
CHURCH GROVE
F G H J K
1 2 3 4 5 6 7
99 500 01 200 98 197

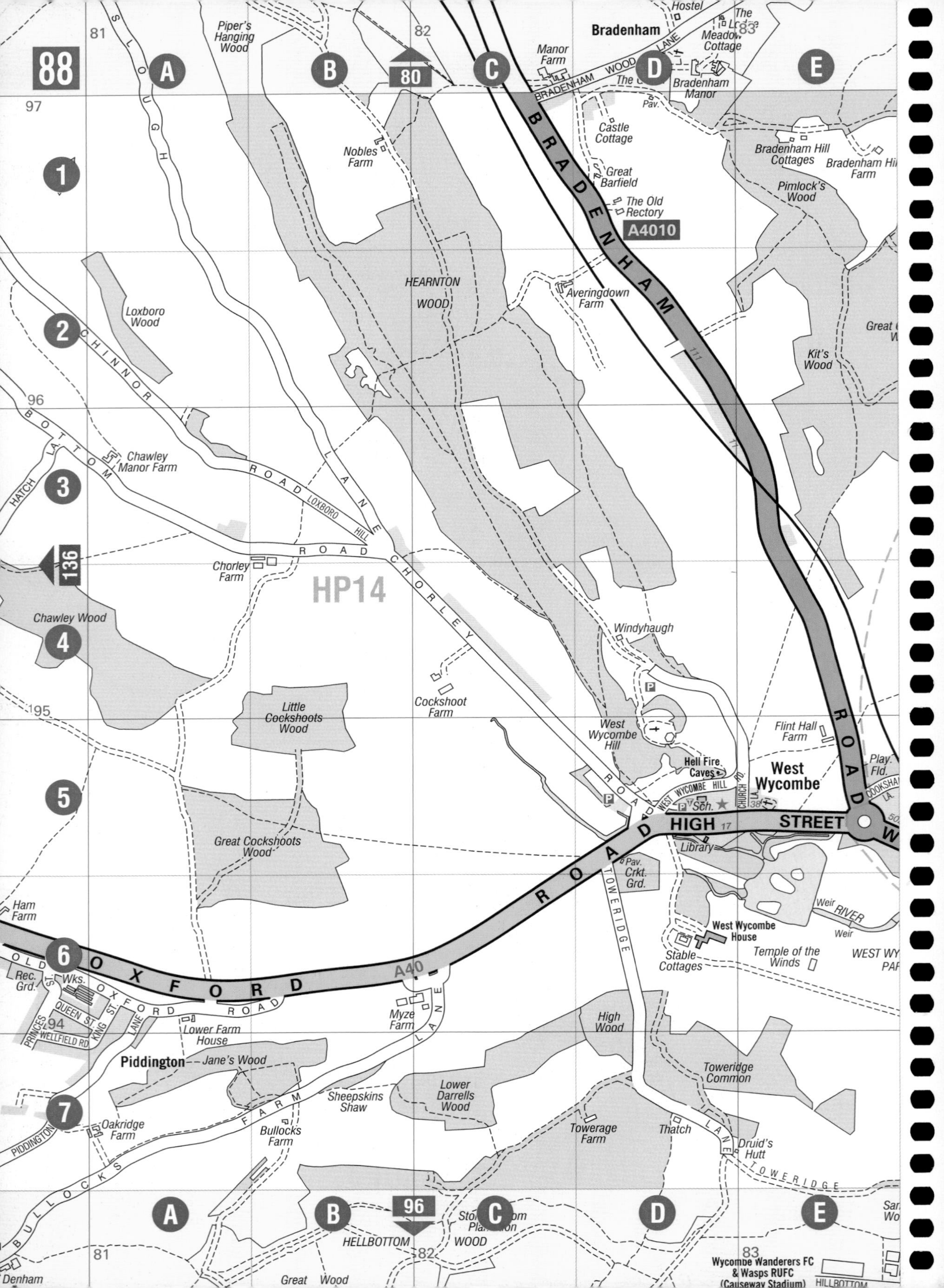

88
80
96
136
Bradenham
Hostel
Meadow Cottage
Manor Farm
Bradenham Manor
BRADENHAM WOOD LANE
Piper's Hanging Wood
Nobles Farm
Castle Cottage
Great Barfield
The Old Rectory
A4010
BRADENHAM ROAD
Bradenham Hill Cottages
Bradenham Hill Farm
Pimlock's Wood
HEARNTON WOOD
Averingdown Farm
Kit's Wood
Loxboro Wood
CHINNOR ROAD
SLOUGH LANE
BOTTOM ROAD
HATCH LANE
Chawley Manor Farm
LOXBORO HILL
Chorley Farm
HP14
CHORLEY ROAD
Chawley Wood
Windyhaugh
Cockshoot Farm
Little Cockshoots Wood
West Wycombe Hill
Hell Fire Caves
Flint Hall Farm
West Wycombe
WEST WYCOMBE HILL
CHURCH LA.
Play. Fld.
HIGH STREET
Library
Pav.
Crkt. Grd.
TOWERIDGE LANE
Great Cockshoots Wood
West Wycombe House
Temple of the Winds
Stable Cottages
RIVER
Weir
Ham Farm
OXFORD ROAD
A40
Rec. Grd.
Wks.
QUEEN ST.
KING ST.
PRINCES
WELLFIELD RD
Lower Farm House
Myze Farm
Piddington
Jane's Wood
High Wood
Toweridge Common
Sheepskins Shaw
Lower Darrells Wood
Oakridge Farm
Bullocks Farm
FARM LANE
PIDDINGTON
BULLOCKS
Towerage Farm
Thatch
Druid's Hutt
TOWERIDGE
HELLBOTTOM WOOD
Great Wood
Denham
Wycombe Wanderers FC & Wasps RUFC (Causeway Stadium)
HILLBOTTOM

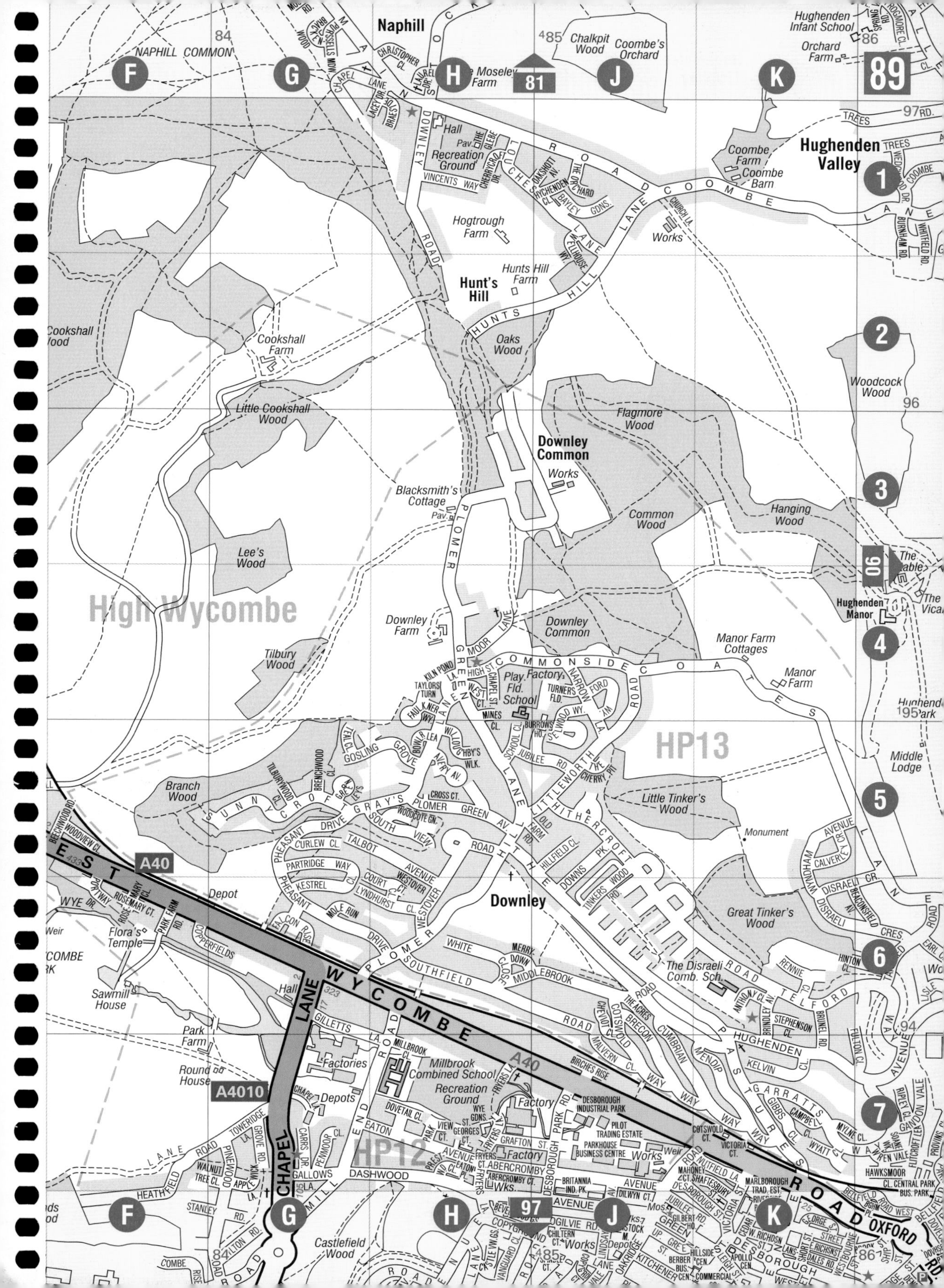
Naphill
NAPHILL COMMON
Hughenden Infant School
Orchard Farm
Chalkpit Wood
Coombe's Orchard
Moseley Farm
81
Hughenden Valley
Coombe Farm
Coombe Barn
Recreation Ground
Hogtrough Farm
Hunts Hill Farm
Hunt's Hill
Works
Cookshall Wood
Cookshall Farm
Oaks Wood
Woodcock Wood
Little Cookshall Wood
Flagmore Wood
Downley Common
Blacksmith's Cottage
Common Wood
Hanging Wood
Lee's Wood
High Wycombe
Downley Farm
Hughenden Manor
Tilbury Wood
Manor Farm Cottages
Manor Farm
HP13
Middle Lodge
Branch Wood
Little Tinker's Wood
Monument
Downley
Great Tinker's Wood
A40
Depot
Flora's Temple
Sawmill House
The Disraeli Comb. Sch.
Park Farm
Round House
Millbrook Combined School
Recreation Ground
A4010
Factories
Depots
Factory
DESBOROUGH INDUSTRIAL PARK
PILOT TRADING ESTATE
PARKHOUSE BUSINESS CENTRE
HP12
97
Castlefield Wood
WEST WYCOMBE ROAD
OXFORD ROAD
90

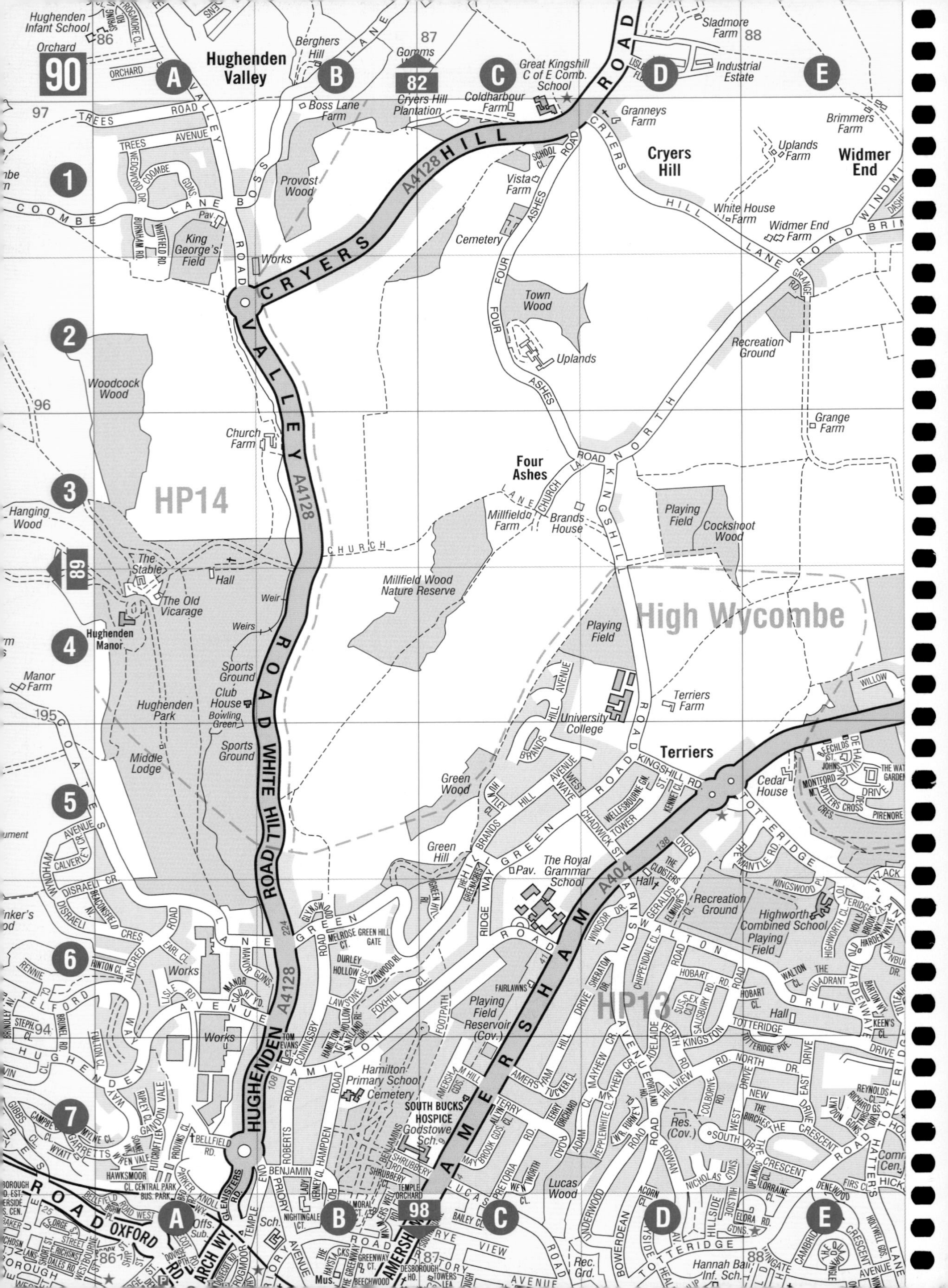
Hughenden Valley
Hughenden Infant School
Orchard
Berghers Hill
Gomms Wood
82
Great Kingshill C of E Comb. School
Sladmore Farm
Industrial Estate
Coldharbour Farm
Cryers Hill Plantation
Boss Lane Farm
Granneys Farm
Brimmers Farm
Cryers Hill
Widmer End
Uplands Farm
Provost Wood
Vista Farm
White House Farm
Widmer End Farm
King George's Field
Cemetery
Works
Town Wood
Uplands
Recreation Ground
Woodcock Wood
Church Farm
Grange Farm
Four Ashes
HP14
Hanging Wood
Millfield Farm
Brands House
Playing Field
Cockshoot Wood
89
The Stable
Hall
The Old Vicarage
Millfield Wood Nature Reserve
Hughenden Manor
Manor Farm
High Wycombe
Sports Ground
Club House
Bowling Green
Hughenden Park
Middle Lodge
University College
Terriers Farm
Terriers
Green Wood
Cedar House
Green Hill
The Royal Grammar School
Recreation Ground
Highworth Combined School Playing Field
Works
HP13
Playing Field Reservoir (Cov.)
Hall
Hamilton Primary School
Cemetery
SOUTH BUCKS HOSPICE
Godstowe Sch.
Res. (Cov.)
Lucas Wood
98
Rec. Grd.
Hannah Ball Inf. Sch.
Mus.
Sch.
Offs.
A4128
A404
CRYERS HILL
VALLEY ROAD
WHITE HILL
HUGHENDEN ROAD
AMERSHAM HILL
OXFORD ROAD
KINGSHILL ROAD
NORTH ROAD
FOUR ASHES ROAD
TOTTERIDGE ROAD
HAMILTON ROAD
GREEN ROAD
WALTON DRIVE

91
F
G
H
J
K
83
99
92
1
2
3
4
5
6
7
89
490
91
97
96
195
94
HP15
HP10
HAZLEMERE
HOLMER GREEN
TYLERS GREEN
Totteridge
PENN
A404
B474
AMERSHAM ROAD
PENN ROAD
HAZLEMERE ROAD
ELM ROAD
CHURCH ROAD
BRACKLEY ROAD
WYCOMBE RD.
HOGG LANE
COMMON WOOD ROAD
MANOR ROAD
KINGSWOOD ROAD
MAGNOLIA DENE
EASTERN DENE
PARK LANE
GREEN STREET
BEAUMONT WAY
HOLMER GREEN ROAD
SAWPIT HILL
WIDE DENE
HILL CREST
WATCHET LANE
POND ROAD
ORCHARD WAY
HOWE ROAD
CEDAR AVENUE
CUMMERS HILL
UPPER LODGE LA.
LOWER LODGE LA.
ROBERTS RIDE
PRIMROSE HILL
HONEYSUCKLE RD.
GEORGE'S HILL
QUEENSWAY
CURZON AV.
ASHLEY DRIVE
MEADOW DRIVE
RAYS LANE
KINGS RIDE
ST. JOHNS RD.
SOUTHCOTE WAY
KINGSWOOD AV.
WYCOMBE
CHILTERN
Primrose Farm
Depot
Holmer Green Senior Sch.
Inf. Sch.
Holmer Green Jun. Sch.
Factory
Tralee Farm
Riding School
Orchard End Farm
Stables
Inkerman Farm
Two Sisters Plantation
Keeper's Cottage
Gravelly Way Plantation
HAZLEMERE GOLF COURSE
Club House
Craig's Wood
Cedar Park School
Wks.
Hall
Recreation Ground
Pav.
War Meml.
Lib.
Hazlemere C of E Combined School
Community Centre
Youth Centre
Sir William Ramsey School
Schs.
COMMON WOOD
The Larches
Works
Recreation Ground
Potter's Cross
Pugh's Wood
Kingswood House
KING'S WOOD
Totteridge Common
The Common
Cricket Grd.
Football Grd.
Council Offices
Depot
Middle Sch.
Tylers Green First School
Playing Field
Penn School
The Old Park
Hangingcroft Wood
King's Wood School
Community Centre
Ash Hill Primary School
Highfield Wood
Comm. Cen.

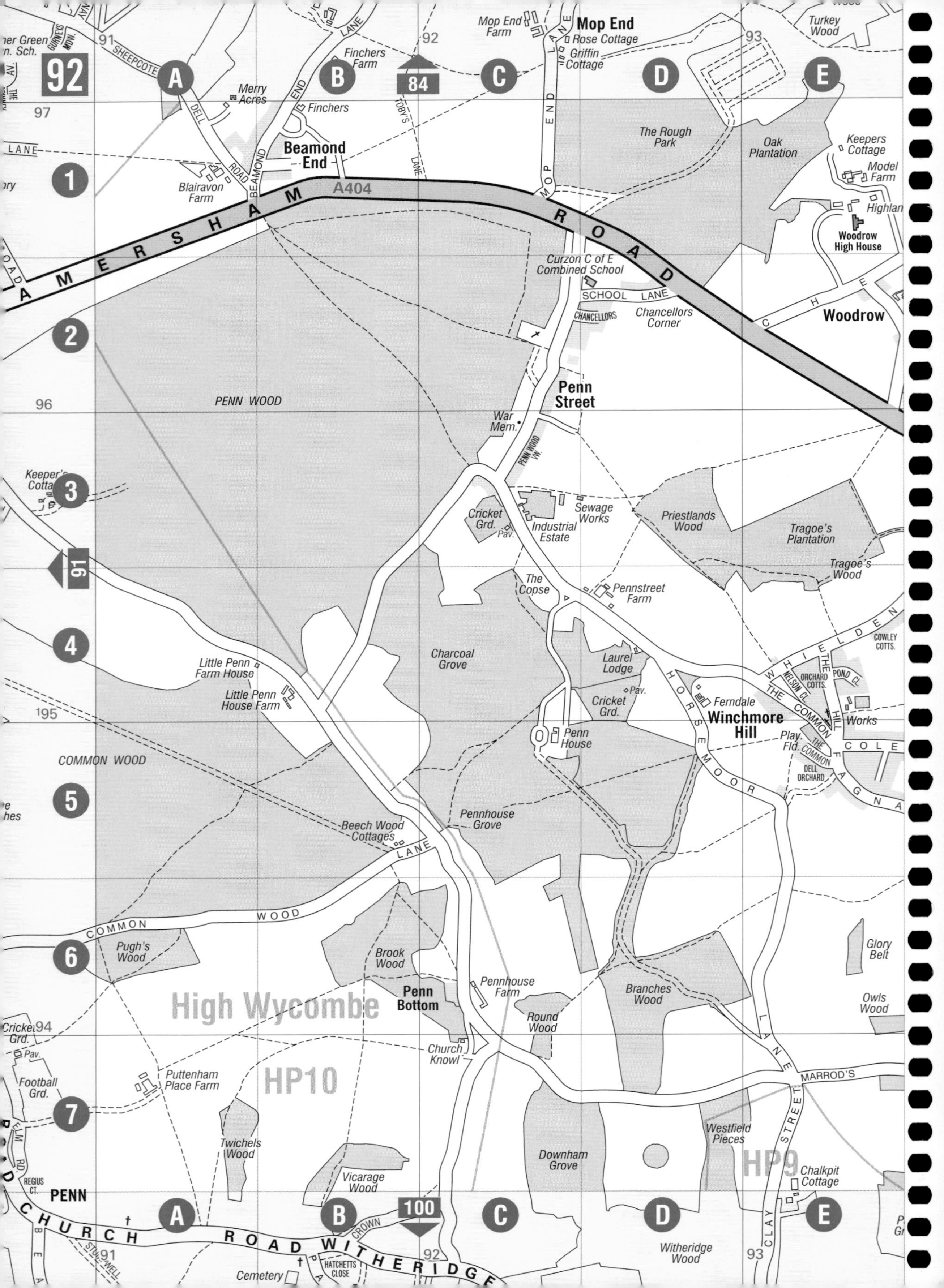
Mop End
Mop End Farm
Rose Cottage
Griffin Cottage
Finchers Farm
Merry Acres
Finchers
Beamond End
Blairavon Farm
Turkey Wood
The Rough Park
Oak Plantation
Keepers Cottage
Model Farm
Woodrow High House
Woodrow
A404
AMERSHAM ROAD
Curzon C of E Combined School
SCHOOL LANE
CHANCELLORS
Chancellors Corner
PENN WOOD
Penn Street
War Mem.
PENN WOOD VW.
Keeper's Cotta
Cricket Grd.
Pav.
Sewage Works
Industrial Estate
Priestlands Wood
Tragoe's Plantation
Tragoe's Wood
The Copse
Pennstreet Farm
Charcoal Grove
Laurel Lodge
Little Penn Farm House
Little Penn House Farm
Cricket Grd.
Pav.
Ferndale
Winchmore Hill
Penn House
COMMON WOOD
Beech Wood Cottages
Pennhouse Grove
HORSEMOOR LANE
WHIELDEN
THE COMMON
ORCHARD COTTS.
NELSON CL.
POND CL.
COWLEY COTTS.
Works
Play. Fld.
DELL ORCHARD
COLE
FAGNA
COMMON WOOD LANE
Pugh's Wood
Brook Wood
Pennhouse Farm
Penn Bottom
Round Wood
Branches Wood
Glory Belt
Owls Wood
High Wycombe
HP10
Church Knowl
Puttenham Place Farm
Cricket Grd.
Football Grd.
Pav.
MARROD'S
Twichels Wood
Downham Grove
Westfield Pieces
CLAY STREET
HP9
Chalkpit Cottage
Vicarage Wood
REGIUS CT.
PENN
ELM RD.
CHURCH ROAD
WITHERIDGE
CROWN
HATCHETTS CLOSE
Cemetery
Witheridge Wood
STUBWELL
SHEEPCOTE
GURNEYS MDW.
DELL
BEAMOND END
TOBY'S LANE
84
100
91
92
93
94
95
96
97
A B C D E
1 2 3 4 5 6 7

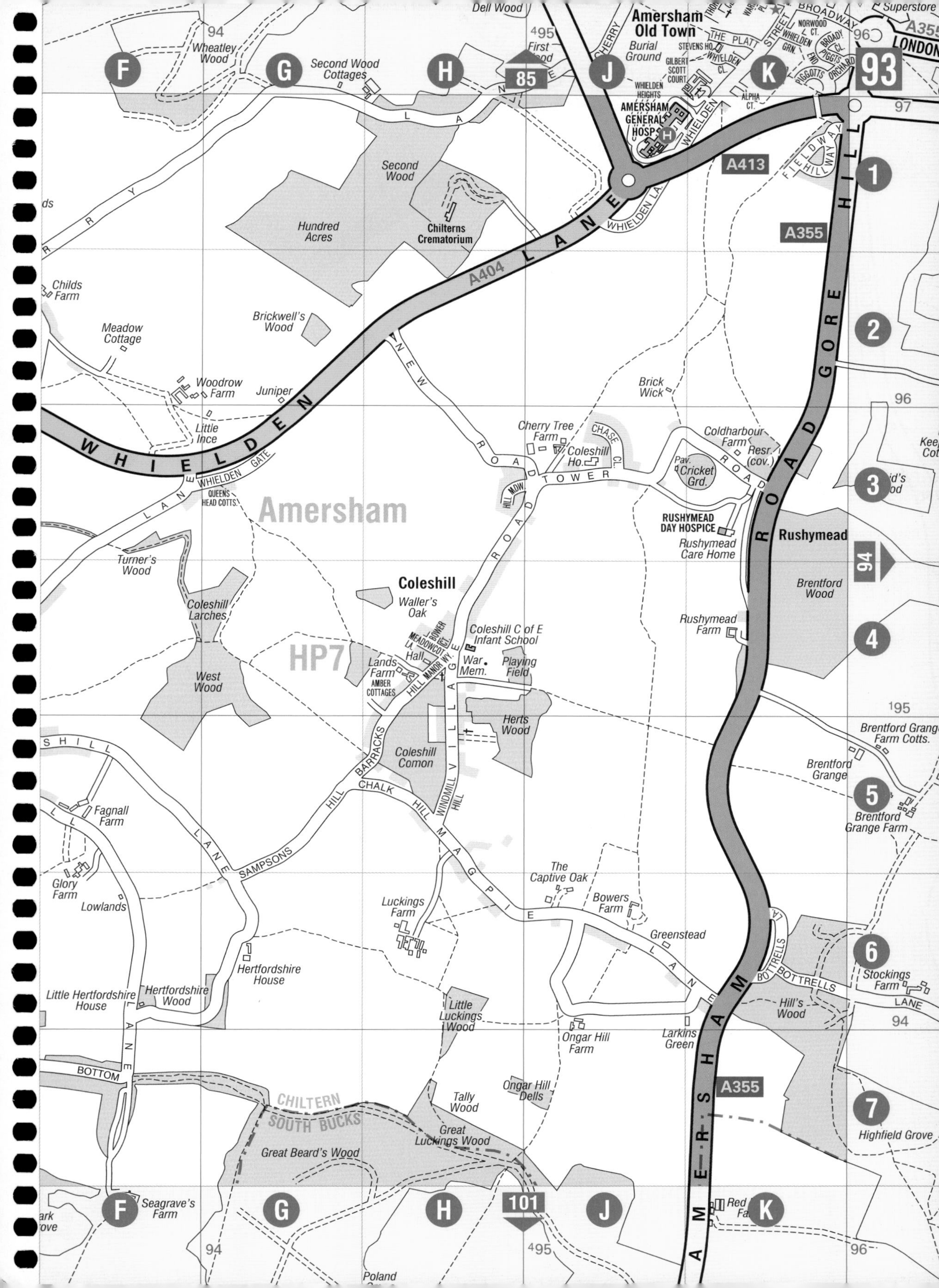

Amersham Old Town
Burial Ground
Amersham General Hosp.
Second Wood Cottages
Wheatley Wood
Dell Wood
First Wood
85
93
LONDON
Superstore
A355
A413
A404
WHIELDEN LANE
GORE HILL
AMERSHAM ROAD
Second Wood
Hundred Acres
Chilterns Crematorium
Childs Farm
Meadow Cottage
Brickwell's Wood
Woodrow Farm
Juniper
Little Ince
WHIELDEN GATE
QUEENS HEAD COTTS.
Amersham
Turner's Wood
Coleshill Larches
West Wood
HP7
Coleshill
Waller's Oak
Coleshill C of E Infant School
War Mem.
Playing Field
Lands Farm
AMBER COTTAGES
Herts Wood
Coleshill Comon
Cherry Tree Farm
Coleshill Ho.
CHASE CL.
TOWER ROAD
NEW ROAD
Brick Wick
Coldharbour Farm
Resr. (cov.)
Pav.
Cricket Grd.
RUSHYMEAD DAY HOSPICE
Rushymead Care Home
Rushymead
94
Brentford Wood
Rushymead Farm
Brentford Grange Farm Cotts.
Brentford Grange
Brentford Grange Farm
CHALK HILL
WINDMILL HILL
SAMPSONS HILL
BARRACKS HILL
MAGPIE LANE
Fagnall Farm
Glory Farm
Lowlands
Luckings Farm
The Captive Oak
Bowers Farm
Greenstead
Hertfordshire House
Little Hertfordshire House
Hertfordshire Wood
Little Luckings Wood
Ongar Hill Farm
Larkins Green
Stockings Farm
BOTTRELLS LANE
Hill's Wood
BOTTOM
CHILTERN
SOUTH BUCKS
Tally Wood
Ongar Hill Dells
Great Luckings Wood
Great Beard's Wood
Highfield Grove
Seagrave's Farm
101
Poland
F G H J K
1 2 3 4 5 6 7

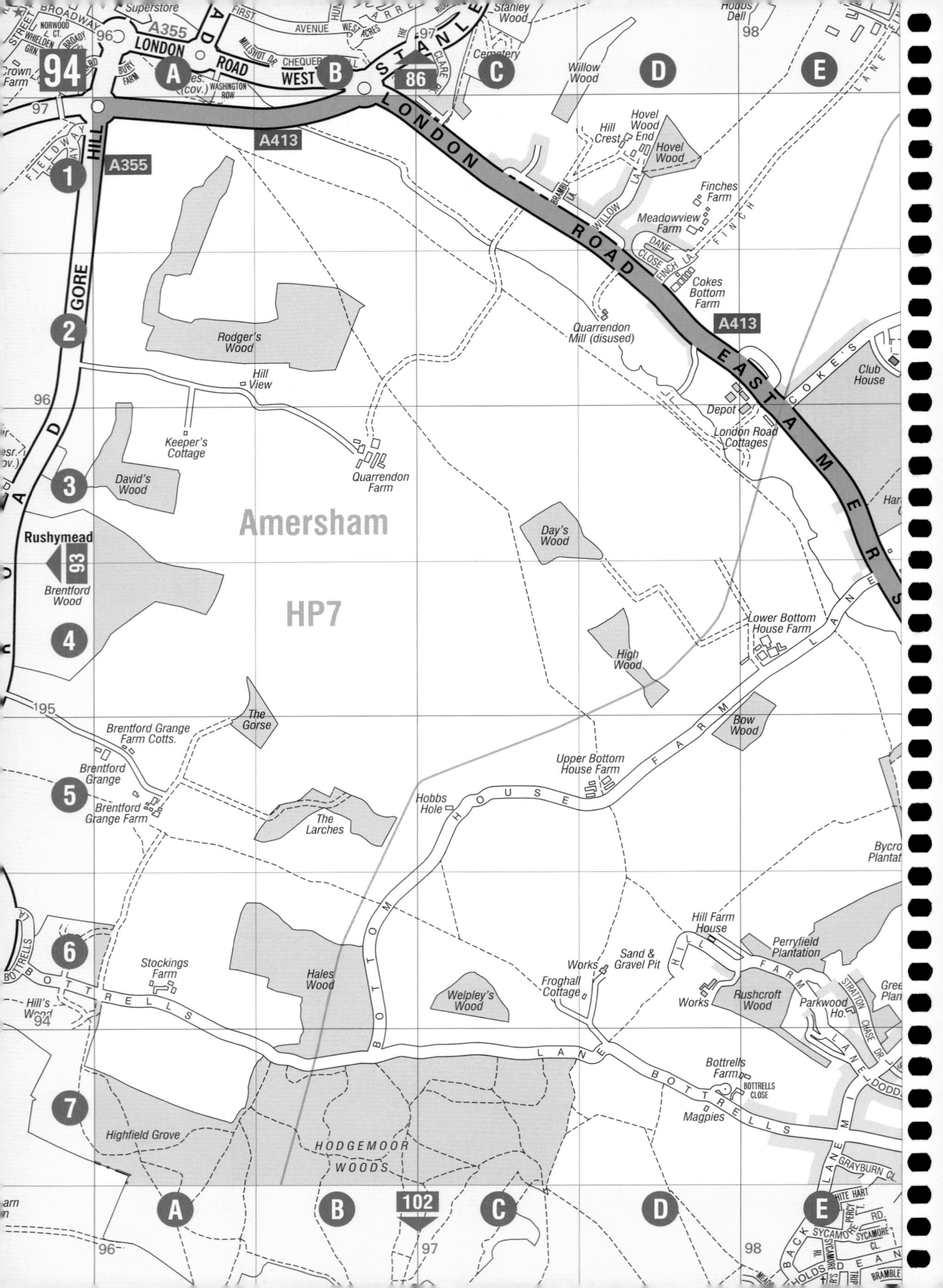

94
86
93
Rushymead
102
A
B
C
D
E
1
2
3
4
5
6
7
Amersham
HP7
London Road
Broadway
Superstore
A355
London Road West
Chequers Hill
First Avenue
West Acres
Millshot Dr.
Washington Row
Bury Farm
Stanley Hill
Stanley Wood
Cemetery
Willow Wood
Hobbs Dell
A413
Gore Hill
Fieldway
A355
London Road
Hill Crest
Hovel Wood End
Hovel Wood
Bramble La.
Willow La.
Finches Farm
Meadowview Farm
Dane Close
Finch La.
Cokes Bottom Farm
Quarrendon Mill (disused)
Rodger's Wood
Hill View
Keeper's Cottage
Quarrendon Farm
David's Wood
A413
London Road East
Coke's
Club House
Depot
London Road Cottages
Day's Wood
Brentford Wood
Lower Bottom House Farm
High Wood
195
96
97
Brentford Grange Farm Cotts.
The Gorse
Brentford Grange
Brentford Grange Farm
The Larches
Upper Bottom House Farm
Bow Wood
Hobbs Hole
Bottom House Farm Lane
Byc
Plantat
Stockings Farm
Hales Wood
Welpley's Wood
Works
Sand & Gravel Pit
Froghall Cottage
Hill Farm House
Hill Farm Lane
Perryfield Plantation
Rushcroft Wood
Works
Parkwood Ho.
Stratton Chase Dr.
Bottrells Lane
Bottrells
Hill's Wood
94
Bottrells Farm
Bottrells Close
Magpies
Highfield Grove
Hodgemoor Woods
Grayburn Cl.
White Hart
Percy Rd.
Sycamore Rd.
Sycamore Cl.
Back
Holds St.
Dean
Bramble
98
96
97
98

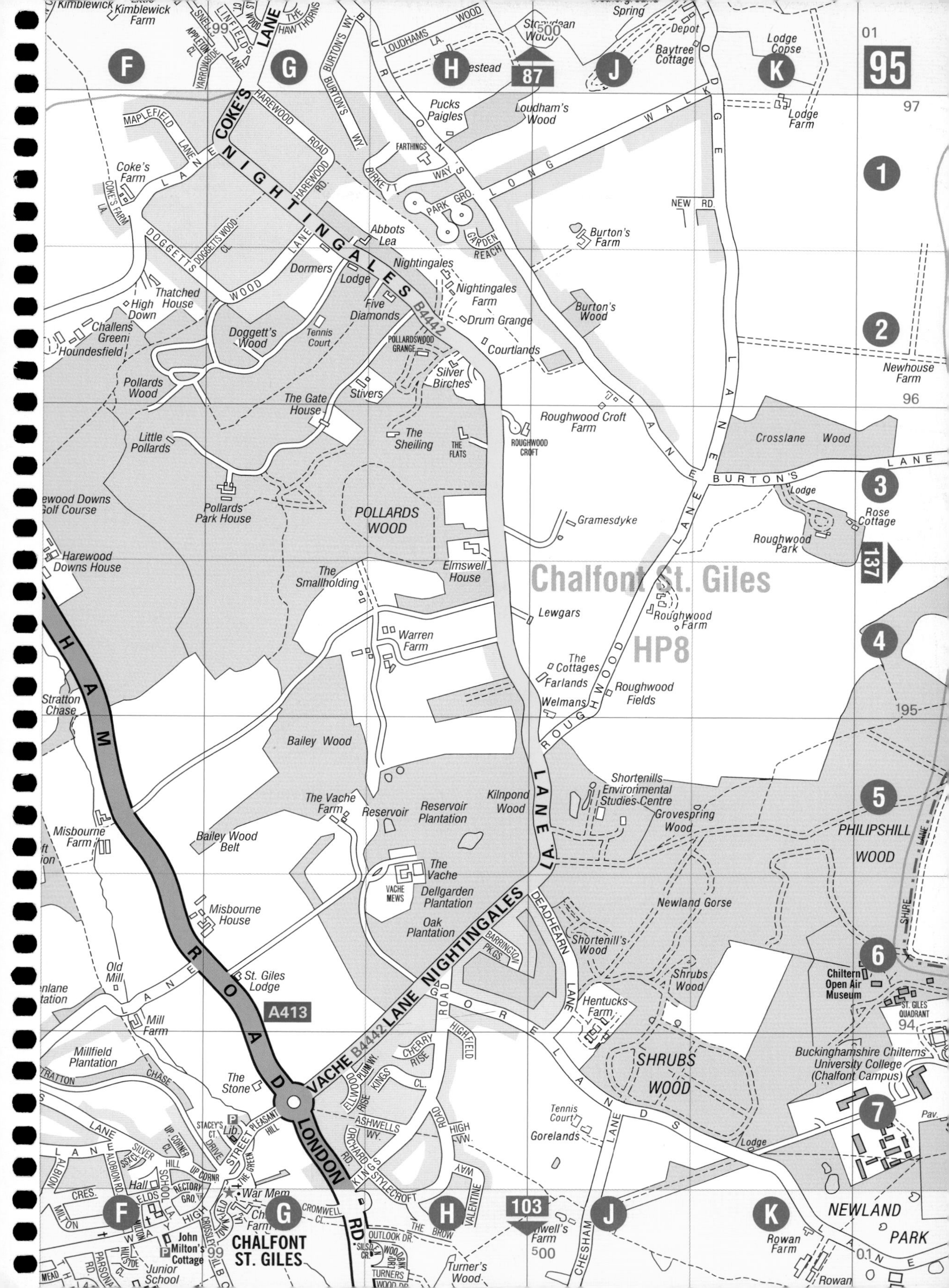
Chalfont St. Giles
HP8
NIGHTINGALES
B4442
A413
LONDON RD.
VACHE LANE NIGHTINGALES
COKE'S LANE
HAREWOOD ROAD
BURTON'S LANE
LODGE LANE
LONG WALK
ROUGHWOOD LANE
DEADHEARN LANE
GORELANDS LANE
CHESHAM LANE
POLLARDS WOOD
Bailey Wood
SHRUBS WOOD
PHILIPSHILL WOOD
Crosslane Wood
Chiltern Open Air Museum
Buckinghamshire Chilterns University College (Chalfont Campus)
NEWLAND PARK
CHALFONT ST. GILES
Shortenills Environmental Studies Centre
The Vache
Newland Gorse
Misbourne House
Stratton Chase
Harewood Downs House
Pollards Park House
Roughwood Park
Newhouse Farm
Lodge Farm
Burton's Farm
Roughwood Croft Farm
Roughwood Farm
Warren Farm
Elmswell House
The Smallholding
Reservoir Plantation
Kilnpond Wood
Grovespring Wood
Hentucks Farm
Gorelands
Mill Farm
Old Mill
St. Giles Lodge
John Milton's Cottage
Junior School
War Mem.
Rowan Farm
87
103
137

Oakridge Farm
Bullocks Farm
Sheepskins Shaw
Darrells Wood
Towerage Farm
Thatch
Druid's Hutt
TOWERIDGE
LANE
BULLOCKS
FARM
LANE
88
104
73
Stoneybottom Plantation
HELLBOTTOM WOOD
Great Wood
Denham Farm
Denham Wood
Wycombe Wanderers FC & Wasps RUFC (Causeway Stadium)
HILLBOTTOM
SANDS INDUSTRIAL ESTATE
Pyatts Farm
Fryers Farm
SUNTERS WOOD
High Barbers Wood
HP14
M40
M40 MOTORWAY
Grove Farm
Sandage Wood
Spring Coppice
LANE END
SPRING COPPICE
LANE END LANE
Booker Common
Millennium Park
Resr. (covered)
Underpass
WIDDENTON PARK WOOD
Cricket Ground
GLADE VW.
MARLOW
B482
TA Centre
OLD HORNS LA.
HORNS LANE
CRESS
WYCOMBE AIR PARK
Hazel Grove
Clay Lane Farm
Council Depot
CLAYHILL
CLAYMOOR PARK
MOOR WOOD
ROAD
CLAY
LANE
BEACON
Round Wood
Pav.
Sports Grd.
Roundwood Farm
Strawberry Grove
MEADOW
ROAD
Bottom Wood
Red Barn Farm
Beacon Farm
Dane Hill Plantation
MOOR WOOD
SIDNEY HOUSE
PARK CL.
PUSEY WY.
DENHAM RD.
MT. PLEASANT
RUSTLINGS GA.
WIDDENTON
BEECH
CORONATION CRES.
OAK TREE DR.
SIMMONS
SLAYTER RD.
SAXHORN RD.
CATER RD.
GRAY'S DORMER
PHILLIPS CL.
SIMMONS WAY
BASSET RD.
RIDGE CL.
ELLIS WY.
FRAMERS COURT
Wycombe Ct.Fm.
HIGH ST.
Ind. Est.
Sch.
WRIGHTS
ARCHERS
BLACKWELL
Management Centre
91
92
93
190
81
82
83
A
B
C
D
E
1
2
3
4
5
6
7

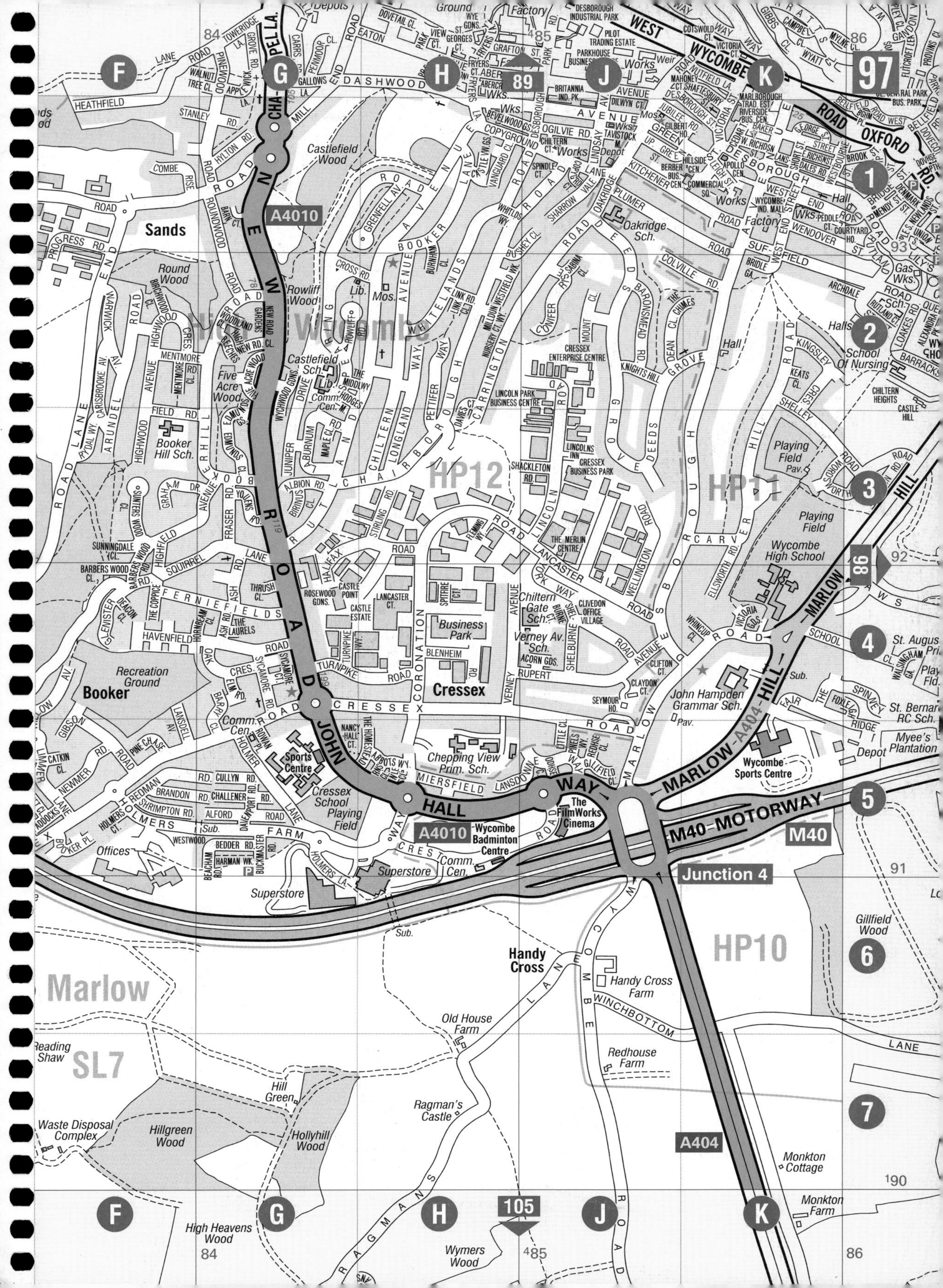

89
High Wycombe
Sands
Booker
Cressex
HP12
HP11
HP10
SL7
Marlow
Handy Cross
NEW ROAD
JOHN HALL WAY
A4010
MARLOW HILL
A404
M40 MOTORWAY
M40
Junction 4
Castlefield Wood
Rowliff Wood
Five Acre Wood
Round Wood
Booker Hill Sch.
Recreation Ground
Sports Centre
Cressex School Playing Field
Business Park
Chepping View Prim. Sch.
John Hampden Grammar Sch.
Wycombe High School
Wycombe Sports Centre
Wycombe Badminton Centre
The FilmWorks Cinema
Superstore
Handy Cross Farm
Old House Farm
Redhouse Farm
Hill Green
Ragman's Castle
Hillgreen Wood
Hollyhill Wood
Waste Disposal Complex
Reading Shaw
High Heavens Wood
Wymers Wood
Monkton Cottage
Monkton Farm
Gillfield Wood
WINCHBOTTOM LANE
WYCOMBE ROAD
RAGMANS LANE
98
105

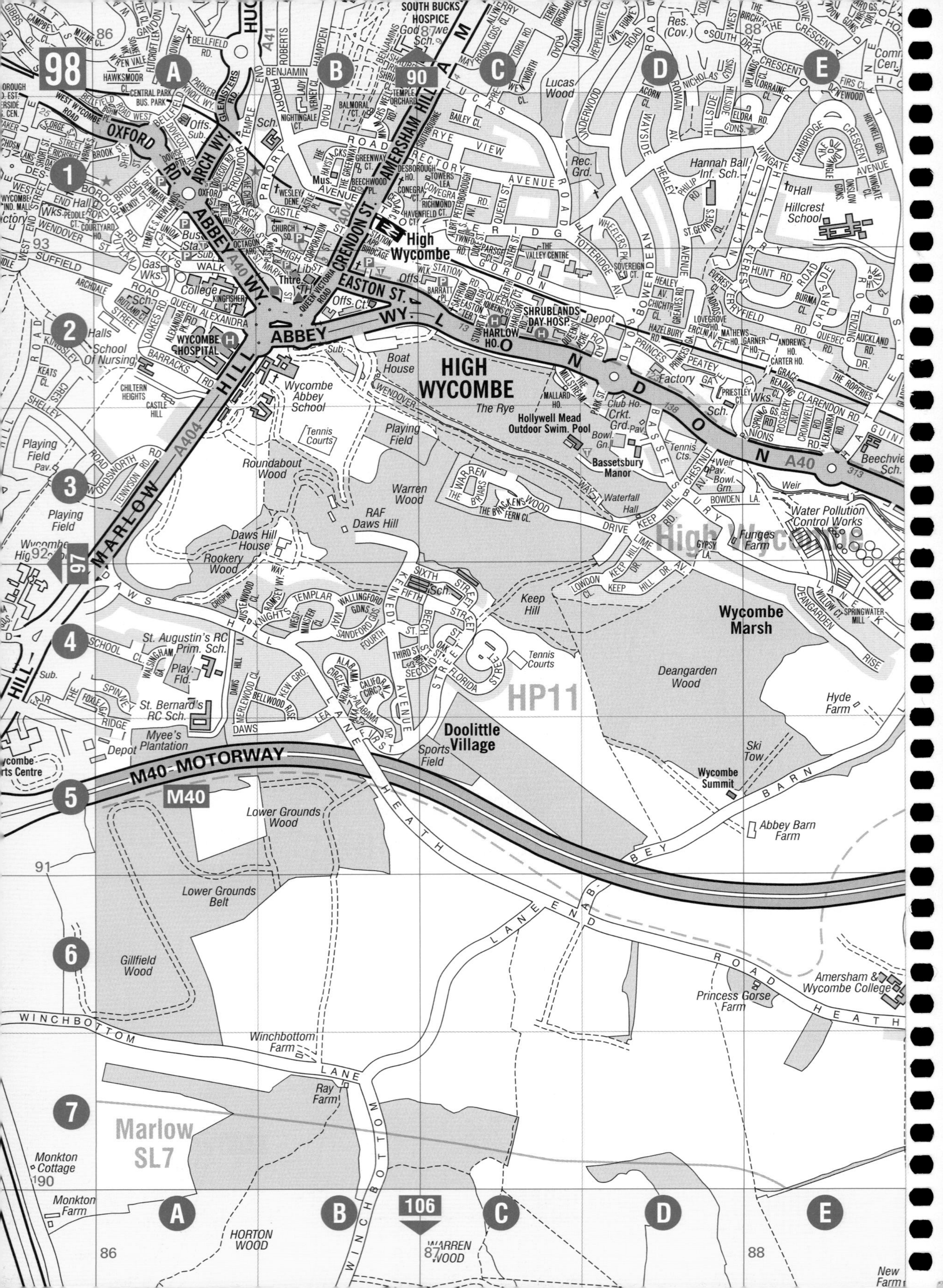

A
B
C
D
E
1
2
3
4
5
6
7
86
87
88
93
92
91
90
SOUTH BUCKS HOSPICE
90
97
106
HIGH WYCOMBE
High Wycombe
OXFORD RD.
ARCH WY.
ABBEY WY.
ABBEY
EASTON ST.
CRENDON ST.
AMERSHAM HILL
MARLOW HILL
A404
A40
A41
LONDON RD.
BENJAMIN RD.
PRIORY
HAMPDEN
LUCAS RD.
RYE VIEW
RECTORY AVENUE
TOTTERIDGE RD.
GORDON RD.
QUEEN ST.
BOWERDEAN RD.
WAYSIDE
HEALEY AV.
LICHFIELD
WINGATE
CAMBRIDGE CRESCENT
HOLLYWELL GDS.
THE CRESCENT
UPLANDS
SOUTH DR.
ROWAN AV.
ACORN CL.
UNDERWOOD
HILLSIDE
ELORA RD.
EVEREST RD.
HUNT RD.
BURMA CL.
CAIRNSIDE
TENZING
QUEBEC RD.
AUCKLAND RD.
CARTER HO.
ANDREWS HO.
GARNER HO.
MATHEWS HO.
GRACE
READING
CLARENDON RD.
THE ROPERIES
SPRING GS.
ROSEBERY
CROMWELL
ALEXANDRA RD.
PRINCES GA.
PEATEY
PRIESTLEY CT.
GUINIONS
Beechview Sch.
ERYFIELD
HAZELBURY RD.
Res. (Cov.)
Lucas Wood
Rec. Grd.
Hannah Ball Inf. Sch.
Hillcrest School
Hall
Mus.
Sch.
Offs.
Sub.
Bus Sta.
Lib.
Thtr.
Gas Wks.
College
Halls
School Of Nursing
WYCOMBE HOSPITAL
QUEEN ALEXANDRA RD.
SUFFIELD
WENDOVER ST.
BOROUGH
PEDDLE CT.
COURTYARD
RUTLAND
LOAKES RD.
BARRACKS RD.
CHILTERN HEIGHTS
CASTLE HILL
KINGSLEY
KEATS CL.
SHELLEY
TENNYSON RD.
WORDSWORTH RD.
Playing Field
Pav.
Wycombe Abbey School
Tennis Courts
Boat House
The Rye
Hollywell Mead Outdoor Swim. Pool
Bassetsbury Manor
Club Ho.
Crkt. Grd.
Bowl. Gn.
SHRUBLANDS DAY HOSP.
HARLOW HO.
MALLARD HO.
Depot
Factory
Wks.
Roundabout Wood
Warren Wood
RAF Daws Hill
Daws Hill House
Rookery Wood
WARREN
THE FRIARS
THE BRACKENS
WOOD
FERN CL.
Waterfall Hall
BASSETSBURY LA.
CHESTNUT AV.
KEEP HILL DRIVE
LIME AV.
LOWDON CL.
KEEP HILL DR.
GYPSY LA.
Weir
Bowl. Grn.
BOWDEN LA.
Water Pollution Control Works
Funges Farm
Wycombe Marsh
DEANGARDEN RISE
WILLOW CT.
SPRINGWATER MILL
Keep Hill
DAWS HILL
SIXTH
FIFTH
FOURTH
THIRD ST.
SECOND
KENNEDY AVENUE
BEECH
OAK
FLORIDA
TEMPLAR
WALLINGFORD GDS.
SANDFORD GDS.
KNIGHTS
WESTMINSTER CL.
ROMSEY WAY
AUSTENWOOD CL.
CRISPIN
ALABAMA
CALIFORNIA CIRC.
Tennis Courts
HP11
Deangarden Wood
Hyde Farm
St. Augustin's RC Prim. Sch.
Play. Fld.
St. Bernard's RC Sch.
SCHOOL CL.
WALSINGHAM
SPINNEY
FOXLEA
RIDGE
FAIR
MERLEWOOD CL.
BELLWOOD RISE
KEW GRO.
LEA
DAWS LEA
Myee's Plantation
Depot
Doolittle Village
Sports Field
M40 MOTORWAY
M40
Wycombe Sports Centre
Sub.
Ski Tow
Wycombe Summit
ABBEY BARN LANE
Abbey Barn Farm
Lower Grounds Wood
HEATH END RD.
Lower Grounds Belt
LANE END ROAD
Gillfield Wood
Princess Gorse Farm
Amersham & Wycombe College
WINCHBOTTOM LANE
Winchbottom Farm
Ray Farm
WINCHBOTTOM
Marlow SL7
Monkton Cottage
Monkton Farm
HORTON WOOD
WARREN WOOD
New Farm

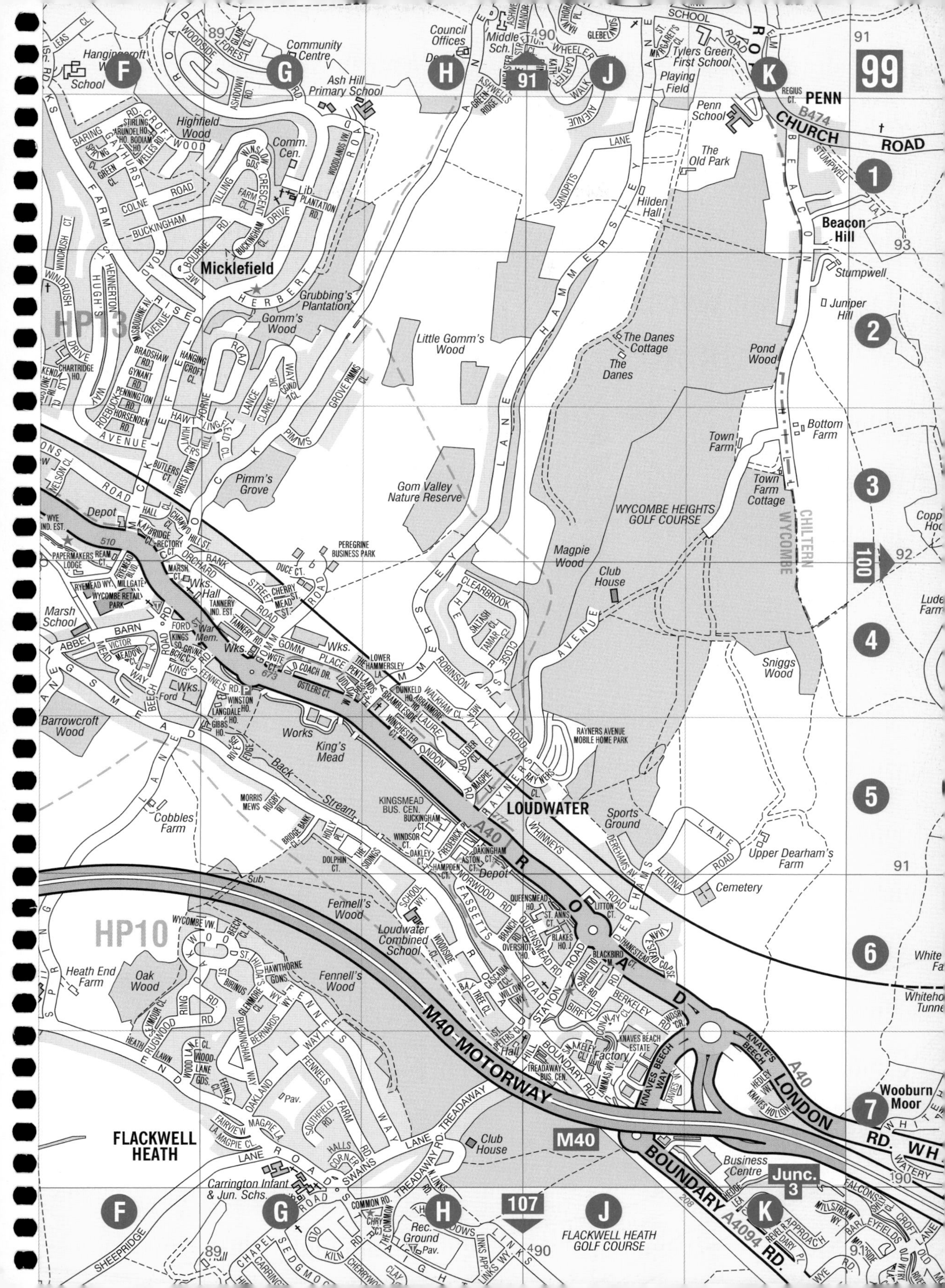

99
F
G
H
J
K
1
2
3
4
5
6
7
91
100
107
M40
Junc. 3
HP13
HP10
PENN
Micklefield
LOUDWATER
FLACKWELL HEATH
Beacon Hill
Wooburn Moor
Hangingcroft School
Community Centre
Council Offices
Middle Sch.
Tylers Green First School
Playing Field
Ash Hill Primary School
Penn School
The Old Park
Highfield Wood
Comm. Cen.
Lib.
Hilden Hall
Stumpwell
Juniper Hill
Grubbing's Plantation
Gomm's Wood
Little Gomm's Wood
The Dames Cottage
The Danes
Pond Wood
Bottom Farm
Town Farm
Town Farm Cottage
Pimm's Grove
Gom Valley Nature Reserve
WYCOMBE HEIGHTS GOLF COURSE
CHILTERN WYCOMBE
Magpie Wood
Club House
Depot
PEREGRINE BUSINESS PARK
WYCOMBE RETAIL PARK
Marsh School
War Mem.
Wks.
Hall
TANNERY IND. EST.
Sniggs Wood
Barrowcroft Wood
Works
King's Mead
Back Stream
RAYNERS AVENUE MOBILE HOME PARK
Cobbles Farm
KINGSMEAD BUS. CEN.
Sports Ground
Upper Dearham's Farm
Cemetery
Fennell's Wood
Loudwater Combined School
Heath End Farm
Oak Wood
Factory
KNAVES BEACH ESTATE
TREADAWAY BUS. CEN.
M40 MOTORWAY
A40 LONDON RD.
BOUNDARY RD. A4094
Business Centre
Club House
Pav.
Carrington Infant & Jun. Schs.
Rec. Ground
FLACKWELL HEATH GOLF COURSE
CHURCH ROAD
B474
White Fa
Whiteho Tunne
Copp Hoo
Lude Farm

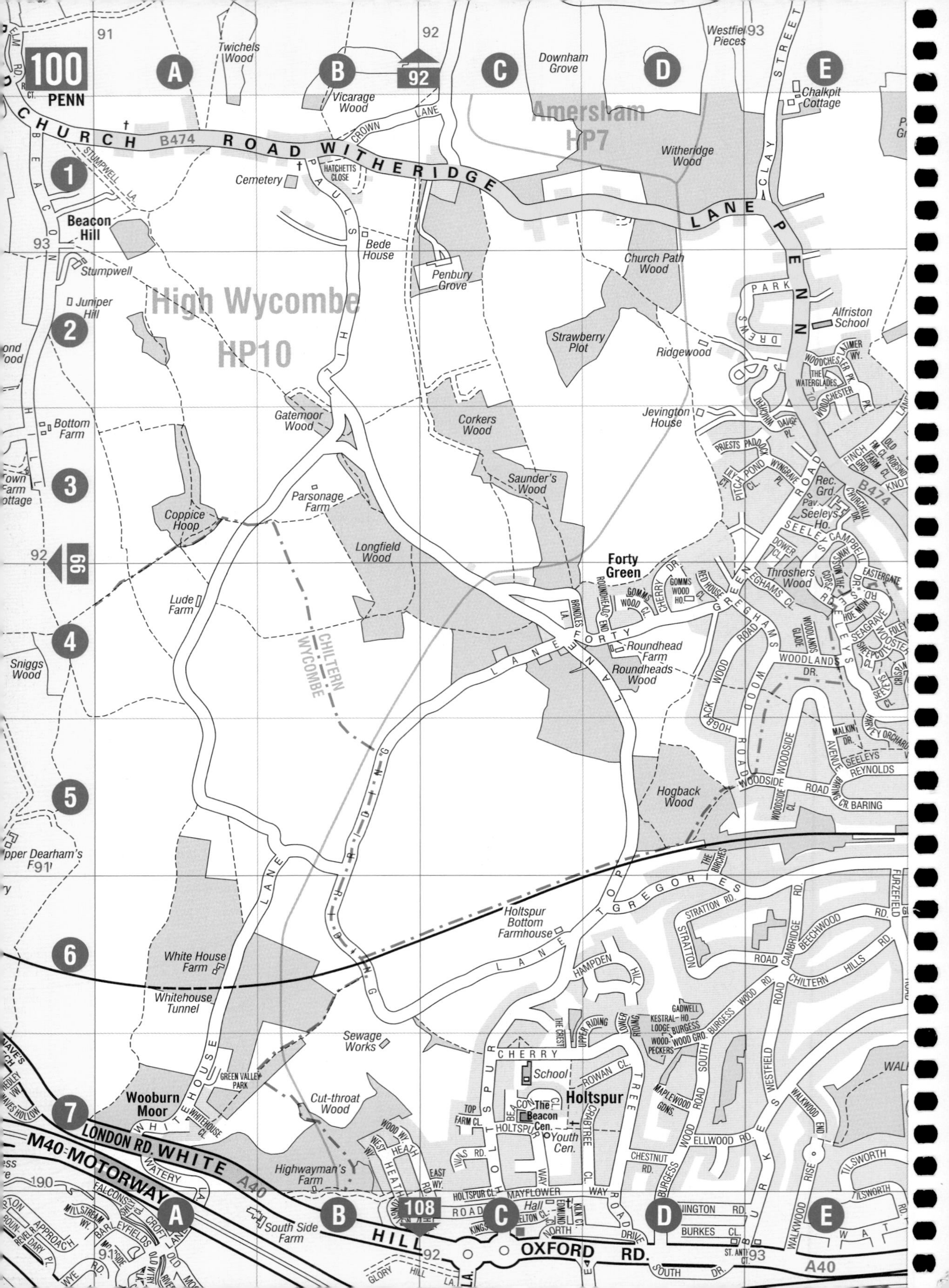
PENN
A
B
C
D
E
91
92
93
92
Twichels Wood
Downham Grove
Westfie Pieces
Vicarage Wood
Chalkpit Cottage
Amersham HP7
CHURCH ROAD WITHERIDGE LANE
B474
CROWN LANE
STUMPWELL LA.
HATCHETTS CLOSE
Cemetery
Witheridge Wood
CLAY STREET
PENN ROAD
Beacon Hill
Stumpwell
Bede House
Penbury Grove
Church Path Wood
PARK
DREWS
Juniper Hill
High Wycombe HP10
Alfriston School
Strawberry Plot
Ridgewood
PAULS HILL
Gatemoor Wood
Corkers Wood
Jevington House
Bottom Farm
Saunder's Wood
Parsonage Farm
Coppice Hoop
Longfield Wood
Forty Green
Throshers Wood
Lude Farm
Sniggs Wood
CHILTERN WYCOMBE
FORTY LANE
Roundhead Farm
Roundheads Wood
WOODLANDS DR.
HOGBACK WOOD ROAD
WOODSIDE ROAD
REYNOLDS
BARING
Hogback Wood
Upper Dearham's F
RIDING LANE
TOP GREGORIES LANE
THE BIRCHES
STRATTON RD.
STRATTON ROAD
BEECHWOOD RD.
CHILTERN HILLS RD.
CAMBRIDGE ROAD
FURZEFIELD RD.
Holtspur Bottom Farmhouse
HAMPDEN HILL
White House Farm
Whitehouse Tunnel
Sewage Works
WHITEHOUSE LANE
CHERRY
School
Holtspur
The Beacon Cen.
Youth Cen.
ROWAN CL.
TREE
SOUTH BURGESS WOOD RD.
BURGESS WOOD ROAD
WESTFIELD
BURKES ROAD
WALKWOOD END
WALKWOOD RISE
TILSWORTH
GREEN VALLEY PARK
Wooburn Moor
Cut-throat Wood
Highwayman's Farm
HOLTSPUR
MAYFLOWER WAY
CRABTREE CL.
ELLWOOD RD.
CHESTNUT RD.
LONDON RD. WHITE HILL
A40
M40 MOTORWAY
South Side Farm
OXFORD RD.
NORTH DRIVE
SOUTH DR.
GLORY HILL LA.
108
99
100

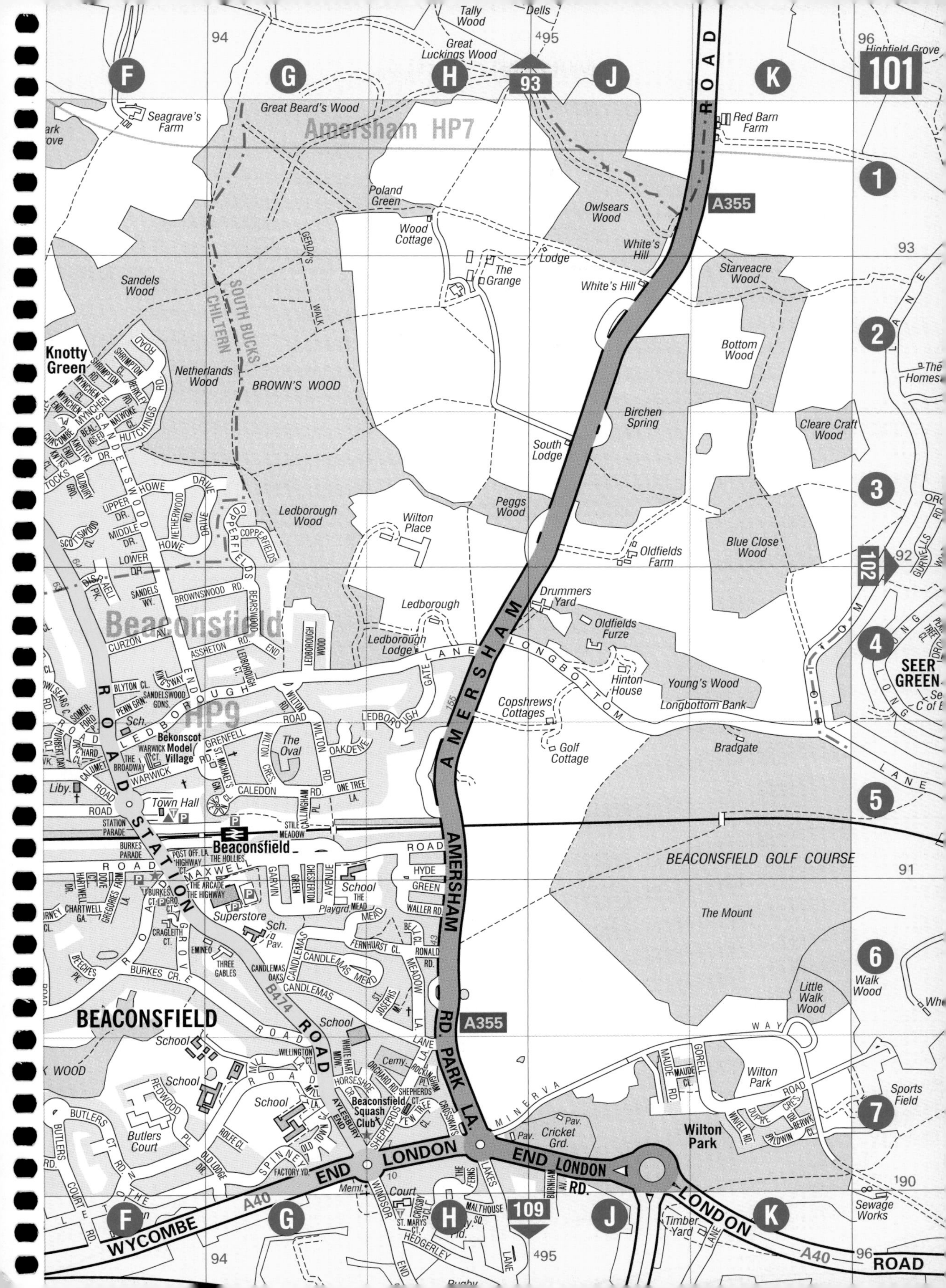
101
Amersham HP7
Beaconsfield
HP9
BEACONSFIELD
Knotty Green
SEER GREEN
A355
A40
B474
93
102
109
Tally Wood
Dells
Great Luckings Wood
Seagrave's Farm
Great Beard's Wood
Red Barn Farm
Poland Green
Wood Cottage
Owlsears Wood
White's Hill
Lodge
The Grange
Starveacre Wood
Sandels Wood
SOUTH BUCKS CHILTERN
Bottom Wood
Netherlands Wood
BROWN'S WOOD
Birchen Spring
Cleare Craft Wood
South Lodge
Peggs Wood
Ledborough Wood
Wilton Place
Oldfields Farm
Blue Close Wood
Drummers Yard
Ledborough
Oldfields Furze
Ledborough Lodge
Hinton House
Young's Wood
Longbottom Bank
Copshrews Cottages
Golf Cottage
Bradgate
Bekonscot Model Village
The Oval
Town Hall
Liby.
Beaconsfield
BEACONSFIELD GOLF COURSE
The Mount
School
Superstore
Playgrd.
Little Walk Wood
Walk Wood
Wilton Park
Sports Field
Butlers Court
Beaconsfield Squash Club
Cemy.
Cricket Grd.
Pav.
Timber Yard
Sewage Works
AMERSHAM ROAD
AMERSHAM RD.
PARK LA.
LONDON END
WYCOMBE END
LONDON ROAD
STATION ROAD
LONGBOTTOM LANE
LEDBOROUGH LANE
MINERVA WAY

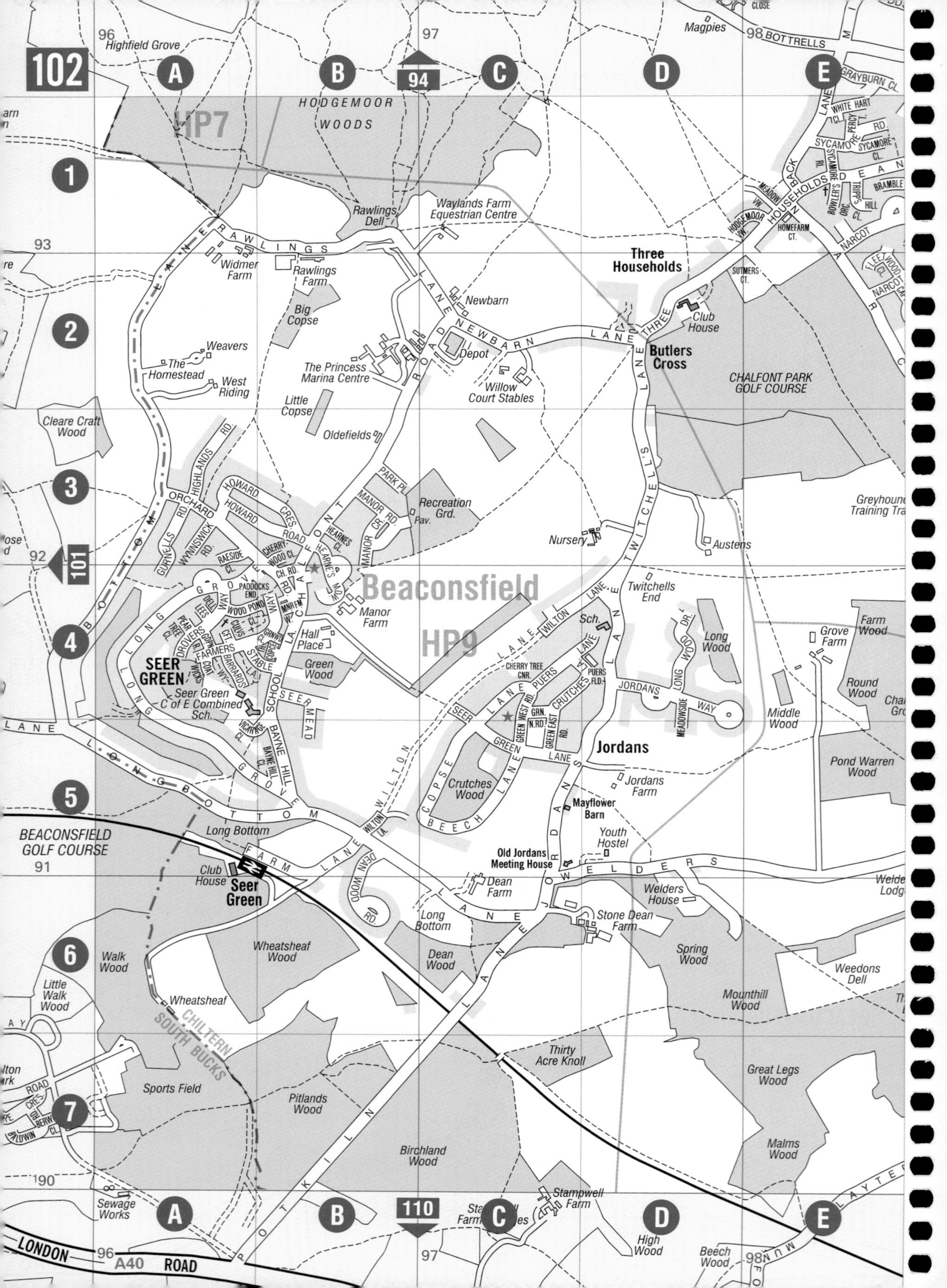

HODGEMOOR WOODS
HP7
Highfield Grove
Rawlings Dell
Waylands Farm Equestrian Centre
RAWLINGS
Widmer Farm
Rawlings Farm
Big Copse
Newbarn
NEWBARN LANE
Three Households
Club House
Butlers Cross
CHALFONT PARK GOLF COURSE
Weavers
The Homestead
West Riding
The Princess Marina Centre
Depot
Willow Court Stables
Little Copse
Oldefields
Cleare Craft Wood
Recreation Grd.
Pav.
Nursery
Austens
Greyhound Training Track
Beaconsfield
HP9
Manor Farm
Hall Place
Green Wood
Twitchells End
Long Wood
Grove Farm
Farm Wood
Round Wood
Middle Wood
Pond Warren Wood
SEER GREEN
Seer Green C of E Combined Sch.
Jordans
Jordans Farm
Crutches Wood
Mayflower Barn
Youth Hostel
Old Jordans Meeting House
BEACONSFIELD GOLF COURSE
Long Bottom
Club House
Seer Green
Dean Farm
Welders House
Stone Dean Farm
Welders Lodge
Walk Wood
Little Walk Wood
Wheatsheaf Wood
Dean Wood
Spring Wood
Weedons Dell
Mounthill Wood
Wheatsheaf
CHILTERN SOUTH BUCKS
Thirty Acre Knoll
Great Legs Wood
Sports Field
Pitlands Wood
Birchland Wood
Malms Wood
Stampwell Farm
Sewage Works
High Wood
Beech Wood
LONDON ROAD
A40
POTKILN LANE
JORDANS LANE
WELDERS LANE
FARM LANE
LONG BOTTOM
LONG GROVE
SCHOOL LA.
CHALFONT ROAD
TWITCHELL'S LANE
WILTON LANE
SEER GREEN LANE
BEECH LANE
COPSE LANE
JORDANS WAY
BOTTRELLS
HOUSEHOLDS
BACK LANE
Magpies

94
101
110

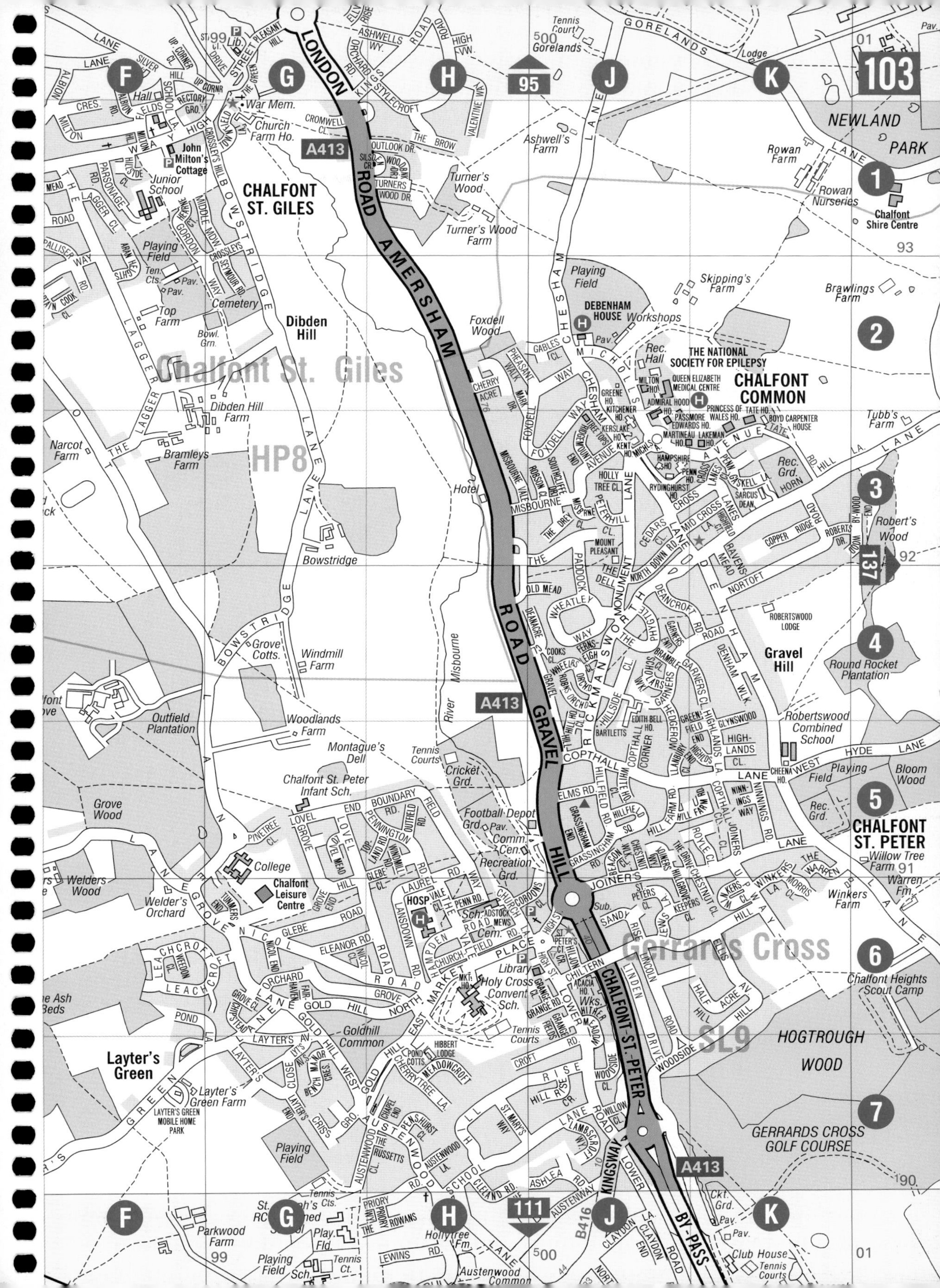
CHALFONT ST. GILES
Chalfont St. Giles
Dibden Hill
HP8
CHALFONT COMMON
THE NATIONAL SOCIETY FOR EPILEPSY
NEWLAND PARK
Gravel Hill
CHALFONT ST. PETER
Gerrards Cross
SL9
HOGTROUGH WOOD
GERRARDS CROSS GOLF COURSE
Layter's Green
Goldhill Common
AMERSHAM ROAD
GRAVEL HILL
LONDON ROAD
CHALFONT ST. PETER BY-PASS
A413
95
111
137

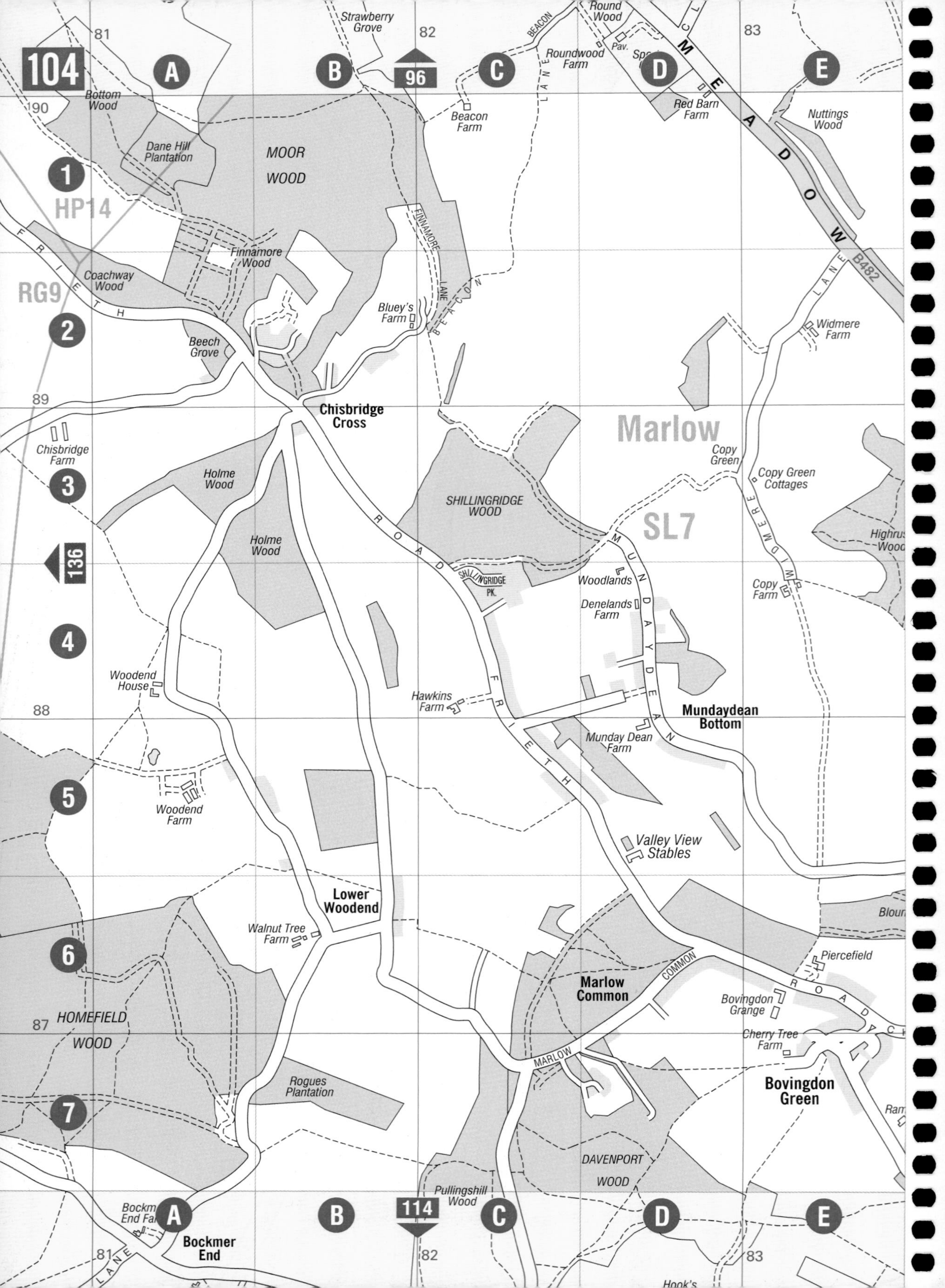

Strawberry Grove
Round Wood
Roundwood Farm
Pav.
Red Barn Farm
Nuttings Wood
Bottom Wood
Beacon Farm
Dane Hill Plantation
MOOR WOOD
HP14
Finnamore Wood
FINNAMORE LANE
BEACON LANE
MEADOW
B482
Coachway Wood
RG9
FRIETH
Bluey's Farm
Widmere Farm
Beech Grove
Chisbridge Cross
Chisbridge Farm
Marlow
Copy Green
Copy Green Cottages
Holme Wood
SHILLINGRIDGE WOOD
SL7
ROAD
SHILLINGRIDGE PK.
MUNDAYDEAN
Woodlands
Denelands Farm
Copy Farm
WIDMERE
Highrus Wood
Woodend House
Hawkins Farm
Mundaydean Bottom
Munday Dean Farm
Woodend Farm
Valley View Stables
Lower Woodend
Walnut Tree Farm
Blour
Pierceﬁeld
Marlow Common
COMMON
Bovingdon Grange
HOMEFIELD WOOD
Cherry Tree Farm
MARLOW
Rogues Plantation
Bovingdon Green
Ram
DAVENPORT WOOD
Pullingshill Wood
Bockmer End Fa
Bockmer End
LANE
Hook's

96
136
114

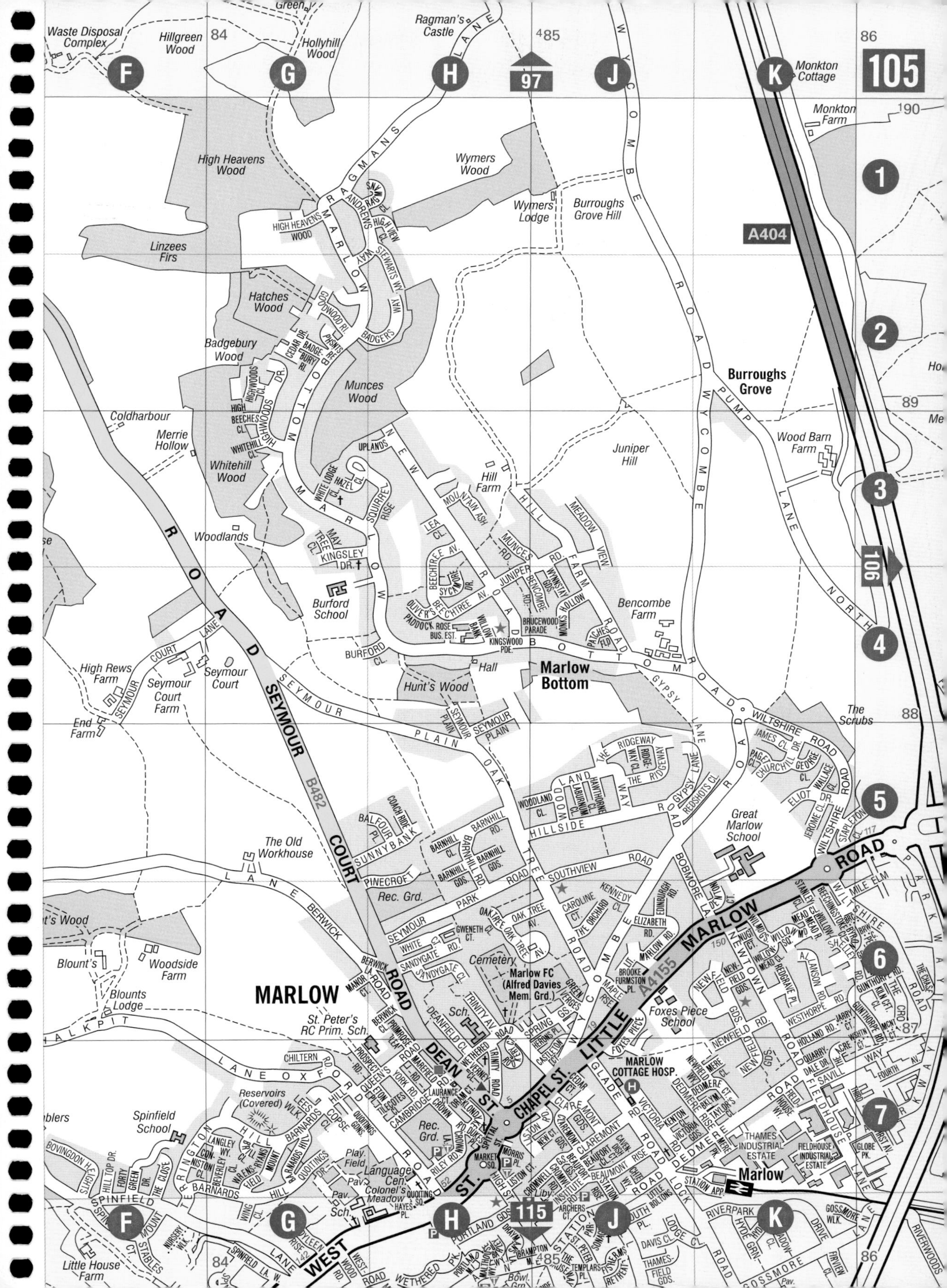

Waste Disposal Complex
Hillgreen Wood
Hollyhill Wood
Ragman's Castle
Monkton Cottage
Monkton Farm
High Heavens Wood
Wymers Wood
Wymers Lodge
Burroughs Grove Hill
Linzees Firs
Hatches Wood
Badgebury Wood
Munces Wood
Burroughs Grove
Coldharbour
Merrie Hollow
Whitehill Wood
Wood Barn Farm
Juniper Hill
Hill Farm
Woodlands
Burford School
Bencombe Farm
High Rews Farm
Seymour Court
Seymour Court Farm
End Farm
Hunt's Wood
Hall
Marlow Bottom
The Scrubs
The Old Workhouse
Great Marlow School
Rec. Grd.
Blount's
Woodside Farm
Blounts Lodge
MARLOW
Cemetery
Marlow FC (Alfred Davies Mem. Grd.)
St. Peter's RC Prim. Sch.
Foxes Piece School
Marlow Cottage Hosp.
Reservoirs (Covered)
Spinfield School
Thames Industrial Estate
Fieldhouse Industrial Estate
Marlow
Language Cen.
Colonel's Meadow
Little House Farm
SEYMOUR COURT ROAD
B482
WYCOMBE ROAD
LITTLE MARLOW ROAD
A4155
A404
MARLOW BOTTOM
CHAPEL ST.
DEAN ST.
WEST ST.
HIGH ST.
97
106
115

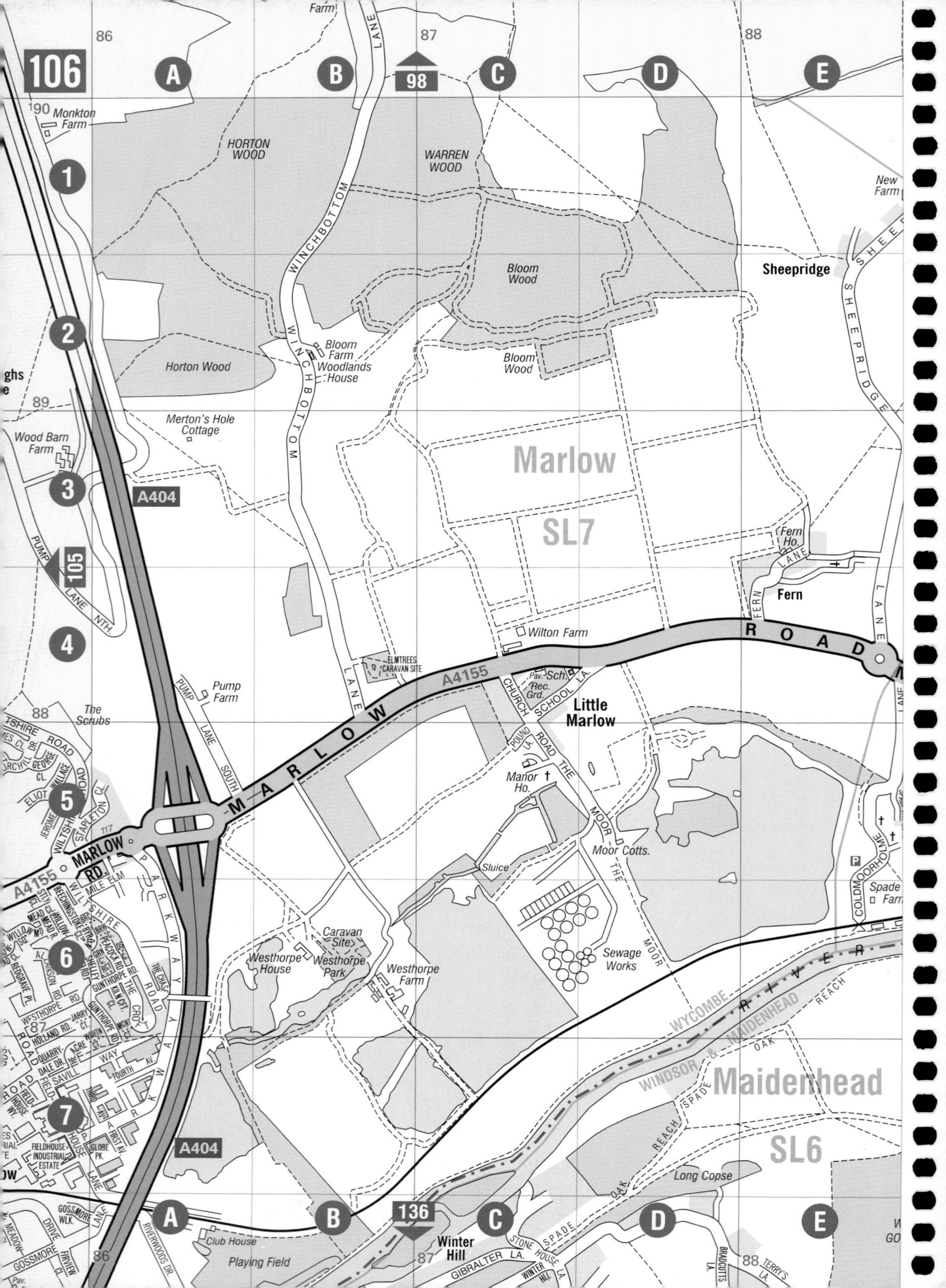

Marlow
SL7
Maidenhead
SL6
Horton Wood
HORTON WOOD
WARREN WOOD
Bloom Wood
Monkton Farm
Bloom Farm
Woodlands House
Merton's Hole Cottage
Wood Barn Farm
Sheepridge
New Farm
Fern Ho.
Fern
Wilton Farm
ELMTREES CARAVAN SITE
Pump Farm
The Scrubs
Little Marlow
Manor Ho.
Moor Cotts.
Sluice
Sewage Works
Caravan Site
Westhorpe House
Westhorpe Park
Westhorpe Farm
Spade Farm
Long Copse
Winter Hill
Club House
Playing Field
FIELDHOUSE INDUSTRIAL ESTATE
GLOBE PK.
MARLOW ROAD
A4155
A404
WINCHBOTTOM LANE
SHEEPRIDGE LANE
FERN LANE
CHURCH ROAD
SCHOOL LA.
POUND LA.
THE MOOR
PUMP LANE SOUTH
PUMP LANE NTH.
PARKWAY
WYCOMBE
WINDSOR & MAIDENHEAD
RIVER
OAK REACH
SPADE OAK REACH
STONE HOUSE LA.
GIBRALTER LA.
WINTER HILL
BRADCUTTS LA.
TERRY'S LA.
COLDMOORHOLME LA.
RIVERWOODS DR.
GOSSMORE WLK.
GOSSMORE LANE
MEADOW DRIVE
FIRVIEW CL.
Farm
98
105
136
86
87
88
89
90
117

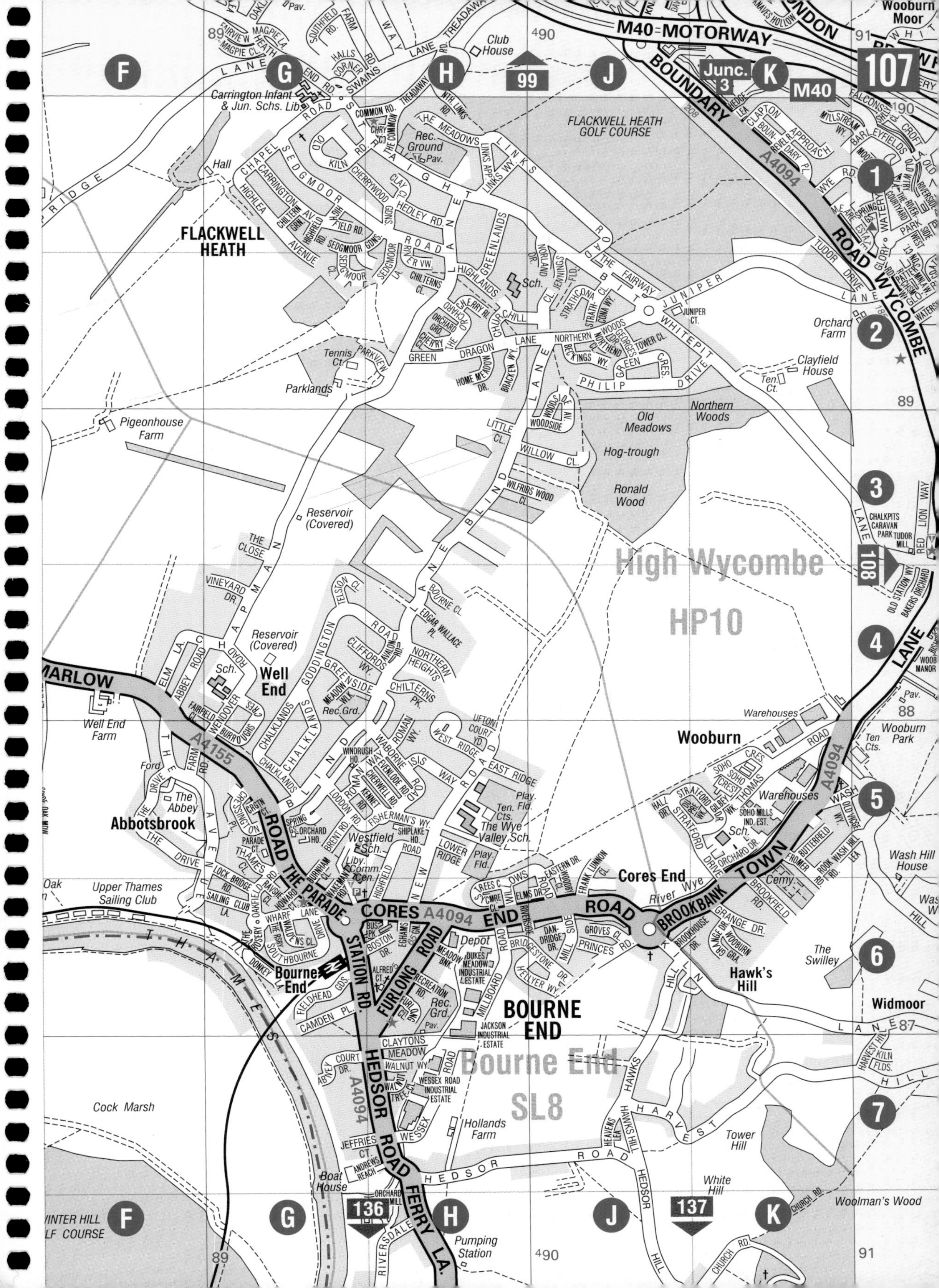

107
M40 MOTORWAY
Junc. 3
M40
BOUNDARY ROAD
WYCOMBE ROAD
A4094
FLACKWELL HEATH
FLACKWELL HEATH GOLF COURSE
Club House
99
108
136
137
Carrington Infant & Jun. Schs. Lib.
Rec. Ground
Pav.
Hall
Sch.
Tennis Ct.
Parklands
Pigeonhouse Farm
Reservoir (Covered)
Old Meadows
Northern Woods
Hog-trough
Ronald Wood
Orchard Farm
Clayfield House
High Wycombe
HP10
Well End
Well End Farm
MARLOW ROAD
A4155
Abbotsbrook
The Abbey
Upper Thames Sailing Club
Rec. Grd.
Westfield Sch.
Liby. Comm. Cen.
The Wye Valley Sch.
Play. Fld.
Warehouses
Wooburn
Wooburn Park
Wooburn Moor
Cores End
CORES END ROAD
BROOKBANK
TOWN LANE
River Wye
Cemy.
Hawk's Hill
The Swilley
Widmoor
Wash Hill House
Bourne End
BOURNE END
Bourne End
SL8
Depot
Dukes Meadow Industrial Estate
Jackson Industrial Estate
Wessex Road Industrial Estate
HEDSOR ROAD
STATION RD.
FURLONG ROAD
FERRY LA.
THE PARADE
Hollands Farm
Tower Hill
White Hill
Woolman's Wood
Cock Marsh
Boat House
Pumping Station
THAMES
WINTER HILL GOLF COURSE
F G H J K
1 2 3 4 5 6 7
89 490 91 88 87 190

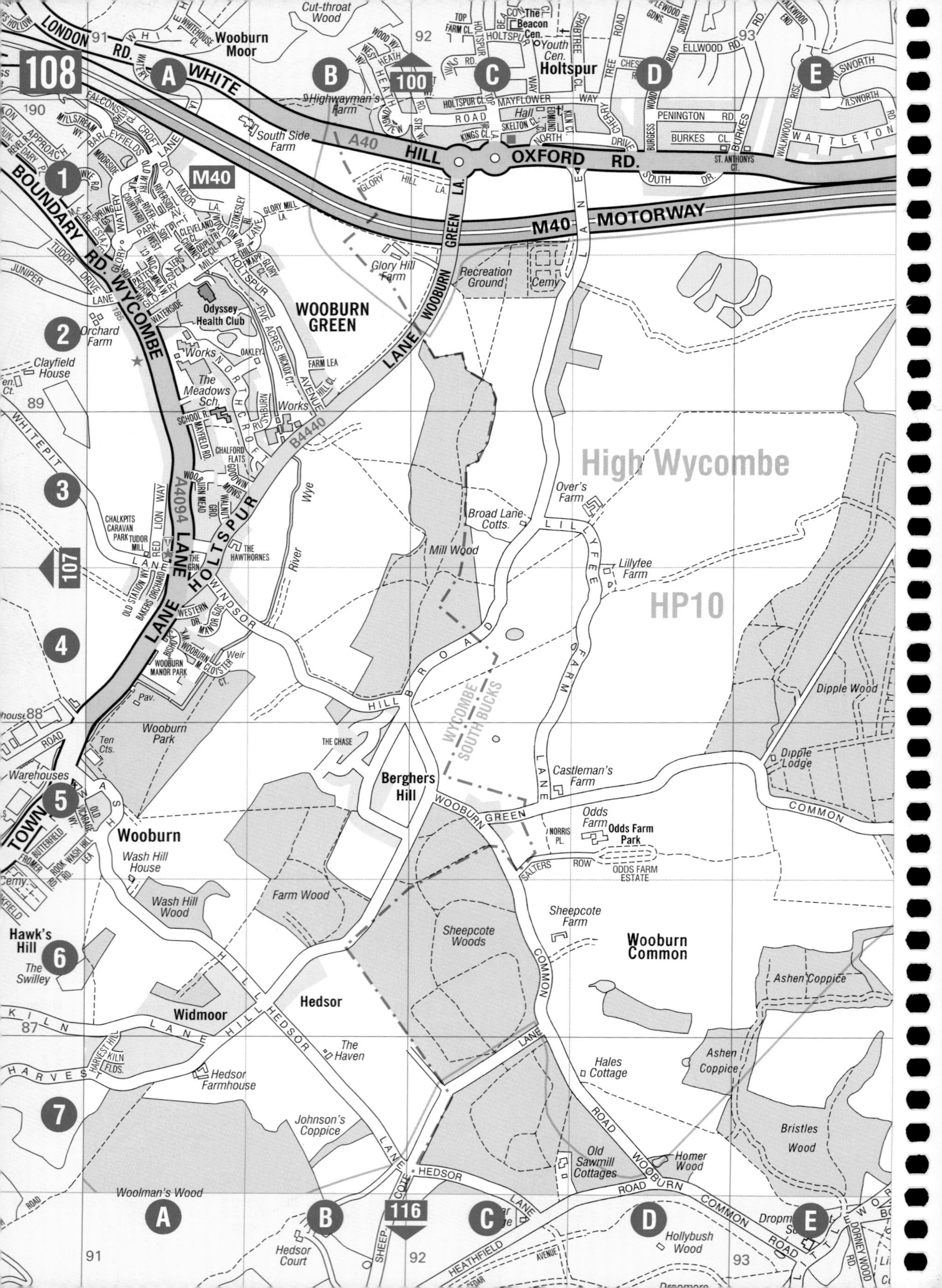
Wooburn Moor
Holtspur
WOOBURN GREEN
High Wycombe
HP10
Berghers Hill
Wooburn
Hedsor
Widmoor
Wooburn Common
M40 MOTORWAY
OXFORD RD.
LONDON RD.
WYCOMBE LANE
HOLTSPUR LANE
WOOBURN GREEN LANE
BROAD LANE
Odyssey Health Club
The Meadows Sch.
Recreation Ground
Glory Hill Farm
South Side Farm
Highwayman's Farm
Over's Farm
Lillyfee Farm
Broad Lane Cotts.
Mill Wood
Castleman's Farm
Odds Farm Park
Sheepcote Farm
Sheepcote Woods
Farm Wood
Wash Hill House
Wash Hill Wood
Wooburn Park
Hawk's Hill
The Swilley
Dipple Wood
Dipple Lodge
Ashen Coppice
Bristles Wood
Homer Wood
Old Sawmill Cottages
Hales Cottage
Hedsor Farmhouse
The Haven
Johnson's Coppice
Woolman's Wood
Hedsor Court
Hollybush Wood
Cut-throat Wood
Chalkpits Caravan Park
Orchard Farm
Clayfield House
WYCOMBE
SOUTH BUCKS

100
107
116

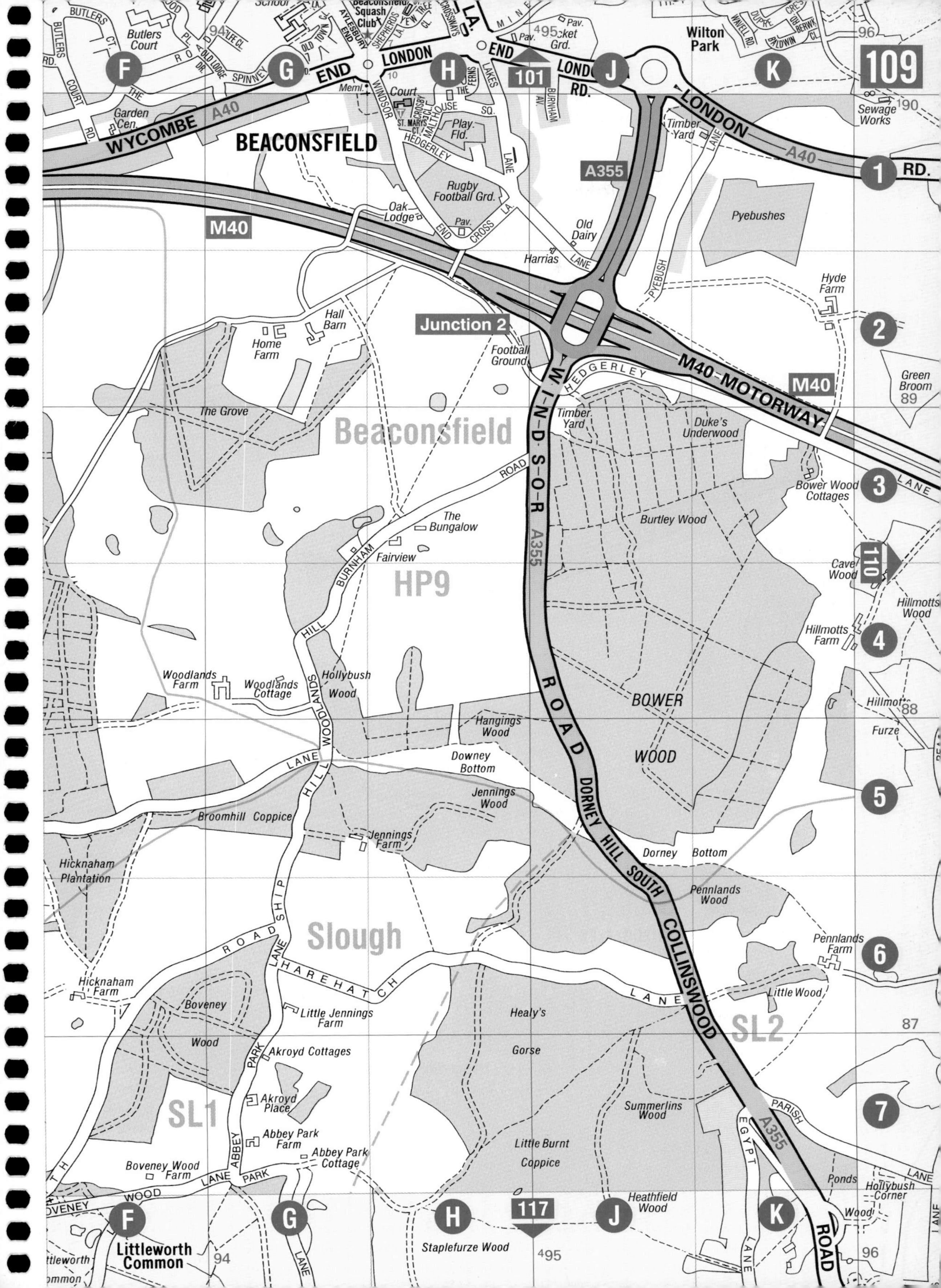
BEACONSFIELD
Beaconsfield
HP9
Slough
SL1
SL2
Wilton Park
Butlers Court
Beaconsfield Squash Club
Garden Cen.
Rugby Football Grd.
Play. Fld.
Oak Lodge
Old Dairy
Harrias
Timber Yard
Sewage Works
Pyebushes
Hyde Farm
Junction 2
M40 MOTORWAY
M40
A40
A355
WYCOMBE END
LONDON END
LONDON RD.
WINDSOR ROAD
HEDGERLEY LANE
Hall Barn
Home Farm
Football Ground
Green Broom
The Grove
Duke's Underwood
Bower Wood Cottages
Burtley Wood
The Bungalow
Fairview
BURNHAM ROAD
Cave Wood
Hillmotts Wood
Hillmotts Farm
Woodlands Farm
Woodlands Cottage
Hollybush Wood
BOWER WOOD
Hangings Wood
Downey Bottom
Jennings Wood
Broomhill Coppice
Jennings Farm
Hicknaham Plantation
Dorney Bottom
DORNEY HILL SOUTH
Pennlands Wood
COLLINSWOOD ROAD
Pennlands Farm
HAREHATCH LANE
SHIP LANE
Hicknaham Farm
Boveney Wood
Little Jennings Farm
Healy's Gorse
Little Wood
Akroyd Cottages
Akroyd Place
Summerlins Wood
Abbey Park Farm
Abbey Park Cottage
Little Burnt Coppice
Boveney Wood Farm
Heathfield Wood
Ponds
Hollybush Corner
Staplefurze Wood
Littleworth Common
EGYPT LANE
PARISH LANE
101
110
117

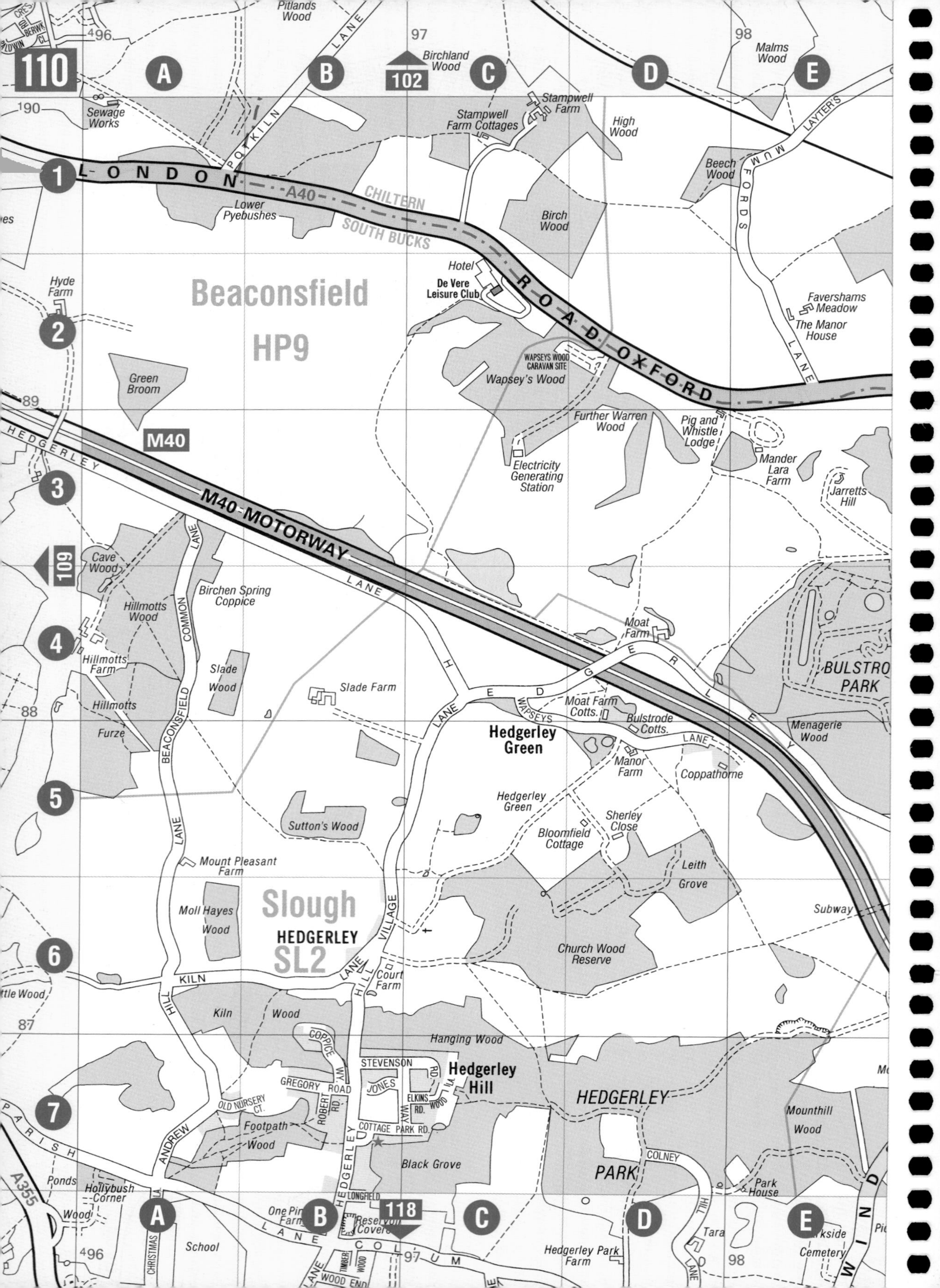

102
109
118
Beaconsfield
HP9
Slough
SL2
HEDGERLEY
Hedgerley Green
Hedgerley Hill
LONDON ROAD OXFORD ROAD
A40
CHILTERN
SOUTH BUCKS
M40 MOTORWAY
M40
HEDGERLEY LANE
BEACONSFIELD COMMON LANE
KILN LANE
VILLAGE LANE
HEDGERLEY HILL
ANDREW HILL
PARISH LANE
COLUM LANE
A355
Pitlands Wood
Birchland Wood
Sewage Works
Stampwell Farm
Stampwell Farm Cottages
High Wood
Malms Wood
Beech Wood
Lower Pyebushes
Birch Wood
Hotel
De Vere Leisure Club
Hyde Farm
Faversham Meadow
The Manor House
Green Broom
WAPSEYS WOOD CARAVAN SITE
Wapsey's Wood
Further Warren Wood
Pig and Whistle Lodge
Mander Lara Farm
Jarretts Hill
Electricity Generating Station
Cave Wood
Birchen Spring Coppice
Hillmotts Wood
Hillmotts Farm
Hillmotts
Furze
Slade Wood
Slade Farm
Moat Farm
Moat Farm Cotts.
Bulstrode Cotts.
BULSTRODE PARK
Menagerie Wood
Manor Farm
Coppathorne
Sutton's Wood
Sherley Close
Bloomfield Cottage
Leith Grove
Mount Pleasant Farm
Moll Hayes Wood
Subway
Church Wood Reserve
Court Farm
Kiln Wood
Hanging Wood
HEDGERLEY PARK
Mounthill Wood
Footpath Wood
Black Grove
Park House
Ponds
Hollybush Corner
One Pin Farm
Reservoir Covered
School
Hedgerley Park Farm
Tara
Cemetery
STEVENSON RD.
GREGORY ROAD
JONES WAY
ELKINS RD.
WOOD LA.
ROBERT RD.
COPPICE WAY
OLD NURSERY CT.
COTTAGE PARK RD.
LONGFIELD
COLNEY HILL LANE
CHRISTMAS LA.
TIMBER
WOOD END
POTKILN LANE
MUMFORDS LANE
LAYTER'S
WAPSEYS LANE

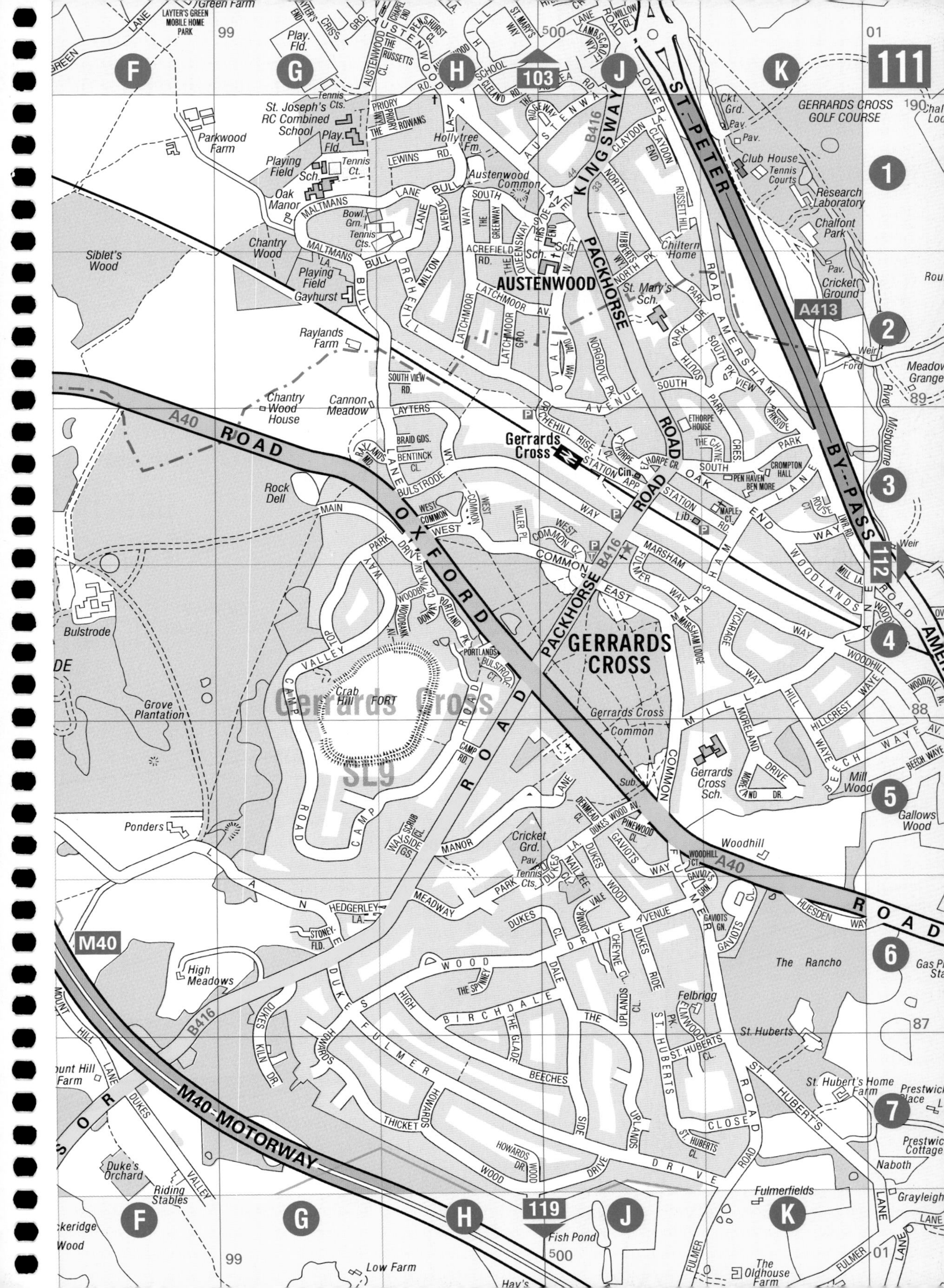
Green Farm
LAYTER'S GREEN MOBILE HOME PARK
99
500
01
F
G
H
J
K
103
Play. Fld.
AUSTENWOOD
THE RUSSETTS
PENSHURST CL.
ST. MARY'S WAY
LAMBSCROFT WY.
WILLOW CL.
SCHOOL
CLELAND RD.
ST. PETER
GERRARDS CROSS GOLF COURSE
Ckt. Grd.
Pav.
Club House
Tennis Courts
Research Laboratory
Chalfont Park
1
Tennis Cts.
St. Joseph's RC Combined School
PRIORY WY.
PRIORY
THE ROWANS
Play. Fld.
Parkwood Farm
Hollytree Fm.
LEWINS RD.
Playing Field
Sch.
Tennis Ct.
Austenwood Common
KINGSWAY
B416
CLAYDON LA.
CLAYDON END
NORTH
RUSSETT HILL
Oak Manor
MALTMANS
LANE
BULL
SOUTH
THE GREENWAY
Bowl. Grn.
Tennis Cts.
MILTON AVENUE
ACREFIELD RD.
THE QUEENSWAY
FIRS END
Sch.
PACKHORSE
HIBBERTS WY.
NORTH PK.
Chiltern Home
Chantry Wood
Siblet's Wood
MALTMANS LA.
Playing Field
Gayhurst
ORCHEHILL
AUSTENWOOD
St. Mary's Sch.
AMERSHAM ROAD
Pav.
Cricket Ground
A413
LATCHMOOR AV.
LATCHMOOR GRO.
OVAL WAY
NORGROVE PK.
PARK DR.
SOUTH PK.
VIEW
2
Raylands Farm
Weir
Ford
Meadow Grange
River Misbourne
89
SOUTH VIEW RD.
SOUTH PARK
AVENUE
PARKSIDE
Chantry Wood House
Cannon Meadow
LAYTERS
ETHORPE HOUSE
THE CHYNE
A40
ROAD
BRAID GDS.
BENTINCK CL.
RAYLANDS MD.
Gerrards Cross
ORCHEHILL RISE
STATION APP
Cin.
ETHORPE CR.
SOUTH
PARK CRES.
CROMPTON HALL
PEN HAVEN
BEN MORE
OAK
LANE
BY-PASS
3
Rock Dell
BULSTRODE WY.
MAIN
OXFORD
WEST COMMON
WEST
MILLER PL.
WEST COMMON CL.
STATION
MAPLE CT.
Lib.
ROUSE CT.
END
WAY
LWR. RD.
Weir
112
COMMON
MARSHAM
FULMER WAY
MARSHAM LANE
WOODLANDS
MILL LA.
PARK DRIVE
WAY
TOP
VALLEY
WOODBURY AV.
WOODBANK AV.
DONNAY CL.
PORTLAND PK.
EAST
VICARAGE WAY
MARSHAM LODGE
WOODHILL
AMERSHAM
4
Bulstrode
PORTLANDS
BULSTRODE CT.
GERRARDS CROSS
Crab Hill
FORT
Gerrards Cross
CAMP
ROAD
Grove Plantation
Gerrards Cross Common
HILL
MILL
MORELAND
HILLCREST
WAYE
WOODHILL AV.
88
BEECH WAYE
AV.
SL9
CAMP RD.
Gerrards Cross Sch.
MORELAND DR.
DRIVE
Mill Wood
5
Gallows Wood
Ponders
LANE
DENMEAD CL.
DUKES WOOD AV.
PINEWOOD CL.
Sub.
CAMP ROAD
WAYSIDE GS.
SCRUB CL.
MANOR
Cricket Grd.
Pav.
Tennis Cts.
DUKES LA.
NAIL ZEE CL.
DUKES WOOD
GAVIOTS WAY
WOODHILL CT.
Woodhill
GAVIOTS GRN.
GAVIOTS CL.
HUESDEN WAY
HEDGERLEY LA.
MEADWAY
PARK
DUKES CL.
COOMBE VALE
AVENUE
GAVIOTS GN.
GAVIOTS
STONEY-FLD.
M40
DRIVE
CHEYNE CL.
DUKES RIDE
The Rancho
6
Gas Pr Sta
High Meadows
WOOD
THE SPINNEY
DALE
THE UPLANDS CL.
Felbrigg
ELMWOOD PK.
87
MOUNT HILL
DUKES
HIGH
BIRCHDALE
THE GLADE
ST. HUBERTS
St. Huberts
B416
DUKES KILN DR.
HOWARDS
FULMER
ST. HUBERTS CL.
Mount Hill Farm
BEECHES
CLOSE
ST. HUBERT'S LANE
St. Hubert's Home Farm
Prestwick Place
7
DUKES VALLEY
M40 MOTORWAY
THICKET
HOWARDS
SIDE
UPLANDS
ST. HUBERTS CL.
Prestwick Cottage
Duke's Orchard
Riding Stables
HOWARDS DR.
WOOD
DRIVE
Naboth
Fulmerfields
Grayleigh
119
Fish Pond
Wood
99
500
Low Farm
FULMER ROAD
The Oldhouse Farm
FULMER
01
LANE
Hay's

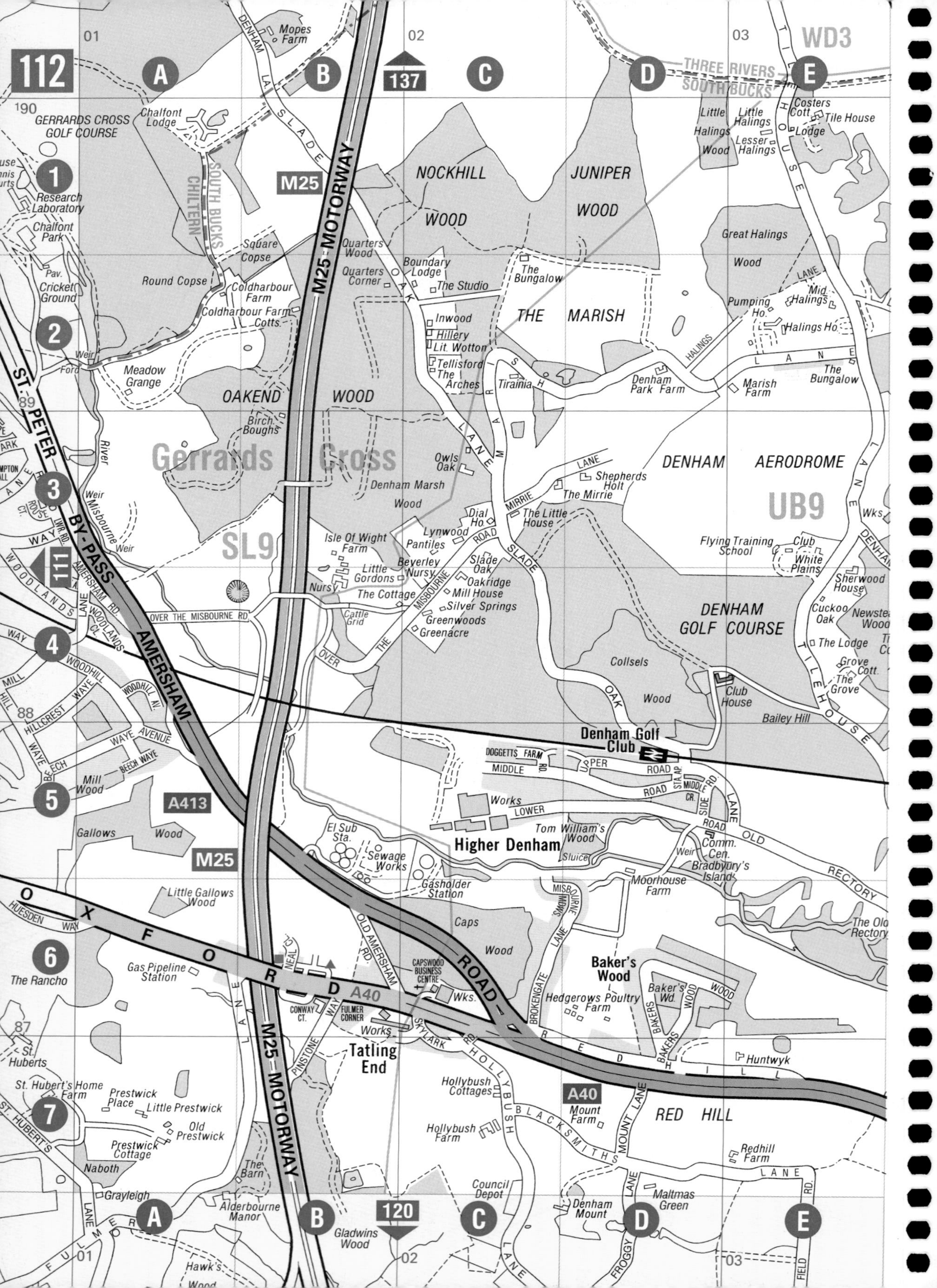

112
137
120
111
WD3
UB9
SL9
THREE RIVERS
SOUTH BUCKS
CHILTERN
Gerrards Cross
GERRARDS CROSS GOLF COURSE
Mopes Farm
Chalfont Lodge
Research Laboratory
Chalfont Park
Cricket Ground
Square Copse
Round Copse
Coldharbour Farm
Coldharbour Farm Cotts.
Meadow Grange
OAKEND WOOD
Birch Boughs
NOCKHILL WOOD
JUNIPER WOOD
Quarters Wood
Quarters Corner
Boundary Lodge
The Studio
The Bungalow
THE MARISH
Inwood
Hillery
Lit. Wotton
Tellisford
The Arches
Tirainia
Denham Park Farm
Marish Farm
Little Halings Wood
Little Halings
Lesser Halings
Costers Cott.
Tile House
Lodge
Great Halings Wood
Pumping Ho.
Mid Halings
Halings Ho.
DENHAM AERODROME
Flying Training School
Club
White Plains
Sherwood House
Cuckoo Oak
The Lodge
Grove Cott.
The Grove
Club House
Bailey Hill
DENHAM GOLF COURSE
Collsels Wood
Owls Oak
Denham Marsh Wood
Shepherds Holt
The Mirrie
Dial Ho.
The Little House
Lynwood
Pantiles
Isle Of Wight Farm
Beverley Nursy.
Little Gordons
Nursy.
The Cottage
Cattle Grid
Slade Oak
Oakridge
Mill House
Silver Springs
Greenwoods
Greenacre
Denham Golf Club
Works
Higher Denham
Tom William's Wood
Sluice
Comm. Cen.
Bradbury's Island
Moorhouse Farm
El Sub Sta.
Sewage Works
Gasholder Station
Caps Wood
Baker's Wood
Baker's Wd.
Hedgerows Poultry Farm
Huntwyk
The Old Rectory
Mill Wood
Gallows Wood
Little Gallows Wood
The Rancho
Gas Pipeline Station
CAPSWOOD BUSINESS CENTRE
Wks.
CONWAY CT.
FULMER CORNER
Works
Tatling End
St. Huberts
St. Hubert's Home Farm
Prestwick Place
Little Prestwick
Old Prestwick
Prestwick Cottage
Naboth
Grayleigh
The Barn
Alderbourne Manor
Hollybush Cottages
Hollybush Farm
Council Depot
Gladwins Wood
Hawk's Wood
Mount Farm
RED HILL
Redhill Farm
Maltmas Green
Denham Mount
M25 MOTORWAY
M25
A413
A40
ST. PETER BY-PASS
AMERSHAM ROAD
OXFORD ROAD
RED HILL
DENHAM LANE
SLADE OAK LANE
MARSH LANE
MIRRIE LANE
HALINGS LANE
TILEHOUSE LANE
OVER THE MISBOURNE RD.
OVER THE MISBOURNE ROAD
DOGGETTS FARM RD.
MIDDLE ROAD
UPPER ROAD
LOWER ROAD
STA. AP.
MIDDLE CR.
SIDE RD.
OLD RECTORY LANE
MISBOURNE MDWS.
BROKENGATE LANE
BAKERS WOOD
BAKERS
OLD AMERSHAM RD.
NEAL CT.
SKYLARK RD.
PINSTONE WAY
HOLLYBUSH LANE
BLACKSMITHS LANE
MOUNT LANE
FROGGY LANE
FIELD RD.
FULMER LANE
ST. HUBERT'S LANE
HUESDEN WAY
WOODLANDS
AMERSHAM RD.
WOODHILL
WOODHILL AV.
HILLCREST WAYE
WAYE AVENUE
BEECH WAYE
MILL HILL
Weir
Ford
River Misbourne
01
02
03
190
89
88
87
A
B
C
D
E
1
2
3
4
5
6
7

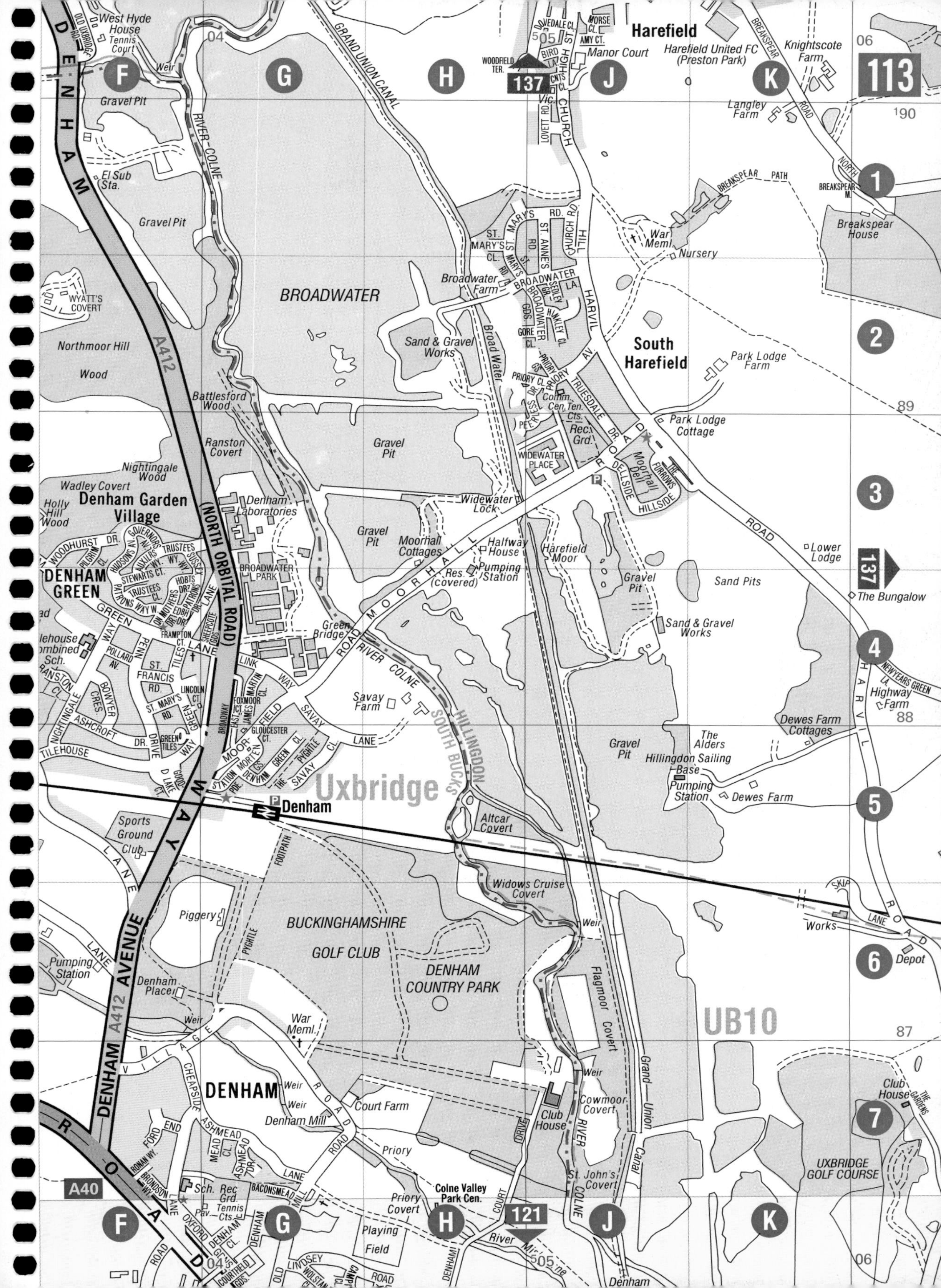

Harefield
South Harefield
Denham Garden Village
DENHAM GREEN
DENHAM
Uxbridge
UB10
BROADWATER
BUCKINGHAMSHIRE GOLF CLUB
DENHAM COUNTRY PARK
UXBRIDGE GOLF COURSE
Harefield United FC (Preston Park)
Manor Court
Knightscote Farm
Langley Farm
Breakspear House
West Hyde House
Gravel Pit
Northmoor Hill Wood
Battlesford Wood
Ranston Covert
Nightingale Wood
Wadley Covert
Holly Hill Wood
Denham Laboratories
Broadwater Park
Sand & Gravel Works
Widewater Lock
Moorhall Cottages
Halfway House
Pumping Station
Harefield Moor
Sand Pits
Lower Lodge
The Bungalow
Highway Farm
Dewes Farm Cottages
The Alders
Hillingdon Sailing Base
Dewes Farm
Savay Farm
Green Bridge
Denham
Altcar Covert
Widows Cruise Covert
Sports Ground Club
Piggery
Denham Place
War Meml.
Denham Mill
Court Farm
Priory
Club House
Cowmoor Covert
Flagmoor Covert
St. John's Covert
Colne Valley Park Cen.
Priory Covert
Playing Field
Park Lodge Farm
Park Lodge Cottage
Moorhall Dell
Works
Depot
A412
A40
DENHAM WAY (NORTH ORBITAL ROAD)
DENHAM AVENUE
OXFORD ROAD
MOORHALL ROAD
HARVIL ROAD
CHURCH HILL
GRAND UNION CANAL
RIVER COLNE
137
121

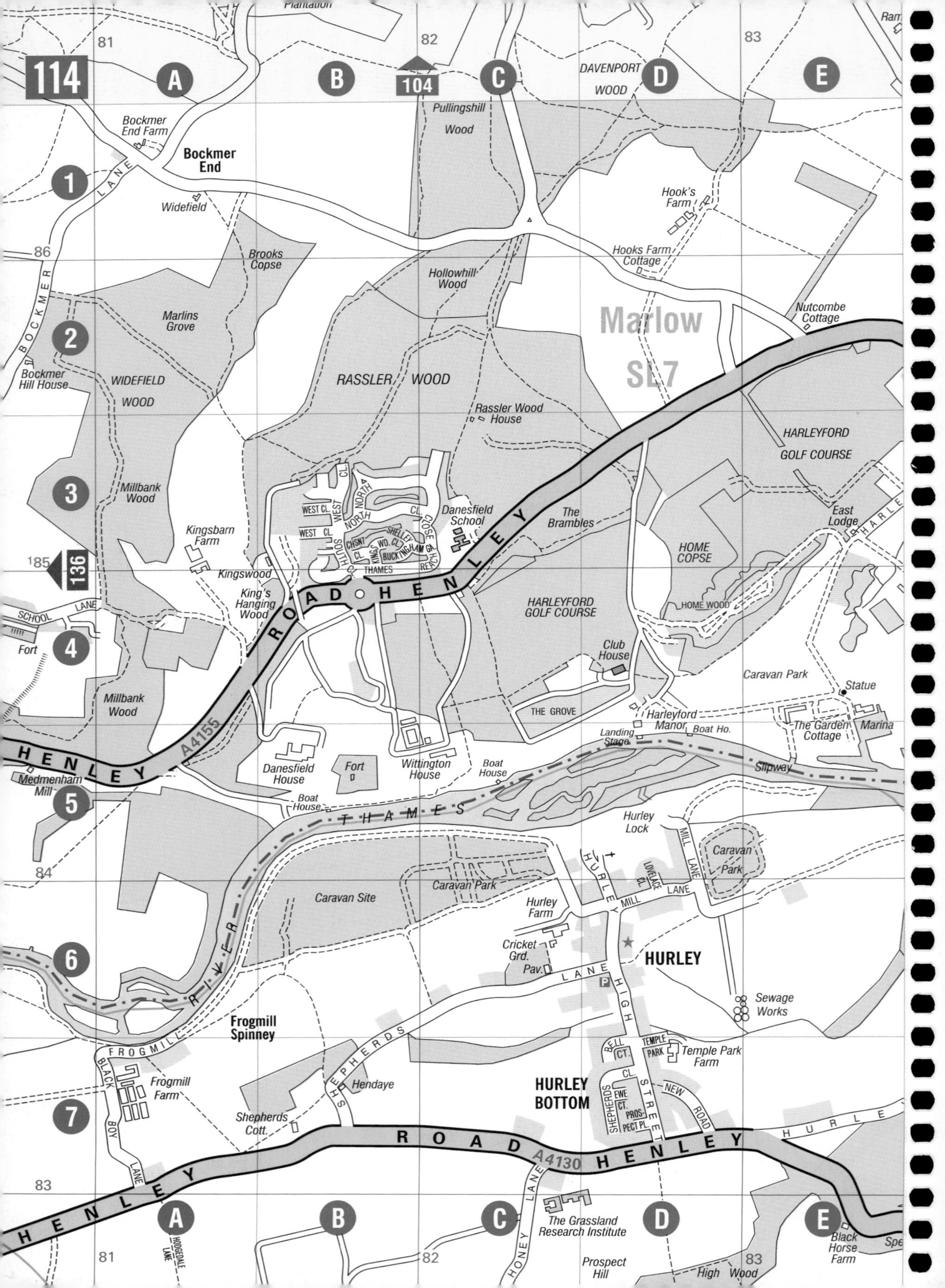
Plantation
81
82
83
Ram
A
B
C
D
E
104
DAVENPORT
WOOD
Pullingshill
Wood
Bockmer
End Farm
Bockmer
End
1
LANE
Widefield
Hook's
Farm
86
Brooks
Copse
Hooks Farm
Cottage
Hollowhill
Wood
BOCKMER
Marlins
Grove
2
Marlow
SL7
Nutcombe
Cottage
Bockmer
Hill House
WIDEFIELD
WOOD
RASSLER
WOOD
Rassler Wood
House
HARLEYFORD
GOLF COURSE
3
Millbank
Wood
Danesfield
School
The
Brambles
East
Lodge
Kingsbarn
Farm
HOME
COPSE
185
136
Kingswood
King's
Hanging
Wood
THAMES
ROAD
HENLEY
HARLEYFORD
GOLF COURSE
HOME WOOD
SCHOOL
LANE
Fort
4
Club
House
Caravan Park
Statue
Millbank
Wood
THE GROVE
Harleyford
Manor
Boat Ho.
The Garden
Cottage
Marina
Landing
Stage
A4155
Danesfield
House
Fort
Wittington
House
Boat
House
Slipway
Medmenham
Mill
5
Boat
House
THAMES
Hurley
Lock
MILL LANE
Caravan
Park
84
HURLEY
LOVELACE
CL.
MILL
LANE
Caravan Site
Caravan Park
Hurley
Farm
Cricket
Grd.
Pav.
6
HURLEY
LANE
HIGH
Sewage
Works
RIVER
Frogmill
Spinney
SHEPHERDS
FROGMILL
BLACK
BELL
CT.
TEMPLE
PARK
Temple Park
Farm
Frogmill
Farm
Hendaye
CL.
HURLEY
BOTTOM
STREET
NEW
ROAD
7
BOY
LANE
Shepherds
Cott.
SHEPHERDS
EWE
CT.
PROS-
PECT PL.
HURLE
ROAD
A4130
HENLEY
83
HENLEY
HONEY LANE
The Grassland
Research Institute
HOGGEDALE
LANE
Black
Horse
Farm
Spe
81
82
83
Prospect
Hill
High Wood

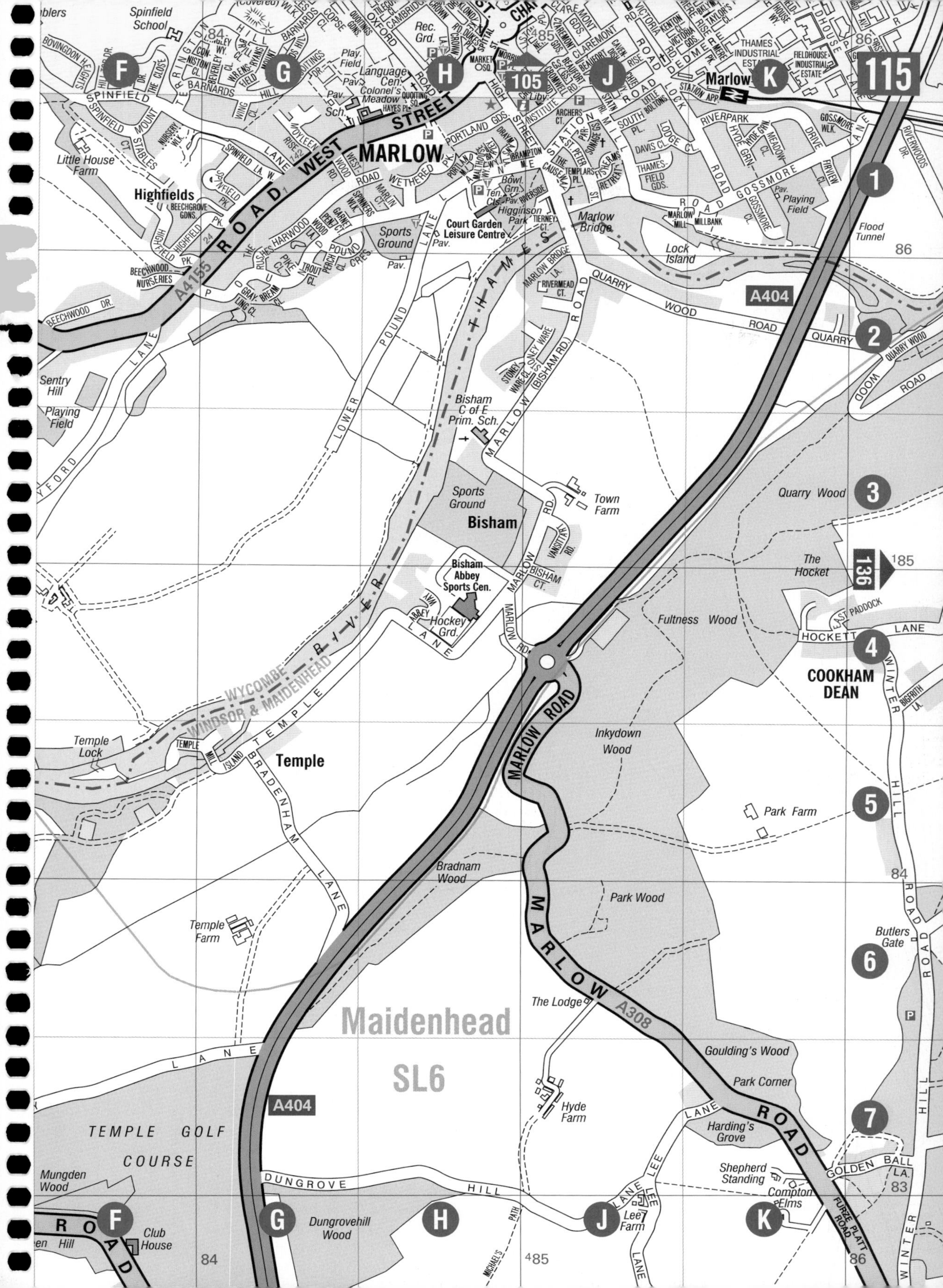

115
MARLOW
West Street
A4155
Highfields
Little House Farm
Spinfield School
Court Garden Leisure Centre
Higginson Park
Marlow Bridge
Lock Island
Marlow
Thames Industrial Estate
Fieldhouse Industrial Estate
Flood Tunnel
Quarry Wood Road
A404
Sentry Hill
Playing Field
Lower Pound Lane
River Thames
Bisham C of E Prim. Sch.
Marlow Road (Bisham Rd)
Sports Ground
Town Farm
Bisham
Bisham Abbey Sports Cen.
Hockey Grd.
Abbey Lane
Quarry Wood
The Hocket
136
Fultness Wood
Hockett Lane
COOKHAM DEAN
Wycombe
Windsor & Maidenhead
Temple Lock
Temple
Temple Lane
Bradenham Lane
Marlow Road
Inkydown Wood
Park Farm
Bradnam Wood
Park Wood
Temple Farm
Butlers Gate
Winter Hill Road
The Lodge
A308
Maidenhead
SL6
Goulding's Wood
Park Corner
Hyde Farm
Harding's Grove
TEMPLE GOLF COURSE
Mungden Wood
Dungrove Hill
Dungrovehill Wood
Lee Lane
Lee Farm
Shepherd Standing
Compton Elms
Golden Ball La.
Furze Platt Road
Club House
84
485
86

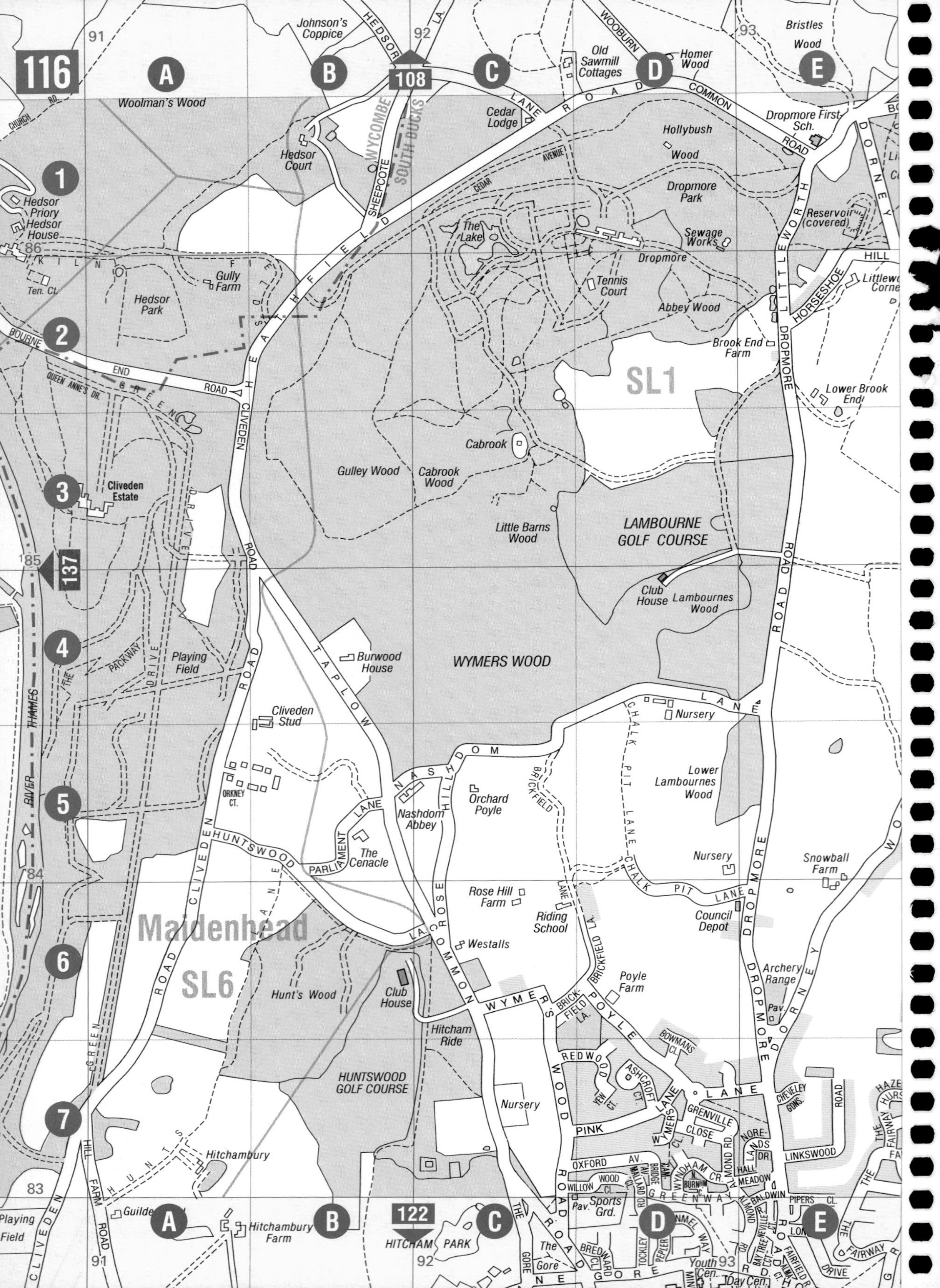
116
108
137
122
Johnson's Coppice
Woolman's Wood
Hedsor Court
Hedsor Priory
Hedsor House
Ten. Ct.
Gully Farm
Hedsor Park
Cedar Lodge
Old Sawmill Cottages
Homer Wood
Bristles Wood
Hollybush Wood
Dropmore First Sch.
Dropmore Park
The Lake
Sewage Works
Reservoir (covered)
Dropmore
Tennis Court
Abbey Wood
Littlewort Corner
Brook End Farm
SL1
Lower Brook End
Cliveden Estate
Cabrook
Gulley Wood
Cabrook Wood
Little Barns Wood
LAMBOURNE GOLF COURSE
Club House
Lambournes Wood
Playing Field
Burwood House
WYMERS WOOD
Cliveden Stud
Nursery
Lower Lambournes Wood
Orchard Poyle
Nashdom Abbey
The Cenacle
Nursery
Snowball Farm
Rose Hill Farm
Riding School
Council Depot
Maidenhead
Westalls
SL6
Hunt's Wood
Club House
Poyle Farm
Archery Range
Pav.
Hitcham Ride
HUNTSWOOD GOLF COURSE
Nursery
Hitchambury
Guildens
Hitchambury Farm
HITCHAM PARK
Playing Field
Pav.
Sports Grd.
The Gore
Youth Cen.
Day Cen.
RIVER THAMES
CLIVEDEN ROAD
TAPLOW COMMON ROAD
DROPMORE ROAD
HEATHFIELD ROAD
BOURNE END ROAD
WOOBURN COMMON ROAD
LITTLEWORTH ROAD
NASHDOM LANE
HUNTSWOOD LANE
PARLIAMENT LANE
WYMERS WOOD ROAD
PINK LANE
POYLE LANE
CHALK PIT LANE
BRICKFIELD LA.
OXFORD AV.
GREENWAY
GORE ROAD
HILL FARM ROAD

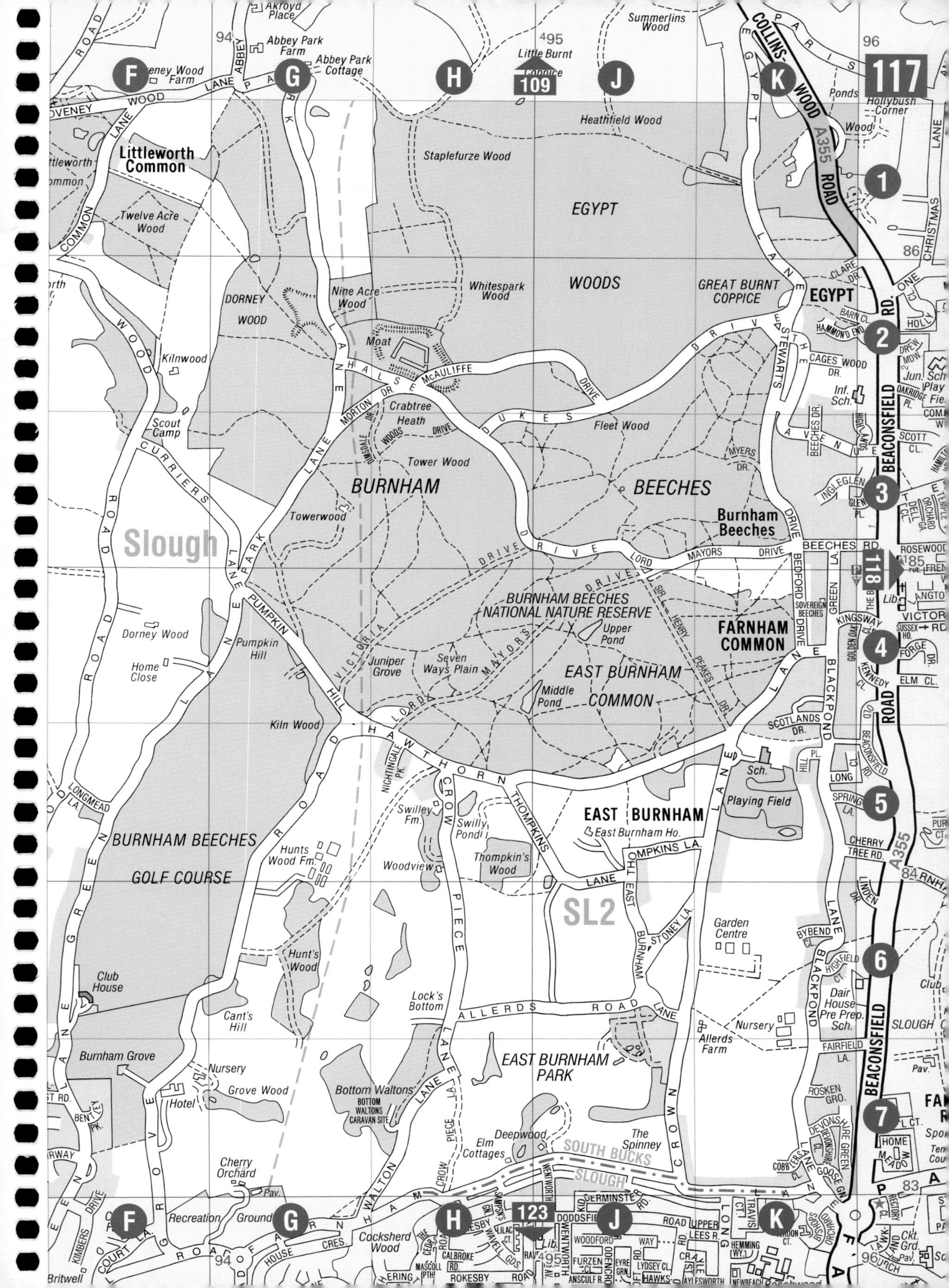
117
109
118
123
F
G
H
J
K
1
2
3
4
5
6
7
Littleworth Common
Slough
EGYPT
WOODS
BURNHAM
BEECHES
Burnham Beeches
BURNHAM BEECHES NATIONAL NATURE RESERVE
EAST BURNHAM COMMON
FARNHAM COMMON
EAST BURNHAM
SL2
BURNHAM BEECHES GOLF COURSE
EAST BURNHAM PARK
Staplefurze Wood
Heathfield Wood
Summerlins Wood
Little Burnt Coppice
Abbey Park Farm
Abbey Park Cottage
Akroyd Place
Twelve Acre Wood
DORNEY WOOD
Kilnwood
Scout Camp
Nine Acre Wood
Whitespark Wood
GREAT BURNT COPPICE
Moat
Crabtree Heath
Tower Wood
Towerwood
Fleet Wood
Dorney Wood
Home Close
Pumpkin Hill
Juniper Grove
Seven Ways Plain
Upper Pond
Middle Pond
Kiln Wood
Swilley Fm.
Swilly Pond
Thompkin's Wood
Hunts Wood Fm.
Woodview
East Burnham Ho.
Playing Field
Sch.
Inf. Sch.
Garden Centre
Hunt's Wood
Lock's Bottom
Cant's Hill
Club House
Burnham Grove
Nursery
Grove Wood
Hotel
Bottom Waltons
BOTTOM WALTONS CARAVAN SITE
Elm Cottages
Deepwood
The Spinney
Cherry Orchard
Recreation Ground
Cocksherd Wood
Allerds Farm
Dair House Pre Prep. Sch.
Hollybush Corner
Ponds
SOUTH BUCKS
SLOUGH
A355
COLLINS-WOOD ROAD
BEACONSFIELD RD.
BEACONSFIELD ROAD
PARK LANE
LORD MAYORS DRIVE
DUKES DRIVE
McAULIFFE DRIVE
HALSE DRIVE
MORTON DR.
DIMSDALE DR.
WOODS DRIVE
VICTORIA DRIVE
SIR HENRY PEAKES DR.
PUMPKIN HILL
HAWTHORN LANE
HAWTHORN ROAD
CROW PIECE LANE
THOMPKINS LANE
EAST BURNHAM LANE
STONEY LA.
ALLERDS ROAD
CROWN LANE
BLACKPOND LANE
EGYPT LANE
STEWART'S DRIVE
BEDFORD DRIVE
GREEN LA.
KINGSWAY
SOVEREIGN BEECHES
SCOTLANDS DR.
BEECHES RD.
CURRIERS LANE
DORNEY WOOD ROAD
COMMON LANE
WOOD LANE
ABBEY PARK LANE
LONGMEAD LA.
GREEN LANE
GROVE ROAD
WALTON LANE
FARNHAM ROAD
KIMBERS DRIVE
COURT LA.
CLARE DR.
BARN CL.
HAMMOND END
CAGES WOOD DR.
BEECHES DR.
BEECHES AVENUE
HIGHLANDS
MYERS DR.
INGLEGLEN
OLD BEACONSFIELD RD.
LONG RD.
SPRING LA.
CHERRY TREE RD.
LINDEN DR.
BYBEND CL.
HIGHFIELD CT.
FAIRFIELD LA.
ROSKEN GRO.
DEVONSHIRE GREEN
GOOSE GN
COBBLERS CL.
KENNEDY CL.
ELM CL.
SCOTT CL.
HILL PL.
CHRISTMAS
NIGHTINGALE PK.
KIDDERMINSTER RD.
DODDSFIELD ROAD
UPPER LEES R
WOODFORD WAY
FURZEN CL.
LYDSEY CL.
HAWKS
HEMMING WY.
TRAVIS CT.
ROKESBY ROAD
CALBROKE RD.
MASCOLL PTH.
LILAC CT.
WENTWORTH
ANSCULF R.
HOUSE CRES.
Britwell
BENTLEY PK.
ONE
HOLLY
DREW MDW.
OAKRIDGE PL.
Jun. Sch
Play
Fie
ROSEWOOD
Lib.
SUSSEX HO.
FORGE DR.
VICTORIA
SLOUGH
HOME MEADOW
Pav.
RECTORY CL.
Ckt. Grd.
CHURCH
94
495
96
86
85
84
83

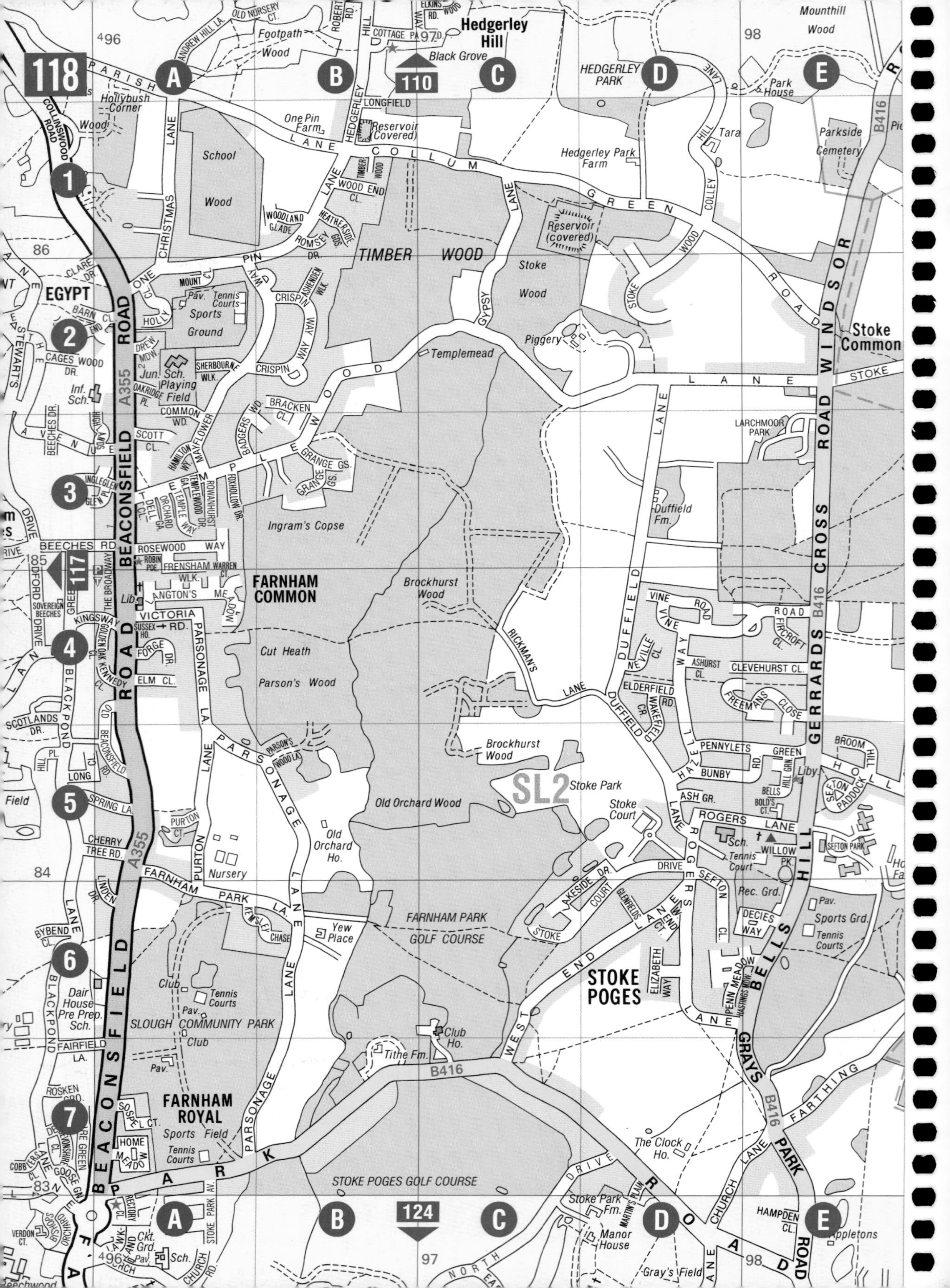
Hedgerley Hill
Black Grove
110
HEDGERLEY PARK
Mounthill Wood
Park House
Hollybush Corner
One Pin Farm
Reservoir (Covered)
COLLUM GREEN ROAD
School Wood
Hedgerley Park Farm
Tara
Parkside Cemetery
B416
TIMBER WOOD
Reservoir (covered)
Stoke Wood
EGYPT
Sports Ground
Piggery
Stoke Common
Templemead
WOOD LANE
STOKE
Jun. Sch. Playing Field
A355
BEACONSFIELD ROAD
LARCHMOOR PARK
WINDSOR ROAD
GERRARDS CROSS ROAD
Ingram's Copse
Duffield Fm.
BEECHES RD
ROSEWOOD WAY
117
FARNHAM COMMON
Brockhurst Wood
VICTORIA RD.
Cut Heath
Parson's Wood
DUFFIELD LANE
RICKMAN'S LANE
Brockhurst Wood
SL2
Stoke Park
Stoke Court
Old Orchard Wood
Old Orchard Ho.
ROGERS LANE
Nursery
FARNHAM PARK LA.
FARNHAM PARK GOLF COURSE
Yew Place
STOKE POGES
Rec. Grd.
Sports Grd.
BELLS HILL
Dair House Pre Prep. Sch.
SLOUGH COMMUNITY PARK
Club Ho.
Tithe Fm.
B416
GRAYS PARK ROAD
FARTHING
FARNHAM ROYAL
Sports Field
The Clock Ho.
PARK ROAD
STOKE POGES GOLF COURSE
Stoke Park Fm.
Manor House
Gray's Field
124
Appletons
CHURCH LANE
HAMPDEN CL.
A B C D E
1 2 3 4 5 6 7
496 97 98
86 85 84 83

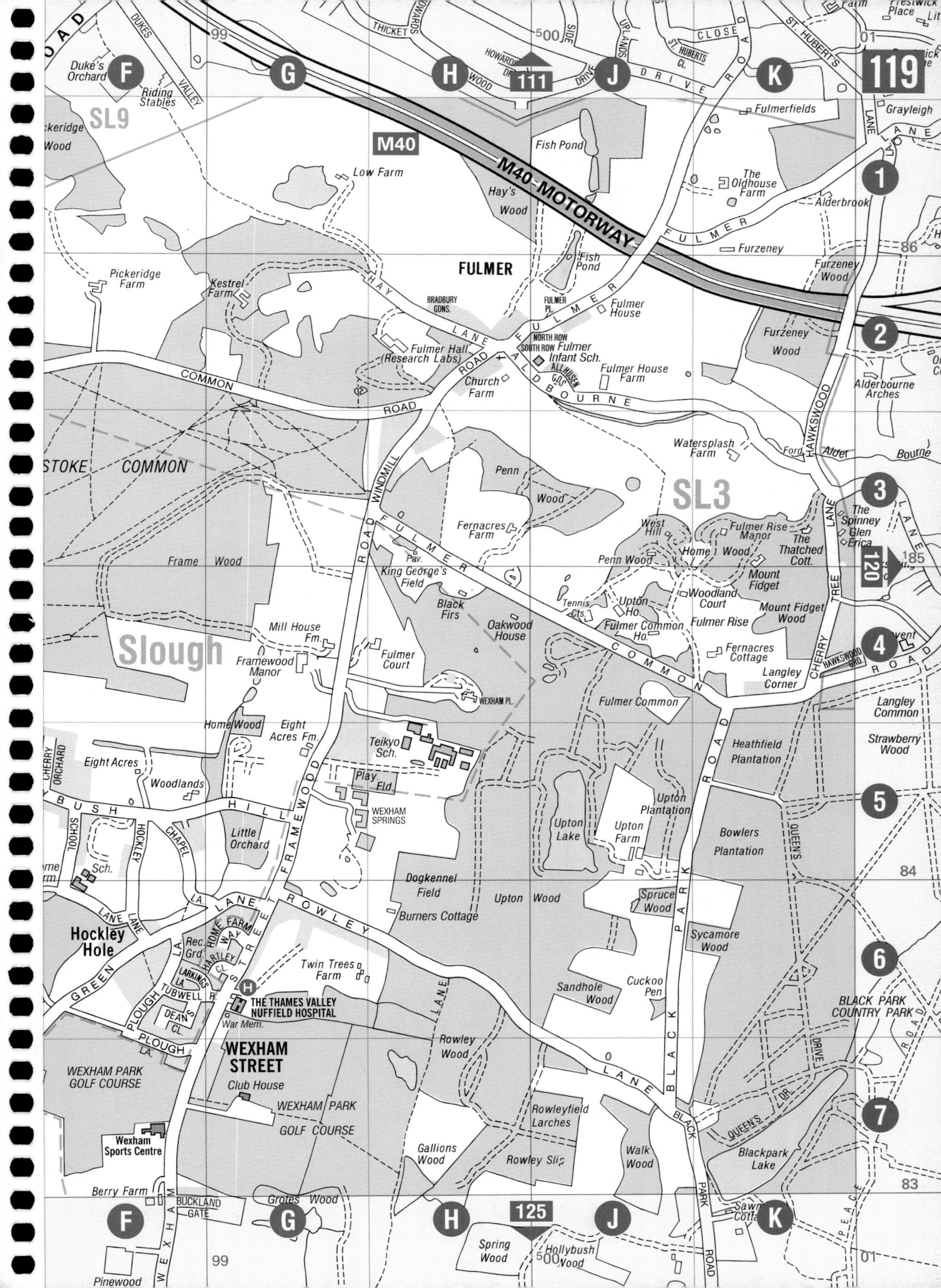
119
111
125
120
M40
M40 MOTORWAY
FULMER
Slough
STOKE COMMON
SL9
SL3
WEXHAM STREET
Hockley Hole
Duke's Orchard
Riding Stables
Pickeridge Wood
Low Farm
Fish Pond
Hay's Wood
Pickeridge Farm
Kestrel Farm
HAY LANE
BRADBURY GDNS.
FULMER PL.
Fulmer House
NORTH ROW
SOUTH ROW
Fulmer Infant Sch.
ALLHUSEN GDS.
Fulmer Hall (Research Labs)
COMMON ROAD
Church Farm
ALDBOURNE
Fulmer House Farm
FULMER ROAD
Fulmerfields
The Oldhouse Farm
Alderbrook
Furzeney
Furzeney Wood
Grayleigh
Alderbourne Arches
HAWKSWOOD
Watersplash Farm
Ford
Alder Bourne
Penn Wood
Fernacres Farm
Frame Wood
WINDMILL ROAD
FULMER COMMON ROAD
Pav.
King George's Field
Black Firs
Oakwood House
Mill House Fm.
Framewood Manor
Fulmer Court
WEXHAM PL.
West Hill
Home Wood
Fulmer Rise Manor
The Thatched Cott.
The Spinney
Glen Erica
Mount Fidget
Woodland Court
Mount Fidget Wood
Tennis Cts.
Upton Ho.
Fulmer Common Ho.
Fulmer Rise
Fernacres Cottage
Langley Corner
CHERRY TREE LANE
HAWKSWOOD GRO.
Langley Common
Strawberry Wood
Fulmer Common
Eight Acres Fm.
Teikyo Sch.
Play. Fld.
WEXHAM SPRINGS
CHERRY ORCHARD
Eight Acres
Woodlands
HOLLYBUSH HILL
SCHOOL LANE
HOCKLEY LANE
CHAPEL LANE
Little Orchard
FRAMEWOOD ROAD
Sch.
Heathfield Plantation
Upton Lake
Upton Farm
Upton Plantation
Bowlers Plantation
QUEEN'S DRIVE
Dogkennel Field
Upton Wood
Burners Cottage
Spruce Wood
BLACK PARK ROAD
Sycamore Wood
ROWLEY LANE
LANE
HOME FARM WAY
STREET
Rec. Grd.
HARTLEY CL.
LARKINGS LA.
TUBWELL R.
DEANS CL.
GREEN LANE
PLOUGH LANE
Twin Trees Farm
THE THAMES VALLEY NUFFIELD HOSPITAL
War Mem.
Sandhole Wood
Cuckoo Pen
BLACK PARK COUNTRY PARK
Rowley Wood
WEXHAM PARK GOLF COURSE
Club House
Rowleyfield Larches
Walk Wood
Blackpark Lake
Gallions Wood
Rowley Slip
Wexham Sports Centre
Berry Farm
BUCKLAND GATE
Grotes Wood
Spring Wood
Hollybush Wood
Sawmill Cotta.
PEACE ROAD
WEXHAM ROAD
Pinewood
THICKET
HOWARDS
HOWARDS WOOD DRIVE
SIDE
UPLANDS
CLOSE
ST. HUBERTS CL.
DRIVE
ST. HUBERT'S LANE
DUKES VALLEY
ROAD
F G H J K
1 2 3 4 5 6 7
99 500 01
86 185 84 83

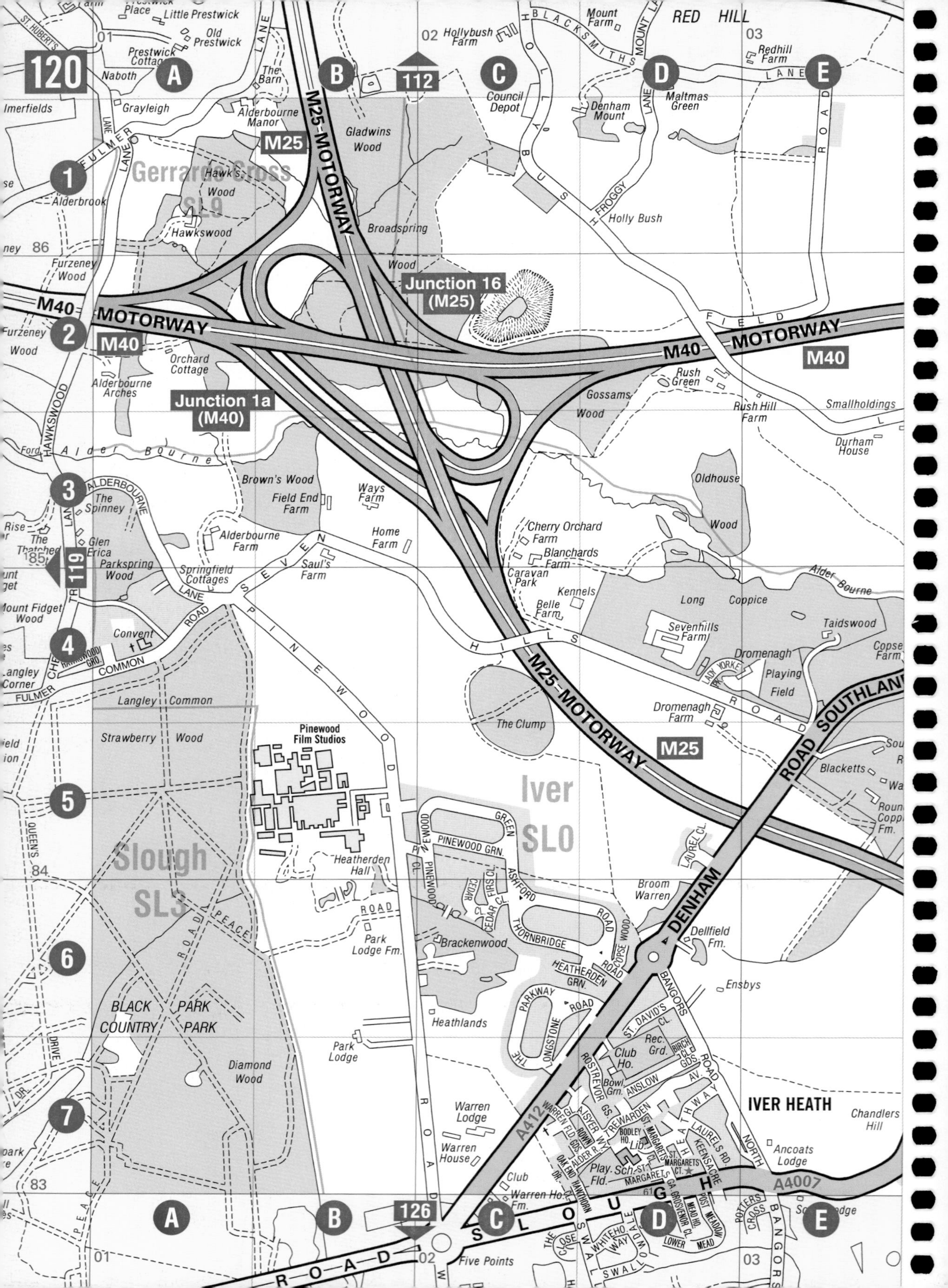

120
112
119
126
A
B
C
D
E
1
2
3
4
5
6
7
01
02
03
86
85
84
83
Place
Little Prestwick
Old Prestwick
Prestwick Cottage
ST. HUBERT'S
Naboth
The Barn
Imerfields
Grayleigh
Alderbourne Manor
Gladwins Wood
Hollybush Farm
Council Depot
Mount Farm
BLACKSMITHS LANE
MOUNT LANE
RED HILL
Redhill Farm
Denham Mount
Maltmas Green
LANE
ROAD
HOLLY BUSH
FROGGY
Holly Bush
FULMER LANE
Gerrards Cross
SL9
Hawk's Wood
Hawkswood
Alderbrook
M25
M25-MOTORWAY
Broadspring
Wood
Furzeney Wood
Junction 16 (M25)
M40
M40 MOTORWAY
MOTORWAY
FIELD
Orchard Cottage
Alderbourne Arches
Junction 1a (M40)
Rush Green
Gossams Wood
Rush Hill Farm
Smallholdings
Durham House
HAWKSWOOD
Ford
Alder Bourne
ALDERBOURNE LANE
The Spinney
Brown's Wood
Field End Farm
Ways Farm
Oldhouse
Wood
Rise
The Thatched
Glen Erica
Parkspring Wood
Alderbourne Farm
Home Farm
Cherry Orchard Farm
Blanchards Farm
Caravan Park
Kennels
Springfield Cottages
Saul's Farm
SEVEN HILLS
Alder Bourne
Mount Fidget Wood
Belle Farm
Long
Coppice
Taidswood
Sevenhills Farm
Convent
HARWOOD GRO.
COMMON
ROAD
FULMER
Langley Corner
Dromenagh
LADY YORKE PK.
Playing Field
Copse Farm
Langley Common
PINEWOOD ROAD
M25-MOTORWAY
Dromenagh Farm
ROAD
SOUTHLANDS ROAD
Strawberry Wood
Pinewood Film Studios
The Clump
Blacketts
Iver
SL0
QUEEN'S
Slough
SL3
GREEN
PINEWOOD GRN.
PINEWOOD CL.
Heatherden Hall
ASHFORD
CEDAR CL.
FIRS CL.
LAUREL CL.
DENHAM
Broom Warren
ROAD
PEACE ROAD
Park Lodge Fm.
Brackenwood
THORNBRIDGE
COPSE WOOD
HEATHERDEN GRN.
Dellfield Fm.
Ensbys
BANGORS ROAD
BLACK COUNTRY PARK
PARK
Heathlands
THE PARKWAY
LONGSTONE ROAD
ST. DAVID'S CL.
Rec. Grd.
BIRCH GDS.
DRIVE
DR.
Diamond Wood
Park Lodge
Club Ho.
ROSTREVOR GS.
Bowl. Grn.
ANSLOW AV.
HEATHWAY
Warren Lodge
Warren House
IVER HEATH
Chandlers Hill
A412
GLAISYER WY.
TREWARDEN
WARREN FLD.
ROWAN GDS.
ALDER R.
BODLEY HO.
Lib.
ST. MARGARETS CL.
ST. MARGARETS CT.
KEENSACRE
LAURELS RD.
NORTH
Ancoats Lodge
Club
OAK END DR.
HAWTHORN
Play. Fld.
Sch.
ST. MARGARET'S GA.
GROSVENOR CL.
MEAD HO.
POST MEADOW
Warren Ho. Fm.
SLOUGH
A4007
POTTERS CROSS
BANGORS
ROAD
Five Points
THE CLOSE
SWALLOW
WHITE HO. WAY
LOWDALE
LOWER MEAD
PEACE

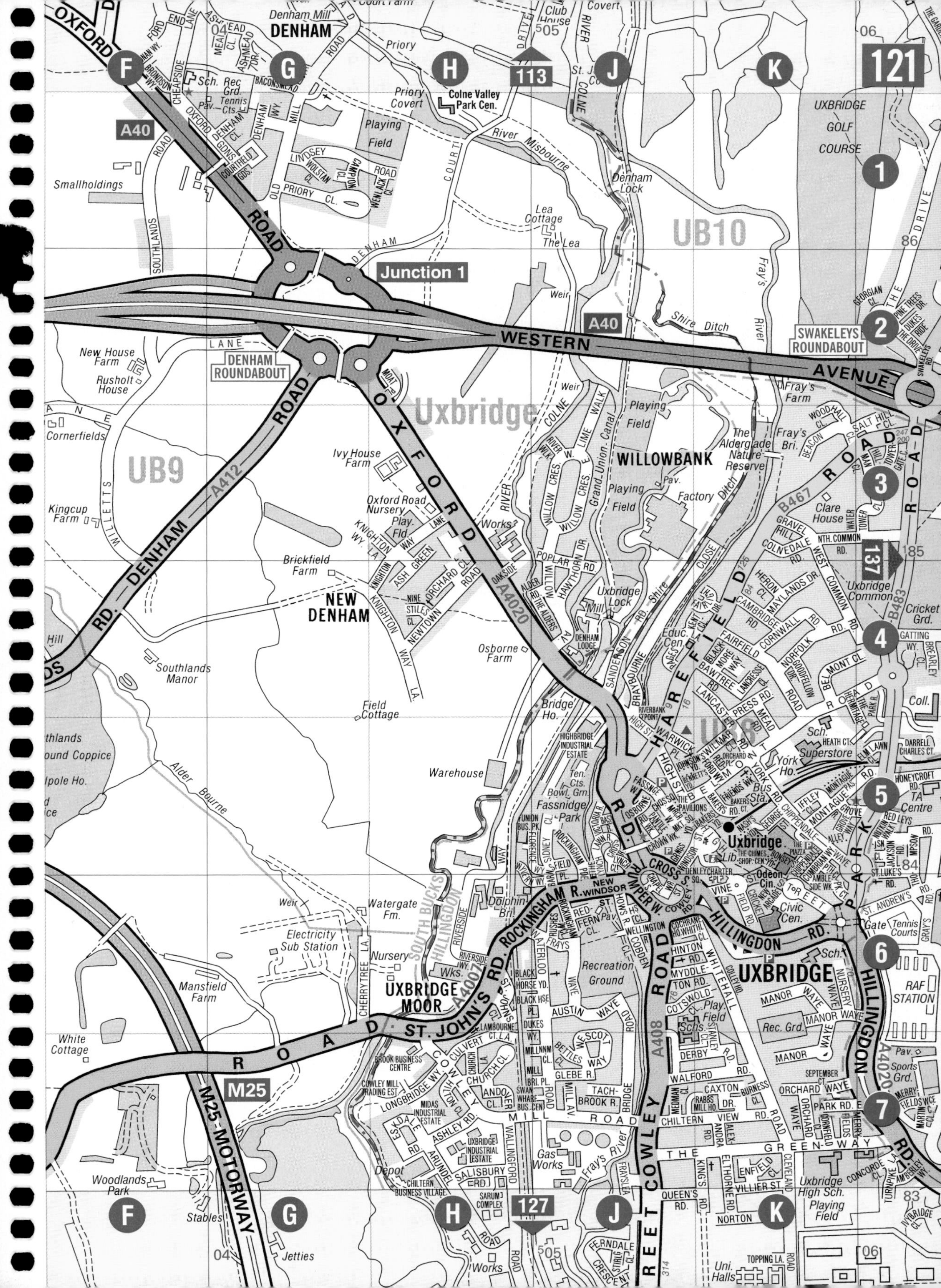
DENHAM
Junction 1
DENHAM ROUNDABOUT
SWAKELEYS ROUNDABOUT
WESTERN AVENUE
Uxbridge
UB9
UB10
WILLOWBANK
NEW DENHAM
UXBRIDGE MOOR
UXBRIDGE
M25 MOTORWAY
113
137
127

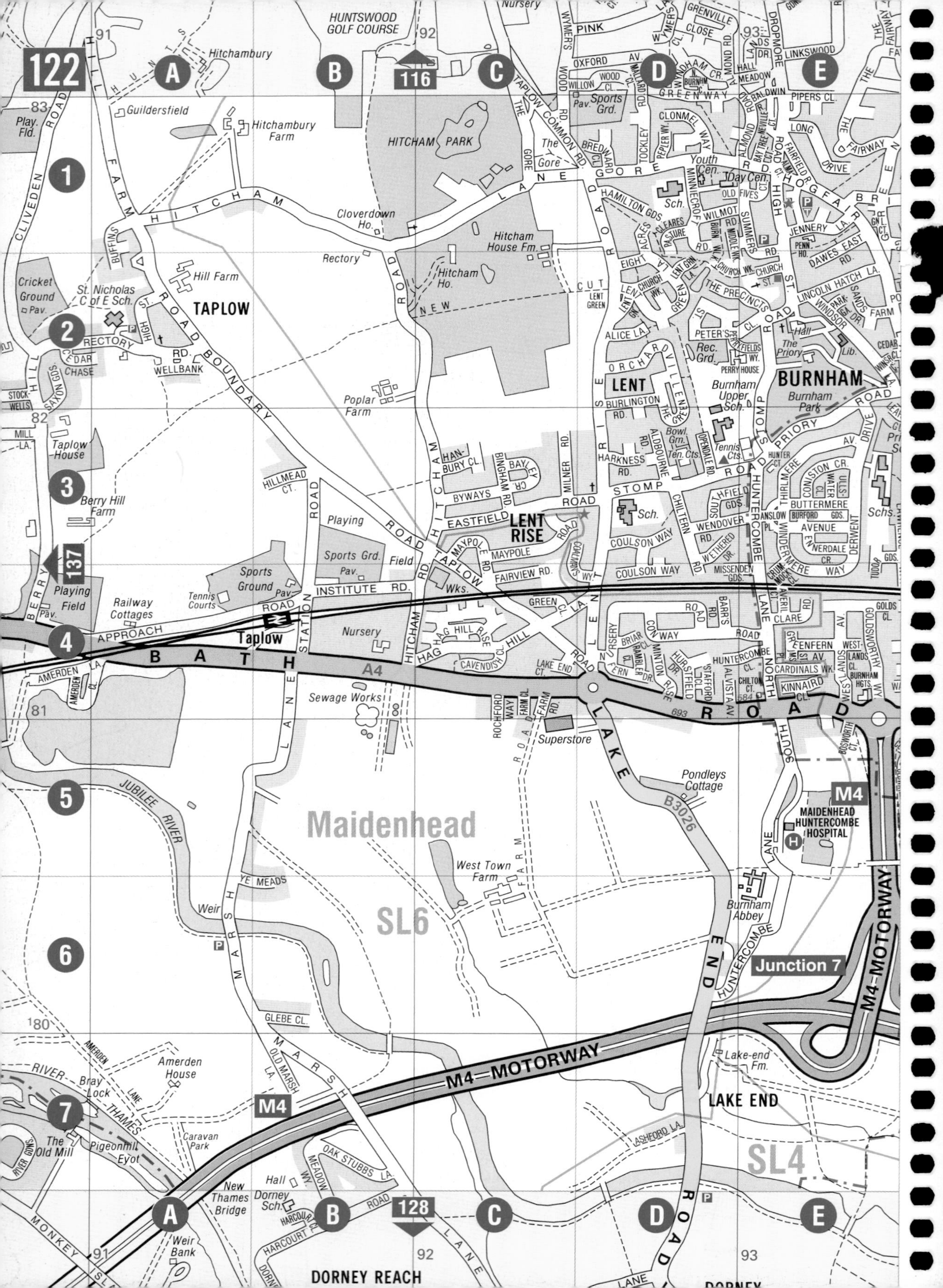

HUNTSWOOD GOLF COURSE
116
Hitchambury
Guildersfield
Hitchambury Farm
HITCHAM PARK
Cloverdown Ho.
Rectory
Hitcham Ho.
Hitcham House Fm.
Hill Farm
TAPLOW
Cricket Ground
St. Nicholas C of E Sch.
Poplar Farm
Taplow House
Berry Hill Farm
137
Playing Field
Railway Cottages
Sports Ground
Tennis Courts
Sports Grd.
Playing Field
Taplow
Nursery
BATH ROAD A4
Sewage Works
Superstore
Maidenhead
SL6
West Town Farm
JUBILEE RIVER
Weir
M4 MOTORWAY
Amerden House
Bray Lock
RIVER THAMES
The Old Mill
Pigeonhill Eyot
Caravan Park
New Thames Bridge
Dorney Sch.
Hall
Weir Bank
DORNEY REACH
128
LAKE END
Lake-end Fm.
SL4
Junction 7
Burnham Abbey
Pondleys Cottage
MAIDENHEAD HUNTERCOMBE HOSPITAL
LENT RISE
LENT
BURNHAM
Burnham Park
Burnham Upper Sch.
The Priory
Lib.
Rec. Grd.
Youth Cen.
Day Cen.
Sports Grd.
LAKE END ROAD B3026
HUNTERCOMBE LANE
STOMP ROAD
PRIORY ROAD
GORE ROAD
CLIVEDEN ROAD
HITCHAM LANE
BOUNDARY ROAD
MARSH LANE
STATION ROAD

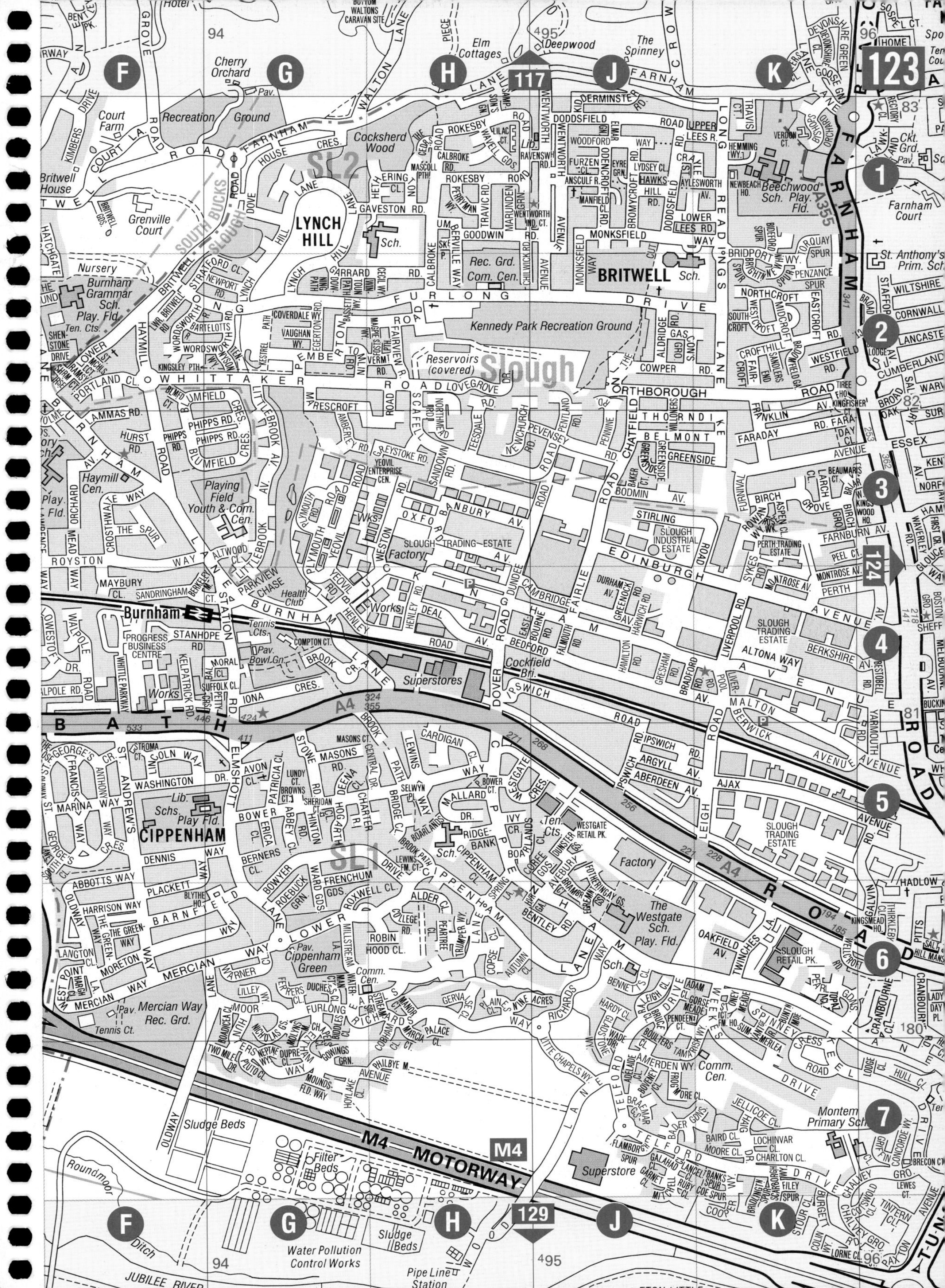

123
117
124
129
F
G
H
J
K
1
2
3
4
5
6
7
94
495
96
SL2
SL1
Slough
BRITWELL
LYNCH HILL
CIPPENHAM
Burnham
Cherry Orchard
Elm Cottages
Deepwood
The Spinney
Court Farm
Recreation Ground
Cocksherd Wood
Britwell House
Grenville Court
Nursery
Burnham Grammar Sch.
Play. Fld.
Haymill Cen.
Kennedy Park Recreation Ground
Reservoirs (covered)
Rec. Grd.
Com. Cen.
Beechwood Sch. Play. Fld.
Farnham Court
St. Anthony's Prim. Sch.
Playing Field
Youth & Com. Cen.
SLOUGH TRADING ESTATE
SLOUGH INDUSTRIAL ESTATE
PERTH TRADING ESTATE
Health Club
Tennis Cts.
PROGRESS BUSINESS CENTRE
Superstores
Cockfield Bri.
WESTGATE RETAIL PK.
The Westgate Sch. Play. Fld.
Factory
SLOUGH RETAIL PK.
Cippenham Green
Comm. Cen.
Mercian Way Rec. Grd.
Tennis Ct.
Sludge Beds
Filter Beds
Water Pollution Control Works
Pipe Line Station
Superstore
Montem Primary Sch.
Roundmoor Ditch
JUBILEE RIVER
M4 MOTORWAY
BATH ROAD
A4
A355
FARNHAM ROAD
FARNHAM LANE
FURLONG DRIVE
WHITTAKER ROAD
NORTHBOROUGH ROAD
EDINBURGH AVENUE
BURNHAM LANE
BURNHAM ROAD
STATION ROAD
IPSWICH ROAD
LIVERPOOL ROAD
LEIGH ROAD
FAIRLIE ROAD
DOVER ROAD
CIPPENHAM LANE
LOWER CIPPENHAM LANE
MERCIAN WAY
ST. ANDREW'S WAY
TELFORD DRIVE
WEEKES DRIVE
LONG READINGS LANE
DODDSFIELD ROAD
MONKSFIELD WAY
WENTWORTH AVENUE
GAVESTON RD.
LYNCH HILL LANE
PEMBERTON ROAD
LOVEGROVE
MARESCROFT
THORNDIKE
BELMONT
GREENSIDE
FARADAY
FRANKLIN AV.
ESSEX AVENUE
BIRCH GROVE
FARNBURN AV.
MALTON AVENUE
BERWICK AVENUE
AJAX AVENUE
ARGYLL AV.
ABERDEEN AV.
ALTONA WAY
BERKSHIRE AV.
OXFORD AV.
BANBURY AV.
BUCKINGHAM AV.
CAMBRIDGE AV.
ROYSTON WAY
MAYBURY CL.
SANDRINGHAM
STANHOPE RD.
IONA CRES.
WASHINGTON
PLACKETT WAY
BARNFIELD
MARINA WAY
DENNIS WAY
ABBOTTS WAY
HARRISON WAY
MORETON WAY
WARNER
FURLONG
NINE ACRES
RICHARDS WAY
AMERDEN WY.
JELLICOE CL.
LOCHINVAR CL.
CHARLTON CL.
BAIRD CL.
MOORE CL.
CHALVEY GRO.
LEWES CT.
TINTERN CL.
BRECON CT.

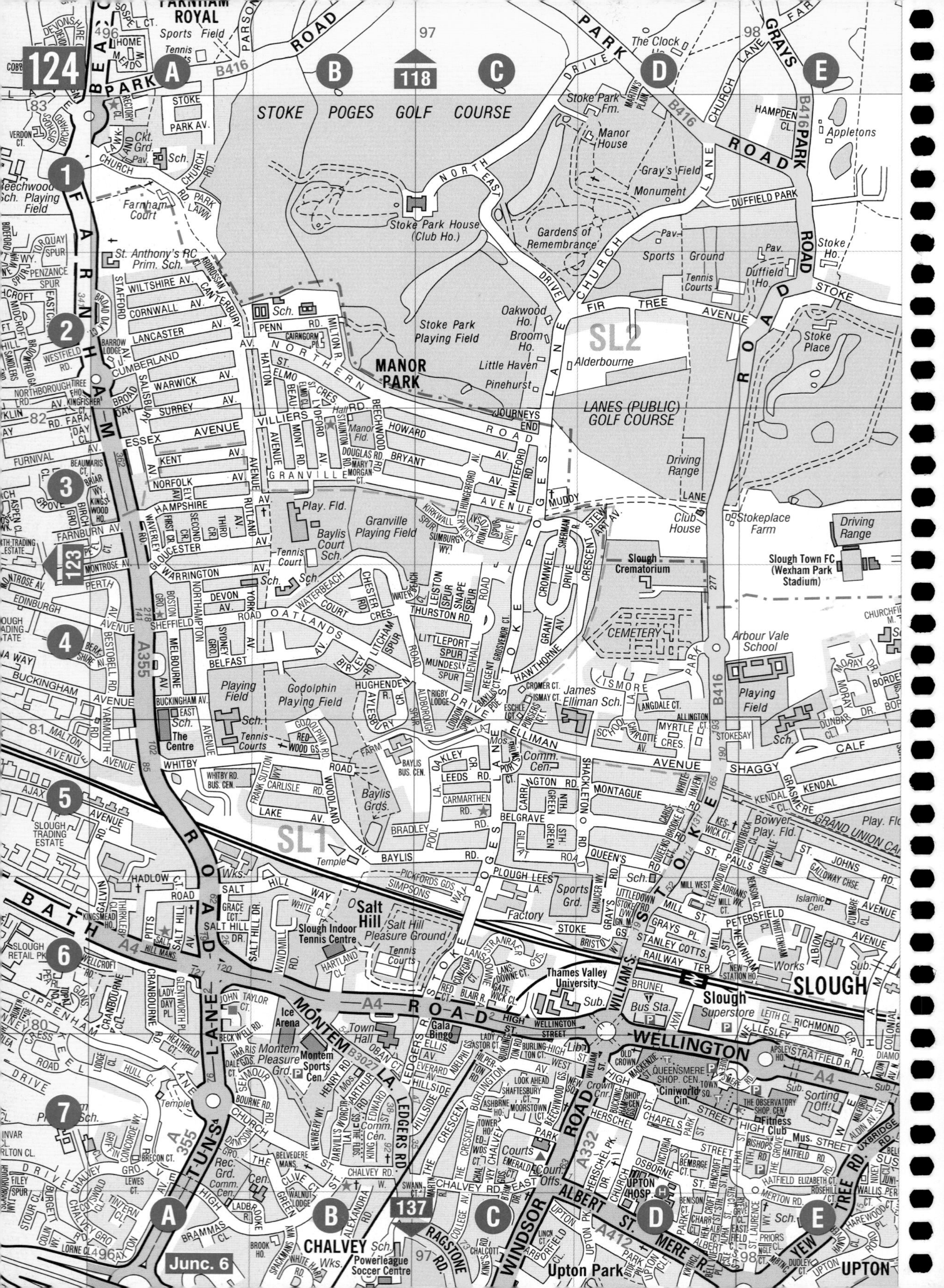

124
FARNHAM ROYAL
118
123
137
97
98
SL1
SL2
STOKE POGES GOLF COURSE
Stoke Park House (Club Ho.)
Gardens of Remembrance
Stoke Park Playing Field
MANOR PARK
LANES (PUBLIC) GOLF COURSE
Driving Range
Slough Crematorium
CEMETERY
Slough Town FC (Wexham Park Stadium)
Arbour Vale School
James Elliman Sch.
Granville Playing Field
Godolphin Playing Field
Baylis Court Sch.
Salt Hill
Salt Hill Pleasure Ground
Slough Indoor Tennis Centre
Thames Valley University
Slough Superstore
SLOUGH
QUEENSMERE SHOP. CEN.
THE OBSERVATORY SHOP. CEN.
Ciniworld Cin.
Ice Arena
Town Hall
Montem Sports Cen.
Montem Pleasure Grd.
Gala Bingo
UPTON HOSP.
Upton Park
UPTON
CHALVEY
Powerleague Soccer Centre
Junc. 6
FARNHAM ROAD
A355
A4
BATH ROAD
WELLINGTON STREET
HIGH STREET
STOKE POGES LANE
STOKE ROAD
STOKE PARK ROAD
B416
A332
WINDSOR ROAD
A412
ALBERT ST.
TUNS LANE
MONTEM LA.
LEDGERS RD.
GRAND UNION CANAL
SLOUGH TRADING ESTATE
SLOUGH RETAIL PK.

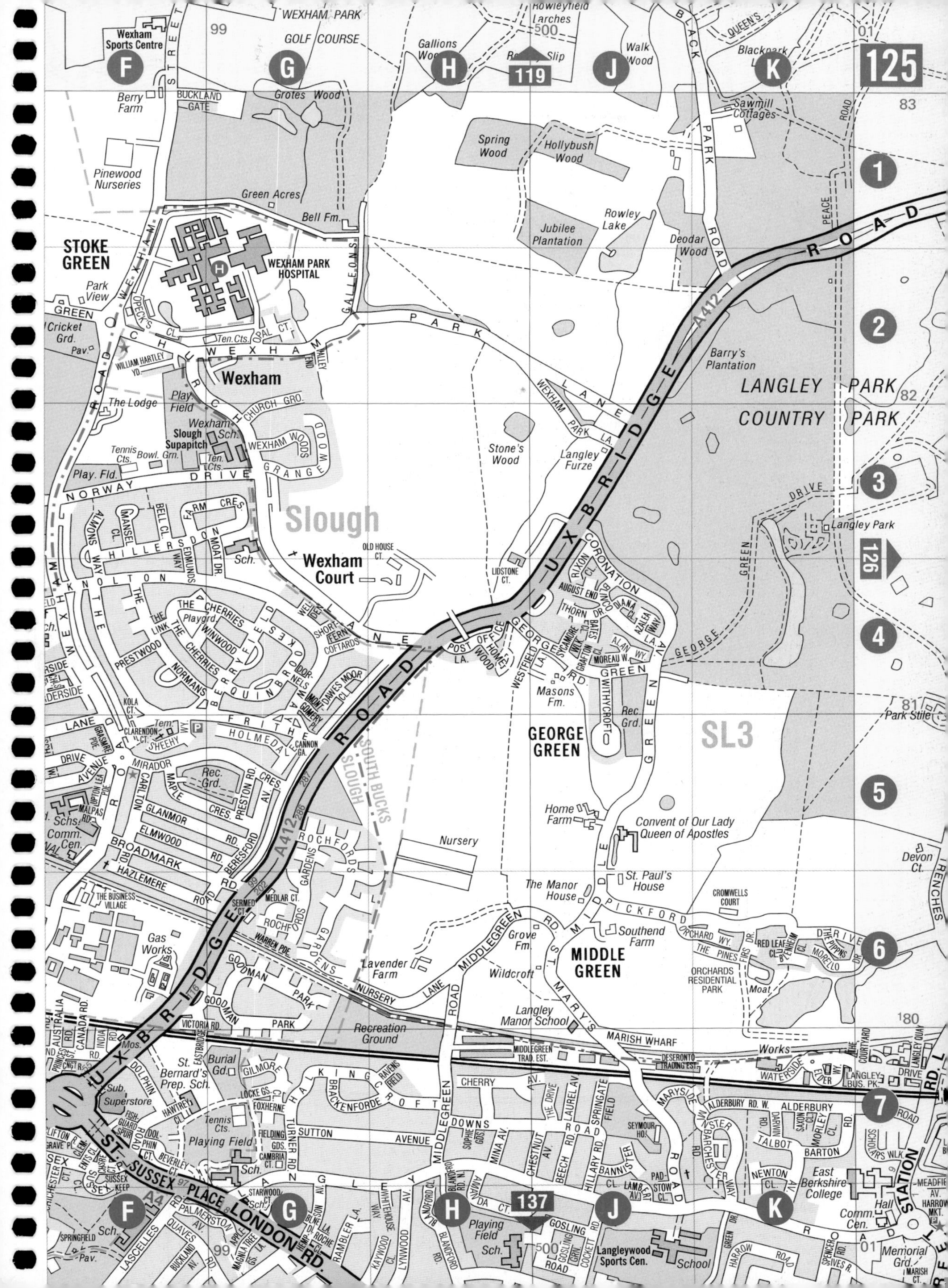
STOKE GREEN
WEXHAM PARK HOSPITAL
Wexham
Slough
Wexham Court
GEORGE GREEN
SL3
LANGLEY PARK COUNTRY PARK
MIDDLE GREEN
UXBRIDGE ROAD
A412
Wexham Sports Centre
WEXHAM PARK GOLF COURSE
Grotes Wood
Spring Wood
Hollybush Wood
Jubilee Plantation
Rowley Lake
Deodar Wood
Pinewood Nurseries
Green Acres
Bell Fm.
Barry's Plantation
Stone's Wood
Langley Furze
Convent of Our Lady Queen of Apostles
Nursery
Recreation Ground
Langley Manor School
East Berkshire College
Langleywood Sports Cen.
ST. SUSSEX PLACE LONDON RD.
119
126
137

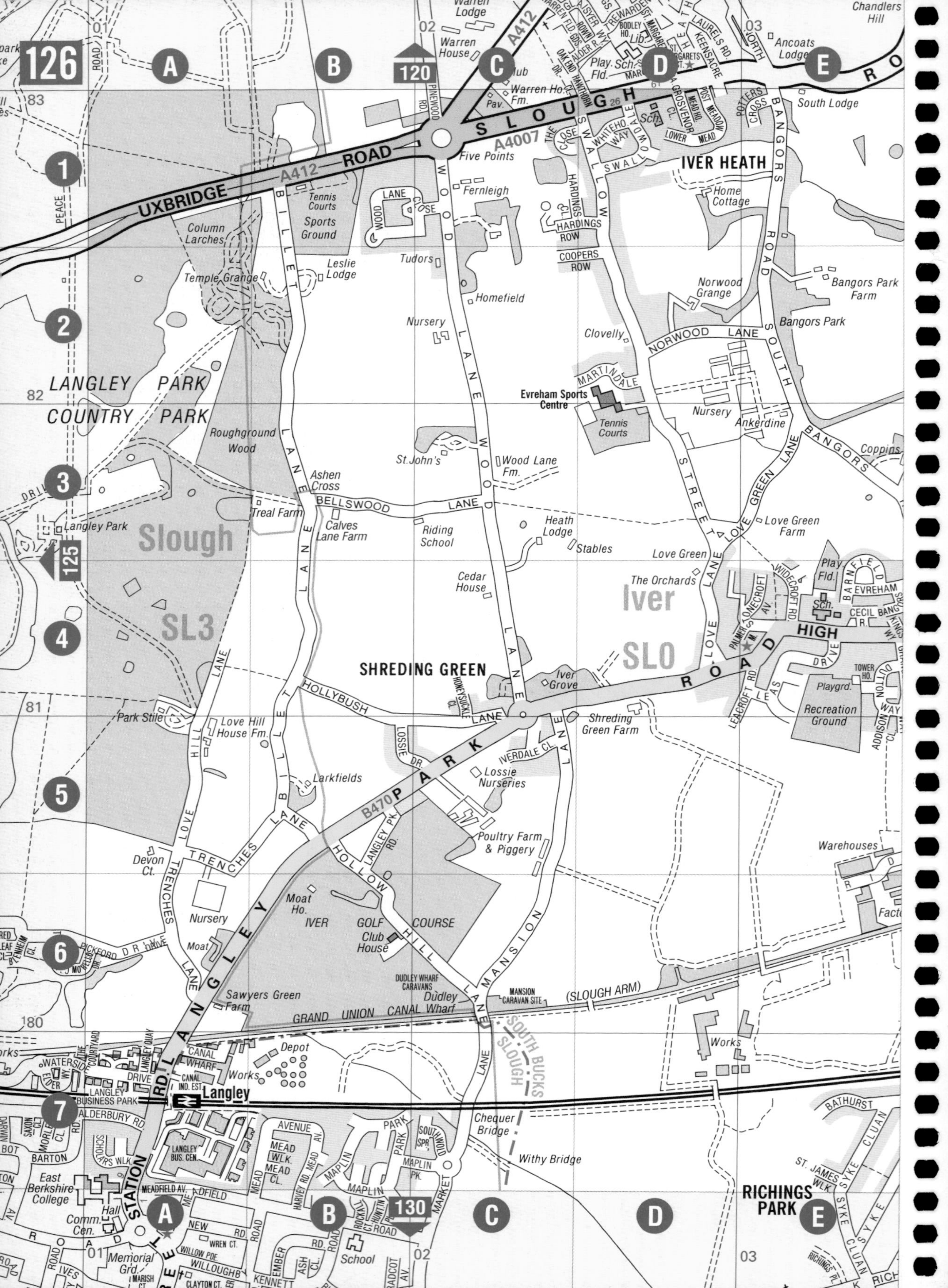

120
125
130
A B C D E
1 2 3 4 5 6 7
LANGLEY PARK COUNTRY PARK
Slough
SL3
SL0
Iver
IVER HEATH
SHREDING GREEN
UXBRIDGE ROAD
A412
SLOUGH ROAD
A4007
Five Points
WOOD LANE
BILLET LANE
BELLSWOOD LANE
HOLLYBUSH LANE
PARK ROAD
B470
LANGLEY PARK RD.
HOLLOW HILL LANE
MANSION LANE
LOVE HILL LANE
TRENCHES LANE
LOVE LANE
LOVE GREEN LANE
BANGORS ROAD SOUTH
BANGORS ROAD
NORWOOD LANE
STREET
HIGH STREET
SWALLOW STREET
Evreham Sports Centre
Tennis Courts
IVER GOLF COURSE
Club House
Moat Ho.
Sawyers Green Farm
GRAND UNION CANAL
(SLOUGH ARM)
Dudley Wharf
SOUTH BUCKS
SLOUGH
Langley
LANGLEY BUSINESS PARK
STATION RD.
East Berkshire College
Comm. Cen.
Memorial Grd.
RICHINGS PARK
Chequer Bridge
Withy Bridge
Works
Warehouses
Depot
Roughground Wood
Temple Grange
Column Larches
Treal Farm
Langley Park
Calves Lane Farm
Riding School
Heath Lodge
Stables
Cedar House
Love Green
The Orchards
Love Green Farm
Bangors Park
Bangors Park Farm
Norwood Grange
Home Cottage
Clovelly
Nursery
Ankerdine
Warren Lodge
Warren House
Warren Ho. Fm.
South Lodge
Ancoats Lodge
Chandlers Hill
Fernleigh
Tudors
Homefield
Leslie Lodge
Tennis Courts
Sports Ground
St. John's
Wood Lane Fm.
Ashen Cross
Park Stile
Love Hill House Fm.
Larkfields
Devon Ct.
Nursery
Moat
Lossie Nurseries
Poultry Farm & Piggery
Shreding Green Farm
Iver Grove
Recreation Ground
Playgrd.
MANSION CARAVAN SITE
DUDLEY WHARF CARAVANS
School
83 82 81 180 01 02 03

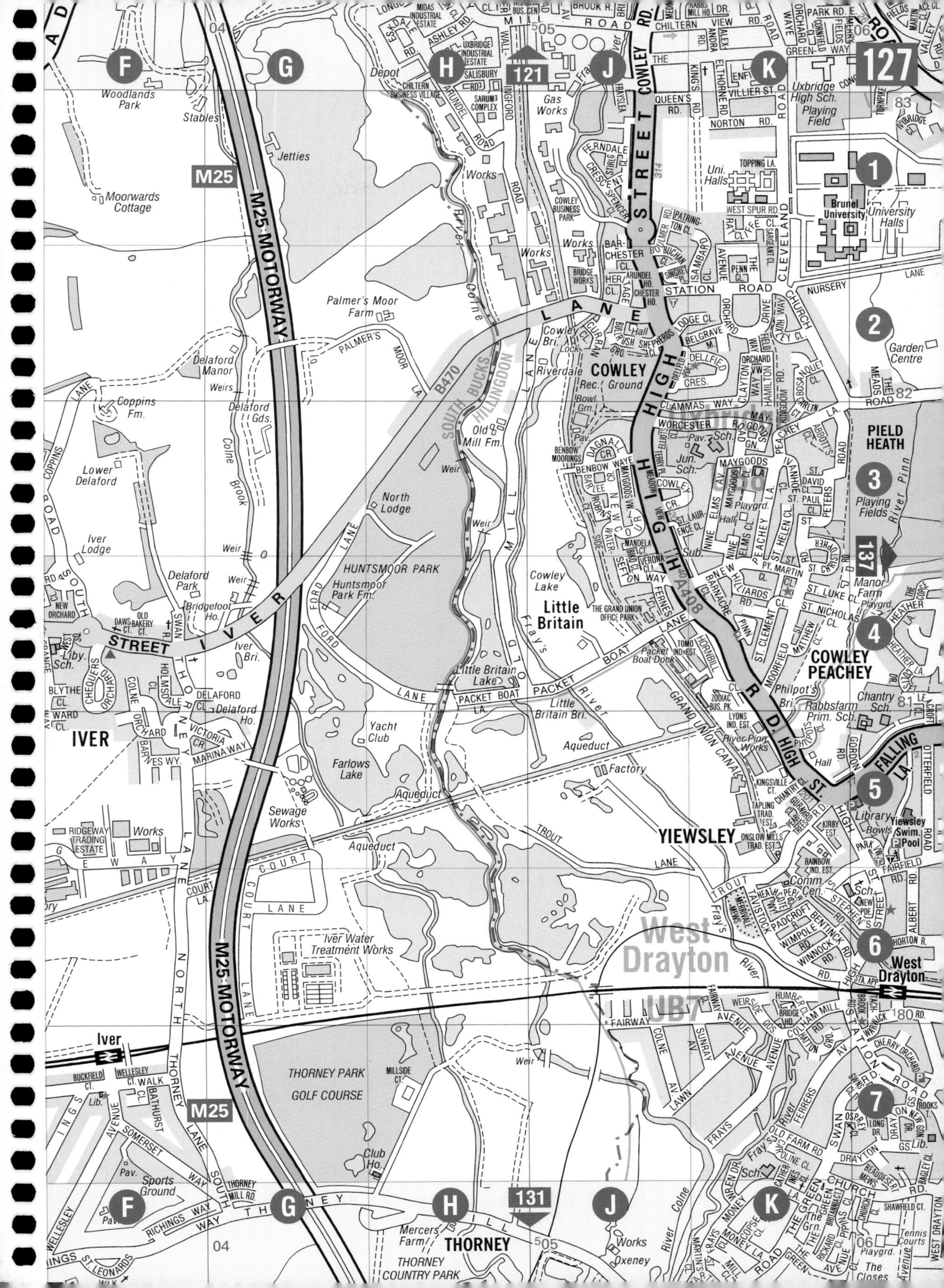

127
F
G
H
J
K
1
2
3
4
5
6
7
04
05
06
121
131
137
M25
M25 MOTORWAY
M25
Woodlands Park
Stables
Jetties
Moorwards Cottage
Depot
CHILTERN BUSINESS VILLAGE
MIDAS INDUSTRIAL ESTATE
ASHLEY RD.
UXBRIDGE INDUSTRIAL ESTATE
SALISBURY RD.
SARUM COMPLEX
ARUNDEL ROAD
INGFORD ROAD
Gas Works
Works
COWLEY BUSINESS PARK
BRIDGE WORKS
FERNDALE CRESCENT
SPENCER CL.
COWLEY ROAD
CHILTERN VIEW RD.
THE GREEN WAY
QUEEN'S RD.
NORTON RD.
VILLIER ST.
Uxbridge High Sch. Playing Field
TOPPING LA.
Uni. Halls
WEST SPUR RD.
Brunel University
University Halls
NURSERY LANE
CLEVELAND ROAD
STATION ROAD
CHURCH
Garden Centre
MEADS ROAD
82
83
PIELD HEATH
Playing Fields
River Pinn
Manor Farm
Playgrd.
HEATHER LA.
COWLEY PEACHEY
Chantry Sch.
Rabbsfarm Prim. Sch.
FALLING LA.
81
OTTERFIELD
Library
Yiewsley Bowls
Yiewsley Swim. Pool
FAIRFIELD RD.
ALBERT RD.
HORTON R.
West Drayton
STA. APP.
180 RD.
CHERRY ORCHARD
BROOKS
Lib.
WEST DRAYTON
Tennis Courts
Playgrd.
The Closes
SHAWFIELD CT.
CHURCH RD.
Palmer's Moor Farm
PALMER'S MOOR LA.
Delaford Manor
Weirs
Delaford Gds.
Coppins Fm.
Lower Delaford
Iver Lodge
Colne Brook
Weir
Delaford Park
Bridgefoot Ho.
Iver Bri.
IVER LANE
B470
SOUTH BUCKS
HILLINGDON
River Colne
Old Mill Fm.
North Lodge
HUNTSMOOR PARK
Huntsmoor Park Fm.
FORD LANE
Cowley Bri.
Lock
Riverdale
COWLEY
Rec. Ground
Bowl Grn.
MILL LANE
HIGH STREET
HIGH ROAD
A408
CLAMMAS WAY
WORCESTER RD.
Uxbridge
Sch.
Pav.
Jun. Sch.
MAYGOODS LA.
BENBOW MOORINGS
BENBOW WAY
DAGNALL CR.
COWLEY CR.
Playgrd.
Hall
Sub.
Cowley Lake
Little Britain
THE GRAND UNION OFFICE PARK
TOMO IND. EST.
Packet Boat Dock
PACKET BOAT LANE
Little Britain Lake
Little Britain Bri.
Frays River
GRAND UNION CANAL
ZODIAC BUS. PK.
LYONS IND. EST.
River Pinn Works
Aqueduct
Factory
KINGSVILLE CT.
TAPLING TRAD. EST.
ONSLOW MILLS TRAD. EST.
YIEWSLEY
KIRBY EST.
RAINBOW IND. EST.
Comm. Cen.
TROUT LANE
Yacht Club
Farlows Lake
Sewage Works
Aqueduct
IVER
STREET
Liby.
Sch.
CHEQUERS
ORCHARD
BLYTHE CL.
WARD CL.
COLNE
HOLMSDALE CL.
DELAFORD CL.
Delaford Ho.
VICTORIA CR.
MARINA WAY
BARNES WY.
RIDGEWAY TRADING ESTATE
Works
RIDGEWAY
COURT LANE
Iver Water Treatment Works
West Drayton
UB7
FAIRWAY
COLNE AV.
SUNRAY AV.
LAWN AV.
AVENUE
FRAYS
FERRERS
Frays River
OLD FARM RD.
DRAYTON
SWAN RD.
River Colne
Sch.
Iver
THORNEY PARK GOLF COURSE
MILLSIDE CT.
Weir
Club Ho.
BUCKFIELD CT.
WELLESLEY CT.
WALK
Lib.
AVENUE
SOMERSET WAY
BATHURST
THORNEY LANE
THORNEY MILL RD.
Sports Ground
Pav.
RICHINGS WAY
WELLESLEY
ST. LEONARDS
THORNEY MILL
Mercers Farm
THORNEY
THORNEY COUNTRY PARK
Works
Oxeney
MONEY LA.
THE GREEN
CHURCH

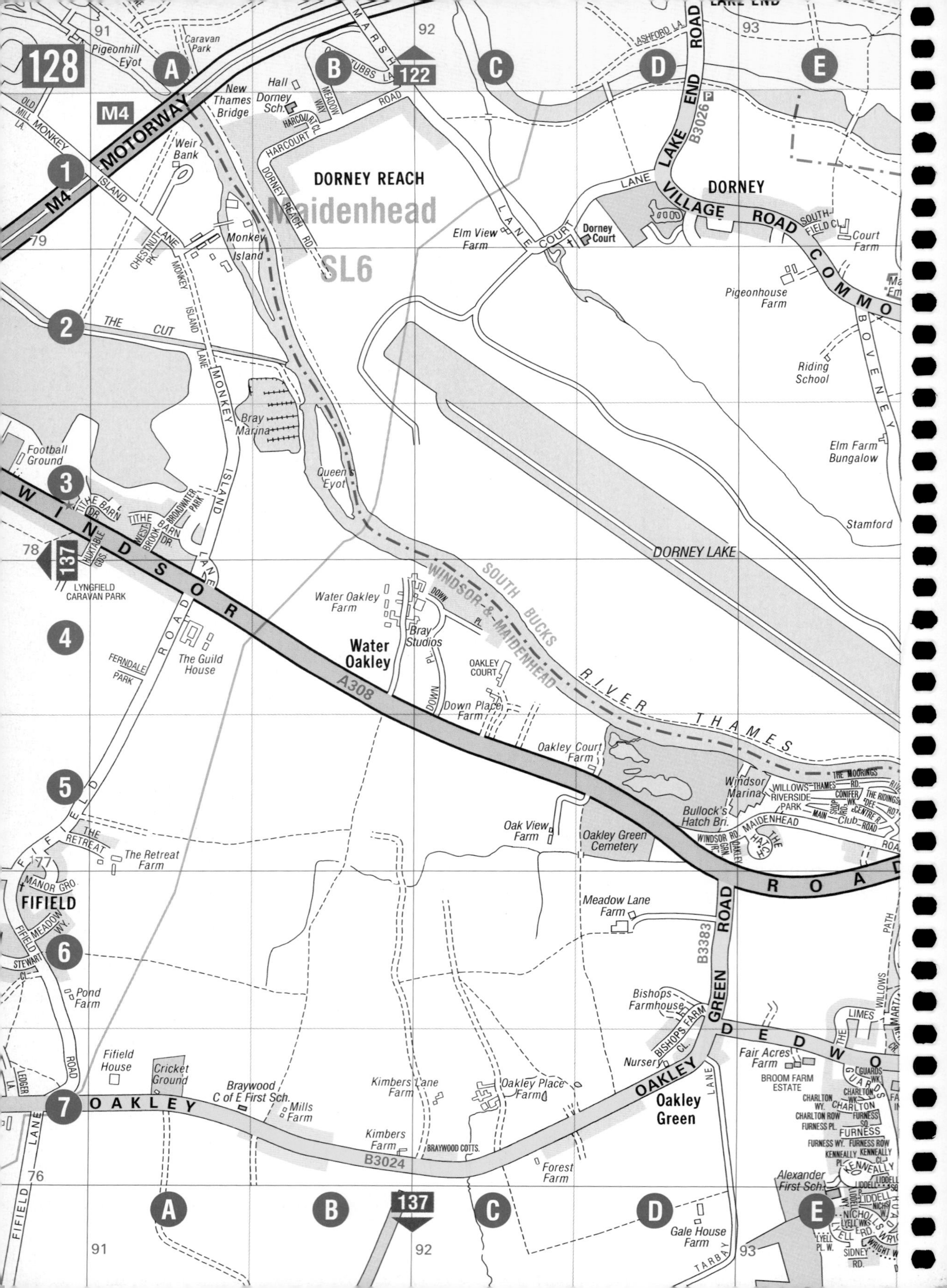

122
137
M4
MOTORWAY
DORNEY REACH
Maidenhead
SL6
DORNEY
Pigeonhill Eyot
Caravan Park
New Thames Bridge
Dorney Sch.
Hall
Weir Bank
Monkey Island
MONKEY ISLAND LANE
OLD MILL LA.
CHESTNUT PK.
HARCOURT CL.
HARCOURT ROAD
MEADOW WAY
STUBBS LA.
MARSH
DORNEY REACH RD.
LAKE END ROAD
B3026
ASHFORD LA.
LAKE END
COURT LANE
VILLAGE ROAD
COMMON
SOUTHFIELD CL.
Court Farm
Dorney Court
Elm View Farm
Pigeonhouse Farm
BOVENEY
Riding School
Elm Farm Bungalow
Stamford
DORNEY LAKE
THE CUT
Bray Marina
Football Ground
Queen's Eyot
TITHE BARN DR.
TITHE BARN DR.
WESTBROOK
BROADWATER PARK
HUXTABLE GDS.
LYNGFIELD CARAVAN PARK
WINDSOR ROAD
A308
ROAD
FERNDALE PARK
The Guild House
Water Oakley Farm
Water Oakley
Bray Studios
DOWN PL.
OAKLEY COURT
Down Place Farm
WINDSOR & MAIDENHEAD
SOUTH BUCKS
RIVER THAMES
Oakley Court Farm
Windsor Marina
WILLOWS RIVERSIDE PARK
THE MOORINGS
THAMES RD.
CONIFER WK.
THE RIDINGS
DEE RD.
CENTRE R.
SHOP RD.
MAIN
Club Road
Bullock's Hatch Bri.
MAIDENHEAD ROAD
WINDSOR RD.
OAKLEY GRN. R.
THE HATCH
Oak View Farm
Oakley Green Cemetery
FIFIELD
THE RETREAT
The Retreat Farm
MANOR GRO.
MEADOW WY.
FIFIELD
STEWART CL.
Pond Farm
FIFIELD ROAD
LEDGER LA.
Fifield House
Cricket Ground
OAKLEY
Braywood C of E First Sch.
Mills Farm
Kimbers Lane Farm
Kimbers Farm
BRAYWOOD COTTS.
B3024
Oakley Place Farm
Forest Farm
Meadow Lane Farm
B3383
GREEN ROAD
Bishops Farmhouse
BISHOPS FARM CL.
Nursery
OAKLEY
Oakley Green
LANE
TARBAY
Gale House Farm
DEDWORTH
Fair Acres Farm
BROOM FARM ESTATE
GUARDS WK.
CHARLTON WY.
CHARLTON WK.
CHARLTON
CHARLTON ROW
FURNESS PL.
FURNESS SQ.
FURNESS
FURNESS WY.
FURNESS ROW
KENNEALLY PL.
KENNEALLY CL.
KENNEALLY
Alexander First Sch.
LIDDELL
LIDDELL WY.
NICHOLLS WK.
LYELL WK.
LYELL RD.
LYELL PL. W.
WRIGHT
SIDNEY RD.
LIMES
WILLOWS
THE
PATH
FIFIELD LANE
A B C D E
1 2 3 4 5 6 7
91 92 93
76 77 78 79

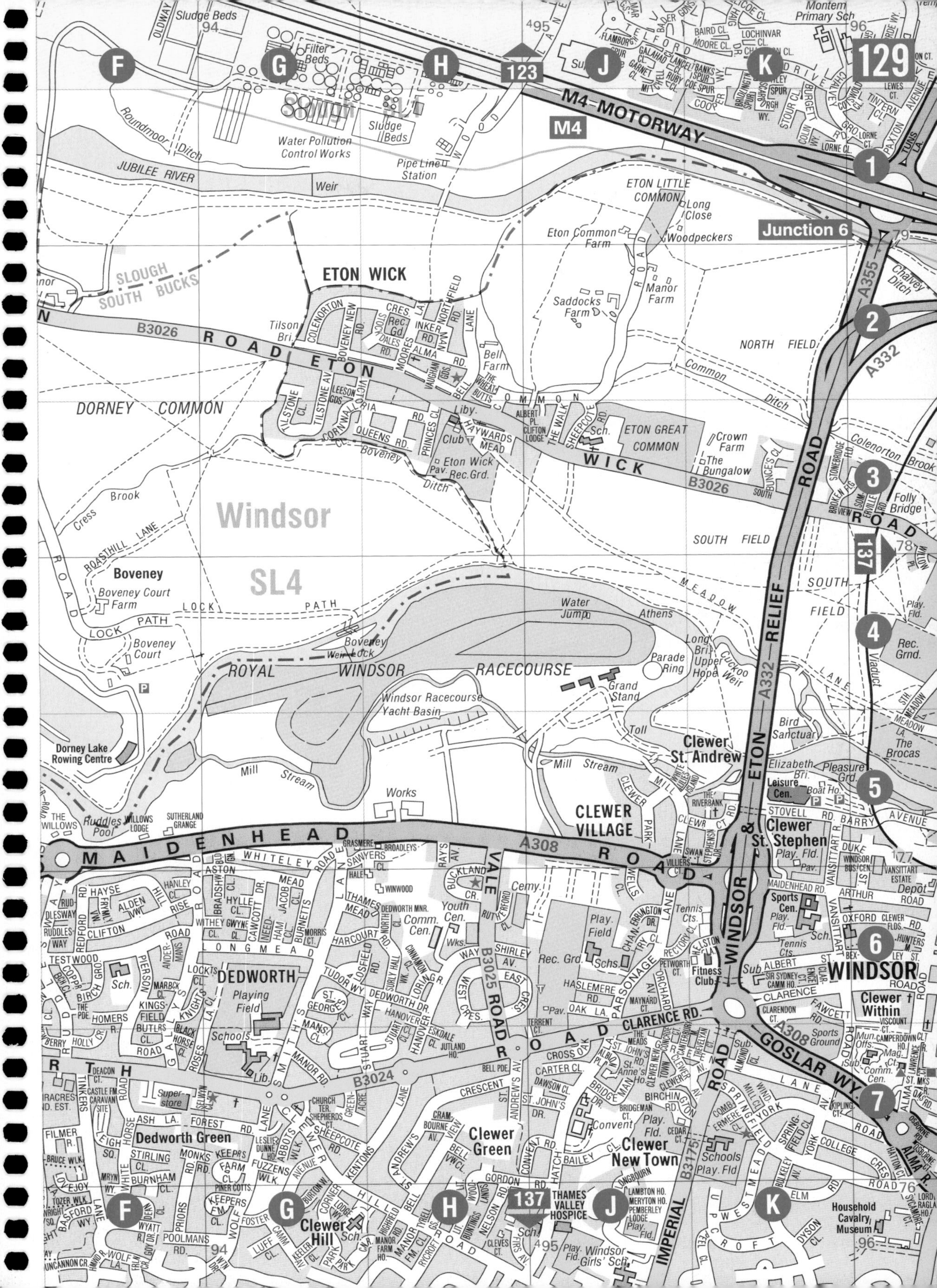

129
123
137
M4 MOTORWAY
M4
Junction 6
Sludge Beds
Filter Beds
Water Pollution Control Works
Pipe Line Station
JUBILEE RIVER
Roundmoor Ditch
Weir
ETON LITTLE COMMON
Long Close
Eton Common Farm
Woodpeckers
SLOUGH
SOUTH BUCKS
ETON WICK
Saddocks Farm
Manor Farm
NORTH FIELD
B3026
ROAD
ETON
WICK
Tilson Bri.
Bell Farm
Common Ditch
Colenorton Brook
DORNEY COMMON
ETON GREAT COMMON
Crown Farm
The Bungalow
Eton Wick Rec. Grd.
Boveney Ditch
Windsor
SL4
Cress Brook
ROASTHILL LANE
Boveney
Boveney Court Farm
LOCK PATH
Boveney Court
Folly Bridge
SOUTH FIELD
MEADOW
Water Jump
Athens
Boveney Lock
Weir Lock
ROYAL WINDSOR RACECOURSE
Parade Ring
Upper Hope
Cuckoo Weir
Grand Stand
Windsor Racecourse Yacht Basin
Toll
Bird Sanctuary
The Brocas
Clewer St. Andrew
Dorney Lake Rowing Centre
Mill Stream
Works
Elizabeth Bri.
Pleasure Grd.
Leisure Cen.
Boat Ho.
THE WILLOWS
Ruddles Pool
WILLOWS LODGE
SUTHERLAND GRANGE
CLEWER VILLAGE
Clewer St. Stephen
MAIDENHEAD ROAD
A308
ETON RELIEF ROAD
A332
A355
WINDSOR
DEDWORTH
Playing Field
Schools
Lib.
Super-store
Dedworth Green
Clewer Green
Clewer New Town
Clewer Hill
Clewer Within
Rec. Grd.
Play. Field
Fitness Club
Sports Cen.
Sports Ground
GOSLAR WY.
CLARENCE RD.
B3024
B3025
VALE ROAD
B3175
IMPERIAL ROAD
Convent
THAMES VALLEY HOSPICE
Windsor Girls' Sch.
Household Cavalry Museum
F G H J K
1 2 3 4 5 6 7

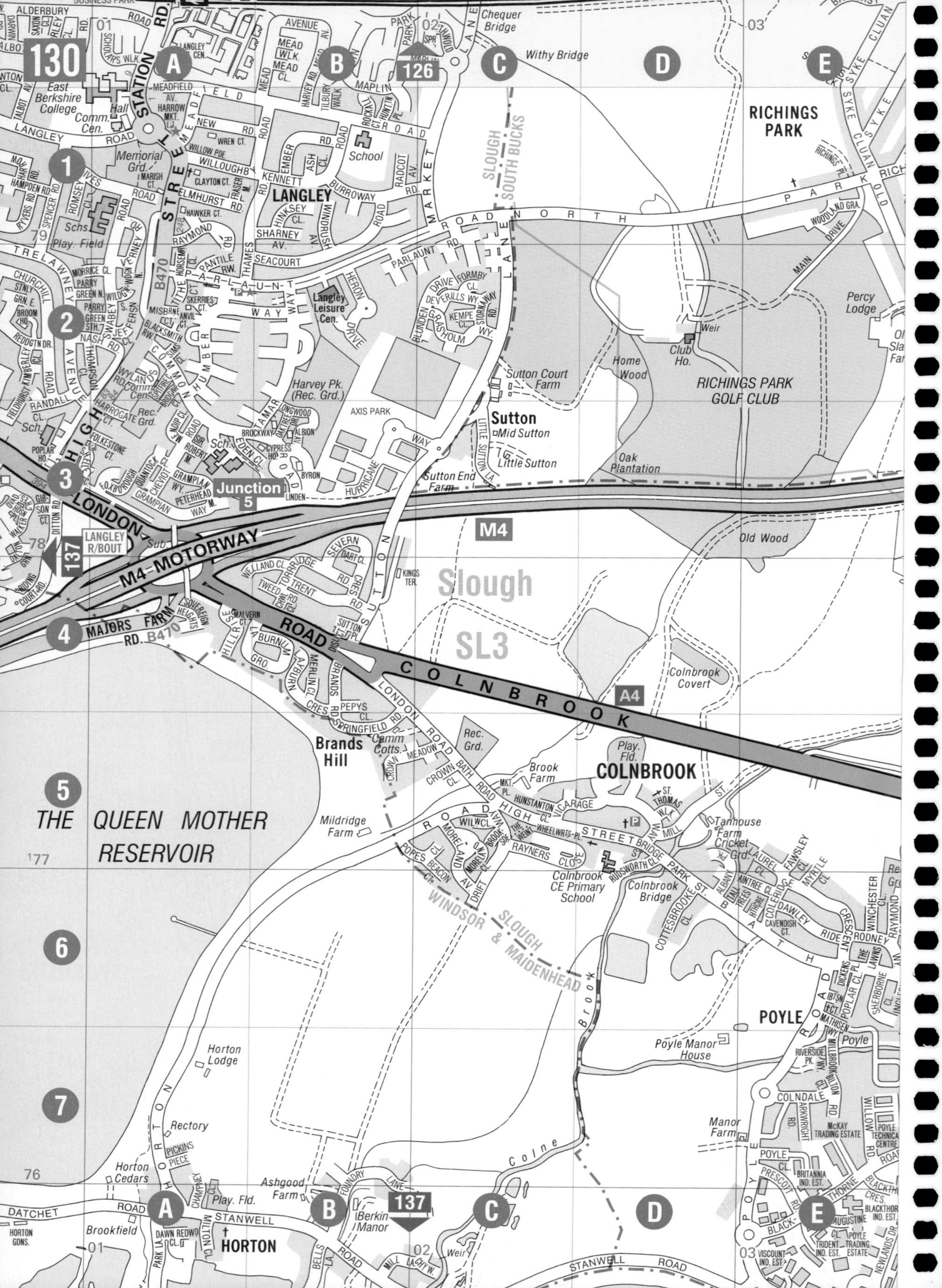

LANGLEY
RICHINGS PARK
Sutton
Slough
SL3
Brands Hill
COLNBROOK
POYLE
HORTON
THE QUEEN MOTHER RESERVOIR
RICHINGS PARK GOLF CLUB
East Berkshire College
Langley Leisure Cen.
Harvey Pk. (Rec. Grd.)
AXIS PARK
Sutton Court Farm
Mid Sutton
Little Sutton
Sutton End Farm
Oak Plantation
Old Wood
Home Wood
Percy Lodge
Club Ho.
Weir
Chequer Bridge
Withy Bridge
Colnbrook Covert
Brook Farm
Mildridge Farm
Colnbrook CE Primary School
Colnbrook Bridge
Tanhouse Farm
Cricket Grd.
Poyle Manor House
Manor Farm
Horton Lodge
Rectory
Horton Cedars
Ashgood Farm
Berkin Manor
Brookfield
SLOUGH SOUTH BUCKS
WINDSOR & MAIDENHEAD SLOUGH
Junction 5
M4
M4-MOTORWAY
A4
B470
COLNBROOK ROAD
LONDON ROAD
MAJORS FARM RD.
STATION RD.
HIGH STREET
PARK ROAD NORTH
MARKET LANE
DATCHET ROAD
STANWELL ROAD
LANGLEY R/BOUT
126
137
McKAY TRADING ESTATE
POYLE TECHNICAL CENTRE
BRITANNIA IND. EST.
BLACKTHORNE IND. EST.
POYLE TRADING ESTATE
TRIDENT IND. EST.
VISCOUNT IND. EST.
Colne
Brook

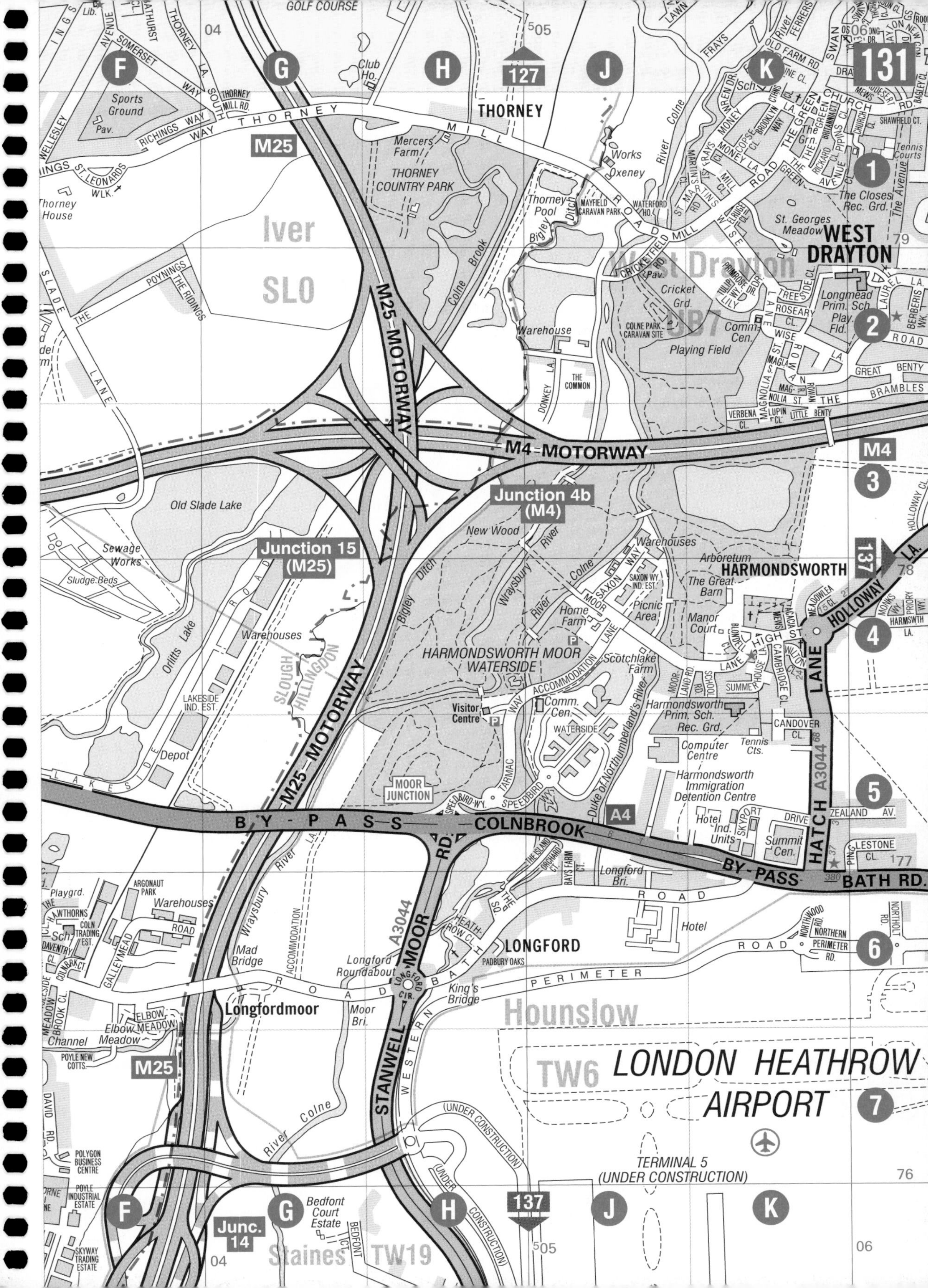
GOLF COURSE
Club Ho.
127
THORNEY
Sports Ground
Pav.
RICHINGS WAY
THORNEY MILL RD.
WAY THORNEY MILL
M25
Mercers Farm
THORNEY COUNTRY PARK
Thorney House
ST. LEONARDS WLK.
Iver
SLO
POYNINGS
THE RIDINGS
SLADE LANE
Colne Brook
M25 MOTORWAY
Works
Oxeney
River Colne
Thorney Pool
Bigley Ditch
MAYFIELD CARAVAN PARK
WATERFORD HO.
MILL ROAD
WEST DRAYTON
West Drayton
UB7
Cricket Grd.
Pav.
CRICKETFIELD RD.
COLNE PARK CARAVAN SITE
Playing Field
Comm. Cen.
Warehouse
DONKEY LA.
THE COMMON
St. Georges Meadow
The Closes Rec. Grd.
Tennis Courts
SHAWFIELD CT.
CHURCH RD.
OLD FARM RD.
FRAYS
Sch.
Longmead Prim. Sch. Play. Fld.
ROSEARY CL.
WISE LA.
GREAT BENTY
THE BRAMBLES
LITTLE BENTY
VERBENA CL.
LUPIN CL.
MAGNOLIA ST.
M4 MOTORWAY
M4
Junction 4b (M4)
Old Slade Lake
Sewage Works
Sludge Beds
Junction 15 (M25)
New Wood
Wraysbury River
River Colne
Warehouses
SAXON WAY
SAXON WY IND. EST.
Arboretum
HARMONDSWORTH
137
The Great Barn
Picnic Area
Home Farm
MOOR LANE
Manor Court
HIGH ST.
HOLLOWAY LA.
HARMONDSWORTH MOOR WATERSIDE
Scotchlake Farm
Orlitts Lake
Warehouses
SLOUGH
HILLINGDON
LAKESIDE IND. EST.
Depot
LAKESIDE
Visitor Centre
ACCOMMODATION WAY
Comm. Cen.
WATERSIDE
Harmondsworth Prim. Sch. Rec. Grd.
CANDOVER CL.
Computer Centre
Tennis Cts.
Harmondsworth Immigration Detention Centre
HATCH LANE
A3044
ZEALAND AV.
MOOR JUNCTION
SPEEDBIRD WY.
TARMAC
Duke of Northumberland's River
BY-PASS COLNBROOK BY-PASS
A4
Hotel Ind. Units
SKYPORT DRIVE
Summit Cen.
PINGLESTONE CL.
BATH RD.
Longford Bri.
BAYS FARM CT.
ROAD
Hotel
NORTHERN PERIMETER RD.
ARGONAUT PARK
Warehouses
Playgrd.
COLN TRADING EST.
Sch.
GALLEYMEAD ROAD
Wraysbury River
ACCOMMODATION LA.
A3044
MOOR RD.
STANWELL MOOR
LONGFORD
PADBURY OAKS
Mad Bridge
Longford Roundabout
LONGFORD CIR.
BATH ROAD
King's Bridge
PERIMETER
Longfordmoor
Moor Bri.
Hounslow
WESTERN
ELBOW MEADOW
Elbow Meadow
Channel
POYLE NEW COTTS.
M25
TW6
LONDON HEATHROW AIRPORT
River Colne
(UNDER CONSTRUCTION)
TERMINAL 5 (UNDER CONSTRUCTION)
POLYGON BUSINESS CENTRE
POYLE INDUSTRIAL ESTATE
SKYWAY TRADING ESTATE
Junc. 14
Bedfont Court Estate
BEDFONT CT.
Staines
TW19
137
F
G
H
J
K
1
2
3
4
5
6
7
04
05
06
79
78
77
76

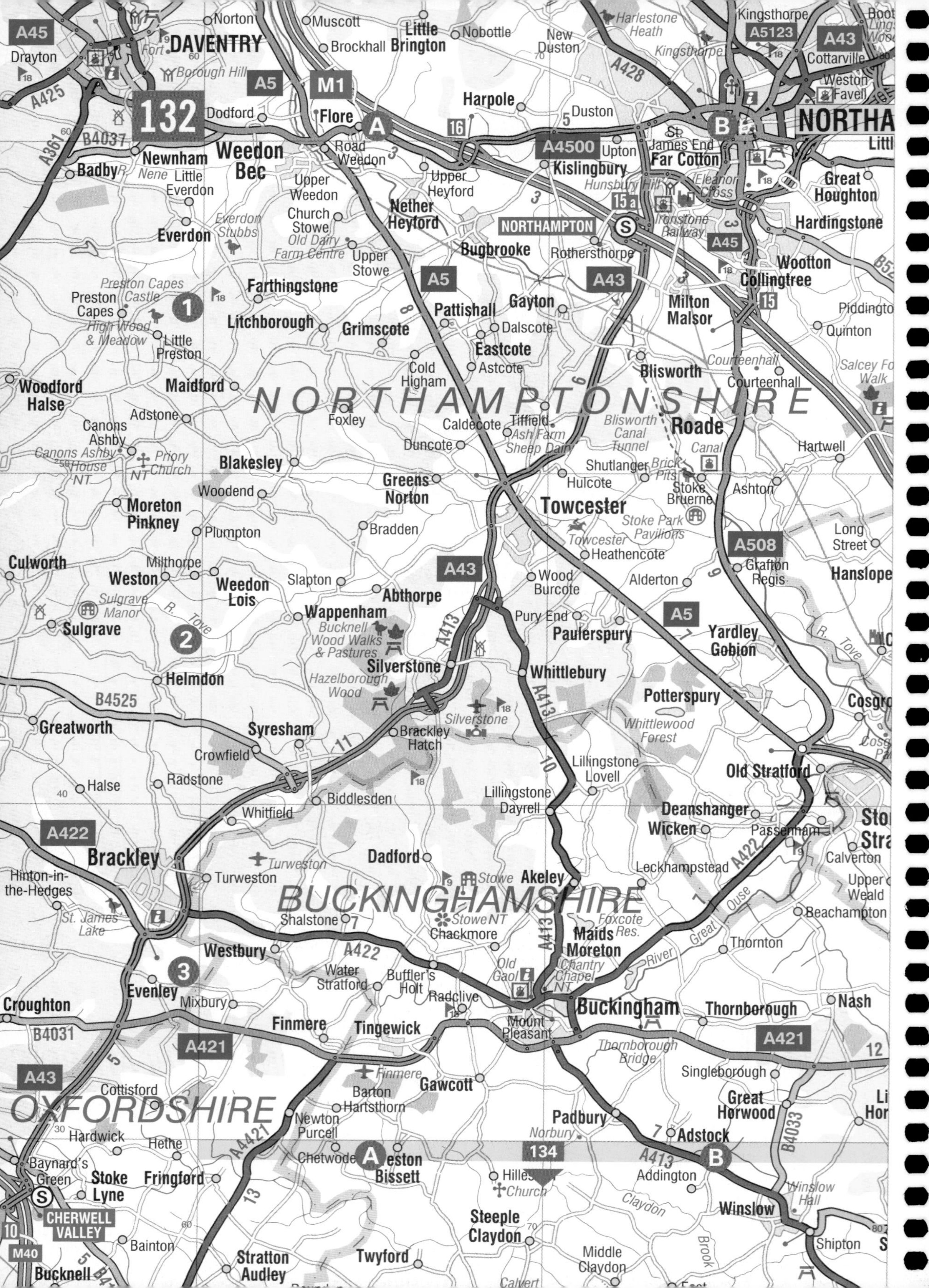

A45
Drayton
Norton
DAVENTRY
Fort
Borough Hill
Muscott
Brockhall
Little Brington
Nobottle
New Duston
Harlestone Heath
Kingsthorpe
A5123
A43
Cottarville
Weston Favell
A425
132
Dodford
A5
M1
Flore
A
Harpole
Duston
NORTHA
A361
B4037
Newnham
Weedon Bec
Road Weedon
16
A4500
Upton
St James End
Far Cotton
B
Badby
Nene
Little Everdon
Upper Weedon
Upper Heyford
Kislingbury
Hunsbury Hill
Eleanor Cross
Great Houghton
Church Stowe
Nether Heyford
15a
NORTHAMPTON
Ironstone Railway
Hardingstone
Everdon
Everdon Stubbs
Old Dairy Farm Centre
Upper Stowe
Bugbrooke
Rothersthorpe
A45
Wootton
Collingtree
Preston Capes
Preston Capes Castle
1
Farthingstone
A5
A43
Milton Malsor
15
Piddington
High Wood & Meadow
Little Preston
Litchborough
Grimscote
Pattishall
Gayton
Dalscote
Eastcote
Quinton
Cold Higham
Astcote
Blisworth
Courteenhall
Salcey Forest Walk
Woodford Halse
Maidford
NORTHAMPTONSHIRE
Adstone
Foxley
Tiffield
Caldecote
Ash Farm Sheep Dairy
Blisworth Canal Tunnel
Roade
Canons Ashby
Canons Ashby House NT
Priory Church
Duncote
Canal
Hartwell
Blakesley
Greens Norton
Shutlanger
Brick Pits
Hulcote
Stoke Bruerne
Ashton
Woodend
Moreton Pinkney
Towcester
Stoke Park Pavilions
Plumpton
Bradden
Towcester
Heathencote
Long Street
A508
Culworth
Milthorpe
Weston
Weedon Lois
Slapton
A43
Wood Burcote
Alderton
Grafton Regis
Hanslope
Abthorpe
Sulgrave Manor
Wappenham
Pury End
Paulerspury
A5
Sulgrave
2
R. Tove
Bucknell Wood Walks & Pastures
A413
Yardley Gobion
Silverstone
Whittlebury
Helmdon
Hazelborough Wood
B4525
Potterspury
Silverstone
Whittlewood Forest
Greatworth
Syresham
Brackley Hatch
Crowfield
Lillingstone Lovell
Old Stratford
Halse
Radstone
Biddlesden
Lillingstone Dayrell
Whitfield
Deanshanger
Passenham
A422
Wicken
Brackley
Turweston
Dadford
Leckhampstead
Calverton
Hinton-in-the-Hedges
Turweston
Stowe
Akeley
Upper Weald
BUCKINGHAMSHIRE
St. James Lake
Shalstone
Stowe NT
Chackmore
Foxcote Res.
Maids Moreton
Beachampton
Westbury
A422
River Great Ouse
Thornton
3
Water Stratford
Buffler's Holt
Old Gaol
Chantry Chapel NT
Evenley
Radclive
Croughton
Mixbury
Buckingham
Thornborough
Nash
B4031
Finmere
Tingewick
Mount Pleasant
A421
A421
Thornborough Bridge
A43
Finmere
Gawcott
Singleborough
Cottisford
Barton Hartshorn
Great Horwood
B4033
OXFORDSHIRE
Newton Purcell
Padbury
Hardwick
Hethe
A4421
Norbury
Adstock
Baynard's Green
Chetwode
A
Preston Bissett
134
A413
B
Stoke Lyne
Fringford
Hillesden
Church
Addington
Winslow Hall
CHERWELL VALLEY
Claydon
Winslow
M40
Bainton
Steeple Claydon
Shipton
Stratton Audley
Twyford
Middle Claydon
Brook
Bucknell

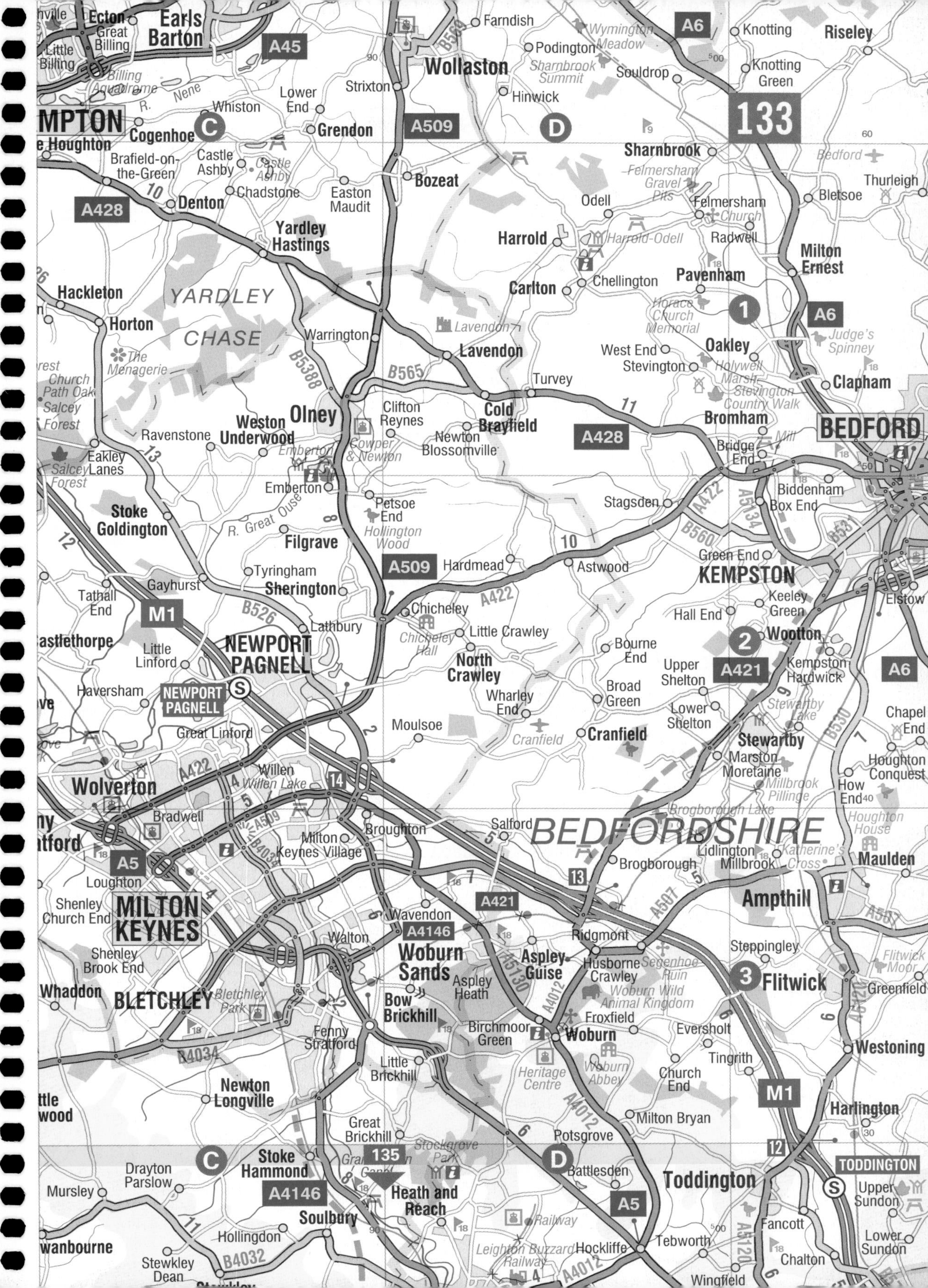

133
Ecton
Earls Barton
Great Billing
Little Billing
A45
Billing Aquadrome
R. Nene
MPTON
Whiston
Cogenhoe
C
Brafield-on-the-Green
Castle Ashby
Chadstone
Denton
A428
Lower End
Grendon
Strixton
Wollaston
A509
B569
Farndish
Podington
Wymington Meadow
Sharnbrook Summit
Hinwick
Souldrop
A6
Knotting
Knotting Green
Riseley
D
Sharnbrook
Felmersham Gravel Pits
Felmersham
Church
Bedford
Thurleigh
Bletsoe
Odell
Harrold
Harrold-Odell
Radwell
Milton Ernest
Bozeat
Easton Maudit
Yardley Hastings
Hackleton
Horton
YARDLEY CHASE
The Menagerie
Church Path Oak
Salcey Forest
Warrington
B5388
Lavendon
B565
Carlton
Chellington
Pavenham
Horace Church Memorial
1
Oakley
West End
Stevington
Holywell Marsh
Stevington Country Walk
Judge's Spinney
Clapham
Turvey
Cold Brayfield
Clifton Reynes
Newton Blossomville
Olney
Weston Underwood
Ravenstone
Eakley Lanes
Emberton
Cowper & Newton
A428
Bromham
Bridge End
Mill
BEDFORD
Biddenham
Box End
Stagsden
A422
A5134
B560
Petsoe End
Hollington Wood
R. Great Ouse
Stoke Goldington
Filgrave
Tyringham
Sherington
Hardmead
Astwood
Green End
KEMPSTON
Keeley Green
Hall End
Elstow
Wootton
2
Gayhurst
B526
Tathall End
M1
Castlethorpe
Little Linford
Lathbury
Chicheley
Chicheley Hall
Little Crawley
NEWPORT PAGNELL
North Crawley
Bourne End
Upper Shelton
A421
Kempston Hardwick
Haversham
NEWPORT PAGNELL
Broad Green
Wharley End
Lower Shelton
Stewartby Lake
Stewartby
Chapel End
Great Linford
Moulsoe
Cranfield
Marston Moretaine
Houghton Conquest
Millbrook Pillinge
How End
Wolverton
Willen
Willen Lake
14
Brogborough Lake
Houghton House
Bradwell
A422
A509
B4034
Milton Keynes Village
Broughton
Salford
BEDFORDSHIRE
Lidlington
Millbrook
Katherine's Cross
Maulden
Brogborough
A5
Loughton
13
A507
Ampthill
Shenley Church End
MILTON KEYNES
Wavendon
A421
A4146
Ridgmont
Steppingley
Shenley Brook End
Walton
Woburn Sands
Aspley Guise
Husborne Crawley
Segenhoe Ruin
3
Flitwick
Flitwick Moor
Greenfield
Whaddon
BLETCHLEY
Bletchley Park
Aspley Heath
A5130
A4012
Woburn Wild Animal Kingdom
Bow Brickhill
Froxfield
Eversholt
Fenny Stratford
Birchmoor Green
Woburn
Westoning
B4034
Little Brickhill
Heritage Centre
Woburn Abbey
Tingrith
Church End
Newton Longville
M1
Harlington
Milton Bryan
Great Brickhill
Potsgrove
12
Stoke Hammond
135
Stockgrove Park
D
Battlesden
TODDINGTON
Drayton Parslow
C
Toddington
Mursley
A4146
Heath and Reach
A5
Upper Sundon
Soulbury
Railway
Fancott
Swanbourne
Hollingdon
Tebworth
A5120
Lower Sundon
Stewkley Dean
B4032
Leighton Buzzard Railway
Hockliffe
A4012
Chalton
Wingfield

134
132
136
Croughton
Mixbury
Finmere
Tingewick
Buckingham
Thornborough
Mount Pleasant
Thornborough Bridge
Singleborough
Great Horwood
B4031
A421
A43
Cottisford
Barton Hartshorn
Gawcott
Newton Purcell
Padbury
Adstock
Hardwick
Hethe
Baynard's Green
Stoke Lyne
Fringford
Chetwode
Preston Bissett
Hillesden
Church
Addington
A413
B4033
Winslow Hall
Winslow
Claydon
Brook
CHERWELL VALLEY
Bainton
Stratton Audley
Twyford
Steeple Claydon
Middle Claydon
East Claydon
Shipton
Granborough
Bucknell
B4100
Poundon
Grebe Lake
Calvert Jubilee
Calvert
NT
Claydon House
Botolph Claydon
Caversfield
Bicester
Charndon
Marsh Gibbon
M40
A4095
B4030
Woodfield
Launton
Edgcott
North Marston
A4421
Chesterton
Grendon Underwood
Oving
Quainton
Bolebec
Pitchcott
A41
Ambrosden
Wendlebury
Blackthorn
Kingswood
Buckinghamshire Railway Centre
OXFORDSHIRE
Merton
Lower Arncott
Ray
Upper Arncott
Ludgershall
Piddington
B4011
BUCKINGHAM
A34
The Lake
Wotton House
Westcott
Waddesdon
Waddesdon Manor
Wotton Underwood
Charlton-on-Otmoor
Fencott
Murcott
Oddington
Duck Decoy
Boarstall Decoy
Boarstall
Pushreeds Wood
Dorton
Upper Winchendon
DANGER AREA
OT MOOR
Whitecross Green Wood
NT Tower
Brill
Dorton House
Ashendon
Pollicott
Noke
Horton-cum-Studley
Little London
Nether Winchendon House
Lower Winchendon
Stone
B4027
Beckley
Oakley
Cuddington
Dinton Castle
Upton
Gibraltar
Dinton
Chilton
Chearsley
Westlington
Bernwood Meadows
Easington
OXFORD
Stanton St. John
Long Crendon
Worminghall
A418
Aylesbury (Thame)
Bishopstone
Ford
Barton
Forest Hill
Courthouse
Haddenham
Aston Sandford
Kimble Wick
Ickford
Thame
Kingsey
A40
Holton
Waterperry
R. Thame
Shabbington
Owlswick
A4142
Wheatley
Waterstock
North Weston
A4129
Shotover
Draycot
Towersey
Ilmer
Horspath
Tiddington
Chapel
A329
Moreton
Longwick
OXFORD
Cowley
Milton Common
B4012
B4445
Pitch Green
Skittle Green
Blenheim
Cuddesdon
Denton
Great Milton
Emmington
Henton
Horsenden
Littlemore
Great Haseley
Tetsworth
Sydenham
Chinnor & Princes Risborough Railway
Garsington
Bledlow
Saunderton
B480
Little Milton
Latchford
Kingston Stert
B4009
Cross
Chinnor
A4074
Toot Baldon
Little Haseley
Kingston Blount
Chinnor Hill
Nuneham Courtenay
Marsh Baldon
Chislehampton
Stoke Talmage
Adwell
Postcombe
University Arboretum
Stadhampton
Chalgrove
Chalgrove 1643
South Weston
Aston Rowant
Rout's Green
CHILTERN
B4015
Berinsfield
Drayton St. Leonard
Easington
Lewknor
Radnage
A415
Chalgrove
Newington
Pyrton
Shirburn
The City
Stokenchurch

135
133
137
BEDFORDSHIRE
HERTFORDHIRE
Bow Brickhill
Fenny Stratford
Little Brickhill
Birchmoor Green
Woburn
Woburn Abbey
Heritage Centre
Froxfield
Eversholt
Animal Kingdom
Church End
Tingrith
Westoning
Harlington
Milton Bryan
Newton Longville
Great Brickhill
Stockgrove Park
Grand Union Canal
Potsgrove
Battlesden
Toddington
TODDINGTON
M1
Stoke Hammond
Drayton Parslow
Mursley
A4146
Heath and Reach
Railway
Soulbury
Hollingdon
Fancott
Lower Sundon
Chalton
Swanbourne
Stewkley Dean
Stewkley
B4032
Leighton Buzzard Railway
Hockliffe
A4012
Tebworth
Wingfield
A5120
Hoggeston
Littlecote
Linslade
Eggington
Tilsworth
Houghton Regis
Dunton
Burcott
Leighton Buzzard
A505
Stanbridge
Maiden Bower
Sewell
Leagrave
Wing
Ascott
Ledburn
Billington
Little Billington
DUNSTABLE
Cublington
Whitchurch
A418
Slapton
R. Ouzel
Honeywick
Totternhoe
Church End
Chaul End
Aston Abbotts
Eaton Bray
Northall
Dunstable Downs
B489
Crafton
Mentmore
Mentmore Towers
Edlesborough
Kensworth
Hardwick
Weedon
Wingrave
Horton
Ivinghoe Aston
Tree Cath.
Whipsnade Heath
Rowsham
Cheddington
Beacon Hill
White Lion
Whipsnade
Kensworth Common
A413
A5
Hulcott
Watermill
Ivinghoe
Ivinghoe Beacon
Dagnall
Studham
Bierton
Long Marston
Farm
Gubblecote
Ashridge Park
Aylesbury
AYLESBURY
Puttenham
Marsworth
Pitstone
Bridgewater Monument
Ringshall
Little Gaddesden
Jockey End
Grand Union Canal
Wilstone
B488
B4506
A4146
Oak Farm
A41
Bulbourne
Ashridge Estate
Kings Head
Buckland
Drayton Beauchamp
New Mill
B486
Upper Dunsley
Aldbury
County
Southcourt
Weston Turville
Aston Clinton
Tring
St. Margaret's
Great Gaddesden
Stoke Mandeville
B4443
Halton
Buckinghamshire Goat Centre
Halton
Weston Turville
West Leith
Dancers End
Zoological
Wigginton
Water End
Nettleden
Frithsden
Marsh
Nash Lee
B4009
Hastoe
Northchurch
Potten End
Piccotts End
North Lee
Wendover Woods
A4010
Terrick
Wendover
A4251
Berkhamsted Castle
Warners End
Little Kimble
Ellesborough
Cholesbury Camp
Cholesbury
St. Leonards
BERKHAMSTED
Bourne End
Chaulden
Meadle
Great Kimble
Coombe Hill
Kingsash
Buckland Common
A416
Askett
THREE HILLS
Dunsmore
HUNDREDS
Bellingdon
Ashley Green
Monks Risborough
Chequers
Whiteleaf Cross
The Lee
Whelpley Hill
Lye Green
B4505
Felden
Lee Clump
Little Hampden
Princes Risborough
Chartridge
Bovingdon
OF AYLESBURY
Great Hampden
Hampden Monument
Ballinger Common
Botley
Ley Hill
South Heath
B485
CHESHAM
Chipperfield
A4128
Loosley Row
Lacey Green
Prestwood
Great Missenden
A413
Hyde Heath
Waterside
Flaunden
Belsize
Bucks Hill
Langley
Speen
Lacey Green
Little Kingshill
Chesham Bois
Sarratt
R. Chess
Upper North Dean
Bryant's Bottom
Great Kingshill
Little Missenden
Latimer
Manor
Chenies
Micklefield Green
Walter's Ash
Beamond End
Bradenham
Naphill
Cryers Hill
Holmer Green
AMERSHAM
A404
M25
Bledlow Ridge
Hughenden Valley
Widmer End
Penn Street
Little Chalfont
CHORLEYWOOD
A4010

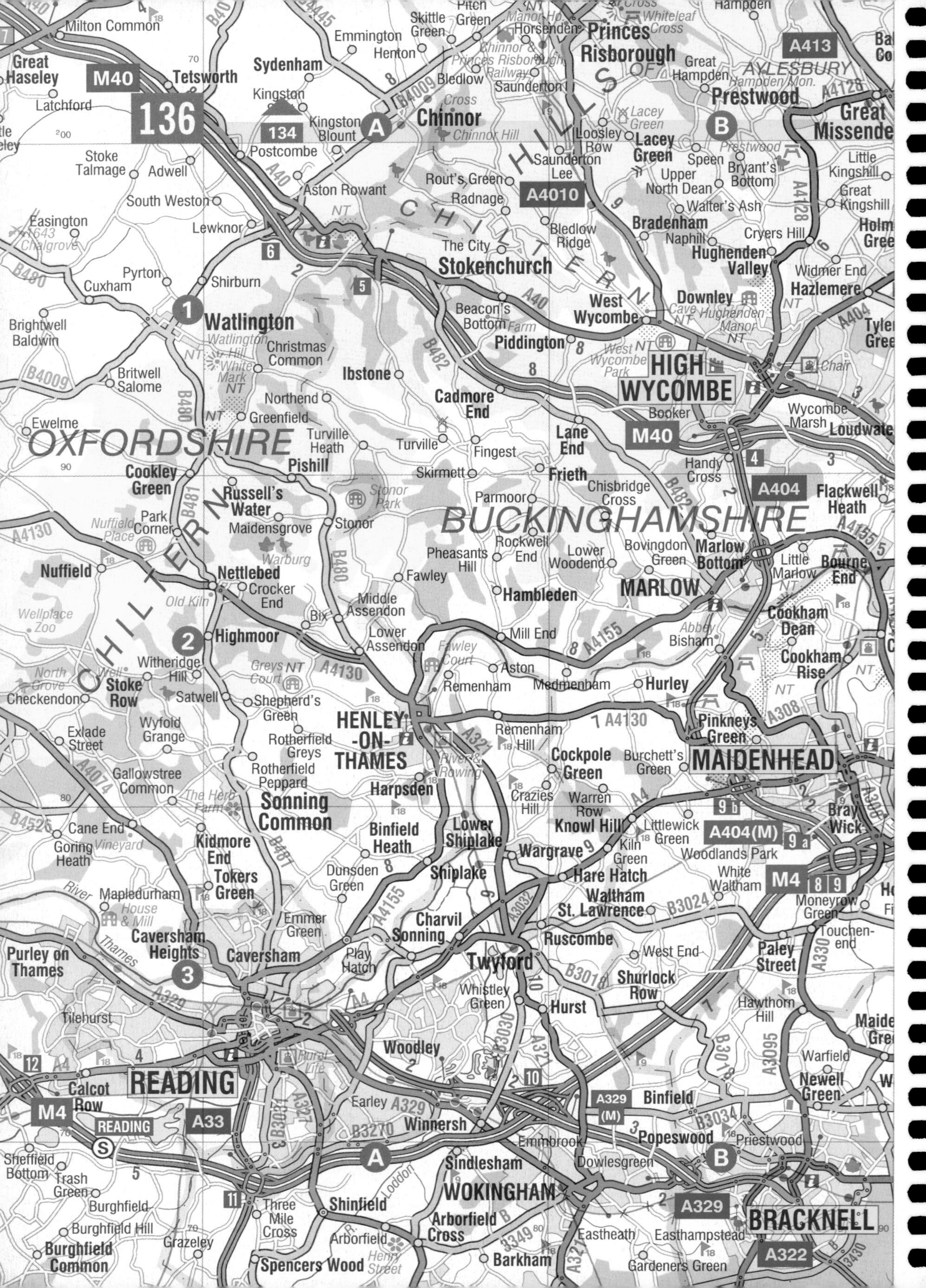
136
134
Milton Common
Great Haseley
M40
Tetsworth
Latchford
Sydenham
Emmington
Henton
Skittle Green
Pitch Green
Horsenden
Princes Risborough
Whiteleaf Cross
Hampden
A413
Great Hampden
AYLESBURY
Prestwood
Great Missenden
Kingston
Kingston Blount
Chinnor
Bledlow
Saunderton
Postcombe
Stoke Talmage
Adwell
Aston Rowant
South Weston
Lewknor
Easington
Chalgrove
Pyrton
Cuxham
Shirburn
Watlington
Brightwell Baldwin
Britwell Salome
Christmas Common
Ibstone
Northend
Greenfield
Ewelme
OXFORDSHIRE
Turville Heath
Turville
Pishill
Cookley Green
Russell's Water
Park Corner
Maidensgrove
Stonor
Nuffield
Nettlebed
Crocker End
Wellplace Zoo
Highmoor
Witheridge Hill
Stoke Row
Satwell
Checkendon
Exlade Street
Wyfold Grange
Gallowstree Common
Cane End
Goring Heath
Kidmore End
Tokers Green
Mapledurham
Caversham Heights
Purley on Thames
Caversham
Tilehurst
READING
Calcot Row
Sheffield Bottom
Trash Green
Burghfield
Burghfield Hill
Burghfield Common
Grazeley
Three Mile Cross
Spencers Wood
Shinfield
Arborfield
Arborfield Cross
Barkham
WOKINGHAM
Sindlesham
Winnersh
Earley
Woodley
Sonning Common
Rotherfield Greys
Rotherfield Peppard
Shepherd's Green
HENLEY -ON- THAMES
Harpsden
Binfield Heath
Dunsden Green
Emmer Green
Play Hatch
Sonning
Charvil
Shiplake
Lower Shiplake
Twyford
Whistley Green
Hurst
Ruscombe
Wargrave
Hare Hatch
Waltham St. Lawrence
Shurlock Row
West End
Binfield
Popeswood
Emmbrook
Dowlesgreen
Eastheath
Easthampstead
Gardeners Green
BRACKNELL
Priestwood
Newell Green
Warfield
Hawthorn Hill
Paley Street
Touchen-end
Moneyrow Green
White Waltham
Woodlands Park
Littlewick Green
Kiln Green
Knowl Hill
Warren Row
Crazies Hill
Cockpole Green
Remenham Hill
Remenham
Aston
Medmenham
Hurley
Burchett's Green
Pinkneys Green
MAIDENHEAD
Bray Wick
Cookham Rise
Cookham Dean
Bisham
MARLOW
Marlow Bottom
Little Marlow
Bourne End
Hambleden
Mill End
Lower Assendon
Middle Assendon
Bix
Fawley
Pheasants Hill
Rockwell End
Lower Woodend
Bovingdon Green
BUCKINGHAMSHIRE
Parmoor
Chisbridge Cross
Frieth
Skirmett
Fingest
Lane End
Cadmore End
Piddington
Beacon's Bottom
Stokenchurch
The City
Radnage
Rout's Green
Bledlow Ridge
West Wycombe
HIGH WYCOMBE
Booker
Handy Cross
Downley
Hughenden Valley
Naphill
Walter's Ash
Bradenham
Upper North Dean
Speen
Lacey Green
Loosley Row
Saunderton Lee
Bryant's Bottom
Cryers Hill
Widmer End
Hazlemere
Little Kingshill
Great Kingshill
Wycombe Marsh
Loudwater
Flackwell Heath
CHILTERN HILLS
M4
A4010
A404
A4130
A4155
A329
A33
A322
A404(M)
A329 (M)
Reading

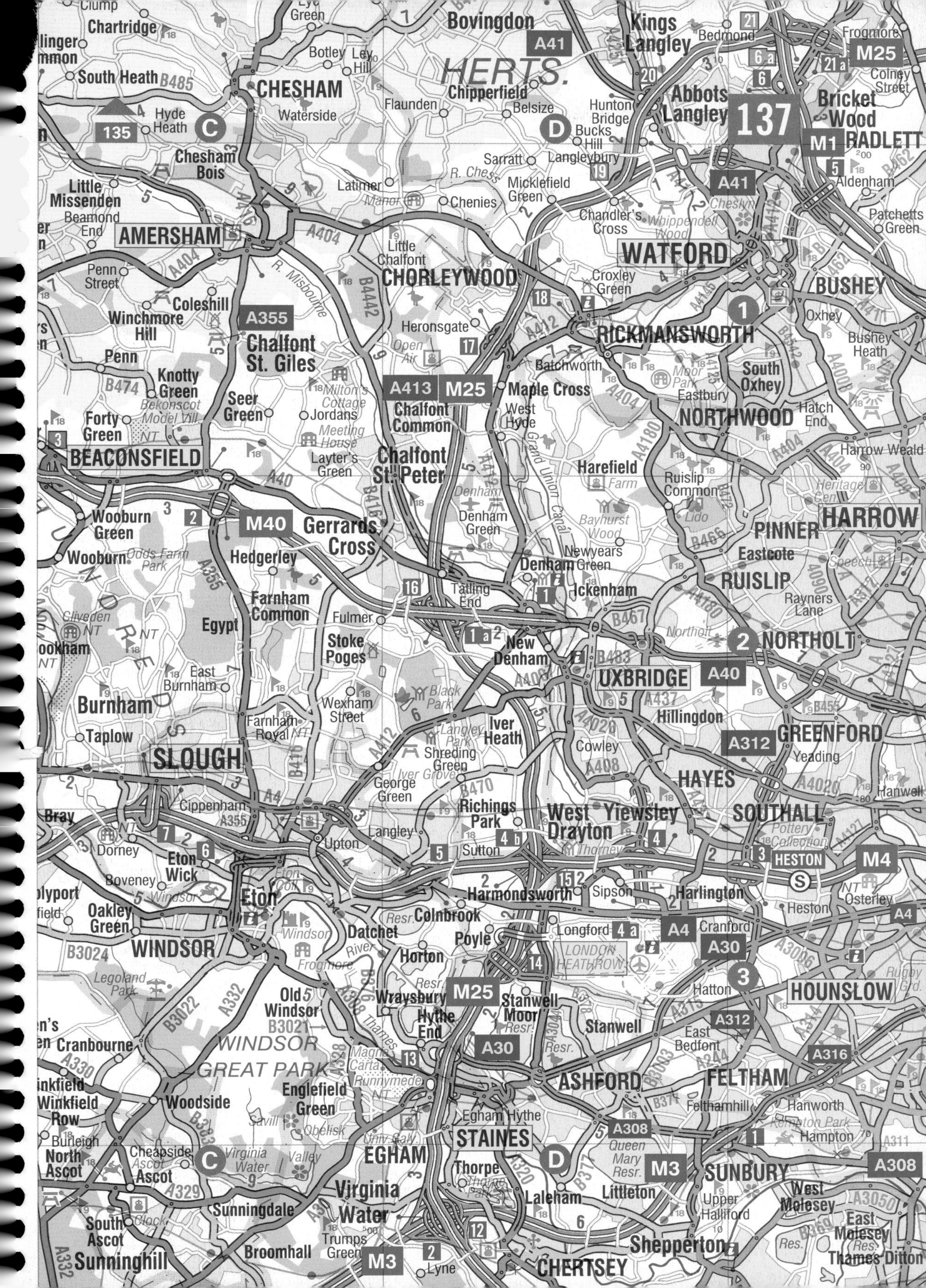

137
HERTS.
Chartridge
South Heath
Chesham
Chesham Bois
Bovingdon
Kings Langley
Abbots Langley
Bricket Wood
Radlett
Frogmore
Colney Street
Bedmond
Botley
Ley Hill
Chipperfield
Flaunden
Belsize
Hunton Bridge
Bucks Hill
Hyde Heath
Waterside
Sarratt
Langleybury
Little Missenden
Beamond End
Amersham
Latimer
Chenies
Micklefield Green
Chandler's Cross
Whippendell Wood
Watford
Aldenham
Patchetts Green
Penn Street
Coleshill
Winchmore Hill
Little Chalfont
Chorleywood
Croxley Green
Rickmansworth
Bushey
Oxhey
Bushey Heath
Heronsgate
Chalfont St. Giles
Penn
Knotty Green
Seer Green
Jordans
Milton's Cottage
Meeting House
Batchworth
Moor Park
South Oxhey
Eastbury
Maple Cross
West Hyde
Chalfont Common
Northwood
Hatch End
Harrow Weald
Forty Green
Beaconsfield
Bekonscot Model Vill
Layter's Green
Chalfont St. Peter
Denham
Harefield
Farm
Ruislip Common
Lido
Heritage Cen.
Harrow
Pinner
Wooburn Green
Wooburn
Odds Farm Park
Hedgerley
Gerrards Cross
Denham Green
Bayhurst Wood
Newyears Green
Eastcote
Ruislip
Rayners Lane
Tatling End
Ickenham
Cliveden NT
Egypt
Farnham Common
Fulmer
Stoke Poges
Northolt
New Denham
Uxbridge
East Burnham
Burnham
Black Park
Wexham Street
Farnham Royal
Langley Park
Iver Heath
Shreding Green
Hillingdon
Cowley
Greenford
Yeading
Taplow
Slough
George Green
Iver Grove
Richings Park
West Drayton
Yiewsley
Hayes
Southall
Hanwell
Bray
Cippenham
Dorney
Eton Wick
Upton
Langley
Sutton
Thorney
Pottery Collection
Heston
Boveney
Eton
Eton Coll
Windsor
Harmondsworth
Sipson
Harlington
Osterley
Oakley Green
Colnbrook
Datchet
Longford
Cranford
Windsor
B3024
Frogmore
Horton
Poyle
London Heathrow
Legoland Park
Old Windsor
Wraysbury
Hythe End
Stanwell Moor
Stanwell
Hatton
Hounslow
Rugby Grd.
Cranbourne
Windsor Great Park
Magna Carta
Runnymede NT
East Bedfont
Ashford
Feltham
Winkfield
Winkfield Row
Woodside
Englefield Green
Savill
Obelisk
Egham Hythe
Felthamhill
Hanworth
Kempton Park
Hampton
Burleigh
North Ascot
Cheapside
Ascot
Virginia Water
Valley
Egham
Staines
Queen Mary Resr.
Sunbury
Thorpe
Thorpe Park
Laleham
Littleton
West Molesey
Sunningdale
South Ascot
Clock
Virginia Water
Trumps Green
Upper Halliford
East Molesey
Sunninghill
Broomhall
Lyne
Chertsey
Shepperton
Thames Ditton
M25
M1
M40
M4
M3
A41
A413
A355
A40
A312
A4
A30
A308
A316
Heston
135
C
D

INDEX

Including Streets, Places & Areas, Industrial Estates,
Flats & Walkways, Stations and Places of Interest.

HOW TO USE THIS INDEX

1. Each street name is followed by its Postcode District and then by its Locality abbreviation(s) and then by its map reference; e.g. **Abbey Barn Rd.** HP11: W Mar . . . .4F **99** is in the HP11 Postcode District and the Wycombe Marsh Locality and is to be found in square 4F on page **99**. The page number is shown in bold type.

2. A strict alphabetical order is followed in which Av., Rd., St., etc. (though abbreviated) are read in full and as part of the street name; e.g. **Abbots Cl.** appears after **Abbotsbury** but before **Abbotsfield**

3. Streets and a selection of flats and walkways too small to be shown on street map pages **6-131**, appear in the index with the thoroughfare to which it is connected shown in brackets; e.g. **Alexandra Ct.** *MK13: B'ell . . . . 2A **22** (off Vicarage Rd.)*

4. Addresses that are in more than one part are referred to as not continuous.

5. Places and areas are shown in the index in BLUE TYPE and the map reference is to the actual map square in which the town centre or area is located and not to the place name shown on the map. Map references for entries that appear on street map pages **6-131** are shown first, with references to road map pages **132-137** shown in brackets; e.g. AMERSHAM 5A 86 (1C 137)

6. An example of a selected place of interest is Amersham Mus. 7K 85

7. An example of a station is Amersham Station (Rail) . . . . 5A 86. Included are Rail (Rail)

8. Junction names are shown in the index in **BOLD CAPITAL TYPE; e.g. ASHLAND 2K 29**

GENERAL ABBREVIATIONS

All. : Alley
App. : Approach
Arc. : Arcade
Av. : Avenue
Blvd. : Boulevard
Bri. : Bridge
Bldgs. : Buildings
Bungs. : Bungalows
Bus. : Business
Cvn. : Caravan
Cen. : Centre
Circ. : Circle
Cir. : Circus
Cl. : Close
Comn. : Common
Cnr. : Corner
Cott. : Cottage
Cotts. : Cottages
Ct. : Court
Cres. : Crescent
Cft. : Croft
Dr. : Drive
E. : East
Ent. : Enterprise
Est. : Estate
Fld. : Field
Flds. : Fields
Gdn. : Garden
Gdns. : Gardens
Gth. : Garth
Ga. : Gate
Gt. : Great
Grn. : Green
Gro. : Grove
Hgts. : Heights
Ho. : House
Ind. : Industrial
Info. : Information
Junc. : Junction
La. : Lane
Lit. : Little
Lwr. : Lower
Mnr. : Manor
Mans. : Mansions
Mkt. : Market
Mdw. : Meadow
Mdws. : Meadows
M. : Mews
Mt. : Mount
Mus. : Museum
Nth. : North
Pde. : Parade
Pk. : Park
Pas. : Passage
Pl. : Place
Res. : Residential
Ri. : Rise
Rd. : Road
Rdbt. : Roundabout
Shop. : Shopping
Sth. : South
Sq. : Square
Sta. : Station
St. : Street
Ter. : Terrace
Twr. : Tower
Trad. : Trading
Up. : Upper
Va. : Vale
Vw. : View
Vs. : Villas
Vis. : Visitors
Wlk. : Walk
W. : West
Yd. : Yard

LOCALITY ABBREVIATIONS

Ads : **Adstock**
Amer : **Amersham**
Ash : **Ashland**
A Grn : **Ashley Green**
Ask : **Askett**
A Gui : **Aspley Guise**
A H'th : **Aspley Heath**
A Abb : **Aston Abbotts**
Ast C : **Aston Clinton**
A San : **Aston Sandford**
Att : **Atterbury**
Ayle : **Aylesbury**
Ball : **Ballinger**
Ban : **Bancroft**
B Pk : **Bancroft Park**
B'ton : **Beachampton**
Bea : **Beaconsfield**
Bea E : **Beamond End**
Bean : **Beanhill**
Bier : **Bierton**
Bish : **Bishopstone**
Blak : **Blakelands**
Blea : **Bleak Hall**
Bled : **Bledlow**
Bled R : **Bledlow Ridge**
Blet : **Bletchley**
Blue B : **Blue Bridge**
Bolb : **Bolbeck Park**
Bolt E : **Bolter End**
Book : **Booker**
Bou E : **Bourne End**
Bov : **Bovingdon**
Bow B : **Bow Brickhill**
Brad : **Bradenham**
B'lle : **Bradville**
B'ell : **Bradwell**
B Abb : **Bradwell Abbey**
B Com : **Bradwell Common**
Bra : **Bray**
Bril : **Brill**
Brin : **Brinklow**
Bro : **Broughton**
Brow : **Browns Wood**
Buck : **Buckingham**
B'land : **Buckland**
Buld : **Bulbourne**
Burc : **Burcott**
Burn : **Burnham**
Cadm : **Cadmore End**
Cald : **Caldecotte**
Calv : **Calverton**
Camp : **Campbell Park**
Cast : **Castlethorpe**
C Key : **Central Milton Keynes**
Chac : **Chackmore**
D Gil : **Chalfont St Giles**
C Pet : **Chalfont St Peter**
Char : **Chartridge**
Che : **Chearsley**
Ched : **Cheddington**
Ches : **Chesham**
Chic : **Chicheley**
Chil : **Chilton**
Chor : **Chorleywood**
C Rey : **Clifton Reynes**
Coff : **Coffee Hall**
Cole : **Coleshill**
Coln : **Colnbrook**
Conn : **Conniburrow**
Cook : **Cookham**
Cosg : **Cosgrove**
Cowl : **Cowley**
C'ill : **Crownhill**
Crye : **Cryers Hill**
Cubl : **Cublington**
Cudd : **Cuddington**
Dag : **Dagnall**
Dat : **Datchet**
Den : **Denham**
Dint : **Dinton**
Dorn : **Dorney**
Dorn R : **Dorney Reach**
D Park : **Downhead Park**
Down : **Downley**
D Barn : **Downs Barn**
Dray : **Draycot**
Dray P : **Drayton Parslow**
Eagl : **Eaglestone**
E Wes : **Eaglestone West**
E Bra : **Eaton Bray**
Edle : **Edlesborough**
Emb : **Emberton**
E Val : **Emerson Valley**
Eto : **Eton**
E Wick : **Eton Wick**
Farn C : **Farnham Common**
Farn R : **Farnham Royal**
F Str : **Fenny Stratford**
Fifi : **Fifield**
Fing : **Fingest**
Fish : **Fishermead**
F Hea : **Flackwell Heath**
Flau : **Flaunden**
Fleet M : **Fleet Marston**
Ford : **Ford**
F Mil : **Fox Milne**
Fri : **Frieth**
F Sla : **Fullers Slade**
Fulm : **Fulmer**
Fur : **Furzton**
Gaw : **Gawcott**
Gayh : **Gayhurst**
G Grn : **George Green**
G Cro : **Gerrards Cross**
G Par : **Giffard Park**
G Far : **Grange Farm**
G Bri : **Great Brickhill**
G Ham : **Great Hampden**
G Hol : **Great Holm**
G Hor : **Great Horwood**
Gt Kim : **Great Kimble**
G Kin : **Great Kingshill**
G Lin : **Great Linford**
G Mis : **Great Missenden**
Gree : **Greenleys**
G Und : **Grendon Underwood**
Gubb : **Gubblecote**
Hadd : **Haddenham**
Halt : **Halton**
H'ope : **Hanslope**
H'ick : **Hardwick**
Hare : **Harefield**
Harm : **Harmondsworth**
Hart : **Hartwell**
H'ham : **Haversham**
H'ley : **Hazeley**
Haz : **Hazlemere**
H Rea : **Heath and Reach**
Hedg : **Hedgerley**
Hee : **Heelands**
H Wyc : **High Wycombe**
Hill : **Hillingdon**
H Lea : **Hodge Lea**
Holl : **Hollingdon**
H Grn : **Holmer Green**
Hor : **Horton**
H Vall : **Hughenden Valley**
Hur : **Hurley**
H Hea : **Hyde Heath**
I'ham : **Ickenham**
Ick : **Ickford**
Ive : **Iver**
I Hea : **Iver Heath**
I'hoe : **Ivinghoe**
I Ast : **Ivinghoe Aston**
Jord : **Jordans**
K Hil : **Kents Hill**
K Par : **Kents Hill Park**
Kiln : **Kiln Farm**
K'ash : **Kingsash**
K'ead : **Kingsmead**
K'ton : **Kingston**
Know : **Knowlhill**
L Grn : **Lacey Green**
L End : **Lane End**
Lang : **Langley**
Lath : **Lathbury**
Lati : **Latimer**
Lave : **Lavendon**
Lead : **Leadenhall**
L Com : **Lee Common**
L Hil : **Ley Hill**
L Woo : **Linford Wood**
L Bric : **Little Brickhill**
L Chal : **Little Chalfont**
L Ham : **Little Hampden**
L Hor : **Little Horwood**
L Kin : **Little Kingshill**
L Lin : **Little Linford**
L Mar : **Little Marlow**
L Miss : **Little Missenden**
L Hea : **London Heathrow Airport**
Long C : **Long Crendon**
Long : **Longford**
Long M : **Long Marston**
Long : **Longwick**
Loos : **Loosely Row**
Loud : **Loudwater**
Lough : **Loughton**
L Lodg : **Loughton Lodge**
Ludg : **Ludgershall**
Lye G : **Lye Green**
Maid : **Maidenhead**
M M'ton : **Maids Moreton**
Marl : **Marlow**
M Gib : **Marsh Gibbon**
M'rth : **Marsworth**
Mead : **Meadle**
Medb : **Medbourne**
Medm : **Medmenham**
Midd : **Middleton**
Mil K : **Milton Keynes**
M Vill : **Milton Keynes Village**
Mon R : **Monks Risborough**
Monk : **Monkston**
Monk P : **Monkston Park**
Moul : **Moulsoe**
Mur : **Mursley**
Nap : **Naphill**
Nas : **Nash**
N Hill : **Neath Hill**
Neth : **Netherfield**
New B : **New Bradwell**
New : **Newlands**
New P : **Newport Pagnell**
New L : **Newton Longville**
N'all : **Northall**
N Craw : **North Crawley**
N Dean : **North Dean**
Nort : **Northfield**
N Mar : **North Marston**
N West : **North Weston**
O'ill : **Oakhill**
Oak : **Oakley**

Oak G : **Oakley Green**
Old : **Oldbrook**
Old P : **Old Farm Park**
O Stra : **Old Stratford**
O Wol : **Old Wolverton**
Oln : **Olney**
O L'gh : **Orchard Leigh**
Ovi : **Oving**
Owls : **Owlswick**
O Pk : **Oxley Park**
Pad : **Padbury**
Par H : **Parslows Hillock**
P Bri : **Peartree Bridge**
Pen : **Penn**
Penn S : **Penn Street**
Penny : **Pennyland**
Pidd : **Piddington**
Pits : **Pitstone**
Poy : **Poyle**
Pres : **Prestwood**
Prin R : **Princes Risborough**
Q'ton : **Quainton**
Rad : **Radnage**
Red : **Redmoor**
R Pk : **Richings Park**
Ring : **Ringshall**
Rook : **Rooksley**
Salf : **Salford**
Saun : **Saunderton**
S Grn : **Seer Green**
Shab : **Shabbington**
S Broo : **Shenley Brook End**
S Chur : **Shenley Church End**
S Lod : **Shenley Lodge**
S Woo : **Shenley Wood**
Sher : **Sherington**
Simp : **Simpson**
Sing : **Singleborough**
Skir : **Skirmett**
Slou : **Slough**
S Wes : **Snelshall West**
Soul : **Soulbury**
S Hea : **South Heath**
Spee : **Speen**
Sprin : **Springfield**
S Bus : **Stacey Bushes**
Stan : **Stantonbury**
S Moor : **Stanwell Moor**
S Clay : **Steeple Claydon**
Stew : **Stewkley**
S Gold : **Stoke Goldington**
S Ham : **Stoke Hammond**
Sto M : **Stoke Mandeville**
Stoke : **Stokenchurch**
S Pog : **Stoke Poges**
Sto : **Stone**
Stone : **Stonebridge**
S Strat : **Stony Stratford**
Tapl : **Taplow**
Tatt : **Tattenhoe**
Tatt P : **Tattenhoe Park**
Terr : **Terrick**
Tha : **Thame**
T Lee : **The Lee**
T'ough : **Thornborough**
Thor : **Thorney**
Tilb : **Tilbrook**
Ting : **Tingewick**
T Bri : **Tinkers Bridge**
Tong : **Tongwell**
Tring : **Tring**
T Ash : **Two Mile Ash**
T Grn : **Tylers Green**
Tyr : **Tyringham**
Upt : **Upton**
Uxb : **Uxbridge**
Wadd : **Waddesdon**
Waln : **Walnut Tree**
Walt A : **Walters Ash**
Walt H : **Walton Hall**
Walt P : **Walton Park**
W Oak : **Water Oakley**
Water : **Waterstock**
Wave : **Wavendon**
W Gat : **Wavendon Gate**
W'don : **Weedon**
Wend : **Wendover**
W Ash : **West Ashland**
W Dra : **West Drayton**
W Hyd : **West Hyde**
W Wyc : **West Wycombe**
West : **Westcroft**
West T : **Weston Turville**
Wex : **Wexham**
Whad : **Whaddon**
Whee : **Wheeler End**
Whel : **Whelpley Hill**
Whip : **Whipsnade**
W'urch : **Whitchurch**
Whit : **Whiteleaf**
W End : **Widmer End**
Will : **Willen**
W Lak : **Willen Lake**
W Par : **Willen Park**
Wils : **Wilstone**
Winc : **Winchmore Hill**
Wind : **Windsor**
Wing : **Wing**
W'rave : **Wingrave**
Wink : **Winkfield**
Wins : **Winslow**
Wint : **Winterhill**
Wob : **Woburn**
W San : **Woburn Sands**
Wolv : **Wolverton**
W Mil : **Wolverton Mill**
Woob G : **Wooburn Green**
Wood : **Woodhill**
Wool : **Woolstone**
Worm : **Worminghall**
W Grn. : **Woughton on the Green**
Wough : **Woughton Park**
W Mar : **Wycombe Marsh**
Wym : **Wymbush**
Yiew : **Yiewsley**

A

Abbey Barn La. HP11: W Mar 6D **98**
Abbey Barn Rd. HP11: W Mar 4F **99**
Abbey Cl. SL1: Slou 5G **123**
Abbeydore Gro. MK10: Monk 5B **24**
ABBEY HILL 3H **21**
Abbey Pk. La. SL1: Burn 7G **109**
Abbey Rd. HP19: Ayle 4G **61**
MK6: Simp 2A **30**
MK13: B'ell 2A **22**
SL8: Bou E 4F **107**
Abbey Ter. MK16: New P 1K **17**
Abbey Wlk. HP16: G Mis 6H **75**
Abbey Way HP11: H Wyc 1A **98**
MK13: B'lle 7A **16**
SL7: Marl 4H **115**
Abbot Ridge HP18: Long C 7D **56**
ABBOTSBROOK 5F **107**
Abbotsbury MK4: West 5J **27**
Abbots Cl. MK13: B'lle 7B **16**
Abbotsfield MK6: Eagl 6H **23**
ABBOTS LANGLEY 1D **137**
Abbots Wlk. SL4: Wind 7G **129**
Abbots Way HP12: H Wyc 5H **97**
HP27: Mon R 3H **71**
Abbotswood HP27: Spee 2G **81**
Abbotts Cl. HP20: Ayle 5K **61**
UB8: Cowl 3K **127**
Abbotts Rd. HP20: Ayle 5K **61**
Abbotts Va. HP5: Ches 2A **78**
Abbotts Way HP22: W'rave 6B **48**
SL1: Slou 6F **123**
Abbot Wlk. HP18: Long C 7D **56**
Abercromby Av. HP12: H Wyc 7H **89**
Abercromby Ct. HP12: H Wyc 7H **89**
Aberdeen Av. SL1: Slou 5J **123**
Aberdeen Cl. MK3: Blet 5F **29**
Abney Ct. Dr. SL8: Bou E 7G **107**
Abraham Cl. MK15: W Par 7J **17**
ABTHORPE 2A **132**
Acacia Ho. SL9: C Pet 6J **103**
Acacia M. UB7: Harm 4K **131**
Accommodation La. UB7: Harm 4J **131**
UB7: Long 6G **131**
Ackerman Cl. MK18: Buck 4K **37**
Ackroyd Pl. MK5: S Lod 2B **28**
Acorn Cl. HP13: H Wyc 1D **98**
Acorn Gdns. HP12: H Wyc 4J **97**
Acorn Ho. MK9: C Key 4D **22**
Acorn Wlk. MK9: C Key 4E **22**
Acre, The SL7: Marl 7K **105**
Acrefield Rd. SL9: C Pet 1H **111**
Acres, The HP13: Down 6J **89**
Acres End HP7: Amer 6C **86**
Activity World 5J 29
(off Saxon St.)
Adam Cl. HP13: H Wyc 7C **90**
SL1: Slou 6J **123**
Adams Cl. MK18: Buck 3G **37**
Adams Ct. MK6: W Grn. 6J **23**
ADDINGTON 1B **134**
Addington Cotts. HP22: Wend 3H **69**
Addington Rd. MK18: Buck 3H **37**
Addington Ter. MK18: Buck 3H **37**
Addison Cl. SL0: Ive 5E **126**
Addison Rd. HP5: Ches 3A **78**
MK18: S Clay 3B **42**
Adelaide Cl. SL1: Slou 7J **123**
Adelaide Rd. HP13: H Wyc 7D **90**
Adelphi Gdns. SL1: Slou 7C **124**
Adelphi St. MK9: Camp 2F **23**
Adkins Cl. HP19: Ayle 3E **60**
Adkins Ct. HP14: Stoke 5C **72**
Admiral Hood Ho. SL9: C Pet 2J **103**
Adrians Wlk. SL2: Slou 6D **124**
ADSTOCK 6E 38 (3B 132)
Adstock M. SL9: C Pet 6H **103**
ADSTONE 1A **132**
ADWELL 3A **134**
Agora Cen. MK2: Blet 7J **29**
MK12: Wolv 6H **15**
Aidan Cl. HP21: Ayle 3B **66**
Ailward Rd. HP19: Ayle 4E **60**
Ainsdale Cl. MK3: Blet 6D **28**
Aintree Cl. MK3: Blet 2C **32**
SL3: Poy 6E **130**
Aiston Pl. HP20: Ayle 4A **62**
Ajax Av. SL1: Slou 5K **123**
AKELEY 3B **132**
Akerman Cl. MK12: Gree 1F **21**
Akister Cl. MK18: Buck 4J **37**
Alabama Circ. HP11: H Wyc 4B **98**
Alabama Dr. HP11: H Wyc 4B **98**
Alan Way SL3: G Grn 4J **125**
Alaska St. HP11: H Wyc 4B **98**
Albany Ct. MK14: Stan 6D **16**
Albany Ga. HP5: Ches 4K **77**
Albany Pk. SL3: Coln 6D **130**
Albany Pl. HP19: Ayle 4F **61**
Albert Cl. SL1: Slou 7D **124**
Albert Pl. SL4: E Wick 3J **129**
Albert Rd. HP5: Ches 5A **78**
UB7: Yiew 6K **127**
Albert St. HP13: H Wyc 1C **98**
HP20: Ayle 6B **62**
MK2: Blet 7J **29**
SL1: Slou 7D **124**
(not continuous)
SL4: Wind 6K **129**
Albion SL3: Lang 3B **130**
Albion Cl. SL2: Slou 6E **124**
Albion Cres. HP8: D Gil 7F **95**
Albion Pl. MK9: Camp 3G **23**
SL4: Wind 7J **129**
Albion Rd. HP8: D Gil 7F **95**
HP12: H Wyc 3G **97**
LU7: Pits 4F **51**
Albury Ct. MK8: G Hol 5K **21**
Aldborough Spur SL1: Slou 4C **124**
Aldbourne Rd. SL1: Burn 3D **122**
ALDBURY 2D **135**
Aldene Rd. MK19: H'ope 1E **8**
ALDENHAM 1D **137**
Aldenham MK6: T Bri 2K **29**
Alden Vw. SL4: Wind 6F **129**
Alderbourne La. SL0: I Hea 3A **120**
SL3: Fulm 2J **119**
Alderbury Rd. SL3: Lang 7K **125**
Alderbury Rd. W. SL3: Lang 7K **125**
Alder Cl. SL1: Slou 6H **123**
Aldergill MK13: Hee 1C **22**
Alderglade Nature Reserve, The 3K **121**
Aldermead MK12: S Bus 1J **21**
Alderney Pl. MK5: S Broo 3K **27**
Alder Rd. SL0: I Hea 7D **120**
UB9: Den 4J **121**
Alders, The UB9: Den 4J **121**
Alderson Cl. HP19: Ayle 4F **61**
ALDERTON 2B **132**
Aldin Av. Nth. SL1: Slou 7E **124**
Aldin Av. Sth. SL1: Slou 7E **124**
Aldrich Dr. MK15: Will 6K **17**
(not continuous)
Aldridge Rd. SL2: Slou 2J **123**
Aldwycks Cl. MK5: S Chur 1K **27**
Alexander Ho. HP5: Ches 1B **86**
MK2: Blet 7J **29**
Alexander Rd. HP20: Ayle 5J **61**
Alexander St. HP5: Ches 4A **78**
Alexandra Ct. *MK13: B'ell 2A 22*
(off Vicarage Rd.)
Alexandra Dr. MK16: New P 2J **17**
Alexandra Pk. HP11: H Wyc 2A **98**
Alexandra Rd. HP13: H Wyc 3E **98**
SL1: Slou 7B **124**
UB8: Uxb 7K **121**
Alford Rd. HP12: Book 5G **97**
Alfred Ct. SL8: Bou E 6H **107**
Alfred Davies Memorial Ground 6H **105**
Alham Rd. HP21: Ayle 1H **65**
Alice Cl. HP15: H Grn 7J **83**
Alice La. SL1: Burn 2D **122**
Alladale Pl. MK12: H Lea 2H **21**
Allanson Rd. SL7: Marl 6K **105**
Allen Cl. MK2: Blet 3J **33**
Allen Dr. HP14: Walt A 6G **81**
Allerds Rd. SL2: Farn R 6H **117**
Allerford Ct. MK4: Fur 3C **28**
Alley Way UB8: Uxb 5K **121**
Allhusen Gdns. SL3: Fulm 2J **119**
Allington Circ. MK4: K'ead 6J **27**
Allington Ct. SL2: Slou 4D **124**
Allison Ct. MK15: Wool 5J **23**
Allonby Way HP21: Ayle 7C **62**
All Saints Vw. MK5: Lough 6B **22**
Allyn Cl. HP13: H Wyc 7C **90**
Alma Ct. SL1: Burn 1E **122**
Alma Rd. HP5: Ches 3A **78**
SL4: E Wick 2H **129**
SL4: Wind 7K **129**
Almond Cl. MK16: New P 2H **17**
SL4: Wind 7K **129**
Almond Rd. SL1: Burn 1E **122**
Almond Wlk. HP15: Haz 4H **91**
Almond Way HP27: Prin R 6F **71**
Almons Way SL2: Slou 3F **125**
Alpha Ct. HP7: Amer 1K **93**
Alpha St. Nth. SL1: Slou 7E **124**
Alpha St. Sth. SL1: Slou 7D **124**
Alpine Cft. MK5: S Broo 4A **28**
ALSCOT 3F **71**
Alscot La. HP27: Prin R 3F **71**
Alston Dr. MK13: B Abb 2K **21**
Alstonefield MK4: E Val 4B **28**
Althorpe Cres. MK13: B'lle 7A **16**
Altona Rd. HP10: Loud 5J **99**
Altona Way SL1: Slou 4K **123**
Alton Ga. MK4: West 5K **27**
Alton Ho. Office Pk. HP19: Ayle 5G **61**
Altwood Cl. SL1: Slou 3G **123**
Alverton MK14: G Lin 5F **17**
Alvista Av. SL6: Tapl 4D **122**
Alwin Cl. HP21: Ayle 3H **65**
Amanda Ct. SL3: Lang 7H **125**
Amber Cotts. HP7: Cole 4H **93**
Ambergate MK16: Bro 2D **24**
Amberley Rd. SL2: Slou 3G **123**
Amberley Wlk. MK4: K'ead 6J **27**
Amberley Way UB10: Uxb 7K **121**
Amblers Way MK18: Pad 6A **38**
Ambleside *HP6: Amer 4A 86*
(off Rickmansworth Rd.)
HP21: Ayle 2C **66**
Ambleside Wlk. *UB8: Uxb 6K 121*
(off Cumbrian Way)
Ambridge Gro. MK6: P Bri 5H **23**
AMBROSDEN 2A **134**
Ambrose Ct. MK15: Wool 4J **23**
Amelas La. MK9: Camp 3G **23**
Amerden Cl. SL6: Tapl 4A **122**
Amerden La. SL6: Tapl 4A **122**
(Amerden Cl.)
SL6: Tapl 7A **122**
(River Gdns.)
Amerden Way SL1: Slou 7J **123**
AMERSHAM 5A 86 (1C 137)
AMERSHAM COMMON 6B **86**
Amersham Ct. *HP6: Amer 4B 86*
(off Woodside Rd.)
Amersham Hill HP13: H Wyc 1B **98**
Amersham Hill Dr. HP13: H Wyc 7C **90**
Amersham Hill Gdns. HP13: H Wyc 7C **90**
Amersham Mus. 7K **85**
AMERSHAM OLD TOWN 7K **85**
AMERSHAM ON THE HILL 4B **86**
Amersham Pl. HP7: L Chal 6G **87**
Amersham Rd. HP5: Ches 7A **78**
HP6: Amer 2K **85**
HP6: L Chal 6H **87**
HP7: Bea E, Penn S 3G **91**
HP7: Cole 5H **101**
HP7: L Chal 6H **87**
HP8: D Gil 2H **103**
(Cherry Acre, not continuous)
HP8: D Gil 3E **94**
(Coke's La.)
HP9: Bea 5H **101**
HP13: H Wyc 7C **90**
HP15: Haz, Bea E 3G **91**
SL9: C Pet 2H **103**
SL9: G Cro 2K **111**
(not continuous)
UB9: Den 4A **112**
Amersham Station (Rail) 5A **86**
Amersham Way HP6: L Chal 6H **87**
Ames Cl. MK6: Old 6F **23**
Amherst Ct. MK15: Will 6J **17**
Amos Ct. MK13: B'lle 7A **16**
Ampleforth MK10: Monk 5C **24**
AMPTHILL 3D **133**
Amy La. HP5: Ches 6K **77**
Ancell Rd. MK11: S Strat 1C **20**
Anchor Ct. MK16: New P 1K **17**
Anchor La. HP20: Ayle 6K **61**
Ancona Gdns. MK5: S Broo 4K **27**
Andermans SL4: Wind 6F **129**
Anderson Cl. HP14: Stoke 6D **72**
Anderson Ga. MK4: S Wes 1A **32**
Anding Cl. MK46: Oln 3G **7**
Andover Cl. UB8: Uxb 7H **121**
Andrewes Cft. MK14: G Lin 5F **17**
(not continuous)
Andrew Hill La. SL2: Hedg 7A **110**
Andrews Cl. LU7: Soul 6H **41**
Andrews Ho. HP13: H Wyc 2E **98**
Andrews Reach SL8: Bou E 7G **107**
Andrews Way HP19: Ayle 7F **61**
SL7: Marl 1G **105**
Anershall HP22: W'rave 6C **48**
Angel Cl. MK15: Penny 6G **17**
Angelica Ct. MK7: Waln 2C **30**
Angels Cl. MK18: Wins 6H **39**
Angleset Ct. HP14: Stoke 5C **72**
Anglesey Ct. MK8: G Hol 6K **21**
Angood Cl. HP27: Prin R 5F **71**
Angora Cl. MK5: S Broo 4A **28**
Angstrom Cl. MK5: S Lod 2B **28**
Angus Dr. MK3: Blet 4F **29**
Angus Rd. HP19: Ayle 3F **61**
Annes Gro. MK14: G Lin 4D **16**

Annesley Rd. MK16: New P 2H **17**
Anns Cl. HP21: Ayle 3B **66**
Anscuff Rd. SL2: Slou 1J **123**
Anslow Gdns. SL0: I Hea 7D **120**
Anslow Pl. SL1: Slou 3E **122**
Anson Cl. HP3: Bov 1K **79**
HP21: Ayle 3K **65**
Anson Rd. MK12: Wolv 6G **15**
Anstey Brook HP22: West T 4H **67**
Anstey Cl. HP18: Wadd 6D **52**
Anstey Ct. HP18: Wadd 5D **52**
Anthony Cl. HP13: Down 6K **89**
Anthony Ct. MK11: S Strat 1B **20**
Anthony Way SL1: Slou 5F **123**
Anton Way HP21: Ayle 3H **65**
Anvil Ct. SL3: Lang 2A **130**
Anxey Way HP17: Hadd 6B **58**
Aplin Rd. HP21: Ayle 1D **66**
Apollo Cen. HP11: H Wyc 1K **97**
Appleacres MK17: S Ham 1G **41**
Appleby Heath MK2: Blet 2K **33**
Applecroft MK17: New L 4D **32**
Applefield HP7: L Chal 6G **87**
Appleton Cl. HP7: L Chal 7F **87**
Appleton M. MK4: E Val 4B **28**
Apple Tree Cotts. HP16: L Com 1A **76**
Appletree La. SL3: Lang 7G **125**
Appletree Wlk. *HP5: Ches* *1B* ***86***
(off Cresswell Rd.)
Applewick La. HP12: H Wyc 7G **89**
Appleyard Pl. MK6: Old 5E **22**
Approach, The MK8: T Ash 3H **21**
Approach Rd. SL6: Tapl 4A **122**
Apsley Ct. HP19: Ayle 5J **61**
Apsley Ho. SL1: Slou 7E **124**
Aquavale Swimming Cen. 6A **62**
Aran Hgts. HP8: D Gil 1F **103**
ARBORFIELD 3A **136**
Arborfield Cl. SL1: Slou 7C **124**
ARBORFIELD CROSS 3A **136**
Arbour Vw. HP7: L Chal 6F **87**
Arbroath Cl. MK3: Blet 4E **28**
Arbrook Av. MK13: B Com 4C **22**
Arcade, The HP9: Bea 6F **101**
Archdale HP11: H Wyc 2K **97**
Archer Ct. *HP6: Amer* *4A* ***86***
(off Chesham Rd.)
Archer Dr. HP20: Ayle 4B **62**
Archers Ct. SL7: Marl 1J **115**
Archers Way HP14: L End 3K **73**
Archers Wells MK3: Blet 5H **29**
Archford Cft. MK4: E Val 4C **28**
Archive Cl. HP22: Ast C 2A **68**
Arch Way HP13: H Wyc 1A **98**
HP27: Spee 2F **81**
Archways *HP20: Ayle* *6J* ***61***
(off Castle St.)
Ardenham La. HP19: Ayle 5J **61**
Ardenham St. HP19: Ayle 5H **61**
Ardley M. MK10: Bro 3D **24**
Ardrossan Cl. SL2: Slou 2A **124**
Ardwell La. MK12: Gree 1E **20**
Ardys Ct. MK5: Lough 6B **22**
Argonaut Pk. SL3: Poy 6F **131**
Argyle Av. HP19: Ayle 4F **61**
Argyll Av. SL1: Slou 5J **123**
Arizona St. HP11: H Wyc 4B **98**
Arkwright Rd. SL3: Poy 7E **130**
Arlington Ct. MK4: Fur 4E **28**
Arlott Cres. MK6: Old 6F **23**
Armourer Dr. MK14: N Hill 7F **17**
Armstrong Cl. MK8: C'ill 1J **27**
Arncliffe Dr. MK13: Hee 1B **22**
(not continuous)
Arncott Way HP19: Ayle 5E **60**
Arne La. MK7: Old P 2F **31**
Arnison Av. HP13: H Wyc 6D **90**
Arnold Cl. HP22: Sto M 4D **66**
Arnold Ct. HP21: Ayle 1A **66**
Arnolds Cl. MK18: Pad 6A **38**
Arnold's Cotts. HP5: Char 1D **76**
Arnos Gro. MK10: Monk P 5B **24**
Arnott's Yd. HP18: Long C 6D **56**
Arranmore Ho. HP13: H Wyc 4H **99**
Arrow Pl. MK2: Blet 4K **33**
Arthur Rd. SL1: Slou 7B **124**
SL4: Wind 6K **129**
Arundel Grn. HP20: Ayle 4A **62**
Arundel Gro. MK3: Blet 7E **28**
Arundel Ho. HP13: H Wyc 1F **99**
UB8: Cowl 2J **127**
Arundel Rd. HP12: Book 3F **97**
UB8: Uxb 7H **121**
ASCOT 3C **137**
Ascot Pl. MK3: Blet 1D **32**
Ascott Ct. HP20: Ayle 5K **61**
Ascott House & Gardens 3E **48**
Ascott Rd. HP20: Ayle 5K **61**
Ashbourne End HP21: Ayle 3H **65**
Ashbourne Ho. SL1: Slou 7C **124**
Ashburnham Cl. MK3: Blet 6D **28**
Ashburnham Dr. HP14: Walt A 5F **81**
Ashby MK6: Eagl 6G **23**
Ashby Vs. LU7: I Ast 1J **51**
Ash Cl. HP14: Walt A 6F **81**
HP20: Ayle 4B **62**
SL3: Lang 1B **130**
Ashcroft Ct. SL1: Burn 7D **116**
Ashcroft Dr. UB9: Den 4F **113**
Ashdown Cl. MK14: G Par 5G **17**
Ashdown Rd. HP13: H Wyc 1G **99**
Ashdown Way HP6: Amer 4B **86**
Ashenden Wlk. SL2: Farn C 2B **118**
ASHENDON 2B **134**
ASHERIDGE 1F **77**
Asheridge Bus. Cen. *HP5: Ches* *3J* ***77***
(off Asheridge Rd.)
Asheridge Rd. HP5: Ches 2H **77**
Ashfield MK14: Stan 5C **16**
Ashfield Cl. HP15: Haz 5H **91**
Ashfield Gro. MK2: Blet 1J **33**
Ashfield Ri. HP18: Oak 5H **53**
Ashfield Rd. HP5: Ches 3B **78**
Ashfield Way HP15: Haz 5H **91**
ASHFORD 3D **137**
Ashford Cl. HP21: Ayle 2B **66**
Ashford Cres. MK8: G Far 1H **27**
Ashford La. SL4: Dorn 7D **122**
Ashford Rd. SL0: I Hea 6C **120**
Ash Grn. UB9: Den 4H **121**
Ash Gro. HP6: Amer 3J **85**
HP21: Ayle 7B **62**
SL2: S Pog 5D **118**
Ashgrove MK18: S Clay 3B **42**
Ashgrove Gdns. HP22: W'urch 5E **44**
(not continuous)
Ash Hill Rd. MK16: New P 1H **17**
ASHLAND 2K **29**
ASHLAND 2J **29**
Ash La. SL4: Wind 7F **129**
Ashlea MK46: Oln 3G **7**
Ashlea Rd. SL9: C Pet 7J **103**
Ashleigh Cl. HP7: Amer 6C **86**
Ashley Cl. LU7: Ched 1C **50**
Ashley Ct. HP10: T Grn 6H **91**
Ashley Dr. HP10: T Grn 5J **91**
ASHLEY GREEN 3D **135**
Ashley Grn. Rd. HP5: Ches 2B **78**
Ashley Rd. UB8: Uxb 7H **121**
Ashley Row HP20: Ayle 5B **62**
Ashmead Dr. UB9: Den 7G **113**
Ashmead La. UB9: Den 7G **113**
Ashpole Furlong MK5: Lough 7A **22**
Ashridge Cl. HP3: Bov 2K **79**
MK3: Blet 1D **32**
Ashridge La. HP5: L Hil 6G **79**
Ash Rd. HP12: Book 4G **97**
HP27: Prin R 5G **71**
ASHTON 2B **132**
Ashtree Wlk. HP15: Haz 5H **91**
Ashwells HP10: T Grn 7H **91**
Ashwells Mnr. Dr. HP10: T Grn 7H **91**
Ashwells Way HP8: D Gil 7H **95**
Ashwood MK13: B'lle 6A **16**
Ashwood Dr. HP5: Ches 4K **77**
ASKETT 1J 71 (3C **135**)
Askett La. HP27: Ask 1J **71**
Aspen Cl. HP20: Ayle 4B **62**
SL2: Slou 3K **123**
Asplands Cl. MK17: W San 3K **31**
Aspley Ct. MK17: A H'th 4K **31**
ASPLEY GUISE 3D **133**
ASPLEY HEATH 5J 31 (3D **133**)
Aspley Hill MK17: W San 3K **31**
Aspreys MK46: Oln 4G **7**
Assheton Rd. HP9: Bea 4F **101**
ASTCOTE 1A **132**
Astlethorpe MK8: T Ash 4K **21**
ASTON 2A **136**
ASTON ABBOTTS 6J 47 (1C **135**)
Aston Abbotts Rd. HP22: W'don 7J **45**
LU7: Cubl 2H **47**
ASTON CLINTON 2A 68 (2C **135**)
Aston Clinton By-Pass
HP22: Ast C, B'land 1D **68**
Aston Clinton Rd. HP22: West T 7E **62**
Aston Cl. HP19: Ayle 3F **61**
MK5: S Lod 2B **28**
Aston Ct. HP11: W Mar 5H **99**
Aston Mead SL4: Wind 6G **129**
Aston Rd. HP17: Hadd 7C **58**
ASTON ROWANT 1A **136**
ASTON SANDFORD 7F 59 (3B **134**)
Astronomey Way *HP19: Ayle* *6F* ***61***
(off Queensgate)
ASTWOOD 2D **133**
Atherstone Ct. MK8: T Ash 4G **21**
Atkins Cl. MK13: B'ell 3B **22**
Atlas Ho. HP5: Ches 4K **77**
Atterbrook MK13: B'ell 2A **22**
ATTERBURY 2B **24**
Attingham Hill MK8: G Hol 6K **21**
Atwell Cl. MK8: C'ill 7J **21**
Auckland Pk. MK1: Blet 4K **29**
Auckland Rd. HP13: H Wyc 2E **98**
Auden Cl. MK16: New P 7G **11**
Audley Mead MK13: B'ell 3B **22**
August End SL3: G Grn 4J **125**
Augustine Cl. SL3: Poy 7E **130**
Augustine M. HP16: G Mis 6H **75**
Augustus Rd. MK11: S Strat 2B **20**
Austen Av. MK46: Oln 3J **7**
Austen Pl. HP19: Ayle 4E **60**
Austenway SL9: C Pet 1J **111**
AUSTENWOOD 7H **103**
Austenwood Cl.
HP11: H Wyc 4A **98**
SL9: C Pet 7G **103**
Austenwood La. SL9: C Pet 7H **103**
Austin Waye UB8: Uxb 6J **121**
Australia Rd. SL1: Slou 7F **125**
Austwick La. MK4: E Val 5B **28**
Autumn Cl. HP19: Ayle 3F **61**
SL1: Slou 6H **123**
Auxiliaries Way UB9: Den 3F **113**
Avalon Rd. SL8: Bou E 4H **107**
Avant Bus. Cen. MK1: Blet 5J **29**
AVEBURY 5D **22**
Avebury SL1: Slou 5J **123**
Avebury Blvd. MK9: C Key 6C **22**
Aveling Rd. HP13: H Wyc 2C **98**
Avenue, The HP7: Amer 5A **86**
HP18: Worm 3C **54**
HP27: Prin R 4H **71**
SL2: Farn C 2K **117**
SL8: Bou E 5F **107**
UB8: Cowl 2K **127**
Avenue Cl. UB7: W Dra 1K **131**
Avenue Ho. *HP5: Ches* *5K* ***77***
(off Park Rd.)
Avenue Rd. MK18: M M'ton 1J **37**
MK18: Wins 6H **39**
Averil Ct. SL6: Tapl 4E **122**
Avery Av. HP13: Down 5H **89**
Avery Ct. MK16: New P 3J **17**
Avington MK8: G Hol 5J **21**
Avocet Way HP19: Ayle 3K **61**
Avon Cl. MK16: New P 2K **17**
SL1: Slou 5G **123**
Avon Gro. MK3: Blet 7E **28**
Avon Pl. HP21: Ayle 3J **65**
Axis Pk. SL3: Lang 3B **130**
AYLESBURY 6K 61 (2C **135**)
Aylesbury Bus. Cen. HP19: Ayle 5G **61**
Aylesbury College Sports Cen. 7H **61**
Aylesbury Cres. SL1: Slou 4B **124**
Aylesbury End HP9: Bea 7G **101**
Aylesbury Ind. Est. HP19: Ayle 5H **61**
Aylesbury Rd. HP16: G Mis 2F **75**
HP17: Dint, Hadd 3C **58**
HP18: Che 2H **57**
HP18: Cudd 1B **58**
HP22: Ast C 1H **67**
HP22: Bier 4B **62**
HP22: Wend 1F **69**
HP27: Ask, Mon R, Prin R 4G **71**
LU7: Wing 4C **48**
OX9: Hadd, Tha 7H **57**
Aylesbury Station (Rail) 7J **61**
Aylesbury St. MK2: Blet, F Str 7A **30**
MK12: Wolv 7G **15**
Aylesbury St. W. MK12: Wolv 7F **15**
Aylesbury United FC 3J **61**
Ayleswater HP19: Ayle 2K **61**
Aylesworth Av. SL2: Slou 1K **123**
Aylsford Gro. MK10: Monk 5C **24**
Aylward Gdns. HP5: Ches 4J **77**
Aynho Ct. MK8: G Hol 6K **21**
Ayres Cl. HP21: Ayle 1G **65**
Ayrshire Cl. HP19: Ayle 3F **61**
Ayrton Cl. MK8: G Far 1H **27**
Ayr Way MK3: Blet 5E **28**
Azalea Cl. HP15: Haz 4G **91**
Azalea Way SL3: G Grn 4J **125**

B

Babbington Cl. MK10: Midd 3C **24**
Babington Rd. HP22: Halt 2K **69**
Baccara Gro. MK2: Blet 2J **33**
Back Dr. MK16: Tyr 1F **11**
Back La. HP8: D Gil 1E **102**
HP16: G Mis 6H **75**
MK18: Ting 2B **36**
Backleys MK7: Cald 5C **30**
Back St. HP22: Wend 4H **69**
MK18: Gaw 6C **36**
MK18: T'ough 2C **38**
Bacombe Hill Nature Reserve 5G **69**
Bacombe La. HP22: Wend 5G **69**
Bacon Hill MK46: Oln 4G **7**
Bacons Mead UB9: Den 7G **113**
BADBY 1A **132**
Bader Gdns. SL1: Slou 7J **123**
Badgebury Ri. SL7: Marl 2G **105**
Badgemore Ct. MK8: T Ash 4G **21**
Badgers, The 5J **37**
Badgers Mdw. HP22: Halt 3J **69**
Badgers Oak MK7: K Hil 7D **24**
Badgers Ri. HP17: Sto 2B **64**
Badgers Way MK18: Buck 5J **37**
SL7: Marl 2H **105**
Badgers Wood SL2: Farn C 3A **118**
Badger Way HP15: Haz 2H **91**
Badminton Ct. *HP7: Amer* *7K* ***85***
(off Church St.)
Badminton Vw. MK8: G Hol 5A **22**
Badrick Rd. HP19: Ayle 4E **60**
Bagley Cl. UB7: W Dra 7K **127**
Bagshot Ct. MK2: Blet 1J **33**
Bailey Cl. HP13: H Wyc 1C **98**
SL4: Wind 7J **129**
Baily Ct. MK5: S Chur 2A **28**
Baines Wlk. *HP5: Ches* *5K* ***77***
(off High St.)
BAINTON 1A **134**
Baird Cl. SL1: Slou 7K **123**
Baisley Ho. MK2: F Str 7K **29**
Bakers Cl. MK16: S Gold 7C **6**
Bakers Ct. UB8: Uxb 5K **121**
Bakers Orchard HP10: Woob G 4A **108**
Bakers Rd. UB8: Uxb 5K **121**
Baker St. HP11: H Wyc 1K **97**
HP18: Wadd 6C **52**
Bakers Wlk. HP22: West T 5G **67**
BAKERS WOOD 6D **112**
Bakers Wood UB9: Den 7D **112**
Bakers Yd. UB8: Uxb 5K **121**
Bakery Cl. HP18: G Und 2H **43**
Bala Cl. MK2: Blet 3J **33**
Bala Way MK2: Blet 2J **33**
Balcary Gro. MK4: Tatt 7K **27**
Baldways Cl. HP22: W'rave 6D **48**
Baldwin Cres. MK16: New P 2J **17**
Baldwin Rd. HP9: Bea 7K **101**
SL1: Burn 1E **122**
Balfe M. MK7: Old P 3F **31**
Balfour M. HP3: Bov 1K **79**
Balfour Pl. SL7: Marl 5H **105**
Balfour Way HP20: Ayle 4K **61**
Ballard Cl. HP21: Ayle 2C **66**
Ballard Grn. SL4: Wind 5G **129**
BALLINGER BOTTOM 2A **76**
BALLINGER BOTTOM (SOUTH) 3A **76**
BALLINGER COMMON 2A 76 (3D **135**)
Ballinger Rd. HP16: S Hea 5K **75**
Ballinger Row HP16: Ball 2K **75**
Ball Moor MK18: Buck 6H **37**
Balmer Bri. MK18: Buck 7H **37**
Balmer Cut MK18: Buck 6J **37**
Balmerino Cl. MK10: Monk 4D **24**
Balmoral Cl. SL1: Slou 4G **123**
Balmoral Ct. HP13: H Wyc 1B **98**
MK16: New P 2H **17**
Balsam Cl. MK7: Waln 1D **30**
Bampton Cl. MK4: Fur 5E **28**
Banburies Cl. MK3: Blet 5G **29**
Banbury Av. SL1: Slou 3H **123**
BANCROFT 1A **22**
BANCROFT 1A **22**
BANCROFT PARK 1K **21**
Bangors Cl. SL0: Ive 4E **126**
Bangors Rd. Nth. SL0: I Hea 6D **120**
Bangors Rd. Sth. SL0: Ive, I Hea 1E **126**
BANKFIELD 3F **23**
Bank Rd. HP10: T Grn 7K **91**
Bankside HP22: Wend 3H **69**
Banks Pde. HP17: Hadd 6C **58**
Banks Rd. HP17: Hadd 6C **58**
Banks Spur SL1: Slou 7K **123**
Bank St. HP13: H Wyc 3G **99**
Banktop Pl. MK4: E Val 4C **28**
Banner Ct. *HP12: H Wyc* *7H* ***89***
(off Eaton Av.)
Bannister Cl. SL3: Lang 7J **125**
Bantock Cl. MK7: Brow 2E **30**
Barbers M. MK14: N Hill 7F **17**
Barbers Wood Cl. HP12: Book 4F **97**
Barbers Wood Rd. HP12: Book 4F **97**
Barbury Ct. MK14: G Par 5G **17**
Barchester Cl. UB8: Cowl 1J **127**
Barchester Rd. SL3: Lang 7K **125**
Bardolphs Cl. HP27: Prin R 4H **71**
Bardon Grn. HP20: Ayle 4K **61**
Bardsey Ct. MK10: Monk 4C **24**
Barford MK11: S Strat 2D **20**
Baring Rd. HP9: Bea 5E **100**
HP13: H Wyc 1F **99**
Barkers Cft. MK12: Gree 1G **21**
Barkestone Cl. MK4: E Val 6C **28**
BARKHAM 3A **136**
Barkham Cl. LU7: Ched 2B **50**
Bar La. HP27: Long, Owls 1C **70**
Barlee Cres. UB8: Cowl 3J **127**
Barley Cl. HP15: Haz 4G **91**
HP22: West T 5G **67**
Barley Cres. HP21: Ayle 4J **65**
Barleycroft MK4: Fur 3E **28**
Barleyfields HP10: Woob G 1A **108**
Barley Way SL7: Marl 1H **115**
Barlow Rd. HP22: Wend 3J **69**
Barnacre Cl. UB8: Cowl 4K **127**
Barnard Cres. HP21: Ayle 2A **66**
Barnards Hill SL7: Marl 7F **105**
Barn Cl. SL2: Farn C 2K **117**
Barn Ct. HP12: H Wyc 1G **97**
Barnes Av. HP5: Ches 4A **78**
Barnes La. HP15: Haz 4F **91**
Barnes Pl. MK6: Old 6E **22**
Barnes Way SL0: Ive 5F **127**
Barnet Cl. MK5: O'ill 2H **27**
Barnett Way HP22: Bier 2C **62**
Barnfield SL0: Ive 4E **126**
SL1: Slou 6F **123**
Barnfield Dr. MK6: Neth 2J **29**
Barnhill Cl. SL7: Marl 5H **105**
Barnhill Gdns. SL7: Marl 5H **105**

Barnhill Rd. SL7: Marl 5H 105
Barn Rd. HP27: Long 2C 70
Barns, The LU7: Burc 1B 48
Barnsbury Av. HP20: Ayle 6C 62
Barnsbury Gdns. MK16: New P 2J 17
Barnsdale Dr. MK4: West 5K 27
Barnsfield Pl. UB8: Uxb 6J 121
Barnstaple Ct. MK4: Fur 4D 28
Barn Theatre 4E 16
Barons Cl. MK2: Blet 7J 29
Barons Ct. HP18: Wadd 6C 52
Baronsmead Rd. HP12: H Wyc 2J 97
Barracks Hill HP7: Cole 5H 93
Barracks Rd. HP11: H Wyc 2A 98
Barrards Way HP9: S Grn 4A 102
Barratt Pl. HP13: H Wyc 2C 98
Barrett Pl. MK5: S Chur 1K 27
Barrie Cl. HP19: Ayle 4E 60
Barrington M. MK6: Old 5E 22
(off Shackleton Pl.)
Barrington Pk. Gdns. HP8: D Gil 6H 95
Barrow Lodge SL2: Slou 2A 124
Barr's Rd. SL6: Tapl 4D 122
Barrus Way HP14: Stoke 5D 72
Barry Av. MK13: B'lle 6C 16
SL4: Wind 5K 129
Barry Cl. HP12: Book 4G 97
Bartelotts Rd. SL2: Slou 2F 123
Bartholomew Cl. MK7: Walt P 2C 30
Bartholomew Tipping Way
HP14: Stoke 5D 72
Bartlett Pl. MK18: Buck 3J 37
Bartletts SL9: C Pet 5J 103
BARTON 3A 134
BARTON HARTSTHORN 3A 132
Barton Rd. MK2: Blet 2J 33
SL3: Lang 7K 125
Bartons Rd. HP10: T Grn 6G 91
Barton Way HP13: H Wyc 6E 90
Bascote MK6: T Bri 2K 29
Base Cl. HP20: Ayle 4B 62
Basford Way SL4: Wind 7F 129
Basildon Ct. MK8: G Hol 6K 21
Baskerfield Gro. MK6: W Grn. 6J 23
Basset Rd. HP14: L End 4A 96
Bassetsbury La. HP11: H Wyc 3D 98
Bassetsbury Manor 3D 98
Bassett Ct. MK16: New P 1J 17
Bassett Rd. UB8: Uxb 5J 121
Bassett Way SL2: Slou 2G 123
Batchelor Cl. HP20: Ayle 4A 62
Batchelors Way HP5: Ches 3K 77
HP7: Amer 6B 86
BATCHWORTH 1D 137
Bateman Cft. MK5: S Chur 1K 27
Bateman Dr. HP21: Ayle 1K 65
Bates Cl. MK15: Will 6K 17
SL3: G Grn 4J 125
Bates Ct. HP20: Ayle 4A 62
Bates Gdns. MK17: Dray P 6C 40
Bates La. HP22: West T 5G 67
Bath La. MK18: Buck 4G 37
Bath La. Ter. MK18: Buck 4G 37
Bath Rd. SL1: Slou 5F 123
SL3: Coln 5C 130
SL3: Coln, Poy 6E 130
SL6: Tapl 4A 122
UB7: Harm 6K 131
UB7: Long 6H 131
Bathurst Cl. SL0: R Pk 7F 127
Bathurst Wlk. SL0: R Pk 7E 126
Battersby M. HP21: Ayle 7H 61
Batt Furlong HP21: Ayle 4K 65
Batting Cl. HP14: Bled R 3C 72
Battingswood Gdns. HP14: Nap 6G 81
Battle Cl. MK46: Emb 7H 7
BATTLESDEN 1D 135
Baulk, The LU7: Ched 2B 50
LU7: I'hoe 4H 51
Bawtree Rd. UB8: Uxb 4K 121
Baxter Cl. MK8: C'ill 7J 21
Bayard Av. MK14: D Barn 1F 23
(not continuous)
Bayley Cres. SL1: Burn 3C 122
Bayley Gdns. HP14: Nap 1J 89
Bayley Hatch HP16: S Hea 5K 75
Baylis Bus. Cen. SL1: Slou 5B 124
Baylis Pde. SL1: Slou 4C 124
Baylis Rd. SL1: Slou 5B 124
Bayman Mnr. HP5: Ches 3C 78
BAYNARD'S GREEN 1A 134
Bayne Hill HP9: S Grn 5B 102
Bayne Hill Cl. HP9: S Grn 5B 102
Baynham Mead MK7: K Hil 6D 24
Bays Farm Ct. UB7: Long 6J 131
Bay Tree Cl. MK17: New L 4D 32
Bay Tree Ct. SL1: Burn 1E 122
Bay Treet Cl. HP11: W Mar 6H 99
BEACHAMPTON 3B 132
Beachampton Bus. Pk. MK19: B'ton 3A 26
Beacham Rd. HP12: Book 5G 97
BEACON 6K 29
Beacon Cen., The 7C 100
Beacon Cl. HP9: Bea 7C 100
HP17: Sto 2B 64
SL9: C Pet 5J 103
UB8: Uxb 3K 121
Beacon Ct. MK4: Fur 5D 28
SL3: Coln 5C 130
BEACON HILL 1K 99
Beacon Hill HP10: Pen 1K 99
Beacon La. SL7: Marl 2C 104
Beacon Retail Pk. MK1: F Str 5K 29
BEACON'S BOTTOM 1A 136
BEACONSFIELD 6G 101 (1C 137)
Beaconsfield Av. HP13: Down 6A 90
Beaconsfield Comn. La. HP9: Bea 5A 110
Beaconsfield Golf Course 5A 102
Beaconsfield Pl. MK16: New P 1J 17
Beaconsfield Rd. HP21: Ayle 7K 61
HP22: Ast C 2B 68
SL2: Farn C, Farn R 7A 118
Beaconsfield Squash Club
Beaconsfield 7G 101
Beaconsfield Station (Rail) 5G 101
Beadlemead MK6: Neth 1J 29
Beales La. MK7: Walt P 2C 30
Bealings End HP9: Bea 3F 101
Beamish Way MK18: Wins 5K 39
BEAMOND END 1B 92 (1C 137)
Beamond End La.
HP7: Bea E, L Miss 1B 92
Beanfare MK6: Bean 3H 29
(not continuous)
BEANHILL 2H 29
BEANSHANGER 3B 132
Bearbrook Cl. HP19: Ayle 7H 61
Bearswood End HP9: Bea 4G 101
Beauchamp Cl. MK14: N Hill 6E 16
Beaudesert M. UB7: W Dra 7K 127
Beaufort Cl. HP21: Ayle 7E 62
SL7: Marl 7J 105
Beaufort Dr. MK15: Will 6J 17
Beaufort Gdns. SL7: Marl 7J 105
Beaumaris Ct. SL2: Slou 3K 123
Beaumaris Gro. MK5: S Chur 1A 28
Beaumont Ri. SL7: Marl 7J 105
Beaumont Rd. SL2: Slou 2B 124
Beaumont Way HP15: Haz 3F 91
Beaverbrook Ct. MK3: Blet 6F 29
Beaver Cl. MK18: Buck 5J 37
Beckings Way HP10: F Hea 2J 107
Beckinsale Gro. MK8: C'ill 7J 21
BECKLEY 2A 134
Beckton Ri. MK10: Monk P 5A 24
Beckwell Rd. SL1: Slou 7A 124
Bec La. MK15: Bolb 6H 17
Bedder Rd. HP12: Book 5G 97
Beddoes Cft. MK5: Medb 3J 27
Bedfont Ct. TW19: S Moor 7G 131
BEDFORD 2D 133
Bedford Av. HP6: L Chal 6G 87
SL1: Slou 4H 123
Bedford Ct. HP6: L Chal 6H 87
Bedford Dr. SL2: Farn C 3K 117
Bedford Rd. MK16: Sher 3C 12
Bedford St. MK2: Blet 7J 29
MK12: Wolv 7H 15
Bedgebury Pl. MK7: K Hil 6C 24
BEDGROVE 2C 66
Bedgrove HP21: Ayle 1D 66
Bedlam La. MK16: Chic 3E 12
Bedlam Wlk. MK16: Chic 3E 12
BEDMOND 1D 137
Bedwyn Wlk. HP21: Ayle 3H 65
Beechams, The MK17: Mur 2C 40
Beech Av. HP14: L End 3A 96
MK46: Oln 4G 7
Beech Cl. HP10: F Hea 6G 99
HP11: W Mar 4F 99
HP14: Stoke 7D 72
HP22: Bier 3C 62
MK18: Buck 2H 37
Beech Ct. HP6: Amer 4A 86
(off Chesham Rd.)
Beechcroft Rd. HP5: Ches 4J 77
MK3: Blet 2E 32
Beeches, The HP22: Wend 3J 69
MK1: F Str 6K 29
Beeches Dr. SL2: Farn C 3K 117
Beeches Gro. HP10: T Grn 5G 91
Beeches Pk. HP9: Bea 6F 101
Beeches Rd. SL2: Farn C 3K 117
Beechfern MK7: Waln 2C 30
Beechfield Way HP15: Haz 4H 91
(Lowfield Way)
HP15: Haz 4G 91
(Rose Av.)
Beech Grn. HP21: Ayle 1J 65
Beech Gro. HP7: Amer 6B 86
Beechgrove Gdns. SL7: Marl 1F 115
Beechingstoke SL7: Marl 6K 105
Beechlands HP15: Haz 5E 90
Beech La. HP9: Jord 5C 102
HP16: Pres 6B 74
Beech Leys MK18: S Clay 2C 42
Beech Pk. HP6: L Chal 5F 87
HP14: Walt A 5E 80
Beech Rd. HP11: W Mar 4F 99
HP27: Prin R 5H 71
MK16: New P 2H 17
SL3: Lang 7J 125
Beech St. HP11: H Wyc 4C 98
Beechtree Av. SL7: Marl 4H 105
Beech Tree Cl. MK19: H'ham 3H 15
Beech Tree Ct. HP22: W'urch 2G 45
Beech Tree Rd. HP15: H Grn 7H 83
Beech Waye SL9: G Cro 5K 111
Beechwood Av. HP6: L Chal 5G 87
Beechwood Cl. HP6: L Chal 6G 87
Beechwood Dr. SL7: Marl 2F 115
Beechwood Gdns. SL1: Slou 7C 124
Beechwood Ho. HP22: Ast C 2C 68
(off Beechwood Way)
Beechwood La. HP22: Halt, Wend 3K 69
Beechwood Nurseries SL7: Marl 2F 115
Beechwood Pl. HP13: H Wyc 1B 98
Beechwood Rd. HP9: Bea 6E 100
HP12: H Wyc 5F 89
SL2: Slou 3B 124
Beechwood Way HP22: Ast C 2C 68
Beel Cl. HP7: L Chal 6G 87
Beethoven Cl. MK7: Old P 3G 31
Beeward Cl. MK12: Gree 1E 20
Bekonscot Ct. MK14: G Par 4F 17
Bekonscot Model Village
Beaconsfield 5F 101
Belfast Av. SL1: Slou 4A 124
Belgrave M. UB8: Cowl 2K 127
Belgrave Pde. SL1: Slou 5C 124
(off Bradley Rd.)
Belgrave Pl. SL1: Slou 7E 124
Belgrave Rd. HP19: Ayle 3E 60
SL1: Slou 5C 124
Bell Bus. Pk. HP19: Ayle 5E 60
Bell Cl. HP9: Bea 6H 101
HP27: Prin R 5G 71
LU7: Cubl 2G 47
MK17: Dray P 7B 40
SL2: Slou 3F 125
Bell Ct. SL6: Hur 7D 114
Bell Cres. HP27: Long 2D 70
Belle Vue HP17: Sto 2B 64
(not continuous)
Bellfield Rd. HP13: H Wyc 7A 90
Bellfield Rd. W. HP13: H Wyc 1K 97
Bellfield Way HP13: H Wyc 1A 98
Bellfounder Ho. MK13: B'ell 2B 22
BELLINGDON 3D 135
Bellingdon Rd. HP5: Ches 5K 77
Bellini Cl. MK7: Old P 2F 31
Bellis Gro. MK6: W Grn. 6J 23
Bell La. HP6: L Chal 6F 87
HP7: L Chal 6F 87
HP27: Prin R 5G 71
SL4: E Wick 2H 129
Bell Leys HP22: W'rave 6C 48
Bell Pde. SL4: Wind 7H 129
Bellsfield Ct. SL4: E Wick 2H 129
(off Bell La.)
Bells Hill SL2: S Pog 6E 118
Bells Hill Grn. SL2: S Pog 5E 118
Bells La. SL3: Hor 7B 130
Bells Mdw. MK15: W Par 6H 17
Bell St. HP27: Prin R 5G 71
Bellswood La. SL0: Ive 3B 126
Bell Vw. SL4: Wind 7H 129
Bell Vw. Cl. SL4: Wind 7H 129
Bell Vue Pl. SL1: Slou 7D 124
Bell Wlk. HP22: W'rave 6C 48
MK18: Wins 6H 39
Bellway MK17: W San 1H 31
Bellwether MK11: F Sla 2E 20
Bellwood Ri. HP11: H Wyc 4B 98
Belmont SL2: Slou 3J 123
Belmont Cl. UB8: Uxb 4K 121
Belmont Cotts. SL3: Coln 5C 130
(off High St.)
Belmont Ct. MK8: T Ash 4G 21
Belmont Rd. HP5: Ches 2K 77
UB8: Uxb 5K 121
BELSIZE 3D 135
Belsize Av. MK6: Sprin 5H 23
BELVEDERE
2F 23
Belvedere Cl. HP6: Amer 4D 86
Belvedere La. MK17: Bow B 6B 30
Belvedere Mans. SL1: Slou 7B 124
Belvoir Av. MK4: E Val 6C 28
Bembridge Ct. SL1: Slou 7D 124
Benacre Cft. MK4: Tatt 7A 28
Benbow Ct. MK5: S Chur 7A 22
Benbow Moorings UB8: Cowl 3J 127
Benbow Waye UB8: Cowl 3J 127
Bench Mnr. Cres. SL9: C Pet 7G 103
Bencombe Rd. SL7: Marl 4J 105
Benham Cl. HP5: Ches 4K 77
Benison Ct. SL1: Slou 7D 124
(off Hencroft St. Sth.)
Benjamin Ho. HP13: H Wyc 1B 98
(off Malmers Well Rd.)
Benjamin Rd. HP13: H Wyc 7B 90
Benjamins Footpath HP13: H Wyc 7B 90
Ben More SL9: G Cro 3K 111
Bennet Cl. MK11: S Strat 2B 20
Bennett End Rd. HP14: Rad 4A 72
Bennetts HP5: Ches 4B 78
Bennetts Cl. MK18: Pad 6A 38
SL1: Slou 6J 123
Bennett's Yd. UB8: Uxb 5J 121
Bens Cl. MK19: Cast 7D 8
Bensheim Way HP6: Amer 5B 86
Benson Cl. SL2: Slou 6E 124
Bentall Cl. MK15: Will 6J 17
Bentinck Cl. SL9: G Cro 3H 111
Bentinck Rd. UB7: Yiew 6K 127
Bentley Pk. SL1: Burn 7F 117
Bentley Rd. SL1: Slou 6J 123
Benwell Cl. MK13: Ban 1K 21
Berber Bus. Cen. HP11: H Wyc 1J 97
Berberis Cl. MK7: Waln 2C 30
Berberis Wlk. UB7: W Dra 2K 131
Bercham MK8: T Ash 4J 21
Beresford Av. HP19: Ayle 3H 61
SL2: Slou 5G 125
Beresford Cl. MK4: E Val 4B 28
Beretun MK8: T Ash 5J 21
Bereville Ct. MK10: Midd 3A 24
Berevilles La. MK10: Midd 3A 24
Bergamot Gdns. MK7: Waln 2D 30
BERGHERS HILL 5C 108
Berington Gro. MK4: West 5J 27
BERINSFIELD 3A 134
Berkeley Av. HP5: Ches 3H 77
Berkeley Cl. HP5: Ches 4J 77
LU7: Pits 7F 51
MK16: S Gold 6C 6
Berkeley M. SL1: Slou 4F 123
Berkeley Ri. HP19: Ayle 4G 61
Berkeley Rd. HP10: Loud 6J 99
Berkhampstead Rd. HP5: Ches 4A 78
BERKHAMSTED 3D 135
Berkley M. SL7: Marl 7K 105
Berkley Rd. HP9: Bea 2F 101
Berkshire Av. SL1: Slou 4K 123
Berkshire Grn. MK5: S Broo 4K 27
Berling Rd. MK8: Wym 4K 21
Bernard Cl. HP18: Cudd 2B 58
Bernardines Way MK18: Buck 5H 37
Bernards Cl. HP16: G Mis 6G 75
HP18: Che 2H 57
Bernards Way HP10: F Hea 7G 99
Bernay Gdns. MK15: Bolb 6H 17
(not continuous)
Berndene Ri. HP27: Prin R 4G 71
Berners Cl. SL1: Slou 5G 123
Bernewode Cl. HP18: Long C 5C 56
Bernstein Cl. MK7: Brow 3E 30
Berrell's Ct. MK46: Oln 4H 7
Berryfield LU7: Ched 2B 50
SL2: Slou 4G 125
Berry Fld. Pk. HP6: Amer 4K 85
Berryfield Rd. HP19: Ayle 3G 61
HP27: Prin R 4H 71
Berry Hill SL6: Tapl 4A 122
Berrystead MK7: Cald 4D 30
Berry Way MK17: New L 4C 32
Bertram Cl. MK13: New B 5B 16
Berwald Cl. MK7: Brow 3F 31
Berwick Av. SL1: Slou 5K 123
Berwick Cl. HP9: Bea 7K 101
SL7: Marl 6H 105
Berwick Dr. MK3: Blet 5F 29
Berwick La. SL7: Marl 6H 105
Berwick Rd. SL7: Marl 6G 105
Bessemer Ct. MK14: Blak 4G 17
Bessemer Cres. HP19: Ayle 5D 60
Bestobell Rd. SL1: Slou 4A 124
Betjeman Ct. UB7: Yiew 6K 127
Bettina Gro. MK2: Blet 1J 33
Bettles Cl. UB8: Uxb 7J 121
Betty's Cl. MK17: New L 5C 32
Bevan Ct. MK18: Wins 6H 39
Bevan Hill HP5: Ches 3K 77
Bevelwood Gdns. HP12: H Wyc 1H 97
Beverley Cl. SL7: Marl 7G 105
Beverley Ct. SL1: Slou 7F 125
Beverley Pl. MK6: Sprin 4H 23
Bewcastle Row MK4: K'ead 7J 27
Bewdley Gro. MK10: Bro 2C 24
Bexley St. SL4: Wind 6K 129
BICESTER 1A 134
Bicester Rd. HP18: Long C 5B 56
HP18: Ludg 1C 52
HP18: Oak 4H 53
HP19: Ayle 3E 60
OX27: M Gib 5A 42
Bickleigh Cres. MK4: Fur 4C 28
BIDDENHAM 2D 133
Biddles Cl. SL1: Slou 6G 123
BIDDLESDEN 2A 132
Bideford Spur SL2: Slou 1K 123
BIERTON 3C 62 (2C 135)
Bierton Rd. HP20: Ayle 5K 61
Bierton Sports Cen. 3D 62
Bigfrith La. SL6: Cook 4K 115
Biggs La. HP17: Dint 2G 59
Bignell Cft. MK5: Lough 5B 22
Biko Cl. UB8: Cowl 4J 127
Bilbrook La. MK4: Fur 3C 28
Billet La. SL0: I Hea 1B 126
SL3: Lang 5B 126
Billings Cl. HP14: Stoke 5D 72
BILLINGTON 1D 135
Billingwell Pl. MK6: Sprin 4H 23
Billwell HP18: Long C 6C 56
Bilsworth MK6: T Bri 2K 29
Bilton Cl. SL3: Poy 7E 130

Bilton Rd. MK1: F Str 6K 29
BINFIELD .3B 136
BINFIELD HEATH 3A 136
Bingham Cl. MK4: E Val 6C 28
Bingham Rd. SL1: Burn 3C 122
Birch Cl. HP6: Amer 4C 86
SL0: I Hea 7D 120
Birch Ct. HP21: Ayle 2J 65
Birchdale SL9: G Cro 6H 111
Birchen Lee MK4: E Val 5C 28
Birches, The HP9: Bea 5D 100
HP13: H Wyc 7E 90
Birches Ri. HP12: H Wyc 7J 89
Birchfield Gro. MK2: Blet 1J 33
Birch Gdns. HP7: Amer 6C 86
Birch Gro. SL2: Slou 3K 123
SL4: Wind 6F 129
Birchington Rd. SL4: Wind 7J 129
BIRCHMOOR GREEN 3D 133
Birch St. HP11: H Wyc 4B 98
Birch Tree Gro. HP5: L Hil 4F 79
Birch Way HP5: Ches 3B 78
Birchway HP10: T Grn 5H 91
Birchwood Chase HP15: G Kin 5D 82
Birchwood Cl. HP12: Book 2F 97
Birdcage Wlk. HP13: H Wyc 1B 98
Bird La. UB9: Hare 1J 113
Birdlip La. MK7: K Hil 7D 24
Birds La. MK16: S Gold 6C 6
Birfield Rd. HP10: Loud 6J 99
Birinus Cl. HP12: H Wyc 3G 97
Birkdale Cl. MK3: Blet 1D 32
Birkett Way HP8: D Gil 1H 95
Birley Rd. SL1: Slou 4B 124
BISHAM 3H 115 (2B 136)
Bisham Abbey Sports Cen. 4H 115
Bisham Ct. *SL1: Slou* *7D 124*
(off Park St.)
SL7: Marl 4J 115
Bisham Rd. SL7: Marl 2J 115
Bishops Farm Cl. SL4: Oak G 7D 128
Bishops Fld. HP22: Ast C 3D 68
Bishops Mdw. HP22: Bier 3B 62
Bishops Orchard SL2: Farn R 1K 123
Bishops Rd. SL1: Slou 7E 124
BISHOPSTONE 6F 65 (2C 135)
Bishopstone HP17: Bish 5F 65
MK13: B'lle 1B 22
Bishopstone Rd. HP17: Sto 2B 64
Bishops Wlk. HP10: Woob G 4A 108
HP21: Ayle 1A 66
MK17: A H'th 4K 31
Bittenham Cl. HP17: Sto 3D 64
Bittern Way HP19: Ayle 3K 61
BIX 2A 136
Black Acre Cl. HP7: Amer 6C 86
Blackberry Ct. MK7: Waln 1D 30
Blackbird M. HP10: Loud 6J 99
Black Boy La. SL6: Hur 7A 114
Blackdown MK11: F Sla 2D 20
Blackfield La. HP16: Ball 2A 76
Blackham Ct. MK6: Old 7E 22
Blackheath Cres. MK13: B Com 3D 22
Blackhill Dr. MK12: W Mil 7E 14
Black Horse Av. HP5: Ches 7B 78
Black Horse Cl. HP6: Amer 5C 86
SL4: Wind 7F 129
Black Horse Cres. HP6: Amer 5C 86
Blackhorse Pl. UB8: Uxb 6H 121
Black Horse Yd. UB8: Uxb 6H 121
Blackmoor Ga. MK4: Fur 5D 28
Blackmore Ga. HP22: B'land 3D 68
Blackmore Way UB8: Uxb 4K 121
Black Pk. Country Pk. 6A 120
Black Pk. Rd. SL3: Fulm, Wex 7J 119
Blackpond La. SL2: Farn C, Farn R . . .4K 117
Blacks, The HP5: Ches 5A 78
Blacksmith La. HP16: Pres 7C 74
Blacksmith Row SL3: Lang 2A 130
Blacksmiths La. UB9: Den 7C 112
Blacksmiths Rd. HP27: Long 1C 70
BLACKTHORN 2A 134
Blackthorne Cres. SL3: Poy 7E 130
Blackthorne Dell SL3: Lang 7G 125
Blackthorne Ind. Est. SL3: Poy 7E 130
Blackthorne La. HP16: Ball 2A 76
Blackthorne Rd. OX27: M Gib 7A 42
SL3: Poy 7E 130
Blackthorn Gro. MK17: W San 3J 31
Blackwater Dr. HP21: Ayle 3H 65
Blackwell Hall La.
HP5: Ches, Lati, L Hil 5G 79
Blackwell Pl. MK5: S Broo 3A 28
Blackwell Rd. HP14: L End 3K 73
Blackwood Cres. MK13: Blue B 7J 15
Blairmont St. MK9: Camp 2F 23
Blair Rd. SL1: Slou 6C 124
BLAKELANDS 3G 17
BLAKELANDS 5H 17
Blakeney Ct. MK4: Tatt 7B 28
Blakes Ho. HP10: Loud 6J 99
BLAKESLEY 1A 132
Blanchland Circ. MK10: Monk 5C 24
Blandford Cl. SL3: Lang 7H 125
Blandford Rd. MK13: B'lle 6B 16
Blandford Rd. Nth. SL3: Lang 7H 125
Blandford Rd. Sth. SL3: Lang 7H 125
Blansby Chase MK4: E Val 4C 28
Blatherwick Ct. MK5: S Chur 7K 21
Blaydon Cl. MK3: Blet 2D 32
BLEAK HALL 2F 29
BLEAK HALL 2G 29
Bleasdale MK13: Hee 1C 22
BLEDLOW 7B 70 (3B 134)
BLEDLOW RIDGE 3C 72 (1A 136)
Bledlow Ridge Rd. HP27: Bled 7B 70
Bledlow Rd. HP27: Saun 7D 70
BLENHEIM 3A 134
Blenheim Av. MK11: S Strat 2C 20
Blenheim Cl. HP27: Long 1C 70
LU7: Ched .1B 50
SL3: Lang 6K 125
Blenheim Pl. HP21: Ayle 2K 65
Blenheim Rd. HP12: H Wyc 4H 97
BLETCHAM .4A 30
Bletcham Way (H10) MK1: Mil K 5H 29
MK7: Mil K 4B 30
BLETCHLEY 5F 29 (3C 133)
Bletchley Leisure Cen. 6J 29
BLETCHLEY PARK 7G 29
Bletchley Pk. Mus. 7G 29
Bletchley Rd. LU7: Stew . . . . . .1A 46 & 7E 40
MK5: S Broo 3B 28
MK17: New L 4D 32
Bletchley Station (Rail) 7H 29
BLETSOE .1D 133
Blinco La. SL3: G Grn 4J 125
Blind La. HP5: Ches 5C 76
HP10: F Hea 3H 107
HP16: H Hea 5C 76
SL8: Bou E 5G 107
Blind Pond Ind. Est. MK17: Bow B 5F 31
Bliss Ct. MK7: Brow 3E 30
BLISWORTH 1B 132
Blondell Cl. UB7: Harm 4K 131
Blucher St. HP5: Ches 5K 77
Bluebell Cft. MK7: Waln 1D 30
BLUE BRIDGE 7J 15
Blumfield Ct. SL1: Slou 2F 123
Blumfield Cres. SL1: Slou 2F 123
Blundells Rd. MK13: B'lle 7B 16
Blunden Dr. SL3: Lang 2C 130
Blyth Cl. HP21: Ayle 2J 65
Blyth Ct. MK4: Tatt 7A 28
Blythe Cl. MK16: New P 1K 17
SL0: Ive .4F 127
Blythe Ho. SL1: Slou 6F 123
Blyton Cl. HP9: Bea 4F 101
Boadicea Cl. SL1: Slou 6G 123
Boarlands Cl. SL1: Slou 5H 123
Boarlands Path SL1: Slou 5H 123
BOARSTALL 2A 134
Bobmore La. SL7: Marl 5J 105
BOCKMER END 1A 114
Bockmer La. SL7: Medm 2A 114
Boddington Rd. HP22: Wend 4J 69
Bodenham Cl. MK18: Buck 4K 37
Bodiam Cl. HP21: Ayle 2C 66
MK5: S Chur 2A 28
Bodiam Ho. HP13: H Wyc 1F 99
Bodle Cl. MK15: Penny 6G 17
Bodley Ho. SL0: I Hea 7D 120
Bodmin Av. SL2: Slou 3J 123
Bodnant Ct. MK4: West 5K 27
Bois Av. HP6: Amer 3K 85
Bois Hill HP5: Ches 1C 86
Bois La. HP6: Amer 3B 86
Bois Moor Rd. HP5: Ches 7A 78
Bolan Ct. MK8: C'ill 1J 27
BOLBECK PARK 6H 17
Bold's Ct. SL2: S Pog 5E 118
BOLTER END 3H 73
Bolter End La. HP14: Bolt E 3H 73
Bolton Cl. MK3: Blet 5G 29
Boltwood Gro. MK5: Medb 2J 27
Bond Av. MK1: Blet 4K 29
(not continuous)
Bond Cl. HP21: Ayle 1H 65
Bone Hill MK18: Buck 5G 37
Bonham Carter Rd. HP22: Halt 1K 69
Bonham Cl. HP21: Ayle 1G 65
Bonnards Rd. MK17: New L 4D 32
Bonnersfield HP18: Long C 5C 56
Bonsey's Yd. UB8: Uxb 5K 121
BOOKER 3G 97 (1B 136)
Booker Av. MK13: B Com 3C 22
Bookerhill Rd. HP12: Book 3G 97
Booker La. HP12: H Wyc 1H 97
Booker Pl. HP12: Book 5F 97
Booth Pl. LU6: E Bra 1J 49
BOOTHVILLE 1B 132
Boot La. HP17: Dint 2G 59
Borderside SL2: Slou 4E 124
Borodin Ct. MK7: Old P 2F 31
(not continuous)
Boroughbridge MK5: O'ill 2H 27
Borough Wlk. *MK9: C Key* *3E 22*
(off Silbury Boulevd.)
Bosanquet Cl. UB8: Cowl 2K 127
Bossiney Pl. MK6: Fish 5F 23
Boss La. HP14: H Vall 1B 90
HP15: G Kin 1B 90
Bostock Ct. MK18: Buck 4G 37
Boston Dr. SL8: Bou E 6H 107
Boston Gro. SL1: Slou 4A 124
Boswell Ct. MK18: Buck 2J 37
Bosworth Cl. MK3: Blet 5E 28
Bosworth Ct. SL1: Slou 5E 122
Botham Dr. SL1: Slou 7C 124
BOTLEY 4E 78 (3D 135)
Botley Ho. *HP5: Ches* *5A 78*
(off East St.)
Botley La. HP5: Ches 4E 78
Botley Rd. HP5: Ches, L Hil 4C 78
BOTOLPH CLAYDON 1B 134
Botrells Cl. HP8: D Gil 7E 94
Botrells La. HP7: Cole, D Gil 6K 93
Bottesford Cl. MK4: E Val 6D 28
Bottom Alley HP15: H Grn 1J 91
Bottom Ho. Farm La. HP8: D Gil 6B 94
Bottom La. HP5: Ches 5D 78
HP9: S Grn 4K 101
Bottom Orchard HP18: Che 3J 57
Bottom Rd. HP14: Rad . . . . . . .3A 88 & 4A 72
Bottom Waltons Cvn. Site
SL2: Farn R 7G 117
Bottrells La. HP8: D Gil 7D 94
Boughton Way HP6: L Chal 5G 87
Boulevard, The MK9: C Key 4E 22
Boulmer Rd. UB8: Cowl 1J 127
Boulters Cl. SL1: Slou 6J 123
Boulters Ct. *HP6: Amer* *5D 86*
(off Plantation Rd.)
Boulters Lock MK14: G Par 3F 17
Boundary, The MK6: Old 6F 23
Boundary Cres. MK11: S Strat 7C 14
Boundary Pl. HP10: Woob G 1K 107
Boundary Rd.
HP10: Loud, Woob G 7J 99
SL6: Tapl 2A 122
SL9: C Pet 5H 103
Bounds Cft. MK12: Gree 2F 21
Bounty St. MK13: New B 6K 15
Bouquet Cl. HP16: Pres 1C 82
Bourbon St. HP20: Ayle 6J 61
Bourne, The HP3: Bov 1K 79
Bourne Cl. SL8: Bou E 4H 107
BOURNE END
Bourne End 6H 107 (2B 136)
Cranfield 2D 133
Hemel Hempstead 3D 135
Bourne End Bus. Pk. SL8: Bou E 6H 107
Bourne End Rd. SL6: Tapl 2A 116
Bourne End Station (Rail) 6G 107
Bourne Rd. SL1: Slou 7A 124
BOURTON .4K 37
Bourton Ho. *HP7: Amer* *6E 86*
(off Repton Pl.)
Bourton Low MK7: Waln 2D 30
Bourton Mill Health Club 5K 37
Bourton Rd. MK18: Buck 4H 37
Bourtonville MK18: Buck 5H 37
Bouverie Sq. MK9: C Key 5D 22
BOVENEY 4F 129 (3C 137)
Boveney Cl. SL1: Slou 7J 123
Boveney New Rd. SL4: E Wick 2G 129
Boveney Rd. SL4: Dorn 2E 128
Boveney Wood La. SL1: Burn 1F 117
BOVINGDON 3D 135
Bovingdon Ct. HP3: Bov 2K 79
BOVINGDON GREEN
Hemel Hempstead 3K 79
Marlow 6E 104 (2B 136)
Bovingdon Grn. La. HP3: Bov 2K 79
Bovingdon Hgts. SL7: Marl 7F 105
BOW BRICKHILL 5F 31 (3D 133)
Bow Brickhill Rd. MK17: Bow B 4G 31
Bow Brickhill Station (Rail) 5D 30
Bowden La. HP11: H Wyc 3D 98
Bowen Cl. MK7: Brow 3E 30
Bowerbank Ct. HP20: Ayle 5K 61
Bower Cl. LU6: E Bra 1K 49
Bower Ct. SL1: Slou 5H 123
Bowerdean Rd. HP13: H Wyc 2D 98
Bower La. LU6: E Bra 1K 49
Bowers La. HP14: Rad 4A 72
Bower Way SL1: Slou 5G 123
Bowes Cl. MK16: New P 2J 17
BOWL, THE .2E 28
BOWL, THE .2D 28
Bowland Dr. MK4: E Val 6B 28
Bowler Lea HP13: Down 5H 89
Bowler Rd. HP21: Ayle 4K 65
Bowler's Orchard HP8: D Gil 1E 102
Bowles Pl. MK6: W Grn. 7K 23
Bowling All. HP22: Ovi 5D 44
Bowling Grn. HP14: Stoke 5B 72
Bowling Leys MK10: Midd 4C 24
Bowmans Cl. SL1: Burn 7D 116
Bowmont Dr. HP21: Ayle 4J 65
Bowood Ct. MK8: G Hol 5K 21
Bowood La. HP22: Wend 1F 75
Bowstridge La. HP8: D Gil 1G 103
Bowyer Cres. UB9: Den 4F 113
Bowyer Dr. SL1: Slou 6G 123
Bowyers M. MK14: N Hill 7F 17
Boxberry Gdns. MK7: Waln 1C 30
BOX END .2D 133
Boxer Rd. HP27: Long 2D 70
Boxgrove Ct. MK10: Monk 5B 24
Box Tree Cl. HP5: Ches 7B 78
Boyce Cres. MK7: Old P 2F 31
Boycott Av. MK6: Old 5E 22
Boyd Carpenter Ho. SL9: C Pet 3K 103
BOZEAT 1D 133
Bracken Cl. SL2: Farn C 2B 118
Brackenforde SL3: Lang 7G 125
Brackens, The HP11: H Wyc 3C 98
Bracken Way HP10: F Hea 2H 107
HP19: Ayle 7G 61
Brackenwood HP14: Nap 7G 81
BRACKLEY 3A 132
Brackley Dr. HP15: Haz 1G 91
BRACKLEY HATCH 2A 132
Brackley Rd. HP15: Haz 1G 91
MK18: Buck 3F 37
BRACKNELL 3B 136
Bradbourne Dr. MK7: Tilb 3E 30
Bradbury Cl. MK13: B'ell 3A 22
Bradbury Gdns. SL3: Fulm 2H 119
Bradcutts La. SL6: Cook 7D 106
BRADDEN .2A 132
Braddons Furlong HP18: Long C 6D 56
Braden Cl. HP21: Ayle 1B 66
BRADENHAM 7D 80 (1B 136)
Bradenham Beeches HP14: Walt A 6E 80
Bradenham La. SL7: Marl 5G 115
Bradenham Rd. HP14: Brad, W Wyc . . .1C 88
Bradenham Wlk. HP21: Ayle 3K 65
Bradenham Wood La.
HP14: Brad, Walt A 8C 80
Bradfield Av. MK18: Buck 2H 37
Bradford Rd. SL1: Slou 4J 123
Bradley Cl. HP18: Oak 5H 53
Bradley Gro. MK4: E Val 5B 28
Bradley Rd. SL1: Slou 5B 124
Bradshaw Cl. SL4: Wind 6G 129
Bradshaw Rd. HP13: H Wyc 2F 99
BRADVILLE .6A 16
BRADVILLE .7A 16
Bradvue Cres. MK13: B'lle 7A 16
BRADWELL 2A 22 (3C 133)
BRADWELL ABBEY 2K 21
BRADWELL COMMON 3C 22
Bradwell Comn. Blvd. MK13: B Com . . .4C 22
Bradwell Rd. MK5: Lough 7A 22
MK8: L Lodg 4A 22
MK13: B'lle, New B 6A 16
Bradwell Sports & Social Club 2K 21
Bradwell Windmill 6A 16
Brae Hill HP18: Bril 3H 53
Brae Hill Cl. HP18: Bril 3H 53
Braemar Gdns. SL1: Slou 7J 123
Braeside HP14: Nap 1H 89
BRAFIELD-ON-THE-GREEN 1C 133
Braford Gdns. MK5: S Broo 3B 28
Bragenham Side MK17: S Ham 2H 41
Brahms Cl. MK7: Old P 2E 30
Braid, The HP5: Ches 4C 78
Braid Gdns. SL9: C Pet 3H 111
Bramber Cl. MK3: Blet 1E 32
Bramber Ct. SL1: Slou 6J 123
Bramble Av. MK14: Conn 2E 22
Bramble Cl. SL9: C Pet 4J 103
Bramble Cres. HP15: H Grn 1J 91
Bramble La. HP7: Amer 1C 94
Bramble Mead HP8: D Gil 1E 102
Brambles, The UB7: W Dra 2K 131
Brambleside HP11: W Mar 4H 99
Brambling HP19: Ayle 3K 61
Bramcote Cl. HP20: Ayle 6D 62
Bramley End HP14: H Vall 5A 82
Bramley Grange MK2: Blet 4K 33
Bramley Mdws. MK16: New P 2H 17
Bramley Rd. MK1: Blet 4J 29
Brammas Cl. SL1: Slou 7A 124
Brampton Ct. MK13: B'lle 7A 16
Brampton M. SL7: Marl 1H 115
Branch Rd. HP10: Loud 6H 99
Brandon Rd. HP12: Book 5F 97
BRANDS HILL
. . . . .4B 130
Brands Hill Av. HP13: H Wyc 5C 90
Brands Rd. SL3: Lang 4B 130
Bransgill Ct. MK13: Hee 2B 22
Bransworth Av. MK10: Brin 6E 24
Brantham Cl. MK7: Cald 4C 30
Braunston MK6: Wough 1K 29
BRAY 3C 137
Braybourne Cl. UB8: Uxb 4J 121
Braybrooke Dr. MK4: Fur 4E 28
Bray Ct. *HP6: Amer* *5D 86*
(off Plantation Rd.)
Brays Cl. HP6: H Hea 2D 84
Brays Grn. La. HP6: H Hea 2E 84
Brays La. HP6: H Hea 2E 84
Brays Mdw. HP6: H Hea 2E 84
Brayton Ct. MK5: S Lod 1C 28
BRAY WICK 3B 136
Braywood Cotts. SL4: Oak G 7C 128
Breachwell Pl. LU7: Ched 1C 50
Breakspear M. UB9: Hare 1K 113
Breakspear Path UB9: Hare 1K 113
Breakspear Rd. Nth. UB9: Hare 1K 113
Bream Cl. SL7: Marl 2G 115
Breamore Ct. MK8: G Hol 5K 21
Brearley Av. MK6: Old 7E 22
Brearley Cl. UB8: Uxb 4K 121

Breckland MK14: L Woo 1C 22
Brecon Ct. MK10: Monk 5B 24
SL1: Slou 7A 124
Brecon Way HP13: Down 6J 89
Bredward Cl. SL1: Burn 1D 122
Bremen Gro. MK5: S Broo 3A 28
Brenchwood Cl. HP13: Down 5G 89
Brendon Ct. MK4: Fur 5D 28
Brent MK6: T Bri 2K 29
Brent Path HP21: Ayle 3J 65
Brent Rd. SL8: Bou E 5G 107
Brentwood Way HP21: Ayle 1C 66
Bretby Chase MK4: West 4K 27
Breton MK11: S Strat 7C 14
Brewster Cl. MK5: Medb 2H 27
Briar Cl. SL6: Tapl 4D 122
Briar Hill MK12: S Bus 1H 21
Briars, The HP11: H Wyc 3C 98
HP15: H Grn 7J 83
Briars Cl. HP19: Ayle 4G 61
Briarswood HP15: Haz 4H 91
Briarswood Cl. HP14: Stoke 5C 72
Briar Way SL2: Slou 3K 123
Briary Vw. MK17: Whad 7G 27
Brices Mdw. MK5: S Broo 4A 28
Brick Cl. MK11: Kiln 4G 21
BRICKET WOOD 1D 137
Brickfield La. SL1: Burn 5C 116
Brickhill Mnr. Ct. MK17: L Bric 3F 35
Brickhill St. (V10) MK7: Mil K 6B 24
MK10: Mil K 3K 23
MK14: Mil K 3F 17
MK15: Mil K 1J 23
Brick Kiln La. HP22: Bier 2D 62
Brickstock HP22: A Abb 7J 47
Brickwell Wlk. HP15: Haz 4H 91
Bridens Way HP17: Hadd 6B 58
Bri. Bank Cl. HP11: W Mar 5G 99
Bridge Cl. SL1: Slou 5H 123
BRIDGE END 1D 133
Bridgeford Ct. MK6: Old 6E 22
Bridgegate Bus. Pk. HP19: Ayle 5G 61
Bridge Ho. UB7: W Dra 6K 127
Bridgeman Ct. SL4: Wind 7J 129
Bridgeman Dr. SL4: Wind 7J 129
Bridgemere Cl. MK4: West 6J 27
Bridge Pl. HP6: Amer 5D 86
Bridge Rd. HP18: Ick 6D 54
MK19: Cosg 3C 14
UB8: Uxb 7J 121
Bridgestone Dr. SL8: Bou E 6H 107
Bridge St. HP11: H Wyc 1A 98
MK13: New B 6K 15
MK18: Buck 4H 37
MK18: T'ough 3C 38
MK46: Emb, Oln 5H 7
SL3: Coln 5D 130
Bridgeturn Av. MK12: O Wol 5H 15
Bridgewater Ct. SL3: Lang 2A 130
Bridgeway HP18: Cudd 1K 57
MK13: New B 6A 16
Bridge Works UB8: Cowl 2J 127
Bridgnorth Dr. MK4: K'ead 6J 27
Bridle Cl. MK13: B'lle 7A 16
Bridle Ga. HP11: H Wyc 2K 97
Bridleway HP22: West T 5G 67
Bridleways HP22: Wend 3G 69
Bridlington Cres. MK10: Monk 5B 24
Bridlington Spur SL1: Slou 1K 129
Bridport Way SL2: Slou 2K 123
Briery Way HP6: Amer 4C 86
Brighton Spur SL2: Slou 2K 123
BRIGHTWELL BALDWIN 1A 136
BRILL 3H 53 (2A 134)
Brill Cl. SL7: Marl 7G 105
Brill Pl. MK13: B Com 3B 22
Brill Rd. HP18: Chil 1A 56
HP18: Ludg 3B 52
HP18: Oak 5J 53
Brill Windmill 2H 53
Brimmers Hill HP15: W End 1E 90
Brimmers Rd. HP27: Prin R 6H 71
Brimmers Way HP19: Ayle 5E 60
Brindlebrook MK8: T Ash 5J 21
Brindles La. HP9: Bea 4C 100
Brindley Av. HP13: Down 6K 89
Brinkburn Chase MK10: Monk 5C 24
BRINKLOW 6E 24
BRINKLOW 5D 24
Briskman Way HP21: Ayle 1G 65
Bristle Hill MK18: Buck 4G 37
Bristol Way SL1: Slou 6D 124
Bristow Cl. MK2: F Str 6A 30
Bristow Ct. SL7: Marl 6A 106
Britannia Ct. UB7: W Dra 1K 131
Britannia Ind. Est. SL3: Poy 7E 130
Britannia Ind. Pk. HP12: H Wyc 7J 89
Britannia Rd. HP5: Ches 3A 78
Britannia St. HP20: Ayle 6K 61
Britannia Wlk. HP20: Ayle 6K 61
Britnell Ct. HP14: Stoke 5C 72
Britten Gro. MK7: Old P 2F 31
BRITWELL 1J 123
Britwell Gdns. SL1: Burn 1F 123
Britwell Rd. SL1: Burn 1E 122
BRITWELL SALOME 1A 136
Broad Arrow Cl. MK14: N Hill 6E 16
Broad Dean MK6: Eagl 6G 23
Broadfields HP19: Ayle 5F 61
Broadfields Ct. HP19: Ayle 5F 61
Broadfields Retail Pk.
HP19: Ayle 4F 61
BROAD GREEN 2D 133
Broadlands MK6: Neth 1H 29
Broadlands Av. HP5: Ches 2A 78
Broad La. HP9: Bea 4C 108
HP10: Woob G 4C 108
Broad Leys HP27: Prin R 5F 71
Broadleys SL4: Wind 5H 129
Broadmark Rd. SL2: Slou 5F 125
Broad Oak SL2: Slou 2A 124
Broad Oak Ct. SL2: Slou 2A 124
Broadpiece MK15: Penny 6G 17
Broad St. HP5: Ches 4A 78
HP16: New P 2J 17
Broadview Rd. HP5: Ches 1K 77
Broadwater MK6: T Bri 1K 29
Broadwater Gdns. UB9: Hare 2J 113
Broadwater La. UB9: Hare 2H 113
Broadwater Pk. SL6: Bra 3A 128
UB9: Den 4G 113
Broadway HP7: Amer 7K 85
Broadway, The *HP5: Ches* *5K 77*
(off High St.)
HP9: Bea 5F 101
HP18: G Und 2G 43
SL2: Farn C 4A 118
SL9: C Pet *6H 103*
(off Market Pl.)
Broadway Av. MK14: G Par 3F 17
Broadway Cl. HP7: Amer 7K 85
Broadway Ct. *HP5: Ches* *5K 77*
(off High St.)
Broadway E. UB9: Den 4G 113
BROCKHALL 1A 132
Brockhampton MK15: D Park 7H 17
Brocks Crest Rd. HP5: Ches 3A 78
Brockway SL3: Lang 3B 130
Brockwell MK16: New P 2J 17
Broddick Ho. *HP11: W Mar* *4H 99*
(off Brambleside)
BROGBOROUGH 3D 133
Broken Furlong SL4: Eto 3K 129
Brokengate La. UB9: Den 6C 112
BROMHAM 1D 133
Bromham Mill MK14: G Par 3F 17
Bromley La. HP6: H Hea 1E 84
Brompton Cl. HP19: Ayle 4G 61
Brompton Cres. HP19: Ayle 4G 61
Bromycroft Rd. SL2: Slou 1J 123
Bronsdon Way UB9: Den 7F 113
Bronte Cl. HP19: Ayle 4E 60
Brookbank HP10: Woob G 6J 107
Brook Bus. Cen. UB8: Uxb 7H 121
Brook Cl. HP18: Ludg 2C 52
HP22: Ast C 2A 68
Brook Cres. SL1: Slou 4G 123
Brooke Cl. MK3: Blet 1F 33
Brooke Furmston Pl. SL7: Marl 6J 105
BROOK END
Aylesbury 4H 67
Leighton Buzzard 5G 51
Newport 7H 13
Brook End HP22: West T 4G 67
MK16: N Craw 7H 13
Brook End Sports Cen. 5A 28
Brooke Rd. HP27: Prin R 4G 71
Brookfield La. MK18: Buck 5H 37
Brookfield Rd. HP10: Woob G 6K 107
MK17: New L 5D 32
MK19: H'ham 3H 15
BROOK FURLONG 7C 18
Brook Ho. SL1: Slou 7B 124
Brookhouse Dr. HP10: Woob G 6J 107
Brooklands Rd. MK2: Blet 7J 29
Brooklyn Way UB7: W Dra 1K 131
Brook Path SL1: Slou 5H 123
(not continuous)
Brooks Ct. MK18: Buck 4H 37
Brookside HP18: Oak 5H 53
HP22: Halt 6K 67
HP22: West T 5H 67
MK12: H Lea 2H 21
SL3: Coln 5C 130
Brookside Ter. *HP20: Ayle* *6K 61*
(off High St.)
Brook St. HP11: H Wyc 1A 98
HP22: Ast C 2A 68
LU6: Edle 2K 49
Broombarn La. HP16: G Mis 6E 74
Broom Cl. HP15: Haz 4G 91
Broom Farm Est. SL4: Wind 7E 128
Broomfield MK12: S Bus 2H 21
Broomfield Cl. HP16: G Mis 6E 74
Broomfield Ga. SL2: Slou 2K 123
Broomfield Hill HP16: G Mis 6E 74
BROOMHALL 3C 137
Broom Hill SL2: S Pog 5E 118
Broom Ho. SL3: Lang 2A 130
Broomlee MK13: Ban 1A 22
Broomstick La. HP5: Ches 5D 78
Brora Cl. MK2: Blet 3J 33
Brotheridge Ct. HP21: Ayle 1G 65
Brough Cl. MK5: S Chur 2A 28
BROUGHTON
Aylesbury 6D 62
Milton Keynes 3D 24 (3C 133)
Broughton Av. HP20: Ayle 6C 62
Broughton Bus. Pk. HP6: L Chal 6F 87
Broughton Cl. HP22: Bier 3C 62
Broughton Crossing HP22: Bro 4D 62
Broughton Grounds La. MK16: Bro 2D 24
Broughton La. HP20: Ayle 6D 62
HP22: Bier 3D 62
HP22: Bro 5D 62
Broughton Mnr. Bus. Pk. MK16: Bro 2D 24
Broughton Rd. MK10: M Vill 3C 24
Brow, The HP8: D Gil 1H 103
Brownbaker Ct. MK14: N Hill 7F 17
Browne Willis Cl. MK2: Blet 7K 29
Browning Cl. MK16: New P 1G 17
Browning Cres. MK3: Blet 1G 33
Brownlow Av. LU6: Edle 3K 49
Brownlow La. LU7: Ched 2C 50
Browns Ct. SL1: Slou 5G 123
Browns Hedge LU7: Pits 6E 50
Browns Rd. HP15: H Grn 1H 91
HP16: H Hea 6C 76
BROWNS WOOD 3F 31
BROWNS WOOD 2E 30
Brownswood Rd. HP9: Bea 4F 101
Broxbourne Cl. MK14: G Par 3F 17
Bruce Cl. SL1: Slou 6J 123
Bruce Wlk. SL4: Wind 7F 129
Brucewood Pde. SL7: Marl 4J 105
Bruckner Gdns. MK7: Old P 2F 31
Brudenell Dr. HP22: Sto M 6C 66
MK10: Brin 6D 24
Brunel Cen. *MK2: Blet* *7J 29*
(off Albert St.)
MK2: Blet 1J 33
(Osborne St.)
Brunel Rd. HP13: Down 6K 89
HP19: Ayle 5E 60
Brunel University
Uxbridge Campus 1K 127
Brunel Way SL1: Slou 6D 124
Brunleys MK11: Kiln 3F 21
Brunswick Cl. HP19: Ayle 3F 61
Brunswick Ct. MK14: Blak 4H 17
Brushford Cl. MK4: Fur 4D 28
Brushmakers Ct. HP5: Ches 4A 78
Brushwood Rd. HP5: Ches 3C 78
Bryans Cres. MK16: N Craw 6J 13
Bryanston Av. HP20: Ayle 4A 62
Bryant Av. SL2: Slou 3B 124
Bryants Acre HP22: Wend 3H 69
BRYANT'S BOTTOM 2J 81 (1B 136)
Bryants Bottom Rd. HP16: G Ham 1J 81
Bryne La. MK18: Pad 5A 38
Bryony Pl. MK14: Conn 1E 22
Buchan Cl. UB8: Cowl 2J 127
Buckby MK6: T Bri 1K 29
Bucken Ho. MK46: Lave 2C 6
Buckfast Av. MK3: Blet 5F 29
(not continuous)
Buckfield Ct. SL0: R Pk 7F 127
BUCKINGHAM 3H 37 (3A 132)
Buckingham Av. SL1: Slou 4G 123
Buckingham Av. E. SL1: Slou 4A 124
Buckingham Cl. HP13: H Wyc 1G 99
Buckingham Ct. HP6: Amer 4C 86
HP11: W Mar 5H 99
MK16: New P 2H 17
Buckingham Dr. HP13: H Wyc 1F 99
Buckingham Gdns. SL1: Slou 7D 124
Buckingham Ga. MK6: Eagl 5H 23
SL7: Medm 3B 114
Buckingham Ind. Pk. MK18: Buck 6H 37
Buckingham Pde. *SL9: C Pet* *6J 103*
(off Market Pl.)
Buckingham Pl. HP13: H Wyc 1A 98
Buckingham Ring Rd. MK18: Buck 5F 37
Buckingham Rd. HP19: Ayle 5J 61
MK3: Blet 2B 32
MK18: Gaw 6D 36
MK18: S Clay 3C 42
MK18: Wins 5H 39
Buckingham School Sports Hall *5H 37*
(off London Rd.)
Buckinghamshire County Mus., The 6J 61
Buckinghamshire Goat Cen. &
Obsidian Art Gallery 7B 66
Buckinghamshire Railway Cen. 7G 43
Buckingham St. HP20: Ayle 5J 61
MK12: Wolv 6H 15
MK18: Ting 2C 36
Buckingham Way HP10: F Hea 6G 99
BUCKLAND 1C 68 (2C 135)
Buckland Av. SL3: Slou 7F 125
BUCKLAND COMMON 3D 135
Buckland Cres. SL4: Wind 6H 129
Buckland Dr. MK6: Neth 1H 29
Buckland Ga. SL3: Wex 1F 125
Buckland Rd. HP22: B'land 2D 68
Bucklandwharf HP22: B'land 3E 68
Buckley Ct. MK11: S Strat 2D 20
Buckman Cl. MK12: Gree 1F 21
Buckmaster Rd. HP12: Book 5G 97
BUCKNELL 1A 134
BUCKS HILL 3D 135
Buckthorn MK12: S Bus 1J 21
Buffins SL6: Tapl 1A 122
BUFFLER'S HOLT 3A 132
BUGBROOKE 1A 132
BULBOURNE 2D 135
Bulkeley Av. SL4: Wind 7K 129
Bullbaiters La. HP6: H Hea 1D 84
Bullfinch Gdns. HP19: Ayle 3A 62
BULLINGTON END 5G 9
Bullington End Rd. MK19: Cast, H'ope 6E 8
Bull La. HP11: H Wyc 1A 98
MK2: F Str 7K 29
SL9: C Pet, G Cro 2G 111
Bullocks Farm La. HP14: Whee 2K 73
Bullrush Gro. UB8: Cowl 2J 127
Bulls La. HP18: Ick 5E 54
Bulmer Cl. MK10: Bro 3D 24
Bulstrode Ct. SL9: G Cro 4H 111
Bulstrode Pl. SL1: Slou 7D 124
Bulstrode Way SL9: G Cro 3H 111
Bunby Rd. SL2: S Pog 5D 118
Bunce's Cl. SL4: E Wick 3K 129
Bungalows, The HP5: Char 1D 76
Bunn's La. HP5: Lati 1E 86
Bunsen Pl. MK5: S Lod 3C 28
Bunsty Ct. MK11: S Strat 2D 20
Bunten Meade SL1: Slou 6K 123
Burano Gro. MK7: W Gat 1E 30
Burchard Cres. MK5: S Chur 7A 22
BURCHETT'S GREEN 2B 136
BURCOTT
Aylesbury 3D 62
Leighton Buzzard 1B 48 (1C 135)
Burcott Cl. HP22: Bier 3C 62
Burcott La. HP22: Bier 2D 62
Burdeleys La. MK5: S Broo 3A 28
Burdett Dr. HP14: Walt A 6F 81
Burdock Ct. MK16: New P 1F 17
Burewelle MK8: T Ash 5H 21
Burford Cl. SL7: Marl 4G 105
Burford Gdns. SL1: Slou 3E 122
Burgess Gdns. MK16: New P 3H 17
Burgess La. HP17: Ford 5K 59
Burgess Wood Gro. HP9: Bea 6D 100
Burgess Wood Rd. HP9: Bea 6D 100
Burgess Wood Rd. Sth. HP9: Bea 1D 108
Burgett Rd. SL1: Slou 1K 129
BURGHFIELD 3A 136
BURGHFIELD COMMON 3A 136
BURGHFIELD HILL 3A 136
Burghley Ct. MK8: G Hol 6K 21
Burholme MK4: E Val 4C 28
Burke Rd. HP22: Wend 3J 69
Burkes Cl. HP9: Bea 1D 108
Burkes Ct. HP9: Bea 6F 101
Burkes Cres. HP9: Bea 6F 101
Burkes Pde. HP9: Bea 5F 101
Burkes Rd. HP9: Bea 1E 108
BURLEIGH 3C 137
Burleigh Ct. *MK18: Buck* *4K 37*
(off Burleigh Piece)
Burleigh Piece MK18: Buck 3J 37
Burleys Rd. MK18: Wins 6H 39
Burlington Av. SL1: Slou 7C 124
Burlington Ct. SL1: Slou 7C 124
Burlington Rd. SL1: Burn 2D 122
SL1: Slou 7C 124
Burma Cl. HP13: H Wyc 2E 98
Burners La. MK11: Kiln 3F 21
Burners La. Sth. MK11: Kiln 3F 21
Burness Cl. UB8: Uxb 7K 121
Burnet MK14: Stan 6C 16
Burnetts Ct. HP16: Pres 1C 82
Burnetts Rd. SL4: Wind 6G 129
BURNHAM 2E 122 (2C 137)
Burnham Av. HP9: Bea 1J 109
BURNHAM BEECHES 3K 117
Burnham Beeches National Nature Reserve
. . . . 4H 117
Burnham Cl. HP12: H Wyc 2H 97
SL4: Wind 7F 129
SL8: Bou E 5G 107
Burnham Dr. MK13: B Com 2C 22
Burnham Hgts. SL1: Slou 4E 122
Burnham La. SL1: Slou 3F 123
Burnham Rd. HP9: Bea 4G 109
HP14: H Vall 1A 90
Burnhams, The HP18: Shab 5H 55
HP22: Ast C 2K 67
Burnhams Rd. HP22: West T 1F 67
Burnham Station (Rail) 4F 123
Burnmoor Cl. MK2: Blet 4K 33
Burns Cl. HP18: Long C 5D 56
MK16: New P 1G 17
Burns Ct. HP21: Ayle 1A 66
Burns Rd. MK3: Blet 1G 33
Burn Wlk. SL1: Burn 1D 122
Burrell Cl. HP21: Ayle 1H 65
Burren, The *HP6: Amer* *4B 86*
(off Sycamore Rd.)
Burroughs Cres. SL8: Bou E 5G 107
BURROUGHS GROVE 2K 105
Burroway Rd. SL3: Lang 1B 130
Burrows Cl. HP10: T Grn 5J 91
MK17: W San 2K 31
Burrows Ho. HP13: Down 5J 89
Burton La. HP27: Mon R 3H 71

Burton's La. HP8: D Gil 7G 87
Burton's Way HP8: D Gil 7G 87
Burton Way SL4: Wind 7G 129
Burtree Cl. MK12: S Bus 1H 21
Burt's La. HP18: Long C 6D 56
BURY, THE 5J 77
Bury Av. MK16: New P 1J 17
Bury Cl. MK16: New P 1J 17
Bury Farm HP7: Amer 7A 86
Buryfield La. HP16: G Mis 6H 75
Bury La. HP5: Ches 5K 77
Bury St. MK16: New P 1J 17
Busby Cl. MK18: Buck 3K 37
Buscot Pl. MK8: G Hol 6K 21
Bush, The HP17: Hadd 7B 58
BUSHEY 1D 137
Bushey Bartrams MK5: S Broo 4A 28
Bushey Cl. HP12: H Wyc 1H 97
MK18: Buck 3K 37
BUSHEY HEATH 1D 137
Bushmead Cl. HP22: W'urch 3H 45
Bushmead Rd. HP22: W'urch 3H 45
Bushy Cl. MK3: Blet 4G 29
Business Village, The SL2: Slou 6F 125
Buslins La. HP5: Ches 2G 77
Butcher La. MK4: West 5K 27
MK5: West 5K 27
Bute Brae MK3: Blet 5E 28
Butler Ct. SL7: Marl 6K 105
Butlers Cl. HP6: Amer 4J 85
SL4: Wind 6F 129
Butlers Ct. HP13: H Wyc 3F 99
Butlers Ct. Rd. HP9: Bea 7F 101
BUTLERS CROSS 2D 102
Butlers Gro. MK14: G Lin 5D 16
Butler Wlk. HP19: Ayle 7F 61
Butterfield HP10: Woob G 5K 107
Butterfield Cl. MK15: Wool 4J 23
Butterly Rd. HP14: Stoke 6D 72
Buttermere HP21: Ayle 7C 62
Buttermere Av. SL1: Slou 3E 122
Buttermere Cl. MK2: Blet 2K 33
Buttfurlong HP17: Hadd 5C 58
Button Gro. MK6: Coff 7G 23
Buzzacott La. MK4: Fur 4C 28
Bybend Cl. SL2: Farn R 6K 117
BYE GREEN 4H 67
Bye Grn. HP22: West T 4H 67
Byerley Ho. MK14: D Barn 1F 23
Byerly Pl. MK14: D Barn 1F 23
Byford Way MK18: Wins 6H 39
Byrd Cres. MK7: W Gat 1F 31
Byres, The HP17: Hadd 6B 58
Byron SL3: Lang 3B 130
Byron Cl. MK3: Blet 1F 33
SL7: Marl 6K 105
Byron Dr. MK16: New P 1G 17
Byron Rd. HP21: Ayle 1A 66
Byward Cl. MK14: N Hill 6E 16
Byways SL1: Burn 3C 122
Bywell Ct. MK4: K'ead 7J 27
By-Wood End SL9: C Pet 3K 103

C

Cadeby Ct. MK10: Bro 3D 24
Cadman Sq. MK5: S Lod 2C 28
CADMORE END 2F 73 (1A 136)
Cadsden Rd. HP27: Whit 1J 71
Caernarvon Cres. MK3: Blet 1D 32
Caesars Cl. MK13: Ban 1A 22
Cages Wood Dr. SL2: Farn C 2K 117
Cairngorm Ga. MK6: Wint 7D 22
Cairngorm Pl. SL2: Slou 2B 124
Cairnside HP13: H Wyc 2E 98
Caister Ct. MK4: K'ead 7J 27
Caithness Ct. MK3: Blet 4E 28
Calamus Ct. MK7: Waln 1D 30
Calbroke Rd. SL2: Slou 2H 123
CALCOT ROW 3A 136
CALDECOTE 4K 17
CALDECOTE 4B 30
Caldecote La. MK16: New P 3A 18
Caldecote St. MK16: New P 1J 17
CALDECOTTE 4C 30
Caldecotte Lake Dr. MK7: Cald 5C 30
Caldecotte La. MK7: Cald 4C 30
Calder Va. MK3: Blet 6E 28
CALDESCOTE 1A 132
Caldewell MK8: T Ash 5H 21
Caldicot Cl. HP21: Ayle 1C 66
Caledon Cl. HP9: Bea 5G 101
Caledonian Rd. MK13: New B 6J 15
Caledon Rd. HP9: Bea 5G 101
Calewen MK8: T Ash 5J 21
CALIFORNIA 7J 61
California Circ. HP11: H Wyc 4B 98
Callingham Pl. HP9: Bea 5G 101
Calluna Dr. MK3: Blet 4G 29
Calumet HP9: Bea 5F 101
Calvards Cft. MK12: Gree 2G 21
Calverleigh Cres. MK4: Fur 4D 28
Calverley Cres. HP13: Down 5K 89
CALVERT 1A 134
CALVERTON 3B 20 (3B 132)
CALVERTON END 2C 20
CALVERTON LANE 4F 21
Calverton La. MK19: Calv 6E 20
Calverton Rd. MK11: S Strat 1B 20
Calves Cl. MK5: S Broo 4A 28
Camber Cl. MK3: Blet 1E 32
Cambourne Av. HP21: Ayle 2B 66
Cambria Ct. SL3: Lang 7G 125
Cambridge Av. SL1: Burn 7D 116
SL1: Slou 4J 123
Cambridge Cl. HP20: Ayle 5K 61
UB7: Harm 4K 131
Cambridge Cl. Trad. Est.
HP20: Ayle 5K 61
Cambridge Cres. HP13: H Wyc 1E 98
Cambridge Pl. HP20: Ayle 6J 61
Cambridge Rd. HP9: Bea 6E 100
SL7: Marl 7H 105
UB8: Uxb 4K 121
Cambridge St. HP20: Ayle 6J 61
MK2: Blet 7J 29
MK12: Wolv 6G 15
Cambron MK8: T Ash 4H 21
Cam Ct. MK3: Blet 7E 28
Camden Pl. SL8: Bou E 6G 107
Cameron Ct. HP5: Ches 4A 78
(off Cameron Rd.)
Cameron Rd. HP5: Ches 4A 78
(not continuous)
Camlet Gro. MK14: Stan 6D 16
Camm Av. SL4: Wind 7G 129
Cam Mead HP21: Ayle 1C 66
Camomile Ct. MK7: Waln 2D 30
Campania Cl. MK10: Midd 4C 24
Campbell Cl. HP13: Down 7K 89
MK18: Buck 4K 37
Campbell Dr. HP9: Bea 3E 100
CAMPBELL PARK 3G 23
CAMPBELL PARK 3F 23
Campbells Ride HP15: H Grn 7K 83
Camperdown Ho. SL4: Wind 7K 129
Campion MK14: G Lin 3E 16
Campion Cl. HP20: Ayle 6D 62
UB9: Den 1G 121
Campion Rd. HP15: W End 1F 91
Camp Rd. SL9: G Cro 4G 111
Canada Rd. SL1: Slou 7F 125
Canal Ind. Est. SL3: Lang 7A 126
CANALSIDE 2H 23
Canal Side HP21: Ayle 6K 61
(off Highbridge Rd.)
Canalside MK19: O Stra 6A 14
Canal Wharf SL3: Lang 7A 126
Candlemas La. HP9: Bea 6G 101
Candlemas Mead HP9: Bea 6G 101
Candlemas Oaks HP9: Bea 6G 101
Candlewicks MK7: Waln 1D 30
Candover Cl. UB7: Harm 5K 131
Candy La. MK5: S Broo 3B 28
Candytoft Grn. HP15: W End 1F 91
CANE END 3A 136
Cane End HP27: Prin R 5F 71
Canford Ct. HP21: Ayle 2A 66
Cannock Rd. HP20: Ayle 3J 61
Cannon Ct. MK16: New P 1K 17
Cannon Ga. SL2: Slou 5G 125
Cannon Mill Av. HP5: Ches 1C 86
Cannon Pl. HP27: Prin R 4G 71
Cannons Health & Fitness Club 5F 61
Cannons Orchard HP22: Q'ton 6J 43
Canonbury MK10: Monk P 5A 24
Canon Harnett Ct. MK12: W Mil 7D 14
Canons, The MK16: New P 2A 18
CANONS ASHBY 1A 132
Canons Rd. MK12: O Wol 6G 15
Cantell Cl. MK18: Buck 3H 37
Canterbury Av. SL2: Slou 2A 124
Canterbury Cl. HP7: Amer 6C 86
HP27: Mon R 3G 71
Canterbury M. SL4: Wind 7J 129
Cantle Av. MK14: D Barn 1G 23
Cantley Cl. HP20: Ayle 4K 61
Capel Dr. MK14: D Barn 1F 23
Capian Wlk. MK8: T Ash 5J 21
Capital Dr. MK14: L Woo 7E 16
Capps La. HP5: Char 1C 76
Capron MK6: Bean 2G 29
Capswood Bus. Cen. UB9: Den 6C 112
Captain Cook Cl. HP8: D Gil 2F 103
Captain's Cl. HP5: Ches 1J 77
Caraway Cl. MK7: Waln 3D 30
Cardigan Cl. MK3: Blet 6F 29
SL1: Slou 5H 123
Cardinals Wlk. SL6: Tapl 4E 122
Cardwell Cl. MK4: E Val 5C 28
Carey Cl. HP21: Ayle 3J 65
Carey Way MK46: Oln 3J 7
Carhampton Ct. MK4: Fur 4D 28
Carisbrooke Av. HP12: Book 3F 97
Carisbrooke Ct. MK18: Buck 2J 37
SL1: Slou 5D 124
Carisbrooke Ho. HP13: H Wyc 1F 99
(off Gayhurst Rd.)
Carisbrooke Way MK4: K'ead 6J 27
Carleton Ga. MK15: Will 6A 18
Carlina Pl. MK14: Conn 3D 22
Carlisle Rd. SL1: Slou 5B 124
CARLTON 1D 133
Carlton Cl. HP19: Ayle 4F 61
MK16: New P 1A 18
Carlton Ct. HP27: Prin R 5G 71
(off Bell St.)
UB8: Cowl 3K 127
Carlton Rd. SL2: Slou 5F 125
Carlyle Av. HP21: Ayle 1K 65
Carlyle Cl. MK16: New P 1G 17
Carmarthen Rd. SL1: Slou 5C 124
Carnation Way HP21: Ayle 2K 65
Carne, The MK11: S Strat 1C 20
Carnot Cl. MK5: S Lod 3C 28
Carnoustie Gro. MK3: Blet 1C 32
Carnweather Ct. MK4: Tatt 7B 28
Caroline Cl. UB7: W Dra 7K 127
Caroline Ct. SL7: Marl 6J 105
Carolus Creek MK15: Penny 6G 17
Carpenter Ct. MK14: N Hill 7F 17
Carr Cl. HP19: Ayle 4F 61
Carrick Rd. MK6: Fish 5F 23
Carriers Cl. MK19: H'ope 2E 8
Carrington Av. HP10: F Hea 1G 107
Carrington Cres. HP22: Wend 1G 69
Carrington Hall Rd. MK17: Dray P 6C 40
Carrington Pl. HP15: H Grn 7J 83
Carrington Rd. HP12: H Wyc 2H 97
HP21: Ayle 1J 65
MK16: New P 2H 17
SL1: Slou 5C 124
Carrington Way HP16: Pres 1C 82
Carroll Cl. MK16: New P 7G 11
Carron Ct. MK2: Blet 4J 33
Carrs Dr. HP12: H Wyc 7G 89
Carter Cl. SL4: Wind 7J 129
Carteret Cl. MK15: Will 6A 18
Carter Ho. HP13: H Wyc 2E 98
Carters Cl. MK16: Sher 3B 12
Carters La. HP18: Long C 5B 56
MK11: Kiln 3E 20
Carters Mdw. MK18: N Mar 2A 44
Carters Ride HP22: Sto M 5C 66
Carter Wlk. HP10: T Grn 7J 91
Cartmel Cl. MK3: Blet 2C 32
Cartwright Pl. MK6: Old 6E 22
Carver Hill Rd. HP11: H Wyc 3K 97
Carvers M. MK14: N Hill 7F 17
Cascadia Cl. HP11: W Mar 6H 99
Cashmere Cl. MK5: S Broo 3A 28
Casterton Cl. MK13: Hee 2C 22
Castle Acre MK10: Monk 5B 24
CASTLE ASHBY 1C 133
Castle Cl. HP20: Ayle 6J 61
(off Castle St.)
LU7: Pits 6F 51
LU7: Wing 2C 48
OX27: M Gib 5D 42
Castle Ct. HP20: Ayle 6J 61
(off Castle St.)
MK18: Buck 4H 37
(off Castle St.)
Castle Est. HP12: H Wyc 4G 97
Castle Farm Cvn. Site SL4: Wind 7F 129
Castlefields HP22: Sto M 4D 66
Castle Hill HP11: H Wyc 2A 98
Castle La. HP22: W'urch 2F 45
Castle Mdw. Cl. MK16: New P 1A 18
Castle Pk. Rd. HP22: Wend 2G 69
Castle Pl. HP13: H Wyc 1B 98
Castle Point HP12: H Wyc 4G 97
Castle Rd. MK46: Lave 1B 6
Castle Rose MK6: Wough 1K 29
Castlesteads MK13: Ban 1K 21
Castle St. HP13: H Wyc 1B 98
HP20: Ayle 6J 61
HP22: W'rave 7C 48
MK18: Buck 4H 37
OX27: M Gib 5C 42
SL1: Slou 7D 124
CASTLETHORPE 7D 8 (2B 132)
Castlethorpe Rd. MK19: H'ope 2D 8
Castleton Ct. SL7: Marl 7J 105
Castle Vw. Gdns. HP12: H Wyc 1H 97
Catchpole Cl. MK12: Gree 1F 21
Cater Rd. HP14: L End 4A 96
Catesby Cft. MK5: Lough 6C 22
Cathay Cl. MK3: Blet 1H 33
Catherine Ct. MK18: Buck 2J 37
Catherines Cl. UB7: W Dra 7K 127
Catkin Cl. HP12: Book 5F 97
Caucutts Yd. MK19: H'ope 2E 8
Causeway, The SL7: Marl 1J 115
Causeway Stadium 1D 96
Cautley Cl. HP22: Q'ton 5H 43
Cavendish Cl. HP6: L Chal 6F 87
HP22: Wend 2H 69
SL6: Tapl 4C 122
Cavendish Ct. HP6: Amer 5A 86
(off Hill Av.)
MK5: Lough 6A 22
SL3: Poy 6E 130
SL7: Marl 7J 105
Cavendish Rd. HP5: Ches 6B 78
Cavenham MK8: T Ash 4K 21
CAVERSFIELD 1A 134
CAVERSHAM 3A 136
Caversham Grn. HP20: Ayle 5J 61
CAVERSHAM HEIGHTS 3A 136
Cawarden MK14: Stan 6C 16
Cawcott Dr. SL4: Wind 6G 129
Cawdor Ri. MK4: West 5J 27
Cawkwell Way MK2: Blet 7J 29
Caxton Dr. UB8: Uxb 7K 121
Caxton Rd. MK12: O Wol 6F 15
Cecil Rd. SL0: Ive 4E 126
Cecil Way SL2: Slou 2H 123
Cecily Ct. MK5: S Chur 2A 28
Cedar Av. HP15: Haz 1F 91
SL1: Burn 1C 116
Cedar Chase SL6: Tapl 2A 122
Cedar Cl. HP5: Ches 4C 78
HP20: Ayle 4B 62
SL0: I Hea 6C 120
SL1: Burn 2E 122
Cedar Ct. HP13: H Wyc 1B 98
SL4: Wind 7J 129
SL7: Marl 7J 105
Cedar Dr. SL7: Marl 2G 105
Cedar Gro. HP7: Amer 6B 86
Cedar Lodge Dr. MK12: Wolv 6H 15
Cedar Ridge HP6: H Hea 1E 84
Cedars, The HP22: Wend 3G 69
SL2: Slou 1H 123
Cedars Cl. SL9: C Pet 3J 103
Cedars Way MK16: New P 1J 17
Cedar Ter. HP11: H Wyc 1K 97
Ceely Rd. HP21: Ayle 1J 65
Celandine Ct. MK7: Waln 1C 30
Celina Cl. MK2: Blet 1J 33
Centenary Cotts. HP27: Long 1C 70
Centenary Way HP6: Amer 5D 86
Central Dr. SL1: Slou 5H 123
CENTRAL MILTON KEYNES 3E 22
Central Pk. Bus. Pk. HP13: H Wyc 7A 90
Central Retail Pk. MK13: Rook 4B 22
Centre, The MK9: C Key 3E 22
Centre Pde. HP27: Mon R 3G 71
Centre Rd. SL4: Wind 5E 128
Centre Wlk. HP15: Haz 4G 91
Centurion Ct. MK11: Kiln 4G 21
Century Av. MK6: Old 6E 22
Cesteham Cres. HP5: Ches 3B 78
CHACKMORE 1F 37 (3A 132)
Chacombe Pl. HP9: Bea 3F 101
Chadbone Cl. HP20: Ayle 6J 61
Chadds La. MK6: P Bri 6J 23
CHADSTONE 1C 133
Chadwell Path HP21: Ayle 1D 66
(off Long Mdw.)
Chadwick Dr. MK6: E Wes 7H 23
Chadwick St. HP13: H Wyc 5D 90
Chaffinch HP19: Ayle 2A 62
Chaffron Way (H7) MK4: Mil K 7K 27
MK5: Mil K 3C 28
MK6: Mil K 5H 23
MK6: Mil K 5H 23
Chairborough Rd. HP12: H Wyc 3H 97
Chalcot Pl. MK8: G Hol 6K 21
Chalcott SL1: Slou 7C 124
Chalfont & Latimer Station (Rail & Tube)
6H 87
Chalfont Av. HP6: L Chal 6H 87
Chalfont Cl. MK13: B'lle 7A 16
CHALFONT COMMON 3K 103 (1D 137)
Chalfont Ho. HP7: L Chal 7H 87
Chalfont Leisure Cen. 6G 103
Chalfont Rd. HP9: S Grn 4B 102
CHALFONT ST GILES 1F 103 (1C 137)
CHALFONT ST PETER 6J 103 (2D 137)
Chalfont St Peter By-Pass
SL9: C Pet 6J 103
Chalfont Shire Cen. 1K 103
Chalfont Sta. Rd. HP7: L Chal 7G 87
Chalford Flats HP10: Woob G 3A 108
Chalford Way HP19: Ayle 6E 60
CHALGROVE 3A 134
Chalgrove End HP22: Sto M 5C 66
Chalgrove Wlk. HP21: Ayle 1H 65
Chalkdell Dr. MK5: S Woo 3K 27
Chalk Farm Rd. HP14: Stoke 5B 72
Chalk Hill HP5: Ches 3K 77
HP7: Cole 5H 93
Chalklands SL8: Bou E 5G 107
Chalk La. HP6: H Hea 3C 84
Chalk Pit La. SL1: Burn 4D 116
(not continuous)
Chalkpit La. SL7: Marl 6F 105
Chalkpits Cvn. Pk. HP10: Woob G 3A 108
Chalkstream Way HP10: Woob G 2A 108
Challacombe MK4: Fur 5D 28
Challener Rd. HP12: Book 5G 97
Challenge Ho. MK3: Blet 6H 29
Chalmers Av. MK19: H'ham 3H 15
Chaloner Pl. HP21: Ayle 1J 65
Chaloner Rd. HP21: Ayle 1J 65
Chaloners Hill MK18: S Clay 2B 42
CHALTON 1D 135
CHALVEY 7B 124
Chalvey Gdns. SL1: Slou 7C 124
Chalvey Gro. SL1: Slou 1K 129
Chalvey Pk. SL1: Slou 7C 124
Chalvey Rd. E. SL1: Slou 7C 124
Chalvey Rd. W. SL1: Slou 7B 124
Chalwell Ridge MK5: S Broo 3B 28
Chamberlain Rd. HP19: Ayle 5G 61

Champflower MK4: Fur 4D 28
Champney Cl. SL3: Hor 7A 130
Chancellors HP7: Penn S 2D 92
Chancery Cl. MK13: B'lle 7A 16
Chandler Ct. MK6: Simp 2A 30
CHANDLER'S CROSS 1D 137
Chandos Cl. HP6: L Chal 5G 87
MK18: Buck 5H 37
Chandos Ct. MK18: Buck 4H 37
Chandos Mall SL1: Slou 7D 124
(off High St.)
Chandos Pl. HP22: Wend 4H 69
MK2: Blet 7H 29
Chandos Rd. MK18: Buck 5H 37
Channer Dr. HP10: T Grn 6H 91
Channory Cl. MK4: Tatt 6A 28
Chantry, The HP20: Ayle 6J 61
(off Church St.)
Chantry Cl. MK17: W San 1J 31
SL4: Wind 6J 129
UB7: Yiew 5K 127
Chantry Rd. HP19: Ayle 3H 61
Chapel Dr. HP22: Ast C 2B 68
CHAPEL END 2D 133
Chapel End SL9: C Pet 7H 103
Chapel Hill HP27: Spee 2G 81
LU7: Soul 6H 41
Chapel La. HP5: Char 1E 76
HP12: H Wyc 7G 89
HP14: Nap 7G 81
HP18: Chil 1B 56
HP22: Sto M 6B 66
HP22: Wend 5H 69
HP27: Bled 5A 70
LU7: I Ast 1J 51
MK17: Dray P 7B 40
MK18: T'ough 2C 38
SL2: S Pog 5F 119
Chapel Path LU7: Cubl 2G 47
(off Silver St.)
Chapel Rd. HP10: F Hea 1G 107
HP17: Ford 6J 59
Chapels Cl. SL1: Slou 6G 123
Chapel Sq. LU7: Stew 3C 46
Chapel St. HP13: Down 4H 89
MK17: W San 3K 31
SL1: Slou 7D 124
SL7: Marl 7H 105
UB8: Uxb 6J 121
Chaplin Gro. MK8: C'ill 7H 21
Chapman Av. MK14: D Barn 1G 23
Chapman Cl. HP21: Ayle 1G 65
Chapman La. HP10: F Hea 4G 107
SL8: Bou E 4G 107
Chapmans Cres. HP5: Ches 3J 77
Chapmans Dr. MK19: O Stra 6A 14
Chapter MK6: Coff 2G 29
Chapter Ho. MK6: Coff 2G 29
Charbray Cres. MK5: S Broo 3A 28
Chardacre MK8: T Ash 5J 21
Charles Cl. HP21: Ayle 3C 66
Charles Gdns. SL2: Slou 4F 125
Charles Way MK16: New P 1J 17
Charlewood Ho. MK17: A H'th 4K 31
Charlock Ct. MK16: New P 1F 17
Charlotte Av. SL2: Slou 5D 124
Charlotte Cl. LU7: Wing 3C 48
(off Stewkley Rd.)
Charlotte Way SL7: Marl 7J 105
Charlton SL4: Wind 7E 128
Charlton Cl. SL1: Slou 7K 123
CHARLTON-ON-OTMOOR 2A 134
Charlton Pl. SL4: Wind 7E 128
(off Charlton Way)
Charlton Row SL4: Wind 7E 128
Charlton Sq. SL4: Wind 7E 128
(off Guards Rd.)
Charlton Wlk. SL4: Wind 7E 128
Charlton Way SL4: Wind 7E 128
Charmfield Rd. HP21: Ayle 2B 66
CHARNDON 1A 134
Charnwood Cl. HP13: H Wyc 3F 99
Charsley Cl. HP6: L Chal 6G 87
Charter Cl. SL1: Slou 7D 124
Charter Dr. HP6: Amer 5D 86
Charter Pl. UB8: Uxb 5K 121
Charter Rd. SL1: Slou 5G 123
Chartidge Ho. HP13: H Wyc 2F 99
Chartley Ct. MK5: S Broo 3B 28
CHARTRIDGE 1E 76 (3D 135)
Chartridge La. HP5: Char, Ches 1D 76
Chartwell Ga. HP9: Bea 6F 101
Chartwell Rd. MK16: New P 2A 18
CHARVIL 3A 136
Chase, The HP5: Ches 3K 77
HP10: T Grn 6J 91
HP10: Woob G 5B 108
MK17: New L 4D 32
SL7: Marl 6A 106
Chase Av. MK7: Walt P 3C 30
Chase Cl. HP7: Cole 3J 93
Chaseside Cl. LU7: Ched 2C 50
Chatfield SL2: Slou 3J 123
Chatham Ct. SL1: Slou 7E 124
(off Grove Cl.)
Chatsworth MK8: G Hol 5K 21
Chaucer Cl. MK16: New P 1G 17
Chaucer Dr. HP21: Ayle 1K 65
Chaucer Rd. MK3: Blet 1G 33
Chaucer Way SL1: Slou 6D 124
CHAULDEN 3D 135
CHAUL END 1D 135
Chawton Cres. MK8: G Hol 5K 21
CHEAPSIDE 3C 137
Cheapside La. UB9: Den 7F 113
CHEARSLEY 2H 57 (2B 134)
Chearsley Rd. HP18: Long C 6C 56
CHECKENDON 2A 136
CHEDDINGTON 2C 50 (2D 135)
Cheddington La. HP23: Long M 3A 50
Cheddington Rd. LU7: Pits 4D 50
Cheena Ho. SL9: C Pet 5K 103
CHELLINGTON 1D 133
Cheltenham Gdns. MK3: Blet 2D 32
Cheney Cl. LU7: Cubl 2H 47
Cheneys Wlk. MK3: Blet 4G 29
(not continuous)
Cheney Wlk. HP20: Ayle 4A 62
(off Cheney Way)
Cheney Way HP20: Ayle 4A 62
CHENIES 1D 137
Chenies Av. HP6: L Chal 6G 87
Chenies Pde. HP7: L Chal 7G 87
Chepping Cl. HP10: T Grn 6G 91
Chepstow Dr. MK3: Blet 2D 32
Chequers, The LU6: E Bra 1K 49
MK19: Cast 7D 8
Chequers Cl. LU7: Pits 5E 50
Chequers Ct. HP21: Ayle 3K 65
Chequers Dr. HP16: Pres 7C 74
Chequers End MK18: Wins 6J 39
Chequers Hill HP7: Amer 7B 86
Chequers La. HP16: Pres 7C 74
LU7: Pits 5E 50
MK16: N Craw 6K 13
Chequers Orchard SL0: Ive 4F 127
Chequers Sq. UB8: Uxb 5J 121
Cheriton MK4: Fur 4E 28
Cherleton MK8: T Ash 5J 21
Cherries, The SL2: Slou 4F 125
Cherry Acre SL9: C Pet 2H 103
Cherry Av. SL3: Lang 7H 125
Cherry Cl. HP10: F Hea 2H 107
HP16: Pres 7D 74
Cherry Cnr. HP10: F Hea 1H 107
Cherrycroft Dr. HP14: Nap 1H 89
Cherry Dr. HP9: Bea 4D 100
Cherry Gth. HP15: H Grn 1J 91
Cherry Gro. HP15: H Grn 1J 91
Cherry La. HP7: Amer 2E 92
Cherry Leys MK18: S Clay 2C 42
Cherry Orchard HP6: Amer 4C 86
HP16: Pres 7C 74
MK46: Oln 3G 7
SL2: S Pog 5F 119
UB7: W Dra 7K 127
Cherry Pit, The HP13: Down 5J 89
Cherry Ri. HP8: D Gil 7H 95
HP10: F Hea 2H 107
Cherry Rd. MK16: New P 2H 17
Cherry St. HP13: H Wyc 4G 99
Cherry Tree Cl. HP14: H Vall 7A 82
HP15: G Kin 5D 82
HP27: Spee 1F 81
Cherry Tree Cnr. HP9: Jord 4C 102
Cherry Tree La. HP16: L Com 1K 75
SL3: Fulm 4K 119
Cherrytree La. SL0: I Hea 6G 121
SL9: C Pet 7H 103
Cherry Tree Rd. HP9: Bea 7C 100
SL2: Farn R 5A 118
Cherry Tree Wlk. HP5: Ches 3B 78
HP22: Wend 3G 69
Cherry Tree Way HP10: T Grn 6J 91
Cherry Way HP15: Haz 1G 91
SL3: Hor 7C 130
Cherrywood Cl. HP9: S Grn 3B 102
Cherrywood Gdns. HP10: F Hea 1G 107
CHERTSEY 3D 137
Chervil MK6: Bean 2H 29
(not continuous)
Cherwell Cl. SL3: Lang 4B 130
Cherwell Ho. MK3: Blet 7E 28
Cherwell Rd. HP21: Ayle 1H 65
SL8: Bou E 5H 107
CHESHAM 5K 77 (3D 135)
Chesham Av. MK13: B Com 3C 22
CHESHAM BOIS 3B 86 (1C 137)
Chesham Bois Lawn Tennis & Squash Club 3J 85
Chesham La. HP8: D Gil 2J 103
SL9: C Pet 2J 103
Chesham Leisure Cen. 5B 78
Chesham Rd. HP3: Bov 2H 79
HP5: Bov, Whel 2H 79
HP5: Ches 6J 75
HP6: Amer 4A 86
HP16: G Mis, H Hea 6J 75
HP22: Wend 7K 69
Chesham Station (Rail) 5A 78
Cheshire Ct. SL1: Slou 7F 125
Cheshire Ri. MK3: Blet 6E 28
Cheslyn Gdns. MK14: G Par 5G 17
Chesney Wold MK6: Blea 1E 28
Chessbury Cl. HP5: Ches 6K 77
Chessbury Rd. HP5: Ches 6J 77
Chess Cl. HP5: Lati 3H 87
HP21: Ayle 4J 65
Chessfield Pk. HP6: L Chal 6J 87
CHESSMOUNT 7B 78
Chessmount Ri. HP5: Ches 7B 78
Chess Valley Sports & Leisure Cen. 7A 78
Chester Cl. MK3: Blet 1D 32
Chesterfield Cres. LU7: Wing 2C 48
Chesterfield Pl. HP19: Ayle 6G 61
Chesterholm MK13: Ban 1K 21
Chester Ho. UB8: Cowl 2J 127
Chester Rd. SL1: Slou 4B 124
CHESTERTON 1A 134
Chesterton Cl. HP5: Ches 3K 77
Chesterton Grn. HP9: Bea 5G 101
Chestnut Av. HP5: Ches 3C 78
HP11: H Wyc 3D 98
HP22: Halt 7K 67
SL3: Lang 7J 125
Chestnut Cl. HP4: Dag 6H 49
HP6: Amer 4B 86
(not continuous)
HP18: Wadd 6C 52
HP22: Ast C 2C 68
HP27: Mon R 3H 71
MK11: S Strat 1B 20
MK17: New L 6D 32
SL7: Medm 3B 114
SL9: C Pet 6K 103
Chestnut Cotts. MK18: Buck 5G 37
(off Mitre St.)
Chestnut Ct. HP6: Amer 4C 86
Chestnut Cres. HP21: Ayle 1K 65
MK2: Blet 1K 33
(not continuous)
Chestnut End HP22: Halt 6K 67
Chestnut La. HP6: Amer 3B 86
HP15: Haz 2H 91
Chestnut Leys MK18: S Clay 2C 42
Chestnut Pk. SL6: Bra 2A 128
Chestnut Rd. HP9: Bea 7D 100
HP27: Prin R 5G 71
Chestnuts, The MK19: Cast 7D 8
Chestnut Vw. HP18: Che 2H 57
Chestnut Wlk. SL9: C Pet 5J 103
Chestnut Way HP22: Sto M 6B 66
HP27: Long 2D 70
CHETWODE 1A 134
Chetwode Av. MK10: Monk 5C 24
Chetwode Cl. MK18: Buck 2J 37
Chevalier Gro. MK8: C'ill 7H 21
Cheveley Gdns. SL1: Burn 7E 116
Cheviot Cl. HP13: Down 6J 89
Cheviot Rd. SL3: Lang 3A 130
Cheyne Cl. HP6: Amer 2B 86
LU7: Pits 5F 51
MK18: Buck 3K 37
SL9: G Cro 6J 111
Cheyne Wlk. HP5: Ches 5B 78
CHICHELEY 4E 12 (2D 133)
Chicheley Hill MK16: Sher 4B 12
Chicheley Rd. MK16: N Craw, Chic 4E 12
Chicheley St. MK16: New P 1A 18
Chichester Cl. HP13: H Wyc 2D 98
Chichester Ct. SL1: Slou 7F 125
Chichester Row HP6: Amer 5B 86
Chicksands Av. MK10: Monk 5C 24
Chievely Ct. MK4: E Val 6C 28
Chilcote La. HP7: L Chal 6F 87
Childs Way (H6) MK4: Mil K 5J 27
MK5: Mil K 2B 28
MK9: Mil K 6D 22
MK10: Mil K 2B 24
MK15: Mil K 4G 23
Chillery Leys MK15: Will 6A 18
Chillingham Ct. MK5: S Broo 3A 28
Chiltern Av. HP6: Amer 5A 86
HP12: H Wyc 3H 97
HP17: Sto 2C 64
LU6: Edle 3J 49
Chiltern Bus. Cen. HP6: Amer 4B 86
Chiltern Bus. Village UB8: Uxb 7H 121
Chiltern Cl. HP17: Sto 2C 64
HP22: Wend 3H 69
HP27: Prin R 5F 71
Chiltern Commerce Cen. HP5: Ches 3J 77
(off Asheridge Rd.)
Chiltern Ct. HP5: Ches 3J 77
HP6: Amer 4A 86
HP12: H Wyc 1J 97
HP22: Wend 4H 69
MK18: Wins 7H 39
SL4: Wind 6K 129
(off Fawcett Rd.)
Chiltern Ct. M. SL4: Wind 6K 129
(off Fawcett Rd.)
Chiltern Grn. HP10: F Hea 1G 107
Chiltern Hgts. HP7: L Chal 6E 86
HP11: H Wyc 2A 98
Chiltern Hill SL9: C Pet 6J 103
Chiltern Hills Rd. HP9: Bea 6E 100
Chiltern Mnr. Pk. HP16: G Mis 6F 75
Chiltern Open Air Mus. 6K 95
Chiltern Pde. HP6: Amer 4A 86
Chiltern Pools, The 5B 86
Chiltern Ridge HP14: Stoke 6A 72
Chiltern Rd. HP6: Amer 1K 85
HP16: Ball 2A 76
HP22: Wend 3H 69
HP22: W'rave 6B 48
SL1: Burn 3D 122
SL7: Marl 7G 105
Chiltern Rugby Club 3J 85
Chilterns, The HP13: H Wyc 1A 98
Chilterns Cl. HP10: F Hea 2H 107
Chilterns Crematorium HP7: Amer 1H 93
Chilterns Pk. SL8: Bou E 4H 107
Chiltern St. HP21: Ayle 1K 65
Chiltern Vw. HP14: Saun 5A 80
HP17: Sto 3B 64
Chiltern Vw. Cvn. Pk. LU6: E Bra 1G 49
Chiltern Vw. Rd. UB8: Uxb 7J 121
Chiltern Way HP22: Ast C 5C 68
CHILTON 1B 56 (2A 134)
Chilton Cl. HP10: T Grn 5J 91
HP15: H Grn 7J 83
Chilton Ct. SL6: Tapl 4E 122
Chilton Rd. HP5: Ches 3A 78
HP18: Che 1F 57
HP18: Long C 3B 56
Chilwick Rd. SL2: Slou 2H 123
Chimes, The HP12: H Wyc 2J 97
Chimes Shop. Cen., The UB8: Uxb 5K 121
Chimney La. HP10: Woob G 1A 108
Chingle Cft. MK4: E Val 5B 28
CHINNOR 3B 134
Chinnor Rd. HP14: Bled R 2A 88
HP27: Bled 6A 70
Chippendale All. UB8: Uxb 5K 121
Chippendale Cl. HP13: H Wyc 6D 90
Chippendale Waye UB8: Uxb 5K 121
Chippenham Dr. MK10: K'ton 4D 24
CHIPPERFIELD 3D 135
Chipperfield Cl. MK13: New B 6A 16
Chipping Va. MK4: E Val 5B 28
Chipps Hill HP14: Whee 1J 73
Chipstead SL9: C Pet 6G 103
Chirlbury Cl. MK10: Monk 5B 24
CHISBRIDGE CROSS 3B 104 (2B 136)
CHISLEHAMPTON 3A 134
Chislehampton MK15: Wool 3J 23
CHISWELL GREEN 1D 137
Chiswick Cl. MK4: West 5K 27
CHOLESBURY 3D 135
Chorley Rd. HP14: W Wyc 4C 88
CHORLEYWOOD 1D 137
Christchurch Gro. MK12: Wolv 7F 15
Christian Ct. MK15: Will 6J 17
Christie Cl. MK16: New P 7G 11
Christine Ho. MK2: Blet 7J 29
(off Mikern Cl.)
CHRISTMAS COMMON 1A 136
Christmas La. SL2: Farn C 1A 118
Christopher Cl. HP14: Nap 7H 81
Church Cl. HP18: Cudd 1B 58
HP22: Ast C 2A 68
MK5: Lough 6B 22
MK18: M M'ton 1K 37
UB7: W Dra 1K 131
UB8: Uxb 7H 121
Church Ct. HP19: Ayle 6F 61
(off Wedgewood St.)
Church Cft. LU6: Edle 3J 49
CHURCH END
Aylesbury 7C 58
Dunstable 4J 49 (1D 135)
Leighton Buzzard 7G 51
Milton Keynes 3D 133
Princes Risborough 7A 70
Church End HP27: Bled 7A 70
HP27: Prin R 5G 71
LU6: Edle 3J 49
MK16: Sher 2C 12
MK17: Dray P 7B 40
MK17: New L 5D 32
MK17: Wave 7G 25
MK18: Ads 6E 38
Church End Rd. MK5: S Broo 3A 28
Church Farm Cl. HP22: Bier 3B 62
Church Farm Cres.
MK14: G Lin 5E 16
Church Farm La. HP23: M'rth 6B 50
Churchfield M. SL2: Slou 4E 124
Churchfield Rd. SL9: C Pet 6H 103
CHURCH GATE 3H 49
Church Grn. Rd. MK3: Blet 7F 29
Church Gro. HP6: L Chal 6J 87
SL3: Wex 3G 125
Church Headland La.
HP22: W'urch 2G 45
Church Hill LU7: Ched 1B 50
MK8: T Ash 5J 21
MK17: Whad 6F 27
UB9: Hare 1J 113
Churchill Av. HP21: Ayle 7H 61
Churchill Cl. HP10: F Hea 2H 107
Churchill Ct. HP21: Ayle 7K 61
(off Beaconsfield Rd.)
Churchill Dr. HP9: Bea 3E 100
SL7: Marl 5K 105
Churchill Rd. SL3: Lang 2A 130
Church La. HP27: L Grn 2C 80

Church La. HP14: Bled R 3C 72
(not continuous)
HP14: Nap 1J 89
HP14: Rad 3A 72
HP14: W Wyc 5E 88
HP15: Crye 3B 90
HP16: G Mis 6H 75
HP18: Che 3H 57
HP18: Ludg 3C 52
HP22: Ast C 3A 68
HP22: Ovi 5C 44
HP22: Wend 5J 69
HP22: West T 6G 67
HP22: W'urch 2G 45
HP23: M'rth 7B 50
HP27: Prin R 4G 71
HP27: Saun 7E 70
LU6: E Bra 1J 49
LU7: Ched 2C 50
LU7: Soul 7H 41
MK5: Lough 6B 22
MK7: Walt H 1B 30
MK16: Lath 5K 11
MK16: S Gold 5B 6
MK17: G Bri 6E 34
MK17: G Hor 2J 39
MK17: Mur 3B 40
MK17: Whad 6F 27
MK18: Pad 5B 38
MK18: Ting 2C 36
MK18: T'ough 2C 38
MK46: C Rey 4K 7
MK46: Emb 7H 7
SL2: S Pog 2D 124
SL3: Wex 2F 125
SL9: C Pet 6H 103
UB8: Uxb 7H 121
Church Lees MK14: G Lin 4D 16
Churchmere Wlk. *HP21: Ayle 2H 65*
(off Hamble Dr., not continuous)
Church Pas. MK16: New P 1K 17
Church Path HP14: L End 4K 73
HP14: Stoke 5B 72
HP16: Pres 1D 82
LU7: Cubl 2G 47
Church Piece HP18: Che 2H 57
Church Rd. HP9: S Grn 4B 102
HP10: Pen 1K 99
HP10: T Grn 7J 91
HP14: L End 7J 73
HP18: Ick 5D 54
LU7: I'hoe 4H 51
LU7: Pits 6G 51
MK17: A H'th 5K 31
MK17: Bow B 5F 31
MK17: S Ham 1G 41
RG9: L End 7J 73
SL0: I Hea 1C 126
SL2: Farn R 1A 124
SL7: L Mar 4C 106
SL8: Bou E 7K 107
UB7: W Dra 1K 131
UB8: Cowl 2K 127
UB9: Hare 1J 113
Church Row HP22: A Abb 6J 47
Churchside HP15: H Grn 7K 83
Church Sq. HP11: H Wyc 1B 98
CHURCH STOWE 1A 132
Church St. HP5: Ches 6K 77
HP7: Amer 7K 85
HP11: H Wyc 1A 98
HP14: Stoke 5B 72
HP16: G Mis 6H 75
HP18: Bril 3H 53
HP20: Ayle 6J 61
HP22: Q'ton 5J 43
HP22: W'rave 7C 48
HP27: Prin R 5G 71
LU7: Wing 3C 48
MK2: F Str 6A 30
MK11: S Strat 1B 20
MK12: Wolv 6G 15
MK13: New B 6K 15
MK18: Buck 4G 37
MK18: Gaw 6D 36
MK18: M M'ton 1K 37
MK18: N Mar 2B 44
MK18: Wins 6H 39
MK46: Oln 4H 7
OX27: M Gib 5C 42
SL1: Burn 2E 122
SL1: Slou 7A 124
(Damson Gro.)
SL1: Slou 7D 124
(Osborne St.)
Church Ter. SL4: Wind 7G 129
Church Vw. HP22: Halt 6K 67
MK16: New P 1K 17
MK18: S Clay 3C 42
Church Wlk. HP22: West T 6G 67
LU7: Wing 3C 48
MK3: Blet 1F 33
MK16: N Craw 6K 13
MK18: Wins 6H 39
SL1: Burn 2D 122
(not continuous)
Church Way HP17: Sto 2B 64
Churchway HP17: Hadd 3C 58
Church Wood Reserve 6D 110
Chyne, The SL9: G Cro 3K 111
Cineworld Cinema 7D 124
Cinnamon Cl. SL4: Wind 6H 129
Cinnamon Gro. MK7: Waln 2C 30
CIPPENHAM 5G 123 (2C 137)
Cippenham Cl. SL1: Slou 5H 123
Cippenham La. SL1: Slou 5H 123
City Discovery Cen. 3K 21
CITY, THE 1A 136
Clailey Ct. MK11: S Strat 1D 20
Clammas Way UB8: Cowl 3J 127
CLAPHAM 1D 133
Clapham Pl. MK13: B Com 4C 22
Clappins La. HP14: Nap 6G 81
Clapton App. HP10: Woob G 1K 107
Clare Cft. MK10: Midd 3C 24
Clare Dr. SL2: Farn C 2K 117
Claremont Av. MK11: S Strat 2C 20
Claremont Cl. HP21: Ayle 2A 66
Claremont Gdns. SL7: Marl 7J 105
Claremont Rd. SL4: Wind 7K 129
SL7: Marl 7J 105
Clarence Ct. HP22: Wend 4H 69
SL4: Wind 6K 129
Clarence Rd. MK11: S Strat 1C 20
SL4: Wind 7J 129
Clarendon Ct. SL2: Slou 5F 125
SL4: Wind 6K 129
Clarendon Dr. MK8: Wym 4K 21
Clarendon Rd. HP13: H Wyc 2E 98
HP16: Pres 7B 74
Clare Pk. HP7: Amer 7C 86
Clare Rd. HP16: Pres 7C 74
SL6: Tapl 4E 122
Claridge Dr. MK10: Midd 4C 24
Clarke Dr. HP13: H Wyc 3G 99
Clarke Rd. MK1: Blet 3J 29
Clarkes Fld. Cl. HP18: Bril 3J 53
Clarke Wlk. *HP20: Ayle 4A 62*
(off Bryanston Av.)
Clauds Cl. HP15: Haz 2G 91
Claverton Cl. HP3: Bov 2K 79
Clay Acre HP5: Ches 4B 78
Clay Cl. HP10: F Hea 1H 107
Claycutters MK18: Wins 6J 39
Claydon Cl. HP21: Ayle 2J 65
Claydon Ct. HP12: H Wyc 4J 97
Claydon End SL9: C Pet 1J 111
Claydon La. SL9: C Pet 1J 111
Claydons Pl. HP27: Long 1C 70
Clayfield Rd. HP22: Halt 7K 67
Clayfields HP10: T Grn 5J 91
Clay Hill MK8: T Ash 4J 21
Clayhill SL7: Book 6E 96
Clay La. HP22: Wend 3J 69
SL7: Book 7D 96
Claymoor Pk. SL7: Book 6D 96
Clays, The HP17: Hadd 5C 58
Clay St. HP9: Bea 1E 100
Clayton Ct. SL3: Lang 1A 130
Clayton Ga. MK14: G Par 5G 17
Clayton Path HP21: Ayle 4K 65
Claytons Mdw. SL8: Bou E 7H 107
Clayton Wlk. HP7: L Chal 6G 87
Clayton Way UB8: Cowl 2K 127
Clearbrook Cl. HP13: H Wyc 4H 99
Cleares Pasture SL1: Burn 1D 122
Cleavers Av. MK14: Conn 3D 22
Cleeve Cres. MK3: Blet 5G 29
Clegg Sq. MK5: S Lod 3B 28
Cleland Rd. SL9: C Pet 7H 103
Clementi Av. HP15: H Grn 7K 83
Clements Cl. SL1: Slou 7F 125
Clements La. OX27: M Gib 5C 42
Clerkenwell Pl. MK6: Sprin 3H 23
Clevehurst Cl. SL2: S Pog 4E 118
Cleveland MK13: B'lle 7B 16
Cleveland Cl. HP10: Woob G 1A 108
Cleveland Pk. HP20: Ayle 3A 62
Cleveland Rd. HP20: Ayle 3K 61
UB8: Cowl 2K 127
Cleves Ct. SL4: Wind 7H 129
Clewer Av. SL4: Wind 7J 129
Clewer Ct. Rd. SL4: Wind 5K 129
CLEWER GREEN 7H 129
CLEWER HILL 7G 129
Clewer Hill Rd. SL4: Wind 7G 129
CLEWER NEW TOWN 7K 129
Clewer New Town SL4: Wind 7J 129
Clewer Pk. SL4: Wind 5J 129
CLEWER ST ANDREW 5J 129
CLEWER ST STEPHEN 5K 129
CLEWER VILLAGE 6J 129
CLEWER WITHIN 6K 129
Clickers Yd. MK46: Oln 3H 7
Clifden Rd. HP18: Worm 3B 54
Clifford Av. MK2: Blet 1J 33
Clifford Rd. HP27: Prin R 5G 71
Cliffords Way SL8: Bou E 4G 107
Clifton Bus. Pk. HP19: Ayle 5F 61
Clifton Ct. HP11: H Wyc 4J 97
MK46: Oln 4J 7
Clifton Grn. HP19: Ayle 4G 61
Clifton Lawns HP6: Amer 2A 86
Clifton Lodge SL4: E Wick 3J 129
Clifton Moor MK5: O'ill 2H 27
CLIFTON REYNES 4K 7 (1D 133)
Clifton Ri. SL4: Wind 6F 129
Clifton Rd. HP6: Amer 2K 85
SL1: Slou 7F 125
Climb, The *5B 86*
(in The Chiltern Pools)
Cline Ct. MK8: C'ill 1J 27
Clinkard Pl. HP14: L End 5J 73
Clinton Cres. HP21: Ayle 6B 62
Clive Ct. SL1: Slou 7B 124
Cliveden Estate 3A 116
Cliveden Rd. SL6: Tapl 2A 116
Clivedon Office Village HP12: H Wyc 4J 97
Clock Ho., The MK17: L Bric 3F 35
Cloebury Paddock MK15: Wool 3J 23
Cloisters, The HP13: H Wyc 5D 90
HP20: Ayle 6J 61
(off Gt. Western St.)
SL1: Slou 7B 124
Clonmel Way SL1: Burn 1D 122
Close, The HP22: Bier 2B 62
HP22: Halt 6B 68
HP22: H'ick 5H 45
MK6: W Grn. 7K 23
MK13: B'ell 2A 22
MK16: Lath 5K 11
MK17: G Hor 2K 39
MK17: W San 3K 31
SL0: I Hea 1C 126
SL1: Slou 5F 123
SL7: Marl 7F 105
SL8: Bou E 3G 107
Closes, The HP17: Hadd 5C 58
Cloudberry MK7: Waln 1C 30
Cloutsham Cl. MK4: Fur 4C 28
Clover Cl. MK5: Lough 6A 22
Clover La. HP21: Ayle 2K 65
Club La. MK17: W San 3K 31
Cluny Ct. MK7: W Gat 1F 31
Clyde Pl. MK3: Blet 6E 28
Clydesdale Pl. MK14: D Barn 2F 23
Coachmaker Ct. MK14: N Hill 7G 17
Coach Ride SL7: Marl 5H 105
Coalmans Way SL1: Burn 3C 122
Coates La. HP13: Down, H Wyc 4J 89
Coat Wicks HP9: S Grn 4A 102
Cobbetts Mt. MK18: S Clay 3B 42
Cobb Hall Rd. MK17: New L 5C 32
Cobblers Cl. SL2: Farn R 7K 117
Cobblers Ct. HP5: Ches 3B 78
COBBLERSHILL 1C 74
Cobblershill La. HP16: L Ham 3A 74
HP22: Wend 1B 74
Cobblers Wick HP22: W'rave 6C 48
Cobbs Gdn. MK46: Oln 3H 7
Cobden Cl. UB8: Uxb 6J 121
Coberley Cl. MK15: D Park 7H 17
Cobham Cl. MK18: Buck 3G 37
SL1: Slou 7H 123
Cochran Cl. MK8: C'ill 7J 21
Cochrane Ho. UB8: Uxb 6J 121
Cockerell Gro. MK5: S Lod 2C 28
Cockett Rd. SL3: Lang 7J 125
Cock La. HP10: T Grn 3F 99
HP13: H Wyc 3F 99
HP20: Ayle 5J 61
(shown as Lucky La.)
Cockpit Cl. HP15: G Kin 6E 82
Cockpit Rd. HP15: G Kin 6D 82
COCKPOLE GREEN 2B 136
Cock's Yd. *UB8: Uxb 5K 121*
(off Bakers Rd.)
Coddimoor La. MK17: Whad 7F 27
CODMORE 4C 78
Codmore Cres. HP5: Ches 4C 78
Codmore Cross HP5: Ches 4B 78
Codmore Wood Rd. HP5: Lati 7G 79
Coe Spur SL1: Slou 7K 123
COFFEE HALL 1G 29
COFFEE HALL 1H 29
Cofferidge Cl. MK11: S Strat 1B 20
Coftards SL2: Slou 4G 125
Cogan Ct. MK8: C'ill 7J 21
Cogdells Cl. HP5: Char 1D 76
Cogdells La. HP5: Char 1D 76
COGENHOE 1C 133
Coggeshall Gro. MK7: W Gat 7E 24
Coin Cl. MK10: Midd 3B 24
Coke's Farm La. HP8: D Gil 1F 95
Coke's La. HP7: L Chal 7G 87
HP8: D Gil 2E 94
Colborne Rd. HP13: H Wyc 7D 90
Colchester Ct. MK3: Blet 1E 32
COLD BRAYFIELD 1D 133
Coldeaton La. MK4: E Val 4B 28
Coldharbour Way HP19: Ayle 5F 61
COLD HIGHAM 1A 132
Coldmoorholme La. SL8: Bou E 6E 106
Coleheath Bottom HP27: Spee 1G 81
Colenorton Cres. SL4: E Wick 2G 129
Coleridge Cl. MK3: Blet 1G 33
MK16: New P 1F 17
Coleridge Cres. SL3: Poy 6E 130
Cole Rd. HP21: Ayle 2H 65
Colesbourne Dr. MK15: D Park 7G 17
COLESHILL 4H 93 (1C 137)
Coleshill La. HP7: Winc 5E 92
Coleshill Pl. MK13: B Com 3C 22
Colet Rd. HP22: Wend 3J 69
Colgrain St. MK9: Camp 2G 23
Colham Mill Rd. UB7: W Dra 7K 127
Colindale St. MK10: Monk P 5A 24
Colin Way SL1: Slou 1K 129
College, The OX27: M Gib 5C 42
College Av. SL1: Slou 7C 124
College Cres. HP18: Oak 6H 53
SL4: Wind 7K 129
College Rd. HP22: Ast C 1A 68
SL1: Slou 6H 123
College Rd. Nth. HP22: Ast C 5K 63
College Rd. Sth. HP22: Ast C 1A 68
Colley Hill MK13: B'ell 2A 22
Colley Hill La. SL2: Hedg 1D 118
Colley Ho. UB8: Uxb 6K 121
Collings Wlk. *HP16: Pres 1C 82*
(off Lodge La.)
COLLINGTREE 1B 132
Collingwood Cl.
HP13: H Wyc 2G 99
Collins Ho *HP11: H Wyc 1A 98*
(off Desborough Rd.)
Collins Wlk. MK16: New P 1G 17
Collinswood Rd. SL2: Farn C 6J 109
Collum Grn. Rd.
SL2: Farn C, S Pog, Hedg 1B 118
Colly Cl. HP18: Bril 3H 53
Collyer Rd. HP14: Stoke 6C 72
COLNBROOK 5D 130 (3D 137)
Colnbrook By-Pass SL3: Coln, Lang 4C 130
UB7: Harm 5H 131
Colnbrook Ct. SL3: Poy 6F 131
Colndale Rd. SL3: Poy 7E 130
Colne MK6: T Bri 1K 29
Colne Av. UB7: W Dra 7J 127
Colnedale Rd. UB8: Uxb 3K 121
Colne Orchard SL0: Ive 4F 127
Colne Pk. Cvn. Site UB7: W Dra 2J 131
Colne Rd. HP13: H Wyc 1F 99
Colne Valley Pk. Cen. 1H 121
COLNEY STREET 1D 137
Coln Trad. Est. SL3: Poy 6F 131
Colonial Rd. SL1: Slou 7E 124
Colsons Way MK46: Oln 2H 7
Colston Bassett MK4: E Val 6C 28
Coltman Av. HP18: Long C 6C 56
Coltsfoot Dr. UB7: Yiew 4K 127
Coltsfoot Pl. MK14: Conn 3D 22
Colts Holm Rd. MK12: O Wol 5G 15
Columbia Pl. MK9: Camp 3G 23
Columbine Rd. HP15: W End 1F 91
Colville Ct. *HP16: G Mis 6H 75*
(off High St.)
Colville Rd. HP11: H Wyc 2J 97
Combe Martin MK4: Fur 5D 28
Combe Ri. HP12: H Wyc 1F 97
Combermere Cl. SL4: Wind 7K 129
Comerford Way MK18: Wins 5J 39
Comfrey, The HP19: Ayle 2K 61
Comfrey Cl. MK7: Waln 2C 30
Commercial Sq. HP11: H Wyc 1K 97
COMMON, THE 1K 39
Common, The HP7: Winc 4E 92
(not continuous)
HP10: F Hea 1H 107
HP14: Stoke 5B 72
HP15: G Kin 5D 82
HP15: H Grn 7K 83
UB7: W Dra 2J 131
Common La. MK5: Lough 6C 22
MK13: B'ell 2A 22
SL1: Burn 1F 117
Common Rd. HP10: F Hea 1G 107
HP15: G Kin 5D 82
SL3: Lang 2A 130
SL4: Dorn, E Wick 2E 128
SL4: E Wick 3H 129
Commonside HP13: Down 4H 89
Common Wood SL2: Farn C 2A 118
Common Wood La.
HP10: Pen, T Grn 6K 91
Como Rd. HP20: Ayle 6C 62
Compton Ct. MK16: Moul 5F 19
SL1: Slou 4G 123
Compton Rd. HP22: Wend 3J 69
Concorde Cl. UB10: Uxb 7K 121
Concorde Ct. SL4: Wind 7J 129
Concorde Way SL1: Slou 7A 124
Concourse, The MK2: Blet 7J 29
Concra Pk. MK17: W San 3K 31
Concrete Cows 2K 21
Condor Cl. MK6: Eagl 6G 23
Conegar Ct. SL1: Slou 6C 124
Conegra Ct. HP13: H Wyc 1B 98
Conegra Rd. HP13: H Wyc 1C 98
Coneygere MK46: Oln 4J 7
Congreve MK6: T Bri 2K 29
Conifer Ri. HP12: H Wyc 2J 97
Conifer Wlk. SL4: Wind 5E 128
Coningsby Rd. HP13: H Wyc 7B 90
Coniston Cl. SL7: Marl 7F 105
Coniston Cres. SL1: Slou 3E 122
Coniston Grn. HP20: Ayle 3J 61
Coniston Way MK2: Blet 2K 33

Connaught Rd. HP20: Ayle . . . 6D 62
SL1: Slou . . . 7F 125
CONNIBURROW . . . 2F 23
Conniburrow Blvd. MK14: Conn . . . 3D 22
Conspec Ho. HP19: Ayle . . . 5H 61
Constable Cl. MK14: N Hill . . . 6F 17
Constable Pl. HP19: Ayle . . . 4E 60
Constantine Way MK13: B Pk . . . 1K 21
Conventon HP19: Ayle . . . 4G 61
Convent Rd. SL4: Wind . . . 7H 129
Conway Cl. HP10: Loud . . . 6J 99
HP21: Ayle . . . 7A 62
MK3: Blet . . . 7F 29
Conway Ct. SL9: G Cro . . . 6B 112
Conway Cres. MK3: Blet . . . 7E 28
Conway Rd. SL6: Tapl . . . 4D 122
Cook Cl. MK7: Walt P . . . 3D 30
COOKHAM . . . 2B 136
Cookham Ct. *HP6: Amer* . . . *5D 86*
(off Plantation Rd.)
COOKHAM DEAN . . . 2B 136
COOKHAM RISE . . . 2B 136
COOKLEY GREEN . . . 1A 136
Cooks Cl. SL9: C Pet . . . 4J 103
Cookshall La. HP12: H Wyc . . . 5E 88
Cooks La. MK17: Mur . . . 2C 40
Cook's Mdw. LU6: Edle . . . 2J 49
Cooks Rd. HP19: Ayle . . . 6E 60
Cooks Wharf Cotts. LU7: Ched . . . 4D 50
Coombe Av. HP22: Wend . . . 4G 69
Coombe Cl. HP22: Sto M . . . 5D 66
Coombe Gdns. HP14: H Vall . . . 1A 90
Coombe La. HP14: H Vall, Nap . . . 1J 89
HP19: Ayle . . . 5E 60
Coombe Va. SL9: G Cro . . . 6J 111
Coopers Ct. MK16: New P . . . 1J 17
Coopers Ct. Rd. HP14: Stoke . . . 5B 72
Coopers M. MK14: N Hill . . . 7F 17
Coopers Row SL0: I Hea . . . 2C 126
Cooper's Yd. HP20: Ayle . . . 5J 61
Cooper Way SL1: Slou . . . 1K 129
Coots Cl. MK18: Buck . . . 5J 37
Copeland Cl. MK7: Brow . . . 2E 30
Copes Haven MK5: S Broo . . . 4B 28
Copes Rd. HP15: G Kin . . . 5E 82
Copes Shroves HP15: Haz . . . 2F 91
Copners Dr. HP15: H Grn . . . 1J 91
Copners Way HP15: H Grn . . . 1H 91
Copper Beech Cl. SL4: Wind . . . 6F 129
Copperfields HP9: Bea . . . 3G 101
HP12: H Wyc . . . 6F 89
Copperfield Ter. *SL2: Slou* . . . *5F 125*
(off Mirador Cres.)
SL2: Slou . . . *5F 125*
(off Mirador Cres.)
Copperkins Gro. HP6: Amer . . . 3K 85
Copperkins La. HP6: Amer . . . 2H 85
Copper Ridge SL9: C Pet . . . 3K 103
Coppice, The HP9: S Grn . . . 4B 102
HP12: Book . . . 4F 97
HP14: Stoke . . . *5D 72*
(off Wycombe Rd.)
HP14: Walt A . . . 6F 81
HP15: G Kin . . . 5E 82
UB7: Yiew . . . 4K 127
Coppice Cl. HP20: Ayle . . . 4B 62
Coppice Farm Rd. HP10: T Grn . . . 5J 91
Coppice Way HP20: Ayle . . . 4B 62
SL2: Hedg . . . 7B 110
Coppidwell Dr. HP21: Ayle . . . 2B 66
Coppin La. MK13: B'ell . . . 3A 22
Coppins La. SL0: Ive . . . 3F 127
Copse, The HP7: Amer . . . 5A 86
HP9: Bea . . . 4E 100
Copse Cl. SL1: Slou . . . 6H 123
SL7: Marl . . . 7G 105
UB7: W Dra . . . 1K 131
Copse Ga. MK18: Wins . . . 6J 39
Copse La. HP9: Jord . . . 5C 102
Copse Way HP5: Ches . . . 1J 77
Copse Wood SL0: I Hea . . . 6D 120
Copthall Cl. SL9: C Pet . . . 5K 103
Copthall Cnr. SL9: C Pet . . . 5J 103
Copthall La. SL9: C Pet . . . 5J 103
Copthorne Cl. *MK7: K Hil* . . . *6D 24*
(off Tunbridge Gro.)
Copyground Ct. HP12: H Wyc . . . 1J 97
Copyground La. HP12: H Wyc . . . 1H 97
Corbett Cl. MK15: Will . . . 6K 17
Cordons Cl. SL9: C Pet . . . 6H 103
Cordwainer Ct. MK14: N Hill . . . 7F 17
CORES END . . . 6J 107
Cores End Rd. SL8: Bou E . . . 6H 107
Corfe Cl. HP21: Ayle . . . 2C 66
Corfe Cres. MK3: Blet . . . 7F 29
Corfe Gdns. SL1: Slou . . . 5J 123
Coriander Ct. MK7: Waln . . . 2D 30
Corin Cl. MK2: Blet . . . 3K 33
Corinium Ind. Est. HP6: Amer . . . 5D 86
Cork Pl. MK3: Blet . . . 5E 28
Cornbrook Rd. HP21: Ayle . . . 2H 65
Cornbury Cres. MK15: D Park . . . 7G 17
Corncrake HP19: Ayle . . . 3K 61
Cornel Cl. HP15: Haz . . . 4H 91
Cornelia Cl. MK2: Blet . . . 2J 33
Cornerways HP27: Spee . . . 1G 81
Cornfield Cl. UB8: Uxb . . . 7K 121
Corn Hill MK8: T Ash . . . 5J 21
Cornwall Av. SL2: Slou . . . 2A 124
Cornwall Cl. SL4: E Wick . . . 3G 129
Cornwall Gro. MK3: Blet . . . 6E 28
(not continuous)
Cornwallis Mdw. MK18: Buck . . . 3H 37
Cornwall Pl. MK18: Buck . . . 3H 37
Cornwall Rd. UB8: Uxb . . . 4K 121
Coronation Av. SL3: G Grn . . . 3J 125
Coronation Cres. HP14: L End . . . 3K 73
Coronation Pl. MK18: S Clay . . . 3B 42
Coronation Rd. HP12: H Wyc . . . 4H 97
MK11: S Strat . . . 1C 20
Coronation Vs. *HP21: Ayle* . . . *6K 61*
(off High St.)
Corporation St. HP13: H Wyc . . . 2B 98
Corrid Ind. Pk. HP19: Ayle . . . 5G 61
Corrigan Cl. MK3: Blet . . . 7G 29
Corsewall Pl. MK4: Tatt . . . 6K 27
Corsham Ct. MK8: G Hol . . . 5K 21
COSGROVE . . . 3C 14 (2B 132)
Cosgrove Rd. MK19: O Stra . . . 6A 14
Cosway Pl. MK8: G Far . . . 1H 27
Cosy Cnr. HP22: Ast C . . . 2A 68
Cotes Way LU7: Wing . . . 2D 48
Cotman Cl. MK12: Gree . . . 1F 21
Cotswold Cl. SL1: Slou . . . 7A 124
UB8: Uxb . . . 6J 121
Cotswold Ct. HP11: H Wyc . . . 7K 89
Cotswold Grn. *HP20: Ayle* . . . *4K 61*
(off Hilton Av.)
Cotswold Way HP13: Down . . . 6J 89
Cottage Comn. MK5: Lough . . . 6B 22
Cott. Farm Way HP27: Spee . . . 2G 81
Cott. Grounds HP17: Sto . . . 2D 64
Cottage Pk. Rd. SL2: Hedg . . . 7B 110
COTTARVILLE . . . 1B 132
Cottesbrooke Cl. SL3: Coln . . . 6D 130
Cottesloe Cl. LU7: Wing . . . 2C 48
Cottesloe Ct. MK11: S Strat . . . 1D 20
Cottesloe Rd. HP21: Ayle . . . 2J 65
Cottingham Gro. MK3: Blet . . . 1G 33
COTTISFORD . . . 3A 132
Cottisford Cres. MK14: G Lin . . . 4E 16
(not continuous)
Cottland Clay HP17: Hadd . . . 5C 58
Coulson Av. MK5: Medb . . . 1J 27
MK8: G Far . . . 1J 27
Coulson Ct. HP16: Pres . . . 7D 74
Coulson Way SL1: Burn . . . 3D 122
Countess Cl. UB9: Hare . . . 1J 113
Countisbury MK4: Fur . . . 5D 28
Country La. HP15: G Kin . . . 5F 83
Cours La Ville Cl. MK18: Wins . . . 7G 39
Court Cl. HP13: Down . . . 6H 89
HP21: Ayle . . . 7K 61
HP27: Prin R . . . 5F 71
Court Cnr. MK46: Oln . . . 4G 7
Court Cres. SL1: Slou . . . 4B 124
COURTEENHALL . . . 1B 132
Courteneys Lodge *MK4: Fur* . . . *4E 28*
(off Blackmoor Ga.)
Court Farm Ho. SL1: Slou . . . 6K 123
Courtfield Gdns. UB9: Den . . . 1G 121
Court Garden Leisure Cen. . . . 1H 115
Courthouse Cl. MK18: Wins . . . 5H 39
Courthouse M. MK16: New P . . . 1J 17
Court La. SL0: Ive . . . 6F 127
(not continuous)
SL1: Burn . . . 1F 123
SL4: Dorn . . . 1C 128
Court Lawns HP10: T Grn . . . 6J 91
Courtmoor Cl. HP27: Mon R . . . 2H 71
Courtneidge Cl. LU7: Stew . . . 4C 46
Courtyard, The HP10: Woob G . . . 1A 108
MK14: G Lin . . . 4E 16
SL3: Lang . . . 7A 126
Courtyard Arts Cen., The . . . 4D 16
Courtyard Cl. HP6: Amer . . . 5A 86
Courtyard Ho. HP11: H Wyc . . . 1K 97
Courtyards, The HP22: Ast C . . . 3B 68
Cousins Dr. HP20: Ayle . . . 4A 62
Cousins Piece HP18: Che . . . 2H 57
Coverack Pl. MK4: Tatt . . . 7B 28
Coverdale MK13: Hee . . . 1C 22
Coverdale Way SL2: Slou . . . 2G 123
Cowdray Cl. MK15: Wool . . . 3J 23
Cow La. LU6: Edle . . . 1H 49
MK18: Gaw . . . 6C 36
COWLEY
Oxford . . . 3A 134
West Drayton . . . 2J 127 (2D 137)
Cowley Bus. Pk. UB8: Cowl . . . 1J 127
Cowley Cl. HP22: Bier . . . 3C 62
Cowley Cotts. HP7: Winc . . . 4E 92
Cowley Cres. UB8: Cowl . . . 3J 127
Cowley Mill Rd. UB8: Uxb . . . 7H 121
Cowley Mill Trad. Est. UB8: Uxb . . . 7H 121
COWLEY PEACHEY . . . 4K 127
Cowley Rd. UB8: Uxb . . . 7J 121
Cowper & Newton Mus., The . . . 4H 7
Cowper Cl. MK16: New P . . . 1G 17
Cowper Rd. HP5: Ches . . . 3K 77
SL2: Slou . . . 2J 123
Cowper St. MK46: Oln . . . 2J 7
Cowslip Rd. HP15: W End . . . 1F 91
Coxfield Cl. HP14: Stoke . . . 5D 72
Coxwell Cl. MK18: Buck . . . 3K 37
Coy Ct. HP20: Ayle . . . 6B 62
Crabbe Cres. HP5: Ches . . . 3B 78
Crabs Gro. HP22: W'urch . . . 1F 45
Crab Tree Cl. MK46: Oln . . . 2G 7
Crabtree Cl. HP9: Bea . . . 7D 100
Crabtree La. MK17: Wave . . . 6K 25
Crabtree Rd. HP17: Hadd . . . 7B 58
Craddocks Cl. MK13: B'ell . . . 3B 22
Cradle Footpath HP27: Whit . . . 2K 71
Cradley Wlk. HP20: Ayle . . . 3K 61
CRAFTON . . . 2C 135
Crafton Pl. HP19: Ayle . . . 5E 60
Cragleith Ct. HP9: Bea . . . 6F 101
Craigmore Av. MK3: Blet . . . 7F 29
Craigwell Av. HP21: Ayle . . . 7D 62
Crambourne Av. SL4: Wind . . . 7H 129
Cranberry Cl. MK7: Waln . . . 1D 30
Cranborne Av. MK4: West . . . 6K 27
(Chaffron Way, not continuous)
MK4: West . . . 5J 27
(Whaddon Rd.)
CRANBOURNE . . . 3C 137
Cranbourne Cl. SL1: Slou . . . 6A 124
Cranbourne Rd. SL1: Slou . . . 6A 124
Cranbrook MK17: W San . . . 2K 31
Crane Ct. MK5: Lough . . . 5B 22
Cranesbill Pl. MK14: Conn . . . 2E 22
CRANFIELD . . . 2D 133
Cranfield Rd. MK16: Moul . . . 5F 19
MK17: Wave, W San . . . 2K 31
CRANFORD . . . 3D 137
Cranwell Cl. MK5: S Broo . . . 4B 28
Craven, The MK13: Hee . . . 2C 22
Crayle St. SL2: Slou . . . 1J 123
CRAZIES HILL . . . 2A 136
CR Bates Ind. Est. HP14: Stoke . . . 5C 72
Creed St. MK12: Wolv . . . 6H 15
Crendon Ho. *HP6: Amer* . . . *4A 86*
(off Sycamore Rd.)
Crendon Rd. HP18: Che . . . 3H 57
HP18: Shab . . . 5H 55
Crendon St. HP13: H Wyc . . . 2B 98
Crendon Way HP18: Long C . . . 7E 56
Crescent, The HP13: H Wyc . . . 7E 90
HP23: M'rth . . . 7C 50
HP27: Prin R . . . 5H 71
LU7: Pits . . . 5E 50
MK2: Blet . . . 6J 29
MK14: G Lin . . . 3E 16
MK19: H'ham . . . 3J 15
SL1: Slou . . . 7C 124
(not continuous)
CRESLOW . . . 1H 45
Creslow Ct. MK11: S Strat . . . 1D 20
Creslow Way HP17: Sto . . . 3A 64
CRESSEX . . . 4H 97
Cressex Bus. Pk. HP12: H Wyc . . . 3J 97
Cressex Ent. Cen. HP12: H Wyc . . . 2J 97
Cressex Rd. HP12: Book, H Wyc . . . 5E 96
Cressex School Sports Cen. . . . 5G 97
Cressey Av. MK5: S Broo . . . 3B 28
Cressington Ct. SL8: Bou E . . . 5G 107
Cressington Pl. SL8: Bou E . . . 5G 107
Cress Rd. SL1: Slou . . . 7K 123
Cresswell Rd. HP5: Ches . . . 1B 86
Cresswell Way HP15: H Grn . . . 7K 83
Crest, The HP9: Bea . . . 6C 100
HP14: Bled R . . . 3C 72
Crest Rd. HP11: H Wyc . . . 5H 97
Creswick Mdw. HP21: Ayle . . . 2B 66
Cricketers Row MK18: Wins . . . 6J 39
Cricket Fld. Rd. UB8: Uxb . . . 6K 121
Cricketfield Rd. UB7: W Dra . . . 2J 131
CRICKET GREEN . . . 2H 23
Cricket Ground HP14: Stoke . . . 5B 72
Cricklebeck MK13: Hee . . . 1B 22
Crispin Cl. HP9: Bea . . . 4E 100
Crispin Fld. LU7: Pits . . . 5E 50
Crispin Rd. MK13: B'lle . . . 6A 16
Crispin Way HP11: H Wyc . . . 4A 98
SL2: Farn C . . . 2B 118
Criss Gro. SL9: C Pet . . . 7G 103
CROCKER END . . . 2A 136
Crocketts La. HP16: L Com . . . 1K 75
Crocus Dr. HP21: Ayle . . . 2G 65
Croft, The HP6: Amer . . . 4C 86
HP17: Hadd . . . 7B 58
SL7: Marl . . . 6A 106
Croft Ct. HP21: Ayle . . . 7K 61
Croft Courtyard HP17: Hadd . . . 7B 58
Crofthill Rd. SL2: Slou . . . 2K 123
Croft Ho. HP21: Ayle . . . 7K 61
Croft Mdws. LU7: Ched . . . 2C 50
Croft Pas. HP21: Ayle . . . 7K 61
Croft Rd. HP21: Ayle . . . 7K 61
SL9: C Pet . . . 7H 103
Crofts End MK16: Sher . . . 3B 12
Crofts La. MK17: New L . . . 5D 32
Croftwood HP13: H Wyc . . . 1F 99
Cromarty Ct. MK3: Blet . . . 4E 28
Cromer Ct. SL1: Slou . . . 4C 124
Cromhamstone HP17: Sto . . . 2C 64
Crompton Hall SL9: G Cro . . . 3K 111
Cromwell Av. HP19: Ayle . . . 4H 61
MK16: New P . . . 2G 17
Cromwell Cl. HP8: D Gil . . . 1G 103
Cromwell Ct. MK18: Buck . . . 2J 37
Cromwell Dr. SL1: Slou . . . 4C 124
Cromwell Gdns. SL7: Marl . . . 7J 105
Cromwell Ho. *HP5: Ches* . . . *4K 77*
(off Townsend Rd.)
Cromwell Rd. HP13: H Wyc . . . 3E 98
SL7: Marl . . . 7J 105
Cromwells Ct. SL3: Lang . . . 6K 125
Cropredy Ct. MK18: Buck . . . 2J 37
Cropton Ri. MK4: E Val . . . 5A 28
Cropwell Bishop MK4: E Val . . . 6C 28
Crosby Cl. HP9: Bea . . . 1H 109
Crosby Ct. MK8: C'ill . . . 1J 27
Crosland Rd. HP21: Ayle . . . 1C 66
Cross Ct. HP13: Down . . . 5H 89
CROSS END . . . 7H 25
Cross End MK17: Wave . . . 6H 25
Crossfield Rd. HP27: Prin R . . . 4H 71
Crosshills MK11: S Strat . . . 2B 20
Crosslands MK14: Stan . . . 5D 16
CROSS LANE . . . 6A 70
Cross La. HP9: Bea . . . 1H 109
MK18: Ting . . . 2C 36
Cross Lanes SL9: C Pet . . . 3J 103
Cross Lanes Cl. SL9: C Pet . . . 3K 103
Crossleys HP8: D Gil . . . 1G 103
Crossley's Hill HP8: D Gil . . . 1G 103
Crosslow Bank MK4: E Val . . . 4C 28
Cross Mdw. HP5: Ches . . . 3H 77
Cross Oak SL4: Wind . . . 7J 129
Cross Rd. HP12: H Wyc . . . 2G 97
UB8: Uxb . . . 5J 121
Cross St. MK16: New P . . . 1J 17
UB8: Uxb . . . 5J 121
Crossway HP5: Ches . . . 4C 78
Crossways HP9: Bea . . . 7H 101
Crosthwaite Way SL1: Slou . . . 3F 123
CROUGHTON . . . 3A 132
Crowborough La. MK7: K Hil . . . 6C 24
Crowbrook Rd. HP27: Mon R . . . 2G 71
Crowell M. HP19: Ayle . . . 6E 60
CROWFIELD . . . 2A 132
Crow La. MK17: Wave . . . 6K 25
Crown Bus. Est. HP5: Ches . . . 4A 78
Crown Cl. SL3: Coln . . . 5C 130
Crown Cotts. HP5: L Hil . . . 5F 79
Crownfield HP27: Saun . . . 3A 80
CROWNHILL . . . 7J 21
CROWNHILL . . . 6J 21
Crownhill Crematorium MK8: C'ill . . . 6J 21
Crown La. HP10: Pen . . . 1B 100
HP11: H Wyc . . . 1B 98
SL2: Farn R . . . 7J 117
SL7: Marl . . . 7H 105
Crown Leys HP20: Ayle . . . 5J 61
(not continuous)
Crown Mdw. SL3: Coln . . . 5B 130
Crown Rd. SL7: Marl . . . 7H 105
Crown Wlk. MK9: C Key . . . 3E 22
UB8: Uxb . . . 5J 121
Crow Piece La. SL2: Farn R . . . 5H 117
(not continuous)
Crowther Ct. MK5: S Lod . . . 2C 28
CROXLEY GREEN . . . 1D 137
Croydon Cl. MK4: Fur . . . 4C 28
Cruickshank Gro. MK8: C'ill . . . 7H 21
Crummock Cl. SL1: Slou . . . 4E 122
Crummock Pl. MK2: Blet . . . 2K 33
Crutches La. HP9: Jord . . . 4C 102
CRYERS HILL . . . 1D 90 (1B 136)
Cryers Hill La. HP15: Crye . . . 1D 90
Cryers Hill Rd. HP15: Crye . . . 2B 90
Cubb Fld. HP19: Ayle . . . 7G 61
CUBLINGTON . . . 2G 47 (1C 135)
Cublington Rd. HP22: A Abb . . . 4H 47
LU7: Wing . . . 3A 48
Cuckoo Way HP19: Ayle . . . 6E 60
CUDDESDON . . . 3A 134
CUDDINGTON . . . 1B 58 (2B 134)
Cuddington Hill HP18: Cudd . . . 1A 58
Cuddington Rd. HP18: Dint . . . 1E 58
Cudsdens Ct. HP16: G Mis . . . 6K 75
Cuff La. MK17: G Bri . . . 7F 35
Culbertson La. MK13: Blue B . . . 7J 15
Cullen Pl. MK2: Blet . . . 3K 33
Cullyn Rd. HP12: Book . . . 5G 97
Culmstock Cl. MK4: E Val . . . 5D 28
Culrain Pl. MK12: H Lea . . . 2H 21
Culross Gro. MK10: Monk . . . 4C 24
Culvert Cft. HP9: S Grn . . . 4A 102
Culvert La. UB8: Uxb . . . 7H 121
Culverton Hill HP27: Prin R . . . 5G 71
Culverton La. HP27: Prin R . . . 7F 71
CULWORTH . . . 2A 132
Cumberland Av. SL2: Slou . . . 2A 124
Cumberland Cl. HP7: L Chal . . . 6F 87
HP21: Ayle . . . 7C 62
Cumbrae Cl. SL2: Slou . . . 6E 124
Cumbria Cl. MK3: Blet . . . 6F 29
Cumbrian Way HP13: Down . . . 6J 89
UB8: Uxb . . . 5K 121
Curlew HP19: Ayle . . . 3A 62
Curlew Cl. HP13: Down . . . 5G 89
Curran Cl. UB8: Cowl . . . 2J 127
Currier Dr. MK14: N Hill . . . 7E 16
Curriers La. SL1: Burn . . . 3F 117
Cursley Path HP19: Ayle . . . 6F 61

Curtis Cft. MK5: S Broo .4B 28
Curzon Av. HP9: Bea .4F 101
HP15: Haz .5J 91
Curzon Cl. HP15: Haz .5J 91
Curzon Mall SL1: Slou .7D 124
(off Wellington St.)
Curzon Pl. MK7: Old P .3G 31
Cut, The SL2: Slou .2J 123
Cutlers Ct. HP12: H Wyc .1J 97
(off Copyground La.)
Cutlers M. MK14: N Hill .7F 17
Cut Throat Av. LU6: Whip .4J 49
CUXHAM .1A 136
Cyclamen Pl. HP21: Ayle .2G 65
Cypress MK16: New P .2G 17
Cypress Ho. SL3: Lang .3B 130
Cypress Wlk. HP15: Haz .4H 91
(off Elder Way)

D

Dadbrook HP18: Cudd .1B 58
Dadbrook Cl. HP18: Cudd .2B 58
Dadfield Cl. HP18: Cudd .2B 58
DADFORD .3A 132
Dag La. MK16: S Gold .5B 6
DAGNALL .6H 49 (2D 135)
Dagnall Cres. UB8: Cowl .3J 127
Dagnall Rd. MK46: Oln .4G 7
Dairymede HP27: Spee .2G 81
Dale Ct. SL1: Slou .7A 124
Dalesford Rd. HP21: Ayle .3B 66
Dale Side SL9: G Cro .6J 111
Dalgin Pl. MK9: Camp .3G 23
DALSCOTE .1A 132
Dalston Cl. HP20: Ayle .4A 62
Dalton Ga. MK10: Midd .3B 24
Dalton Grn. SL3: Lang .4A 130
Dalvina Pl. MK12: H Lea .2H 21
Dalwood M. HP19: Ayle .6F 61
Daly Way HP20: Ayle .7C 62
Damson Gro. SL1: Slou .7A 124
Danbury Ct. MK14: L Woo .1E 22
Dancers End & Crong Meadow
Nature Reserve .7D 68
Dancers End La. HP23: Tring .4E 68
Dandridge Ct. MK8: G Far .1G 27
Dandridge Dr. SL8: Bou E .6J 107
Dane Cl. HP7: Amer .1D 94
Dane Ct. HP21: Ayle .3J 65
Dane Rd. MK1: F Str .5K 29
Danesborough Dr. MK17: A H'th .5J 31
Danesbrook Cl. MK4: Fur .3D 28
Daneswood MK17: A H'th .6J 31
Daniels Welch MK6: Coff .7G 23
Dansteed Way (H4) MK13: Mil K .3B 22
MK14: Mil K .2D 22
MK15: Mil K .7G 17
Darby Cl. MK5: S Lod .2B 28
Darin Ct. MK8: C'ill .6K 21
Dark La. HP18: Che .2H 57
HP22: Ovi .5C 44
HP22: W'rave .6C 48
Darley Cl. HP21: Ayle .1C 66
Darley Ga. MK14: D Barn .1F 23
Darley's Cl. HP18: G Und .2H 43
Darlington Cl. HP6: Amer .5B 86
Darnel Cl. MK6: Bean .2G 29
Darrell Charles Ct. UB8: Uxb .5K 121
Darsham Wlk. HP5: Ches .5K 77
(off High St.)
Dart Cl. HP21: Ayle .2H 65
MK16: New P .1K 17
SL3: Lang .3B 130
Dartmouth Rd. MK46: Oln .3H 7
Darvell Dr. HP5: Ches .3J 77
Darvill Rd. HP17: Sto .2A 64
DARVILLSHILL .2E 80
Darvill's La. SL1: Slou .7B 124
Darvills Mdw. HP15: H Grn .7J 83
Darwin Cl. MK5: Medb .2H 27
Darwin Rd. SL3: Lang .7K 125
Dashwood Av. HP12: H Wyc .7G 89
Dashwood Works Ind. Est.
HP12: H Wyc .7H 89
(off Fryers La.)
DATCHET .3C 137
Datchet Rd. SL3: Hor .7A 130
Daubeney Ga. MK5: S Chur .1K 27
Davenport Lea MK7: Old P .3G 31
Davenport Rd. HP12: Book .5G 97
DAVENTRY .1A 132
Daventry Cl. SL3: Poy .6F 131
David Bishop Ct. HP5: Ches .1B 86
(off Woodley Hill)
David Cl. HP21: Ayle .3B 66
Davidge Pl. HP8: D Gil .1F 103
(off Milton Flds.)
HP9: Bea .3E 100
David Lloyd Leisure .1J 23
David Rd. SL3: Poy .7F 131
Davies Cl. HP20: Ayle .6J 61
Davies Ct. HP12: H Wyc .3H 97
Davies Way HP10: Loud .7J 99
Davis Cl. SL7: Marl .1J 115
Davison Ct. MK8: G Far .1H 27
Davy Av. MK5: Know .7C 22
Dawes Cl. HP5: Ches .6K 77
Dawes E. Rd. SL1: Burn .2E 122
Dawes Moor Cl. SL2: Slou .4G 125
Dawley Ride SL3: Poy .6E 130
Dawney Cl. HP19: Ayle .4H 61
Dawn Redwood Cl. SL3: Hor .7A 130
Daws Ct. SL0: Ive .4F 127
Daws Hill La. HP11: H Wyc .4A 98
Daws Lea HP11: H Wyc .5A 98
Dawson Cl. SL4: Wind .7J 129
Dawson Rd. MK1: Blet .4J 29
Daylesford Ct. MK15: D Park .7H 17
Daytona International Karting Circuit
.4B 22
Deacon Cl. HP12: Book .4F 97
Deacon Ct. SL4: Wind .7F 129
Deacon Pl. MK10: Midd .3A 24
Deadhearn La. HP8: D Gil .6J 95
Deal Av. SL1: Slou .4H 123
Dean, The HP22: W'rave .6C 48
Deanacre Cl. SL9: C Pet .4J 103
Dean Cl. HP12: H Wyc .2J 97
HP21: Ayle .2B 66
SL4: Wind .7F 129
Deancroft Rd. SL9: C Pet .4J 103
Dean Farm La. LU7: Soul .4H 41
Dean Fld. HP3: Bov .1K 79
Deanfield HP14: Saun .2D 72
Deanfield Cl. HP14: Saun .5A 80
SL7: Marl .6H 105
Deangarden Ri. HP11: H Wyc .4E 98
Dean Rd. LU7: Stew .2A 46
Deans Cl. HP6: Amer .4D 86
SL2: S Pog .6F 119
DEANSHANGER .3B 132
Deanshanger Rd. MK19: O Stra .7A 14
Deans Mdw. HP4: Dag .6H 49
Dean's Rd. MK12: O Wol .6G 15
Dean St. SL7: Marl .7H 105
Deansway HP5: Ches .3J 77
Dean Way HP8: D Gil .1E 102
HP15: H Grn .1H 91
HP22: Ast C .3C 68
Dean Wood Rd. HP9: Jord .5B 102
Dearing Cl. HP20: Ayle .4A 62
Dearmer Ho. SL9: C Pet .3J 103
(off Micholls Av.)
Debbs Cl. MK11: S Strat .1C 20
Deben Cl. MK16: New P .2A 18
Decies Way SL2: S Pog .6E 118
De Clare Ct. MK18: Buck .3J 37
Dedmere Ct. SL7: Marl .7K 105
Dedmere Ri. SL7: Marl .7J 105
Dedmere Rd. SL7: Marl .7J 105
DEDWORTH .7G 129
Dedworth Dr. SL4: Wind .6H 129
DEDWORTH GREEN .7F 129
Dedworth Mnr. SL4: Wind .6H 129
Dedworth Rd. SL4: Wind .7E 128
Deeds Gro. HP12: H Wyc .1J 97
Deena Cl. SL1: Slou .5G 123
Deep Acres HP6: Amer .3J 85
Deepdale MK13: Hee .1C 22
Deep Mill La. HP16: L Kin .3K 83
Deerfern Cl. MK14: G Lin .4E 16
Deerfield Cl. MK18: Buck .5J 37
Deermead HP16: L Kin .2H 83
Dee Rd. SL4: Wind .5E 128
Deer Pk. Wlk. HP5: Ches .2C 78
Deer Wlk. MK9: C Key .3E 22
Deethe Cl. MK17: W San .1K 31
De Havilland Dr. HP15: Haz .5E 90
Delafield Cl. HP14: Stoke .6D 72
Delaford Cl. SL0: Ive .4G 127
Delamere Cl. HP20: Ayle .4A 62
Delaware Dr. MK15: Blak .4H 17
(not continuous)
Delius Cl. MK7: Brow .3E 30
Dell, The HP10: T Grn .6J 91
HP14: Stoke .6D 72
HP20: Ayle .4B 62
SL9: C Pet .4J 103
Dell Cl. SL2: Farn C .3A 118
Dell Fld. HP16: Pres .1D 82
Dellfield HP5: Ches .3J 77
Dellfield Cres. UB8: Cowl .2K 127
Dellfield Pde. UB8: Cowl .2J 127
Dell Lees HP9: S Grn .4A 102
Dell Orchard HP7: Winc .5E 92
Dells MK46: Oln .3H 7
Dellside UB9: Hare .3J 113
Delmeade Rd. HP5: Ches .6J 77
Deltic Av. MK13: Rook .4B 22
Demoram Cl. MK18: Wins .7H 39
DENBIGH .5K 29
DENBIGH EAST .5K 29
Denbigh E. Ind. Est. MK1: F Str .5A 30
DENBIGH HALL .4F 29
Denbigh Hall MK3: Blet .4F 29
Denbigh Hall Dr. MK3: Blet .4F 29
Denbigh Hall Ind. Est. MK3: Blet .4F 29
DENBIGH NORTH .4H 29
Denbigh North Leisure .5J 29
Denbigh Rd. MK1: Blet .4H 29
Denbigh Way MK2: Blet .6J 29
DENBIGH WEST .5H 29
Denbigh W. Ind. Est. MK1: Blet .5H 29
(Denbigh Rd.)
MK1: Blet .6J 29
(Watling St.)
Denby Wlk. HP20: Ayle .6B 62
Denchworth Ct. MK4: E Val .5C 28
Dene, The MK18: S Clay .2B 42
Dene Cl. MK17: W San .4K 31
MK18: Wins .7J 39
Denewood HP13: H Wyc .7E 90
DENHAM
Aylesbury .5K 43
Uxbridge .1F 121 (2D 137)
Denham Aerodrome .3D 112
Denham Av. UB9: Den .7F 113
Denham Cl. MK3: Blet .7D 28
UB9: Den .1G 121
Denham Cotts. HP22: Q'ton .5K 43
Denham Country Pk. .6H 113
Denham Ct. Dr. UB9: Den .2G 121
DENHAM GARDEN VILLAGE .3F 113
Denham Golf Club Station (Rail) .5D 112
DENHAM GREEN .4F 113 (2D 137)
Denham Grn. Cl. UB9: Den .5G 113
Denham Grn. La. UB9: Den .3E 112
Denham La. SL9: C Pet .1B 112
Denham Lodge UB9: Den .4J 121
Denham Pde. UB9: Den .1F 121
(off Oxford Rd.)
Denham Rd. HP14: L End .3A 96
SL0: I Hea .6D 120
UB9: Den .4F 121
DENHAM RDBT. .2G 121
Denham Station (Rail) .5G 113
Denham Wlk. SL9: C Pet .4K 103
Denham Way UB9: Den .1G 121
(Old Mill Rd.)
UB9: Den .1F 113
(Wyatt's Covert)
WD3: W Hyd .1F 113
Denison Ct. MK7: W Gat .1F 31
Denley Sq. UB8: Uxb .5K 121
Denmark St. HP11: H Wyc .1A 98
MK2: F Str .7A 30
Denmead MK8: T Ash .4J 21
Denmead Cl. SL9: G Cro .5J 111
Dennis Cl. HP22: Ast C .3D 68
Dennis Way SL1: Slou .5F 123
DENTON
Northampton .1C 133
Oxford .3A 134
Denton Ct. SL7: Marl .6K 105
De Pirenore HP15: Haz .5E 90
Derby Rd. UB8: Uxb .7J 121
Derehams Av. HP10: Loud .5J 99
Derehams La. HP10: Loud .6J 99
Dere Pl. MK2: Blet .4A 34
Derwent Cl. HP7: L Chal .6F 87
MK16: New P .1K 17
Derwent Dr. MK3: Blet .7E 28
SL1: Slou .3E 122
Derwent Rd. HP21: Ayle .1C 66
Desborough Av. HP11: H Wyc .4J 97
Desborough Grn. HP20: Ayle .5J 61
(off Dusham La.)
Desborough Ho. HP13: H Wyc .1B 98
Desborough Ind. Pk. HP12: H Wyc .7J 89
Desborough Pk. Rd. HP12: H Wyc .1J 97
Desborough Rd. HP11: H Wyc .1K 97
Desborough St. HP11: H Wyc .7J 89
Deseronto Trad. Est. SL3: Lang .7J 125
Develin Cl. MK14: N Hill .6F 17
De Vere Leisure Club .2C 110
Devereux Pl. HP19: Ayle .4F 61
Deverill Rd. HP21: Ayle .4H 65
Deverills Way SL3: Lang .2C 130
Devon Av. SL1: Slou .4A 124
Devon Cl. MK3: Blet .6E 28
Devon Rd. HP19: Ayle .3F 61
Devonshire Av. HP6: Amer .4K 85
Devonshire Cl. HP6: Amer .4A 86
SL2: Farn R .7K 117
Devonshire Grn. SL2: Farn R .7K 117
Dexter Av. MK6: Old .6F 23
Dexter Ho. MK6: Old .6F 23
Diamond Rd. SL1: Slou .7E 124
Diana Cl. SL3: G Grn .4J 125
Diane Cl. HP21: Ayle .3B 66
Diane Wlk. HP21: Ayle .3B 66
DIBDEN HILL .2G 103
Dickens Pl. SL3: Poy .6E 130
Dickens Rd. MK12: O Wol .5G 15
Dickens Spinney MK46: Oln .3G 7
Dickens Way HP19: Ayle .4E 60
Dicks Way HP19: Ayle .3E 60
Diddington Cl. MK2: Blet .5J 33
Digby Cft. MK10: Midd .3A 24
Dilwyn Ct. HP12: H Wyc .1J 97
Dimsdale Dr. SL2: Farn C .3G 117
Dingledderry MK46: Oln .3H 7
Dinmore HP3: Bov .2K 79
DINTON .2G 59 (2B 134)
Disraeli Ct. SL3: Lang .4B 130
Disraeli Cres. HP13: Down .6K 89
Disraeli Pk. HP9: Bea .4F 101
Disraeli Sq. HP19: Ayle .6F 61
DITCHFIELD .4J 73
Ditchfield Comn. HP14: L End .5J 73
Ditchingham Cl. HP19: Ayle .7G 61
Ditton Rd. SL3: Lang .4A 130
Dixie La. MK7: W Gat .1E 30
Dixon Cl. HP21: Ayle .1G 65
Dobbins La. HP22: Wend .3G 69
Docton Mill MK4: West .5J 27
Doddsfield Rd. SL2: Slou .1J 123
Dodds La. HP8: D Gil .7E 94
DODFORD .1A 132
Dodkin MK6: Bean .2H 29
(not continuous)
Dodman Grn. MK4: Tatt .7B 28
Doggetts Farm Rd. UB9: Den .5C 112
Doggetts Wood Cl. HP8: D Gil .2F 95
Doggetts Wood La. HP8: D Gil .1F 95
Dolben Ct. MK15: Will .5K 17
Dollicott HP17: Hadd .6B 58
Dolphin Ct. HP11: W Mar .5G 99
SL1: Slou .7F 125
Dolphin Pl. HP21: Ayle .1K 65
Dolphin Rd. SL1: Slou .7F 125
Don, The MK3: Blet .6D 28
Donkey La. SL8: Bou E .6G 107
UB7: W Dra .2J 131
Donnay Cl. SL9: G Cro .4H 111
Donnington MK13: B'lle .7B 16
DOOLITTLE VILLAGE .4B 98
Doon Way MK2: Blet .3J 33
(not continuous)
Dorchester Av. MK3: Blet .5F 29
(not continuous)
Dorchester Cl. HP22: Sto M .5C 66
Doreen Cl. MK2: Blet .1J 33
Dorking Pl. MK5: S Broo .3B 28
Dormans Cl. MK10: M Vill .4C 24
Dormer Av. LU7: Wing .2C 48
Dormer Cl. HP21: Ayle .1G 65
Dormer Ct. HP20: Ayle .4A 62
Dormer La. HP15: G Kin .7H 83
Dornels SL2: Slou .4G 125
DORNEY .1D 128 (3C 137)
Dorney Court .1D 128
Dorney End HP5: Ches .4J 77
Dorney Hill Nth. HP9: Bea .3J 109
Dorney Hill Sth. HP9: Bea .5J 109
Dorney Lake .3D 128
Dorney Pl. MK13: B Com .3C 22
DORNEY REACH .1B 128
Dorney Reach Rd. SL6: Dorn R .1B 128
Dorney Wood Rd. SL1: Burn .1E 116
Dorrels Rd. HP27: Long .2C 70
Dorset Cl. MK3: Blet .6F 29
Dorset Pl. HP21: Ayle .1D 66
Dorsey Cl. MK8: C'ill .1J 27
DORTON .2A 134
Dorton Cl. MK8: G Hol .5K 21
Dorton Rd. HP18: Chil .1B 56
Douglas Ct. SL7: Marl .6A 106
Douglas Pl. MK6: Old .6D 22
Douglas Rd. HP20: Ayle .4A 62
SL2: Slou .3B 124
Doune Ho. MK3: Blet .5F 29
Dove Cl. HP21: Ayle .2H 65
MK16: New P .1K 17
MK18: Buck .5J 37
Dovecote HP17: Hadd .6B 58
MK16: New P .1J 17
Dovecote Cl. HP17: Hadd .6B 58
HP27: Mon R .3H 71
Dovecote Cft. MK14: G Lin .4E 16
Dovecot Rd. HP13: H Wyc .1A 98
(not continuous)
Dove Ct. HP9: Bea .5F 101
Dovedale Cl. UB9: Hare .1J 113
Dove Ho. HP19: Ayle .2A 62
(off Dove Pl.)
Dove Ho. Cl. MK18: Wins .6J 39
Dovehouse Cl. LU6: Edle .2K 49
Dove Ho. Cres. SL2: Slou .1G 123
Dovehouse M. MK16: S Gold .6C 6
Dovehouse Path HP11: H Wyc .1A 98
Dove Pl. HP19: Ayle .2A 62
Dover Cl. LU7: Pits .7F 51
Dover Ga. MK3: Blet .1F 33
Dover Hedge HP21: Ayle .7D 62
Dover Rd. SL1: Slou .4H 123
Dove St. LU7: Stew .4C 46
Dovetail Cl. HP12: H Wyc .7H 89
Dower Cl. HP9: Bea .3E 100
DOWLESGREEN .3B 136
Downdean MK6: Eagl .6G 23
Downderry Cft. MK4: Tatt .7B 28
Downer Cl. MK18: Buck .4K 37
Downham Rd. MK17: W San .3K 31
DOWNHEAD PARK .1H 23
Downhill Cl. MK5: S Chur .1A 28
Downing Path SL2: Slou .2G 123
Download MK8: T Ash .4J 21
DOWNLEY .5H 89 (1B 136)
Downley Av. MK13: B Com .3C 22
DOWNLEY COMMON .3J 89
Downley Rd. HP14: Nap .1H 89
Down Pl. SL4: W Oak .4C 128
DOWNS BARN .1G 23
DOWNS BARN .1F 23
Downs Barn Blvd. MK14: D Barn .2F 23

Downs Pk. HP13: Down 6J 89
Downs Rd. SL3: Lang 7H 125
Downs Vw. MK17: Bow B 5E 30
Dragons Health Club 4G 123
(off Bunrham La.)
Dragon Tail HP17: Hadd 7C 58
Drake Cl. HP21: Ayle 1G 65
Drakes Dr. HP18: Long C 7D 56
Drakes Farm HP18: Long C 7E 56
Drakes M. MK8: C'ill 7J 21
Drake's Rd. HP7: Amer 6C 86
Drakewell Rd. MK17: Bow B 6F 31
Drawing Room, The 5K 77
(off East St.)
DRAYCOT 7D 54 (3A 134)
Draymans La. SL7: Marl 1H 115
DRAYTON 1A 132
DRAYTON BEAUCHAMP 2E 68 (2D 135)
Drayton Gdns. UB7: W Dra 7K 127
DRAYTON PARSLOW 6C 40 (1C 135)
Drayton Rd. HP20: Ayle 4J 61
MK2: Blet 2J 33
MK17: New L 6C 32
DRAYTON ST LEONARD 3A 134
Dresser Rd. HP16: Pres 1C 82
Drew Ct. MK6: Red 3G 29
Drew Mdw. SL2: Farn C 2A 118
Drews Pk. HP9: Bea 2E 100
Drey, The SL9: C Pet 3J 103
Drift Way MK46: Oln 2H 7
SL3: Coln 6C 130
Drive, The HP7: Amer 5B 86
LU7: I Ast 1J 51
SL3: Lang 7J 125
SL8: Bou E 5F 107
SL9: C Pet 5J 103
UB10: I'ham 2K 121
Dropmore Rd. SL1: Burn 2E 116
Drovers Cft. MK12: Gree 2F 21
Drovers Way HP9: S Grn 4A 102
MK17: New L 6D 32
Drummond Hay MK15: Will 6J 17
Drydell La. HP5: Ches 4G 77
Dryden Cl. HP20: Ayle 4K 61
MK16: New P 1G 17
Dsahfield Gro. HP15: W End 1E 90
Duchess Gro. MK7: W Gat 7E 24
Duchess St. SL1: Slou 6G 123
Duchie's Piece Nature Reserve 7H 51
Duck End MK17: G Bri 7F 35
Duck Farm Ct. HP20: Ayle 6J 61
Duck Lake MK18: M M'ton 1J 37
Duck Lake Cl. MK18: M M'ton 1J 37
Duck La. HP18: Ludg 2C 52
Duckworth Ct. MK6: Old 7E 22
Dudley Cl. MK18: N Mar 2A 44
Dudley Ct. SL1: Slou 7E 124
Dudley Hill MK5: S Chur 1A 28
Dudley Wharf Caravans SL0: Lang 6B 126
Duffield La. SL2: S Pog 4D 118
Duffield Pk. SL2: S Pog 1E 124
Dukes Cl. HP18: Shab 6G 55
SL9: G Cro 6H 111
Dukes Dr. MK2: Blet 6J 29
SL2: Farn C 3H 117
Dukes Kiln Dr. SL9: G Cro 6G 111
Dukes La. SL9: G Cro 5J 111
Dukes Mdw. Ind. Est. SL8: Bou E 6H 107
Dukes Piece MK18: Buck 4K 37
Dukes Pl. SL7: Marl 7H 105
Dukes Ride SL9: G Cro 6J 111
UB10: I'ham 2K 121
Duke St. HP13: H Wyc 1C 98
HP27: Prin R 4G 71
SL4: Wind 5K 129
Dukes Valley SL9: G Cro 7F 111
Dukes Way UB8: Uxb 6H 121
Dukes Wood Av. SL9: G Cro 5J 111
Dukes Wood Dr. SL9: G Cro 6G 111
Dulverton Dr. MK4: Fur 4C 28
Dulwich Cl. MK16: New P 3J 17
Dumfries Cl. MK3: Blet 4F 29
Dunbar Cl. MK3: Blet 7D 28
SL2: Slou 5E 124
Duncan Gro. MK5: S Chur 1K 27
Duncannon Cres. SL4: Wind 7F 129
Dunchurch Dale MK7: Waln 2C 30
Duncombe Cl. HP6: Amer 5C 86
Duncombe St. MK2: Blet 7H 29
DUNCOTE 1A 132
Dundee Rd. SL1: Slou 4H 123
Dungeness Ct. MK4: Tatt 6K 27
Dungrove Hill La. SL6: Maid 7G 115
Dunkeld Ho. HP13: H Wyc 4H 99
Dunkery Beacon MK4: Fur 4D 28
Dunnet Cl. MK4: Tatt 7A 28
Dunsby Rd. MK6: Red 3G 29
DUNSDEN GREEN 3A 136
Dunsham La. HP19: Ayle 3A 62
HP20: Ayle 4J 61
DUNSMORE 3C 135
Dunsmore Av. HP27: Mon R 3H 71
Dunsmore Ride HP27: Mon R 3G 71
DUNSTABLE 1D 135
Dunstable Rd. HP4: Dag 6H 49
LU6: E Bra 1K 49
Dunster Ct. MK4: Fur 4E 28
Dunster Gdns. SL1: Slou 5J 123
Dunthorne Way MK8: G Far 1H 27
DUNTON 1C 135
Dunton Rd. LU7: Stew 7A 46
Dunvedin Pl. MK12: H Lea 2H 21
Dunvegan Cl. MK2: Blet 4K 33
Dunwood Ri. HP13: H Wyc 6B 90
Duparc Cl. MK7: Brow 2E 30
Dupre Cl. SL1: Slou 7G 123
Dupre Cres. HP9: Bea 7K 101
Du Pre Wlk. HP10: Woob G 5K 107
Durgate MK7: K Par 6C 24
Durham Av. SL1: Slou 4J 123
Durley Hollow HP13: H Wyc 6B 90
Durlston End MK4: Tatt 7A 28
Durrans Ct. MK2: F Str 6A 30
Durrans Ho. MK2: F Str 6A 30
(off Durrans Ct.)
Durrants Path HP5: Ches 1J 77
DUSTON 1B 132
Dutton Way SL0: Ive 4E 126
Dyersdale MK13: Hee 1C 22
Dyers M. MK14: N Hill 7F 17
Dyson Cl. SL4: Wind 7K 129

E

Eagle Cl. HP6: Amer 4D 86
Eagles Rd. HP20: Ayle 6B 62
EAGLESTONE 6H 23
EAGLESTONE 6G 23
EAGLESTONE WEST 7H 23
Eagle Wlk. MK9: C Key 3F 23
EAKLEY LANES 1C 133
Ealing Chase MK10: Monk 6B 24
Eames Cl. HP20: Ayle 3A 62
Eardley Pl. MK8: G Far 1H 27
Earl Cl. HP13: Down 6A 90
EARLEY 3A 136
Earl Howe Rd. HP15: H Grn 7J 83
EARLS BARTON 1C 133
Earls Cl. MK2: Blet 7J 29
Earls La. SL1: Slou 6H 123
Earls Willow MK13: New B 5A 16
Earlswood Cl. HP21: Ayle 2B 66
Easby Gro. MK10: Monk 5C 24
EASINGTON
Aylesbury 3B 56 (2A 134)
Watlington 3A 134
Easington La. HP18: Long C 3B 56
EAST BEDFONT 3D 137
Eastbourne Rd. SL1: Slou 4J 123
Eastbridge SL1: Slou 7F 125
EAST BURNHAM 5J 117 (2C 137)
E. Burnham La. SL2: Farn R 6J 117
EASTBURY 1D 137
Eastbury Ct. MK4: E Val 6D 28
East Chapel MK4: Tatt 7B 28
EAST CLAYDON 1B 134
E. Claydon Rd. MK18: Wins 7G 39
East Comn. SL9: G Cro 4J 111
EASTCOTE
Pinner 2D 137
Towcester 1A 132
Eastcote Rd. HP21: Ayle 3C 66
East Cres. SL4: Wind 6H 129
Eastcroft SL2: Slou 2K 123
East Dales MK13: Hee 1C 22
East Dr. HP13: H Wyc 7E 90
SL2: S Pog 1C 124
East End HP22: W'don 7K 45
Eastergate HP9: Bea 4E 100
Eastern Dene HP15: Haz 2G 91
Eastern Dr. SL8: Bou E 5J 107
Eastern St. HP20: Ayle 5K 61
Eastfield Cl. SL1: Slou 7E 124
Eastfield Dr. MK19: H'ope 1E 8
Eastfield Rd. HP20: Ayle 6C 62
HP27: Prin R 5H 71
SL1: Burn 3C 122
Eastgreen Cl. MK5: S Chur 1K 27
EASTHAMPSTEAD 3B 136
EASTHEATH 3B 136
Eastlands HP27: L Grn 1C 80
East La. MK7: Walt H 7B 24
EAST MOLESEY 3D 137
Eastnor HP3: Bov 2K 79
Eastoke Pl. MK4: Tatt 7A 28
EASTON MAUDIT 1C 133
Easton St. HP11: H Wyc 2B 98
Easton Ter. HP13: H Wyc 2C 98
E. Paddock SL6: Cook 4K 115
E. Richardson St. HP11: H Wyc 1K 97
East Ridge SL8: Bou E 5H 107
East Spur MK7: Walt H 7B 24
East St. HP5: Ches 6K 77
MK18: Ads 6E 38
MK46: Oln 3H 7
East Wlk. MK9: C Key 4E 22
East Wlk. Sth. MK9: C Key 4E 22
(off East Wlk.)
East Way HP9: Bea 7C 100
Eastwood Ct. SL7: Marl 6K 105
(off Wiltshire Rd.)
Eastwood Rd. HP14: Stoke 7D 72
Easy Cinema 4F 23
Eaton Av. HP12: H Wyc 7H 89
MK2: Blet 1K 33
EATON BRAY 1J 49 (1D 135)
Eaton Bray Rd. LU6: N'all 2G 49
Eatongate Cl. LU6: E Bra 2J 49
Eaton Pk. LU6: E Bra 1K 49
Eaton Pl. HP12: H Wyc 7H 89
Eaton Rd. HP21: Ayle 1J 65
Ebble Cl. HP21: Ayle 3H 65
Ebbsgrove MK5: Lough 5B 22
ECTON 1C 133
Eddington Ct. MK4: E Val 6D 28
Eden Cl. HP21: Ayle 3J 65
SL3: Lang 3A 130
Eden Wlk. MK3: Blet 6E 28
Edgar Wallace Pl. SL8: Bou E 4H 107
EDGCOTT 1A 134
Edgcott Rd. HP18: G Und 1G 43
Edgecombe Rd. HP21: Ayle 2C 66
Edgecote MK8: G Hol 6A 22
Edge Hill Ct. MK18: Buck 2J 37
Edinburgh Av. SL1: Slou 3J 123
Edinburgh Dr. UB9: Den 4F 113
Edinburgh Ga. UB9: Den 4F 113
(off Patrons Way W.)
Edinburgh Ho. MK3: Blet 1D 32
(off Chester Clo.)
Edinburgh Pl. HP21: Ayle 1H 65
Edinburgh Rd. SL7: Marl 6J 105
Edison Rd. HP19: Ayle 5D 60
Edison Sq. MK5: S Lod 2C 28
Edith Bell Ho. SL9: C Pet 4J 103
EDLESBOROUGH 2J 49 (2D 135)
Edmonds Cl. MK18: Buck 3K 37
Edmonds Rd. HP14: L End 4K 73
Edmonds Shop. Cen. HP14: L End 4K 73
(off Edmonds Rd.)
Edmund Ct. HP9: Bea 1C 108
MK5: S Chur 7K 21
Edmunds Cl. HP12: Book 3G 97
Edmunds Gdns. HP12: Book 3G 97
Edmunds Way SL2: Slou 3F 125
Edrich Av. MK6: Old 6F 23
Edward Cl. HP21: Ayle 3B 66
Edwards Ct. SL1: Slou 7C 124
Edwards Cft. MK13: B'lle 6A 16
Edward Wlk. HP21: Ayle 3B 66
Edwin Allman Pl. HP15: Haz 5E 90
(off Beechlands)
Edwin Cl. MK17: Bow B 5F 31
Edy Ct. MK5: Lough 5A 22
Edzell Cres. MK4: West 5J 27
Eelbrook Av. MK13: B Com 4C 22
Eeles Cl. HP19: Ayle 3E 60
Egerton Ga. MK5: S Broo 3A 28
Egerton Rd. SL2: Slou 2G 123
EGGINGTON 1D 135
EGHAM 3D 137
EGHAM HYTHE 3D 137
Eghams Cl. HP9: Bea 4E 100
Eghams Grn. SL8: Bou E 6H 107
Eghams Wood Rd. HP9: Bea 4E 100
Egmont Av. MK11: S Strat 2C 20
Egremont Gdns. SL1: Slou 6J 123
EGYPT 2K 117 (2C 137)
Egypt La. SL2: Farn C 7K 109
Egypt Way HP19: Ayle 6F 61
Eider Cl. MK18: Buck 4J 37
Eight Acres SL1: Burn 2D 122
Elbow Mdw. SL3: Poy 6F 131
Elder Cl. HP13: H Wyc 5H 99
Elderfield Rd. SL2: S Pog 4D 118
Elder Ga. MK9: C Key 5B 22
(not continuous)
Elder Way HP15: Haz 4G 91
SL3: Lang 7K 125
Eleanor Gdns. HP21: Ayle 2A 66
Eleanor Ho. SL9: C Pet 3J 103
(off Micholls Av.)
Eleanor Rd. SL9: C Pet 6G 103
ELFIELD PARK 3F 29
ELFIELD PARK 3F 29
Elfords MK6: Coff 1G 29
Elgar Gro. MK7: Brow 2E 30
Elgiva, The 5K 77
Elgiva La. HP5: Ches 5K 77
Elham Way HP21: Ayle 3B 66
Eliot Cl. HP19: Ayle 4E 60
MK16: New P 7F 11
Eliot Dr. SL7: Marl 5K 105
Elizabeth Av. HP6: L Chal 6F 87
Elizabeth Cl. HP21: Ayle 3C 66
Elizabeth Ct. HP13: H Wyc 2C 98
SL1: Slou 7E 124
Elizabeth Rd. HP14: Stoke 6D 72
SL7: Marl 6J 105
Elizabeth Way SL2: S Pog 6D 118
Elkins Rd. SL2: Hedg 7C 110
Ellen Pl. HP21: Ayle 2H 65
Ellen Rd. HP21: Ayle 1G 65
Ellenstow MK13: B'ell 2A 22
Ellen Wlk. HP21: Ayle 1G 65
(off Ellen Rd.)
Ellerburn Pl. MK4: E Val 4B 28
Ellery Ri. RG9: Fri 7H 73
ELLESBOROUGH 3C 135
Ellesborough Gro. MK8: T Ash 3H 21
Ellesborough Rd. HP22: Wend 5F 69
Elliman Av. SL2: Slou 5C 124
Elliman Sq. SL1: Slou 7D 124
(off High St.)
Elliots Cl. UB8: Cowl 3J 127
Elliott Ho. HP11: H Wyc 7K 89
(off Shaftesbury St.)
Ellis Av. SL1: Slou 7C 124
SL9: C Pet 6K 103
Ellisgill Ct. MK13: Hee 2B 22
Ellis Way HP14: L End 4K 73
Ellsworth Rd. HP11: H Wyc 4K 97
Ellwood Ri. HP8: D Gil 7G 95
Ellwood Rd. HP9: Bea 7D 100
Elmar Grn. SL2: Slou 1J 123
Elm Brook Cl. HP18: Che 3J 57
Elm Cl. HP6: Amer 5A 86
HP15: Haz 4G 91
HP22: West T 5G 67
MK17: New L 6C 32
SL2: Farn C 4A 118
Elmdale Gdns.
HP27: Prin R 5G 71
Elmers Mdw. MK18: N Mar 2A 44
Elmers Pk. MK3: Blet 7G 29
Elm Farm Rd. HP21: Ayle 2A 66
Elmfields Ga. MK18: Wins 6J 39
Elm Grn. HP21: Ayle 1J 65
Elm Gro. MK17: W San 3K 31
ELMHURST 3K 61
Elmhurst Cl. HP13: H Wyc 6D 90
MK4: Fur 3F 29
Elmhurst Rd. HP20: Ayle 4J 61
SL3: Lang 1A 130
Elm La. SL8: Bou E 4F 107
Elm Lawn Cl. UB8: Uxb 5K 121
Elmlea Dr. MK46: Oln 4G 7
Elmridge Ct. MK4: E Val 5C 28
Elm Rd. HP10: T Grn 6K 91
HP12: Book 4G 97
HP27: Prin R 5G 71
SL4: Wind 7K 129
Elms, The HP20: Ayle 4K 61
MK3: Blet 7F 29
Elms Dr. SL8: Bou E 6H 107
Elmshott Cl. HP10: T Grn 6G 91
Elmshott La. SL1: Slou 5G 123
Elmside MK18: Wins 6J 39
Elms Rd. SL9: C Pet 5J 103
Elm St. MK18: Buck 4H 37
Elmtree Ct. HP16: G Mis 5G 75
Elmtree Grn. HP16: G Mis 5G 75
Elm Tree Hill HP5: Ches 4K 77
Elm Trees HP18: Long C 5B 56
Elmtrees Cvn. Site SL7: L Mar 4B 106
Elmwood Cl. HP18: Oak 5H 53
Elmwood Pk. SL9: G Cro 6J 111
Elmwood Rd. SL2: Slou 5F 125
Elora Rd. HP13: H Wyc 1D 98
Elruge Cl. UB7: W Dra 1K 131
Elsmore Cl. HP21: Ayle 3C 66
ELSTOW 2D 133
Eltham Av. SL1: Slou 7G 123
Elthorne Rd. UB8: Uxb 7K 121
Elthorne Way MK16: New P 2J 17
Elton MK6: Wough 7K 23
Elwes Rd. HP14: L End 4K 73
Ely Av. SL1: Slou 3A 124
Ely Cl. HP7: Amer 6C 86
Ember Path HP21: Ayle 3H 65
Ember Rd. SL3: Lang 1B 130
EMBERTON 7H 7 (2C 133)
Emberton Country Pk. 6G 7
Emberton Country Pk. Vis. Cen. 6G 7
Emerald Ct. SL1: Slou 7C 124
Emerald Ga. MK15: F Mil 1A 24
EMERSON 5D 28
EMERSON VALLEY 5C 28
Emerton Gdns. MK11: S Strat 1B 20
Emineo HP9: Bea 6F 101
EMMBROOK 3A 136
EMMER GREEN 3A 136
Emmett Cl. MK4: E Val 6C 28
EMMINGTON 3B 134
Empingham Cl. MK2: Blet 4K 33
Enborne Cl. HP21: Ayle 3J 65
Enfield Chase MK14: L Woo 1D 22
Enfield Cl. UB8: Uxb 7K 121
Engaine Dr. MK5: S Chur 1K 27
ENGLEFIELD GREEN 3C 137
ENMORE 3G 23
Enmore Ga. MK9: Camp 3G 23
Ennell Gro. MK2: Blet 3J 33
Ennerdale Cl. MK2: Blet 2K 33
Ennerdale Cres. SL1: Slou 3E 122
Ensbury Path HP20: Ayle 4K 61
Enterprise La. MK9: Camp 3G 23
Epsom Gro. MK3: Blet 2D 32
Ercolani Av. HP13: H Wyc 2D 98
Erica Cl. SL1: Slou 5G 123
Erica Rd. MK12: S Bus 2J 21
Eridge Grn. MK7: K Hil 6C 24
Errington Dr. SL4: Wind 6J 129
Eschle Ct. SL2: Slou 4C 124
Eskan Ct. MK9: Camp 2H 23
Eskdale Av. HP5: Ches 4A 78
Eskdale Lodge HP6: Amer 4A 86

Eskdale Rd. HP22: Sto M 5C **66**
UB8: Uxb 7H **121**
Eskdale Way MK10: Bro 3D **24**
Esk Way MK3: Blet 6D **28**
(not continuous)
Essenden Ct. MK11: S Strat 1D **20**
Essex Av. SL2: Slou 3A **124**
Essex Cl. MK3: Blet 6F **29**
Essex Ho. HP20: Ayle 5J **61**
Essex Pl. HP19: Ayle 3F **61**
Essex Rd. HP5: Ches 3A **78**
Estcourt Dr. HP15: W End 1F **91**
Esther Cl. MK13: B'lle 7A **16**
Eston Ct. MK13: B'lle 1A **22**
Etheridge Av. MK10: Brin 6E **24**
Ethorpe MK8: T Ash 5J **21**
Ethorpe Cl. SL9: G Cro 3J **111**
Ethorpe Cres. SL9: G Cro 3J **111**
Ethorpe Ho. SL9: G Cro 3J **111**
ETON 3C **137**
Eton Cres. MK12: Wolv 7G **15**
Eton Pl. SL7: Marl 7H **105**
Eton Wlk. *SL1: Slou* *7C* ***124***
(off Upton Pk.)
ETON WICK 2H 129 (3C 137)
Eton Wick Rd. SL4: E Wick 2G **129**
Eunice Gro. HP5: Ches 6B **78**
Europa Bus. Pk. MK10: K'ton 4E **24**
Evans Cl. HP18: Che 2H **57**
HP21: Ayle 3B **66**
Evans Ga. MK6: Old 6E **22**
Evelyn Cl. LU7: Wing 4C **48**
Evelyn Pl. MK13: B'lle 6A **16**
EVENLEY 3A **132**
Evenlode Cl. HP21: Ayle 2H **65**
Evenlode Rd. SL8: Bou E 5H **107**
Everard Av. SL1: Slou 7C **124**
EVERDON 1A **132**
Everest Cl. HP13: H Wyc 2D **98**
Everest Rd. HP13: H Wyc 2E **98**
Everglade MK6: Eagl 6G **23**
Everley Cl. MK4: E Val 4C **28**
EVERSHOLT 3D **133**
Evesham Grn. HP19: Ayle 3H **61**
Evesham Way MK5: O'ill 2H **27**
Evett Cl. HP20: Ayle 5A **62**
Evreham Rd. SL0: Ive 4E **126**
Evreham Sports Cen. 2C **126**
EWELME 1A **136**
Exbury La. MK4: West 6K **27**
Exchange St. HP20: Ayle 6K **61**
Exebridge MK4: Fur 4C **28**
EXLADE STREET 2A **136**
Exmoor Ga. MK4: Fur 5E **28**
Eynsham Ct. MK15: Wool 4J **23**
Eyre Cl. HP19: Ayle 6E **60**
Eyre Grn. SL2: Slou 1J **123**
Eythrope Rd. HP17: Sto 1A **64**

F

Factory Yd. HP9: Bea 7G **101**
Fadmoor Pl. MK4: E Val 4B **28**
Fagnall La. HP7: Winc 5E **92**
Fair Acres HP16: Pres 1C **82**
Fairacres Ind. Est. SL4: Wind 7E **128**
Faircroft SL2: Slou 2K **123**
Fairfax MK13: B'lle 7C **16**
Fairfax Cres. HP20: Ayle 4K **61**
Fairfax M. HP7: Amer 7J **85**
Fairfield Cl. MK46: Oln 4J **7**
SL8: Bou E 4F **107**
Fairfield La. SL2: Farn R 7K **117**
Fairfield Rd. SL1: Burn 1E **122**
UB7: Yiew 5K **127**
UB8: Uxb 4K **121**
Fairfields HP15: G Kin 5E **82**
Fairford Cres. MK15: D Park 7G **17**
FAIRFORD LEYS 6E **60**
Fairford Leys Way HP19: Ayle 7F **61**
Fairhaven SL9: C Pet 6G **103**
Fairlawns HP13: H Wyc 6C **90**
Fair Leas HP5: Ches 3J **77**
Fairlie Rd. SL1: Slou 4J **123**
Fairlight Dr. UB8: Uxb 4K **121**
Fairmeadow MK18: Wins 6J **39**
Fair Mile HP21: Ayle 7A **62**
Fair Ridge HP11: H Wyc 4K **97**
Fair Vw. Cotts. *SL9: C Pet* *5J* ***103***
(off Gravel Hill)
Fairview Ind. Est. HP6: Amer 5D **86**
Fairview La. HP10: F Hea 7G **99**
Fairview Rd. SL2: Slou 2H **123**
SL6: Tapl 4C **122**
Fairway HP27: Prin R 5F **71**
Fairway, The HP10: F Hea 2J **107**
SL1: Burn 7E **116**
Fairway Av. UB7: W Dra 6J **127**
Fairway Cl. UB7: W Dra 6K **127**
FAIRWAYS 4G **21**
Fairways MK8: T Ash 4G **21**
Faithfull Cl. HP17: Sto 2A **64**
Faithorn Cl. HP5: Ches 4J **77**
Faith Ter. MK19: H'ope 2E **8**
Falaise MK15: Bolb 6H **17**
Falcon, The HP19: Ayle 2A **62**
Falcon Av. MK6: Sprin 4H **23**
Falcon Ri. HP13: Down 6G **89**
Falcons Cft. HP10: Woob G 1A **108**
Falklands Cl. MK18: S Clay 3B **42**
Fall Cl. HP19: Ayle 3J **61**
Falling La. UB7: Yiew 5K **127**
Fallow Fld. HP15: Haz 4H **91**
Falmouth Pl. MK6: Fish 5F **23**
Falmouth Rd. SL1: Slou 4J **123**
FANCOTT 1D **135**
Faraday Cl. SL2: Slou 3K **123**
Faraday Dr. MK5: S Lod 3B **28**
Faraday Rd. HP19: Ayle 5F **61**
SL2: Slou 3K **123**
FAR BLETCHLEY 1D **32**
FAR COTTON 1B **132**
Far Furlong Cl. HP21: Ayle 4J **65**
Farinton MK8: T Ash 4K **21**
Farjeon Ct. MK7: Old P 3F **31**
Farmborough MK6: Neth 1J **29**
Farmbrough Cl. HP20: Ayle 5B **62**
Farm Cl. HP6: L Chal 6H **87**
HP13: H Wyc 1G **99**
HP18: Ick 5D **54**
LU7: Stew 5C **46**
SL6: Tapl 4C **122**
Farm Cl. Gro. HP9: Bea 3E **100**
Farm Cres. SL2: Slou 3F **125**
Farmers Way HP9: S Grn 4A **102**
Farm La. HP9: Jord 5B **102**
SL1: Slou 5B **124**
Farm Lea HP10: Woob G 2B **108**
Farm Rd. SL6: Tapl 4C **122**
SL8: Bou E 5F **107**
Farnborough Cl. MK6: Neth 1J **29**
Farnburn Av. SL1: Slou 3K **123**
Farndale Gdns. HP15: Haz 1G **91**
FARNDISH 1D **133**
Farnell Ct. MK5: Lough 6C **22**
Farnham Cl. HP3: Bov 2K **79**
FARNHAM COMMON 4A 118 (2C 137)
Farnham Ct. MK8: G Hol 5J **21**
Farnham La. SL2: Slou 1G **123**
Farnham Pk. La. SL2: Farn R 5A **118**
Farnham Rd. SL1: Slou 1K **123**
SL2: Farn R, Slou 1K **123**
FARNHAM ROYAL 1A 124 (2C 137)
Farnley Rd. HP20: Ayle 4K **61**
Farrier Pl. MK14: D Barn 7G **17**
Farringdon St. MK10: Monk P 5B **24**
Farthing Grn. La. SL2: S Pog 7E **118**
Farthing Gro. MK6: Neth 1H **29**
Farthings HP8: D Gil 1H **95**
Farthings, The HP6: Amer 3B **86**
FARTHINGSTONE 1A **132**
Fassetts Rd. HP10: Loud 6H **99**
Fassnidge Vw. UB8: Uxb 5J **121**
Faulkner Way HP13: Down 4H **89**
Favell Dr. MK4: Fur 3E **28**
Fawcett Rd. SL4: Wind 6K **129**
FAWLEY 2A **136**
Fawsley Cl. SL3: Poy 5E **130**
Featherbed La. HP15: H Grn 5K **83**
HP16: L Kin 4J **83**
Featherstone Rd. MK12: W Mil 1E **20**
Fegans Ct. MK11: S Strat 7B **14**
Felbridge MK7: K Hil 7C **24**
FELDEN 3D **135**
Fells Cl. HP18: Long C 6D **56**
FELMERSHAM 1D **133**
FELTHAM 3D **137**
FELTHAMHILL 3D **137**
Fences La. MK16: Tyr 1G **11**
FENCOTT 2A **134**
Fennel Dr. MK14: Conn 1E **22**
Fennels Farm Rd. HP10: F Hea 7G **99**
Fennels Rd. HP11: W Mar 4G **99**
Fennels Way HP10: F Hea 6G **99**
Fennemore Cl. HP18: Oak 6H **53**
Fennings, The HP6: Amer 3B **86**
FENNY LOCK 5A **30**
FENNY LOCK 4A **30**
Fenny Lodge Galley 6A **30**
Fennymere MK8: T Ash 5H **21**
FENNY STRATFORD 6A 30 (3C 133)
Fenny Stratford Station (Rail) 6A **30**
Fenton Ct. MK8: G Hol 6K **21**
FERN 4E **106**
Fernan Dell MK8: C'ill 7H **21**
Fernborough Haven MK4: E Val 5C **28**
Ferndale MK6: Eagl 5H **23**
Ferndale Cl. HP14: Stoke 6D **72**
Ferndale Cres. UB8: Cowl 1J **127**
Ferndale Pk. SL6: Bra 4A **128**
Fern Dr. SL6: Tapl 4D **122**
Ferne Furlong MK46: Oln 2H **7**
Fernes Cl. UB8: Cowl 4J **127**
Fern Gro. MK2: Blet 3J **33**
Fernhurst Cl. HP9: Bea 6G **101**
Erniefields HP12: Book 4F **97**
Fern La. HP17: Hadd 6C **58**
SL7: L Mar 4E **106**
Fernlea Cl. HP10: F Hea 7G **99**
Ferns, The HP9: Bea 7H **101**
Fernside HP15: G Kin 5E **82**
Fernsleigh Cl. SL9: C Pet 4J **103**
Fern Wlk. HP15: Haz 4H **91**
Ferrers Av. UB7: W Dra 7K **127**
Ferrers Cl. SL1: Slou 6G **123**
Ferryfield Rd. HP13: H Wyc 2D **98**
Ferry La. SL8: Bou E 7H **107**
(not continuous)
Field Cl. HP5: Ches 2C **78**
HP18: Ick 5E **54**
HP20: Ayle 4B **62**
MK16: Sher 2C **12**
Field End HP18: Long C 7E **56**
Fieldfare HP19: Ayle 2K **61**
Fieldhead Gdns. SL8: Bou E 6G **107**
Fieldhouse Ind. Est.
SL7: Marl 7K **105**
Fieldhouse La. SL7: Marl 7K **105**
Fieldhouse Way SL7: Marl 7K **105**
Fieldhurst SL3: Lang 3A **130**
Fielding Gdns. SL3: Lang 7G **125**
Field La. MK12: Gree 1F **21**
Field Rd. HP12: Book 3F **97**
UB9: Den 2D **120**
Fields, The SL1: Slou 7B **124**
Field Wlk. MK9: C Key 3F **23**
(not continuous)
Field Way HP3: Bov 1K **79**
HP20: Ayle 4B **62**
SL9: C Pet 5H **103**
UB8: Cowl 2K **127**
Fieldway HP7: Amer 1K **93**
Fife Ct. MK4: Tatt 7A **28**
FIFIELD 6A 128 (3C 137)
Fifield La. SL4: Wink 7A **128**
Fifield Rd. SL6: Bra, Fifi 5A **128**
Fifth St. HP11: H Wyc 4B **98**
Filey Spur SL1: Slou 7K **123**
FILGRAVE 2C **133**
Filmer Rd. SL4: Wind 7F **129**
Filmworks Cinema, The 5J **97**
Finch Cl. MK10: M Vill 3B **24**
Finch End HP10: T Grn 7J **91**
Finch La. HP7: Amer, L Chal 2D **94**
HP9: Bea 3E **100**
Findlay Way MK2: Blet 7J **29**
FINGEST 1A **136**
Fingest La. HP14: Bolt E 5F **73**
RG9: Fing 5F **73**
Fingle Dr. MK13: Stone 6J **15**
Finings Rd. HP14: Bolt E 3H **73**
FINMERE 3A **132**
Finmere Cres. HP21: Ayle 2D **66**
Finnamore La. SL7: Marl 1C **104**
Finsbury Chase MK10: Monk P 6B **24**
Fircroft Cl. SL2: S Pog 4E **118**
Firecrest Way HP19: Ayle 5E **60**
Fire La. MK17: New L 5D **32**
Firs, The HP18: Bril 3J **53**
HP22: Bier 2D **62**
Firs Av. SL4: Wind 7H **129**
Firs Cl. HP13: H Wyc 7E **90**
HP14: L End 3K **73**
HP15: Haz 5H **91**
HP22: W'urch 3G **45**
SL0: I Hea 6C **120**
Firs Ct. *HP6: Amer* *4A* ***86***
(off Chesham Rd.)
HP22: Bier 2D **62**
Firs Dr. SL3: Lang 6K **125**
Firs End SL9: C Pet 1J **111**
Firs Ri. HP16: G Mis 6E **74**
First Av. HP7: Amer 7A **86**
MK1: Blet 5H **29**
SL7: Marl 7A **106**
First Cres. SL1: Slou 3A **124**
First St. HP11: H Wyc 5B **98**
Firs Vw. Rd. HP15: Haz 5H **91**
Firs Wlk. HP15: Haz 5H **91**
Fir Tree Av. SL2: S Pog 2D **124**
Fir Tree Bungs. HP14: Walt A 6F **81**
Firview Cl. SL7: Marl 1K **115**
Fishermans Cl. MK46: Oln 3G **7**
Fishermans Retreat SL7: Marl 1J **115**
Fisherman's Way SL8: Bou E 5H **107**
FISHERMEAD 5G **23**
FISHERMEAD 5H **23**
Fishermead Blvd. MK6: Fish 5F **23**
Fishers Fld. MK18: Buck 4G **37**
Fishguard Spur SL1: Slou 7F **125**
Fishweir LU7: Stew 3B **46**
Fitwilliam St. MK3: Blet 7H **29**
Fitzhamon Ct. MK12: W Mil 1E **20**
Five Acres HP5: Ches 7B **78**
HP10: Woob G 2B **108**
Five Acre Wood HP12: Book 2G **97**
FLACKWELL HEATH 1H 107 (2B 136)
Flaggs Mdw. MK46: Oln 3G **7**
Flambard Cl. MK15: Bolb 6G **17**
Flamborough Spur SL1: Slou 7J **123**
Flats, The HP8: D Gil 3H **95**
FLAUNDEN 3D **135**
Flaunden Bottom HP5: Lati 4J **87**
Flaunden Hill HP3: Flau 7K **79**
Flaxbourne Ct. *MK7: W Gat* *7E* ***24***
(off Isaacson Dri.)
Flaxen Fld. HP22: West T 5G **67**
Flaxley Ga. MK10: Monk 4C **24**
Fledgelings Wlk. MK18: Wins 5J **39**
Fleet, The MK6: Sprin 4H **23**
Fleet Cl. HP14: H Vall 7K **81**
MK18: Buck 2K **37**
FLEET MARSTON 2A **60**
Fleet St. HP20: Ayle 5J **61**
Fleetwood Cl. HP8: D Gil 2E **102**
Fleetwood Rd. SL2: Slou 6D **124**
Fleming Dr. MK6: E Wes 1H **29**
Fleming Hall *UB8: Cowl* *1K* ***127***
(off Topping La.)
Fleming Way HP12: H Wyc 3H **97**
Fletcher Cl. HP19: Ayle 3E **60**
Fletchers M. MK14: N Hill 7F **17**
Flintergill Ct. MK13: Hee 2B **22**
Flint St. HP17: Hadd 7B **58**
Flint Way HP16: Pres 6C **74**
Flitcroft Lea HP13: Down 7A **90**
Flitton Ct. MK11: S Strat 1D **20**
FLITWICK 3D **133**
Flora Thompson Dr. MK16: New P 6F **11**
FLORE 1A **132**
Florence Ct. *HP19: Ayle* *5J* ***61***
(off Willow Rd.)
Florence Way UB8: Uxb 5J **121**
Florida St. HP11: H Wyc 4C **98**
Florin Cl. MK15: Penny 6G **17**
FLOWERS BOTTOM 2F **81**
Flowers Bottom La. HP27: Spee 3E **80**
Folding Cl. LU7: Stew 4C **46**
Foley Cl. HP9: Bea 4E **100**
Folkestone Ct. SL3: Lang 3A **130**
Folly La. MK16: N Craw 1K **19**
Fontwell Dr. MK3: Blet 3C **32**
Forbes Pl. MK5: Medb 2J **27**
Forches Cl. MK4: E Val 5D **28**
FORD 5K 59 (3B 134)
FORD, THE 4A **70**
Fordcombe Lea MK7: K Hil 6C **24**
FORD END 3F **51**
Ford End UB9: Den 7F **113**
Ford End Watermill 3F **51**
Ford La. SL0: Ive 4G **127**
Ford Rd. HP17: Ford, Sto 3J **59**
Ford's Cl. HP14: Bled R 3C **72**
Ford St. HP11: W Mar 4F **99**
MK18: Buck 4H **37**
Ford Way HP13: Down 4J **89**
Forelands Way HP5: Ches 6A **78**
Forest Cl. HP22: Wend 4H **69**
HP27: Prin R *5H* ***71***
(off Chestnut Rd.)
FOREST HILL 3A **134**
Forest Point HP13: H Wyc 3F **99**
Forest Ri. MK6: Eagl 6H **23**
Forest Rd. SL4: Wind 7F **129**
Forest Way HP13: H Wyc 7G **91**
Forfar Dr. MK3: Blet 5F **29**
Forge, The MK46: Emb 7H **7**
Forge Cl. HP15: H Grn 1J **91**
HP18: Oak 6H **53**
MK18: S Clay 3C **42**
OX27: M Gib 5C **42**
Forge Dr. SL2: Farn C 4A **118**
Forge End HP7: Amer 7K **85**
Forge Rd. HP14: Nap 6G **81**
Forgetts Rd. HP14: L End 4A **96**
Formby Cl. MK3: Blet 1C **32**
SL3: Lang 2C **130**
Forrabury Av. MK13: B Com 3B **22**
Forscott Rd. MK18: M M'ton 1K **37**
FORT END 5B **58**
Fortescue Dr. MK5: S Chur 1A **28**
Forthill Pl. MK5: S Chur 7K **21**
Fortuna Ct. MK7: W Gat 1E **30**
FORTY GREEN 4D 100 (1C 137)
Forty Grn. Dr. SL7: Marl 7F **105**
Forty Grn. Rd. HP9: Bea 4D **100**
Foscott Way MK18: Buck 2J **37**
Fossey Cl. MK5: S Broo 4K **27**
Foster Av. SL4: Wind 7G **129**
Foster Cl. HP20: Ayle 4A **62**
Fosters La. MK13: B'ell 3A **22**
Fosters Path SL2: Slou 2H **123**
Fotheringay Gdns.
SL1: Slou 5J **123**
Founders M. MK14: N Hill 7F **17**
Foundry La. HP27: Loos 1A **80**
SL3: Hor 7B **130**
Fountain Ct. *HP20: Ayle* *6J* ***61***
(off Buckingham St.)
Fountaine Cl. MK14: G Lin 5E **16**
FOUR ASHES 3C **90**
Four Ashes Rd. HP15: Crye 2C **90**
Four Oaks HP5: Ches 1J **77**
Fourth Av. SL7: Marl 7A **106**
Fourth St. HP11: H Wyc 4B **98**
Fowler MK14: Stan 6C **16**
Fowler Rd. HP19: Ayle 6G **61**
Foxborough Cl. SL3: Lang 3A **130**
Foxcovert Rd. MK5: S Woo 3K **27**
Foxdell Way SL9: C Pet 3J **103**
Foxes Piece SL7: Marl 7J **105**
Fox Farm Rd. MK17: L Bric 2F **35**
Foxgate MK16: New P 1H **17**
Foxglove HP21: Ayle 2G **65**
Foxglove Ct. MK16: New P 1F **17**
Foxherne SL3: Lang 7G **125**
Foxhill MK46: Oln 2G **7**

Foxhill Cl. HP13: H Wyc 6B 90
Foxhollow Dr. SL2: Farn C 3A 118
Foxhunter Dr. MK14: L Woo 7D 16
Fox La. HP15: H Grn 1H 91
Foxleigh HP11: H Wyc 4K 97
FOXLEY 1A 132
Foxley Pl. MK5: Lough 6C 22
FOX MILNE 2B 24
FOX MILNE 2B 24
Foxmoor Ct. UB9: Den 4G 113
Fox Rd. HP15: H Grn 1H 91
Foxton MK6: Wough 1K 29
Fox Way MK18: Buck 5J 37
Frameers Ct. HP14: L End 4K 73
Framewood Rd. SL2: S Pog, Wex 5G 119
SL3: S Pog, Wex 5G 119
Framlingham Ct. MK5: S Chur 2A 28
Frampton Ct. UB9: Den 4F 113
Frampton Gro. MK4: West 6K 27
France Furlong MK14: G Lin 5F 17
Frances St. HP5: Ches 3A 78
Franchise St. HP5: Ches 4A 78
Francis Cotts. HP5: Ches 5A 78
Francis Ct. MK5: S Chur 1A 28
Francis Way SL1: Slou 5F 123
Francis Yd. *HP5: Ches* *5A 78*
(off East St.)
Frank Atter Cft. MK12: Wolv 1G 21
Frank Howe Ct. *MK6: Fish* *5G 23*
(off Penryn Av.)
Franklin Av. SL2: Slou 2K 123
Franklin Cl. HP17: Hadd 5C 58
Franklin Ct. HP7: Amer 5A 86
Franklin Rd. HP17: Hadd 5C 58
Franklins Cft. MK12: Wolv 1G 21
Frank Lunnon Cl. SL8: Bou E 6J 107
Franklyn Cres. SL4: Wind 7F 129
Frankston Av. MK11: S Strat 1C 20
Frank Sutton Way SL1: Slou 5B 124
Fraser Rd. HP12: Book 3G 97
Fraucup Cl. HP17: Ford 5K 59
Frays Av. UB7: W Dra 7K 127
Frays Cl. UB7: W Dra 1K 131
Frayslea UB8: Uxb 7J 121
Frays Waye UB8: Uxb 6J 121
Frederick Pl. HP11: W Mar 5H 99
Frederick Smith Ct. MK12: H Lea 2H 21
Frederick St. HP18: Wadd 6C 52
Freeman Cl. MK12: Gree 1F 21
Freeman Ct. HP5: Ches 4A 78
Freemans Cl. SL2: S Pog 4D 118
Freemans Gdns. MK46: Oln 4J 7
Freestone Yd. *SL3: Coln* *5D 130*
(off Park St.)
Fremantle Rd. HP13: H Wyc 5D 90
HP21: Ayle 2K 65
Frenchum Gdns. SL1: Slou 6G 123
Frensham Dr. MK2: Blet 1J 33
Frensham Wlk. SL2: Farn C 3A 118
Friarage Pas. HP20: Ayle 6J 61
Friarage Rd. HP20: Ayle 6J 61
Friarscroft Way HP20: Ayle 6H 61
Friars Furlong HP18: Long C 5C 56
Friars Gdns. HP14: H Vall 7A 82
Friars Sq. HP20: Ayle 6J 61
Friars Wlk. *HP16: Pres* *1D 82*
(off Fair Acres)
Friary Gdns. MK16: New P 3J 17
Friends Wlk. UB8: Uxb 5K 121
FRIETH 7H 73 (1A 136)
Frieth Rd. RG9: Fri 6H 73 & 1A 104
SL7: Marl 2A 104
FRINGFORD 1A 134
Fripp Gdns. MK8: G Far 1H 27
Frithe, The SL2: Slou 4F 125
FRITH-HILL 6J 75
Frith Hill HP16: G Mis, S Hea 6H 75
FRITHSDEN 3D 135
Frithwood Cres. MK7: K Hil 7C 24
Froggy La. UB9: Den 1D 120
Frog La. HP18: Cudd 1B 58
Frogmill SL6: Hur 7A 114
FROGMILL SPINNEY 7A 114
Frogmoor HP13: H Wyc 1A 98
FROGMORE 1D 137
Frogmore Cl. HP14: H Vall 7A 82
SL1: Slou 7J 123
Frogmore La. HP18: Long C 7B 56
Frogmore Pl. MK4: West 5J 27
Frome Cl. HP21: Ayle 2H 65
Fromer Rd. HP10: Woob G 5K 107
FROXFIELD 3D 133
Froxfield Ct. MK4: E Val 6C 28
Fryday St. MK6: Lead 7E 22
Fryer Cl. HP5: Ches 7B 78
Fryers Ct. HP12: H Wyc 7H 89
Fryers La. HP12: H Wyc 7H 89
(not continuous)
Frymley Vw. SL4: Wind 6F 129
Fuller's Cl. HP5: Ches 6K 77
Fuller's Hill HP5: Ches 1H 85
HP6: H Hea 1H 85
FULLERS SLADE 2D 20
Full Moon Cotts. HP16: L Kin 3G 83
Fulmar Pl. *HP19: Ayle* *3A 62*
(off Watermeadow)
FULMER 2H 119 (2C 137)
Fulmer Comn. Rd. SL0: I Hea 3H 119
SL3: Fulm 3H 119
Fulmer Cnr. SL9: G Cro 6B 112
Fulmer Dr. SL9: G Cro 7H 111
Fulmer La. SL3: Fulm 1K 119
SL9: G Cro 1K 119
Fulmer Pl. SL3: Fulm 2J 119
Fulmer Rd. SL3: Fulm 2J 119
SL9: G Cro 5J 111
Fulmer St. (V3) MK5: Mil K 3B 28
MK8: Mil K 7H 21
Fulmer Way SL9: G Cro 4J 111
Fulton Cl. HP13: Down 7A 90
Fulwell Ct. MK14: G Lin 5E 16
Fulwoods Dr. MK6: Lead 6G 23
Furlong Cl. SL8: Bou E 6H 107
Furlong Cres. HP17: Bish 6F 65
Furlong Rd. SL8: Bou E 6H 107
Furness SL4: Wind 7E 128
Furness Cres. MK3: Blet 6F 29
Furness Pl. SL4: Wind 7E 128
Furness Row SL4: Wind 7E 128
Furness Sq. SL4: Wind 7E 128
Furness Wlk. *SL4: Wind* *7E 128*
(off Furnace Sq.)
Furness Way SL4: Wind 7E 128
Furnival Av. SL2: Slou 3K 123
Furrow Cl. HP21: Ayle 3J 65
Furrows, The UB9: Hare 3J 113
Fury Ct. MK8: C'ill 7K 21
Furzefield Rd. HP9: Bea 6E 100
Furze Ho. MK4: Fur 5E 28
Furze La. MK18: Wins 6G 39
Furzen Cl. SL2: Slou 1J 123
Furze Platt Rd. SL6: Maid 7K 115
Furze Way MK12: Wolv 7G 15
FURZTON 3D 28
FURZTON 3B 28
FURZTON LAKE 2D 28
Fuzzens Wlk. SL4: Wind 7G 129
Fyfield Barrow MK7: Waln 1E 30

G

Gables, The HP17: Hadd 7C 58
MK12: Wolv 7H 15
Gables Cl. HP22: Wend 4G 69
SL9: C Pet 2J 103
Gables Dr. HP14: Saun 5A 80
Gables Mdw. HP15: H Grn 1J 91
Gable Thorne MK7: W Gat 1F 31
Gabriel Cl. MK7: Brow 2E 30
Gaddesden Cres. MK7: W Gat 1E 30
Gadsden Ct. MK17: S Ham 1H 41
Gadwell Ho. HP9: Bea 6D 100
Gainsborough Cl. MK8: G Far 7H 21
Gainsborough Pl. HP19: Ayle 3E 60
Gainsborough Rd. HP21: Ayle 3K 65
Gairloch Av. MK2: Blet 3K 33
Gala Bingo
Aylesbury 6K 61
Slough 7C 124
Galahad Cl. SL1: Slou 7J 123
Gallagher Cl. MK8: C'ill 6J 21
Galleons HP7: Amer 5A 86
Galleons La. SL3: Wex 2G 125
(not continuous)
GALLEY HILL 2D 20
Galley Hill MK11: S Strat 1D 20
Galley Hill Arts Workshop 2D 20
Galley La. MK17: G Bri 4C 34
Galleymead Rd. SL3: Poy 6F 131
Galloway HP19: Ayle 3F 61
Galloway Chase SL2: Slou 5E 124
Galloway Cl. MK3: Blet 5E 28
Gallows La. HP12: H Wyc 7G 89
GALLOWSTREE COMMON 2A 136
Gallys Rd. SL4: Wind 7F 129
Galsworthy Pl. HP19: Ayle 4E 60
Galvin Rd. SL1: Slou 6A 124
Gandon Va. HP13: Down 7A 90
Ganton Cl. MK3: Blet 6D 28
Garamonde Dr. MK8: Wym 3J 21
Garbo Cl. MK8: C'ill 7H 21
Garden Cl. HP22: Halt 7K 67
Garden End HP6: Amer 4C 86
GARDENERS GREEN 3B 136
Gardener Wlk. HP15: H Grn 1J 91
Garden M. SL1: Slou 6D 124
Garden M., The MK16: Gayh 3D 10
Garden Reach HP8: D Gil 1H 95
Gardens, The MK18: Ads 6E 38
UB10: I'ham 7K 113
Gardens Cl. HP14: Stoke 5D 72
Gardiner Ct. MK13: Blue B 7J 15
Gardner Cl. HP15: G Kin 5D 82
HP19: Ayle 3F 61
Garland Ct. MK8: C'ill 6J 21
Garland Way HP22: Ast C 2B 68
Garner Ho. HP13: H Wyc 2E 98
Garners Cl. SL9: C Pet 4K 103
Garners End SL9: C Pet 4J 103
Garners Rd. SL9: C Pet 4J 103
Garnet Cl. SL1: Slou 7J 123
Garnet Ct. SL7: Marl 1G 115
Garrard Rd. SL2: Slou 2G 123
Garratts Way HP13: Down 7K 89
Garraways MK6: Coff 7G 23
Garrett Cl. HP5: Ches 7A 78
Garrick Wlk. MK9: C Key 3F 23
Garron Cl. HP21: Ayle 4J 65
Garrowmore Gro. MK2: Blet 3K 33
Garry Cl. MK2: Blet 3J 33
GARSINGTON 3A 134
Garson Gro. HP5: Ches 3J 77
Garston MK8: T Ash 5K 21
Garth, The HP16: G Mis 5G 75
Garthwaite Cres. MK5: S Broo 4K 27
Garvin Av. HP9: Bea 5G 101
Garwood Cres. MK8: G Far 1H 27
Gascon's Gro. SL2: Slou 2J 123
Gaskin Ct. MK14: D Barn 1G 23
Gatcombe MK8: G Hol 5K 21
Gatehouse Cl. HP19: Ayle 6H 61
Gatehouse Rd. HP19: Ayle 5H 61
Gatehouse Way HP19: Ayle 5G 61
Gatensbury Pl. HP27: Prin R 5G 71
Gatewick Cl. SL1: Slou 6C 124
Gatewick La. MK7: Cald 4C 30
Gaveston Rd. SL2: Slou 1H 123
Gaviots Cl. SL9: G Cro 6K 111
Gaviots Grn. SL9: G Cro 5J 111
(not continuous)
Gaviots Way SL9: G Cro 5J 111
GAWCOTT 6C 36 (3A 132)
Gawcott Rd. MK18: Buck 4E 36
Gawdrey Cl. HP5: Ches 7B 78
Gayal Cft. MK5: S Broo 4A 28
GAYHURST 2D 10 (2C 133)
Gayhurst Rd. HP13: H Wyc 1F 99
GAYTON 1B 132
Gayton Cl. HP6: Amer 2C 86
George Cl. SL7: Marl 5K 105
George Ct. HP18: G Und 3J 43
George Farm Cl. MK17: L Bric 3F 35
GEORGE GREEN 4J 125 (2C 137)
George Grn. Dr. SL3: G Grn 4J 125
George Grn. Rd. SL3: G Grn 4H 125
George Inn Pl. MK16: S Gold 6C 6
George Lee Ct. *HP14: Pidd* *6A 88*
(off King St.)
George Rd. HP14: Stoke 5C 72
Georges Dr. HP10: F Hea 2J 107
George's Hill HP15: W End 1F 91
George St. HP5: Ches 4A 78
HP11: H Wyc 1K 97
HP20: Ayle 6J 61
LU7: Wing 3C 48
MK2: F Str 6A 30
UB8: Uxb 5K 121
George Yd. *MK11: S Strat* *1B 20*
(off High St.)
Geralds Ct. *HP13: H Wyc* *6D 90*
(off Geralds Rd.)
Geralds Rd. HP13: H Wyc 6D 90
Gerard Cl. MK13: B'lle 6A 16
Gerda's Wlk. HP9: Bea 1G 101
Germains Cl. HP5: Ches 6K 77
Germains St. HP5: Ches 6K 77
Germander Pl. MK14: Conn 2D 22
GERRARDS CROSS 3J 111 (2C 137)
Gerrards Cross Golf Course 1K 111
Gerrards Cross Rd. SL2: S Pog 4E 118
Gerrards Cross Station (Rail) 3J 111
Gershwin Ct. MK7: Brow 3E 30
Gervaise Cl. SL1: Slou 6H 123
Gibbings Cl. MK18: N Mar 1A 44
Gibbs Cl. HP13: Down 7K 89
Gibbs Ho. HP11: W Mar 5G 99
Gibbwin MK14: G Lin 5D 16
Gib La. HP22: Bier 2E 62
GIBRALTAR 1F 59 (2B 134)
Gibraltar La. SL6: Cook 7C 106
Gibson Ct. SL3: Lang 3A 130
Gibson La. HP17: Hadd 7C 58
Gibson Rd. HP12: Book 5F 97
Gibsons Grn. MK13: Hee 2B 22
GIFFARD PARK 3F 17
GIFFARD PARK 2F 17
Giffard Way HP18: Long C 5C 56
Gifford Ga. MK14: G Lin 6E 16
Gifford Pl. MK18: Buck 3J 37
Gilbert Cl. MK3: Blet 1H 33
Gilbert Ho. HP11: H Wyc 1J 97
Gilbert Scott Ct. HP7: Amer 7J 85
Gilbert Scott Rd. MK18: Buck 2H 37
Gilby Wlk. HP10: Woob G 5K 107
Gilders M. MK14: N Hill 7F 17
Giles Ga. HP16: Pres 7B 74
Gillamoor Cl. MK4: E Val 4B 28
Gilletts La. HP12: H Wyc 6G 89
Gillfield Cl. HP11: H Wyc 5J 97
Gilliat Rd. SL1: Slou 5C 124
Gilmore Cl. SL3: Lang 7G 125
Gilmore Rd. HP20: Ayle 3K 61
Gilpin Way MK46: Oln 3J 7
Gingers Cl. HP22: Ast C 2B 68
Gisburn Cl. MK13: Hee 1B 22
Glade, The HP10: T Grn 6J 91
SL9: G Cro 6H 111
Glade Rd. SL7: Marl 7J 105
Glade Vw. HP12: Book 5E 96
Gladstone Cl. MK16: New P 2J 17
Gladstone Ri. HP13: H Wyc 2F 99
Gladstone Rd. HP5: Ches 5A 78
Gladstone Way SL1: Slou 6J 123
Glaisyer Way SL0: I Hea 7C 120
Glamis Ho. MK3: Blet 1E 32
Glamorgan Cl. MK3: Blet 6F 29
Glanmor Rd. SL2: Slou 5F 125
Glastonbury Cl. MK3: Blet 5G 29
Glaven Rd. HP21: Ayle 3H 65
Glazier Dr. MK14: N Hill 7F 17
GLEBE 3H 23
Glebe, The HP14: Nap 1H 89
HP16: Pres 6B 74
HP17: Sto 2B 64
HP22: West T 5G 67
MK46: Lave 2C 6
Glebe Cl. HP15: H Grn 7H 83
LU7: Pits 4F 51
MK5: Lough 6A 22
MK18: M M'ton 1J 37
SL6: Tapl 6B 122
SL9: C Pet 5H 103
Glebe Cotts. *HP5: Ches* *6K 77*
(off Germain St.)
Glebe Ho. *SL9: C Pet* *5H 103*
(off Glebe Cl.)
Glebelands HP10: T Grn 7J 91
Glebelands Cl. HP16: Pres 2E 82
Glebe Rd. SL9: C Pet 6G 103
UB8: Uxb 7J 121
Glebe Ter. MK18: M M'ton 1K 37
Glebe Way HP6: Amer 3B 86
Gledfield Pl. MK12: H Lea 2H 21
Gleeman Cl. MK12: Gree 1E 20
Glendurgan Ct. MK4: West 6J 27
Gleneagles Cl. MK3: Blet 1D 32
Glenfield Cl. HP21: Ayle 2B 66
Glenfields SL2: S Pog 6D 118
Glenister Rd. HP5: Ches 2A 78
HP12: Book 4F 97
Glenisters Rd. HP13: H Wyc 1A 98
Glenmoors MK16: New P 2J 17
Glenmore Cl. HP10: F Hea 6G 99
Glenmore Ho. *HP11: W Mar* *5H 99*
(off Brambleside)
Glenstal Pl. MK9: Camp 3G 23
Glentworth Pl. SL1: Slou 6A 124
Globe Pk. SL7: Marl 7A 106
Glory Cl. HP10: Woob G 2B 108
Glory Hill La. HP9: Bea 1B 108
Glory Mill La. HP10: Woob G 2A 108
Glory Watery La. HP10: Woob G 2A 108
Gloucester Av. SL1: Slou 3A 124
Gloucester Ct. UB9: Den 5G 113
Gloucester Rd. MK12: Wolv 1G 21
Glovers La. MK13: Hee 2B 22
Glyn Sq. MK12: Wolv 6H 15
Glyn St. MK13: New B 6K 15
Glynswood HP13: H Wyc 6B 90
SL9: C Pet 5K 103
Glynswood Rd. MK18: Buck 4G 37
Goathland Cft. MK4: E Val 5B 28
Goddards Cft. MK12: Wolv 1G 21
Goddington Rd. SL8: Bou E 4G 107
Godfreys Cl. HP18: Bril 2J 53
Godolphin Rd. HP9: S Grn 4A 102
SL1: Slou 5B 124
Godrevy Gro. MK4: Tatt 7B 28
Godwin Cl. MK7: W Gat 7E 24
Gogh Rd. HP19: Ayle 4D 60
Gold Crest HP19: Ayle 2A 62
Golden Ball La. SL6: Maid 7K 115
Golden Dr. MK6: Eagl 7G 23
Golden Oak Cl. SL2: Farn C 4A 118
Golder's Cl. HP18: Ick 5D 54
Gold Hill E. SL9: C Pet 7H 103
Gold Hill Nth. SL9: C Pet 6G 103
Gold Hill W. SL9: C Pet 6G 103
Goldilocks MK7: Waln 1D 30
Goldmark Cl. MK7: Old P 2F 31
Goldney Ct. MK4: West 5J 27
Gold Oak Wlk. *MK9: C Key* *3F 23*
(off Silbury Boulevd.)
Goldsmith Dr. MK16: New P 1F 17
Gold St. MK19: H'ope 1E 8
Goldsworthy Way SL1: Slou 4E 122
Golspie Cft. MK12: H Lea 2G 21
Gomm Pl. HP13: H Wyc 4G 99
Gomm Rd. HP13: H Wyc 4G 99
Gomms Wood Cl. HP9: Bea 4D 100
Gomms Wood Ho. HP9: Bea 4D 100
Gom Valley Nature Reserve 3H 99
Goodacres La. HP27: L Grn 1C 80
Good Intent LU6: Edle 2J 49
Goodlake Ct. UB9: Den 5F 113
Goodman Gdns. MK6: W Grn. 6K 23
Goodman Pk. SL2: Slou 6G 125
Goodrich Grn. MK4: K'ead 7J 27
Goodwick Gro. MK4: Tatt 7B 28
Goodwin Mdws. HP10: Woob G 3A 108
Goodwin Rd. HP19: Ayle 6H 61
SL2: Slou 1H 123
Goodwins Mead LU7: Ched 2C 50
Goodwood MK8: G Hol 6K 21
Goodwood Ri. SL7: Marl 2G 105
Goose Acre HP5: Ches 4E 78
LU7: Ched 2B 50

Goose Grn. SL2: Farn R .7K 117
Goosen Grn. HP21: Ayle .1D 66
Goran Av. MK11: S Strat .2C 20
Gordale MK13: Hee .1C 22
Gordon Rd. HP5: Ches .6A 78
HP13: H Wyc .2C 98
SL4: Wind .7H 129
UB7: Yiew .5K 127
Gordon Way HP8: D Gil .1F 103
Gore, The SL1: Burn .1C 122
Gore Cl. UB9: Hare .2J 113
Gore Hill HP7: Amer .2K 93
Gorelands La. HP8: D Gil .6H 95
Gorell Rd. HP9: Bea .7K 101
Gore Rd. SL1: Burn .1D 122
Goring MK14: Stan .6C 16
GORING HEATH .3A 136
Gorman Pl. MK2: Blet .4A 34
Gorrell Cl. MK18: Ting .2C 36
Gorrell La. MK18: Ting .2C 36
(off Main St.)
MK18: Ting .2C 36
(Gorrell Cl.)
Gorricks MK11: S Strat .2B 20
Gorse Meade SL1: Slou .6K 123
Gorse Wlk. HP15: Haz .4G 91
Goslar Way SL4: Wind .7K 129
Gosling Grn. SL3: Lang .7J 125
Gosling Gro. HP13: Down .5G 89
Gosling Rd. SL3: Lang .7J 125
Goslington MK1: Blet .5J 29
Goss Av. HP18: Wadd .6D 52
Gossmore Cl. SL7: Marl .1K 115
Gossmore La. SL7: Marl .1K 115
Gossmore Wlk. SL7: Marl .1K 115
Goudhurst Ct. MK7: K Hil .7D 24
Governors Av. UB9: Den .3F 113
Governors Cl. HP6: Amer .5D 86
Gower Ho. HP6: Amer .3C 86
Gowers, The HP6: Amer .3C 86
Gowers Fld. HP20: Ayle .5J 61
Gowings Grn. SL1: Slou .7G 123
Goya Pl. HP19: Ayle .4E 60
Grace Av. MK6: Old .6D 22
Grace Ct. SL1: Slou .6A 124
Grace Reading Cl. HP13: H Wyc .2E 98
Graeme Av. HP16: Pres .7C 74
Grafham Cl. MK14: G Par .5G 17
Grafton Cl. SL3: G Grn .4J 125
Grafton Gate E. MK9: C Key .5C 22
Grafton Ga. (V6) MK9: Mil K .4C 22
Grafton Gate W. MK9: C Key .5C 22
Grafton Pk. MK9: C Key .5D 22
GRAFTON REGIS .2B 132
Grafton Rd. HP19: Ayle .4F 61
Grafton St. HP12: H Wyc .7H 89
Grafton St. (V6) MK6: Mil K .6D 22
MK13: Mil K .5J 15
Graham Dr. HP12: Book .3F 97
Grainges Yd. UB8: Uxb .5J 121
Grampian Ga. MK6: Wint .7D 22
Grampian Way SL3: Lang .3A 130
Gramwell MK5: S Chur .7K 21
Granary, The MK16: Tyr .1E 10
Granary Cl. MK19: H'ham .2K 15
Granary Yd. HP18: Long C .6C 56
GRANBOROUGH .1B 134
Granborough Rd. MK18: N Mar .1A 44
MK18: Wins .7G 39
GRANBY .4G 29
GRANBY .4H 29
Granby Ct. MK1: Blet .4G 29
Granby Ind. Est. MK1: Blet .4H 29
Grand Union Office Pk., The
UB8: Cowl .4J 127
Granes End MK14: G Lin .5E 16
Grange, The SL1: Burn .1E 122
(off Green La.)
Grange Cl. MK18: Buck .1J 37
SL9: C Pet .6J 103
Grange Cotts. HP16: L Kin .3G 83
Grange Ct. MK12: W Mil .7D 14
Grange Dr. HP5: Char .1F 77
HP10: Woob G .6K 107
GRANGE FARM .1H 27
GRANGE FARM .7H 21
Grange Flds. SL9: C Pet .6J 103
Grange Gdns. HP22: Wend .3H 69
SL2: Farn C .3B 118
Grange Rd. HP15: Haz .3F 91
HP15: W End .2E 90
LU7: Pits .4F 51
MK3: Blet .1F 33
SL9: C Pet .6J 103
Grangers Cft. MK12: H Lea .2G 21
Grange Sports Cen., The .7A 62
Grange Vw. HP27: Ask .1K 71
Grange Way SL0: Ive .4F 127
Grangewood SL3: Wex .3G 125
Grant Av. SL1: Slou .4C 124
Grantham Ct. MK5: S Lod .2C 28
Granville Av. SL2: Slou .3B 124
Granville Pl. HP20: Ayle .6J 61
Granville Sq. MK15: Will .6J 17
(not continuous)
Granville St. HP20: Ayle .6J 61
Grapevine Cl. HP11: W Mar .4F 99
Grasholm Way SL3: Lang .2C 130
Grasmere HP21: Ayle .2C 66
SL4: Wind .5G 129
Grasmere Av. SL2: Slou .5E 124
Grasmere Pde. SL2: Slou .5F 125
Grasmere Way MK2: Blet .2K 33
Grasscroft MK4: Fur .3E 28
Grass Hays HP21: Ayle .7D 62
Grassingham End SL9: C Pet .5J 103
Grassingham Rd. SL9: C Pet .5J 103
Grassington MK13: Ban .1A 22
Grasslands HP20: Ayle .5B 62
Grattan Ct. SL7: Marl .6A 106
Gratton Ct. MK4: E Val .4C 28
GRAVEL HILL .4K 103
Gravel Hill SL9: C Pet .4J 103
UB8: Uxb .3K 121
Gravel Wlk. MK46: Emb .7H 7
Graveney Pl. MK6: Sprin .4H 23
Grayburn Cl. HP8: D Gil .7E 94
Grayling Cl. SL7: Marl .2G 115
Gray's Dormer HP14: L End .4A 96
Grays Pk. Rd. SL2: S Pog .7E 118
Grays Pl. SL2: Slou .6D 124
Grays Rd. SL1: Slou .6D 124
UB10: Uxb .6K 121
Grays Wlk. HP5: Ches .3K 77
GRAZELEY .3A 136
Great Benty UB7: W Dra .2K 131
GREAT BILLING .1C 133
GREAT BRICKHILL .7F 35 (3D 133)
Gt. Brickhill La. MK17: L Bric .5F 35
Greatchesters MK13: Ban .1K 21
Gt. Denson MK6: Eagl .6G 23
GREAT GADDESDEN .2D 135
GREATGAP .3F 51
Great Ground MK14: Stan .6E 16
GREAT HAMPDEN .3C 135
GREAT HASELEY .3A 134
Greatheed Dell MK7: Old P .3F 31
GREAT HIVINGS .1J 77
Great Hivings HP5: Ches .1J 77
GREAT HOLM .5A 22
GREAT HORWOOD .2J 39 (3B 132)
Gt. Horwood Rd. MK18: Wins .5H 39
GREAT HOUGHTON .1B 132
GREAT KIMBLE .3C 135
GREAT KINGSHILL .6E 82 (1B 136)
Great La. HP22: Bier .2B 62
HP22: Wend .4H 69
Great Linch MK10: Midd .4C 24
GREAT LINFORD .4E 16 (2C 133)
GREAT LINFORD .6F 17
Great Mdw. Way HP19: Ayle .6E 60
GREAT MILTON .3A 134
GREAT MISSENDEN .6G 75 (3C 135)
Great Missenden Station (Rail) .6G 75
Gt. Monks St. (V5) MK12: Mil K .7E 14
Great Ormes MK4: Tatt .7K 27
Great Pasture MK10: M Vill .3B 24
GREAT SEABROOK .3E 50
Great Slade MK18: Buck .6H 37
Great Stone HP18: Cudd .1B 58
Gt. Western St. HP20: Ayle .6J 61
GREATWORTH .2A 132
Greaves Rd. HP13: H Wyc .2D 98
Grebe Cl. HP19: Ayle .3A 62
Grecian St. HP20: Ayle .6B 62
GREEN, THE .2J 17
Green, The HP7: Amer .5B 86
HP8: D Gil .7G 95
HP10: Woob G .3A 108
HP16: G Mis .6H 75
(off Church St.)
HP18: Bril .3J 53
HP18: Che .2H 57
HP18: Cudd .1B 58
HP18: Ludg .2C 52
HP22: A Abb .6J 47
HP22: Q'ton .5J 43
HP27: Long .2C 70
LU6: Edle .2K 49
LU7: Ched .2C 50
LU7: Pits .5F 51
LU7: Soul .6H 41
MK5: Lough .6A 22
MK6: W Grn. .6J 23
(not continuous)
MK16: New P .1J 17
MK17: G Hor .2J 39
MK17: Nas .7A 26
MK18: T'ough .2C 38
MK19: Cosg .3D 14
(not continuous)
MK19: H'ope .2E 8
SL1: Burn .3D 122
SL1: Slou .7B 124
UB7: W Dra .1K 131
Green Acre HP21: Ayle .7B 62
Greenacre SL4: Wind .7G 129
Greenacres LU7: Pits .5E 50
Greenacres, The HP13: H Wyc .6C 90
Green Acres Cl. HP22: W'urch .5E 44
Greenacres La. HP10: T Grn .6G 91
Green Cl. HP13: H Wyc .1F 99
SL6: Tapl .4C 122
Green Comn. La. HP10: Woob G .5C 108
Green Cres. HP10: F Hea .2J 107
Greendale M. SL2: Slou .5E 124
Grn. Dragon La. HP10: F Hea .2H 107
Green Dr. SL3: Lang .7K 125
(not continuous)
SL6: Tapl .2A 116
Green E. Rd. HP9: Jord .5C 102
Greene Ho. SL9: C Pet .2J 103
GREEN END
Bedford .2D 133
Milton Keynes .5F 35
Green End HP20: Ayle .6J 61
MK17: G Bri .6F 35
Green End La. MK19: H'ope .2D 8
Green End St. HP22: Ast C .2A 68
Green Farm Rd. MK16: New P .1J 17
Greenfell Rd. HP9: Bea .5G 101
Greenfern Av. SL1: Slou .4E 122
GREENFIELD
Bedford .3D 133
Henley-on-Thames .1A 136
Greenfield End SL9: C Pet .5K 103
Greenfield Rd. MK16: New P .1G 17
Greenfields MK18: Ads .6E 38
GREENFORD .2D 137
Green Hill HP13: H Wyc .6B 90
Greenhill Cl. MK5: Lough .6K 21
Green Hill Ga. HP13: H Wyc .6B 90
Green Hill Ri. HP13: H Wyc .6C 90
Greenlands HP10: F Hea .2H 107
HP27: L Grn .1B 80
Greenlands Cl. MK16: New P .2G 17
Greenlands La. HP16: Pres .6B 74
GREEN LANE .2H 23
Green La. HP3: Bov .4G 79
HP5: Ches, Lati .7D 78
HP6: Amer .3B 86
HP14: Stoke .5A 72
HP16: Pres .7D 74
HP17: Hadd .3E 58
LU7: I'hoe .4G 51
MK12: Wolv .7H 15
SL1: Burn .1E 122
SL2: Farn C .4K 117
SL4: Wind .7J 129
Green La. Cl. HP6: Amer .3B 86
Green La. Ct. SL1: Burn .1E 122
Greenlaw Pl. MK3: Blet .4G 29
GREENLEYS .1G 21
GREENLEYS .7F 15
Green Leys HP13: Down .5G 89
Greenleys La. MK12: Gree .2F 21
Green Nth. Rd. HP9: Jord .4C 102
Greenock Rd. SL1: Slou .4J 123
Green Pk. HP16: Pres .7D 74
Green Pk. Dr. MK16: New P .3H 17
Greenridge HP10: T Grn .1H 99
Green Rd. HP5: Ches .1B 78
HP13: H Wyc .5C 90
Greenside HP16: Pres .1D 82
(off Lodge La.)
SL2: Slou .3J 123
SL8: Bou E .4G 107
Greenside Hill MK4: E Val .6B 28
Greens Keep HP17: Hadd .6B 58
GREENS NORTON .2A 132
Green St. HP11: H Wyc .1J 97
HP15: Haz .3F 91
Green Tiles UB9: Den .5F 113
Green Tiles La. UB9: Den .4F 113
Green Valley Pk. HP10: Woob G .7A 100
Green Verges SL7: Marl .6J 105
Green Vw. HP20: Ayle .4B 62
Green Vw. Cl. HP3: Bov .3K 79
Green Way MK17: New L .4D 32
Greenway HP5: Ches .2K 77
HP17: Hadd .7B 58
MK17: G Hor .3J 39
SL1: Burn .7D 116
Greenway, The HP10: T Grn .6H 91
HP13: H Wyc .1B 98
SL1: Slou .6F 123
SL9: C Pet .1H 111
UB8: Uxb .7J 121
Greenway Ct. HP13: H Wyc .1B 98
Greenway Pde. HP5: Ches .2K 77
Greenways MK17: Bow B .5E 30
Greenway Wlk. MK18: Buck .3K 37
Green W. Rd. HP9: Jord .5C 102
Greenwich Gdns.
MK16: New P .3H 17
Greenwood HP14: Walt A .4E 80
Greenwood, The HP22: Ast C .2A 68
Greenwood Cl. HP6: Amer .4C 86
HP9: S Grn .4B 102
Greenwood Pl. MK18: S Clay .2B 42
Greetham Rd. HP21: Ayle .1D 66
Gregories Dr. MK7: W Gat .1E 30
Gregories Farm La. HP9: Bea .6F 101
Gregories Rd. HP9: Bea .6D 100
Gregory Rd. SL2: Hedg .7B 110
GRENDON .1C 133
GRENDON UNDERWOOD .2G 43 (1A 134)
Grendon Way HP22: Bier .2B 62
Grenfell Av. HP12: H Wyc .1H 97
Grenville Av. HP22: Wend .2G 69
Grenville Cl. SL1: Burn .7D 116
Grenville Grn. HP21: Ayle .3J 65
Grenville Rd. HP21: Ayle .2H 65
MK18: Buck .3G 37
Gresham Rd. SL1: Slou .4J 123
Greyfriars Ct. MK10: K'ton .4D 24
Greyhound La. MK18: Wins .6J 39
Greys, The MK6: W Grn. .6J 23
Greystoke Rd. SL2: Slou .3H 123
Greystonley MK4: E Val .5C 28
Griffin Cl. SL1: Slou .7A 124
Griffin Ind. Mall HP19: Ayle .5G 61
Griffin La. HP19: Ayle .5G 61
GRIFFITH GATE .3C 24
Griffith Ga. MK10: Midd .3C 24
Griffiths Acre HP17: Sto .2D 64
Griffiths Yd. HP5: Ches .4K 77
Griffon Cl. MK6: Eagl .6G 23
Griggs Orchard MK16: Sher .2C 12
Grigsby Ri. MK6: Coff .7G 23
Grimbald Ct. MK15: Will .6J 17
Grimmer Cl. HP19: Ayle .3E 60
Grimms Hill HP16: G Mis .6F 75
Grimms Mdw. HP14: Walt A .5F 81
GRIMSCOTE .1A 132
Grimsdell's Cnr. HP6: Amer .4B 86
(off Grimsdell's La.)
Grimsdell's La. HP6: Amer .4B 86
Grizedale MK13: Hee .1B 22
Groombridge MK7: K Hil .7C 24
Groom Rd. HP16: Pres .1C 82
Groomsby Dr. LU7: I'hoe .4G 51
Grooms Cotts. HP5: L Hil .4F 79
Grosmont Cl. MK4: E Val .5B 28
Grosvenor Cl. SL0: I Hea .1D 126
Grosvenor Ct. SL1: Slou .4C 124
Groundsel Cl. MK7: Waln .1D 30
Grove, The HP5: Lati .3H 87
HP6: Amer .3B 86
HP18: Wadd .6C 52
MK3: Blet .7G 29
MK13: B'ell .2A 22
MK16: New P .2H 17
SL1: Slou .7E 124
SL7: Marl .4C 114
Grove Ash MK1: Blet .4K 29
Grove Cl. SL1: Slou .7E 124
SL9: C Pet .6G 103
Grove Ct. HP9: Bea .6F 101
HP22: Bier .1D 62
Grove End SL9: C Pet .6G 103
Grove Hill SL9: C Pet .5G 103
Grove La. HP5: O L'gh, Whel .1E 78
SL9: C Pet .6F 103
Grove Rd. HP6: Amer .4D 86
HP9: Bea .6F 101
HP12: H Wyc .7G 89
HP15: Haz .4F 91
SL1: Burn .1F 123
UB8: Uxb .5K 121
Grovers Ct. HP27: Prin R .6F 71
Grovesbrook MK17: Bow B .5E 30
Groves Cl. SL8: Bou E .6J 107
Groves Rd. HP22: Halt .7B 68
Grove Way HP18: Wadd .6C 52
UB8: Uxb .5K 121
Groveway MK6: Red .4G 29
MK7: Brin, W Gat .7E 24
Groveway (H9) MK6: Mil K .3H 29
Grubbins La. HP27: Spee .1F 81
Gryms Dyke HP16: Pres .7C 74
Guards Rd. SL4: Wind .7E 128
Guards Wlk. SL4: Wind .7E 128
GUBBLECOTE .2D 135
Guernsey Cl. HP19: Ayle .3F 61
Guest Gdns.
MK13: New B .5B 16
Guildford Av. MK4: K'ead .6J 27
Guildford Cl. MK18: Gaw .6D 36
Guillemot Ct. HP19: Ayle .3K 61
Guillemot Way HP19: Ayle .3K 61
Guinea Orchard MK46: Oln .3G 7
Guinions Rd. HP13: H Wyc .3E 98
Gullicott Way LU7: Pits .5F 51
Gulliver's Land Theme Pk. .2J 23
Gull Way HP19: Ayle .3A 62
Gundale Ct. MK4: E Val .5B 28
Gun La. MK16: Sher .1B 12
Gunmaker Ct. MK14: N Hill .7F 17
Gunthorpe Rd. SL7: Marl .6A 106
Gunver La. MK4: Tatt .6B 28
Gurnard Cl. UB7: Yiew .5K 127
Gurnards Av. MK6: Fish .4F 23
Gurnells Rd. HP9: S Grn .3A 102
Gurney Cl. HP9: Bea .6F 101
HP20: Ayle .4A 62
MK5: Lough .7A 22
Gurney Ct. LU6: E Bra .1K 49
Gurneys Mdw.
HP15: H Grn .7K 83
Guttman Rd. HP21: Ayle .2A 66
Gweneth Ct. SL7: Marl .6H 105
Gwynant Ct. MK2: Blet .5K 33
Gwynne Cl. SL4: Wind .6G 129
Gynant Rd. HP13: H Wyc .2F 99
Gypsy La. HP11: H Wyc .3D 98
SL2: S Pog .2C 118
SL7: Marl .4J 105

H

H1 (Ridgeway) MK11: Mil K ... 2D 20
MK12: Mil K ... 1E 20
H2 (Millers Way) MK11: Mil K ... 3E 20
MK12: Mil K ... 1H 21
H3 (Monks Way) MK8: Mil K ... 4G 21
MK12: Mil K ... 2J 21
MK13: Mil K ... 2J 21
MK14: Mil K ... 7C 16
MK15: Mil K ... 6G 17
H4 (Dansteed Way) MK8: Mil K ... 1H 27
MK13: Mil K ... 3B 22
MK14: Mil K ... 2D 22
MK15: Mil K ... 7G 17
H5 (Portway) MK8: Mil K ... 2H 27
MK9: Mil K ... 4B 22
MK15: Mil K ... 1G 23
H6 (Childs Way) MK4: Mil K ... 5J 27
MK5: Mil K ... 2B 28
MK9: Mil K ... 6D 22
MK10: Mil K ... 2B 24
MK15: Mil K ... 4G 23
H7 (Chaffron Way) MK4: Mil K ... 7K 27
MK5: Mil K ... 3C 28
MK6: Mil K ... 5H 23
MK10: Mil K. ... 5H 23
H8 (Standing Way) MK6: Mil K ... 2G 29
MK7: Mil K. ... 7A 24
MK10: Mil K ... 6B 24
H9 (Groveway) MK6: Mil K ... 3H 29
H10 (Bletcham Way) MK1: Mil K ... 5H 29
MK7: Mil K ... 4B 30
Haberley Mead MK13: B'ell ... 3B 22
Hackett Pl. MK16: N Craw ... 6J 13
HACKLETON ... 1C 133
HADDENHAM ... 6B 58 (3B 134)
Haddenham and Thame
Parkway Station (Rail) ... 6A 58
Haddenham Bus. Pk. HP17: Hadd ... 5B 58
Haddington Cl. HP22: Halt ... 3K 69
MK3: Blet ... 5E 28
Haddington Way HP20: Ayle ... 5B 62
Haddon MK8: G Hol ... 6K 21
Hadland Cl. HP3: Bov ... 1K 79
Hadley Ct. *SL3: Poy ... 6E 130*
(off Coleridge Cres.)
Hadley Pl. MK13: B Com ... 3C 22
Hadlow Ct. SL1: Slou ... 6A 124
Hadrians Dr. MK13: Ban ... 7A 16
Haggar St. HP17: Sto ... 2A 64
Hag Hill La. SL6: Tapl ... 4C 122
Hag Hill Ri. SL6: Tapl ... 4C 122
Haglis Dr. HP22: Wend ... 2G 69
Haig Dr. SL1: Slou ... 7K 123
Hainault Av. MK14: G Par ... 4G 17
Haines Cl. HP19: Ayle ... 4E 60
Haithwaite MK8: T Ash ... 5H 21
Haldene MK8: T Ash ... 4J 21
Hale Av. MK11: S Strat ... 1C 20
Hale La. HP22: Wend ... 5J 69
Hale Leys Cen. HP20: Ayle ... 6K 61
Hale Rd. HP22: Wend ... 4J 69
Hales Cres. HP21: Ayle ... 3C 66
Hale St. HP20: Ayle ... 6K 61
Half Acre Hill SL9: C Pet ... 6K 103
Halfway Ho. La. HP5: Ches ... 7G 77
Halifax Ho. HP7: L Chal ... 6G 87
Halifax Rd. HP12: H Wyc ... 4G 97
Halings La. UB9: Den ... 2D 112
Halkingcroft SL3: Lang ... 7G 125
Hall Cl. HP13: H Wyc ... 3F 99
MK18: M M'ton ... 1J 37
HALL END ... 2D 133
Hall La. MK16: Chic ... 4E 12
Hall Mdw. SL1: Burn ... 7E 116
Halls Corner HP10: F Hea ... 7G 99
HALSE ... 2A 132
Halse Dr. SL2: Farn C ... 2G 117
Halswell Pl. MK10: Midd ... 3C 24
HALTON ... 7K 67 (3C 135)
Haltonchesters MK13: Ban ... 7K 15
Halton La. HP22: Halt, Wend ... 1G 69
Halton Stadium Sports Arena ... 7J 67
Halton Wood Rd. HP22: Halt ... 3K 69
Haly Cl. MK13: B'ell ... 2B 22
HAMBLEDEN ... 2A 136
Hambledon Cl. HP21: Ayle ... 2C 66
Hamble Dr. HP21: Ayle ... 2H 65
Hambleton Gro. MK4: E Val ... 5B 28
Hamburgh Cft. MK5: S Broo ... 4B 28
Hambye Cl. HP27: L Grn ... 2C 80
Hamilton Cl. HP4: Dag ... 6H 49
Hamilton Ct. HP13: H Wyc ... 7B 90
HP19: Ayle ... 4J 61
Hamilton Gdns. SL1: Burn ... 1D 122
Hamilton Ho. *HP19: Ayle ... 5F 61*
(off Broadfields)
Hamilton La. MK3: Blet ... 2C 32
Hamilton Rd. HP13: H Wyc ... 7B 90
SL1: Slou ... 4J 123
UB8: Cowl ... 2K 127
Hamilton Way SL2: Farn C ... 3A 118
Hamlins MK6: Coff ... 1G 29
Hammersley La. HP10: Pen ... 2J 99
HP13: H Wyc ... 4H 99
Hammerwood Ga. MK7: K Par ... 7C 24
Hammond Cres. MK15: W Par ... 7H 17
Hammond End SL2: Farn C ... 2K 117
Hampden Av. HP5: Ches ... 4J 77
HAMPDEN BOTTOM ... 3A 74
Hampden Cl. HP21: Ayle ... 1J 65
HP22: Sto M ... 6C 66
SL2: S Pog ... 1E 124
Hampden Ct. HP11: W Mar ... 5H 99
Hampden Gdns. HP21: Ayle ... 1J 65
Hampden Hill HP9: Bea ... 6D 100
Hampden Rd. HP13: H Wyc ... 7B 90
HP16: Pres ... 7A 74
HP21: Ayle ... 1J 65
HP22: Sto M ... 5C 66
HP22: Wend ... 4J 69
HP27: Spee ... 2G 81
SL3: Lang ... 1A 130
SL9: C Pet ... 6H 103
Hampden Sq. HP19: Ayle ... 6F 61
Hampshire Av. SL1: Slou ... 3A 124
Hampshire Ct. MK3: Blet ... 5F 29
Hampshire Ho. SL9: C Pet ... 3J 103
Hampson Cl. MK13: B'ell ... 1A 22
Hampstead Ga. MK13: B Com ... 3C 22
HAMPTON ... 3D 137
Hampton MK8: G Hol ... 6A 22
Hanbury Cl. SL1: Burn ... 3C 122
Handel Mead MK7: Old P ... 2G 31
HANDY CROSS ... 6J 97 (1B 136)
Hanes Rd. HP15: W End ... 1F 91
Hanging Cft. Cl. HP13: H Wyc ... 2F 99
Hangings La. HP16: Pres ... 7A 74
Hanley Cl. SL4: Wind ... 6F 129
Hanmer Rd. MK6: Simp ... 2A 30
Hannon Rd. HP21: Ayle ... 2H 65
Hanover Cl. HP19: Ayle ... 4G 61
SL1: Slou ... 7E 124
SL4: Wind ... 6H 129
Hanover Ct. HP15: Haz ... 4G 91
HP21: Ayle ... 7K 61
(off Croft Rd.)
MK14: Stan ... 6D 16
Hanover Ga. SL1: Slou ... 6J 123
Hanover Way SL4: Wind ... 7H 129
Hanscomb Cl. MK15: Wool ... 4J 23
Hansen Cft. MK5: S Lod ... 2B 28
HANSLOPE ... 2E 8 (2C 133)
Hanslope Rd. MK19: Cast, H'ope ... 4D 8
Hanson Environmental Study Cen. ... 3B 16
Hanson Way HP21: Ayle ... 3B 66
HANWELL ... 2D 137
HANWORTH ... 3D 137
Harborne Ct. MK8: T Ash ... 4G 21
Harborough Cl. SL1: Slou ... 6F 123
Harbourne Cl. HP21: Ayle ... 4H 65
Harby Cl. MK4: E Val ... 6C 28
Harcourt MK13: B'ell ... 3A 22
Harcourt Cl. SL6: Dorn R ... 1B 128
Harcourt Grn. HP19: Ayle ... 4G 61
Harcourt Rd. SL4: Wind ... 6G 129
SL6: Dorn R ... 1B 128
Hardenwaye HP13: H Wyc ... 6E 90
Harding Rd. HP5: Ches ... 4B 78
MK10: Brin ... 6E 24
Hardings Cl. SL0: I Hea ... 1C 126
Hardings Row SL0: I Hea ... 1C 126
HARDINGSTONE ... 1B 132
HARDMEAD ... 2D 133
HARDWICK
Aylesbury ... 5H 45 (2C 135)
Bicester ... 1A 134
Hardwick Gdns. HP6: Amer ... 5C 86
Hardwick M. MK17: W San ... 4K 31
Hardwick Pl. MK17: W San ... 3K 31
Hardwick Rd. MK17: W San ... 3K 31
Hardy Cl. HP21: Ayle ... 7K 61
SL1: Slou ... 6J 123
Harebell Cl. MK7: Waln ... 2D 30
Harebell Wlk. HP15: W End ... 1F 91
Harebridge La. HP22: Halt ... 5B 68
Hare Cl. MK18: Buck ... 5J 37
Hareden Cft. MK4: E Val ... 5B 28
HAREFIELD ... 1J 113 (1D 137)
Harefield Rd. UB8: Uxb ... 5J 121
HARE HATCH ... 3B 136
Harehatch La. SL1: Burn ... 6G 109
SL2: Farn C ... 6G 109
Hare La. HP16: L Kin ... 3G 83
Hare La. End HP16: L Kin ... 3G 83
Harewood Pl. SL1: Slou ... 7E 124
Harewood Rd. HP8: D Gil ... 1G 95
Hargreaves Nook MK14: Blak ... 3G 17
Harkness Cl. MK2: Blet ... 2K 33
Harkness Rd. SL1: Burn ... 3D 122
Harlans Cl. MK6: Eagl ... 6H 23
Harlech Ho. *HP13: H Wyc ... 1F 99*
(off Gayhurst Rd.)
Harlech Pl. MK3: Blet ... 1E 32
Harlequin Pl. MK5: S Broo ... 4K 27
Harlesden Cl. MK10: Monk P ... 5A 24
Harlestone Ct. MK14: G Par ... 4G 17
Harleyford La. SL7: Marl ... 3E 114
Harling Rd. LU6: E Bra ... 2K 49
HARLINGTON
Dunstable ... 3D 133
Hounslow ... 3D 137
Harlow Rd. HP13: H Wyc ... 2C 98
Harman Wlk. HP12: Book ... 5G 97
HARMONDSWORTH ... 4K 131 (3D 137)
Harmondsworth La. UB7: Harm ... 4K 131
Harmondsworth Moor Waterside ... 4H 131
Harmondsworth Moor Waterside Vis. Cen. ... 4H 131
Harnett Dr. MK12: W Mil ... 7D 14
Harpers La. MK14: G Lin ... 5F 17
HARPOLE ... 1A 132
HARPSDEN ... 2A 136
Harrier Cl. HP19: Ayle ... 3A 62
Harrier Ct. MK6: Eagl ... 6G 23
Harrier Dr. MK6: Eagl ... 6G 23
Harries Cl. HP5: Ches ... 3K 77
Harries Way HP15: H Grn ... 1H 91
Harris Cl. HP18: Bril ... 3H 53
HP20: Ayle ... 4A 62
Harris Gdns. SL1: Slou ... 7A 124
Harrison Cl. MK5: Know ... 1D 28
Harrison Way SL1: Slou ... 6F 123
Harris Rd. HP14: L End ... 3K 73
Harroell HP18: Long C ... 6D 56
(not continuous)
Harrogate Ct. SL3: Lang ... 3A 130
HARROLD ... 1D 133
Harrold Rd. MK46: Lave ... 2D 6
HARROW ... 2D 137
Harrow Cl. HP21: Ayle ... 3K 65
Harrowden MK13: B'lle ... 6B 16
Harrow Mkt. SL3: Lang ... 1A 130
Harrow Rd. SL3: Lang ... 1A 130
HARROW WEALD ... 1D 137
Hartdames MK5: S Broo ... 4A 28
Hartfield Cl. MK7: K Hil ... 7C 24
Hartington Gro. MK4: E Val ... 4B 28
Hartland Av. MK4: Tatt ... 7A 28
Hartland Cl. SL1: Slou ... 6B 124
Hartley MK14: G Lin ... 5E 16
Hartley Cl. SL3: S Pog ... 6G 119
Hartmoor Cl. HP14: Stoke ... 6C 72
Harts Rd. HP17: Hadd ... 6D 58
HARTWELL
Aylesbury ... 2E 64
Northampton ... 1B 132
Hartwell Dr. HP9: Bea ... 5F 101
Hartwell End HP21: Ayle ... 7G 61
(not continuous)
Hartwell Rd. MK19: H'ope ... 1D 8
Hartwort Cl. MK7: Waln ... 1D 30
Harvard Cl. MK14: G Par ... 3F 17
Harvest Bank HP6: H Hea ... 2E 84
Harvester Cl. MK12: Gree ... 1F 21
Harvest Hill HP10: Woob G ... 7A 108
SL8: Bou E ... 7J 107
Harvey Dr. MK46: Emb ... 6H 7
Harvey Orchard HP9: Bea ... 5E 100
Harvey Rd. HP21: Ayle ... 2K 65
SL3: Lang ... 1B 130
Harvil Rd. UB9: Hare ... 2J 113
UB10: I'ham ... 4K 113
Harwich Rd. SL1: Slou ... 4J 123
Harwood Rd. SL7: Marl ... 1G 115
Harwood St. MK13: New B ... 6A 16
Hasgill Ct. MK13: Hee ... 2B 22
Haslemere Rd. SL4: Wind ... 6J 129
Haslerig Cl. HP21: Ayle ... 2A 66
Haslow Ct. MK8: T Ash ... 3J 21
Hastings MK11: S Strat ... 1C 20
Hastings Mdw. SL2: S Pog ... 6D 118
HASTOE ... 3D 135
Hastoe Pk. HP20: Ayle ... 4A 62
Hatch, The SL4: Wind ... 5E 128
HATCH END ... 1D 137
Hatches La. HP15: G Kin ... 5A 82
HP16: Pres ... 5A 82
Hatchet Leys La. MK18: T'ough ... 2B 38
Hatchetts Cl. HP10: Pen ... 1B 100
Hatchgate Gdns. SL1: Burn ... 1F 123
Hatchlands MK8: G Hol ... 5K 21
Hatch La. HP14: Rad ... 5K 81
SL4: Wind ... 7J 129
UB7: Harm ... 5K 131
Hatfield Rd. SL1: Slou ... 7E 124
Hathaway Ct. MK8: C'ill ... 7J 21
Hatter's La. HP13: H Wyc ... 3E 98
HATTON ... 3D 137
Hatton MK6: T Bri ... 1K 29
Hatton Av. SL2: Slou ... 2B 124
Hatton Ct. SL4: Wind ... 7K 129
Hatton Gro. UB7: W Dra ... 7K 127
Hauksbee Gdns. MK5: S Lod ... 2C 28
Havelock St. HP20: Ayle ... 5J 61
Havenfield Ct. HP13: H Wyc ... 1B 98
Havenfield Rd. HP12: Book ... 4F 97
Havenshaw Cl. HP21: Ayle ... 2B 66
HAVERSHAM ... 3K 15 (2C 133)
HAVERSHAM ... 5H 15
Haversham Rd. MK12: O Wol ... 5H 15
Hawfinch HP19: Ayle ... 3K 61
Hawker Ct. SL3: Lang ... 1A 130
Hawkhurst Ga. MK7: K Par ... 7B 24
Hawkins Cl. MK11: S Strat ... 1B 20
Hawkmoor Cl. MK6: Eagl ... 6H 23
Hawkridge MK4: Fur ... 4E 28
Hawkshead Dr. MK4: E Val ... 4C 28
HAWKS HILL ... 6K 107
Hawks Hill SL8: Bou E ... 7J 107
Hawkshill Rd. SL2: Slou ... 1J 123
Hawkslade Furlong HP21: Ayle ... 4J 65
Hawksmoor Cl. HP13: Down ... 7A 90
Hawkswood MK46: Oln ... 2H 7
Hawkswood Gro. SL3: Fulm ... 4K 119
Hawkswood La. SL3: Fulm ... 3K 119
SL9: G Cro ... 3K 119
Hawkwell Est. MK19: O Stra ... 7A 14
Haw La. HP14: Bled R ... 3C 72
Hawleys La. HP22: W'urch ... 2G 45
Hawthorn Av. MK2: Blet ... 7A 30
Hawthorn Cl. HP20: Ayle ... 4A 62
SL0: I Hea ... 7C 120
Hawthorn Cotts. HP16: L Com ... 1A 76
Hawthorn Cres. HP15: Haz ... 5H 91
Hawthorn Dr. UB9: Den ... 4J 121
Hawthorne Cl. SL7: Marl ... 5J 105
Hawthorne Cres. SL1: Slou ... 4C 124
Hawthorne Gdns. HP10: F Hea ... 6G 99
Hawthorne Rd. HP13: H Wyc ... 3F 99
Hawthornes, The HP10: Woob G ... 3A 108
HAWTHORN HILL ... 3B 136
Hawthorn La. SL2: Farn C ... 5H 117
Hawthorn Pl. HP10: T Grn ... 7J 91
Hawthorn Rd. HP27: Prin R ... 5H 71
Hawthorns, The HP8: D Gil ... 7G 87
HP27: Mon R ... 1H 71
SL3: Poy ... 6F 131
Hawthorn Wlk. HP15: Haz ... 5H 91
Hawthorn Way HP5: Ches ... 3B 78
LU7: Wing ... 2C 48
Hawtrey Cl. SL1: Slou ... 7F 125
Hay Barn Bus. Pk., The
HP22: A Abb ... 5H 47
Haydock Cl. MK3: Blet ... 2C 32
HAYDON HILL ... 4D 60
Haydon Rd. HP19: Ayle ... 4H 61
HAYES ... 2D 137
Hayes Pl. SL7: Marl ... 1H 115
Hayfield Dr. HP15: Haz ... 5H 91
Hay La. SL3: Fulm ... 2H 119
Haylesfield RG9: Fri ... 7G 73
Hayman Ri. MK8: G Far ... 1H 27
Haymill Rd. SL1: Slou ... 2F 123
SL2: Slou ... 2F 123
Haynes Cl. MK17: Bow B ... 5F 31
Hayse Hill SL4: Wind ... 6F 129
Haystacks, The HP13: H Wyc ... 1B 98
Haythrop Cl. MK15: D Park ... 7H 17
Haywards Cft. MK12: Gree ... 1F 21
Haywards Mead SL4: E Wick ... 3H 129
Haywood Pk. LU7: Stew ... 1A 46
Haywood Way HP19: Ayle ... 3E 60
Hazelbury Rd. HP13: H Wyc ... 2D 98
Hazel Cl. SL7: Marl ... 3G 105
Hazeldene HP22: Wend ... 4J 69
HAZELEY ... 2H 27
Hazel Gro. MK2: Blet ... 1K 33
Hazelhurst MK4: E Val ... 5B 28
Hazelhurst Rd. SL1: Burn ... 7E 116
Hazell Av. HP21: Ayle ... 7B 62
Hazell Pk. HP7: Amer ... 6B 86
Hazell Rd. HP16: Pres ... 1C 82
Hazell Way SL2: S Pog ... 5D 118
Hazel Row MK19: H'ope ... 2F 9
Hazelwood MK14: G Lin ... 5F 17
Hazelwood Cl. HP5: Ches ... 3B 78
Hazlehurst Dr. HP21: Ayle ... 2B 66
HAZLEMERE ... 3G 91 (1B 136)
Hazlemere Ct. HP15: Haz ... 3G 91
Hazlemere Rd. HP10: T Grn ... 5J 91
SL2: Slou ... 6F 125
Hazlemere Vw. HP15: Haz ... 2H 91
Hazley Wlk. MK18: Buck ... 3K 37
Headington Pl. *SL2: Slou ... 6D 124*
(off Mill St.)
Headland Cl. HP16: G Mis ... 5F 75
Healey Av. HP13: H Wyc ... 1D 98
Heaney Cl. MK16: New P ... 7G 11
Hearn Cl. HP10: T Grn ... 5F 91
Hearne Ct. HP8: D Gil ... 1F 103
Hearne Pl. MK6: Old ... 6F 23
Hearnes Cl. HP9: S Grn ... 3B 102
Hearne's Mdw. HP9: S Grn ... 3B 102
Heathacre SL3: Coln ... 6E 130
HEATH AND REACH ... 1D 135
Heath Cl. HP15: H Grn ... 1H 91
HP21: Ayle ... 2C 66
MK17: W San ... 4K 31
Heathcote Way UB7: Yiew ... 6K 127
Heath Ct. UB8: Uxb ... 5K 121
HEATHENCOTE ... 2B 132
HEATH END ... 5E 82
Heath End Cl. HP15: G Kin ... 5E 82
Heath End Rd.
HP10: F Hea, H Wyc ... 5B 98
HP15: G Kin ... 5E 82
HP16: L Kin ... 5E 82
Heather Bank MK17: A H'th ... 5J 31
Heathercroft MK14: G Lin ... 6E 16
Heatherden Grn. SL0: I Hea ... 6C 120
Heather La. UB7: Yiew ... 4K 127
Heather Mead LU6: E Bra ... 1J 49
Heatherside Gdns. SL2: Farn C ... 1B 118
Heatherton Pk. HP6: Amer ... 3K 85
Heather Wlk. HP15: Haz ... 4G 91

Heather Wlk. *HP21: Ayle* 1G 65
(off Primrose Dr.)
Heathfield MK12: S Bus 2J 21
Heathfield Rd. HP12: H Wyc 1F 97
SL1: Burn 2A 116
SL6: Tapl 2B 116
Heath La. MK17: A H'th 5J 31
Heath Lawn HP10: F Hea 7F 99
Heath Rd. HP6: H Hea 1E 84
HP9: Bea 7B 100
LU7: H Rea 7F 35
MK17: G Bri 7F 35
Heathrow Cl. UB7: Long 6H 131
HEATHROW (LONDON) AIRPORT 3D 137
Heathway SL0: I Hea 7D 120
Heavens Lea SL8: Bou E 7J 107
Hedge Lea HP10: Loud 1K 107
HEDGERLEY 6B 110 (2C 137)
HEDGERLEY GREEN 5C 110
HEDGERLEY HILL 7B 110
Hedgerley Hill SL2: Hedg 1B 118
Hedgerley La. HP9: Bea 1H 109
HP9: Bea, Hedg, G Cro 2J 109
SL2: G Cro, Hedg 4C 110
SL9: G Cro 4C 110
Hedgerow SL9: C Pet 4J 103
Hedgerows, The MK4: Fur 3E 28
Hedges Ct. MK5: S Chur 1B 28
Hedingham Ct. MK5: S Chur 2A 28
Hedley Cl. HP22: Ast C 3D 68
Hedley Rd. HP10: F Hea 1H 107
Hedley Vw. HP10: Loud 7K 99
HEDSOR 6B 108
Hedsor Hill SL8: Bou E 7J 107
Hedsor La. HP10: Woob G 6B 108
SL1: Burn 7C 108
Hedsor Rd. SL8: Bou E 7H 107
HEELANDS 2B 22
Hele Ct. MK7: Cald 4D 30
Helford Cl. HP21: Ayle 3J 65
Helford Pl. MK6: Fish 5G 23
Hell Fire Caves 5D 88
Hellyer Way SL8: Bou E 6H 107
HELMDON 2A 132
Helmsley Ri. MK4: K'ead 6J 27
Helston La. SL4: Wind 6K 129
Helston Pl. MK6: Fish 5F 23
Hemingway Cl. MK16: New P 1F 17
Hemingway Rd. HP19: Ayle 4E 60
Hemming Way SL2: Slou 1K 123
Hemp Hill HP19: Ayle 6F 61
Hempson Av. SL3: Lang 7G 125
Hemwood Rd. SL4: Wind 7F 129
Hencroft St. Nth. SL1: Slou 7D 124
Hencroft St. Sth. SL1: Slou 7D 124
Henders MK11: S Strat 1C 20
Hendrix Dr. MK8: C'ill 7H 21
Hengistbury La. MK4: Tatt 6K 27
HENLEY-ON-THAMES 2A 136
Henley Rd. SL1: Slou 4G 123
SL6: Hur, Maid 7A 114
SL7: Medm 5A 114
Hennerton Way HP13: H Wyc 2F 99
Henry Rd. HP20: Ayle 6C 62
SL1: Slou 7B 124
Hensman Ga. MK10: Midd 2B 24
HENTON 3B 134
Henton M. HP19: Ayle 6F 61
Hepleswell MK8: T Ash 5J 21
Hepplewhite Cl. HP13: H Wyc 7D 90
Herbert Rd. HP13: H Wyc 2G 99
Herberts Hole HP5: Ches 4C 76
HP16: Ball 4B 76
Herdman Cl. MK12: Gree 1F 21
Herd's Hill MK18: S Clay 2C 42
Hereford Way HP19: Ayle 3F 61
Heritage Cl. UB8: Cowl 2J 127
Hermitage, The *HP16: G Mis* 6G 75
(off High St.)
UB8: Uxb 4K 121
Heron, The HP19: Ayle 2K 61
Heron Cl. HP20: Ayle 6D 62
UB8: Uxb 4K 121
Heron Dr. SL3: Lang 2B 130
Heron Ho. MK7: K Par 6C 24
Heron Path HP22: Wend 4H 69
HERONSGATE 1D 137
Herons Pl. SL7: Marl 7J 105
Herriot Cl. MK16: New P 7G 11
Herschel Pk. Dr. SL1: Slou 7D 124
Herschel St. SL1: Slou 7D 124
Herston Cl. HP21: Ayle 2C 66
Hertford Pl. MK3: Blet 5F 29
Hervines Ct. HP6: Amer 4A 86
Hervines Rd. HP6: Amer 4K 85
HESTON 3D 137
HETHE 1A 134
Hetherington Cl. SL2: Slou 1H 123
Het's Orchard HP27: L Grn 1C 80
Hetton Cl. MK13: Hee 2C 22
Hever Cl. LU7: Pits 7F 51
Hexham Gdns. MK3: Blet 2D 32
Heybridge Cres. MK7: Cald 4C 30
Heydon Ct. MK13: B'lle 6A 16
Hibbert Lodge SL9: C Pet 7H 103
Hibberts Way SL9: G Cro 1J 111
Hickmans Cl. MK18: Ting 2C 36
Hickman St. HP19: Ayle 6E 60
Hickox Ct. HP10: Woob G 2B 108
Hicks Farm Ri. HP13: H Wyc 7E 90
Hide, The MK6: Neth 1J 29
Higgs Ct. MK5: Lough 6A 22
HIGHAM CROSS 1B 8
Higham Cross Rd. MK19: H'ope 1B 8
Higham Mead HP5: Ches 4A 78
Higham Rd. HP5: Ches 4K 77
High Beeches HP12: Book 2G 97
SL9: G Cro 6H 111
High Beeches Cl. SL7: Marl 3G 105
High Bois La. HP6: Amer 2B 86
Highbridge Ind. Est. UB8: Uxb 5J 121
Highbridge Rd. HP21: Ayle 6K 61
Highbridge Wlk. HP20: Ayle 6K 61
Highbury La. MK9: Camp 3G 23
High Coppice HP7: Amer 6A 86
HIGHER DENHAM 5C 112
Highfield HP8: D Gil 6H 95
HP18: Long C 6C 56
Highfield Av. HP12: Book 3F 97
Highfield Cl. HP6: Amer 4B 86
MK3: Blet 5G 29
MK16: New P 1A 18
Highfield Ct. HP15: Haz 4G 91
SL2: Farn R 6K 117
SL9: C Pet 3K 103
Highfield Pk. SL7: Marl 1F 115
Highfield Rd. HP5: Ches 3K 77
HP10: F Hea 1G 107
HP27: Prin R 4H 71
MK18: Wins 5H 39
SL4: Wind 7H 129
SL8: Bou E 6H 107
HIGHFIELDS 1F 115
Highfield Way HP15: Haz 4G 91
Highgate M. HP19: Ayle 5E 60
Highgate Over MK7: Waln 7D 24
Highgrove Hill MK8: G Hol 6K 21
High Halden MK7: K Hil 6D 24
High Heavens Wood SL7: Marl 1G 105
Highland Cl. HP18: Bril 2H 53
MK3: Blet 4F 29
Highlands HP10: F Hea 2H 107
SL2: Farn C 3A 118
Highlands Cl. SL9: C Pet 5K 103
Highlands End SL9: C Pet 5K 103
Highlands La. SL9: C Pet 5K 103
Highlands Rd. HP9: S Grn 3A 102
MK18: Buck 2J 37
Highlea Av. HP10: F Hea 1G 107
Highley Ct. MK10: Bro 3D 24
HIGHMOOR 2A 136
Highmoor HP7: Amer 6B 86
High Moors HP22: Halt 7J 67
Highmore Cotts. HP7: L Miss 4B 84
Highmore Cft. MK8: G Far 1H 27
Highover Pk. HP7: Amer 7B 86
High Pk. Dr. MK12: W Mil 7E 14
High Rd. LU7: Soul 6H 41
UB8: Cowl 3J 127
High St. HP5: Ches 5K 77
(not continuous)
HP7: Amer 6J 85
HP8: D Gil 1F 103
HP11: H Wyc 2B 98
HP13: Down 4H 89
(Abbey Way)
HP13: Down 4H 89
(Plomer Grn. La.)
HP14: L End 4K 73
HP14: W Wyc 5D 88
HP16: G Mis 5G 75
HP16: Pres 7C 74
HP17: Dint 2G 59
HP17: Hadd 7B 58
HP18: Bril 3H 53
HP18: Long C 6C 56
HP18: Ludg 3B 52
HP18: Wadd 5B 52
HP20: Ayle 6J 61
HP22: W'don 7J 45
HP22: Wend 4H 69
HP22: W'urch 2G 45
HP27: Prin R 5G 71
LU6: E Bra 1J 49
LU6: Edle 3J 49
LU7: Burc 1B 48
LU7: Ched 2C 50
LU7: Cubl 2G 47
LU7: I'hoe 4G 51
LU7: Wing 3C 48
MK11: S Strat 7A 14
MK13: New B 6K 15
MK14: G Lin 4E 16
MK16: N Craw 6K 13
MK16: New P 1J 17
MK16: S Gold 4B 6
MK16: Sher 2B 12
MK17: G Hor 2J 39
MK17: Nas 6A 26
MK17: W San 3K 31
MK17: Whad 5F 27
MK18: Buck 3H 37
MK18: N Mar 2A 44
MK18: T'ough 2C 38
High St. MK18: Wins 5H 39
MK19: H'ham 3K 15
MK19: H'ope 2E 8
MK46: Emb 7H 7
MK46: Lave 2C 6
MK46: Oln 3H 7
SL0: Ive 4E 126
SL1: Burn 1E 122
SL1: Slou 7A 124
(Chalvey)
SL1: Slou 7D 124
(Slough, not continuous)
SL3: Coln 5C 130
SL3: Lang 3A 130
SL6: Tapl 2A 122
SL7: Marl 7H 105
SL9: C Pet 6J 103
UB7: Harm 4K 131
UB7: Yiew 5K 127
UB8: Cowl 2J 127
UB8: Uxb 5J 121
UB9: Hare 1J 113
High St., The MK8: T Ash 4G 21
(not continuous)
High St. Nth. LU7: Stew 1A 46
High St. Sth. LU7: Stew 4C 46
MK46: Oln 4H 7
High St. W. SL1: Slou 7C 124
High Trees MK6: Eagl 6H 23
Highveer Cft. MK4: Tatt 6B 28
High Vw. HP8: D Gil 7H 95
MK17: L Bric 3F 35
High Vw. Cl. SL7: Marl 1H 105
Highway, The HP9: Bea 6F 101
MK17: Dray P 6C 40
Highway Ct. HP5: Ches 4B 78
HP9: Bea 5F 101
Highwood Av. HP12: Book 3F 97
Highwood Bottom HP27: Spee 1E 80
Highwood Cres. HP12: Book 2F 97
Highwoods Cl. SL7: Marl 2G 105
Highwoods Dr. SL7: Marl 3G 105
Highworth Cl. HP13: H Wyc 6E 90
HIGH WYCOMBE 1B 98 (1B 136)
High Wycombe Station (Rail) 1B 98
Hikers Way HP18: Long C 7F 57
Hilbre Ct. MK4: Tatt 6K 27
Hilda Wharf HP20: Ayle 6K 61
Hildreth Rd. HP16: Pres 1C 82
Hiljon Cres. SL9: C Pet 6J 103
Hill, The HP7: Winc 4E 92
Hillary Cl. HP13: H Wyc 2E 98
HP21: Ayle 2B 66
Hillary Rd. HP13: H Wyc 1E 98
SL3: Lang 7J 125
Hill Av. HP6: Amer 5A 86
HP15: Haz 2G 91
Hillbeck Gro. MK10: Midd 3A 24
Hillbottom Rd. HP12: H Wyc 1E 96
Hillbury Cl. HP6: Amer 2A 86
Hill Cl. HP10: Woob G 2B 108
Hillcrest Cl. MK5: Lough 1B 28
Hillcrest Ct. *HP6: Amer* 5A 86
(off Hill Av.)
Hillcrest Ri. MK18: Buck 7J 37
Hillcrest Way MK18: Buck 7J 37
Hillcrest Waye SL9: G Cro 5K 111
Hillcroft Rd. HP5: Ches 3B 78
HP10: T Grn 6J 91
Hillersdon SL2: Slou 3F 125
Hillersdon Chase MK17: S Ham 2G 41
HILLESDEN 1A 134
Hillesden Way MK18: Buck 3J 37
Hill Farm MK18: N Mar 2A 44
Hill Farm App. HP10: Woob G 2B 108
Hill Farm La. HP8: D Gil 6D 94
Hill Farm Rd. HP5: Ches 1B 86
SL6: Tapl 7A 116
SL7: Marl 3H 105
SL9: C Pet 5J 103
Hill Farm Way HP15: Haz 5H 91
Hillfield Cl. HP13: Down 5J 89
Hillfield Rd. SL9: C Pet 5J 103
Hillfield Sq. SL9: C Pet 5J 103
Hillgrove SL9: C Pet 6J 103
Hill Ho. Cl. SL9: C Pet 5J 103
Hilliard Dr. MK13: B'ell 3A 22
Hilliards Rd. UB8: Cowl 4K 127
Hillier Rd. HP21: Ayle 4J 65
HILLINGDON 2D 137
Hillingdon Rd. UB8: Uxb 6K 121
UB10: Uxb 6K 121
Hillington Cl. HP19: Ayle 7G 61
Hillman Cl. UB8: Uxb 3K 121
Hillmead Ct. SL6: Tapl 3B 122
Hill Mdw. HP7: Cole 3H 93
Hill Pl. SL2: Farn C 5K 117
Hill Ri. SL9: C Pet 7H 103
Hillrise SL3: Lang 4A 130
Hill Ri. Cres. SL9: C Pet 7J 103
Hills Cl. MK14: G Lin 6E 16
Hill Side LU7: Ched 2B 50
Hillside HP5: Ches 2J 77
HP13: H Wyc 1D 98
MK18: Gaw 6C 36
SL1: Slou 7C 124
UB9: Hare 3J 113
Hillside Cen. HP11: H Wyc 1K 97
Hillside Cl. HP8: D Gil 1F 103
SL9: C Pet 4J 103
Hillside Cotts. HP18: Cudd 2B 58
Hillside Gdns. HP7: Amer 7C 86
HP13: H Wyc 1D 98
Hillside Pk. HP27: Spee 2F 81
Hillside Rd. HP10: T Grn 5G 91
SL7: Marl 5J 105
Hill St. HP13: H Wyc 3F 99
HILLTOP 3C 78
Hilltop HP18: Long C 7D 56
Hilltop Av. MK18: Buck 2J 37
Hill Top Dr. SL7: Marl 7F 105
HILL VIEW 2G 17
Hill Vw. HP18: Oak 5H 53
MK16: New P 2G 17
Hillview HP14: Saun 5A 80
MK16: Sher 3C 12
Hillview Rd. HP13: H Wyc 7D 90
Hillway HP7: Amer 1K 93
MK17: W San 1J 31
Hill Waye SL9: G Cro 4K 111
Hillyer Ct. MK6: P Bri 5J 23
Hilperton Rd. SL1: Slou 7C 124
Hilton Av. HP20: Ayle 4K 61
Hilton Cl. UB8: Uxb 7H 121
Hindemith Gdns. MK7: Old P 2F 31
Hindhead Knoll MK7: Waln 1D 30
Hinds Way HP21: Ayle 1G 65
Hinkley Cl. UB9: Hare 2J 113
Hinksey Cl. SL3: Lang 1B 130
Hinton Cl. HP13: Down 6K 89
Hinton Ct. MK3: Blet 6F 29
HINTON-IN-THE-HEDGES 3A 132
Hinton Rd. SL1: Slou 5G 123
UB8: Uxb 6J 121
HINWICK 1D 133
Hipwell Ct. MK46: Oln 4H 7
Hitcham La. SL1: Burn 1A 122
SL6: Burn, Tapl 1A 122
Hitcham Rd. SL1: Burn 3C 122
SL6: Tapl 4B 122
Hithercroft Rd. HP13: Down 5J 89
Hither Mdw. SL9: C Pet 6J 103
Hiving's Hill HP5: Ches 2J 77
Hivings Pk. HP5: Ches 2K 77
HM Young Offenders Institution Aylesbury
HP20: Ayle 5A 62
Hoathly M. MK7: K Hil 6D 24
Hobart Cl. HP13: H Wyc 6E 90
Hobart Cres. MK15: W Par 7H 17
Hobart Rd. HP13: H Wyc 6D 90
Hobarts Dr. UB9: Den 4F 113
Hobbshill Rd. HP16: G Mis 7H 75
Hockett La. SL6: Cook 4K 115
HOCKLEY HOLE 6F 119
Hockley La. SL2: S Pog 5F 119
HOCKLIFFE 1D 135
Hockliffe Brae MK7: Waln 2D 30
Hodder La. MK4: E Val 5C 28
Hodgedale La. SL6: Hur 7A 114
HODGE LEA 2G 21
HODGE LEA 1H 21
Hodge Lea La. MK12: H Lea 2G 21
Hodgemoor Vw. HP8: D Gil 1D 102
Hodgemore Ct. MK14: G Par 3F 17
Hodges M. HP12: H Wyc 2G 97
Hoe Mdw. HP9: Bea 4E 100
Hogarth Cl. SL1: Slou 5G 123
Hogarths Ct. MK8: G Hol 5K 21
Hogback Wood Rd. HP9: Bea 5D 100
Hogfair La. SL1: Burn 1E 122
HOGGESTON 1C 135
Hogg La. HP15: H Grn 1K 91
Hog Hall La. HP4: Dag 7F 49
Hogthrough La. HP22: Wend 5J 69
Hogtrough La. HP16: K'ash 5J 69
Holborn Cres. MK4: Tatt 7A 28
Holdom Av. MK1: F Str 5K 29
Holes La. MK46: Oln 3H 7
Holiday La. MK19: H'ope 1D 8
Holland Cl. HP22: Wend 4H 69
Holland Rd. HP19: Ayle 4G 61
SL7: Marl 7K 105
Holland Way MK16: New P 2J 17
Holliday Cl. MK8: C'ill 1J 27
Hollies, The HP9: Bea 5G 101
HOLLINGDON 5F 41 (1C 135)
Hollingdon Depot LU7: Soul 6G 41
Hollingdon Rd.
LU7: Soul, Holl 1D 46 & 6F 41
Hollin La. MK12: S Bus 2J 21
Hollinwell Cl. MK3: Blet 6D 28
Hollis Rd. HP13: H Wyc 7E 90
Hollister Chase MK5: S Lod 3B 28
Holloway, The HP27: Whit 2J 71
Holloway Cl. UB7: Harm 3K 131
Holloway Dr. MK18: Buck 2J 37
Holloway La. UB7: Harm, W Dra 4K 131
Hollow Hill La. SL0: Ive 5B 126
Hollow Ri. HP13: H Wyc 6B 90
Hollow Way HP5: Ches 4G 77
Hollow Way La. HP5: Ches 2D 86
HP6: Amer 2C 86
Hollow Wood MK46: Oln 4G 7
Hollyberry Gro. HP15: H Grn 7J 83

Hollybrook Way HP13: H Wyc 6E **90**
Hollybush Hill SL2: S Pog 5E **118**
Hollybush La. HP6: Amer 3B **86**
Hollybush La. SL0: Ive 4B **126**
UB9: Den .7C **112**
Hollybush Rd. HP5: Ches 1J **77**
Holly Cl. MK8: C'ill 1J **27**
SL2: Farn C 2A **118**
Holly Ct. HP22: Wend 3J **69**
Holly Cres. SL4: Wind 7F **129**
Holly Dr. HP21: Ayle 1K **65**
Holly End HP14: Nap 6G **81**
HOLLY GREEN 4A **70**
Holly Grn. La. HP27: Bled 4A **70**
Holly Pl. HP11: W Mar 5G **99**
Holly Tree Cl. HP5: L Hil 5F **79**
SL9: C Pet 3J **103**
Holly Tree La. HP18: Cudd 1B **58**
Holly Wlk. MK17: A H'th 5K **31**
Hollywell Mead Outdoor Swimming Pool 3C **98**
Holman St. HP19: Ayle 3H **61**
Holmedale SL2: Slou 5G **125**
HOLMER GREEN 1J **91** (1C **137**)
Holmer Grn. Rd. HP15: Haz 3G **91**
Holmer La. HP12: Book 5G **97**
Holmer Pl. HP15: H Grn 7J **83**
Holmers Ct. HP12: Book 5F **97**
Holmers Farm Way
HP12: Book, H Wyc 5F **97**
Holmers La. HP12: H Wyc 5G **97**
Holmes Place Health and Fitness Club 7E **124**
Holmewood MK4: Fur 3E **28**
Holmfield Cl. MK6: T Bri 2A **30**
Holmgate MK8: Lough 6A **22**
Holmoak Wlk. HP15: Haz 4H **91**
Holmsdale Cl. SL0: Ive 4F **127**
Holst Cres. MK7: Brow 3E **30**
Holt, The MK18: Buck 5J **37**
Holt Gro. MK5: Lough 6A **22**
HOLTON 3A **134**
Holton Hill MK4: E Val 5C **28**
Holton Rd. MK18: Buck 2H **37**
Holts Grn. MK17: G Bri 7E **34**
HOLTSPUR .7C **100**
Holtspur Av. HP10: Woob G 2A **108**
Holtspur Cl. HP9: Bea 1C **108**
Holtspur La. HP10: Woob G 4A **108**
Holtspur Pde. *HP9: Bea* *1C* ***108***
(off Holtspur Top La.)
Holtspur Top La. HP9: Bea 1C **108**
Holtspur Way HP9: Bea 7C **100**
Holyhead Cres. MK4: Tatt 7C **28**
HOLYPORT .3B **136**
Holyrood MK8: G Hol 6J **21**
Holy Thorn La. MK5: S Chur 2A **28**
Holywell Gdns. HP13: H Wyc 1E **98**
Holywell Pl. MK6: Sprin 4J **23**
Home Cl. HP18: Shab 5H **55**
HP22: West T 5G **67**
MK3: Blet .5H **29**
Home Farm MK17: New L 4D **32**
Home Farm Ct. HP3: Bov 4J **79**
MK46: Emb 7G **7**
Homefarm Ct. HP8: D Gil 1E **102**
Home Farm La. MK17: G Bri 6F **35**
Home Farm Way SL3: S Pog 6G **119**
Home Fld. HP19: Ayle 7F **61**
MK7: Cald 4C **30**
Homefield Cl. HP14: Stoke 5C **72**
Homeground MK18: Buck 6J **37**
Homelands Gdns. HP15: G Kin 6D **82**
Home Mdw. SL2: Farn R 7A **118**
Home Mdw. Dr. HP10: F Hea 2H **107**
Home of Rest for Horses 3F **81**
Homeridings Ho. MK13: Hee 2B **22**
Homers Rd. SL4: Wind 6F **129**
Homerton St. MK3: Blet 7H **29**
Homestall MK18: Buck 6H **37**
Homestall Cl. MK5: Lough 7A **22**
Homestead HP17: Upt 1J **59**
Homestead, The HP12: H Wyc 5H **97**
HP15: G Kin 5C **82**
MK5: S Chur 1A **28**
Homestead Pl. HP19: Ayle 6F **61**
Homeward Ct. MK5: Lough 7A **22**
Home Wood SL7: Marl 4D **114**
Homewood SL3: G Grn 4H **125**
Honey Banks HP22: Wend 4J **69**
Honeycroft Hill UB10: Uxb 5K **121**
Honey Hill MK46: Emb 7H **7**
Honey La. SL6: Hur 7C **114**
Honeypot Cl. MK13: B'ell 2B **22**
Honeysuckle Cl. SL0: Ive 4C **126**
Honeysuckle Fld. HP5: Ches 4A **78**
Honeysuckle Rd. HP15: W End 7F **83**
Honey Way HP14: Walt A 6F **81**
HONEYWICK 1D **135**
Honiton Ct. *MK7: W Gat* *7E* ***24***
(off Isaacson Dri.)
Honor End La. HP16: Pres 4A **74**
Honor Rd. HP16: Pres 7C **74**
Honorwood Cl. HP16: Pres 7B **74**
Honour Cl. HP20: Ayle 4A **62**
Honours Mead HP3: Bov 1K **79**
Hoods Farm Cl. HP22: Bier 2D **62**
Hoods Wood Rd. HP5: Ches 7A **78**
Hooke, The MK15: Will 6K **17**
Hooper Ga. MK15: Will 6J **17**
Hopkins Cl. MK10: M Vill 4C **24**
Hopkins Ct. HP20: Ayle 4A **62**
Hoppers Mdw. MK5: Lough 6A **22**
Hoppers Way HP15: G Kin 6D **82**
Hopton Gro. MK16: New P 2B **18**
Hordern Cl. HP17: Hadd 6B **58**
Hornbeam MK16: New P 2G **17**
Hornbeam Cl. HP12: Book 4G **97**
Hornbeam Wlk. *HP15: Haz* *4G* ***91***
(off Rose Av.)
Hornbill Cl. UB8: Cowl 4K **127**
Hornby Chase MK4: E Val 5B **28**
Horners Cft. MK12: Wolv 1G **21**
Horn Hill La. SL9: C Pet 3K **103**
Horn La. MK11: S Strat 1B **20**
Horns La. HP12: Book 5E **96**
HP27: Prin R 5G **71**
Horn St. MK18: Wins 6H **39**
Horsefair Grn. MK11: S Strat 1B **20**
Horse Hill HP5: L Hil 6H **79**
Horsemoor Cl. SL3: Lang 2A **130**
Horsemoor La. HP7: Winc 4D **92**
HORSENDEN 5D **70** (3B **134**)
Horsenden La. HP27: Prin R 6D **70**
Horsenden Rd. HP13: H Wyc 3F **99**
Horsepond MK17: G Bri 6E **34**
Horseshoe Cl. LU7: Ched 2B **50**
Horseshoe Cres. HP9: Bea 7G **101**
Horseshoe Hill SL1: Burn 2E **116**
Horseshoe Rd. HP14: Rad 3A **72**
HORSPATH .3A **134**
HORTON
Leighton Buzzard 2D **135**
Northampton 1C **133**
Slough 7A **130** (3D **137**)
Horton Cl. HP19: Ayle 7F **61**
HORTON-CUM-STUDLEY 2A **134**
Horton Ga. MK14: G Par 3F **17**
Horton Pde. UB7: Yiew 6K **127**
Horton Rd. SL3: Coln, Hor 7A **130**
UB7: Yiew 6K **127**
Horwood Ct. MK1: F Str 5K **29**
HOSPITAL .1H **29**
Hospital Circular Rd. HP22: Halt 2K **69**
(not continuous)
Hospital Hill HP5: Ches 6A **78**
HOTLEY BOTTOM 5C **74**
Hotley Bottom La. HP16: Pres 4C **74**
HOUGHTON CONQUEST 2D **133**
Houghton Ct. MK8: G Hol 6K **21**
HOUGHTON REGIS 1D **135**
HOUNSLOW .3D **137**
Household Cavalry Mus. 7K **129**
Housman Cl. MK16: New P 7G **11**
Howard Agne Cl. HP3: Bov 1K **79**
Howard Av. HP21: Ayle 7C **62**
SL2: Slou .3B **124**
Howard Ct. SL8: Bou E 6G **107**
Howard Cres. HP9: S Grn 3A **102**
Howard Ind. Est. *HP5: Ches* *3A* ***78***
(off Chilton Rd.)
Howard Rd. HP5: Ches 2K **77**
Howards Thicket SL9: G Cro 7G **111**
Howards Wood Dr. SL9: G Cro 7H **111**
Howard Way MK16: New P 2B **18**
Howe Ct. MK10: Midd 3C **24**
Howe Dr. HP9: Bea 3F **101**
Howe Hill La. HP15: H Grn 6H **83**
HOW END 2D **133**
Howe Rock Pl. MK4: Tatt 6B **28**
Howitt Dr. MK13: B'lle 6B **16**
Howletts Cl. HP19: Ayle 7F **61**
Hows Cl. UB8: Uxb 6J **121**
Hows Rd. UB8: Uxb 6J **121**
Hoylake Cl. MK3: Blet 1D **32**
SL1: Slou .7G **123**
Hoyton Ga. MK8: G Far 1H **27**
Hubbard Cl. MK18: Buck 3K **37**
Huckleberry Cl. MK7: Waln 1D **30**
Hudson La. MK8: C'ill 7H **21**
Hudson Pl. SL3: Lang 3A **130**
Hudsons Av. UB9: Den 3F **113**
Huesden Way SL9: G Cro 6K **111**
Hughenden Av. HP13: Down, H Wyc . . .7K **89**
Hughenden Grn. HP21: Ayle 3K **65**
Hughenden Manor 4A **90**
Hughenden Rd. HP13: H Wyc 7A **90**
SL1: Slou .4B **124**
HUGHENDEN VALLEY 7A **82** (1B **136**)
Hughes Cft. MK3: Blet 1F **33**
Hugh Parke Cl. MK5: Lough 6C **22**
Hulbert End HP21: Ayle 2E **66**
Hulcombe Wlk. HP20: Ayle 4K **61**
HULCOTE 1B **132**
HULCOTT 1E **62** (2C **135**)
Hulcott La. HP22: Bier 2E **62**
Hull Cl. HP21: Ayle 1K **65**
SL1: Slou .7A **124**
Hulton Dr. MK46: Emb 7H **7**
Humber Cl. UB7: W Dra 6K **127**
Humber Dr. HP21: Ayle 2H **65**
Humber Way MK3: Blet 6E **28**
SL3: Lang 2A **130**
Hundred Acres La. HP7: Amer 7B **86**
HUNGATE END 2B **8**
Hungerford Av. SL2: Slou 3C **124**
Hungerford Ho. *MK4: E Val* *6D* ***28***
(off Eastbury Ct.)
Hunsbury Chase MK10: Bro 3C **24**
Hunsdon Cl. MK14: Stan 7D **16**
Hunstanton Cl. SL3: Coln 5C **130**
Hunstanton Way MK3: Blet 7D **28**
Huntercombe Cl. SL6: Tapl 4D **122**
Huntercombe La. Nth. SL1: Slou 3E **122**
Huntercombe La. Sth. SL6: Tapl 6D **122**
Hunter Ct. SL1: Slou 3E **122**
Hunter Dr. MK2: Blet 2J **33**
Hunters Cl. HP3: Bov 3K **79**
HP5: Ches 4J **77**
Hunters Hill HP13: H Wyc 3F **99**
Hunters M. SL4: Wind 6K **129**
Hunters Reach MK13: B'ell 3A **22**
Hunter St. MK18: Buck 5G **37**
Hunters Way SL1: Slou 6G **123**
Huntingbrooke MK8: G Hol 6K **21**
Huntingdon Cres. MK3: Blet 2C **32**
Huntley Cl. HP13: H Wyc 5C **90**
Huntley Cres. MK9: Camp 3G **23**
HUNTON BRIDGE 1D **137**
Hunt Rd. HP13: H Wyc 2E **98**
HUNT'S GREEN 1H **75**
Hunt's Grn. Cotts. HP16: T Lee 1H **75**
HUNT'S HILL 2H **89**
Hunts Hill La. HP14: Nap 2H **89**
Hunts La. SL6: Tapl 7A **116**
Huntsman Gro. MK14: Blak 3G **17**
Huntsmans Cl. HP4: Dag 6H **49**
Huntswood La. SL6: Tapl 5A **116**
Hurbert Day Cl. HP9: Bea 5F **101**
HURLEY 6D **114** (2B **136**)
HURLEY BOTTOM 7D **114**
Hurley Cft. MK10: Monk 5D **24**
Hurley High St. SL6: Hur 5D **114**
Hurley La. SL6: Hur 7E **114**
Hurlstone Gro. MK4: Fur 4D **28**
Hurricane Way SL3: Lang 3B **130**
HURST 3A **136**
Hurstfield Dr. SL6: Tapl 4D **122**
Hurst Rd. SL1: Slou 3F **123**
HUSBORNE CRAWLEY 3D **133**
Hutchings Cl. MK5: Lough 6A **22**
Hutchings Rd. HP9: Bea 3F **101**
Hutton Av. MK6: Old 5E **22**
Hutton Ct. MK17: W San 2K **31**
Hutton Way MK17: W San 2K **31**
Huxley Cl. MK16: New P 1F **17**
UB8: Cowl 2K **127**
Huxtable Gdns. SL6: Bra 3A **128**
Hychenden Cl. HP14: Nap 1J **89**
Hyde, The HP22: West T 5G **67**
Hyde Cl. MK16: New P 3J **17**
Hyde Grn. HP9: Bea 5H **101**
SL7: Marl 1K **115**
HYDE HEATH 2E **84** (3D **135**)
Hyde Heath Rd. HP6: H Hea 6C **76**
HP16: H Hea 6C **76**
Hyde La. HP3: Bov 1K **79**
HP16: H Hea, L Kin 2K **83**
Hylle Cl. SL4: Wind 6G **129**
Hylton Rd. HP12: H Wyc 1G **97**
Hyrons Cl. HP6: Amer 5C **86**
Hyrons La. HP6: Amer 5B **86**
Hythe, The MK8: T Ash 3H **21**
HYTHE END .3D **137**

I

Ibbotson Ct. SL3: Poy 6E **130**
IBSTONE 1A **136**
Ibstone Av. MK13: B Com 2C **22**
Ibstone Rd. HP14: Stoke 7A **72**
ICKENHAM .2D **137**
ICKFORD 5D **54** (3A **134**)
Ickford Rd. HP18: Shab, Worm, Ick 2C **54**
OX9: Dray 7D **54**
Icknield Cl. HP22: Wend 3J **69**
Idaho Pk. HP16: Pres 7B **74**
Iffley Cl. UB8: Uxb 5K **121**
Ilex Cl. HP15: Haz 4G **91**
Illingworth Pl. MK6: Old 6F **23**
ILMER 3B **134**
Imperial Ct. *HP10: Loud* *6J* ***99***
(off London Rd.)
Imperial Rd. SL4: Wind 7J **129**
Independent Bus. Pk.
HP14: Stoke 5A **72**
India Rd. SL1: Slou 7F **125**
Ingleglen SL2: Farn C 3K **117**
Ingleside SL3: Poy 6E **130**
Ingleton Cl. MK13: Hee 2C **22**
Ingram Av. HP21: Ayle 1D **66**
Inkerman Dr. HP15: Haz 2H **91**
Inkerman Rd. SL4: E Wick 2H **129**
Inkerman Ter. HP5: Ches 7A **78**
Innes Ct. MK8: G Far 1J **27**
Inn Farm Ct. MK16: Lath 5K **11**
Innholder Ct. MK14: N Hill 7F **17**
Innings Ga. RG9: Fri 7G **73**
Institute Rd. SL6: Tapl 4B **122**
SL7: Marl .1J **115**
Intalbury Av. HP19: Ayle 4F **61**
Inverewe Pl. MK4: West 5J **27**
Inverness Cl. MK3: Blet 5F **29**
Iona Cres. SL1: Slou 4G **123**
Ipswich Rd. SL1: Slou 4H **123**
Ireland Cl. MK7: Brow 3F **31**
Iris Cl. HP21: Ayle 2G **65**
Iris Ct. HP20: Ayle 6C **62**
Ironmonger Ct. MK14: N Hill 7F **17**
Irvine Dr. HP22: Sto M 5B **66**
Irving Cres. LU7: Ched 1C **50**
Irving Dale MK7: Old P 2G **31**
Isaacson Dr. MK7: W Gat 1E **30**
Isambard Cl. UB8: Cowl 2K **127**
Isis Cl. HP21: Ayle 4J **65**
Isis Wlk. MK3: Blet 6E **28**
Isis Way SL8: Bou E 5H **107**
Island, The MK18: S Clay 3B **42**
UB7: Long 5J **131**
Islingbrook MK5: S Broo 4B **28**
Ismay Ct. SL2: Slou 4C **124**
Ivanhoe Cl. UB8: Cowl 3K **127**
IVER 4E **126**
Iverdale Cl. SL0: Ive 5C **126**
IVER HEATH 7D **120** (2D **137**)
Iver La. SL0: Ive 4G **127**
UB8: Cowl 4G **127**
Iver Station (Rail) 7F **127**
Ives Ho. *HP13: H Wyc* *2D* ***98***
(off Ercolani Ho.)
Ives Rd. SL3: Lang 7K **125**
IVINGHOE 4G **51** (2D **135**)
IVINGHOE ASTON 1J **51** (2D **135**)
Ivinghoe Vw. HP20: Ayle 5A **62**
Ivins Rd. HP9: Bea 7C **100**
Ivybridge Cl. UB8: Uxb 1K **127**
Ivy Cl. HP27: Long 3D **70**
MK16: New P 1A **18**
Ivy Cotts. *HP8: D Gil* *7F* ***95***
(off Up Corner)
Ivy Cres. SL1: Slou 5H **123**
Ivy La. HP22: Bro 5E **62**
LU7: Burc .1B **48**
LU7: Stew .3C **46**
MK17: New L 5C **32**
Ivy Pl. HP14: L End 3A **96**

J

Jacks Cl. MK46: Lave 3B **6**
Jackson Cl. UB10: Uxb 5K **121**
Jackson Ct. HP15: Haz 4G **91**
Jackson Ind. Est. SL8: Bou E 6H **107**
Jackson Rd. HP19: Ayle 3E **60**
UB10: Uxb 5K **121**
Jacksons Cl. LU6: Edle 2J **49**
Jacob Cl. SL4: Wind 6G **129**
Jacobs Cl. MK14: Stan 6D **16**
Jacob's Ladder *HP5: Ches* *6A* ***78***
(off Punch Bowl La.)
Jakeman Way HP21: Ayle 1G **65**
Jamaica MK6: Coff 1G **29**
James Cl. HP15: Haz 1G **91**
SL7: Marl .5K **105**
James Martin Cl. UB9: Den 4G **113**
James Rd. HP14: L End 4K **73**
James Way MK1: Blet 6H **29**
Jane Cl. HP21: Ayle 3B **66**
Jansel Sq. HP21: Ayle 1C **66**
Japonica La. MK15: W Par 7J **17**
Jardines Ten Pin Bowling Club *6J* ***61***
(off Silver St.)
Jarman Cl. MK18: Buck 4K **37**
Jarry Ct. SL7: Marl 6K **105**
Jarvis Cl. HP21: Ayle 1B **66**
Jasmine Cl. HP21: Ayle 3B **66**
Jasmine Cres. HP27: Prin R 5G **71**
Jasmine Wlk. HP5: Ches 4J **77**
Jasons Hill HP5: O L'gh 4F **79**
Jeeves Cl. MK6: P Bri 7J **23**
Jefferies Rd. HP17: Sto 2A **64**
Jefferson Cl. SL3: Lang 2A **130**
Jeffrey Wlk. HP19: Ayle 7F **61**
Jeffries Ct. SL8: Bou E 7G **107**
Jellicoe Cl. SL1: Slou 7K **123**
Jenkins Cl. MK5: S Chur 2K **27**
Jenkins Ct. HP22: W'rave 6D **48**
Jenna Way MK16: New P 2C **18**
Jenner Rd. HP21: Ayle 2K **65**
Jennery La. SL1: Burn 1E **122**
Jennings MK14: Stan 6C **16**
Jennings Fld. HP10: F Hea 2J **107**
Jerome Cl. SL7: Marl 5K **105**
Jersey Rd. MK12: Wolv 6G **15**
Jesse's La. HP18: Long C 6D **56**
JOCKEY END 2D **135**
John Hall Way HP12: H Wyc 5G **97**
John Hampden Way HP16: Pres 6B **74**
John Horncapps La. MK17: G Bri 6E **34**
John Mills Ct. *UB9: Den* *4F* ***113***
(off Stewarts Ct.)
John Milton's Cottage 1F **103**
Johnson Rd. HP14: L End 3K **73**
Johnsons Fld. MK46: Oln 3G **7**
Johnson's Yd. UB8: Uxb 5J **121**
Johnston Pl. MK6: Old 6E **22**

John Taylor Ct. SL1: Slou 6A 124
Joiners Cl. HP5: L Hil 4F 79
Joiners Cl. SL9: C Pet 5K 103
Joiner's La. SL9: C Pet 6J 103
Joiners Way MK46: Lave 2C 6
SL9: C Pet 5J 103
Jonathans MK6: Coff 7G 23
Jonathans Ct. MK6: Coff 1G 29
Jones Way SL2: Hedg 7B 110
Joplin Ct. MK8: C'ill 7K 21
JORDANS 4C 102 (1C 137)
Jordans La. HP9: Jord 6C 102
Jordans Way HP9: Jord 4D 102
Joules Ct. MK5: S Lod 2C 28
Journeys End SL2: S Pog 3C 124
Jubilee Homes *HP8: D Gil* 7F 95 (off School La.)
Jubilee Rd. HP11: H Wyc 1J 97
HP13: Down 5H 89
HP14: Stoke 7D 72
Jubilee Ter. MK11: S Strat 1C 20
Juniper Cl. HP15: Haz 4H 91
Juniper Ct. HP10: F Hea 2K 107
SL1: Slou 7E 124
Juniper Dr. HP12: H Wyc 3G 97
Juniper Gdns. MK7: Waln 7D 24
Juniper La. HP10: F Hea, Woob G 2J 107
Juniper Rd. SL7: Marl 4H 105
Juson's Glebe HP22: Wend 3J 69
Jutland Ho. SL4: Wind 7H 129

K

Kalman Gdns. MK7: Old P 2F 31
Kanton Ct. HP19: Ayle 4H 61
Kaplan Cl. MK5: S Lod 2B 28
Kates Cl. HP16: Pres 7C 74
Katherine Cl. HP10: T Grn 7J 91
MK7: Walt P 3C 30
Katrine Pl. MK2: Blet 3K 33
Kaybridge Cl. HP13: H Wyc 3F 99
Kaywood Cl. SL3: Lang 7H 125
Keach Cl. MK18: Wins 5J 39
Keasden Ct. MK4: E Val 5B 28
Keaton Cl. MK8: C'ill 7H 21
Keats Cl. HP11: H Wyc 2K 97
HP21: Ayle 1A 66
MK16: New P 1G 17
Keats Way MK3: Blet 1F 33
Keble Cl. HP19: Ayle 6G 61
Keel Dr. SL1: Slou 7K 123
Keeler Cl. SL4: Wind 7G 129
KEELEY GREEN 2D 133
Keen Cl. HP19: Ayle 6F 61
Keensacre SL0: I Hea 7D 120
Keen's Cl. HP13: H Wyc 6E 90
Keepers Cl. LU7: Ched 2C 50
Keepers Farm Cl. SL4: Wind 7G 129 (not continuous)
Keepers La. HP6: H Hea 4E 84
HP7: L Miss 4E 84
Keep Hill Dr. HP11: H Wyc 4D 98
Keep Hill Rd. HP11: H Wyc 3D 98
Keinches La. HP22: W'urch 2G 45
Kellan Dr. MK6: Fish 5G 23
Keller Cl. MK11: Kiln 4F 21
Kelmarsh Ct. MK8: G Hol 5K 21
Kelpatrick Rd. SL1: Slou 4F 123
Kelsey Cl. MK4: Tatt 7K 27
Kelso Cl. MK3: Blet 2D 32
Kelvin Cl. HP13: Down 7K 89
Kelvin Dr. MK5: Know 1C 28
Kemble Ct. MK15: D Park 7H 17
Kempe Cl. SL3: Lang 2C 130
Kempson Cl. HP19: Ayle 5G 61
Kemps Piece HP17: Hadd 6C 58
KEMPSTON 2D 133
KEMPSTON HARDWICK 2D 133
Kempton Gdns. MK3: Blet 2D 32
Kemsley Chase
SL2: Farn R 6A 118
Kenchester MK13: Ban 1K 21
Kendal Cl. HP21: Ayle 1C 66
SL2: Slou 5E 124
Kendal Dr. SL2: Slou 5E 124
Kendall Pl. MK5: Medb 2J 27
Kendalls Cl. HP13: H Wyc 2F 99
Kenilworth Cl. SL1: Slou 7D 124
Kenilworth Dr. HP19: Ayle 4J 61
MK3: Blet 1E 32
Kenneally SL4: Wind 7E 128
Kenneally Cl. SL4: Wind 7E 128
Kenneally Pl. SL4: Wind 7E 128
Kenneally Row *SL4: Wind* 7E 128 (off Liddell Sq.)
Kenneally Wlk. *SL4: Wind* 7E 128 (off Guards Rd.)
Kennedy Av. HP11: H Wyc 4B 98
Kennedy Cl. SL2: Farn C 4A 118
SL7: Marl 6J 105
Kennedy Ho. *SL1: Slou* 6F 123 (off Harrison Way)
Kennet Cl. HP13: H Wyc 5D 90
HP21: Ayle 3H 65
Kennet Dr. MK3: Blet 7E 28
Kennet Pl. MK3: Blet 7E 28
Kennett Rd. SL3: Lang 1B 130
SL8: Bou E 5H 107
Kennington Cl. MK16: New P 2H 17
Kennish Cl. *MK18: Wins* 7H 39 (off Walk, The)
Kensal Grn. MK10: Monk P 5A 24
Kensington Dr. MK8: G Hol 5K 21
Kensington Path *HP19: Ayle* 5E 60 (off Arncott Way)
Kensington Pl. MK46: Oln 2H 7
KENSWORTH 2D 135
KENSWORTH COMMON 2D 135
Kent Av. SL1: Slou 3A 124
Kent Cl. UB8: Uxb 4J 121
Kent Ho. SL9: C Pet 3J 103
Kentmere Rd. HP21: Ayle 7C 62
Kenton Cl. SL7: Marl 7J 105
Kentons La. SL4: Wind 7G 129
KENTS HILL 6D 24
KENTS HILL 6B 24
KENTS HILL PARK 6C 24
Kents Rd. MK14: Stan 5D 16
Kenway Dr. HP7: L Chal 6F 87
Kenwell Ct. MK15: Wool 3J 23
Kenwood Ga. MK6: Sprin 3H 23
Keppel Av. MK19: H'ham 3H 15
Kepwick MK8: T Ash 5J 21
Kercroft MK8: T Ash 4J 21
Kernow Cres. MK6: Fish 5G 23
Kerria Pl. MK3: Blet 4G 29
Kerry Cl. HP19: Ayle 3F 61
Kersey MK14: Stan 5C 16
Kerslake Ho. SL9: C Pet 3J 103
Kesters Rd. HP5: Ches 6B 78
Kestral Lodge HP9: Bea 6D 100
Kestrel Cl. HP13: Down 6G 89
Kestrel Dr. HP15: Haz 2H 91
Kestrel Ho. MK7: K Par 6C 24
Kestrel Path SL2: Slou 2G 123
Kestrel Way HP19: Ayle 1K 61
MK18: Buck 5J 37
Keswick Ct. SL2: Slou 5D 124
Keswick Rd. MK19: H'ope 2E 8
Ketchmere Cl. HP18: Long C 6C 56
Ketelbey Nook MK7: Old P 2F 31
Ketton Cl. MK15: Will 6K 17
Kew Ct. MK8: G Hol 5K 21
Kew Gro. HP11: H Wyc 4B 98
Keyes Way MK18: Buck 2J 37
Keynes Cl. MK16: New P 1A 18
Khasiaberry MK7: Waln 2D 30
Kidd Cl. MK8: C'ill 1J 27
Kidderminster Rd. SL2: Slou 1J 123
Kidderminster Wlk. MK10: Bro 4D 24
KIDMORE END 3A 136
Kildonan Pl. MK12: H Lea 2H 21
Kilkenny Ho. MK4: West 5J 27
Killerton Cl. MK4: West 5K 27
Kiln Av. HP6: L Chal 5G 87
Kiln Cl. HP16: Pres 6C 74
KILN COMMON 6C 74
Kiln Ct. HP9: Bea 1C 108
Kiln Cft. Cl. SL7: Marl 6A 106
Kilner Rd. HP21: Ayle 2K 65
KILN FARM 4G 21
KILN FARM 3E 20
Kiln Farm Ind. Est. MK11: Kiln 3G 21
Kiln Flds. HP10: Woob G 7A 108
SL6: Tapl 2A 116
SL8: Bou E 2A 116
KILN GREEN 3B 136
Kiln La. HP5: L Hil 5F 79
HP10: Woob G 6K 107
HP27: L Grn 1C 80
SL2: Hedg 6A 110
SL8: Bou E 6J 107
Kilnpond La. HP13: Down 4H 89
Kiln Rd. HP16: Pres 6B 74
Kilnwood HP14: Walt A 5F 81
Kilpin Grn. MK16: N Craw 6K 13
Kilwinning Dr. MK10: Monk 5B 24
Kimbells Cl. HP18: Shab 6H 55
Kimberley Cl. SL3: Lang 2A 130
Kimbers Dr. SL1: Burn 1F 123
KIMBLE WICK 3C 135
Kimbolton Ct. MK14: G Par 5G 17
Kincardine Dr. MK3: Blet 4F 29
Kindermann Ct. MK5: S Lod 2B 28
Kindleton MK14: G Lin 5F 17
King Charles Cl. MK18: Buck 2J 37
Kingdom Way UB8: Cowl 3K 127
King Edward Av. HP21: Ayle 7B 62
King Edward St. MK13: New B 6K 15
SL1: Slou 7B 124
Kingfisher HP19: Ayle 2K 61
Kingfisher Cl. HP16: Pres 1C 82
Kingfisher Ct. HP11: H Wyc 2A 98
SL2: Slou 2K 123
Kingfisher Ho. MK7: K Par 6C 24
Kingfisher Rd. MK18: Buck 5J 37
King George V Rd. HP6: Amer 5B 86
King George Cres. MK11: S Strat 7C 14
KINGSASH 3C 135
Kingsash Rd. HP19: Ayle 6E 60
Kingsbridge MK4: Fur 5D 28
Kingsbury Sq. HP20: Ayle 6J 61
Kings Cl. HP8: D Gil 7H 95
Kings Cl. HP9: Bea 1C 108
HP18: Worm 3B 54
KINGSEY 3B 134
Kingsfield SL4: Wind 6F 129
Kingsfold MK13: B'lle 6B 16
Kingsgate Way HP19: Ayle 6F 61
King's Head Inn 6J 61 (off King's Head Yd.)
King's Head Pas. *HP20: Ayle* 6J 61 (off Market St.)
Kingshill Rd. HP13: H Wyc 5D 90
HP15: H Wyc 3D 90
Kingsland Rd. HP21: Ayle 3B 66
Kings La. HP16: L Ham 2C 74
HP16: S Hea 5K 75
HP16: T Lee 1G 75
KINGS LANGLEY 1D 137
Kingsley Cl. MK16: New P 1F 17
Kingsley Cres. HP11: H Wyc 2K 97
Kingsley Dr. SL7: Marl 3G 105
Kingsley Path SL2: Slou 2F 123
Kings Lodge *HP6: Amer* 5B 86 (off King George V Rd.)
KINGSMEAD 7K 27
Kings Mead LU6: Edle 3J 49
Kingsmead HP27: Mon R 2G 71
Kingsmead Bus. Cen. HP11: W Mar 5H 99
Kingsmead Ho. SL1: Slou 6A 124
Kings Mdw. HP22: Bier 2D 62
Kingsmead Rd. HP11: W Mar 4E 98
Kings Oak Cl. HP27: Mon R 2H 71
Kingsoe Leys MK10: Midd 4C 24
Kings Ride HP10: T Grn 6H 91
Kings Rd. HP8: D Gil 7G 95
HP11: W Mar 4F 99
HP21: Ayle 6A 62
SL1: Slou 7C 124
UB8: Uxb 7K 121
Kings Sq. HP11: W Mar 4F 99
Kings St. LU7: Stew 5C 46
Kings Ter. SL3: Lang 4B 130
KINGSTHORPE 1B 132
KINGSTON 4E 24
KINGSTON 6F 25
Kingston Av. MK11: S Strat 1C 20
KINGSTON BLOUNT 1A 136
Kingston Gymnastics Cen. 5E 24
Kingston Ind. Est. MK10: K'ton 5E 24
Kingston Rd. HP13: H Wyc 7D 90
KINGSTON STERT 3B 134
King St. HP5: Ches 6K 77
HP14: Pidd 7A 88
MK11: S Strat 7C 14
Kingstreet La. HP15: H Grn 6K 83
HP16: L Kin 6K 83
Kingsville Ct. UB7: Yiew 5K 127
Kingsway HP9: Bea 4F 101
SL0: Ive 4E 126
SL2: Farn C 4K 117
SL9: C Pet 1J 111
KINGSWOOD 2A 134
Kings Wood SL7: Medm 3B 114
Kingswood Av. HP10: T Grn 7H 91
Kingswood Ho. SL2: Slou 3A 124
Kingswood Pde. SL7: Marl 4H 105
Kingswood Pl. HP13: H Wyc 6E 90
Kingswood Rd. HP10: T Grn 6G 91
Kinloch Pl. MK2: Blet 3K 33
Kinnaird Cl. SL1: Tapl 4E 122
Kinnear Cl. MK8: C'ill 7H 21
Kinross Dr. MK3: Blet 5E 28
Kinson Grn. HP20: Ayle 3K 61
Kipling Ct. SL4: Wind 7K 129
Kipling Dr. MK16: New P 1F 17
Kipling Rd. MK3: Blet 1G 33
Kippell Hill MK46: Oln 2H 7
Kirby Est. UB7: Yiew 5K 127
Kirkeby Cl. MK14: Stan 7D 16
Kirke Cl. MK5: S Chur 2A 28
Kirkham Ct. MK5: Lough 6C 22
Kirkstall Pl. MK6: Old 6D 22
Kirkwall Spur SL1: Slou 3C 124
Kirkwood Gro. MK5: Medb 2H 27
Kirtle Rd. HP5: Ches 5A 78
Kirtlington MK15: D Park 1H 23
KISLINGBURY 1A 132
Kitchener Cl. MK46: Oln 4J 7
Kitchener Ho. SL9: C Pet 2J 103
Kitchener Rd. HP11: H Wyc 1J 97
Kite Hill MK6: Eagl 6H 23
Kitelee Cl. MK19: H'ope 1E 8
Kite Wood Rd. HP10: T Grn 6H 91
Kittiwake HP19: Ayle 2K 61
Klee Cl. HP22: Q'ton 5H 43
Klondyke SL7: Marl 7H 105
Klub Kart Racing 6A 62
Knapp Ga. MK5: S Chur 7K 21
Knaresborough Ct. MK3: Blet 1D 32
Knaves Beech HP10: Loud 7K 99
Knaves Beech Est. HP10: Loud 7J 99
Knaves Beech Way HP10: Loud 7J 99
Knaves Hollow HP10: Woob G 7K 99
KNEBWORTH 4G 17
Knebworth Ga. MK14: G Par 4G 17
Knighton Way La. UB9: Den 4H 121
Knightsbridge Ct. *SL3: Lang* 2A 130 (off High St.)
Knights Cl. LU6: E Bra 1J 49
MK17: G Bri 7F 35
SL4: Wind 6F 129
Knights Ct. LU6: E Bra 1J 49
Knights Hill HP12: H Wyc 2J 97
Knights Templar Way HP11: H Wyc 4B 98
KNOLHILL 1C 28
Knoll, The MK16: Sher 3B 12
MK17: A H'th 5J 31
Knoll Cl. MK16: Sher 2B 12
Knolls Cl. HP22: W'rave 6C 48
Knolton Way SL2: Slou 4F 125
KNOTTING 1D 133
KNOTTING GREEN 1D 133
Knottocks Cl. HP9: Bea 3F 101
Knottocks Dr. HP9: Bea 3E 100
Knottocks End HP9: Bea 3F 101
KNOTTY GREEN 3F 101 (1C 137)
Knowles Grn. MK2: Blet 1J 33
Knowl Ga. MK5: Lough 7C 22
KNOWL HILL 3B 136
KNOWLHILL 1C 28
Knox Bri. MK7: K Hil 6D 24
Kola Ct. SL2: Slou 4F 125
Kop Hill HP27: Prin R 5J 71
Kramer Ct. MK8: G Far 1H 27
Krohn Cl. MK18: Buck 4K 37
Krypton Cl. MK5: S Lod 2C 28
Kynaston Av. HP21: Ayle 4K 65

L

Laburnum Cl. SL7: Marl 5J 105
Laburnum Gro. MK2: Blet 1A 34
SL3: Lang 4B 130
Laburnum Rd. HP12: H Wyc 3G 97
Lacemaker Ct. *HP7: Amer* 7A 86 (off Piggotts Orchard)
Lacemakers HP18: Long C 6C 56
Lace M. MK46: Oln 3H 7
Lacey Dr. HP14: Nap 1H 89
LACEY GREEN 1C 80 (3C 135)
Laceys Dr. HP15: Haz 1H 91
Lacey's Yd. *HP5: Ches* 5K 77 (off High St.)
Lacy Dr. MK15: Bolb 6G 17 (not continuous)
Ladbroke Cl. HP20: Ayle 4K 61
Ladbroke Gro. MK10: Monk P 6B 24
Ladbrooke Rd. SL1: Slou 7A 124
Lady Astor Ct. SL1: Slou 7C 124
Ladyday Pl. SL1: Slou 6A 124
Ladymead Cl. MK17: Whad 7F 27
Ladymeadow Ct. MK10: Midd 3A 24
Ladysmith Rd. LU7: I'hoe 4G 51
Lady Verney Cl. HP13: H Wyc 7B 90
Lady Yorke Pk. SL0: I Hea 4D 120
Laggan Ct. MK2: Blet 4K 33
Lagger, The HP8: D Gil 1F 103
Lagger Cl. HP8: D Gil 1F 103
Lagonda Cl. MK16: New P 1A 18
Laidon Cl. MK2: Blet 4K 33
Lake Av. SL1: Slou 5B 124
Lake Cl. MK18: Wins 4K 39
LAKE END 7D 122
Lake End Ct. SL6: Tapl 4C 122
Lake End Rd. SL4: Dorn 5D 122
SL6: Dorn R, Tapl 5D 122
Lakeman Ho. SL9: C Pet 3K 103
Laker Ct. MK6: Old 7E 22
LAKESIDE 2J 23
Lakeside HP19: Ayle 2K 61
Lakeside Dr. SL2: S Pog 6C 118
Lakeside Ind. Est. SL3: Coln 4F 131
Lakeside Rd. SL0: R Pk 5F 131
SL3: Coln, R Pk 5F 131
Lakes La. HP9: Bea 7H 101
MK16: New P 6F 11
LALEHAM 3D 137
Lamb Cl. MK16: New P 1G 17
Lamberhurst Gro. MK7: K Hil 6C 24
Lambe Rd. HP22: Halt 2K 69
Lambert Av. SL3: Lang 7J 125
Lamberts Cft. MK12: Gree 1G 21
Lamb La. MK7: W Gat 7E 24
Lambourn Ct. MK4: E Val 5D 28
Lambourne Av. HP21: Ayle 4J 65
Lambourne Ct. UB8: Uxb 6H 121
Lambscroft Way SL9: C Pet 7J 103
Lambton Ho. SL4: Wind 7J 129
Lambtons Way MK18: Wins 5K 39
Lammas MK6: Bean 2G 29 (not continuous)
Lammas La. HP18: Che 2H 57
Lammas Path HP18: Che 2H 57
Lammas Rd. LU7: Ched 2C 50
SL1: Slou 3F 123
Lammas Way HP10: Loud 7J 99
HP14: L End 4J 73
Lampitts Cross MK6: E Wes 1H 29
Lamport Ct. MK8: G Hol 6A 22
Lamva Ct. MK11: S Strat 1D 20
Lancaster Av. SL2: Slou 2A 124
Lancaster Ct. HP12: H Wyc 4H 97
Lancaster Dr. HP3: Bov 1K 79
Lancaster Ga. MK3: Blet 1E 32

Lancaster Ride HP10: T Grn 7H 91
Lancaster Rd. HP12: H Wyc 3J 97
HP21: Ayle 1C 66
UB8: Uxb 4K 121
Lancelot Cl. SL1: Slou 7J 123
Lance Way HP13: H Wyc 3G 99
Lancresse Cl. UB8: Uxb 4K 121
Lander Rd. HP19: Ayle 3E 60
Landrace Ct. MK5: S Broo 4K 27
Lands, The LU7: Wing 2D 48
Landsborough Ga. MK15: Will 6J 17
Lands End Gro. MK4: Tatt 7K 27
Lane, The MK17: Mur 2C 40
LANE END 4K 73 (1B 136)
Lane End Rd. HP12: H Wyc, Book 3F 97
HP14: L End 3D 96
Lanercost Cres. MK10: Monk 5D 24
Lane Wood Cl. HP7: Amer 6D 86
Lanfranc Gdns. MK15: Bolb 6H 17
Langcliffe Dr. MK13: Hee 2B 22
Langdale Cl. MK2: Blet 4K 33
Langdale Ho. HP11: W Mar 4G 99
Langdon Av. HP21: Ayle 2C 66
Langerstone La. MK4: Tatt 6B 28
Langford Pl. MK7: Cald 4C 30
Langland Ho. MK6: Neth 1J 29
Langland Rd. MK6: Neth 1J 29
Langlands MK46: Lave 3B 6
LANGLEY 1A 130 (3D 137)
LANGLEYBURY 1D 137
Langley Bus. Cen. SL3: Lang 7A 126
Langley Bus. Pk. SL3: Lang 7A 126
Langley Cl. MK18: Wins 6G 39
Langley Hall *1A 130*
(off Langley Rd.)
Langley Leisure Cen. 2B 130
Langley Pk. Country Pk. 2K 125
Langley Pk. La. SL0: Ive 5B 126
Langley Pk. Rd. SL0: Ive 7A 126
SL3: Lang 7A 126
Langley Quay SL3: Lang 7A 126
Langley Rd. SL3: Lang 7G 125
LANGLEY RDBT. 4A 130
Langley Station (Rail) 7A 126
Langley Way SL7: Marl 7G 105
Langleywood Sports & Playcentre 7J 125
Langmuir Ct. MK5: S Lod 3C 28
Langport Cres. MK5: O'ill 2H 27
Langstone Cl. HP20: Ayle 3A 62
Langstone Ct. HP20: Ayle 3A 62
Langton Cl. SL1: Slou 6F 123
Langton Dr. MK8: T Ash 3J 21
Langton's Mdw. SL2: Farn C 4A 118
Lanner Wlk. *MK6: Eagl 6H 23*
(off Montagu Dri.)
Lansdales Rd. HP11: H Wyc 1K 97
Lansdell Av. HP12: Book 4F 97
Lansdowne Av. SL1: Slou 6C 124
Lansdowne Ct. SL1: Slou 6C 124
Lansdowne Rd. HP5: Ches 3A 78
HP20: Ayle 4J 61
Lansdowne Way HP11: H Wyc 5H 97
Lansdown Rd. SL9: C Pet 6H 103
Lanthorn Cl. MK14: N Hill 7E 16
Lappetts La. HP16: S Hea 5K 75
Lapwing Ho. MK7: K Par 6C 24
Larch Cl. HP10: T Grn 5J 91
HP20: Ayle 4B 62
SL2: Slou .3K 123
Larches, The HP6: L Chal 5F 87
HP15: H Grn 7K 83
Larch Gro. MK2: Blet 1K 33
Larchlands, The HP10: T Grn 6K 91
Larchmoor Pk. SL2: S Pog 3E 118
Larchwood HP16: L Kin 2H 83
Lark Cl. MK18: Buck 5J 37
Larkfield Cl. HP13: H Wyc 6F 91
Larkin Cl. MK16: New P 7G 11
Larkings La. SL2: S Pog 6F 119
Lark Ri. HP15: Haz 2H 91
Larkspur Av. MK14: Conn 1E 22
Larkspur Way HP15: W End 1F 91
Larks Ri. HP5: Ches 7B 78
Lark Va. HP19: Ayle 3K 61
La Roche Cl. SL3: Lang 7G 125
Larwood Pl. MK6: Old 5F 23
Lasborough Rd. MK10: K'ton 5E 24
Lascelles Cl. MK15: Bolb 6H 17
Lascelles Rd. SL3: Slou 7F 125
Laser Cl. MK5: S Lod 1C 28
Lastingham Gro. MK4: E Val 5B 28
LATCHFORD 3A 134
Latchmoor Av. SL9: C Pet 2H 111
Latchmoor Gro. SL9: C Pet 2H 111
Latchmoor Way SL9: C Pet 2H 111
LATHBURY 5K 11 (2C 133)
LATIMER 4J 87 (1D 137)
Latimer MK11: S Strat 2C 20
Latimer Cl. HP6: L Chal 6G 87
Latimer Rd. HP5: Ches, Lati 1C 86
Latimer Way HP9: Bea 2E 100
Launceston Ct. MK5: S Chur 1B 28
Launde MK10: Monk 5D 24
LAUNTON 1A 134
Laurance Ct. SL7: Marl 7H 105
Laurel Av. SL3: Lang 7J 125
Laurel Cl. HP16: Pres 6B 74
Laurel Cl. HP27: Spee 2G 81
MK8: C'ill 7H 21
SL0: I Hea 5D 120
SL3: Poy .5E 130
Laurel Ct. HP6: Amer 3A 86
Laurel Dr. HP13: H Wyc 5H 99
HP14: Nap 7H 81
Laurel La. UB7: W Dra 2K 131
Laurel Rd. SL9: C Pet 6H 103
Laurels, The HP12: Book 4G 97
MK1: F Str 6K 29
Laurels Rd. SL0: I Hea 7D 120
Laurel Way HP21: Ayle 7K 61
Lautrec Way HP19: Ayle 4E 60
Lavender Ct. HP21: Ayle 2G 65
Lavender Gro. MK7: Waln 2C 30
Lavender Wlk. *HP21: Ayle 1G 65*
(off Lavender Ct.)
Lavender Way HP15: W End 7F 83
LAVENDON 2C 6 (1D 133)
Lavendon Rd. MK46: Oln 2J 7
Lavric Rd. HP21: Ayle 1H 65
Lawkland SL2: Farn R 1A 124
Lawn Av. UB7: W Dra 7J 127
Lawn Farm Bus. Cen.
HP18: G Und 4K 43
Lawn Rd. UB8: Uxb 5J 121
Lawns, The HP10: T Grn 5H 91
HP18: Bril 2J 53
SL3: Poy .6E 130
Lawnsmead Gdns. MK16: New P 7K 11
Lawrence Cl. HP20: Ayle 4A 62
Lawrence Ct. SL4: Wind 7K 129
Lawrence Gro. HP16: Pres 1D 82
Lawrence Wlk. MK16: New P 7F 11
Lawrence Way SL1: Slou 3E 122
Lawsone Ri. HP13: H Wyc 6B 90
Lawson Pl. MK5: S Lod 2B 28
Layburn Cres. SL3: Lang 4B 130
Lay Rd. HP19: Ayle 4G 61
Layter's Av. SL9: C Pet 7G 103
Layter's Av. Sth. SL9: C Pet 7G 103
Layter's Cl. SL9: C Pet 7G 103
Layter's End SL9: C Pet 7G 103
LAYTER'S GREEN 6G 103 (1C 137)
Layter's Grn. La. SL9: C Pet 1E 110
Layter's Grn. Mobile Home Pk.
SL9: C Pet 7F 103
Layters Way SL9: G Cro 3H 111
Leaberry MK13: New B 5A 16
Leachcroft SL9: C Pet 6F 103
Leach Rd. HP21: Ayle 7H 61
Lea Cl. SL7: Marl 3H 105
Lea Ct. *HP7: Amer 6D 86*
(off Orchard End Av.)
Leacroft Cl. UB7: Yiew 4K 127
Leacroft Rd. SL0: Ive 4E 126
LEADENHALL 7G 23
LEADENHALL 7E 22
Leaders Cl. HP22: W'rave 6C 48
Leafield Ri. MK8: T Ash 4H 21
LEAGRAVE .1D 135
Leaholme Gdns. SL1: Slou 3E 122
Lea La. HP18: Long C 7E 56
Leapingwell La. MK18: Wins 4K 39
Leary Cres. MK16: New P 1A 18
Leas Cl. HP13: H Wyc 7F 91
Leas Dr. SL0: Ive 4E 126
Leaside MK16: S Gold 6C 6
Leasowe Pl. MK13: B Com 3C 22
Leather La. HP16: G Mis 3F 75
LECKHAMPSTEAD 3B 132
Ledborough Ct. HP9: Bea 4G 101
Ledborough Ga. HP9: Bea 4H 101
Led Borough La. HP9: Bea 5F 101
Ledborough Wood HP9: Bea 4G 101
LEDBURN 1D 135
Ledbury MK14: G Lin 4D 16
Ledger La. SL6: Fifi 7A 128
Ledgers Rd. SL1: Slou 7B 124
LEE, THE 1H 75 (3D 135)
Lee Bottom HP16: L Com 1K 75
Leeches Way LU7: Ched 2C 50
LEE CLUMP 1A 76 (3D 135)
LEE COMMON 1K 75
Lee Cres. HP17: Sto 2C 64
Leeds Rd. SL1: Slou 5C 124
Lee Farm Cl. HP5: Ches 4E 78
Lee Ho. MK2: Blet 7J 29
Lee La. SL6: Maid 7J 115
Lee Rd. HP21: Ayle 1J 65
HP22: Q'ton 4G 43
Leeson Gdns. SL4: E Wick 2G 129
Lees Wlk. SL7: Marl 7G 105
Leigh Hill MK4: E Val 5D 28
Leigh Rd. SL1: Slou 5K 123
Leigh Sq. SL4: Wind 7F 129
Leigh St. HP11: H Wyc 1K 97
LEIGHTON BUZZARD 1D 135
Leighton Rd. HP22: W'rave 6C 48
LU6: Edle, N'all 1F 49
LU7: Soul .7K 41
LU7: Wing 3C 48
MK17: S Ham 2H 41
Leiston Spur SL1: Slou 4C 124
Leisure Plaza 6C 22
Leith Cl. SL1: Slou 6E 124
Leith Rd. HP19: Ayle 6F 61
Lembrook Wlk. HP21: Ayle 1H 65
LENBOROUGH 7H 37
Lenborough Cl. MK18: Buck 5G 37
Lenborough Ct. MK15: Wool 4J 23
Lenborough Rd. MK18: Buck 5G 37
(not continuous)
Lennon Dr. MK8: C'ill 7J 21
Lennox Rd. MK2: Blet 7J 29
LENT 2D 122
Lent Grn. SL1: Burn 2D 122
(not continuous)
Lent Grn. La. SL1: Burn 2D 122
Lenthall Cl. MK13: B'ell 2A 22
LENT RISE .3D 122
Lent Ri. Rd. SL1: Burn 4D 122
SL6: Tapl .4D 122
Leominster Ga. MK10: Monk 5C 24
Leonard Pulham Ho. HP22: Halt 1K 69
Leonardslee MK4: West 5K 27
Leon Av. MK2: Blet 7K 29
Leopard Dr. MK15: Penny 6G 17
Lerwick Dr. SL1: Slou 3C 124
Leslie Dunne Ho. SL4: Wind 7G 129
Lester Ct. MK7: W Gat 7E 24
Lester Gro. HP15: Haz 3G 91
Letchfield HP5: L Hil 5F 79
Letter Box La. HP27: Ask 1J 71
Leven Cl. MK2: Blet 3K 33
Levens Hall Dr. MK4: West 6K 27
Levings Cl. HP19: Ayle 3F 61
Lewes Ct. SL1: Slou 7A 124
Lewes Ho. *MK3: Blet 1D 32*
(off Chester Clo.)
Lewins Farm Ct. SL1: Slou 5H 123
Lewins Rd. SL9: C Pet 1H 111
Lewins Way SL1: Slou 5H 123
Lewins Yd. *HP5: Ches 6K 77*
(off High St.)
Lewis Cl. MK16: New P 7F 11
Lewis La. SL9: C Pet 6J 103
LEWKNOR 1A 136
Lexham Ct. *HP6: Amer 4A 86*
(off Rickmansworth Rd.)
Lexham Gdns. HP6: Amer 4A 86
Leyfield Rd. HP21: Ayle 1K 65
LEY HILL 4F 79 (3D 135)
Ley Hill Rd. HP3: Bov 3J 79
Leyland Pl. MK6: Old 6E 22
Leys, The HP6: Amer 2K 85
HP22: Halt 6K 67
MK17: W San 3K 31
Leys Rd. MK5: Lough 6B 22
Leys Vw. MK16: Sher 3B 12
Leywood Cl. HP7: Amer 7C 86
Lichfield Down MK7: Waln 1D 30
Liddell SL4: Wind 7E 128
Liddell Pl. SL4: Wind 7E 128
Liddell Sq. SL4: Wind 7E 128
Liddell Way SL4: Wind 7E 128
LIDLINGTON 3D 133
Lidstone Ct. SL3: G Grn 4H 125
Liffre Dr. HP22: Wend 2H 69
Lightfoot Ct. MK7: Walt P 2B 30
Ligo Av. HP22: Sto M 5D 66
Lilac Cl. MK17: New L 5C 32
Lilac Ct. SL2: Slou 1H 123
Lilies, The HP22: W'don 7J 45
Lilleshall Av. MK10: Monk 5B 24
Lilley Way SL1: Slou 6G 123
LILLINGSTONE DAYRELL 3B 132
LILLINGSTONE LOVELL 2B 132
Lillyfee Farm La. HP10: Woob G 3C 108
Lilly Hill MK46: Oln 2H 7
Lily Dr. UB7: W Dra 2K 131
Lily's Wlk. HP11: H Wyc 2A 98
Limbaud Cl. MK7: Walt P 2C 30
Lime Av. HP11: H Wyc 3D 98
MK18: Buck 5K 37
Lime Cl. HP15: Haz 4G 91
MK16: New P 1H 17
Lime Gro. MK17: W San 3K 31
Limelight Theatre *6A 62*
(in Queens Pk. Arts Cen.)
Limerick La. MK9: Camp 3H 23
Lime Rd. HP27: Prin R 5G 71
Limes, The HP6: Amer 2K 85
HP22: Sto M 5C 66
MK2: Blet .7A 30
MK11: S Strat 1C 20
SL4: Wind 7E 128
Limes Av. HP21: Ayle 7C 62
Lime St. MK46: Oln 4H 7
Limes Way HP18: Shab 5H 55
Lime Tree Cl. HP15: G Kin 6D 82
Lime Tree Wlk. HP7: Amer 6D 86
Lime Wlk. UB9: Den 3J 121
Limmer La. HP12: Book 5F 97
Limmers Mead HP15: G Kin 6C 82
Linceslade Gro. MK5: Lough 6A 22
Linchfield HP13: H Wyc 2D 98
Lincoln MK14: Stan 5C 16
Lincoln Cl. HP22: Sto M 5C 66
Lincoln Ct. MK19: H'ope 2E 8
SL1: Slou .7C 124
UB9: Den .4F 113
Lincoln Hatch La. SL1: Burn 2E 122
Lincoln Pk. HP7: Amer 6C 86
Lincoln Pk. Bus. Cen. HP12: H Wyc . . .2H 97
Lincoln Rd. HP12: H Wyc 3J 97
SL9: C Pet 6J 103
Lincolns, The HP16: L Kin 3G 83
Lincolns Hill HP12: H Wyc 3J 97
Lincolnshire Cl. MK3: Blet 6E 28
Lincoln Way SL1: Slou 5F 123
Linden SL3: Lang 3B 130
Linden Dr. SL2: Farn R 6A 118
SL9: C Pet 6J 103
Linden End HP21: Ayle 1A 66
Linden Gro. MK14: G Lin 5E 16
Linden Lea HP22: Wend 2H 69
LINDEN VILLAGE 4J 37
Linden Wlk. HP15: Haz 4H 91
Linden Way HP17: Ford 5K 59
Lindisfarne Dr. MK10: Monk 5C 24
Lindo Cl. HP5: Ches 4K 77
Lindores Cft. MK10: Monk 5D 24
Lindsay Av. HP12: H Wyc 1J 97
Lindsey Rd. UB9: Den 1G 121
Lines, The HP22: A Abb 7H 47
Lines Rd. HP14: L End 3K 73
Linfields HP7: L Chal 7G 87
Linford Av. MK16: New P 1G 17
Linford La. MK15: Will 6K 17
MK15: Wool 3J 23
LINFORD WOOD 7E 16
Linford Wood Bus. Cen.
MK14: L Woo 7E 16
Lingfield MK12: S Bus 2J 21
Lingfield Cvn. Pk. SL6: Bra 4A 128
Lingfield Cl. HP13: H Wyc 3G 99
Linington HP5: Ches 4E 78
Link, The HP15: Haz 2G 91
SL2: Slou .4F 125
Link Cl. HP12: H Wyc 2H 97
Link Rd. HP12: H Wyc 2H 97
HP16: G Mis 6G 75
Links App. HP10: F Hea 1H 107
Links Rd. HP10: F Hea 1H 107
Links Way HP10: F Hea 1H 107
Linkswood Rd. SL1: Burn 7E 116
Link Way UB9: Den 4G 113
Linnet Cl. HP12: Book 5E 96
Linney Ct. MK4: Tatt 6A 28
LINSLADE 1D 135
Lintlaw Pl. MK3: Blet 4G 29
Linton Cl. MK13: Hee 2C 22
Linx, The MK3: Blet 5G 29
Lionel Av. HP22: Wend 3G 69
Lionel Cl. HP22: Wend 3G 69
Lipscombe Dr. MK18: Buck 3J 37
Lipscomb La. MK5: S Chur 7A 22
Lisburn Pl. HP20: Ayle 4A 62
Lisle Rd. HP13: H Wyc 6A 90
Lisleys Fld. HP15: Crye 7D 82
Lismore Pk. SL2: Slou 4D 124
Lissel Rd. MK6: Simp 2A 30
Lister Grn. *HP21: Ayle 2K 65*
(off Jenner Rd.)
Liston Ct. SL7: Marl 7H 105
Liston Rd. SL7: Marl 7H 105
Litcham Spur SL1: Slou 4B 124
LITCHBOROUGH 1A 132
Little Balmer MK18: Buck 6J 37
Little Benty UB7: W Dra 3K 131
LITTLE BILLING 1C 133
LITTLE BILLINGTON 1D 135
Little Boltons SL7: Marl 1J 115
LITTLE BOYS HEATH 3J 83
LITTLE BRICKHILL 3F 35 (3D 133)
Lit. Brickhill La. MK17: G Bri 6F 35
LITTLE BRINGTON 1A 132
LITTLE BRITAIN 4J 127
Little Britain HP18: Wadd 5D 52
Littlebrook Av. SL2: Slou 2G 123
Little Buntings SL4: Wind 7H 129
LITTLE CHALFONT 6H 87 (1C 137)
Lit. Chapels Way SL1: Slou 7J 123
Lit. Chartridge Ct. HP5: Ches 4J 77
Little Cl. HP10: F Hea 3H 107
HP12: H Wyc 5J 97
HP20: Ayle 5J 61
LITTLECOTE 1C 135
Littlecote MK8: G Hol 5A 22
LITTLE CRAWLEY 5J 13 (2D 133)
Littledown Rd. SL1: Slou 6D 124
Little Dunmow MK10: Monk 5C 24
LITTLE END .4D 12
LITTLE EVERDON 1A 132
LITTLE GADDESDEN 2D 135
Little Greencroft HP5: Ches 1J 77
Little Habton MK4: E Val 5B 28
Little Hame MK10: M Vill 3B 24
Little Ham La. HP27: Mon R 3G 71
LITTLE HAMPDEN 1A 74 (3C 135)
Lit. Hampden Cl. HP22: Wend 4H 69
LITTLE HASELEY 3A 134
Little Hivings HP5: Ches 1J 77
Little Hollis HP16: G Mis 6E 74
LITTLE HORWOOD 3B 132
Lit. Horwood Rd. MK17: G Hor 2J 39
LITTLE HOUGHTON 1C 133
Lit. Hundridge La. HP5: Ches 4C 76
HP16: H Hea 4C 76

LITTLE ICKFORD 5E 54
LITTLE KIMBLE 3C 135
LITTLE KINGSHILL 2H 83 (1B 136)
Little La. HP27: Saun 2A 80
LITTLE LINFORD 7C 10 (2C 133)
Lit. Linford La. MK19: L Lin 7C 10
LITTLE LONDON
HP18 5K 53 (2A 134)
HP22 7J 69
Little London HP22: W'urch 3G 45
Lit. London Grn. HP18: Oak 5K 53
LITTLE MARLOW 4C 106 (2B 136)
Lit. Marlow Rd. SL7: Marl 7J 105
LITTLE MARSH 5D 42
Lit. Marsh Rd. OX27: M Gib 5D 42
Little Mdw. MK5: Lough 1B 28
Littlemere MK8: T Ash 5H 21
LITTLE MILTON 3A 134
LITTLE MISSENDEN 4C 84 (1C 137)
Little Mollards HP22: W'rave 6B 48
LITTLEMORE 3A 134
Little Orchard HP20: Ayle 3A 62
Lit. Orchard Cl. HP27: Long 3D 70
Little Pk. HP3: Bov 2K 79
HP27: Prin R 5H 71
Littleport Spur SL1: Slou 4C 124
LITTLE PRESTON 1A 132
Lit. Reeves Av. HP7: Amer 6D 86
LITTLE SEABROOK 3B 50
Little Shardeloes HP7: Amer 6J 85
Little Springs HP5: Ches 2K 77
Little Stanton MK14: Stan 6D 16
Little Stocking MK5: S Broo 4A 28
Lit. Sutton La. SL3: Lang 3C 130
LITTLETON 3D 137
LITTLEWICK GREEN 3B 136
Little Wood HP14: Stoke 5C 72
LITTLE WOOD CORNER 5A 76
Little Woodlands SL4: Wind 7H 129
Littleworth LU7: Wing 2C 48
LITTLEWORTH COMMON 1F 117
Littleworth Rd. HP13: Down 5J 89
SL1: Burn 1E 116
Litton Ct. HP10: Loud 6J 99
Liverpool Rd. SL1: Slou 4K 123
Livesey Hill MK5: S Lod 2B 28
Livingstone Dr. MK15: New 1J 23
Llanbury Cl. SL9: C Pet 5J 103
Lloyds MK6: Coff 7G 23
Lloyd's Ct. MK9: C Key 3E 22
Loakes Rd. HP11: H Wyc 2A 98
Lochinvar Cl. SL1: Slou 7K 123
Lock Bri. Rd. SL8: Bou E 5G 107
Locke Cl. HP19: Ayle 4F 61
Locke Gdns. SL3: Lang 7G 125
Locke Rd. MK2: Blet 7J 29
(not continuous)
Lockets Cl. SL4: Wind 6F 129
Lock La. MK19: Cosg 3C 14
Lock Path SL4: Dorn, E Wick 4F 129
Lock Rd. SL7: Marl 7J 105
Lockton Ct. MK4: E Val 4B 28
Lock Vw. Cotts. *MK1: F Str* *6A 30*
(off Lock Vw. La.)
Lock Vw. La. MK1: F Str 6A 30
Lodden Cl. HP21: Ayle 4J 65
Loddon Rd. SL8: Bou E 5G 107
Loddon Spur SL1: Slou 5C 124
LODGE 5K 21
Lodge, The MK46: Lave 2C 6
Lodge Cl. LU7: Ched 2C 50
MK18: Pad 5B 38
SL1: Slou 7A 124
SL7: Marl 1J 115
UB8: Cowl 2J 127
Lodge Farm Cl. HP22: West T 5F 67
Lodge Farm Ct. MK19: Cast 6D 8
Lodge Ga. MK14: G Lin 6E 16
Lodge La. HP8: D Gil 6J 87
HP16: Pres 1C 82
MK17: S Ham 2H 41
Lodge Pk., The MK16: New P 1J 17
Lodge Path HP19: Ayle 6E 60
Lodge Way SL4: Wind 7G 129
Logan Rock MK4: Tatt 7B 28
Lollards Cl. HP6: Amer 4A 86
Lomond Dr. MK2: Blet 5J 33
London Ct. HP21: Ayle 7A 62
London End HP9: Bea 7H 101
MK17: New L 4D 32
London End La. MK17: Bow B 6F 31
LONDON HEATHROW AIRPORT 3D 137
London Rd. HP8: D Gil 7G 95
HP9: Bea 7J 101
HP10: Woob G 7K 99
HP11: H Wyc, W Mar 2C 98
HP16: G Mis 7H 75
HP22: Ast C 2A 68
HP22: Wend 5J 69 & 1E 74
MK5: Lough 7A 22
MK11: S Strat 1B 20
MK16: Bro 1C 24
MK16: New P 2B 18
MK18: Buck 4H 37
MK19: O Stra 6A 14
SL3: Lang 7G 125 & 3A 130
London Rd. E. HP7: Amer 1B 94
London Rd. W. HP7: Amer 7A 86
Long Ayres MK7: Cald 4C 30
Longbottom La.
HP9: Bea, S Grn, Jord 4J 101
Longbourn SL4: Wind 7J 129
Longbridge Way UB8: Uxb 7H 121
Long Cl. SL2: Farn C 5K 117
LONG CRENDON 6C 56 (3A 134)
Long Crendon Court House 5D 56
Long Crendon Ind. Est. HP18: Long C 7E 56
Long Crendon Rd.
HP18: Shab, Long C 5H 55 & 7A 56
Longcroft HP22: Ast C 2C 68
Longcroft Av. HP22: Halt 2K 69
Longcross MK15: Penny 7G 17
Longdown Hill HP27: Whit 2K 71
Longdown M. HP19: Ayle 6E 60
Long Dr. SL1: Burn 1E 122
UB7: W Dra 7K 127
Longfellow Dr. MK16: New P 1G 17
Longfield HP16: L Kin 2H 83
SL2: Hedg 1B 118
Longfield Dr. HP6: Amer 5K 85
Longfield Rd. HP5: Ches 3H 77
LONGFORD 6H 131 (3D 137)
Longford Cir. UB7: Long 6H 131
LONGFORDMOOR 6G 131
Long Furlong HP17: Hadd 6B 58
HP17: Sto 2A 64
Long Furlong Dr. SL2: Slou 2F 123
Long Gro. HP9: S Grn 4A 102
Long Hale LU7: Pits 6E 50
Long Hedge LU7: Pits 5E 50
Longhedge MK7: Cald 5C 30
Long Hide HP27: Prin R 4H 71
Longlands Ct. MK18: Wins 5J 39
Longlands Wlk. MK18: Wins 5J 39
Longland Way HP12: H Wyc 3H 97
Long La. HP3: Bov, Flau 5K 79
MK46: Oln 3F 7
Longleat Ct. MK8: G Hol 5K 21
Long Ley LU7: Ched 2C 50
Long Leys HP19: Ayle 6F 61
Long Lional HP20: Ayle 6K 61
LONG MARSTON 2C 135
Long Marston Rd. HP23: M'rth 6A 50
LU7: Ched 2A 50
Long Massey MK46: Oln 2G 7
Longmead SL4: Wind 6G 129
Longmead La. SL1: Burn 5F 117
Long Mdw. HP5: Ches 2A 78
HP21: Ayle 1C 66
Longmeadow Cl. HP27: Mon R 2H 71
Longmire MK46: Lave 2C 6
Long Orchard Dr. HP10: T Grn 7J 91
Long Pk. Cl. HP6: Amer 3A 86
Long Pk. Way HP6: Amer 3A 86
Longpeak Cl. MK4: Tatt 6B 28
Long Plough HP22: Ast C 2A 68
Long Readings La. SL2: Slou 1K 123
Long Row HP16: Pres 7D 74
Longstone Rd. SL0: I Hea 7C 120
LONG STREET 1C 8 (2B 132)
Long St. Rd. MK19: H'ope 1D 8
Longview HP9: Bea 1B 108
Longville MK12: O Wol 6F 15
Long Wlk. HP8: D Gil 1H 95
Long Wall HP17: Hadd 7B 58
LONGWICK 2C 70 (3B 134)
Longwick Rd. HP27: Long, Mon R 2E 70
Longwood Av. SL3: Lang 3B 130
Long Wood Dr. HP9: Jord 4D 102
Longwood La. HP7: Amer 6B 86
Look Ahead SL1: Slou 7C 124
Loosley Hill HP27: Loos 1B 80
LOOSLEY ROW 1B 80 (3C 135)
Lord Mayor's Dr. SL2: Farn C 4H 117
(not continuous)
Lord Raglan Ho. SL4: Wind 7K 129
Lords Cl. MK2: Blet 6J 29
Lords Mill Ct. HP5: Ches 6A 78
Loriner Pl. MK14: D Barn 7G 17
Loring Rd. SL4: Wind 6H 129
Lorne Cl. SL1: Slou 1K 129
Lorne Ct. SL1: Slou 7A 124
Lorraine Cl. HP13: H Wyc 7E 90
Loseley Ct. MK8: G Hol 5K 21
Losfield Rd. SL4: Wind 6G 129
Lossie Dr. SL0: Ive 5B 126
Lothersdale MK13: Hee 1B 22
Lothian Cl. MK3: Blet 5E 28
Lott Mdw. HP21: Ayle 4J 65
Lott Wlk. *HP21: Ayle* *4J 65*
(off Lott Mdw.)
Louches La. HP14: Nap 1H 89
Loudhams Rd. HP7: L Chal 6G 87
Loudhams Wood La. HP8: D Gil 7H 87
LOUDWATER 6J 99 (1C 137)
LOUGHTON 6B 22 (3C 133)
LOUGHTON 6K 21
LOUGHTON LODGE 5K 21
Loughton Manor Equestrian Cen. 7B 22
Loughton Rd. MK13: B'ell 2A 22
Lovat Mdw. Cvn. Site MK16: New P 2A 18
Lovat St. MK16: New P 1J 17
Lovatt Dr. MK3: Blet 7D 28
Love Grn. La. SL0: Ive 3D 126
Lovegrove Dr. SL2: Slou 2H 123
Lovegrove Ho. HP13: H Wyc 2D 98
Love Hill La. SL3: Lang 5A 126
Lovejoy La. SL4: Wind 7F 129
Lovelace Cl. SL6: Hur 5D 114
Love La. SL0: Ive 4D 126
Lovel End SL9: C Pet 5G 103
Lovel Mead SL9: C Pet 5G 103
Lovel Rd. SL9: C Pet 5G 103
Lovers Wlk. HP20: Ayle 6K 61
Lovett Rd. UB9: Hare 1J 113
Lovetts End LU7: Stew 4C 46
Lowbrook Cl. HP21: Ayle 3B 66
Lowden Cl. HP11: H Wyc 4C 98
LOWER ARNCOTT 2A 134
LOWER ASSENDON 2A 136
LOWER BOIS 1B 86
Lwr. Britwell Rd. SL2: Slou 2F 123
(not continuous)
LOWER CADSDEN 2K 71
Lwr. Church St. HP14: Stoke 5C 72
HP18: Cudd 1B 58
Lwr. Cippenham La. SL1: Slou 6G 123
Lower Cl. HP19: Ayle 7G 61
Lower Dr. HP9: Bea 3F 101
Lwr. Eighth St. MK9: C Key 4E 22
LOWER END
Aylesbury 5B 56
Milton Keynes 6K 25
Northampton 1C 133
Tring 7B 50
Lower End HP22: W'rave 7C 48
MK17: New L 5C 32
MK18: T'ough 2B 38
Lwr. End Rd. MK17: Wave 6H 25
Lwr. Farm Cl. HP18: Shab 5H 55
Lwr. Farm Ga. HP17: Upt 1J 59
Lwr. Fourth St. MK9: C Key 5D 22
Lwr. Furney Cl. HP13: H Wyc 7D 90
Lower Grn. HP18: Cudd 1B 58
HP22: West T 4H 67
Lower Grn. La. HP18: Che 2H 57
Lwr. Hammersley La.
HP13: H Wyc 4H 99
LOWER HARTWELL 1D 64
Lwr. Icknield Way HP17: Gt Kim 2E 70
HP22: Ast C, B'land 3C 68
HP23: Wils 7C 50 & 1D 68
HP27: Bled, Long, Owls 5A 70
Lwr. Lees Rd. SL2: Slou 1J 123
Lwr. Lodge La. HP15: Haz 1G 91
Lower Mead SL0: I Hea 1D 126
Lwr. Ninth St. MK9: C Key 4E 22
LOWER NORTH DEAN 5J 81
Lwr. Pound La. SL7: Marl 3G 115
Lower Ridge SL8: Bou E 5H 107
Lwr. Riding HP9: Bea 6D 100
Lower Rd. HP17: Hadd, Ford 6D 58
HP21: Ayle 3K 65
HP22: H'ick 5H 45
HP22: Sto M 3K 65
HP27: Loos 1B 80
SL9: C Pet 6J 103
(not continuous)
SL9: G Cro 3K 111
UB9: Den 5C 112
Lwr. Second St. MK9: C Key 5D 22
(not continuous)
LOWER SHELTON 2D 133
LOWER SHIPLAKE 3A 136
Lwr. Stonehayes MK14: G Lin 6F 17
Lower St. HP22: Q'ton 5H 43
LOWER SUNDON 1D 135
Lwr. Tenth St. MK9: C Key 4F 23
Lwr. Third St. MK9: C Key 5D 22
(not continuous)
Lwr. Twelfth St. MK9: C Key 3F 23
Lower Way MK17: G Bri 6E 34
MK18: Pad 5A 38
LOWER WEALD 4C 20
LOWER WINCHENDON 2B 134
LOWER WOODEND 6B 104 (2B 136)
Lowes Cl. HP14: Stoke 5A 72
Lowestoft Dr. SL1: Slou 4F 123
Lowfield Cl. HP15: Haz 4G 91
Lowfield Way HP15: Haz 4H 91
Lowick Pl. MK4: E Val 5B 28
Lowland Rd. MK4: Tatt 7C 28
Lowlands Av. HP5: Ches 4K 77
Lowlands Cres. HP15: G Kin 5D 82
Low La. HP18: Cudd 1C 58
Lowman Way HP21: Ayle 3J 65
Lowndes Av. HP5: Ches 4K 77
Lowndes Gro. MK5: S Chur 7K 21
Lowndes Path *HP19: Ayle* *6E 60*
(off Meadow Way)
Lowndes Way MK18: Wins 5J 39
Loxbeare Dr. MK4: Fur 3C 28
Loxboro Hill HP14: Bled R 3B 88
Lucas Pl. MK6: W Grn. 6K 23
Lucas Rd. HP13: H Wyc 7C 90
Luccombe MK4: Fur 4D 28
Lucky La. HP20: Ayle 5J 61
Lucy La. MK5: Lough 6B 22
Ludgate MK6: Lead 7E 22
LUDGERSHALL 2C 52 (2A 134)
Ludlow Cl. MK3: Blet 1F 33
Ludlow M. HP11: W Mar 4G 99
Ludlow Pl. HP20: Ayle 6D 62
Luff Cl. SL4: Wind 7G 129
Lufford Pk. MK14: G Lin 4F 17
Luke Pl. MK10: Midd 3B 24
Lukes La. HP23: Gubb 6A 50
Lukes Lea HP23: M'rth 7C 50
Lullingstone Dr. MK13: B Pk 1J 21
Lum's Yd. *HP5: Ches* *5K 77*
(off high St.)
Lundbeck Ho. MK7: Cald 5C 30
Lundholme MK13: Hee 1B 22
Lundy Ct. SL1: Slou 5G 123
Lupin Cl. UB7: W Dra 3K 131
Lupin Ct. *HP21: Ayle* *1G 65*
(off Ellen Rd.)
Lupin Wlk. HP21: Ayle 2G 65
Luttlemarsh MK7: Walt P 2B 30
Lutyens Gro. MK7: Old P 2F 31
Luxborough Gro. MK4: Fur 3C 28
Lycrome La. HP5: Ches 2B 78
Lycrome Rd. HP5: Ches, Lye G 2B 78
Lyde End HP27: Bled 7A 70
Lydford Av. SL2: Slou 3B 124
Lydiard MK8: G Hol 5J 21
Lydiard Cl. HP21: Ayle 3C 66
Lydsey Cl. SL2: Slou 1J 123
LYE GREEN 2D 78 (3D 135)
Lye Grn. Rd. HP5: Ches 4B 78
Lyell Pl. E. *SL4: Wind* *7E 128*
(off Lyell Rd.)
Lyell Pl. W. *SL4: Wind* *7E 128*
(off Lyell Rd.)
Lyell Rd. SL4: Wind 7E 128
Lyell Wlk. E. SL4: Wind 7E 128
Lyell Wlk. W. SL4: Wind 7E 128
Lynch, The UB8: Uxb 5J 121
Lynch Cl. UB8: Uxb 5J 121
LYNCH HILL 1G 123
Lynch Hill La. SL2: Slou 2G 123
Lynden Ho. HP5: Ches 4B 78
Lyndhurst Cl. HP13: Down 6G 89
Lyndhurst Rd. HP5: Ches 2K 77
Lyndon Cl. HP16: Pres 6C 74
Lyndon Gdns. HP13: H Wyc 7E 90
LYNE 3D 137
Lynford Pde. HP15: H Grn 1J 91
Lynher Cl. HP21: Ayle 3H 65
Lynmouth Cres. MK4: Fur 3C 28
Lynott Cl. MK8: C'ill 1J 27
Lynton Rd. HP5: Ches 2K 77
Lynwood Av. SL3: Lang 7H 125
Lynwood Rd. HP21: Ayle 2B 66
Lyon Rd. MK1: Blet 5H 29
Lyons Ind. Est. UB8: Cowl 5K 127
Lysander Cl. HP3: Bov 1K 79

M

McAuliffe Dr. SL2: Farn C 2H 117
McConnell Dr. MK12: Wolv 6H 15
Macdonald Cl. HP6: Amer 2A 86
McEwen Ride HP22: Halt 7K 67
McKay Trad. Est. SL3: Poy 7E 130
McKenzie Cl. MK18: Buck 4H 37
Mackenzie Mall *SL1: Slou* *7D 124*
(off Wellington St.)
Mackenzie St. SL1: Slou 7D 124
McLernon Way MK18: Wins 5J 39
Madeley Cl. HP6: Amer 3B 86
Madeley Rd. HP21: Ayle 1K 65
Magdalen Cl. MK11: S Strat 7B 14
Magdalen Ho. MK11: S Strat 7B 14
Magenta Cl. MK2: Blet 2K 33
Magna Karta 5J 29
Magnolia Dene HP15: Haz 5F 91
Magnolia Gdns. SL3: Lang 7G 125
Magnolia St. UB7: W Dra 2K 131
Magnolia Way HP10: Woob G 2A 108
Magpie Cl. HP10: F Hea 7G 99
MK5: S Broo 3B 28
Magpie La. HP7: Cole 5H 93
HP10: F Hea 7G 99
HP13: H Wyc 5H 99
Magpie Way MK18: Wins 5J 39
SL2: Slou 2H 123
Mahler Cl. MK7: Brow 2E 30
Mahoney Ct. HP11: H Wyc 7J 89
MK8: G Far 1H 27
MAIDENHEAD 2B 136
Maidenhead Av. MK13: B Com 3C 22
Maidenhead Rd. SL4: Wind 5E 128
MAIDEN'S GREEN 3B 136
MAIDENSGROVE 2A 136
MAIDFORD 1A 132
MAIDS MORETON 1K 37 (3B 132)
Maids Moreton Av. MK18: Buck 3H 37
Maidstone Rd. MK10: K'ton 4E 24
Main Dr. SL0: R Pk 2E 130
SL9: G Cro 3G 111
Main Rd. HP14: Walt A 5F 81
HP27: L Grn 1B 80
MK17: Dray P 7B 40
SL4: Wind 5E 128
Main Rd. Nth. HP4: Dag 4F 49
Main Rd. Sth. HP4: Dag 6H 49

Main St. HP18: G Und 2G 43
HP22: West T 5F 67
MK17: Mur 2C 40
MK18: Ads 7E 38
MK18: Gaw 6C 36
MK18: M M'ton 1J 37
MK18: Pad 6A 38
MK18: Ting 2B 36
MK19: Cosg 3C 14
Maitland Dr. HP13: H Wyc 7B 90
Maitland Rd. HP22: Halt 1K 69
Majors Farm Rd. SL3: Dat 4A 130
Malbons Ct. MK6: Lead 7E 22
Malden Cl. HP6: Amer 5D 86
Malet Cl. HP14: Stoke 5D 72
Malins Ga. MK14: G Lin 5E 16
Malkin Dr. HP9: Bea 5E 100
Mallard Cl. HP19: Ayle 2K 61
SL1: Burn 7D 116
Mallard Cft. HP17: Hadd 5C 58
Mallard Dr. MK18: Buck 4J 37
SL1: Slou 5H 123
Mallard Ho. HP11: H Wyc 2C 98
Mallets End HP22: Q'ton 6J 43
Malletts Cl. MK11: S Strat 1C 20
Mallow Ga. MK14: Conn 2E 22
Malmers Well Rd. HP13: H Wyc 1B 98
Malpas Rd. SL2: Slou 5F 125
Malthouse Sq. HP9: Bea 1H 109
HP27: Prin R 4G 71
Malthouse Way SL7: Marl 1H 115
Malting Cl. MK16: S Gold 6C 6
Malting La. HP4: Dag 6H 49
Maltings, The HP7: Amer 6K 85
MK18: Ting 2C 36
MK46: Oln 4J 7
(off Silver End)
Maltings Cl. LU7: Stew 4C 46
Maltings Fld. MK19: Cast 7D 8
Maltmans La. SL9: C Pet 1G 111
Malton Av. SL1: Slou 4K 123
Malton Cl. MK10: Monk 5B 24
Malvern Cl. HP13: Down 7J 89
Malvern Ct. SL3: Lang 4A 130
Malvern Dr. MK11: F Sla 2D 20
Malvern Rd. HP20: Ayle 6D 62
Mandela Ct. UB8: Cowl 3J 127
Mandeville Dr. MK10: K'ton 4E 24
Mandeville M. HP21: Ayle 3K 65
Mandeville Rd. HP16: Pres 6B 74
HP21: Ayle 1K 65
Mandeville School Sports Cen., The. 3J 65
Manfield Cl. SL2: Slou 1J 123
Manifold La. MK5: S Broo 4A 28
Manor, The HP18: Long C 7C 56
Manor Cl. HP10: T Grn 5G 91
HP16: Pres 2D 82
HP27: Bled 7A 70
MK10: M Vill 3B 24
MK17: S Ham 2H 41
MK19: Cosg 3C 14
MK19: H'ope 2E 8
Manor Ct. SL1: Slou 6H 123
SL7: Marl 6G 105
Manor Ct. Yd. HP13: H Wyc 6A 90
Manor Courtyard HP17: A San 7F 59
MK16: Sher 3B 12
Manor Cres. HP9: S Grn 3B 102
HP22: Wend 3J 69
Manor Dr. HP6: Amer 3K 85
HP20: Ayle 4A 62
LU7: Stew 4C 46
MK19: H'ham 3J 15
Mnr. Farm Cl. HP17: Sto 2B 64
LU7: Soul 7H 41
SL4: Wind 7H 129
Mnr. Farm Ct. HP22: H'ick 5H 45
Mnr. Farm Ho. SL4: Wind 7H 129
Mnr. Farm Way HP9: S Grn 4B 102
Manorfields Rd. MK19: O Stra 7A 14
Manor Gdns. HP10: Woob G 4A 108
HP13: H Wyc 6A 90
HP18: G Und 2H 43
MK18: M M'ton 2J 37
Manor Gro. SL6: Fifi 6A 128
Manor Ho. Cl. HP20: Ayle 5A 62
Manor La. SL9: G Cro 5H 111
MANOR PARK
Aylesbury 4K 61
Slough 3B 124
Manor Pk. MK18: M M'ton 1K 37
Manor Pk. Av. HP27: Prin R 6F 71
Manor Pk. Est. MK18: M M'ton 1K 37
Mnr. Pound Rd. LU7: Ched 2C 50
Manor Rd. HP5: Ches 3K 77
HP9: S Grn 3B 102
HP10: T Grn 4F 91
HP15: Haz 4F 91
HP18: Oak 5H 53
HP20: Ayle 5K 61
HP22: Ovi 5C 44
HP22: Wend 3J 69
HP27: Prin R 6F 71
LU7: Ched 2B 50
MK2: Blet 1K 33
MK12: O Wol 6F 15
MK16: New P 1G 17
Manor Rd. MK17: New L 5D 32
SL4: Wind 7G 129
Manor St. MK18: Buck 4G 37
Manor Vw. HP15: Haz 5H 91
Manor Vs. HP18: Che 2H 57
Manor Way HP5: Ches 4B 78
HP7: Cole 4H 93
Manor Waye UB8: Uxb 6K 121
Manse Cl. MK11: S Strat 7B 14
Mansel Cl. MK19: Cosg 3B 14
SL2: Slou 3F 125
Mansell Cl. MK5: S Chur 1A 28
SL4: Wind 6G 129
Manshead Ct. MK11: S Strat 1D 20
Mansion Cvn. Site SL0: Ive 6C 126
Mansion Hill HP22: Halt 7B 68
Mansion La. SL0: Ive 6C 126
MANTLES GREEN 6J 85
Maple Cl. HP12: H Wyc 3G 97
HP15: Haz 4G 91
Maple Ct. HP5: Ches 4K 77
HP18: Oak 5K 53
SL9: G Cro 3K 111
Maple Cres. SL2: Slou 5F 125
MAPLE CROSS 1D 137
Mapledean MK12: S Bus 2J 21
MAPLEDURHAM 3A 136
Mapledurham MK7: Cald 4C 30
Maplefield La. HP8: D Gil 1F 95
Maple Gro. MK2: F Str 7A 30
MK17: W San 3J 31
MAPLE HILL 4H 79
Maple Leys MK18: S Clay 2C 42
Maple Ri. SL7: Marl 6J 105
Maplewood Gdns. HP9: Bea 7D 100
Maplin Pk. SL3: Lang 7B 126
Mapridge Grn. La. HP16: G Mis 3D 74
Mara Pl. MK9: Camp 3G 23
Marbeck Cl. SL4: Wind 6F 129
Marchant Ct. SL7: Marl 6A 106
March Edge MK18: Buck 3J 37
March Mdw. MK7: W Gat 7F 25
March Pl. HP19: Ayle 6G 61
Marcia Ct. SL1: Slou 6H 123
Marconi Cft. MK5: S Lod 2C 28
Marcourt Rd. HP14: Stoke 6D 72
Maree Cl. MK2: Blet 3J 33
Marefield Rd. SL7: Marl 7H 105
Mare Leys MK18: Buck 4K 37
Marescroft Rd. SL2: Slou 2G 123
Margam Cres. MK10: Monk 5C 24
Marigold Pl. MK14: Conn 2E 22
Marigold Wlk. HP15: W End 1F 91
MARINA 7J 23
Marina Dr. MK12: Wolv 1H 21
Marina Way SL0: Ive 5G 127
SL1: Slou 5F 123
Marish Ct. SL3: Lang 1A 130
Marish La. UB9: Den 3C 112
(not continuous)
Marish Wharf SL3: Lang 7J 125
Marjoram Pl. MK14: Conn 1E 22
Mark Dr. SL9: C Pet 2H 103
Markenfield Pl. MK4: K'ead 6J 27
Market Hill HP22: W'urch 2F 45
MK6: Eagl 6H 23
MK18: Buck 3H 37
Market Ho. SL9: C Pet 6H 103
Market La. SL3: Lang 1C 130
Market Pde. HP15: Haz 3G 91
Market Pl. MK46: Oln 4H 7
SL3: Coln 5C 130
SL9: C Pet 6H 103
Market Sq. *HP5: Ches 6K 77*
(off High St.)
HP7: Amer 7K 85
HP20: Ayle 6J 61
HP27: Prin R 5G 71
MK11: S Strat 1B 20
MK18: Buck 3H 37
MK18: Wins 6H 39
MK19: H'ope 2E 8
SL7: Marl 7H 105
UB8: Uxb 5J 121
Market St. HP20: Ayle 6J 61
Market Wlk. HP7: Amer 7K 85
Markham Cl. HP19: Ayle 7F 61
Markhams Ct. MK18: Buck 4H 37
MARLBOROUGH 5B 16
Marlborough Ct. MK14: L Woo 7E 16
Marlborough Ga. MK9: C Key 3F 23
Marlborough Rd. HP21: Ayle 3K 65
Marlborough St. (V8)
MK6: Mil K 1J 29
MK9: Mil K 2F 23
(not continuous)
MK14: Mil K 5C 16
Marlborough Trad. Est.
HP11: H Wyc 7K 89
Marley Gro. MK8: C'ill 7J 21
Marlin Ct. SL7: Marl 1H 115
MARLOW 1H 115 (2B 136)
MARLOW BOTTOM 4H 105 (2B 136)
Marlow Bottom SL7: Marl 1G 105
Marlow Bri. La. SL7: Marl 2J 115
MARLOW COMMON 6D 104
Marlow Comn. SL7: Marl 7C 104
Marlow Ct. *HP6: Amer 5D 86*
(off Plantation Rd.)
Marlow Dr. MK16: New P 1G 17
Marlow FC 6H 105
Marlow Hill HP11: H Wyc 5K 97
Marlow Mill SL7: Marl 1J 115
Marlow Rd. HP11: H Wyc 5J 97
HP14: Cadm 2F 73
HP14: L End 4A 96
HP14: Stoke 6C 72
(not continuous)
SL6: Maid 5H 115
SL7: L Mar 5B 106
SL7: Marl 4H 115
(Bisham)
SL7: Marl 4A 96
(Lane End, not continuous)
SL8: Bou E 4F 107
Marlow Station (Rail) 7K 105
Marram Cl. MK6: Bean 2G 29
Marriot's Cl. HP17: Hadd 6B 58
Marriotts Av. HP16: S Hea 4A 76
(not continuous)
Marriott's La. HP17: Hadd 6B 58
Marriott's Way HP17: Hadd 6B 58
Marrod's Bottom HP7: Winc 7E 92
Marron La. MK12: Wolv 1G 21
Marroway HP22: West T 6E 66
MARSH 7J 65 (3C 135)
Marshall Ct. Ind. Pk. MK1: Blet 6H 29
Marshalls La. MK15: Wool 4J 23
Marshalls Lea HP22: Bier 3D 62
Marsham Cl. HP21: Ayle 3B 66
Marsham La. SL9: G Cro 4J 111
Marsham Lodge SL9: G Cro 4J 111
Marsham Way SL9: G Cro 3J 111
Marshaw Pl. MK4: E Val 5C 28
MARSH BALDON 3A 134
Marsh Ct. HP11: H Wyc 4F 99
Marsh Dr. MK14: G Lin 4F 17
MARSH END 3K 17
Marsh End Rd. MK16: New P 1J 17
MARSH GIBBON 5C 42 (1A 134)
Marsh Gibbon Rd. HP18: G Und 1F 43
Marsh La. HP22: Sto M 7K 65
SL4: Dorn 7B 122
SL6: Dorn, Tapl, Dorn R 6A 122
Marshment Cl. HP22: Ast C 2A 68
Marsh Rd. HP18: Shab 5G 55
Marshworth MK6: T Bri 1K 29
Marston Cl. HP5: Ches 1J 77
Marstonfields Rd. MK18: N Mar 2B 44
Marston Hill HP22: Ovi 4C 44
MARSTON MORETAINE 2D 133
Marston Rd. HP23: M'rth 6A 50
MARSWORTH 7B 50 (2D 135)
Marsworth Rd. LU7: Pits 6E 50
Martell Cl. MK7: Cald 3C 30
Martin Cl. MK14: N Hill 7E 16
MK18: Buck 5K 37
SL4: Wind 6E 128
UB10: Uxb 7K 121
Martindale SL0: Ive 2D 126
Martin Dell Cotts. HP16: L Com 1A 76
Martineau Ho. SL9: C Pet 3J 103
Martingale Pl. MK14: D Barn 1F 23
Martin Rd. SL1: Slou 7C 124
Martinsend La. HP16: G Mis 6E 74
Martin's Plain SL2: S Pog 1D 124
Martyrs Ct. HP7: Amer 6A 86
Marunden Grn. SL2: Slou 1H 123
Marwood Cl. MK4: Fur 4D 28
Marygold Wlk. HP6: L Chal 6G 87
Maryland Rd. MK15: Tong 5H 17
Mary Macmanus Dr. MK18: Buck 3H 37
Mary Morgan Ct. SL2: Slou 3B 124
Maryot Cl. MK16: Sher 2B 12
Maryside SL3: Lang 7J 125
Marys Mead HP15: Haz 3F 91
Mascoll Path SL2: Slou 1H 123
Masefield Cl. HP5: Ches 2K 77
MK16: New P 1G 17
Masefield Gro. MK3: Blet 1G 33
Maslin Dr. MK6: Bean 2H 29
Mason MK14: Stan 5C 16
Masons Cl. HP16: Pres 1C 82
Masons Ct. HP5: Ches 4A 78
HP19: Ayle 7G 61
SL1: Slou 5G 123
Masons Rd. SL1: Slou 5G 123
Massie Cl. MK15: W Par 7H 17
Mathews Ho. HP13: H Wyc 2D 98
Mathiesen Rd. MK13: B'lle 7A 16
Mathisen Way SL3: Poy 6E 130
Matilda Gdns. MK5: S Chur 1B 28
Matlock Rd. HP20: Ayle 4A 62
Matthew Ct. MK5: S Chur 1B 28
Matthews Cl. HP20: Ayle 4A 62
Maude Cl. HP9: Bea 7J 101
Maude Rd. HP9: Bea 7J 101
Maud Jane's Cl. LU7: I'hoe 4G 51
Maudsley Cl. MK5: S Lod 1C 28
Mauduit Cl. MK19: H'ope 1E 8
MAULDEN 3D 133
Maulden Gdns. MK14: G Par 5G 17
Maurice Mt. HP15: Haz 1F 91
Mavoncliff Dr. MK4: Tatt 7A 28
Maxham MK5: S Broo 4A 28
Maxwell Dr. HP15: Haz 2H 91
Maxwell Rd. HP9: Bea 5G 101
Maybach Ct. MK5: S Lod 2B 28
Maybrook Gdns. HP13: H Wyc 7C 90
Maybury Cl. SL1: Slou 4F 123
Maybush Gdns. HP16: Pres 7C 74
Maybush Wlk. MK46: Oln 2G 7
May Cl. LU6: E Bra 1J 49
Mayditch Pl. MK13: B Com 3C 22
Mayer Gdns. MK5: S Lod 2C 28
Mayfield Cvn. Pk. UB7: W Dra 1J 131
Mayfield Rd. HP10: Woob G 3A 108
Mayflower Barn 5D 102
Mayflower Cl. HP17: Hart 2E 64
Mayflower Way HP9: Bea 1C 108
SL2: Farn C 3A 118
Maygoods Cl. UB8: Cowl 3K 127
Maygoods Grn. UB8: Cowl 3K 127
Maygoods La. UB8: Cowl 3K 127
Maygoods Vw. UB8: Cowl 3J 127
Mayhall La. HP6: Amer 2K 85
Mayhew Cres. HP13: H Wyc 7D 90
Maylands Dr. UB8: Uxb 4K 121
Maynard Cl. MK13: B'ell 3A 22
Maynard Ct. SL4: Wind 6J 129
Maypole Rd. SL6: Tapl 3C 122
May Tree Cl. SL7: Marl 3G 105
Mead, The HP9: Bea 6G 101
LU7: Soul 6H 41
Mead Acre HP27: Mon R 3G 71
Mead Av. SL3: Lang 7B 126
Mead Cl. HP27: Mon R 2G 71
SL3: Lang 7B 126
SL7: Marl 6K 105
UB9: Den 7G 113
Meades La. HP5: Ches 6K 77
Meadfield Av. SL3: Lang 7A 126
Meadfield Rd. SL3: Lang 1A 130
Mead Ho. SL0: I Hea 1D 126
MEADLE 1F 71 (3C 135)
Meadoway HP17: Hart 3E 64
MK18: S Clay 2B 42
Meadow Bank SL8: Bou E 6H 107
Mdw. Bank Cl. HP18: Long C 5C 56
Mdw. Brook Cl. SL3: Poy 6F 131
Meadow Cl. HP5: Ches 1J 77
HP11: W Mar 4F 99
HP18: Oak 6H 53
HP20: Ayle 5B 62
LU7: Cubl 2H 47
SL7: Marl 1K 115
Meadowcot La. HP7: Cole 4H 93
Meadow Cotts. HP16: L Kin 3H 83
Meadowcroft HP19: Ayle 4F 61
SL9: C Pet 7H 103
Meadow Dr. HP6: Amer 4C 86
HP27: Long 2C 70
Meadow Gdns. MK18: Buck 6J 37
Meadow Ga. HP16: Pres 3C 82
MK18: Pad 5A 38
Meadow La. HP9: Bea 6H 101
HP16: S Hea 4A 76
HP18: Long C 7E 56
LU7: Pits 6G 51
MK10: M Vill 3C 24
SL4: E Wick 4K 129
Meadowlea Cl. UB7: Harm 4K 131
Meadow Pk. HP22: Sto M 5D 66
Meadow Ri. HP27: L Grn 1C 80
Meadow Rd. SL7: Marl 7D 96
Meadows, The HP7: Amer 6C 86
HP10: F Hea 1H 107
HP22: W'urch 1F 45
Meadowside HP9: Jord 5D 102
Meadowsweet MK7: Waln 2D 30
Meadow Vw. HP8: D Gil 1E 102
HP18: Long C 7E 56
SL7: Marl 3J 105
UB8: Cowl 3J 127
Meadow Wlk. HP10: T Grn 6J 91
SL8: Bou E 4G 107
Meadow Way HP6: H Hea 2E 84
HP19: Ayle 6E 60
HP20: Ayle 5B 62
LU7: Wing 2C 48
SL6: Dorn R 7B 122
SL6: Fifi 6A 128
Mead Pk. HP15: H Grn 7J 83
Mead Platt HP14: Stoke 5B 72
Mead Rd. UB8: Uxb 5K 121
Meads, The LU6: E Bra 1J 49
SL4: Wind 7J 129
UB8: Cowl 2K 127
Meads Cl. MK13: New B 5A 16
Mead St. HP13: H Wyc 4G 99
Mead Wlk. SL3: Lang 7B 126
Mead Way HP11: W Mar 4F 99
SL1: Slou 3F 123
Meadway HP22: Ovi 4D 44
MK18: Buck 6H 37
Meadway, The MK5: Lough 7A 22
Meadway Pk. SL9: G Cro 6H 111
Meare Estate HP10: Woob G 1K 107
Meavy Cl. HP13: H Wyc 4H 99
Medale Rd. MK6: Bean 2G 29
MEDBOURNE 2J 27

MEDBOURNE 1J 27
Medeswell MK4: Fur 4E 28
Medhurst MK8: T Ash 4J 21
Medland MK6: Wough 7K 23
Medlar Ct. SL2: Slou 6G 125
Medley Cl. LU6: E Bra 1K 49
Medman Cl. UB8: Uxb 7J 121
MEDMENHAM 2B 136
Medway Cl. MK16: New P 2A 18
Meeting Oak La. MK18: Wins 5K 39
Megdale Pl. HP20: Ayle 4J 61
Melbourne Av. SL1: Slou 4A 124
Melbourne Cl. HP21: Ayle 2K 65
Melbourne Rd. HP13: H Wyc 2F 99
Melbourne Ter. MK13: B'lle 6A 16
Melford Grn. HP19: Ayle 3H 61
Melfort Dr. MK2: Blet 4K 33
Melick Rd. MK6: Bean 3H 29
Mellish Ct. MK3: Blet 5F 29
Mellstock Rd. HP21: Ayle 2A 66
Melrose Av. MK3: Blet 5F 29
Melrose Ct. HP13: H Wyc 6B 90
Melrose Wlk. HP21: Ayle 2A 66
Melton MK14: Stan 5C 16
Mendelssohn Gro. MK7: Brow 3E 30
Mendip Cl. SL3: Lang 3A 130
Mendip Way HP13: Down 7K 89
Mendy St. HP11: H Wyc 1A 98
Menmarsh Rd. HP18: Worm 1A 54
Menteith Cl. MK2: Blet 3J 33
MENTMORE 2D 135
Mentmore Cl. HP12: Book 2F 97
Mentmore Ct. MK8: G Hol 6K 21
Mentmore Grn. HP21: Ayle 4K 65
Mentmore Rd. HP12: Book 2F 97
LU7: Ched 1B 50
Menzies Ct. MK5: S Lod 3B 28
Mercers Dr. MK13: B'lle 6B 16
Mercers Mdw. HP22: Wend 2H 69
Mercer Wlk. UB8: Uxb 5J 121
Merchant Pl. MK10: Midd 3A 24
Mercian Way SL1: Slou 6F 123
Mercury Gro. MK8: C'ill 7J 21
Mere Cl. SL7: Marl 7K 105
Meredith Dr. HP19: Ayle 4E 60
Mere Pk. SL7: Marl 7K 105
Mere Rd. SL1: Slou 7D 124
Meriland Ct. MK2: Blet 4A 34
Merlewood Cl. HP11: H Wyc 4A 98
Merlewood Dr. MK5: S Woo 3J 27
Merlin Cen. HP19: Ayle 6H 61
Merlin Cen., The HP12: H Wyc 3J 97
Merlin Cl. SL3: Lang 4B 130
Merlin Wlk. MK6: Eagl 6H 23
Merrivale M. UB7: Yiew 6K 127
Merrydown HP13: Down 6H 89
Merryfields UB8: Uxb 7K 121
UB10: Uxb 7K 121
MERRYMEAD 7A 40
Mersey Cl. MK3: Blet 6E 28
Mersey Way MK3: Blet 6E 28
Merthen Gro. MK4: Tatt 7B 28
MERTON 2A 134
Merton Dr. MK6: Red 3G 29
Merton Rd. HP27: Prin R 6G 71
SL1: Slou 7E 124
Merwin Way SL4: Wind 7F 129
Meryton Ho. SL4: Wind 7J 129
Messenger Cl. HP21: Ayle 1B 66
Metcalfe Gro. MK14: Blak 3H 17
Michaels M. HP19: Ayle 6F 61
Michael's Path SL6: Maid 7H 115
Michigan Dr. MK15: Tong 4J 17
Micholls Av. SL9: C Pet 2J 103
Micholls Cotts. *SL9: C Pet* *3K 103*
(off Micholls Av.)
MICKLEFIELD 2G 99
MICKLEFIELD GREEN 1D 137
Micklefield Rd. HP13: H Wyc 3F 99
Mickleton MK15: D Park 7G 17
Midas Ind. Est. UB8: Uxb 7H 121
Midcroft SL2: Slou 2K 123
Mid Cross La. SL9: C Pet 3K 103
MIDDLE ASSENDON 2A 136
Middlebrook Rd. HP13: Down 6H 89
MIDDLE CLAYDON 1B 134
Middle Cl. HP6: Amer 4D 86
Middle Cres. UB9: Den 5D 112
Middle Dr. HP9: Bea 3F 101
Middle Fld. HP22: West T 4G 67
Middlefield Cl. MK18: Buck 3J 37
MIDDLE GREEN 6J 125
Middle Grn. SL3: Lang 6J 125
Middlegreen Rd. SL3: Lang 7H 125
Middlegreen Trad. Est. SL3: Lang 7H 125
Middle Mdw. HP8: D Gil 1F 103
Middle Rd. HP21: Ayle 7C 62
UB9: Den 5C 112
Middlesex Dr. MK3: Blet 6F 29
Middle Slade MK18: Buck 6H 37
MIDDLETON 3A 24
Middleton MK14: G Lin 6E 16
Middleton Hall MK9: C Key 3F 23
Middleton Swimming Pool 2A 18
Middle Wlk. SL1: Burn 1D 122
Middleway, The HP12: H Wyc 2G 97
MIDDLE WEALD 4C 20
Midhurst Cl. HP21: Ayle 2C 66
Midland Rd. MK46: Oln 2H 7
Midshires Way MK19: H'ope 1J 9
MIDSUMMER 5C 22
Midsummer Arc. MK9: C Key 4E 22
(not continuous)
Midsummer Blvd. MK9: C Key 5C 22
(not continuous)
Midsummer Dr. HP18: G Und 2G 43
Midsummer Pl. MK9: C Key 4E 22
Miersfield HP11: H Wyc 5H 97
Mikern Cl. MK2: Blet 7J 29
Milburn Av. MK6: Old 6E 22
Mildenhall Rd. SL1: Slou 4C 124
Milecastle MK13: Ban 1A 22
Mile Elm SL7: Marl 6A 106
Milennium Point HP19: Ayle 5F 61
Miles Cl. HP21: Ayle 7B 62
MK14: Blak 2G 17
Miles Ct. HP22: Bier 3C 62
Miles End HP21: Ayle 1G 65
Milesmere MK8: T Ash 5H 21
Milestone Cl. HP14: Stoke 5C 72
Milfoil Av. MK14: Conn 2D 22
Milford Av. MK11: S Strat 2B 20
Milford Ct. SL1: Slou 7E 124
Mill Av. UB8: Uxb 7J 121
Millbank SL7: Marl 1K 115
Millbank Pl. MK7: K Hil 6D 24
Millboard Rd. SL8: Bou E 6H 107
Mill Bri. Pl. UB8: Uxb 7J 121
MILLBROOK 3D 133
Millbrook Cl. HP12: H Wyc 7H 89
Millbrook Way SL3: Poy 7E 130
Mill Cl. HP5: Ches 1C 86
HP22: W'rave 6C 48
UB7: W Dra 1K 131
Mill Ct. MK12: W Mil 1E 20
SL2: Slou 6D 124
Milldun Way HP12: H Wyc 2H 97
MILL END 2A 136
Mill End MK12: O Wol 6E 14
Mill End Cl. LU6: E Bra 2K 49
Mill End Cotts. HP7: L Miss 4D 84
Mill End Rd. HP12: H Wyc 1G 97
Millennium Cl. UB8: Uxb 7J 121
Miller Pl. SL9: G Cro 3H 111
Millers Cl. HP18: G Und 2G 43
Millers Way HP19: Ayle 6F 61
Millers Way (H2) MK11: Mil K 3E 20
MK12: Mil K 1H 21
Millfield Av. OX27: M Gib 5C 42
Millfield Cl. OX27: M Gib 5C 42
Millfield Wood Nature Reserve 4B 90
Millfiields HP5: Ches 7A 78
(not continuous)
Millgate HP11: H Wyc 4F 99
Mill Hall *UB8: Cowl* *1K 127*
(off Topping La.)
Millhayes MK14: G Lin 5F 17
Millholm Ri. MK6: Simp 2K 29
Millington Ga. MK15: Will 5K 17
Mill La. HP7: Amer 6J 85
HP8: D Gil 7E 94
HP9: Bea 7G 101
HP14: Stoke 5A 72
(not continuous)
HP16: G Mis 6J 75
HP22: West T 4G 67
HP22: W'rave 7D 48
HP27: Mon R 2F 71
MK11: S Strat 1A 20
MK13: B'lle 6A 16
MK15: Wool 3J 23
MK17: A Gui, W San 2K 31
MK17: Salf 3K 25
MK18: Buck 4G 37
SL3: Hor 7B 130
SL4: Wind 5J 129
SL6: Hur 5D 114
SL6: Tapl 3A 122
SL9: G Cro 4K 111
Mill Mead HP22: Wend 3H 69
Mill M. HP19: Ayle 6G 61
Mill Path HP22: Wend 3H 69
Mill Rd. HP14: Stoke 6A 72
HP18: Oak 6H 53
HP18: Shab 6H 55
MK2: Blet 1K 33
MK19: H'ham 1B 16
SL7: Marl 1J 115
UB7: W Dra 1J 131
Millshot Dr. HP7: Amer 7A 86
Mill Side SL8: Bou E 6J 107
Millside Ct. SL0: Thor 7H 127
Mill Sq. MK12: W Mil 1D 20
Millstream HP22: West T 5G 67
Millstream, The HP11: H Wyc 2C 98
Mill Stream Cl. HP27: Prin R 6F 71
Millstream La. SL1: Slou 6G 123
Millstream Way HP10: Woob G 1K 107
Mill St. HP20: Ayle 5K 61
MK16: New P 7K 11
SL2: Slou 6D 124
SL3: Coln 5D 130
Mill Ter. MK12: W Mil 7E 14
Mill Vw. MK19: Cast 7D 8
Mill Way HP20: Ayle 6H 61
Mill West SL2: Slou 6D 124
Milner Rd. SL1: Burn 3C 122
MILTHORPE 2A 132
Milton Av. SL9: C Pet 2H 111
MILTON BRYAN 3D 133
Milton Cl. SL3: Hor 7A 130
MILTON COMMON 3A 134
Milton Dr. MK16: New P 1A 18
MILTON ERNEST 1D 133
Milton Flds. HP8: D Gil 1F 103
Milton Gdns. HP27: Prin R 6F 71
Milton Gro. MK3: Blet 1F 33
Milton Hill HP8: D Gil 1F 103
Milton Ho. SL9: C Pet 2J 103
MILTON KEYNES 3E 22 (3C 133)
Milton Keynes Central Station (Rail) 5C 22
Milton Keynes Mus. 1H 15
Milton Keynes Rugby Football Ground 2F 21
Milton Keynes Stadium (Greyhound) 2J 29
Milton Keynes Theatre & Art Gallery 3F 23
MILTON KEYNES VILLAGE 4C 24 (3C 133)
Milton Keynes Water Ski Club 4H 17
Milton Lawns HP6: Amer 3B 86
MILTON MALSOR 1B 132
Milton Rd MK16: Bro 3D 24
Milton Rd. HP5: Ches 3K 77
HP21: Ayle 1A 66
HP22: Ast C 2C 68
MK7: Walt H 7B 24
MK10: Bro 3D 24
MK15: Will 6K 17
SL2: Slou 2B 124
Mimosa Ct. *HP21: Ayle* *1G 65*
(off Primrose Dr.)
Mina Av. SL3: Lang 7H 125
Mineral La. HP5: Ches 6A 78
Minerva Gdns. MK7: W Gat 7E 24
Minerva Way HP9: Bea 7H 101
Mines Cl. HP13: Down 4H 89
Ministry Wharf HP14: Saun 5A 80
Minniecroft Rd. SL1: Burn 1D 122
Minorca Gro. MK5: S Broo 3A 28
Minshull Cl. MK18: Buck 3H 37
Minster Way SL3: Lang 7K 125
Minstrel Ct. MK13: B'lle 6B 16
Minton Cl. MK14: Blak 4G 17
Minton Ri. SL6: Tapl 4D 122
Mirador Cres. SL2: Slou 5F 125
Mirrie La. UB9: Den 3C 112
Misbourne Av. HP13: H Wyc 2F 99
SL9: C Pet 3H 103
Misbourne Cl. HP21: Ayle 4J 65
SL9: C Pet 3J 103
Misbourne Ct. *HP7: Amer* *7K 85*
(off Church St.)
SL3: Lang 2A 130
Misbourne Dr. HP16: G Mis 7H 75
Misbourne Mdws. UB9: Den 6C 112
Misbourne Va. SL9: C Pet 3H 103
Missenden Cl. MK18: Wins 6G 39
Missenden Gdns. SL1: Burn 4D 122
Missenden M. *HP16: G Mis* *6G 75*
(off High St.)
Missenden Rd. HP5: Ches 6G 77
HP15: G Kin 3D 82
MK18: Wins 6G 39
Mitcham Pl. MK13: B Com 3D 22
Mitcham Wlk. HP19: Ayle 4F 61
Mitch Cl. HP20: Ayle 7C 62
Mitchell Cl. HP3: Bov 1K 79
SL1: Slou 7J 123
Mitchell Wlk. HP6: Amer 5C 86
Mithras Gdns. MK7: W Gat 1E 30
Mitre Ct. MK18: Buck 5G 37
Mitre St. MK18: Buck 5G 37
MIXBURY 3A 132
Moat Cl. HP16: Pres 7C 74
HP22: Wend 2H 69
Moat Dr. HP16: Pres 6C 74
SL2: Slou 3G 125
Moat End HP22: Bier 2C 62
Moat La. HP16: Pres 6C 74
HP22: A Abb 7H 47
HP22: W'rave 7C 48
OX27: M Gib 6B 42
Moat Pl. UB9: Den 2H 121
MOBWELL 5G 75
Mobwell Ter. HP16: G Mis 5G 75
Moeran Cl. MK7: Brow 2E 30
Mole Run HP13: Down 6G 89
Molyneaux Av. HP3: Bov 1K 79
Molyns M. SL1: Slou 6G 123
Monellan Cres. MK7: Cald 4C 30
Monellan Gro. MK7: Cald 4C 30
(not continuous)
Monet Pl. HP19: Ayle 4D 60
Money La. UB7: W Dra 1K 131
MONEYROW GREEN 3B 136
Monkey Island La. SL6: Bra 1A 128
Monksfield Way SL2: Slou 2J 123
Monks Hollow SL7: Marl 4J 105
Monks Path *HP19: Ayle* *6F 61*
(off Hemp Hill)
MONKS RISBOROUGH 3H 71 (3C 135)
Monks Risborough Station (Rail) 2G 71
Monks Rd. SL4: Wind 7F 129
MONKSTON 5C 24
MONKSTON 4D 24
MONKSTON PARK 5A 24
Monks Way UB7: Harm 4K 131
Monks Way (H3) MK8: Mil K 4G 21
MK12: Mil K 2J 21
MK13: Mil K 2J 21
MK14: Mil K 7C 16
MK15: Mil K 6G 17
Monkton Way HP27: Spee 1G 81
Monmouth Cl. HP19: Ayle 4F 61
Monmouth Gro. MK4: K'ead 6J 27
Monro Av. MK8: C'ill 1J 27
Montagu Dr. MK6: Eagl 6H 23
Montague Pas. UB8: Uxb 5K 121
Montague Rd. HP21: Ayle 7J 61
SL1: Slou 5D 124
UB8: Uxb 5K 121
Montem La. SL1: Slou 6B 124
Montem Sports Cen. 7B 124
Montford M. HP15: Haz 5E 90
Montgomery Cres. MK15: Bolb 5H 17
Montgomery Pl. SL2: Slou 4G 125
Montrose Av. SL1: Slou 4K 123
(not continuous)
Monument La. SL9: C Pet 4J 103
Moon St. MK12: Wolv 7H 15
Moor, The SL7: L Mar 5C 106
MOOR COMMON 5J 73
Moore Cl. SL1: Slou 7K 123
MOOR END
Dunstable 1J 49
Henley-on-Thames 7J 73
Moor End LU6: E Bra 2K 49
Moor End Cl. LU6: E Bra 2K 49
Moor End La. LU6: E Bra 1K 49
Moores Hill MK46: Oln 2H 7
Moores La. SL4: E Wick 2H 129
Moorfield MK17: New L 5D 32
Moorfield Rd. UB8: Cowl 4K 127
UB9: Den 5G 113
Moorfoot MK11: F Sla 2E 20
Moor Furlong SL1: Slou 6G 123
Moorgate MK6: Lead 7F 23
Moorhall Rd. UB9: Hare 4H 113
Moorhen Ct. HP19: Ayle 3K 61
Moorhen Way MK18: Buck 4J 37
Moorhills Cres. LU7: Wing 3D 48
Moorhills Rd. LU7: Wing 2D 48
Moorings, The SL4: Wind 5E 128
MOOR JUNC. 5H 131
Moorland Rd. UB7: Harm 4J 131
Moorlands LU7: Wing 2C 48
Moorlands Rd. LU7: Wing 2D 48
Moor La. HP13: Down 4H 89
UB7: Harm 4J 131
Moor Pk. HP22: Wend 1H 69
LU7: Wing 3C 48
MK3: Blet 7D 28
Moor Rd. HP5: Ches 7A 78
Moorside HP10: Woob G 1A 108
Moors La. HP5: O L'gh 2F 79
Moorstown Ct. SL1: Slou 7C 124
MOP END 7C 84
Mop End La. HP7: Amer 1C 92
Moray Dr. SL2: Slou 4E 124
Moray Pl. MK3: Blet 5F 29
Mordaunts Ct. MK15: Wool 4J 23
Moreau Wlk. SL3: G Grn 4J 125
More Av. HP21: Ayle 7J 61
Morebath Gro. MK4: Fur 3C 28
Moreland Av. SL3: Coln 5C 130
Moreland Cl. SL3: Coln 5C 130
Moreland Dr. SL9: G Cro 5K 111
Morello Dr. SL3: Lang 6K 125
MORETON 3A 134
Moreton Dr. MK18: Buck 1J 37
Moreton La. HP17: Bish 6F 65
MORETON PINKNEY 2A 132
Moreton Rd. MK18: Buck 3H 37
Moreton Way SL1: Slou 6F 123
Morland Dr. MK8: G Far 1H 27
Morley Cl. SL3: Lang 7K 125
Morley Cres. MK7: Brow 3F 31
Morrell Cl. MK5: S Chur 2B 28
Morrice Cl. SL3: Lang 2A 130
Morris Cl. SL9: C Pet 6K 103
Morris Ct. HP21: Ayle 3J 65
Morris M. HP11: W Mar 5G 99
Morrison Ct. MK8: C'ill 1J 27
Morris Pl. SL7: Marl 7H 105
Morris Wlk. MK16: New P 1F 17
Morse Cl. UB9: Hare 1J 113
Mortain Cl. MK7: Cald 4D 30
Morten Gdns. UB9: Den 5G 113
Mortens Wod HP7: Amer 7C 86
Morton Cl. LU7: Pits 5E 50
MK18: N Mar 2B 44
Morton Dr. SL2: Farn C 3G 117
Morton King Cl. HP18: Shab 5H 55
Mortons Fork MK13: Blue B 7K 15
Moseley Rd. HP14: Nap 7G 81

Moses Plat La. HP27: Spee 1F 81
Moss Ct. *HP9: S Grn* *4B 102*
(off Orchard Rd.)
Mossdale MK13: Hee 1B 22
Mossway HP9: Bea 4E 100
MOULSOE 5F 19 (2D 133)
Moundsfield Way SL1: Slou 7G 123
Mount, The MK6: Simp 3A 30
Mountain Ash SL7: Marl 3H 105
Mount Av. MK1: Blet 4K 29
Mountbatten Cl. SL1: Slou 7E 124
Mount Cl. HP12: H Wyc 2J 97
HP22: Ast C 3C 68
SL2: Farn C 2A 118
MOUNT FARM 5J 29
MOUNT FARM 3K 29
Mt. Farm Ind. Est. MK1: Blet 3K 29
Mounthill Av. MK19: O Stra 6A 14
Mt. Hill La. SL9: G Cro 6F 111
Mount La. UB9: Den 7D 112
Mount Nugent HP5: Ches 1J 77
Mount Pl. HP19: Ayle 5J 61
MOUNT PLEASANT 5G 37 (3A 132)
Mt. Pleasant HP14: L End 3K 73
HP22: W'urch 1F 45
LU7: Soul 6H 41
MK6: Simp 3A 30
MK16: S Gold 5C 6
MK17: S Ham 2H 41
MK18: S Clay 3D 42
SL9: C Pet 3J 103
Mt. Pleasant Cl. MK18: Buck 5G 37
Mountsfield Cl. MK16: New P 2J 17
Mount St. HP20: Ayle 6J 61
Mount Way HP27: Prin R 5F 71
Mowbray Rd. HP20: Ayle 4J 61
Mow Mead MK46: Oln 2H 7
Moyleen Ri. SL7: Marl 1G 115
Mozart Cl. MK7: Brow 3E 30
Muddiford La. MK4: Fur 4D 28
Muddy La. SL2: Slou 3C 124
Muirfield Dr. MK3: Blet 7D 28
Mulberry Cl. HP7: Amer 6D 86
Mulberry Ct. HP15: H Grn 7K 83
Mullen Av. MK14: D Barn 2F 23
Mullins Way HP19: Ayle 4D 60
Mullion Pl. MK6: Fish 5G 23
Mumfords La. SL9: C Pet 1E 110
Munces Rd. SL7: Marl 3H 105
MUNDAYDEAN BOTTOM 5D 104
Mundaydean La. SL7: Marl 4D 104
Mundesley Spur SL1: Slou 4C 124
MURCOTT 2A 134
Murrey Cl. MK5: S Lod 2C 28
MURSLEY 2C 40 (1C 135)
Mursley Ct. MK11: S Strat 1D 20
MUSCOTT 1A 132
Musgrave Wlk. HP14: Stoke 5D 72
Musgrove Pl. MK5: S Chur 1K 27
Myddleton Rd. UB8: Uxb 6J 121
Myers Dr. SL2: Farn C 3K 117
Mylne Cl. HP13: Down 7K 89
Mynchen Cl. HP9: Bea 2F 101
Mynchen End HP9: Bea 2F 101
Mynchen Rd. HP9: Bea 3F 101
Myrtle Bank MK12: S Bus 1H 21
Myrtle Cl. SL3: Poy 6E 130
Myrtle Cres. SL2: Slou 5D 124

N

Nag's Head La. HP16: G Mis 2F 83
(not continuous)
Nailzee Cl. SL9: G Cro 5J 111
Nairdwood Cl. HP16: Pres 2E 82
Nairdwood La. HP16: Pres 7D 74
Nairdwood Way HP16: Pres 2E 82
Nairn Ct. MK3: Blet 5E 28
Naisby Dr. MK17: G Bri 7E 34
Nalders Rd. HP5: Ches 3B 78
Nan Aires HP22: W'rave 6B 48
NAPHILL 7H 81 (1B 136)
Naphill Pl. MK13: B Com 3C 22
Napier Rd. HP19: Ayle 6E 60
Napier St. MK2: F Str 7K 29
Nappin Cl. HP19: Ayle 3E 60
Nappins Cl. HP18: Long C 6D 56
Narbeth Dr. HP20: Ayle 6C 62
Narcot La. HP8: D Gil 1E 102
SL9: C Pet 1E 102
Narcot Rd. HP8: D Gil 1E 102
Narcot Way HP8: D Gil 2E 102
Narrow La. HP13: Down 4J 89
Narrow Path MK17: A H'th 4K 31
Naseby Cl. MK16: New P 2G 17
Naseby Ct. MK13: B'lle 7B 16
MK18: Buck 2J 37
NASH 6A 26 (3B 132)
Nash Cl. HP21: Ayle 3B 66
Nash Cft. MK4: Tatt 7B 28
Nashdom La. SL1: Burn 5C 116
Nash Ho. *HP7: Amer* *6E 86*
(off Repton Pl.)
NASH LEE 3C 135
Nash Lee End HP22: Wend 2F 69
Nash Lee Rd. HP22: Wend 4H 69
Nashleigh Ct. *HP5: Ches* *3A 78*
(off Severalls Rd.)
Nashleigh Hill HP5: Ches 3A 78
Nashleigh Ho. HP5: Ches 2C 78
Nash Pl. HP10: T Grn 6H 91
Nash Rd. MK17: G Hor 2J 39
MK17: Whad 5C 26
MK18: T'ough 2D 38
SL3: Lang 2A 130
Nashs Farm HP22: A Abb 7J 47
Nash's Yd. UB8: Uxb 5K 121
Nathanial Cl. MK5: S Chur 2B 28
National Badminton Cen. 5A 22
National Bowl, The 2E 28
National Hockey Stadium & Milton Keynes Dons FC 4C 22
Natwoke Cl. HP9: Bea 3F 101
Neal Cl. SL9: G Cro 6B 112
Neale Cl. HP12: H Wyc 5H 97
Neapland MK6: Bean 2H 29
(not continuous)
Near Town MK46: Oln 4J 7
Near Town Gdns. MK46: Oln 4J 7
Neath Cres. MK3: Blet 5G 29
NEATH HILL 7G 17
NEATH HILL 7G 17
Needham Cl. SL4: Wind 6G 129
Needham Ct. *HP11: H Wyc* *1K 97*
(off Desborough Rd.)
Needlemakers HP18: Long C 5D 56
Nelson Cl. HP7: Winc 4E 92
HP13: H Wyc 3F 99
MK8: C'ill 1J 27
Nelson Ct. MK18: Buck 4G 37
Nelson Rd. HP4: Dag 6H 49
SL4: Wind 7H 129
Nelson St. MK18: Buck 4G 37
Nelson Ter. HP20: Ayle 6J 61
Nene Cl. HP21: Ayle 3H 65
MK16: New P 2K 17
Nene Dr. MK3: Blet 7E 28
Neptune Way SL1: Slou 7G 123
Ness Way MK2: Blet 3K 33
NETHERFIELD 1H 29
NETHERFIELD 7J 23
Nether Gro. MK5: S Broo 4B 28
NETHER HEYFORD 1A 132
Netherwood Rd. HP9: Bea 3F 101
Netley Ct. MK10: Monk 5C 24
NETTLEBED 2A 136
Nettlecombe MK4: Fur 4C 28
NETTLEDEN 2D 135
Nevill Cl. MK19: H'ope 2F 9
Neville Cl. SL2: S Pog 4D 118
Neville Ct. SL1: Burn 1E 122
Nevis Gro. MK2: Blet 3A 34
New Arc. UB8: Uxb 6K 121
Newark Ct. MK7: Cald 4C 30
Newbarn La. HP9: S Grn 2C 102
Newbeach Ho. SL2: Slou 1K 123
Newberry Cres. SL4: Wind 7F 129
Newbery Way SL1: Slou 7B 124
Newbolt Cl. MK16: New P 7F 11
NEW BRADWELL 6A 16
NEW BRADWELL 5B 16
Newbridge Oval MK4: E Val 4B 28
Newbury Ct. MK3: Blet 2D 32
Newby Pl. MK4: E Val 5B 28
New Chilterns HP7: Amer 6C 86
Newchurch Rd. SL2: Slou 3H 123
New Ct. SL7: Marl 7J 105
Newcourt UB8: Cowl 3J 127
New Cut SL1: Burn 2C 122
NEW DENHAM 4H 121 (2D 137)
New Dr. HP13: H Wyc 7E 90
NEW DUSTON 1B 132
Newell Cl. HP21: Ayle 1B 66
NEWELL GREEN 3B 136
Newells Hedge LU7: Pits 4F 51
Newfield Gdns. SL7: Marl 6K 105
Newfield Rd. SL7: Marl 7K 105
Newfield Way SL7: Marl 7K 105
New Footpath *HP5: Ches* *6K 77*
(off Germaine St.)
New Gdn. Dr. UB7: W Dra 7K 127
Newhaven Spur SL2: Slou 2K 123
Newhouse Rd. HP3: Bov 1K 79
NEWINGTON 3A 134
New Inn La. MK18: Gaw 6C 36
Newland Pk. 1K 103
NEWLANDS 2J 23
NEWLANDS 2J 23
Newlands Dr. SL3: Poy 7E 130
Newlands St. HP11: H Wyc 1A 98
Newlyn Pl. MK6: Fish 4G 23
Newmans Cl. MK14: G Lin 4E 16
Newmans Courtyard MK17: Dray P 6B 40
Newmarket Ct. MK10: K'ton 4E 24
New Mdw. HP21: Ayle 1D 66
Newmer Rd. HP12: Book 5F 97
NEW MILL 2D 135
NEWNHAM 1A 132
Newnham Cl. SL2: Slou 6D 124
New Orchard SL0: Ive 4F 127
New Pde. UB7: Yiew 6K 127
New Peachey La. UB8: Cowl 4K 127
New Pond Rd. HP15: H Grn 7J 83
NEWPORT PAGNELL 1K 17 (2C 133)
Newport Rd. MK6: W Grn. 5J 23
MK13: New B 5J 15
MK15: Will 6K 17
MK15: Wool 3J 23
MK16: Chic 4E 12
MK16: Moul 6C 18
MK17: Wave, W San 6F 25
MK19: H'ope 2F 9
MK46: Emb 7H 7
SL2: Slou 2G 123
Newquay Cl. MK4: Tatt 6K 27
New Rd. HP6: Amer 4C 86
HP7: Cole 2H 93
HP8: D Gil 1J 95
HP10: T Grn 7H 91
HP12: Book, H Wyc 1G 97
HP14: Walt A 5F 81
HP15: G Kin 6C 82
HP16: L Kin 2H 83
HP16: Pres 7D 74
HP17: Dint 2G 59
HP22: Ast C, B'land 2B 68
HP22: W'don 7J 45
HP22: West T 1E 66
HP27: L Grn 2D 80
HP27: Prin R 4G 71
(not continuous)
MK17: Dray P 7C 40
MK19: Cast 7D 8
SL3: Lang 1A 130
SL6: Hur 7D 114
SL7: Marl 3H 105
SL8: Bou E 6H 107
New Rd. Cl. HP12: Book 2G 97
New Rd. Gdns. HP12: Book 2G 97
New Row MK46: Lave 2B 6
New Sq. SL1: Slou 7C 124
New Sta. Ho. SL2: Slou 6D 124
New St. HP18: Wadd 5C 52
HP20: Ayle 5J 61
LU7: Ched 2B 50
MK11: S Strat 1B 20
MK18: Ting 2C 36
NEWTON BLOSSOMVILLE 1D 133
Newton Cl. SL3: Lang 7K 125
NEWTON LONGVILLE 5C 32 (3C 133)
NEWTON PURCELL 3A 132
Newton Rd. MK3: Blet 2E 32
MK17: Dray P 4D 40
MK17: S Ham 2H 41
Newton St. MK46: Oln 3J 7
NEWTOWN 4A 78
Newtown Rd. SL7: Marl 6K 105
UB9: Den 4H 121
Newville HP22: W'don 7J 45
New Windsor St. UB8: Uxb 6J 121
NEWYEARS GREEN 2D 137
Newyears Grn. La. UB9: Hare 4K 113
New Zealand Gdns. LU7: Wing 3C 48
Neyland Dr. HP19: Ayle 3H 61
Nicholas Gdns. HP13: H Wyc 7D 90
SL1: Slou 6G 123
Nicholas Mead MK14: G Lin 5F 17
Nicholls SL4: Wind 7E 128
Nicholls Wlk. SL4: Wind 7E 128
Nicholson Gro. MK8: G Far 1J 27
Nickson Ct. HP15: Haz 4G 91
Nicol Cl. SL9: C Pet 6G 103
Nicol End SL9: C Pet 6G 103
Nicol Rd. SL9: C Pet 6G 103
Nielson Ct. MK7: Old P 2F 31
Nightingale Cl. MK18: S Clay 3C 42
Nightingale Ct. HP13: H Wyc 1B 98
SL1: Slou 7E 124
Nightingale Cres. MK13: B'lle 6K 15
Nightingale Ho. MK7: K Par 6C 24
Nightingale Pk. SL2: Farn C 5H 117
Nightingale Pl. MK18: Buck 3J 37
Nightingale Rd. HP5: Ches 3K 77
HP21: Ayle 1K 65
HP22: Wend 3H 69
Nightingales Cnr. *HP7: L Chal* *7G 87*
(off Coke's La.)
Nightingales Ct. HP8: D Gil 7G 87
Nightingales La. HP8: D Gil 1G 95
Nightingale Way UB9: Den 5F 113
Nightingdale Cl. HP15: Haz 2H 91
Nine Acres SL1: Slou 6H 123
Nine Elms Av. UB8: Cowl 3K 127
Nine Elms Cl. UB8: Cowl 3K 127
Nine Stiles Cl. UB9: Den 4H 121
Ninnings Rd. SL9: C Pet 5K 103
Ninnings Way SL9: C Pet 5K 103
Nixey Cl. SL1: Slou 7E 124
Nixons Cl. MK6: Lead 1E 28
Noble Cl. MK15: Penny 6G 17
Noble Ct. *SL2: Slou* *6D 124*
(off Mill St.)
NOBOTTLE 1A 132
NOKE 2A 134
Noon Layer Dr. MK10: Midd 3A 24
Norbrek MK8: T Ash 4J 21
Norelands Dr. SL1: Burn 7E 116
Norfolk Av. SL1: Slou 3A 124
Norfolk Rd. UB8: Uxb 4K 121
Norfolk Ter. HP20: Ayle 5K 61
Norgrove Pk. SL9: G Cro 2J 111
Norland Dr. HP10: F Hea 1J 107
Norman Cres. MK10: Midd 3A 24
Normandy Ct. MK3: Blet 5E 28
Normandy Way MK3: Blet 5E 28
Normans, The SL2: Slou 4F 125
Normill Ter. HP22: Ast C 1H 67
Norrington MK8: T Ash 4J 21
Norris Pl. HP10: Woob G 5C 108
NORTHALL 1F 49 (1D 135)
Northall Cl. LU6: E Bra 1H 49
Northall Rd. LU6: E Bra 1H 49
NORTHAMPTON 1B 132
Northampton Av. SL1: Slou 4A 124
Northampton Rd. MK16: Lath 5K 11
MK19: Cosg, O Stra 5A 14
MK46: Lave 2B 6
NORTH ASCOT 3C 137
Northborough Rd. SL2: Slou 2J 123
Nth. Burnham Cl. SL1: Burn 7D 116
NORTHCHURCH 3D 135
Northcliffe LU6: E Bra 1J 49
North Cl. MK17: Dray P 7C 40
SL4: Wind 6H 129
SL7: Medm 3B 114
North Comn. Rd. UB8: Uxb 3K 121
NORTH CRAWLEY 6K 13 (2D 133)
Nth. Crawley Rd.
MK16: New P, N Craw 2B 18
North Cft. MK18: Wins 6J 39
Northcroft HP10: Woob G 2A 108
HP22: W'don 7J 45
MK5: S Lod 2B 28
SL2: Slou 2K 123
Nth. Down Rd. SL9: C Pet 4J 103
North Dr. HP9: Bea 1C 108
HP13: H Wyc 7E 90
HP21: Ayle 2K 65
SL2: S Pog 1C 124
Nth. Eastern Rd. HP19: Ayle 4H 61
Nth. Eighth St. MK9: C Key 3E 22
NORTH ELDER 5C 22
Nth. Eleventh St. MK9: C Key 3E 22
NORTHEND 1A 136
NORTH END
Buckingham 2B 42
Leighton 1B 46
Northend Cl. HP10: F Hea 2J 107
North End Rd. HP22: Q'ton 5H 43
MK18: S Clay 2B 42
Northend Sq. MK18: Buck 3H 37
Northern Hgts. SL8: Bou E 4H 107
Northern Rd. HP19: Ayle 5H 61
SL2: Slou 2B 124
Northern Woods HP10: F Hea 2J 107
NORTHFIELD 1B 24
NORTHFIELD 1C 24
Northfield Dr. MK15: Nort 1B 24
Northfield Rd. HP20: Ayle 6C 62
HP27: Prin R 4H 71
SL4: E Wick 2H 129
Nth. Fifth St. MK9: C Key 4D 22
Nth. Fourteenth St. MK9: C Key 2F 23
Nth. Fourth St. MK9: C Key 4C 22
North Ga. MK2: Blet 6J 29
NORTH GRAFTON 4C 22
North Grn. SL1: Slou 5C 124
North Hill HP18: Bril 2H 53
Northlands Rd. MK18: Ads 6E 38
North La. MK7: Walt H 7A 24
NORTH LEE 3C 135
North Lee La. HP22: Terr 7K 65
Northleigh MK4: Fur 5D 28
North Links Rd. HP10: F Hea 7H 99
NORTH MARSTON 2B 44 (1B 134)
North Marston La. HP22: W'urch 5E 44
Northmead Rd. SL2: Slou 2H 123
Northmill HP27: Prin R 5E 70
Nth. Mill Rd. HP27: Bled 3A 70
Nth. Ninth St. MK9: C Key 3E 22
NORTHOLT 2D 137
Northolt Rd. TW6: L Hea 6K 131
Nth. Orbital Rd. UB9: Den 3G 113
NORTH OVERGATE 1G 23
North Pk. SL0: R Pk 1C 130
SL9: C Pet 1J 111
North Ridge MK6: Eagl 5H 23
North Rd. HP6: Amer 3A 86
HP15: W End 3D 90
North Row MK9: C Key 4C 22
(not continuous)
SL3: Fulm 2J 119
NORTH SAXON 3D 22
NORTH SECKLOW 3E 22
Nth. Second St. MK9: C Key 4C 22
Nth. Seventh St. MK9: C Key 4D 22
Nth. Sixth St. MK9: C Key 4D 22
NORTH SKELDON 2G 23
North Sq. MK16: New P 7K 11
North St. MK2: Blet 6J 29
MK13: New B 6A 16
MK19: Cast 7D 8
Nth. Tenth St. MK9: C Key 3E 22
Nth. Third St. MK9: C Key 4C 22
Nth. Thirteenth St. MK9: C Key 2F 23
Nth. Twelfth St. MK9: C Key 3F 23
Northumberland Av. HP21: Ayle 1C 66

NORTH WESTON 7K 55 (3A 134)
Northwich MK6: Wough 7K 23
Northwick Rd. MK10: Monk P 5A 24
NORTH WITAN 4C 22
NORTHWOOD 1D 137
Northwood Rd. TW6: L Hea 6K 131
Nortoft Rd. SL9: C Pet 4K 103
NORTON 1A 132
Norton Leys MK7: W Gat 7E 24
Norton Rd. UB8: Uxb 1K 127
Nortons, The MK7: Cald 4C 30
Norton's Pl. MK18: Buck 4G 37
Norvic Rd. HP23: M'rth 7C 50
Norway Dr. SL2: Slou 3F 125
Norwood Cl. HP20: Ayle 4A 62
Norwood Ct. HP7: Amer 7K 85
Norwood La. MK16: New P 2J 17
SL0: Ive 2D 126
Norwood Rd. HP10: Loud 6H 99
Nottingham Gro. MK3: Blet 6E 28
Nottingham Ho. *HP13: H Wyc* 1F 99
(off Gayhurst Rd.)
Nova Lodge MK4: E Val 5B 28
Novello Cft. MK7: Old P 3F 31
NUFFIELD 2A 136
Nugent Ct. *HP5: Ches* 2J 77
(off Hiving's Hill)
SL7: Marl 6K 105
NUNEHAM COURTENAY 3A 134
Nuneham Gro. MK4: West 4K 27
NUP END 6C 48
Nup End Cl. HP22: W'rave 6C 48
Nup End La. HP22: W'rave 6B 48
Nurseries, The LU6: E Bra 1J 49
Nursery Cl. HP7: Amer 6C 86
HP21: Ayle 2H 65
Nursery Ct. HP12: H Wyc 2H 97
Nursery Dr. HP14: L End 3K 73
Nursery Gdns. MK13: B'ell 2A 22
Nursery La. HP10: T Grn 7J 91
SL3: Lang 6H 125
UB8: Cowl 2K 127
Nursery Rd. SL6: Tapl 4D 122
Nursery Wlk. SL7: Marl 1F 115
Nursery Waye UB8: Uxb 6K 121
Nutfield La. HP11: H Wyc 7K 89
Nuthatch HP19: Ayle 3A 62
Nutkins Way HP5: Ches 3A 78
Nutkin Wlk. UB8: Uxb 5K 121
Nutmeg Cl. MK7: Waln 2D 30
Nymans Ga. MK4: West 6J 27

O

Oak Ct. *MK9: C Key* 4E 22
(off Midsummer Pl.)
Oak Cres. HP12: Book 4G 97
Oakdene HP9: Bea 5G 101
Oakdown Cres. MK46: Oln 4H 7
Oak End Dr. SL0: I Hea 7C 120
Oak End Way SL9: G Cro 3K 111
Oakengrove *HP16: Pres* 1C 82
(off Lodge La.)
Oakengrove Cl. HP15: H Grn 1J 91
Oakengrove La. HP15: Haz 4H 91
Oakengrove Rd. HP15: Haz 4G 91
(not continuous)
Oaken Head MK4: E Val 5C 28
Oak Farm MK16: Tyr 1E 10
Oak Farm Rare Breeds Pk. 6E 62
Oak Fld. HP5: Ches 4K 77
Oakfield Av. SL1: Slou 6K 123
Oakfield Cl. HP6: Amer 4A 86
Oakfield Cnr. *HP6: Amer* 5A 86
(off Chesham Rd.)
Oakfield Rd. HP20: Ayle 6B 62
SL8: Bou E 6G 107
Oak Grn. HP21: Ayle 7H 61
OAKGROVE 5B 24
OAKGROVE 5B 24
Oakham Ri. MK4: K'ead 6J 27
OAKHILL 2H 27
OAKHILL 2H 27
Oakhill Cl. MK5: S Chur 1J 27
Oakhill La. MK19: Calv 5E 20
Oakhill Rd. MK5: O'ill 3H 27
MK5: S Chur 1K 27
Oakingham Ct. HP11: W Mar 5H 99
Oakington Av. HP6: L Chal 6H 87
Oaklands Ct. *HP6: Amer* 5A 86
(off Chesham Rd.)
Oakland Way HP10: F Hea 7G 99
Oak La. SL4: Wind 6J 129
OAKLEY
Aylesbury 5H 53 (2A 134)
Bedford 1D 133
Oakley HP10: Woob G 2B 108
Oakley Ct. HP11: W Mar 5H 99
SL4: W Oak 4C 128
Oakley Cres. SL1: Slou 5C 124
Oakley Gdns. MK15: D Park 1H 23
OAKLEY GREEN 7D 128 (3C 137)
Oakley Grn. Rd. SL4: Oak G, W Oak 7A 128
(not continuous)
Oakley Rd. HP18: Bril 4G 53
Oakridge MK4: Fur 3E 28
Oakridge Pl. SL2: Farn C 2A 118
Oakridge Rd. HP11: H Wyc 1J 97
Oak Rd. HP27: Prin R 5H 71
Oakshott Av. HP14: Nap 1J 89
Oakside UB9: Den 4H 121
Oak St. HP11: H Wyc 4C 98
Oak Stubbs La. SL6: Dorn R 7B 122
Oak Tree Av. SL7: Marl 6H 105
Oaktree Cl. HP10: T Grn 5H 91
SL7: Marl 6H 105
Oaktree Ct. MK15: Will 6J 17
Oak Tree Dr. HP14: L End 3A 96
Oaktree Dr. SL3: Lang 3B 130
Oak Tree Rd. SL7: Marl 5H 105
Oak Vw. HP15: G Kin 6D 82
Oakview HP6: H Hea 2F 85
Oakway HP6: Amer 2K 85
MK18: Wins 6J 39
Oakwood HP10: F Hea 6F 99
Oakwood Dr. MK2: Blet 1A 34
Oakworth Av. MK10: Bro 2C 24
Oat Cl. HP21: Ayle 4H 65
Oatlands Dr. SL1: Slou 4B 124
Oban Ct. SL1: Slou 7B 124
Observatory Shop. Cen., The
SL1: Slou 7E 124
Octagon, The *HP11: H Wyc* 1A 98
(off Oxford St.)
Octagon Arc. HP11: H Wyc 1A 98
Octagon Pde. *HP11: H Wyc* 1A 98
(off Abbey Way)
Octavian Dr. MK13: Ban 1K 21
ODDINGTON 2A 134
Oddley La. HP27: Saun 7D 70
Odds Farm Est. HP10: Woob G 5D 108
Odds Farm Pk. 5D 108
ODELL 1D 133
Odell Cl. MK6: W Grn. 6J 23
Odencroft Rd. SL2: Slou 1J 123
Odeon Cinema
Aylesbury 6K 61
Gerrards Cross 3J 111
Uxbridge 6K 121
Odyssey Health Club 2A 108
Offas La. MK18: Wins 5K 39
Ogilvie Rd. HP12: H Wyc 1J 97
O'Grady Way HP19: Ayle 3F 61
Old Airfield Ind. Est. HP23: Long M 3A 50
Old Amersham Rd. SL9: G Cro 6B 112
Old Bakery Ct. SL0: Ive 4F 127
Old Barn Cl. MK18: Gaw 6D 36
Old Beaconsfield Rd. SL2: Farn C 4A 118
Old Bell's Ct. *HP5: Ches* 6K 77
(off Church St.)
Old Brewery Cl. HP21: Ayle 7K 61
OLDBROOK 6E 22
Oldbrook Blvd. MK6: Old 6E 22
Old Burrs HP21: Ayle 4J 65
Oldbury Gro. HP9: Bea 3F 101
Oldcastle Cft. MK4: Tatt 6A 28
Old Coach Dr. HP11: W Mar 4G 99
Old Crown SL1: Slou 7D 124
Old Dean HP3: Bov 2K 79
Olde Bell Cl. MK17: S Ham 2H 41
Olde Bell La. MK5: Lough 7A 22
OLD END 5A 38
Old End MK18: Pad 6A 38
Old English Cl. MK17: Nas 6A 26
Old Farm LU7: Pits 5F 51
Old Farm Cl. HP9: Bea 3E 100
HP18: Worm 3C 54
OLD FARM PARK 1F 31
Old Farm Rd. HP13: Down 5J 89
UB7: W Dra 7K 127
Old Field Cl. HP6: L Chal 6J 87
Old Fives Ct. SL1: Burn 1D 122
Old Forge Cl. MK18: Ting 2C 36
Old Forge Gdns. HP22: Bier 2C 62
Old Forge Rd. HP10: Loud 6J 99
Old Gaol, The 3H 37
Old Groveway MK6: Simp 2K 29
Oldhams Mdw. HP20: Ayle 4A 62
Old Harden Waye HP13: H Wyc 6E 90
Old Horns La. SL7: Book 5E 96
Oldhouse Cl. HP11: H Wyc 5J 97
Old Ho. Ct. SL3: Wex 3H 125
Old Jordans Meeting House 5C 102
Old Kiln Rd. HP10: F Hea 1G 107
HP10: T Grn 5J 91
Old Lodge Dr. HP9: Bea 7G 101
Old Manor Cl. MK17: Whad 6F 27
Oldmanor Cl. HP27: Ask 1H 71
Old Marsh La. SL6: Tapl 7B 122
Old Mead SL9: C Pet 4J 103
Old Mews, The MK46: Oln 3H 7
Old Mill Cl. HP17: Hadd 6C 58
Old Mill Furlong MK18: Wins 5J 39
Old Mill La. SL6: Bra 1A 128
UB8: Cowl 4H 127
Old Mill Rd. UB9: Den 1G 121
Old Moor La. HP10: Woob G 1A 108
Old Nursery Ct. SL2: Hedg 7A 110
Old Orchards HP22: Bier 3B 62
Old Oxford Rd. HP14: Pidd 6A 88
Old Papermill Cl. HP10: Woob G 1A 108
Old Plough Cl. HP18: Che 2H 57
Old Rectory La. UB9: Den 5E 112
Old Risborough Rd. HP22: Sto M 7B 66
Old Sax La. HP5: Char 1F 77
Old School, The MK18: S Clay 2B 42
Old School Cl. HP14: Stoke 6C 72
HP22: Halt 6K 67
Old School Cotts. HP5: Whel 1H 79
Old School Ct. LU6: E Bra 1K 49
MK18: Buck 4G 37
Old School La. MK17: S Ham 1G 41
Old Slade La. SL0: R Pk 1E 130
Old Stable Yd., The *MK18: Wins* 6H 39
(off Horn St.)
Old Station Cl. MK18: Wins 4J 39
Old Station Way HP10: Woob G 4A 108
Old Stoke Rd. HP21: Ayle 2K 65
OLD STRATFORD 6A 14 (2B 132)
Old Tanyard Cl. MK18: Wins 6H 39
Old Town Cl. HP9: Bea 7G 101
Old Town Farm HP16: G Mis 6G 75
Old Uxbridge Rd. WD3: W Hyd 1F 113
Old Vicarage Way HP10: Woob G 5A 108
Old Watery La. HP10: Woob G 1A 108
Oldway La. SL1: Slou 5E 122
(not continuous)
Old Windmill Way HP18: Long C 5C 56
OLD WINDSOR 3C 137
OLD WOLVERTON 6E 14
OLD WOLVERTON 7E 14
Old Wolverton Rd. MK12: O Wol 6E 14
Oliffe Cl. HP20: Ayle 3J 61
Oliffe Way HP20: Ayle 3J 61
Oliver Rd. MK2: Blet 7J 29
Oliver's Paddock SL7: Marl 4H 105
Olivia Dr. SL3: Lang 3A 130
Olivier Way HP20: Ayle 6B 62
OLNEY 4H 7 (1C 133)
Olney Rd. MK46: Emb 7H 7
MK46: Lave 3B 6
O'Neill Rd. MK8: G Far 1H 27
One Pin La. SL2: Farn C 2A 118
One Tree La. HP9: Bea 5G 101
Onslow Ct. MK7: Cald 3C 30
Onslow Gdns. HP13: H Wyc 1E 98
Onslow Mills Trad. Est. UB7: Yiew 5K 127
Opal Ct. SL3: Wex 2G 125
Opal Dr. MK15: F Mil 2A 24
Opeck's Cl. SL2: S Pog 2F 125
Open Air Theatre 3G 23
Opendale Rd. SL1: Burn 3D 122
Oram Ct. SL7: Marl 7H 105
Orbison Ct. MK8: C'ill 7H 21
Orchard, The HP10: F Hea 2H 107
HP14: Nap 1J 89
HP15: Haz 1G 91
HP22: Ast C 2B 68
HP22: Halt 7K 67
SL7: Marl 6J 105
Orchard Av. SL1: Slou 3F 123
SL4: Wind 6J 129
Orchard Cl. HP9: Bea 5F 101
HP14: H Vall 7A 82
HP18: Oak 6H 53
HP18: Wadd 5C 52
HP20: Ayle 3A 62
HP22: Sto M 5C 66
(not continuous)
HP22: Wend 2G 69
HP22: W'rave 6C 48
HP27: Long 1C 70
MK3: Blet 1F 33
MK17: New L 5C 32
UB9: Den 4H 121
Orchard Cotts. HP7: Winc 4E 92
Orchard Ct. UB7: Long 5J 131
Orchard Dr. HP10: Woob G 5K 107
HP15: Haz 4G 91
HP22: Ast C 2B 68
UB8: Cowl 2K 127
Orchard End HP15: Haz 1H 91
LU6: Edle 2J 49
Orchard End Av. HP7: Amer 6D 86
Orchard Ga. SL2: Farn C 3A 118
Orchard Gro. HP10: F Hea 2H 107
SL9: C Pet 6G 103
Orchard Ho. MK12: Wolv 7H 15
SL8: Bou E 5G 107
Orchard La. HP6: Amer 5B 86
HP16: Pres 7C 74
LU7: Stew 5C 46
ORCHARD LEIGH 2E 78
Orchard M. *HP9: S Grn* 4B 102
(off Orchard Rd.)
Orchard Mill SL8: Bou E 7H 107
Orchard Pk. HP15: H Grn 1J 91
Orchard Pl. HP27: Mon R 3H 71
UB8: Uxb 5K 121
Orchard Ri. MK46: Oln 4H 7
Orchard Rd. HP8: D Gil 7G 95
HP9: Bea 7H 101
HP9: S Grn 3A 102
HP13: H Wyc 3F 99
Orchards, The HP16: L Kin 4G 83
HP17: Sto 2B 64
Orchards Res. Pk. SL3: Lang 6K 125
Orchard Vw. UB8: Cowl 2K 127
Orchardville SL1: Burn 2D 122
Orchard Wlk. MK46: Lave 3C 6
Orchard Way HP15: H Grn 1J 91
HP20: Ayle 4A 62
LU6: E Bra 1K 49
LU7: Pits 4G 51
LU7: Wing 3C 48
MK16: N Craw 6J 13
MK16: S Gold 6C 6
SL3: Lang 6J 125
Orchard Waye UB8: Uxb 7K 121
Orchehill Av. SL9: G Cro 2H 111
Orchehill Ri. SL9: G Cro 3J 111
Orford Ct. MK5: S Chur 1A 28
Oriel Cl. MK12: Wolv 7F 15
Orkney Cl. LU7: Stew 4C 46
MK3: Blet 5F 29
Orkney Ct. SL6: Tapl 5A 116
Ormesby Cl. HP21: Ayle 2B 66
Ormonde MK14: Stan 6D 16
Ormsgill Ct. MK13: Hee 1B 22
Orne Gdns. MK15: Bolb 6G 17
Orpington Gro. MK5: S Broo 3B 28
Ortensia Dr. MK7: W Gat 7E 24
Orwell Cl. HP21: Ayle 3J 65
MK16: New P 7F 11
Orwell Dr. HP21: Ayle 3J 65
Osborne Rd. SL4: Wind 7K 129
UB8: Uxb 5J 121
Osborne St. MK2: Blet 1J 33
MK12: Wolv 7H 15
SL1: Slou 7D 124
Osborn's Ct. MK46: Oln 4H 7
Osier La. MK5: S Lod 3B 28
Osier Way HP20: Ayle 6A 62
MK18: Buck 6G 37
Osprey, The HP19: Ayle 2K 61
Osprey Cl. MK6: Eagl 6G 23
UB7: W Dra 7K 127
Osprey Wlk. HP19: Ayle 2K 61
MK18: Buck 5K 37
OSTERLEY 3D 137
Osterley Cl. MK16: New P 2J 17
Ostlers Ct. HP11: W Mar 4G 99
Ostlers La. MK11: S Strat 7B 14
Otterburn Cres. MK5: O'ill 2H 27
Otter Cl. MK3: Blet 6D 28
Otterfield Rd. UB7: Yiew 5K 127
Otters Brook MK18: Buck 5J 37
Otway Cl. HP21: Ayle 4K 65
Oulton Cl. HP21: Ayle 2B 66
Ousebank St. MK16: New P 7K 11
Ousebank Way MK11: S Strat 1B 20
Outfield Rd. SL9: C Pet 5H 103
Outlook Dr. HP8: D Gil 1H 103
Ouzel Cl. MK3: Blet 6E 28
Oval, The MK6: Old 7E 22
Oval Way SL9: G Cro 2J 111
Overdale Rd. HP5: Ches 2K 77
Overdales HP15: Haz 4F 91
Overend Cl. MK13: B'ell 2A 22
Overgate MK9: Camp 1H 23
(not continuous)
Over Hampden HP16: Pres 6C 74
Overhills MK46: Oln 3G 7
Overn Av. MK18: Buck 3G 37
Overn Cl. MK18: Buck 3H 37
Overn Cres. MK18: Buck 3G 37
Overshot Ho. HP10: Loud 6H 99
Oversley Ct. MK14: G Par 4G 17
Overstrand HP22: Ast C 2B 68
Overstreet (V9) MK14: Mil K 6F 17
Over The Misbourne Rd. SL9: G Cro 4A 112
UB9: Den 4B 112
Oville Ct. MK5: S Chur 2A 28
OVING 5C 44 (1B 134)
Oving Rd. HP22: W'urch 5E 44
Ovitts Cl. MK18: Wins 5J 39
Owl Cl. HP19: Ayle 3A 62
Owlsears Cl. HP9: Bea 4F 101
OWLSWICK 3B 134
Owlswick La. HP27: Owls 1D 70
Oxfield Pk. Dr. MK19: O Stra 6A 14
OXFORD 3A 134
Oxford Av. SL1: Burn 7D 116
SL1: Slou 3H 123
Oxford Gdns. UB9: Den 1F 121
Oxford Rd. HP9: Bea 1C 108
HP11: H Wyc 1A 98
HP14: Pidd 6A 88
HP14: Stoke 4A 72
HP17: Sto, Hart 2A 64
HP18: Oak 5H 53
HP19: Ayle 7G 61
HP21: Ayle 7G 61
SL4: Wind 6K 129
SL7: Marl 7G 105
SL9: G Cro 2D 110
UB8: Uxb 3H 121
UB9: Den 3H 111
Oxford St. HP11: H Wyc 1A 98
HP16: L Com 1K 75
MK2: Blet 7J 29
MK11: S Strat 1B 20
MK12: Wolv 7H 15
OXHEY 1D 137
Oxhouse Ct. MK5: S Broo 4A 28
OXLEY PARK 5J 27
OXLEY PARK 4K 27

Oxleys MK46: Oln 3G 7
Oxman La. MK12: Gree 1E 20
Oxwich Gro. MK4: Tatt 7B 28

P

Packet Boat La. UB8: Cowl 4H 127
Packhorse Rd. SL9: G Cro 2J 111
Packway, The SL6: Tapl 4A 116
PADBURY 6A 38 (3B 132)
Padbury Oaks UB7: Long 6H 131
Padcroft Rd. UB7: Yiew 6K 127
Paddock, The HP21: Ayle 7D 62
SL9: C Pet 3J 103
Paddock Cl. MK14: G Lin 5E 16
Paddocks, The HP12: Book 5F 97
HP16: Pres 1C 82
HP17: Hadd 7C 58
HP22: Wend 3H 69
MK18: S Clay 2B 42
MK46: Emb 7G 7
SL7: Marl 7K 105
(off Savill Way)
Paddocks End HP9: S Grn 4A 102
Paddock Way MK2: F Str 6K 29
Padstow Av. MK6: Fish 5F 23
Padstow Cl. HP20: Ayle 5A 62
SL3: Lang 7J 125
PAGE HILL 2J 37
Page Hill Av. MK18: Buck 3J 37
Pages La. UB8: Uxb 4J 121
Paget Cl. SL7: Marl 5K 105
Paget Ho. *SL9: C Pet 2J 103*
(off Micholls Av.)
Paggs Ct. MK16: New P 1K 17
PAGODA 1J 23
Paines Orchard LU7: Ched 1B 50
Pakenham Cl. HP19: Ayle 6E 60
Palace Cl. SL1: Slou 6H 123
Palace Sq. MK6: Lead 7F 23
PALEY STREET 3B 136
Palliser Rd. HP8: D Gil 1F 103
Palmer Av. HP19: Ayle 5H 61
Palmers Moor MK18: T'ough 2C 38
Palmer's Moor La. SL0: Ive 2G 127
Palmers Rd. MK46: Oln 4J 7
Palmerston Av. SL3: Slou 7F 125
Pank Ridge Dr. HP16: Pres 6C 74
Pannier Pl. MK14: D Barn 1G 23
Panters Cl. MK17: Nas 6A 26
Pantile Row SL3: Lang 2A 130
Pantile Wlk. UB8: Uxb 5J 121
Papermakers Lodge HP11: H Wyc 3F 99
Paprika Ct. MK7: Waln 2D 30
Parade, The SL4: Wind 6F 129
SL8: Bou E 6G 107
Parade Ct. SL8: Bou E 5G 107
Paradise MK17: New L 4D 32
Parchment Cl. HP6: Amer 4C 86
Parish La. SL2: Farn C 7K 109
Parish Piece HP15: H Grn 7J 83
Park & Ride
Milton Keynes 1C 24
Park Av. HP10: Woob G 1A 108
MK16: New P 1H 17
Park Cl. HP14: L End 3A 96
MK19: Cosg 3C 14
PARK CORNER 2A 136
Park Cnr. SL4: Wind 7G 129
Park Ct. UB8: Uxb 6K 121
Parker Cl. MK13: B'lle 7A 16
Parker Knoll Way HP13: H Wyc 7A 90
Parker Wlk. HP19: Ayle 3J 61
Park Farm HP14: L End 3A 96
Park Farm Rd. HP12: H Wyc 6F 89
Parkfield Av. HP6: Amer 4B 86
Parkfield Barn MK16: Tyr 1E 10
Parkfield Ri. HP27: Prin R 6G 71
Park Gdns. MK3: Blet 6G 29
Park Ga. LU7: Wing 4C 48
Parkgate SL1: Burn 2E 122
Park Gro. HP8: D Gil 1H 95
Parkhouse Bus. Cen. HP12: H Wyc 7J 89
Park Ho. Dr. MK5: S Chur 1K 27
Parklands MK14: G Lin 4D 16
Park La. HP9: Bea 7H 101
HP14: L End 3K 73
HP14: Stoke 5C 72
HP15: Haz 3G 91
SL1: Burn 7G 109
SL3: Hor 7A 130
Park La. Ct. HP14: Stoke 5C 72
Park Lawn SL2: Farn R 1A 124
Park Mdw. HP27: Prin R 5F 71
Parkminster MK10: Monk 5C 24
Park Pde. Cen., The HP15: Haz 2G 91
Park Pl. HP6: Amer 5D 86
HP9: S Grn 3B 102
Park Rd. HP5: Ches 5K 77
HP6: Amer 4D 86
MK11: S Strat 1B 20
MK16: Sher 2C 12
MK18: Wins 5H 39
MK19: H'ope 2F 9
SL2: Farn R, S Pog 7A 118
UB8: Uxb 5K 121
Park Rd. E. UB10: Uxb 7K 121
Park Rd. Sth. MK18: Wins 6H 39
Parkside HP14: Walt A 5F 81
MK4: Fur 4E 28
SL9: G Cro 3K 111
Park St. HP20: Ayle 5K 61
HP27: Prin R 5G 71
SL1: Slou 7D 124
(not continuous)
SL3: Coln 6D 130
Park St. Ind. Est. HP20: Ayle 5A 62
Park Vw. HP22: Ast C 3B 68
MK16: New P 1K 17
UB7: Yiew 5K 127
Parkview HP10: F Hea 2H 107
Parkview Chase SL1: Slou 4G 123
Parkview Cotts. HP7: Amer 4E 84
Park Vw. Ct. HP12: H Wyc 7H 89
Parkway MK17: Bow B 5F 31
MK17: W San 1J 31
SL7: Marl 5A 106
Parkway, The SL0: I Hea 7C 120
Parkwood HP14: Walt A 4D 80
Parlaunt Rd. SL3: Lang 2A 130
Parliament Cl. HP16: Pres 6B 74
Parliament La. SL1: Burn 5B 116
Parmiter Cl. HP19: Ayle 6G 61
PARMOOR 2A 136
Parmoor La. RG9: Fri 7G 73
Parneleys MK10: M Vill 4B 24
Parrish's Piece HP22: H'ick 5H 45
Parrock La. MK10: M Vill 4C 24
Parrot Cl. HP21: Ayle 1G 65
Parrs Rd. HP14: Stoke 6C 72
Parry Cotts. *SL9: C Pet 2J 103*
(off Chesham La.)
Parry Grn. Nth. SL3: Lang 2A 130
Parry Grn. Sth. SL3: Lang 2A 130
Parsley Cl. HP22: Ast C 2K 67
MK7: Waln 2D 30
Parslow Cl. HP21: Ayle 4J 65
Parslow Ct. *HP21: Ayle 4J 65*
(off Sheridan Cl.)
PARSLOW'S HILLOCK 7K 71
Parsonage Cl. HP13: H Wyc 2C 98
Parsonage Farm HP22: W'rave 6C 48
Parsonage Gdns. SL7: Marl 1J 115
Parsonage La. SL2: Farn C, Farn R 4A 118
SL4: Wind 6J 129
Parsonage Pl. HP7: Amer 6A 86
Parsonage Rd. HP8: D Gil 1F 103
Parson Cl. MK18: Wins 6H 39
Parsons Cl. LU7: Stew 4C 46
Parsons Cres. MK5: S Lod 2C 28
Parson's Fee HP20: Ayle 6J 61
Parsons La. HP22: Bier 3C 62
Parsons Wlk. HP15: H Grn 1J 91
Parson's Wood La. SL2: Farn C 5B 118
Parton Cl. HP22: Wend 3G 69
Parton Rd. HP20: Ayle 6C 62
Partridge Cl. HP5: Ches 2C 78
MK18: Buck 5K 37
Partridge Way HP13: Down 5G 89
HP19: Ayle 3A 62
Pascal Dr. MK5: Medb 2J 27
Passalewe La. MK7: W Gat 7E 24
PASSENHAM 3A 20 (3B 132)
Passmore MK6: T Bri 7J 23
Passmore Edwards Ho. SL9: C Pet 3J 103
Pastern Pl. MK14: D Barn 1G 23
Pastures, The HP13: Down 5H 89
HP20: Ayle 4C 62
LU6: Edle 3K 49
Patches Fld. SL7: Marl 4J 105
PATCHETTS GREEN 1D 137
Pateman Cl. MK18: Buck 3F 37
Paterson Rd. HP21: Ayle 7H 61
Patricia Cl. SL1: Slou 5G 123
Patrick Way HP21: Ayle 2B 66
Patrington Cl. UB8: Cowl 1J 127
Patriot Dr. MK13: Rook 4B 22
Patrons Dr. UB9: Den 4F 113
Patrons Way W. UB9: Den 4F 113
Patterson Ct. HP10: Woob G 2A 108
Patterson Rd. HP5: Ches 2K 77
PATTISHALL 1A 132
Pattison La. MK15: Wool 3J 23
PAULERSPURY 2B 132
Pauls Hill HP10: Pen 1B 100
Paul's Row HP11: H Wyc 2B 98
PAVENHAM 1D 133
Pavers Ct. HP21: Ayle 4J 65
Pavilion Cl. HP20: Ayle 6B 62
Pavilions, The UB8: Uxb 5J 121
Pavilion Way HP6: L Chal 6G 87
Paxton Av. SL1: Slou 7A 124
Paxton Cl. MK46: Oln 4H 7
Paxton Cres. MK5: S Lod 2B 28
Paynes Dr. MK5: Lough 6A 22
Peace Rd. SL3: Wex 1K 125
Peachey Cl. UB8: Cowl 3K 127
Peachey La. UB8: Cowl 3K 127
Peacock Hay MK4: E Val 5C 28
Peacock Rd. SL7: Marl 6A 106
Pearce Cl. HP21: Ayle 3K 65
Pearce Rd. HP5: Ches 3K 77
Pearl Gdns. SL1: Slou 6K 123
Pearman Ho. *SL9: C Pet 2J 103*
(off Micholls Av.)
Pearse Gro. MK7: Walt P 3C 30
Pearson Cl. HP19: Ayle 1G 65
PEARTREE BRIDGE 6J 23
Pear Tree Cl. HP7: Amer 6D 86
HP9: S Grn 4A 102
Peartree Cl. SL1: Slou 6H 123
Pear Tree Ct. HP15: H Grn 1J 91
Pear Tree Ind. Units OX27: M Gib 6B 42
Pear Tree La. MK6: Coff 7F 23
Peartrees UB7: Yiew 5K 127
Peascroft HP18: Long C 6D 56
Peatey Ct. HP13: H Wyc 2D 98
Pebblemoor LU6: Edle 3J 49
Peckover Ct. MK8: G Hol 5K 21
Pecks Farm Cl. HP22: Bier 2D 62
Peddle Ct. HP11: H Wyc 1K 97
PEDNOR BOTTOM 2F 77
Pednor Bottom HP5: Ches 2D 76
PEDNORMEAD END 6K 77
Pednormead End HP5: Ches 6K 77
Pednor Rd. HP5: Ches 3F 77
Peeble La. HP20: Ayle 6J 61
Peebles Pl. MK3: Blet 4F 29
Peel Cl. SL4: Wind 7K 129
Peel Ct. SL1: Slou 3K 123
Peel Rd. MK12: Wolv 7G 15
Peerless Dr. UB9: Hare 3J 113
Peers La. MK5: S Chur 1B 28
Peggs La. HP22: B'land 2C 68
Pelham Pl. MK14: D Barn 1F 23
Pelton Ct. MK5: S Lod 1B 28
Pemberley Lodge SL4: Wind 7J 129
Pemberton Cl. HP21: Ayle 2A 66
Pemberton Rd. SL2: Slou 2G 123
Pembridge Chase HP3: Bov 2K 79
Pembridge Cl. HP3: Bov 2K 79
Pembridge Gro. MK4: K'ead 6J 27
Pembridge Rd. HP3: Bov 2K 79
Pembroke Rd. HP20: Ayle 5A 62
Pencarrow Pl. MK6: Fish 5F 23
Pendeen Ct. SL1: Slou 6J 123
Pendennis Ct. MK4: Tatt 7A 28
Pendrill Ho. *HP11: H Wyc 1J 97*
(off Oakridge Rd.)
Penfold HP22: West T 5G 67
Penfold Cotts. HP15: H Grn 7K 83
Penfold La. HP7: L Miss 7K 83
HP15: H Grn 7K 83
Pengelly Ct. MK6: Fish 5G 23
Penhale Cl. MK4: Tatt 7B 28
Pen Haven SL9: G Cro 3K 111
Penhow Ri. MK4: K'ead 6J 27
Penina Cl. MK3: Blet 6D 28
Penington Rd. HP9: Bea 1D 108
Penlee Ri. MK4: Tatt 7B 28
Penmon Cl. MK10: Monk 5B 24
Penmoor Cl. HP12: H Wyc 7G 89
PENN 1K 99 (1C 137)
Penn Av. HP5: Ches 4J 77
PENN BOTTOM 6B 92
Penn Cl. UB8: Cowl 2K 127
Penn Dr. UB9: Den 4F 113
Pennefather Ct. HP21: Ayle 7K 61
Penn Gaskell La. SL9: C Pet 3K 103
Penn Grn. HP9: Bea 4F 101
Penn Ho. SL1: Burn 1E 122
SL9: C Pet 3J 103
Pennine Rd. SL2: Slou 3J 123
Pennings, The HP22: Wend 3H 69
Pennington Rd. HP13: H Wyc 2F 99
SL9: C Pet 5H 103
Penningtons, The HP6: Amer 4C 86
Penn Mdw. SL2: S Pog 6D 118
Penn Rd. HP9: Bea 2E 100
HP15: Haz 3G 91
HP21: Ayle 7J 61
MK2: F Str 7A 30
SL2: Slou 2B 124
SL9: C Pet 6H 103
PENN STREET 2C 92 (1C 137)
Pennwood Vw. HP7: Penn S 3C 92
Pennycress Way MK16: New P 7F 11
Pennycuik MK17: G Bri 7E 34
PENNYLAND 6G 17
Pennylets Grn. SL2: S Pog 5D 118
Pennyroyal MK7: Waln 7D 24
Penrith Cl. UB8: Uxb 5K 121
Penrith Way HP21: Ayle 7C 62
Penryn Av. MK6: Fish 5G 23
Penshurst Cl. SL9: C Pet 7H 103
Pentewan Ga. MK6: Fish 4F 23
Pentland Rd. HP21: Ayle 1A 66
SL2: Slou 3J 123
Pentlands MK11: F Sla 2D 20
Pentlands, The HP13: H Wyc 4G 99
Pentlands Ct. HP13: H Wyc 4G 99
Penwood La. SL7: Marl 1G 115
Penzance Spur SL2: Slou 2K 123
Pepler Way SL1: Burn 1D 122
Peplow Cl. UB7: Yiew 6K 127
Peppard Mdw. HP16: Pres 1D 82
PEPPERSHILL 2H 55
Peppiates, The LU6: N'all 1G 49
Pepys Cl. SL3: Lang 4B 130
Pepys Dr. HP16: Pres 7C 74
Perch Cl. SL7: Marl 2G 115
Percheron Pl. MK14: D Barn 1F 23
Perch Mdw. HP22: Halt 7J 67
Percy Ter. HP8: D Gil 1E 102
Peregrine HP19: Ayle 3K 61
Peregrine Bus. Pk. HP13: H Wyc 3G 99
Peregrine Cl. MK6: Eagl 6H 23
Perks La. HP16: Pres 3B 82
Permayne MK13: New B 6A 16
Perracombe MK4: Fur 4E 28
Perran Av. MK6: Fish 5G 23
Perrin Springs La. RG9: Fri 6H 73
Perryfields Way SL1: Burn 2D 122
Perry Ho. SL1: Burn 2D 122
Perry La. HP27: Bled 6A 70
MK16: Sher 3C 12
Perryman Way SL2: Slou 1H 123
Perry Mead LU6: E Bra 1J 49
Perry St. HP22: Wend 3G 69
Pershore Cft. MK10: Monk 5C 24
Perth Av. SL1: Slou 4K 123
Perth Cl. MK3: Blet 5F 29
Perth Rd. HP13: H Wyc 6D 90
Perth Trad. Est. SL1: Slou 3K 123
Peterborough Av. HP13: H Wyc 1C 98
Peterborough Ga. MK15: W Par 7J 17
Peterhead M. SL3: Lang 3A 130
Peterhill Cl. SL9: C Pet 3J 103
Peterley La. HP16: Pres 3D 82
Peterman Wlk. MK14: N Hill 7F 17
Peter's Cl. HP16: Pres 7C 74
Petersfield HP22: Sto M 4D 66
Petersfield Av. SL2: Slou 6E 124
Petersham Cl. MK16: New P 3J 17
Peters La. HP27: Mon R, Par H, Whit 3J 71
PETSOE END 7J 7 (2C 133)
Pettifer Way HP12: H Wyc 3H 97
Pettingrew Cl. MK7: Waln 1D 30
Petty Cross SL1: Slou 4G 123
Petworth MK8: G Hol 6J 21
Petworth Ct. SL4: Wind 6J 129
Petworth Ho. MK8: G Hol 5K 21
Pevensey Cl. HP21: Ayle 2C 66
MK3: Blet 1E 32
Pevensey Rd. SL2: Slou 3J 123
Peverel Dr. MK1: Blet 4G 29
Peveril Cl. HP21: Ayle 2C 66
Pheasant Dr. HP13: Down 5G 89
Pheasant Hill HP8: D Gil 7G 95
Pheasant Ri. HP5: Ches 7B 78
Pheasants Dr. HP15: Haz 2H 91
PHEASANTS HILL 2A 136
Pheasants Ridge SL7: Marl 2G 105
Pheasant Wlk. SL9: C Pet 2H 103
Philbye M. SL1: Slou 7H 123
Philip Dr. HP10: F Hea 2J 107
Philip Rd. HP13: H Wyc 1D 98
Philips Rd. HP19: Ayle 6F 61
Phillimore Cl. MK15: W Par 6H 17
Phillip Ct. MK5: S Chur 1B 28
Philpots Cl. UB7: Yiew 5K 127
Philps Cl. HP14: L End 4A 96
Phipps Cl. HP20: Ayle 4B 62
Phipps Rd. SL1: Slou 3F 123
(not continuous)
Phoebe La. MK17: Wave 1G 31
Phoebe's Orchard MK17: S Ham 2H 41
Phoenix Bus. Cen. *HP5: Ches 4K 77*
(off Higham Rd.)
Phoenix Dr. MK6: Lead 1F 29
Phygtle, The SL9: C Pet 4J 103
Piazza, The UB8: Uxb 5K 121
Picasso Pl. HP19: Ayle 4E 60
PICCOTTS END 3D 135
Pickering Dr. MK4: E Val 5A 28
Pickford Dr. SL3: Lang 6J 125
Pickfords Gdns. SL1: Slou 6C 124
Pickins Piece SL3: Hor 7A 130
Picton St. MK4: K'ead 6J 27
Picts La. HP27: Prin R 7E 70
PIDDINGTON
Bicester 2A 134
High Wycombe 6A 88 (1B 136)
Northampton 1C 133
Piddington La. HP14: Whee 1K 73
Piddington Rd. HP18: Ludg 2A 52
Pierson Rd. SL4: Wind 6F 129
Pigeon Farm Rd. HP14: Stoke 5C 72
Piggotts End HP7: Amer 7K 85
Piggott's Hill HP14: N Dean 4J 81
Piggotts Orchard HP7: Amer 7K 85
Pightle, The HP22: Ovi 5D 44
LU7: Pits 6F 51
MK18: M M'ton 1J 37
Pightle Cres. MK18: Buck 2H 37
Pigott Dr. MK5: S Chur 2A 28
Pigott Orchard HP22: Q'ton 5H 43
Pike Cl. SL7: Marl 2G 115
Pike Cnr. HP21: Ayle 2D 66
Pilch La. MK17: G Hor, Sing 1F 39
Pilgrims Cl. HP27: Mon R 3G 71
Pilgrim St. MK9: Camp 2G 23
Pilot Trad. Est. HP12: H Wyc 7J 89
Pimms Cl. HP13: H Wyc 2G 99
Pimms Gro. HP13: H Wyc 3G 99
Pimpernel Gro. MK7: Waln 1D 30
Pinders Cft. MK12: Gree 1F 21

PINDON END . . . 1A 8
Pineapple Rd. HP7: Amer . . . 6D 86
Pine Chase HP12: Book . . . 5F 97
Pine Cl. HP15: Haz . . . 4H 91
Pine Ct. HP5: Ches . . . 5A 78
Pinecroft SL7: Marl . . . 6H 105
Pine Gro. MK17: W San . . . 3J 31
PINEHAM . . . 6A 18
PINEHAM . . . 1A 24
Pine Hill HP15: Haz . . . 4F 91
Pinels Way HP11: H Wyc . . . 5J 97
Piner Cotts. SL4: Wind . . . 7G 129
Pines, The HP10: T Grn . . . 6H 91
SL3: Lang . . . 6K 125
Pines Cl. HP6: Amer . . . 4K 85
HP16: G Mis . . . 2H 83
Pine St. HP19: Ayle . . . 5E 60
Pinetree Cl. SL9: C Pet . . . 5G 103
Pine Trees Dr. UB10: I'ham . . . 2K 121
Pine Wlk. HP15: Haz . . . 5H 91
Pinewood Cl. SL0: I Hea . . . 5C 120
SL9: G Cro . . . 5J 111
Pinewood Dr. MK2: Blet . . . 1K 33
Pinewood Film Studios . . . 5B 120
Pinewood Grn. SL0: I Hea . . . 5C 120
Pinewood Rd. HP12: H Wyc . . . 7G 89
SL0: I Hea . . . 4B 120
Pinfold MK7: Waln . . . 1D 30
Pinfold Yd. MK18: Ting . . . 2C 36
Pinglestone Cl. UB7: Harm . . . 5K 131
Pinions Rd. HP13: H Wyc . . . 3E 98
Pinkard Ct. MK6: W Grn. . . . 6J 23
Pink Hill HP27: Par H . . . 7K 71
Pink La. SL1: Burn . . . 7D 116
PINKNEYS GREEN . . . 2B 136
Pink Rd. HP27: L Grn, Par H . . . 7K 71 & 1B 80
Pinks Cl. MK5: Lough . . . 6C 22
Pinkworthy MK4: Fur . . . 3D 28
Pinnacle Leisure Cen. . . . 7F 119
Pinn Cl. UB8: Cowl . . . 4K 127
PINNER . . . 2D 137
Pinstone Way SL9: G Cro . . . 7B 112
Pintail Cl. HP19: Ayle . . . 2K 61
Pipard MK14: G Lin . . . 6E 16
Pipers Cl. SL1: Burn . . . 1E 122
Pipers La. HP15: G Kin . . . 6C 82
Pipers Wood Cotts. HP7: L Miss . . . 4E 84
Pipit Gdns. *HP19: Ayle* . . . *2K 61*
(off Aylesswater)
Pipit Wlk. HP19: Ayle . . . 2K 61
Pippin Cl. MK16: New P . . . 2H 17
Pippins, The SL3: Lang . . . 6K 125
Pippins Cl. UB7: W Dra . . . 1K 131
Pipston Grn. MK7: K Hil . . . 7D 24
PISHILL . . . 2A 136
PITCHCOTT . . . 7B 44 (1B 134)
Pitchcott Rd. HP22: Ovi . . . 6B 44
Pitcher La. MK5: Lough . . . 6B 22
Pitcher Wlk. *HP19: Ayle* . . . *7F 61*
(off Jeffrey Wlk.)
Pitchford Av. MK18: Buck . . . 2J 37
Pitchford Wlk. MK18: Buck . . . 3J 37
PITCH GREEN . . . 5A 70 (3B 134)
Pitch Pond Cl. HP9: Bea . . . 3D 100
Pitfield MK11: Kiln . . . 3F 21
PITSTONE . . . 5E 50 (2D 135)
Pitstone Green Farm Mus. . . . 5F 51
Pitstone Windmill . . . 5G 51
Pitt Cl. HP22: Sto M . . . 4D 66
Pitters Piece HP18: Long C . . . 5B 56
Pitt Grn. MK18: Buck . . . 3K 37
Pitts Rd. SL1: Slou . . . 6A 124
Place, The MK9: C Key . . . 5B 22
Place Farm Way HP27: Mon R . . . 2G 71
Plackett Way SL1: Slou . . . 6F 123
Plaines Cl. SL1: Slou . . . 6H 123
Plaistow Cres. MK10: Monk P . . . 5B 24
Plantain Ct. MK7: Waln . . . 1D 30
Plantation Pl. MK5: S Broo . . . 3A 28
Plantation Rd. HP6: Amer . . . 4C 86
HP13: H Wyc . . . 1G 99
Plantation Way HP6: Amer . . . 4C 86
Platt, The HP7: Amer . . . 7K 85
PLAY HATCH . . . 3A 136
Pleasaunce, The HP22: Ast C . . . 2B 68
Pleshey Cl. MK5: S Chur . . . 1B 28
Plested Ct. HP22: Sto M . . . 5D 66
Plomer Green Av. HP13: Down . . . 5H 89
Plomer Grn. La. HP13: Down . . . 3H 89
Plomer Hill HP13: Down . . . 6H 89
Plough Cl. HP21: Ayle . . . 4K 65
Plough La. SL2: S Pog . . . 6F 119
Plough Lees La. SL1: Slou . . . 5C 124
Plover, The HP19: Ayle . . . 2K 61
Plover Cl. MK16: New P . . . 2B 18
MK18: Buck . . . 5J 37
Plover Wlk. *HP19: Ayle* . . . *2K 61*
(off Aylesswater)
Plowman Cl. MK12: Gree . . . 1F 21
Plumer Rd. HP12: H Wyc . . . 1J 97
PLUMPTON . . . 2A 132
Plumstead Av. MK13: B Com . . . 3D 22
Pluto Cl. SL1: Slou . . . 7G 123
Plym Cl. HP21: Ayle . . . 2H 65
Plymouth Gro. MK4: Tatt . . . 6B 28
Plymouth Rd. SL1: Slou . . . 3G 123
Pocketsdell La. HP3: Bov . . . 2H 79
PODINGTON . . . 1D 133
Poets Chase HP21: Ayle . . . 1A 66
Poles Hill HP5: Ches . . . 3J 77
Polidoris La. HP15: H Grn . . . 7J 83
Polish Av. HP22: Halt . . . 7B 68
Pollard Av. UB9: Den . . . 4F 113
Pollardswood Grange HP8: D Gil . . . 2H 95
POLLICOTT . . . 2B 134
Pollys Yd. *MK16: New P* . . . *7K 11*
(off Union St.)
Polmartin Ct. MK6: Fish . . . 5G 23
Polruan Pl. MK6: Fish . . . 5G 23
Polygon Bus. Cen. SL3: Poy . . . 7F 131
Pomander Cres. MK7: Waln . . . 7D 24
Pomeroy Cl. HP7: Amer . . . 7B 86
Pond Approach HP15: H Grn . . . 1J 91
Pond Cl. HP7: Winc . . . 4E 92
MK17: New L . . . 6C 32
Pond Cotts. SL9: C Pet . . . 7H 103
Pondgate MK7: K Hil . . . 6D 24
Pond La. SL9: C Pet . . . 6F 103
POND PARK . . . 2K 77
Pond Pk. Rd. HP5: Ches . . . 3K 77
Pondwicks HP7: Amer . . . 6K 85
Pool La. SL1: Slou . . . 5C 124
Poolmans Rd. SL4: Wind . . . 7F 129
Popes Acre HP17: Hadd . . . 7B 58
Popes Cl. HP6: Amer . . . 4D 86
SL3: Coln . . . 5B 130
POPESWOOD . . . 3B 136
Pope Way HP21: Ayle . . . 3K 65
Poplar Av. HP7: Amer . . . 6D 86
Poplar Cl. HP5: Ches . . . 2A 78
HP20: Ayle . . . 4B 62
MK6: Simp . . . 2A 30
SL3: Poy . . . 6E 130
Poplar Cotts. *HP5: Ches* . . . *6K 77*
(off Amy La.)
Poplar Ho. SL3: Lang . . . 3A 130
Poplar Rd. HP10: Woob G . . . 2A 108
HP20: Ayle . . . 4B 62
UB9: Den . . . 3J 121
Poplars, The HP22: Wend . . . 3J 69
Poplars Cl. HP17: Sto . . . 2B 64
Poplars Rd. MK18: Buck . . . 4H 37
Poppy Rd. HP27: Prin R . . . 6F 71
Porchester Cl. MK3: Blet . . . 7F 29
Porlock La. MK4: Fur . . . 3C 28
Portal Rd. HP22: Halt . . . 2K 69
Portchester Ct. MK8: G Hol . . . 5K 21
Portfield Cl. MK18: Buck . . . 4J 37
Portfields Rd. MK16: New P . . . 1G 17
Portfield Way MK18: Buck . . . 4J 37
Porthcawl Grn. MK4: Tatt . . . 7C 28
Porthleven Pl. MK6: Fish . . . 4G 23
Porthmellin Cl. MK4: Tatt . . . 7B 28
Portishead Dr. MK4: Tatt . . . 7K 27
Portland Cl. SL2: Slou . . . 2F 123
Portland Dr. MK15: Will . . . 6J 17
Portland Gdns. SL7: Marl . . . 1H 115
Portland Ho. HP13: H Wyc . . . 7D 90
Portland M. SL7: Marl . . . 1H 115
Portland Pk. SL9: G Cro . . . 4H 111
Portlands SL9: G Cro . . . 4H 111
Portmarnock Cl. MK3: Blet . . . 6C 28
Portobello Cl. HP5: Ches . . . 3J 77
Portrush Cl. MK3: Blet . . . 7D 28
Portsmouth Ct. SL1: Slou . . . 5C 124
PORTWAY . . . 5B 22
Portway HP17: Sto . . . 3D 64
MK18: N Mar . . . 2B 44
Portway Dr. HP12: H Wyc . . . 6F 89
Portway (H5) MK8: Mil K . . . 2H 27
MK9: Mil K . . . 4B 22
MK15: Mil K . . . 1G 23
Portway Rd. HP17: Sto . . . 2D 64
POSTCOMBE . . . 1A 136
Post Mdw. SL0: I Hea . . . 1D 126
Post Office La. HP9: Bea . . . 5F 101
HP22: W'urch . . . 2G 45
SL3: G Grn . . . 4H 125
Potkiln La. HP9: Jord . . . 1B 110
POTSGROVE . . . 1D 135
POTTEN END . . . 3D 135
Potter Row HP16: G Mis, S Hea . . . 2H 75
Potters Cl. HP16: Pres . . . 6B 74
Potters Cross SL0: I Hea . . . 1E 126
Potters Cross Cres. HP15: Haz . . . 5E 90
Potters Glen MK18: Pad . . . 6A 38
Potters La. MK11: Kiln . . . 2G 21
POTTERSPURY . . . 2B 132
Pottery Cl. HP19: Ayle . . . 7F 61
Pottery Ct. *HP19: Ayle* . . . *7F 61*
(off Pottery Cl.)
Pound, The SL1: Burn . . . 2F 123
Pound Cl. MK18: S Clay . . . 2B 42
Pound Cres. SL7: Marl . . . 1G 115
Pound Hill MK17: G Bri . . . 7E 34
Pound La. MK16: N Craw . . . 5K 13
SL7: L Mar . . . 5C 106
SL7: Marl . . . 2G 115
POUNDON . . . 1A 134
Pound St. HP22: Wend . . . 4H 69
Powell Haven MK10: Midd . . . 3A 24
Powerleague Soccer Cen.
Chalvey . . . 7B 124
Powis La. MK4: West . . . 4J 27
POYLE . . . 7E 130 (3D 137)
Poyle Cl. SL3: Poy . . . 7E 130
Poyle Ind. Est. SL3: Poy . . . 7F 131
Poyle La. SL1: Burn . . . 6D 116
Poyle New Cotts. SL3: Poy . . . 7F 131
Poyle Rd. SL3: Poy . . . 7E 130
Poyle Technical Cen. SL3: Poy . . . 7E 130
Poyle Trad. Est. SL3: Poy . . . 7E 130
Poynings, The SL0: R Pk . . . 2F 131
Pratt Ho. HP6: Amer . . . 5D 86
Prebendal Av. HP21: Ayle . . . 7H 61
Prebendal Cl. HP20: Ayle . . . 6J 61
Prebendal Ct. HP20: Ayle . . . 6J 61
PREBENDAL FARM . . . 7H 61
Prebendal Ho. *HP20: Ayle* . . . *6J 61*
(off Prebendal Cl.)
Precedent Dr. MK13: Rook . . . 4B 22
Precincts, The SL1: Burn . . . 2D 122
Prentice Gro. MK5: S Broo . . . 4B 28
Prescott Rd. SL3: Poy . . . 7E 130
Presley Way MK8: C'ill . . . 7J 21
Press Rd. UB8: Uxb . . . 4K 121
PRESTON BISSETT . . . 1A 134
PRESTON CAPES . . . 1A 132
Preston Ct. MK15: W Par . . . 6H 17
Preston Hill HP5: Ches . . . 3B 78
Preston Rd. SL2: Slou . . . 5G 125
Prestwick Cl. MK3: Blet . . . 1D 32
Prestwold Way HP19: Ayle . . . 7F 61
PRESTWOOD . . . 7C 74 (3C 135)
Prestwood SL2: Slou . . . 4F 125
Prestwood Cl. HP12: H Wyc . . . 7H 89
Prestwood Ho. *HP19: Ayle* . . . *7F 61*
(off Prestwold Way)
Prestwood Pl. HP16: Pres . . . 7C 74
Priestley Ct. HP13: H Wyc . . . 2D 98
Priests Paddock HP9: Bea . . . 3D 100
PRIESTWOOD . . . 3B 136
Primatt Cres. MK5: S Chur . . . 1B 28
Primrose Ct. *HP21: Ayle* . . . *1G 65*
(off Primrose Dr.)
Primrose Dr. HP21: Ayle . . . 1G 65
UB7: W Dra . . . 2K 131
Primrose Grn. HP15: W End . . . 1F 91
Primrose Hill HP15: W End . . . 7F 83
Primrose Lea SL7: Marl . . . 6H 105
Primrose Rd. MK13: B'ell . . . 2A 22
Primrose Ter. *HP18: Bril* . . . *3H 53*
(off Windmill St.)
Princes Cl. HP18: Chil . . . 1B 56
SL4: E Wick . . . 3H 129
PRINCES ESTATE . . . 5E 70
Princes Ga. HP13: H Wyc . . . 2D 98
PRINCES RISBOROUGH . . . 4G 71 (3C 135)
Princes Risborough Station (Rail) . . . 6E 70
Princes Rd. HP21: Ayle . . . 6K 61
SL8: Bou E . . . 6J 107
Princess of Wales Ho. SL9: C Pet . . . 2K 103
Princes St. HP14: Pidd . . . 7A 88
SL1: Slou . . . 7F 125
PRINCES WAY . . . 7H 29
Princes Way MK2: Blet . . . 7J 29
Printers End HP19: Ayle . . . 6G 61
Prior Gro. HP5: Ches . . . 4A 78
Priors Cl. SL1: Slou . . . 7E 124
Priors Pk. MK4: E Val . . . 5D 28
Priors Rd. SL4: Wind . . . 7F 129
Priory Av. HP13: H Wyc . . . 7B 90
UB9: Hare . . . 2J 113
Priory Cl. HP19: Ayle . . . 4H 61
MK16: New P . . . 1A 18
UB9: Den . . . 1G 121
UB9: Hare . . . 2H 113
Priory Ct. MK11: S Strat . . . 7B 14
Priory Cres. HP19: Ayle . . . 4H 61
Priory Gdns. UB9: Hare . . . 2J 113
Priory Rd. HP13: H Wyc . . . 1B 98
SL1: Slou . . . 3E 122
SL9: C Pet . . . 1H 111
Priory St. MK16: New P . . . 1K 17
Priory Way SL9: C Pet . . . 1H 111
UB7: Harm . . . 4K 131
Pritchard Ct. MK14: G Lin . . . 5E 16
Proctor Ri. MK8: G Far . . . 1H 27
Progress Bus. Cen. SL1: Slou . . . 4F 123
Progress Rd. HP12: H Wyc . . . 1F 97
Prospect Cl. MK17: Dray P . . . 6C 40
Prospect Ct. HP14: L End . . . 3K 73
Prospect Pl. LU7: Wing . . . 3C 48
MK19: Cast . . . 7D 8
SL6: Hur . . . 7D 114
Prospect Rd. MK11: S Strat . . . 1A 20
SL7: Marl . . . 7G 105
Protheroe Fld. MK7: Old P . . . 3F 31
Providence Pl. *MK13: B'ell* . . . *2A 22*
(off Loughton Rd.)
Prretoria Rd. HP13: H Wyc . . . 7C 90
PUDDS CROSS . . . 3J 79
Puers Fld. HP9: Jord . . . 4D 102
Puers La. HP9: Jord . . . 4C 102
Puffin Way HP19: Ayle . . . 3A 62
Pulborough Cl. MK3: Blet . . . 6D 28
Pullfields HP5: Ches . . . 4J 77
Pulpit Cl. HP5: Ches . . . 3J 77
Pulpit La. HP22: Ovi . . . 4D 44
Pumpkin Hill SL1: Burn . . . 4G 117
Pump La. HP5: Ches . . . 7C 78
Pump La. Nth. SL7: Marl . . . 2K 105
Pump La. Sth. SL7: L Mar . . . 4A 106
Pump Mdw. HP16: G Mis . . . 5G 75
Pumpus Grn. MK18: Wins . . . 6J 39
Punch Bowl La. HP5: Ches . . . 6A 78
Purbeck MK14: Stan . . . 6C 16
Purbeck Cl. HP21: Ayle . . . 2C 66
Purcel Dr. MK16: New P . . . 2H 17
PURLEY ON THAMES . . . 3A 136
Purse La. MK16: S Gold . . . 4B 6
Pursell Pl. HP27: Prin R . . . 3G 71
Pursells Mdw. HP14: Nap . . . 7G 81
Pursers Ct. SL2: Slou . . . 4C 124
Purton Ct. SL2: Farn R . . . 5A 118
Purton La. SL2: Farn C, Farn R . . . 5A 118
PURY END . . . 2B 132
Pusey Way HP14: L End . . . 3A 96
Putlowes Dr. HP18: Fleet M . . . 2B 60
Putman Ho. MK5: S Lod . . . 2C 28
Putnams Dr. HP22: Ast C . . . 2A 68
PUTTENHAM . . . 2C 135
Pyebush La. HP9: Bea . . . 2J 109
Pyghtle, The MK46: Oln . . . 4H 7
UB9: Den . . . 5G 113
Pyghtle Footpath UB9: Den . . . 6G 113
Pyghtles, The HP22: Q'ton . . . 5J 43
Pyke Hayes MK8: T Ash . . . 3H 21
Pyncombe Cl. HP27: Prin R . . . 3G 71
PYRTON . . . 1A 136
Pyxe Ct. MK7: Walt P . . . 3C 30

Q

Quadrangle, The HP13: H Wyc . . . 1E 98
Quadrans Cl. MK15: Penny . . . 6G 17
Quadrant, The HP13: H Wyc . . . 6E 90
QUAINTON . . . 5J 43 (1B 134)
Quainton Rd. HP18: Wadd . . . 5C 52
MK18: N Mar . . . 2A 44
Quainton Road Station
Buckinghamshire Railway Cen.
. . . 7G 43
Quainton Windmill . . . 5J 43
Quaker Hill *HP5: Ches* . . . *5K 77*
(off Wesley Hill)
Quakers Mead HP22: West T . . . 4G 67
Quakers Mede HP17: Hadd . . . 6C 58
Quantock Cl. SL3: Lang . . . 3A 130
Quantock Cres. MK4: E Val . . . 6D 28
QUARRENDON . . . 4F 61 (2C 135)
Quarrendon Av. HP19: Ayle . . . 4G 61
Quarrendon Rd. HP7: Amer . . . 7B 86
Quarry Cl. HP18: Long C . . . 5C 56
Quarry Ct. LU7: Pits . . . 7E 50
Quarrydale Dr. SL7: Marl . . . 7K 105
Quarry Rd. LU7: Pits . . . 7E 50
Quarry Wood SL6: Cook . . . 2K 115
Quarry Wood Rd. SL6: Cook . . . 2K 115
SL7: Cook, Marl . . . 2J 115
Quaves Rd. SL3: Slou . . . 7F 125
Quebec Rd. HP13: H Wyc . . . 2E 98
Queen Alexandra Rd. HP11: H Wyc . . . 2A 98
Queen Anne's Dr. SL6: Tapl . . . 2A 116
Queen Anne St. MK13: New B . . . 6K 15
Queen Catherine Rd. MK18: S Clay . . . 3C 42
Queen Eleanor St. MK11: S Strat . . . 7A 14
Queen Mothers Dr. UB9: Den . . . 4F 113
Queens Acre HP13: H Wyc . . . 2C 98
Queens Av. MK16: New P . . . 1J 17
Queensbury La. MK10: Monk P . . . 5A 24
Queens Ct. HP13: H Wyc . . . 2C 98
MK9: C Key . . . 3E 22
SL1: Slou . . . 5D 124
Queen's Dr. SL3: Fulm, Wex . . . 5K 119
Queensgate HP19: Ayle . . . 6F 61
Queens Head Cotts. HP7: Winc . . . 3G 93
Queens Mead HP21: Ayle . . . 7D 62
Queensmead Ho. HP10: Loud . . . 6H 99
Queensmead Rd. HP10: Loud . . . 6J 99
Queensmere Rd. SL1: Slou . . . 7D 124
Queensmere Shop. Cen. SL1: Slou . . . 7D 124
Queen's Pk. HP21: Ayle . . . 6A 62
Queens Pk. Arts Cen. . . . 6A 62
Queen Sq. HP11: H Wyc . . . 1A 98
Queens Rd. HP5: Ches . . . 4A 78
HP13: H Wyc . . . 2C 98
HP27: Prin R . . . 4H 71
SL1: Slou . . . 5D 124
SL4: E Wick . . . 3H 129
SL4: Wind . . . 7K 129
SL7: Marl . . . 7H 105
UB8: Uxb . . . 1J 127
Queen St. HP13: H Wyc . . . 1C 98
HP14: Pidd . . . 6A 88
HP18: Wadd . . . 6B 52
HP20: Ayle . . . 6B 62
LU7: Pits . . . 5F 51
MK11: S Strat . . . 7C 14
Queensway HP15: Haz . . . 3G 91
MK2: Blet . . . 7J 29
(not continuous)
Queensway, The SL9: C Pet . . . 2H 111
Queen Victoria Rd. HP11: H Wyc . . . 2B 98
Quickberry Pl. HP7: Amer . . . 6B 86
Quill Hall La. HP6: Amer . . . 4D 86
Quilter Mdw. MK7: Old P . . . 2F 31

Quilters Way HP22: Sto M 7E 66
Quinbrookes SL2: Slou 4G 125
Quince Cl. MK7: Waln 2D 30
QUINTON 1B 132
Quinton Dr. MK13: B'ell 3A 22
Quoitings Dr. SL7: Marl 7G 105
Quoitings Gdns. SL7: Marl 7G 105
Quoiting Sq. SL7: Marl 7H 105

R

Raans Rd. HP6: Amer 5D 86
Rabans Cl. HP19: Ayle 4D 60
Rabans La. HP19: Ayle 5D 60
Rabbs Mill Ho. UB8: Uxb 7K 121
Rachels Way *HP5: Ches 1B 86*
(off Cresswell Rd.)
Rackstraw Gro. MK7: Old P 2F 31
Radcliffe St. MK12: Wolv 6H 15
(not continuous)
RADCLIVE 3A 132
Radclive Rd. MK18: Gaw 4C 36
Radcot Av. SL3: Lang 1B 130
Radcote Lodge MK8: T Ash 4J 21
Radian Ct. MK5: Know 7C 22
RADLETT 1D 137
Radman Gro. MK12: Gree 1F 21
RADNAGE 3A 72 (1A 136)
Radnage La. HP14: Rad 1A 72
Radnor End HP20: Ayle 4K 61
Radstock Cres. MK10: Bro 2C 24
RADSTONE 2A 132
RADWELL 1D 133
Radworthy MK4: Fur 4C 28
Raeside Cl. HP9: S Grn 3A 102
RAF Halton Airfield 4K 67
Raglan Dr. MK4: K'ead 6J 27
Ragmans La. SL7: H Wyc, Marl 1G 105
Ragstone Rd. SL1: Slou 7C 124
Railway Cotts. MK18: S Clay 4E 42
Railway St. HP20: Ayle 6K 61
Railway Ter. SL2: Slou 6D 124
Railway Wlk. MK14: G Lin 4D 16
MK16: New P 1H 17
Rainborough Gdns. HP20: Ayle 4K 61
Rainbow Dr. MK6: Lead 7F 23
(not continuous)
Rainbow Ind. Est. UB7: Yiew 5K 127
Rainsborough MK14: G Par 5G 17
Rake Way HP21: Ayle 4J 65
Raleigh Cl. SL1: Slou 6J 123
Ralphs Retreat HP15: Haz 3F 91
Ram All. MK16: S Gold 7C 6
Rambler Cl. SL6: Tapl 4D 122
Rambler La. SL3: Lang 7G 125
Ramsay Cl. MK13: B'ell 3B 22
(not continuous)
Ramsey Ct. SL2: Slou 2F 123
Ramsey Vw. HP15: Haz 4G 91
Ramsgill Ct. MK13: Hee 2C 22
Ramsons Av. MK14: Conn 2E 22
Ramsthorn Gro. MK7: Waln 1D 30
Ramworth Way HP21: Ayle 1B 66
Randall Cl. SL3: Lang 3A 130
Randolph Cl. MK13: B'lle 7A 16
Ranelagh Gdns. MK16: New P 3J 17
Rangers Ct. MK8: G Hol 5K 21
Rannoch Cl. MK2: Blet 3K 33
Ranston Cl. UB9: Den 4F 113
Rashleigh Pl. MK6: Old 7E 22
Ratcliffe Cl. UB8: Cowl 1K 127
Rathbone Cl. MK8: C'ill 7J 21
Ravel Cl. MK7: Old P 1F 31
Raven Cl. HP19: Ayle 3A 62
Ravenglass Cft. MK10: Bro 3D 24
Raven Rd. HP14: Stoke 6D 72
Ravensbourne Pl. MK6: Sprin 4H 23
Ravensbourne Rd. HP21: Ayle 4J 65
Ravenscar Ct. MK4: E Val 6B 28
Ravenscourt SL7: Marl 6A 106
Ravens Fld. SL3: Lang 7H 125
Ravenshoe Cl. SL8: Bou E 6G 107
Ravensmead SL9: C Pet 3K 103
RAVENSTONE 1C 133
Ravensworth Rd. SL2: Slou 1J 123
Ravigill Pl. MK12: H Lea 2H 21
Rawlings La. HP9: S Grn 1A 102
Rawlins Rd. MK13: B'ell 2A 22
Raylands Mead SL9: G Cro 3G 111
Rayleigh Cl. MK5: S Chur 1B 28
Raymers Av. Mobile Home Pk.
HP10: Loud 5J 99
Raymond Cl. SL3: Poy 6E 130
Raymond Rd. SL3: Lang 1A 130
Rayners Av. HP10: Loud 5H 99
Rayners Cl. HP10: Loud 5J 99
SL3: Coln 5C 130
RAYNERS LANE 2D 137
Rayners La. MK10: Monk P 5A 24
Ray's Av. SL4: Wind 5H 129
Rays La. HP10: T Grn 6J 91
Razzaq Pl. *HP12: H Wyc 1J 97*
(off Lindsay Av.)
Read Dr. HP22: Bier 2D 62
Read Ho. *HP19: Ayle 7F 61*
(off Horton Cl.)
READING 3A 136
Reading Cl. HP19: Ayle 3F 61
Reads La. LU7: Cubl 2H 47
Ream Ct. HP11: H Wyc 3F 99
Recreation Rd. SL8: Bou E 6H 107
Rectory Av. HP13: H Wyc 1C 98
Rectory Cl. OX27: M Gib 5C 42
SL2: Farn R 1A 124
SL4: Wind 6J 129
Rectory Ct. *HP7: Amer 7K 85*
(off Rectory Way)
HP13: H Wyc 3F 99
Rectory Dr. HP18: Wadd 6C 52
Rectory Flds. MK15: Wool 3J 23
Rectory Gro. HP8: D Gil 7F 95
Rectory Hill HP6: Amer 6K 85
HP7: Amer 6K 85
Rectory Orchard MK46: Lave 2B 6
Rectory Rd. MK19: H'ham 3K 15
SL6: Tapl 2A 122
Rectory Way HP7: Amer 6K 85
Redbourne Ct. MK11: S Strat 1D 20
REDBRIDGE 6E 16
Redbridge MK14: Stan 5D 16
Redcliffe Wlk. HP19: Ayle 4G 61
Redcote Mnr. MK7: Walt P 3C 30
Red Ct. SL1: Slou 6C 124
Redding Dr. HP6: Amer 4J 85
Redding Gro. MK8: C'ill 1J 27
Reddings Cl. HP22: Wend 2H 69
Reddington Dr. SL3: Lang 2A 130
Redfern Cl. UB8: Uxb 6J 121
Redford Rd. SL4: Wind 6F 129
Redford Way UB8: Uxb 5K 121
Redgrave Pl. SL7: Marl 6K 105
Red Hill UB9: Den 7D 112
Red Ho. Cl. HP9: Bea 4D 100
MK17: New L 4D 32
Redhouse Cl. HP11: H Wyc 5J 97
Redhuish Cl. MK4: Fur 4D 28
Redland Cl. MK18: S Clay 3B 42
Redland Dr. MK5: Lough 6B 22
Redland Way HP21: Ayle 2B 66
Red Leaf Cl. SL3: Lang 6K 125
Red Leys UB8: Uxb 5K 121
Red Lion Cotts. HP7: L Miss 4C 84
Redlion Dr. HP14: Stoke 5B 72
Red Lion La. HP27: Long 2C 70
Red Lion St. HP5: Ches 6K 77
Red Lion Way HP10: Woob G 3A 108
Redman Rd. HP12: Book 5F 97
REDMOOR 3G 29
REDMOOR 3H 29
Redshaw Cl. MK18: Buck 3J 37
Redshots Cl. SL7: Marl 5J 105
Redvers Ga. MK15: Bolb 6H 17
Red Wing HP19: Ayle 3K 61
Redwing Ho. MK7: K Par 6C 24
Redwood SL1: Burn 7D 116
Redwood Cl. HP15: Haz 4H 91
LU7: Wing 3C 48
Redwood Dr. HP21: Ayle 7K 61
Redwood Gdns. SL1: Slou 5B 124
Redwood Ga. MK5: S Lod 3C 28
Redwood Pl. HP9: Bea 7F 101
Redwood Rd. LU7: Wing 3C 48
Reeves Ct. MK12: H Lea 2G 21
Reflexions Health & Leisure 3J 61
Regency Ct. HP21: Ayle 7C 62
Regent Ct. SL1: Slou 4C 124
Regent Rd. HP21: Ayle 7C 62
Regent St. MK2: Blet 7J 29
Regius Ct. HP10: Pen 7K 91
Reliance La. MK9: Camp 3H 23
Rembrandt End HP19: Ayle 4E 60
REMENHAM 2A 136
REMENHAM HILL 2A 136
Rendlesham MK15: Wool 3J 23
Renfrew Way MK3: Blet 4F 29
Rennie Cl. HP13: Down 6K 89
Repton Pl. HP7: Amer 6E 86
Retreat, The HP6: L Chal 6J 87
HP27: Prin R 4G 71
MK11: S Strat 1B 20
(off High St.)
SL6: Fifi 5A 128
Retreat La. HP14: Bled R 1A 72
Revel Rd. HP10: Woob G 1K 107
Reyners Grn. HP16: L Kin 2H 83
Reynold Dr. HP20: Ayle 4B 62
Reynolds Cl. HP13: H Wyc 7E 90
Reynolds Pl. MK8: G Far 1H 27
Reynolds Rd. HP9: Bea 5E 100
Reynolds Wlk. HP5: Ches 1J 77
Reynold's Yd. *HP5: Ches 6K 77*
(off Church St.)
Rhodes Pl. MK6: Old 7E 22
Rhondda Cl. MK1: F Str 6A 30
Rhoscolyn Dr. MK4: Tatt 7B 28
Rhuddlan Cl. MK5: S Chur 7K 21
Rhymer Cl. MK19: H'ope 1D 8
Ribble Cl. MK16: New P 1A 18
Ribble Cres. MK3: Blet 7D 28
Richard Gdns. HP13: H Wyc 7E 90
Richardson Pl. MK6: Old 5E 22
Richards Way SL1: Slou 6G 123
Richborough MK13: Ban 7A 16
RICHINGS PARK 7F 127 (3D 137)
Richings Pl. SL0: R Pk 1E 130
Richings Way SL0: R Pk 1E 130
Richmond Cl. HP6: Amer 5D 86
MK3: Blet 6D 28
Richmond Ct. HP13: H Wyc 1C 98
Richmond Cres. SL1: Slou 6E 124
Richmond Rd. HP20: Ayle 6D 62
Richmond Way MK16: New P 2J 17
Rickard Cl. HP21: Ayle 4J 65
UB7: W Dra 1K 131
Rickford's Hill HP20: Ayle 6J 61
Rickley La. MK3: Blet 6F 29
Rickman's La. SL2: S Pog 4C 118
RICKMANSWORTH 1D 137
Rickmansworth La. SL9: C Pet 5J 103
Rickmansworth Rd. HP6: Amer 4A 86
Rickman Wlk. *HP19: Ayle 7F 61*
(off Fairford Leys Way)
Rickyard Cl. HP22: W'urch 1F 45
MK13: B'ell 2A 22
Rickyard Gro. HP18: G Und 3J 43
Ridgebank SL1: Slou 5H 123
Ridge Cl. HP14: L End 4A 96
HP21: Ayle 4J 65
Ridgemont End SL9: C Pet 3J 103
Ridge Side HP14: Bled R 3D 72
Ridge Way HP13: H Wyc 6C 90
HP18: Long C 7F 57
Ridgeway LU7: Wing 2C 48
SL0: Ive 6E 126
Ridgeway, The HP7: Amer 7B 86
SL7: Marl 5J 105
SL9: C Pet 1H 111
Ridgeway Cl. HP5: Ches 2K 77
SL7: Marl 5J 105
Ridgeway Ct. *HP20: Ayle 5K 61*
(off Stirling Av.)
Ridgeway (H1) MK11: Mil K 2D 20
MK12: Mil K 1E 20
Ridgeway Ho. *HP6: Amer 4A 86*
(off Rickmansworth Rd.)
Ridgeway Meads HP27: Bled 6A 70
Ridgeway Rd. HP5: Ches 2J 77
Ridgeway Trad. Est. SL0: Ive 5F 127
RIDGMONT 3D 133
Ridgway MK17: W San 1K 31
Riding Ct. Rd. SL3: Dat, Lang 4A 130
Riding La. HP9: Bea 5B 100
Ridings, The HP5: Lati 3H 87
HP6: Amer 2B 86
SL0: R Pk 2F 131
SL4: Wind 5E 128
Ridings Cotts. HP15: H Grn 1K 91
Ridings Way LU7: Cubl 2G 47
Rigby Lodge SL1: Slou 4C 124
Rignall Rd. HP16: G Mis 4C 74
Riley Cl. HP20: Ayle 6H 61
Riley Rd. SL7: Marl 7H 105
Rillington Gdns. MK4: E Val 4B 28
Rimmington Way HP19: Ayle 5G 61
Rimsdale Ct. MK2: Blet 5K 33
Ring Rd. HP10: F Hea 6F 99
Ring Rd. E. MK7: Walt H 7B 24
Ring Rd. Nth. MK7: Walt H 7A 24
Ring Rd. W. MK7: Walt H 7A 24
RINGSHALL 2D 135
Ringshall Rd. HP4: Dag, Ring 7G 49
Ringstead Way HP21: Ayle 2A 66
Riplay Cl. MK4: K'ead 6J 27
Ripley Cl. HP13: Down 7A 90
Ripon Ho. HP21: Ayle 1A 66
Ripon St. HP20: Ayle 6J 61
Risborough Rd. HP17: Gt Kim 1K 71
HP22: Sto M, Terr 6C 66
Risborough Swimming & Fitness Cen.
4F 71
Rise, The HP7: Amer 6A 86
HP13: H Wyc 4H 99
HP15: Haz 2G 91
MK18: Gaw 6C 36
RISELEY 1D 133
Riverbank, The SL4: Wind 5K 129
Riverbank Point UB8: Uxb 4J 121
River Cl. MK16: New P 1K 17
Rivercrest Rd. MK19: O Stra 7A 14
River Gdns. SL6: Bra 7A 122
Rivermead Ct. SL7: Marl 2J 115
Riverpark Dr. SL7: Marl 1K 115
River Rd. SL4: Wind 5E 128
Riversdale SL8: Bou E 7H 107
Rivers Edge HP11: W Mar 5G 99
Riverside HP5: Ches 7A 78
MK16: New P 1K 17
SL7: Marl 1J 115
SL8: Bou E 6H 107
Riverside Bus. Cen.
HP11: H Wyc 1K 97
Riverside E. HP10: Woob G 1A 108
Riverside Pk. SL3: Poy 7E 130
Riverside W HP10: Woob G 1A 108
Riverside Way UB8: Uxb 6H 121
Riverswood Gdns. *HP13: H Wyc 5H 99*
(off Laurel Dr.)
River Vw. HP10: F Hea 1H 107
River Wlk. UB9: Den 3J 121
Riverwoods Dr. SL7: Marl 7A 106
Rivets Cl. HP21: Ayle 1K 65
Rivetts Cl. MK46: Oln 3G 7
Rixband Cl. MK7: Walt P 3C 30
Rixon Cl. SL3: G Grn 4J 125
Rixons Mdw. HP19: Ayle 7F 61
ROADE 1B 132
ROAD WEEDON 1A 132
Roald Dahl Gallery *6J 61*
(in The Buckinghamshire County Mus.)
Roald Dahl Mus., The 6H 75
Roasthill La. SL4: Dorn 4F 129
Robert Rd. SL2: Hedg 7B 110
Roberts Dr. HP19: Ayle 4J 61
Robertson Cl. MK5: S Chur 7K 21
Roberts Ride HP15: Haz 1F 91
Roberts Rd. HP13: H Wyc 7B 90
HP17: Hadd 6C 58
Roberts Way HP21: Ayle 1G 65
Roberts Wood Dr. SL9: C Pet 3K 103
Robertswood Lodge SL9: C Pet 4K 103
Robeson Pl. MK8: C'ill 6J 21
Robin Cl. HP15: G Kin 5D 82
HP19: Ayle 3A 62
MK18: Buck 5K 37
Robin Hood Cl. SL1: Slou 6H 123
Robin Pde. SL2: Farn C 3A 118
Robins Cl. HP12: H Wyc 5H 97
UB8: Cowl 3J 127
Robins Hill MK6: Coff 1G 29
Robinson Cl. HP19: Ayle 3E 60
Robinson Rd. HP13: H Wyc 4H 99
Robinson St. MK3: Blet 7H 29
Robins Orchard SL9: C Pet 4J 103
Robinswood Cl. HP9: Bea 3E 100
Roblin Cl. HP21: Ayle 3K 65
Robson Cl. SL9: C Pet 3J 103
Robson Ct. *HP16: G Mis 5G 75*
(off Aylesham Rd.)
Roche Gdns. MK3: Blet 7G 29
Rochester Ct. MK5: S Chur 2A 28
Rochester Pl. HP19: Ayle 6G 61
Rochfords MK6: Coff 7F 23
Rochfords Gdns. SL2: Slou 5G 125
Rochford Way SL6: Tapl 5C 122
Rockall Ct. SL3: Lang 1B 130
Rockingham Cl. LU7: Pits 6F 51
UB8: Uxb 6J 121
Rockingham Dr. MK14: L Woo 7E 16
(not continuous)
Rockingham Pde. UB8: Uxb 5J 121
Rockingham Pl. HP9: Bea 7H 101
Rockingham Rd. UB8: Uxb 6H 121
Rockspray Gro. MK7: Waln 2D 30
ROCKWELL END 2A 136
Rodney Way SL3: Poy 6E 130
Rodwell Gdns. MK7: Old P 3F 31
Roebuck Av. HP13: H Wyc 3F 99
Roebuck Grn. SL1: Slou 6G 123
Roebuck Way MK5: Know 1C 28
Roeburn Cres. MK4: E Val 6B 28
Rogers Cft. MK6: W Grn. 7K 23
Rogers La. SL2: S Pog 5D 118
Rokesby Rd. SL2: Slou 1H 123
Rolfe Cl. HP9: Bea 7G 101
Rolvenden Gro. MK7: K Hil 7D 24
Roman Way HP19: Ayle 6G 61
SL8: Bou E 5G 107
(not continuous)
Romar Ct. MK1: Blet 5J 29
Romney Rd. HP21: Ayle 3K 65
Romsey Cl. SL3: Lang 1A 130
Romsey Dr. SL2: Farn C 1B 118
Romsey Way HP11: H Wyc 4B 98
Ronald Rd. HP9: Bea 6H 101
Ronaldsay Spur SL1: Slou 3C 124
Ronan Way UB9: Den 7F 113
Rookery Ct. SL7: Marl 7H 105
Rookery Mdw. HP15: H Grn 7J 83
Rookery Way MK18: S Clay 2D 42
Rook Rd. HP10: Woob G 5K 107
ROOKSLEY 4B 22
ROOKSLEY 3B 22
Rooks Ter. UB7: W Dra 7K 127
Rook Wood Way HP16: G Mis 1H 83
Roperies, The HP13: H Wyc 2E 98
Rosary, The HP15: H Grn 7J 83
SL8: Bou E 6G 107
Roseary Cl. UB7: W Dra 2K 131
Rose Av. HP15: Haz 4G 91
HP19: Ayle 4H 61
Rosebay Cl. MK7: Waln 2D 30
Rosebery Av. HP13: H Wyc 3E 98
Rosebery Rd. HP22: Ast C 2B 68
Rose Bus. Est. SL7: Marl 4H 105
Rosecomb Pl. MK5: S Broo 3A 28
Rose Cnr. HP14: Stoke 5C 72
Rose Ct. HP6: Amer 4C 86
MK46: Oln 4J 7
(off East St.)
Rose Dr. HP5: Ches 6B 78
Rose Hill SL1: Burn 6C 116
Rosemary Cl. HP12: H Wyc 6F 89
Rosemary Ct. HP12: H Wyc 6F 89
MK7: Waln 2C 30
Rosemary La. HP17: Hadd 5C 58
Rosemead HP22: Halt 6B 68
Rosemoor M. HP19: Ayle 6E 60

Rosemullion Av. MK4: Tatt 7B 28
Rosery, The SL8: Bou E 6G 107
Roses Cl. LU7: Cubl 2G 47
Roses La. SL4: Wind 7F 129
Rose Ter. HP18: Wadd 6C 52
Rosetree Cl. HP16: Pres 7C 74
Rose Wlk. SL2: Slou 3K 123
Rosewood Gdns. HP12: H Wyc 4G 97
Rosewood Way SL2: Farn C 3A 118
Rosken Gro. SL2: Farn R 7K 117
Roslyn Ct. MK15: Will 6K 17
Rossal Pl. MK12: H Lea 2H 21
Rossendale MK14: Stan 6D 16
Rossetti Pl. HP15: H Grn 7J 83
Rossini Pl. MK7: Old P 2F 31
Ross Rd. HP22: A Abb 6J 47
Ross Way MK3: Blet 5F 29
Rostrevor Gdns. SL0: I Hea 7D 120
ROTHERFIELD GREYS 2A 136
ROTHERFIELD PEPPARD 2A 136
ROTHERSTHORPE 1B 132
Rothersthorpe MK14: G Par 5G 17
Rothesay Cl. HP20: Ayle 5K 61
Rothschild Av. HP22: Ast C 2B 68
Rothschild Rd. LU7: Wing 3C 48
Rotten Row MK17: G Bri 6E 34
Roughwood Cft. HP8: D Gil 3H 95
Roughwood La. HP8: D Gil 5J 95
Roundheads End HP9: Bea 4D 100
Round Hill HP17: Sto 2C 64
Roundhill Ct. HP17: Hadd 4A 58
Roundlands HP27: L Grn 1C 80
Roundwood Rd. HP6: Amer 5C 86
HP12: H Wyc 1G 97
Rouse Ct. SL9: G Cro 3K 111
ROUT'S GREEN 1A 72 (1A 136)
Routs Grn. HP14: Bled R 1A 72
Roveley Ct. MK11: S Strat 1D 20
Row, The HP14: L End 3K 73
Rowan Av. HP13: H Wyc 7D 90
Rowan Cl. HP9: Bea 7D 100
HP15: Haz 4G 91
HP21: Ayle 3K 65
Rowan Cotts. HP16: H Hea 6C 76
Rowan Dr. MK19: H'ham 3H 15
Rowan Gdns. SL0: I Hea 7D 120
Rowanhurst Dr. SL2: Farn C 3A 118
Rowan Pl. HP6: Amer 5D 86
HP12: Book 5G 97
Rowan Rd. UB7: W Dra 2K 131
Rowans, The SL9: C Pet 1H 111
Rowan Way HP5: Ches 4K 77
SL2: Slou 3K 123
Rowborough Rd. HP22: Halt 1K 69
Rowlands Cl. MK2: F Str 7A 30
Rowland Way HP19: Ayle 7G 61
Rowle Cl. MK14: Stan 6D 16
Rowley La. SL3: Wex 6G 119
Rowliff Rd. HP12: H Wyc 2G 97
ROWSHAM 2C 135
Rowsham Dell MK14: G Par 3F 17
Rowsham Rd. HP22: Bier 1D 62
Rowton Heath MK5: O'ill 2G 27
Roxburgh Way MK3: Blet 4F 29
Roxwell Cl. SL1: Slou 6G 123
Roxwell Path *HP20: Ayle* *4A 62*
(off Bryanston Av.)
Royle Cl. SL9: C Pet 5K 103
Royston Way SL1: Slou 3F 123
Rubbra Cl. MK7: Brow 2E 30
Rubens Cl. HP19: Ayle 4E 60
Ruby Cl. SL1: Slou 7J 123
Ruckles Way HP7: Amer 7A 86
Rudchesters MK13: Ban 1K 21
Ruddlesway SL4: Wind 7F 129
(not continuous)
Rudds Cl. MK18: Wins 5J 39
Rudd's La. HP17: Hadd 5C 58
Rudsworth Cl. SL3: Coln 6D 130
Rugby Ri. HP11: W Mar 5G 99
Rugwood Rd. HP10: F Hea 7F 99
RUISLIP 2D 137
RUISLIP COMMON 2D 137
Rumptons Paddock HP18: G Und 2G 43
Runford Ct. MK5: S Lod 2C 28
Run Furrow HP17: Hadd 5C 58
Runnymede MK14: G Par 4F 17
Runrig Hill HP6: Amer 2C 86
Rupert Av. HP12: H Wyc 4J 97
RUSCOMBE 3A 136
Rushbrooke Cl. HP13: H Wyc 5F 91
Rushburn HP10: Woob G 3B 108
Rushendon Furlong LU7: Pits 4G 51
Rushes, The SL7: Marl 2G 115
Rushes Mead UB8: Uxb 6J 121
Rushleys Cl. MK5: Lough 6K 21
Rushmere Cl. MK17: Bow B 5E 30
Rushmere La. HP5: O L'gh 2E 78
Rushmere Retail Pk. MK1: F Str 5K 29
Rushmoor Av. HP15: Haz 5H 91
Rushton Ct. MK8: G Hol 6K 21
RUSHYMEAD 3K 93
Ruskin Ct. MK16: New P 3J 17
Ruskin Way HP20: Ayle 4J 61
Rusland Cir. MK4: E Val 5B 28
Russel Ct. HP14: Nap 6G 81
Russell Av. HP21: Ayle 1H 65
Russell Cl. HP6: L Chal 6H 87
HP10: T Grn 6H 91
Russell Ct. HP5: Ches 3B 78
Russell St. MK11: S Strat 1B 20
MK17: W San 3K 31
RUSSELL'S WATER 2A 136
Russett Hill SL9: C Pet 1J 111
Russetts, The SL9: C Pet 7H 103
Russwell La. MK17: L Bric 2E 34
Rustlings Ga. HP14: L End 3A 96
Rutherford Cl. SL4: Wind 6H 129
Rutherford Ga. MK5: S Lod 2C 28
Rutherford Rd. HP21: Ayle 3K 65
Ruthven Cl. MK2: Blet 4J 33
Rutland Av. HP12: H Wyc 3G 97
SL1: Slou 3A 124
Rutland Ct. HP11: H Wyc 2A 98
Rutland St. HP11: H Wyc 1A 98
Ryans Mt. SL7: Marl 7G 105
Rycroft MK4: Fur 4E 28
Rydal Way HP12: Book 3F 97
MK2: Blet 2K 33
Ryding, The MK5: S Broo 3K 27
Rydinghurst Ho. SL9: C Pet 3J 103
Rydings SL4: Wind 7H 129
Rye Cl. HP21: Ayle 3J 65
Rye Ct. SL1: Slou 7E 124
Ryecroft Rd. HP5: Ches 6J 77
Ryeland MK11: S Strat 7C 14
Ryemead Blvd. HP11: H Wyc 4F 99
Ryemead Way HP11: H Wyc 4F 99
Rye Vw. HP13: H Wyc 1C 98
Rylstone Cl. MK13: Hee 3B 22
Ryton Pl. MK4: E Val 4C 28
Ryvers Rd. SL3: Lang 1A 130

S

Sabina Cl. HP12: H Wyc 2J 97
Saddington MK6: Wough 1K 29
Saddlers Pl. MK14: D Barn 1G 23
Sadleir's Grn. MK17: W San 2K 31
Saffron Ct. *HP13: H Wyc* *2C 98*
(off Saffron Ct.)
Saffron Ri. LU6: E Bra 1J 49
Saffron Rd. HP13: H Wyc 2C 98
Saffron St. MK2: Blet 1K 33
Saham Cft. Cl. MK18: Wins 6G 39
Sailing Club La. SL8: Bou E 6G 107
St Agnes Ga. HP22: Wend 3G 69
St Aiden's Cl. MK3: Blet 2E 32
St Alban's Rd. MK18: Wins 6H 39
St Andrew's Av. MK3: Blet 1E 32
SL4: Wind 7H 129
St Andrew's Cl. HP13: H Wyc 6F 91
St Andrews Cotts. *SL4: Wind* *7J 129*
(off Cross Oak)
St Andrews Ct. *SL1: Slou* *7C 124*
(off Upton Pk.)
St Andrew's Cres. SL4: Wind 7H 129
St Andrews Ho. MK7: Cald 5C 30
St Andrew's Rd. UB10: Uxb 6K 121
St Andrew's Way SL1: Slou 5F 123
St Andrews Way Ind. Est.
HP19: Ayle 5H 61
St Anne's Cl. HP22: Wend 3H 69
St Anne's Ho. MK7: Cald 5C 30
St Anne's Rd. HP19: Ayle 6G 61
UB9: Hare 1J 113
St Anns Ct. HP10: Loud 6J 99
St Anthony Pl. MK4: Tatt 7B 28
St Anthony's Cl. HP19: Ayle 6G 61
St Anthonys Ct. HP9: Bea 1D 108
St Bartholomews MK10: Monk 5C 24
St Bees MK10: Monk 5D 24
St Bernards Ct. *HP13: H Wyc* *2C 98*
(off Harlow Rd.)
St Birinus HP10: F Hea 6G 99
St Botolphs MK10: Monk 5D 24
St Brides Cl. MK6: Sprin 4J 23
St Catherine's Av. MK3: Blet 2D 32
St Catherine's Ct. HP19: Ayle 6G 61
St Christopher Rd. UB8: Cowl 4K 127
St Christophers Cl. HP16: L Kin 3H 83
St Clement Cl. UB8: Cowl 4K 127
St Clements Dr. MK3: Blet 1D 32
St David Cl. UB8: Cowl 3K 127
St David's Cl. SL0: I Hea 6D 120
St David's Rd. MK3: Blet 2E 32
St Dunstans MK6: Coff 7G 23
St Edmund's Cl. HP19: Ayle 6G 61
St Edwards Ct. MK14: N Hill 6F 17
St Elmo Cl. SL2: Slou 2B 124
St Elmo Cres. SL2: Slou 2B 124
St Faith's Cl. MK17: New L 5D 32
St Francis Rd. UB9: Den 4F 113
St Georges Cl. HP13: H Wyc 1D 98
SL4: Wind 6G 129
St Georges Ct. HP12: H Wyc 7H 89
St George's Cres. SL1: Slou 5F 123
St George's Ho. MK7: Cald 5C 30
St Georges Ind. Est. HP7: Amer 6D 86
St George's Rd. MK3: Blet 2D 32
St Georges Way MK12: Wolv 6H 15
St Giles M. MK11: S Strat 7B 14
St Giles Quadrant HP8: D Gil 6K 95
St Giles St. MK13: New B 6K 15
St Govans Cl. MK4: Tatt 7C 28
St Helen Cl. UB8: Cowl 3K 127
St Helens Gro. MK10: Monk 6B 24
St Hilda's Ct. HP19: Ayle 6G 61
St Hilda's Way HP10: F Hea 6G 99
St Huberts Cl. SL9: G Cro 6J 111
St Hubert's La. SL9: G Cro 7K 111
St Hughes Cl. HP14: Stoke 6D 72
St Hughes Pl. HP14: Stoke 6D 72
St Hugh's Av. HP13: H Wyc 2F 99
St Ives Cres. MK4: Tatt 7A 28
St James Cl. MK19: H'ope 2E 8
St James' Courtyard *SL7: Marl* *7J 105*
(off Claremont Gdns.)
ST JAMES END 1B 132
St James Pl. SL1: Slou 4E 122
St James St. MK13: New B 6K 15
St James Wlk. SL0: R Pk 7E 126
St James Way HP22: Bier 3C 62
St Johns HP15: Haz 5E 90
St John's Av. HP10: T Grn 6H 91
St Johns Cl. HP10: T Grn 6H 91
UB8: Uxb 6H 121
St Johns Cres. MK12: Wolv 1H 21
St Johns Dr. HP17: Sto 2A 64
SL4: Wind 7J 129
St Johns Rd. HP10: T Grn 6H 91
HP15: Haz 4F 91
HP20: Ayle 5K 61
MK3: Blet 2D 32
SL2: Slou 5E 124
SL4: Wind 7J 129
UB8: Uxb 6H 121
St John's St. HP20: Ayle 5K 61
St John's Ter. MK16: New P 1K 17
St John St. MK16: New P 1K 17
St Josephs Cl. MK46: Oln 3H 7
St Josephs M. HP9: Bea 6H 101
St Laurence Cl. UB8: Cowl 3J 127
St Laurence Rd. MK18: Wins 6H 39
St Laurence Way SL1: Slou 7E 124
St Lawrence Vw. MK13: B'ell 2A 22
St Leger Ct. MK14: G Lin 5E 16
St Leger Dr. MK14: G Lin 5D 16
ST LEONARDS 3D 135
St Leonard's Rd. HP6: Amer 2C 86
St Leonards Wlk. SL0: R Pk 1F 131
St Luke Cl. UB8: Cowl 4K 127
St Luke's Rd. UB10: Uxb 5K 121
ST MARGARET'S 2D 135
St Margarets Cl. HP10: Pen 7J 91
MK16: New P 1A 18
SL0: I Hea 7D 120
St Margarets Ct. MK2: Blet 7A 30
SL0: I Hea 7D 120
St Margarets Ga. SL0: I Hea 7D 120
St Margarets Gro. HP15: G Kin 5E 82
St Marks Rd. HP21: Ayle 7H 61
SL4: Wind 7K 129
St Martin Cl. UB8: Cowl 4K 127
St Martin's Cl. UB7: W Dra 1K 131
St Martin's Rd. UB7: W Dra 1J 131
St Martin's St. MK2: Blet 7J 29
St Mary's Av. MK3: Blet 1E 32
MK11: S Strat 7C 14
St Mary's Cl. HP16: L Com 1K 75
MK17: Mur 2C 40
MK17: Wave 7G 25
UB9: Hare 1H 113
St Marys Ct. HP7: Amer 7K 85
HP9: Bea 1H 109
MK18: Ting 1C 36
St Mary's Glebe LU6: Edle 3J 49
St Mary's Rd. SL3: Lang 6J 125
UB9: Den 4F 113
UB9: Hare 1H 113
St Mary's Row *HP20: Ayle* *6J 61*
(off St Mary's Sq.)
St Mary's Sq. HP20: Ayle 6J 61
St Mary's St. MK13: New B 6K 15
St Mary St. HP11: H Wyc 2B 98
St Mary's Way HP5: Ches 5K 77
SL9: C Pet 7H 103
St Matthew Cl. UB8: Cowl 4K 127
St Matthews Ct. MK3: Blet 2E 32
St Michaels Cl. HP22: Halt 7K 67
LU7: Stew 3C 46
St Michaels Ct. SL2: Slou 2F 123
St Michaels Dr. MK7: Walt H 1B 30
St Michael's Grn. HP9: Bea 5G 101
St Michaels Way MK18: S Clay 3C 42
St Monica's La. MK14: N Hill 7F 17
St Nicholas Cl. LU7: Cubl 2G 47
UB8: Cowl 4K 127
St Nicholas St. HP7: L Chal 6F 87
St Patrick's Way MK3: Blet 2E 32
St Paul Cl. UB8: Cowl 3K 127
St Pauls Av. SL2: Slou 5D 124
St Pauls Ct. MK11: S Strat 7A 14
St Paul's Rd. MK3: Blet 2D 32
St Peter's Av. HP19: Ayle 3H 61
St Peters Cl. HP11: W Mar 7H 99
HP27: Spee 2G 81
SL1: Burn 2D 122
SL9: C Pet 6J 103
St Peter's Ct. SL9: C Pet 6J 103
St Peters Rd. UB8: Cowl 3K 127
St Peter St. SL7: Marl 1J 115
St Peters Way MK13: New B 5A 16
St Rumbold's La. MK18: Buck 4G 37
St Stephens Dr. MK15: Bolb 6H 17
St Stephen's Rd. UB7: Yiew 6K 127
St Teresas Cl. HP27: Prin R 4G 71
St Thomas Ct. MK4: Tatt 6K 27
St Thomas Wlk. SL3: Coln 5D 130
St Tiggywinkles Wildlife Hospital 7D 58
Salden Cl. MK5: S Chur 1B 28
MK17: Dray P 6C 40
SALFORD 3D 133
Salisbury Av. SL2: Slou 2A 124
Salisbury Cl. HP7: Amer 6C 86
HP27: Prin R 5H 71
Salisbury Gro. MK14: G Par 3F 17
Salisbury Rd. HP13: H Wyc 6D 90
UB8: Uxb 7H 121
Salmons La. HP16: Pres 7D 74
Saltash Cl. HP13: H Wyc 4H 99
Salters Cl. HP18: Ludg 2C 52
Salters La. HP18: Ludg 2C 52
Salters M. MK14: N Hill 7F 17
Salters Row HP10: Woob G 5C 108
SALT HILL 6A 124
Salt Hill Av. SL1: Slou 6A 124
Salt Hill Cl. UB8: Uxb 3K 121
Salt Hill Dr. SL1: Slou 6A 124
Salt Hill Mans. SL1: Slou 6A 124
Salt Hill Way SL1: Slou 6A 124
Salton Link MK4: E Val 5B 28
Saltwood Dr. MK4: K'ead 6H 27
Samphire Ct. MK7: Waln 1C 30
Sampson's Grn. SL2: Slou 1H 123
Sampsons Hill HP7: Cole 5G 93
Samuel Cl. MK16: New P 2B 18
Sanctuary Rd. HP15: Haz 2H 91
Sandage Rd. HP14: L End 3K 73
Sandal Ct. MK5: S Chur 2A 28
Sandbrier Cl. MK7: Waln 1C 30
Sandels Way HP9: Bea 4F 101
Sandelswood End HP9: Bea 3F 101
Sandelswood Gdns. HP9: Bea 4F 101
Sanderson Rd. UB8: Uxb 4J 121
Sandford Gdns. HP11: H Wyc 4B 98
Sandhill Way HP19: Ayle 6F 61
Sandholme MK18: S Clay 2C 42
Sandhurst Dr. MK18: Buck 5G 37
Sandlers End SL2: Slou 2K 123
Sandmartin Cl. MK18: Buck 3J 37
Sandown Ct. MK3: Blet 2D 32
Sandown Rd. SL2: Slou 3H 123
Sandpiper HP19: Ayle 2K 61
Sandpit Hill MK18: Ting 2A 36
Sandpit La. HP27: Bled 4A 70
Sandpits La. HP10: Pen 1J 99
Sandringham Ct. MK16: New P 2H 17
SL1: Slou 4F 123
Sandringham Pl. MK2: Blet 7J 29
SANDS 1F 97
Sands Farm Dr. SL1: Burn 2E 122
Sands Ind. Est. HP12: H Wyc 1E 96
Sandwell Ct. MK8: T Ash 4G 21
Sandy Cl. MK14: G Lin 5D 16
MK18: Buck 4K 37
Sandycroft Rd. HP6: L Chal 5G 87
Sandygate Cl. SL7: Marl 6H 105
Sandygate Rd. SL7: Marl 6H 105
Sandy La. HP18: Long C 6B 56
MK17: A H'th 5K 31
Sandy Ri. SL9: C Pet 6J 103
Sandywell Dr. MK15: D Park 7G 17
Santen Gro. MK2: Blet 4K 33
Saracens Wharf MK2: F Str 6A 30
Sarcus Dean SL9: C Pet 3K 103
Sargeant Cl. UB8: Cowl 1K 127
SARRATT 1D 137
Sarum Complex UB8: Uxb 1H 127
SATWELL 2A 136
Saunders Cl. MK7: W Gat 1F 31
Saunders End HP6: H Hea 1E 84
Saunders Pl. HP19: Ayle 7F 61
Saunders Wood Copse
HP14: Stoke 6D 72
SAUNDERTON 7E 70 (3B 134)
SAUNDERTON LEE 1B 136
Saunderton Station (Rail) 5A 80
Saunderton Va.
HP14: Saun 5A 80
Savage Cft. MK10: Midd 3A 24
Savay Cl. UB9: Den 5G 113
Savay La. UB9: Den 4G 113
Savernake Rd. HP19: Ayle 4H 61
Savill Way SL7: Marl 7K 105
Savoy Cres. MK9: C Key 3F 23
Sawmill Rd. HP27: Long 1C 70
Sawpit Hill HP15: Haz 2G 91
Sawpit La. MK17: G Bri 5E 34
Sawyers Cl. SL4: Wind 5G 129
Saxeway Bus. Cen. HP5: Ches 2G 77
Saxhorn Rd. HP14: L End 4A 96
Saxon Cl. HP6: Amer 5B 86
SL3: Lang 7K 125
Saxon Gdns. SL6: Tapl 2A 122
Saxon Ga. E. MK9: C Key 4E 22
Saxon Ga. (V7) MK9: Mil K 3D 22
Saxon Ga. W. MK9: C Key 4E 22

Saxon St. (V7) MK1: Mil K 6J **29**
MK2: Mil K 7J **29**
MK6: Mil K 5F **23**
MK6: Mil K 3J **29**
MK14: Mil K 5C **16**
Saxon Way UB7: Harm 4J **131**
Saxon Way Ind. Est. UB7: Harm 4J **131**
Saye & Sele Cl. HP18: G Und 2G **43**
Sayward Cl. HP5: Ches 3B **78**
Scafell Rd. SL2: Slou 2H **123**
Scarborough Way SL1: Slou 1K **129**
Scardale MK13: Hee 1C **22**
Scarlett Av. HP22: Halt 2K **69**
Scatterill Cl. MK13: B'ell 2A **22**
Scholars Wlk. SL3: Lang 7A **126**
SL9: C Pet 4J **103**
Scholars Way HP6: Amer 5D **86**
School Cl. HP11: H Wyc 4K **97**
HP13: Down 5H **89**
HP15: Crye 1C **90**
HP15: H Grn 7J **83**
HP18: Ick 5E **54**
School Dr. MK17: New L 5C **32**
School End MK17: G Hor 2J **39**
School Hill MK18: N Mar 2B **44**
School La. HP7: Amer 6H **85**
HP7: Penn S 2D **92**
HP8: D Gil 7F **95**
HP9: S Grn 4B **102**
HP17: Dint 2H **59**
HP18: Che 2H **57**
HP18: Oak 5H **53**
HP18: Shab 6H **55**
HP18: Wadd 6C **52**
HP22: West T 5F **67**
LU6: E Bra 1J **49**
MK5: Lough 6B **22**
MK16: Sher 2C **12**
MK18: Buck 4G **37**
MK19: Cast 7D **8**
SL2: S Pog 5F **119**
SL2: Slou 5D **124**
SL7: L Mar 4C **106**
SL7: Medm 4A **114**
SL9: C Pet 7H **103**
School Rd. HP10: T Grn 7J **91**
HP10: Woob G 3A **108**
UB7: Harm 4K **131**
School St. MK13: New B 6K **15**
School Wlk. SL2: Slou 5F **125**
School Way HP11: W Mar 6H **99**
Schorne La. MK18: N Mar 2B **44**
Schumann Cl. MK7: Brow 3E **30**
Schwarz Ho. HP5: Ches 6A **78**
Scotch Firs MK7: W Gat 1E **30**
Scotlands Dr. SL2: Farn C 4K **117**
Scotney Gdns. MK3: Blet 7E **28**
Scott Cl. SL2: Farn C 3A **118**
Scott Dr. MK16: New P 7G **11**
Scott End HP19: Ayle 4E **60**
Scott Evans Ct. MK18: Wins 5J **39**
Scott Ho. *HP5: Ches 3K* ***77***
(off Pearce Rd.)
Scotts Cl. MK17: S Ham 1H **41**
OX27: M Gib 5D **42**
Scotts Farm Cl. MK18: M M'ton 1J **37**
Scotts La. MK18: Ads 6E **38**
MK18: M M'ton 1J **37**
OX27: M Gib 6B **42**
Scottswood Cl. HP9: Bea 3F **101**
Scriven Ct. MK15: Will 6K **17**
Seabrooke Ct. MK8: G Far 1H **27**
Seacourt Rd. SL3: Lang 2B **130**
Seagrave Ct. MK7: Walt P 3C **30**
Seagrave Rd. HP9: Bea 4E **100**
Sears, The LU6: N'all 1F **49**
Seaton Dr. HP21: Ayle 3J **65**
Seaton Gro. MK10: Bro 2C **24**
Secklow Ga. MK9: C Key 3E **22**
Secklow Ga. E. MK9: C Key 4F **23**
Secklow Ga. W. MK9: C Key 4F **23**
Second Av. MK1: Blet 5J **29**
Second Cres. SL1: Slou 3A **124**
Second St. HP11: H Wyc 4B **98**
Sedgemere MK8: T Ash 5H **21**
Sedgmoor Cl. HP10: F Hea 2G **107**
Sedgmoor Gdns. HP10: F Hea 1G **107**
Sedgmoor La. HP10: F Hea 2H **107**
Sedgmoor Rd. HP10: F Hea 1G **107**
Sedley Gro. UB9: Hare 2J **113**
SEDRUP 3F **65**
Sedrup La. HP17: Hart 3E **64**
Seeleys Cl. HP9: Bea 4E **100**
Seeleys Ct. *HP9: Bea 5F* ***101***
(off Orchard Cl.)
Seeleys La. *HP9: Bea 5F* ***101***
(off Seeleys La.)
Seeleys Rd. HP9: Bea 3E **100**
Seeleys Wlk. HP9: Bea 5E **100**
SEER GREEN 4A **102** (1C **137**)
Seer Grn. La. HP9: Jord 4C **102**
Seer Green Station (Rail) 5A **102**
Seermead HP9: S Grn 4B **102**
Sefton Cl. SL2: S Pog 6D **118**
Sefton Paddock SL2: S Pog 5E **118**
Sefton Pk. SL2: S Pog 5E **118**
Sefton Way UB8: Cowl 4J **127**

Selbourne Av. MK3: Blet 1F **33**
Selby Cotts. *HP16: L Kin 3G* ***83***
(off Hare La.)
Selby Gro. MK5: S Chur 2A **28**
Seldon Ga. MK9: Camp 2G **23**
Selim Ct. *SL1: Slou 7F* ***125***
(off Clifton Rd.)
Selkirk Av. HP19: Ayle 4J **61**
Selkirk Gro. MK3: Blet 5F **29**
Selwood Way
HP13: Down 5J **89**
Selworthy MK4: Fur 4D **28**
Selwyn Cl. SL4: Wind 7F **129**
Selwyn Ct. HP21: Ayle 1C **66**
Selwyn Gro. MK3: Blet 7H **29**
Selwyn Pl. SL1: Slou 5H **123**
September Ct. UB8: Uxb 7K **121**
Serjeants Grn.
MK14: N Hill 7F **17**
Serles Cl. MK6: Coff 1G **29**
Sermed Ct. SL2: Slou 6G **125**
Serpentine Ct. MK2: Blet 3K **33**
Sevenacres HP18: Long C 5B **56**
Seven Hills Rd. SL0: I Hea 3B **120**
Severalls Av. HP5: Ches 4A **78**
Severn Cres. SL3: Lang 3B **130**
Severn Dr. MK16: New P 1K **17**
Severn Way MK3: Blet 6D **28**
SEWELL 1D **135**
Sewell Cl. HP19: Ayle 4E **60**
Seymour Cl. HP10: F Hea 6F **99**
Seymour Ct. La. SL7: Marl 4F **105**
Seymour Ct. Rd. SL7: Marl 4G **105**
Seymour Ho. HP12: H Wyc 4J **97**
SL3: Lang 7J **125**
Seymour Pk. Rd. SL7: Marl 6H **105**
Seymour Plain SL7: Marl 4G **105**
Seymour Rd. HP8: D Gil 2G **103**
SL1: Slou 7A **124**
SHABBINGTON 5H **55** (3A **134**)
Shackleton Pl. MK6: Old 5E **22**
Shackleton Rd. HP12: H Wyc 3H **97**
SL1: Slou 5D **124**
Shaftesbury Ct. MK18: Wins 5H **39**
SL1: Slou 7C **124**
Shaftesbury Cres. MK3: Blet 6G **29**
Shaftesbury Ho. HP21: Ayle 7D **62**
Shaftesbury St. HP11: H Wyc 7K **89**
Shaggy Calf La. SL2: Slou 5E **124**
Shakespeare Cl. MK16: New P 7G **11**
Shakespeare Orchard HP18: G Und 2G **43**
Shakespeare Way HP20: Ayle 6B **62**
Shallowford Gro. MK4: Fur 3D **28**
SHALSTONE 3A **132**
Shamrock Cl. MK7: Waln 1D **30**
Shannon Ct. *HP5: Ches 4A* ***78***
(off Broadlands Av.)
MK14: D Barn 7G **17**
Shantock Hall La. HP3: Bov 3J **79**
Shantock La. HP3: Bov 4H **79**
Shantung Pl. *HP5: Ches 7A* ***78***
(off Moor Rd.)
Sharkham Ct. MK4: Tatt 6B **28**
Sharman Wlk. MK13: B'ell 3A **22**
SHARNBROOK 1D **133**
Sharney Av. SL3: Lang 1B **130**
Sharp Cl. HP21: Ayle 2K **65**
Sharp's Cl. HP18: Wadd 6D **52**
Sharrow Va. HP12: H Wyc 1J **97**
Shaw Cl. HP16: Pres 1D **82**
HP20: Ayle 6B **62**
MK16: New P 7G **11**
Shaw Ct. HP21: Ayle 4K **65**
Shawfield Ct. UB7: W Dra 1K **131**
Shearmans MK11: F Sla 2E **20**
Sheehy Way SL2: Slou 5F **125**
Sheelin Gro. MK2: Blet 4K **33**
Sheepcoat Cl. MK5: S Chur 2A **28**
Sheepcote Cl. HP9: Bea 4E **100**
Sheepcote Dell Rd. HP7: Bea E 7A **84**
HP15: H Grn 7K **83**
Sheepcote Gdns. UB9: Den 4G **113**
Sheepcote La. SL1: Burn 1B **116**
Sheepcote Rd. SL4: E Wick 3J **129**
SL4: Wind 7G **129**
Sheepfold La. HP7: Amer 6B **86**
SHEEPRIDGE 2E **106**
Sheepridge La. HP10: F Hea 2E **106**
SL7: L Mar 2E **106**
Sheep St. MK18: Wins 6J **39**
Sheering Gro. MK13: B'lle 5B **16**
Sheerness Ct. MK4: Tatt 7A **28**
Sheerstock HP17: Hadd 7A **58**
Sheerwater HP19: Ayle 2K **61**
SHEFFIELD BOTTOM 3A **136**
Sheffield Dr. HP21: Ayle 1K **65**
Sheffield Rd. SL1: Slou 4A **124**
Shelburne Ct. HP12: H Wyc 4J **97**
Shelburne Rd. HP12: H Wyc 4J **97**
Sheldon Ct. MK8: G Hol 5K **21**
Sheldon Rd. HP18: Ick 5D **54**
Shellduck Cl. HP19: Ayle 3K **61**
Shelley Cl. HP10: Woob G 1A **108**
MK16: New P 1H **17**
SL3: Lang 3A **130**
SL7: Medm 3B **114**
Shelley Dr. MK3: Blet 1F **33**

Shelley Rd. HP5: Ches 3K **77**
HP11: H Wyc 2K **97**
SL7: Marl 6K **105**
Shelsmore MK14: G Par 5G **17**
Shelton Ct. MK17: W San 3K **31**
SL3: Lang 7G **125**
SHENLEY 2A **28**
SHENLEY BROOK END 3A **28** (3C **133**)
SHENLEY CHURCH END 1K **27** (3C **133**)
Shenley Leisure Cen. 7K **21**
SHENLEY LODGE 2B **28**
Shenley Pavilions MK5: S Woo 3K **27**
Shenley Rd. MK3: Blet 6E **28**
(not continuous)
MK5: S Chur 1A **28**
MK17: Whad 7G **27**
SHENLEY WOOD 3A **28**
Shenstone Dr. SL1: Burn 2F **123**
Shepherd Cl. HP20: Ayle 4B **62**
Shepherds MK11: F Sla 2E **20**
Shepherds Cl. SL6: Hur 7D **114**
UB8: Cowl 2J **127**
Shepherds Ct. HP9: Bea 7H **101**
SL4: Wind 7G **129**
Shepherds Fold HP15: H Grn 7K **83**
Shepherds Ga. HP16: L Kin 3G **83**
SHEPHERD'S GREEN 2A **136**
Shepherds La. HP9: Bea 7H **101**
HP15: Haz 2F **91**
SL6: Hur 7B **114**
Shepherds Row MK18: Wins 6J **39**
Shepherds Way HP5: Ches 7B **78**
Sheppards Cl. MK16: New P 1J **17**
Shepperds Cl. MK18: N Mar 2A **44**
Shepperds Grn. MK5: S Chur 1K **27**
SHEPPERTON 3D **137**
Shepperton Cl. MK19: Cast 7C **8**
Sheraton Dr. HP13: H Wyc 6D **90**
Sherborne Cl. SL3: Poy 6E **130**
Sherbourne Dr. MK7: Tilb 4D **30**
Sherbourne Wlk. SL2: Farn C 2A **118**
Shereway HP19: Ayle 6G **61**
Sheridan Cl. HP21: Ayle 4J **65**
Sheridan Ct. SL1: Slou 5G **123**
Sheriff Cl. HP19: Ayle 6G **61**
SHERINGTON 3B **12** (2C **133**)
Sherington Rd. MK16: New P, Sher 7K **11**
Sherman Rd. SL1: Slou 3C **124**
Shernfold MK7: K Hil 7D **24**
Sherriff Cotts. HP18: Wadd 5C **52**
Sherwood Dr. MK3: Blet 5H **29**
Sherwood Ho. MK3: Blet 6H **29**
Shields Ct. HP10: T Grn 6H **91**
Shilling Cl. MK15: Penny 6G **17**
Shillingridge Pk. SL7: Marl 4C **104**
SHINFIELD 3A **136**
Shinfield Cl. MK18: S Clay 3B **42**
Ship Hill SL1: Burn 6G **109**
SHIPLAKE 3A **136**
Shiplake Ho. SL8: Bou E 5H **107**
Ship La. HP23: M'rth 7B **50**
LU7: Pits 6F **51**
Shipley Rd. MK16: New P 1G **17**
Shipman Ct. MK15: W Par 6H **17**
Ship St. HP11: H Wyc 1A **98**
SHIPTON 7K **39** (1B **134**)
Shipton Hill MK13: B'lle 7B **16**
SHIRBURN 1A **136**
Shire Ct. MK14: D Barn 1G **23**
Shire La. WD3: Chor 6K **95**
Shirley Av. SL4: Wind 6H **129**
Shirley Moor MK7: K Hil 6D **24**
Shirwell Cres. MK4: Fur 2D **28**
Shogmoor La. RG9: Skir 7F **73**
SHOOTACRE CORNER 7F **71**
Shootacre La. HP27: Prin R 7E **70**
Shop Rd. SL4: Wind 5E **128**
Shoreham Ri. SL2: Slou 2F **123**
Shorham Ri. MK8: T Ash 4J **21**
Shortborough Av. HP27: Prin R 3G **71**
Short Ditch HP17: Hadd 5C **58**
Shortfern SL2: Slou 4G **125**
Short Hale LU7: Pits 7F **51**
Short Massey MK46: Oln 2G **7**
Short St. HP11: H Wyc 1K **97**
Shortway HP5: Ches 3K **77**
HP6: Amer 4B **86**
Shotfield Rd. HP14: L End 4A **96**
Shouler Cl. MK5: S Chur 2A **28**
SHREDING GREEN 4C **126** (2D **137**)
Shrewsbury Cl. MK10: Monk 4C **24**
Shrimpton Cl. HP9: Bea 2F **101**
Shrimpton Rd. HP9: Bea 2F **101**
HP12: Book 5F **97**
Shropshire Ct. MK3: Blet 6E **28**
Shrubbery Cl. HP13: H Wyc 7B **90**
Shrubbery Rd. HP13: H Wyc 7B **90**
Shupp's La. HP18: Che 2H **57**
SHURLOCK ROW 3B **136**
SHUTLANGER 2B **132**
Shuttleworth Gro. MK7: W Gat 1F **31**
Sibleys Ri. HP16: S Hea 5K **75**
Side Rd. UB9: Den 5D **112**
Sidings, The HP11: W Mar 5H **99**
Sidlaw Ct. MK11: F Sla 2D **20**
Sidney Cl. UB8: Uxb 5J **121**
Sidney Ho. HP14: L End 3A **96**

Sidney Rd. SL4: Wind 7E **128**
Sidney Ter. HP22: Wend 3H **69**
SILBURY 5C **22**
Silbury Arc. MK9: C Key 4E **22**
Silbury Blvd. MK9: C Key 5C **22**
Silicon Ct. MK5: S Lod 2C **28**
Silk St. HP18: Wadd 6C **52**
Sillswood MK46: Oln 3G **7**
Sills Yd. HP5: Ches 5K **77**
Silsden Cres. HP8: D Gil 1H **103**
Silver Birch Cvn. Pk. HP14: Walt A 5F **81**
Silver Birch Cl. HP27: L Grn 1C **80**
Silverbirches La. MK17: A H'th 5J **31**
Silverdale Cl. HP10: T Grn 6G **91**
HP20: Ayle 5J **61**
Silver End MK46: Oln 4J **7**
Silver Hill HP8: D Gil 7F **95**
Silvermead HP18: Worm 3B **54**
SILVERSTONE 2A **132**
Silver St. HP20: Ayle 6J **61**
LU7: Cubl 2G **47**
MK11: S Strat 1B **20**
MK16: New P 1K **17**
Silverweed Ct. MK7: Waln 1D **30**
Simmons Cl. SL3: Lang 2A **130**
Simmons Ct. HP21: Ayle 3K **65**
Simmons Way HP14: L End 4A **96**
Simms Cft. MK10: Midd 4C **24**
Simnel MK6: Bean 1H **29**
Simon Dean HP3: Bov 1K **79**
Simonsbath MK4: Fur 5D **28**
Simons Lea MK13: B'ell 2B **22**
SIMPSON 2K **29**
SIMPSON 2K **29**
Simpson MK6: Simp 2A **30**
Simpson Dr. MK6: Simp 2A **30**
Simpson Pl. HP21: Ayle 2A **66**
Simpson Rd. MK6: Simp 2A **30**
Simpsons Way SL1: Slou 6B **124**
Sinclair Ct. MK1: Blet 4G **29**
SINDLESHAM 3A **136**
SINGLEBOROUGH 1H **39** (3B **132**)
Singleborough La. MK17: G Hor 2H **39**
Singleton Dr. MK8: G Far 1H **27**
Singleton Way HP19: Ayle 6F **61**
Singret Pl. UB8: Cowl 2J **127**
SIPSON 3D **137**
Sipthorp Cl. MK7: W Gat 1E **30**
Sir Henry Peakes Dr. SL2: Farn C 4J **117**
Sir Robert M. SL3: Lang 3A **130**
Sir Sydney Camm Ho.
SL4: Wind 6K **129**
Sissinghurst Dr. MK4: West 5J **27**
Sitwell Cl. MK16: New P 7F **11**
Sixth St. HP11: H Wyc 4C **98**
Sixty Acres Rd. HP16: Pres 1C **82**
Skeats Wharf MK15: Penny 6G **17**
SKELDON 2G **23**
Skelton Cl. HP9: Bea 1C **108**
Skene Cl. MK2: Blet 4J **33**
Skerries Ct. SL3: Lang 2A **130**
Skimmers Cl. HP15: H Grn 1J **91**
Skimmers End HP15: H Grn 1J **91**
Skimmers Fld. HP15: H Grn 1J **91**
Skip La. UB9: Hare 6K **113**
Skipton Cl. MK15: W Par 7J **17**
SKIRMETT 1A **136**
SKITTLE GREEN 5A **70** (3B **134**)
Skittle Grn. HP27: Bled 6A **70**
Skydmore Path SL2: Slou 1H **123**
Skye Lodge *SL1: Slou 6C* ***124***
(off Lansdowne Av.)
Skylark Rd. UB9: Den 6C **112**
Skyport Dr. UB7: Harm 5K **131**
Skyway Trad. Est. SL3: Poy 7F **131**
Slade, The MK17: New L 5D **32**
Slade Hill HP19: Ayle 7F **61**
Slade La. MK11: F Sla 2D **20**
(not continuous)
Slade Oak La.
SL9: Den, G Cro 1B **112**
UB9: Den 3C **112**
Slade Rd. HP14: Stoke 5B **72**
Slad La. HP27: L Grn, Spee 2D **80**
SLAPTON
Leighton Buzzard 1D **135**
Towcester 2A **132**
Slated Row MK12: O Wol 6F **15**
Slattenham Cl. HP19: Ayle 7G **61**
Slave Hill HP17: Hadd 7B **58**
Slayter Rd. HP14: L End 4A **96**
Slickett's La. LU6: Edle 3K **49**
Slipe, The LU7: Ched 2C **50**
SLOUGH 7D **124** (2C **137**)
Slough Crematorium SL2: Slou 4D **124**
Slough Ice Arena 6B **124**
Slough Indoor Tennis Cen. 6B **124**
Slough Ind. Est. SL1: Slou 3J **123**
(not continuous)
Slough La. HP14: Saun 7A **80**
Slough Mus. *SL1: Slou 7E* ***124***
(off High St.)
Slough Retail Pk. SL1: Slou 6K **123**
Slough Rd. SL0: I Hea 1C **126**
Slough Station (Rail) 6D **124**
Slough Supapitch 3F **125**
Slough Town FC 3E **124**

Slough Trad. Est. SL1: Slou 3H 123
(Banbury Av.)
SL1: Slou 4K 123
(Liverpool Rd., not continuous)
Sly Cnr. HP16: L Com 1A 76
Smabridge Wlk. MK15: Will 6K 17
Small Cres. MK18: Buck 4K 37
Smalldean La. HP14: L Grn, Saun 5B 80
HP22: Wend 7J 69
HP27: L Grn 5B 80
Smarden Bell MK7: K Hil 6D 24
Smeaton Cl. HP19: Ayle 5E 60
MK14: Blak 3G 17
Smithergill Ct. MK13: Hee 2C 22
Smith's La. SL4: Wind 7G 129
Smithsons Pl. MK9: Camp 3H 23
Snaith Cres. MK5: Lough 7B 22
Snakeley Cl. HP10: Loud 7J 99
Snape Spur SL1: Slou 4C 124
Snells La. HP7: L Chal 7F 87
Snells Wood Ct. HP7: L Chal 7G 87
SNELSHALL EAST 1A 32
Snelshall St. (V1) MK4: Mil K 5J 27
SNELSHALL WEST 1A 32
Snowberry Cl. MK12: S Bus 1H 21
Snowdon Dr. MK9: Wint 6D 22
Snowdrop Way HP15: W End 7F 83
Snowshill Ct. MK14: G Par 3F 17
Soames Cl. MK46: Lave 3C 6
Soane Ho. *HP7: Amer 6E 86*
(off Repton Pl.)
Soane Wlk. HP13: Down 7A 90
Soho Cres. HP10: Woob G 5K 107
Soho Mills Ind. Est. HP10: Woob G 5K 107
Sokeman Cl. MK12: Gree 1E 20
Solar Ct. MK14: G Lin 4E 16
Somerford Pl. HP9: Bea 4F 101
Somerset Cl. MK3: Blet 6F 29
Somerset Way SL0: R Pk 7F 127
Somers Lees HP19: Ayle 6F 61
Somerville Rd. SL4: Eto 3K 129
Somerville Way HP19: Ayle 6G 61
SONNING 3A 136
SONNING COMMON 2A 136
Sophie Gdns. SL3: Lang 7H 125
Sorensen Ct. MK5: Medb 3J 27
Sorrell Dr. MK16: New P 7F 11
Soskin Dr. MK14: Stan 7C 16
Sospel Ct. SL2: Farn R 7A 118
SOULBURY 6H 41 (1C 135)
Soulbury Rd. LU7: Stew 3C 46
LU7: Wing, Burc 1B 48
SOULDROP 1D 133
SOUTHALL 3D 137
Southall MK18: M M'ton 1J 37
SOUTH ASCOT 3C 137
Southbourne HP13: H Wyc 1C 98
Southbourne Dr. SL8: Bou E 6G 107
Southbridge Gro. MK7: K Hil 7C 24
Southcliffe Dr. SL9: C Pet 3J 103
South Cl. SL1: Slou 5F 123
SL7: Medm 3B 114
Sth. Concourse MK9: C Key 4E 22
Southcote Way HP10: T Grn 6G 91
SOUTHCOURT 1H 65 (2C 135)
Southcroft SL2: Slou 2K 123
South Dr. HP9: Bea 1D 108
HP13: H Wyc 7D 90
Sth. Eighth St. MK9: C Key 4E 22
SOUTH ELDER 6C 22
SOUTH END 4C 46
South End HP17: Hadd 7B 58
South End La. LU6: N'all 3F 49
SOUTH ENMORE 3H 23
Southern Rd. HP19: Ayle 5H 61
Southern Way MK12: Wolv 1H 21
Southfield Cl. MK15: Will 6K 17
SL4: Dorn 1E 128
Southfield Dr. HP15: Haz 1G 91
Southfield Gdns. SL1: Burn 3D 122
Southfield Rd. HP10: F Hea 7G 99
HP13: Down 6H 89
HP20: Ayle 6C 62
HP27: Prin R 5H 71
Sth. Fifth St. MK9: C Key 5E 22
Sth. Fourth St. MK9: C Key 5D 22
SOUTH GRAFTON 6D 22
South Grn. SL1: Slou 5C 124
SOUTH HAREFIELD 3J 113
SOUTH HEATH 4A 76 (3D 135)
Southlands Rd. SL0: Den, I Hea 4E 120
UB9: Den 2F 121
South La. LU7: Stew 5C 46
South Lawne MK3: Blet 7F 29
South Maundin HP14: H Vall 6A 82
South Mdw. La. SL4: Eto 4K 129
Sth. Ninth St. MK9: C Key 4F 23
SOUTH OVERGATE 3H 23
SOUTH OXHEY 1D 137
South Pk. SL9: G Cro 3K 111
South Pk. Ct. *SL9: G Cro 3K 111*
(off South Pk.)
South Pk. Cres. SL9: G Cro 2J 111
South Pk. Dr. SL9: G Cro 2J 111
South Pk. Vw. SL9: G Cro 2K 111
South Pl. SL7: Marl 1J 115
South Rd. HP6: Amer 3A 86
South Row MK9: C Key 5E 22
(not continuous)
SL3: Fulm 2J 119
SOUTH SAXON 5F 23
SOUTH SECKLOW 4F 23
Sth. Second St. MK9: C Key 5D 22
Sth. Seventh St. MK9: C Key 5E 22
South Side SL9: C Pet 1H 111
Southside La. MK10: M Vill 4B 24
Sth. Sixth St. MK9: C Key 5E 22
South St. HP22: Wend 4H 69
MK19: Cast 7D 8
Sth. Tenth St. MK9: C Key 4F 23
South Ter. MK2: Blet 7J 29
South Vw. HP13: Down 5H 89
SL4: Eto, E Wick 3K 129
Sth. Vw. Rd. SL9: C Pet 2H 111
Southview Rd. SL7: Marl 5J 105
South Way HP9: Bea 1C 108
SOUTH WESTON 1A 136
Southwick Ct. MK8: G Hol 6K 21
SOUTH WITAN 5E 22
Southwold Cl. HP21: Ayle 1B 66
Southwold Spur SL3: Lang 7C 126
Sovereign Beeches SL2: Farn C 4K 117
Sovereign Ct. HP13: H Wyc 2D 98
HP19: Ayle 5J 61
Sovereign Dr. MK15: Penny 6G 17
Sovereign Hgts. SL3: Dat 4A 130
Sovereign Lodge MK15: Penny 6G 17
Spackmans Way SL1: Slou 7B 124
Spa Cl. HP18: Bril 3J 53
Spade Oak Mdw. SL8: Bou E 5E 106
Spade Oak Reach SL6: Cook 7C 106
Span Grn. HP18: Bril 3F 53
Spark Way MK16: New P 7F 11
Sparrow Cl. HP19: Ayle 3A 62
Sparsholt Cl. MK4: E Val 5C 28
Spearing Rd. HP12: H Wyc 2G 97
Spearmint Cl. MK7: Waln 2D 30
Specklands MK5: Lough 6A 22
Speedbird Way UB7: Harm 5H 131
Speedwell Pl. MK14: Conn 2E 22
SPEEN 2G 81 (1B 136)
Speen Rd. HP14: H Vall, N Dean 5J 81
HP27: Spee 2H 81
Speldhurst Ct. MK7: K Hil 7D 24
Spencer MK14: Stan 5C 16
Spencer Cl. UB8: Cowl 1J 127
Spencer Rd. SL3: Lang 1A 130
Spencer St. MK13: New B 6K 15
SPENCERS WOOD 3A 136
Spenlows Rd. MK3: Blet 4G 29
Spenser Rd. HP21: Ayle 1A 66
Spickett's La. HP18: Cudd 1B 58
Spier's La. OX27: M Gib 6C 42
Spiert, The HP17: Sto 2C 64
Spindle Cl. HP15: Haz 4G 91
Spindle Ct. HP12: H Wyc 1J 97
Spinfield La. SL7: Marl 1F 115
Spinfield La. W. SL7: Marl 1G 115
Spinfield Mt. SL7: Marl 1F 115
Spinfield Pk. SL7: Marl 1G 115
Sping Copse HP12: Book 3D 96
Spinners Wlk. SL7: Marl 1G 115
Spinney SL1: Slou 6K 123
Spinney, The HP5: Ches 3B 78
HP9: Bea 1F 109
HP11: H Wyc 4K 97
HP15: H Grn 7K 83
MK13: B'ell 2A 22
MK18: Wins 4J 39
SL9: G Cro 6H 111
Spinney Cl. MK18: S Clay 3C 42
Spinney Hill Rd. MK46: Oln 4G 7
Spinney Pl. HP7: Amer 6B 86
Spirit Health & Fitness Club 7E 62
Spitfire Cl. SL3: Lang 2A 130
Spittal St. SL7: Marl 7H 105
Spoonley Wood MK13: B Pk 1J 21
Sportsman Cl. MK18: S Clay 2B 42
Springate Fld. SL3: Lang 7J 125
Springbank Ct. MK16: S Gold 5C 6
Spring Cl. HP5: Lati 3H 87
HP13: H Wyc 1F 99
MK17: G Hor 3J 39
Spring Coppice La. HP27: Spee 2H 81
Springett Pl. HP6: Amer 4D 86
SPRINGFIELD 4H 23
SPRINGFIELD 4G 23
Springfield MK46: Oln 3H 7
SL1: Slou 7F 125
Springfield Blvd. MK6: Sprin 4H 23
(not continuous)
Springfield Cl. HP5: Ches 6A 78
HP19: Ayle 6H 61
SL4: Wind 7K 129
Springfield Ct. *MK6: Sprin 4H 23*
(off Ravensbourne Pl.)
Springfield Rd. HP5: Ches 7A 78
HP14: Stoke 6D 72
SL3: Lang 5B 130
SL4: Wind 7K 129
Springfields HP6: Amer 4A 86
MK18: Pad 6B 38
Springfields Cl. MK18: Pad 5B 38
Springfields Ct. MK18: Pad 6B 38
Spring Gdns. HP10: Woob G 1A 108
MK16: New P 1J 17
SL7: Marl 6J 105
SL8: Bou E 5G 107
Spring Gdns. Rd. HP13: H Wyc 3E 98
Spring Gro. MK17: W San 2K 31
Springhill Rd. HP18: G Und 1G 43
Spring La. HP10: F Hea, W Mar 6F 99
MK17: G Hor 2J 39
MK46: Oln 4G 7
SL1: Slou 6H 123
SL2: Farn R 5K 117
Spring Valley Rd. HP14: H Vall 7A 82
Springwater Mill HP11: H Wyc 4E 98
Sprinters Sports Cen. 6A 74
Spruce Ct. SL1: Slou 7D 124
Spruce Dene HP15: Haz 5F 91
Spruce Rd. HP19: Ayle 6E 60
Spur, The SL1: Slou 3F 123
Spur Dr. SL1: Slou 3C 124
Spurgrove La. RG9: Fri 6G 73
SPURLANDS END 6G 83
Spurlands End Rd. HP15: G Kin 5E 82
Spurt St. HP18: Cudd 1B 58
Square, The HP16: G Mis 6H 75
HP18: Long C 6C 56
HP18: Wadd 6C 52
MK12: Wolv 7H 15
UB7: Long 6H 131
Squires Cl. MK6: Coff 1G 29
Squirrel La. HP12: Book 4F 97
Squirrel Ri. SL7: Marl 3H 105
Squirrels Way MK18: Buck 5J 37
Stablebridge Rd. HP22: Ast C 3C 68
Stable La. HP9: S Grn 4A 102
Stable Rd. HP22: Halt 1K 69
Stables, The 7F 25
Stables, The MK16: Tyr 1E 10
MK19: H'ham 2K 15
Stables Ct. SL7: Marl 1F 115
Stable Yd. MK14: D Barn 1G 23
Stacey Av. MK12: Wolv 7H 15
STACEY BUSHES 2J 21
STACEY BUSHES 2J 21
Stacey Bushes Trading Cen.
MK12: S Bus 2J 21
Stacey's Ct. HP8: D Gil 7G 95
Staddle Stones HP27: Prin R 4G 71
STADHAMPTON 3A 134
Stadium, The 3J 61
Stafford Av. SL2: Slou 2A 124
Stafford Cl. SL6: Tapl 4D 122
Stafford Gro. MK5: S Chur 1B 28
Stafford Keep HP19: Ayle 6F 61
Stag La. HP15: G Kin 5D 82
STAGSDEN 2D 133
Stagshaw Gro. MK4: E Val 5B 28
STAINES 3D 137
Stainton Dr. MK13: Hee 2C 22
Stamford Av. MK6: Sprin 5H 23
STANBRIDGE 1D 135
Stanbridge Cl. HP17: Hadd 5C 58
Stanbridge Ct. MK11: S Strat 1D 20
Stanbridge Rd. HP17: Hadd 5C 58
Stanbrook Pl. MK10: Monk 5C 24
Standfield Cl. HP19: Ayle 6F 61
Standing Way (H8) MK4: Mil K 2A 32
MK6: Mil K 2G 29
MK7: Mil K 7A 24
MK10: Mil K 6B 24
Standring Pl. HP20: Ayle 4A 62
Stanhope Cl. HP22: Wend 1G 69
Stanhope Rd. HP20: Ayle 6B 62
SL1: Slou 4F 123
Stanier Sq. MK2: Blet 7J 29
Stanley Av. HP7: Amer 6B 86
Stanley Cl. SL7: Marl 6K 105
UB8: Uxb 7K 121
Stanley Cotts. SL2: Slou 6D 124
Stanley Ct. MK46: Oln 4H 7
Stanley Grn. E. SL3: Lang 2A 130
Stanley Hill HP7: Amer 7B 86
Stanley Maude Ho. *SL9: C Pet 2J 103*
(off Micholls Av.)
Stanley Rd. HP5: Ches 5K 77
HP12: H Wyc 1F 97
Stanmore Gdns. MK16: New P 3H 17
Stanstead Pl. HP7: Amer 6A 86
Stanton Av. MK13: B'lle 7A 16
STANTONBURY 6D 16
STANTONBURY 7C 16
STANTONBURY CAMPUS 6C 16
Stantonbury Campus Theatre 7C 16
Stantonbury Cl. MK13: New B 5A 16
STANTONBURY FIELDS 6D 16
Stantonbury Leisure Cen. 7C 16
Stantonbury Stadium 6C 16
Stanton Ga. MK14: Stan 5D 16
STANTON ST JOHN 3A 134
STANTON WOOD 2D 22
Stanway Cl. MK15: D Park 7H 17
STANWELL 3D 137
STANWELL MOOR 3D 137
Stanwell Moor Rd. UB7: Long 7H 131
Stanwell Rd. SL3: Hor 7A 130
Staple Hall Rd. MK1: F Str 6K 29
Stapleton Cl. SL7: Marl 5K 105
Starling M. HP19: Ayle 6E 60
Stars La. HP17: Dint 2G 59
STARTOP'S END 7C 50
Starwood Ct. SL3: Lang 7G 125
Staters Pound MK15: Penny 6G 17
Statham Pl. MK6: Old 6F 23
Station App. HP6: Amer 5A 86
HP7: L Chal 6H 87
HP13: H Wyc 1B 98
HP16: G Mis 6G 75
HP22: Wend 4H 69
SL7: Marl 7K 105
SL9: G Cro 3J 111
UB7: Yiew 6K 127
UB9: Den 5D 112
Station Cotts. MK18: Wins 5J 39
Station Ct. *HP7: Amer 5A 86*
(off The Avenue)
Station Pde. HP9: Bea 5F 101
UB9: Den 5G 113
Station Ri. SL7: Marl 7J 105
Station Rd. HP5: Ches 5A 78
HP6: Amer 5A 86
HP7: Amer 5A 86
HP9: Bea 5F 101
HP10: Loud 6J 99
HP13: H Wyc 2C 98
HP17: Hadd 7K 57
HP22: Q'ton 7G 43
HP22: Sto M 6C 66
HP27: Prin R 6F 71
LU7: Ched 1B 50
LU7: I'hoe 4G 51
MK16: New P 1J 17
MK17: Bow B 5D 30
MK17: L Hor, Mur 1A 40
MK17: W San 2K 31
MK18: Buck 5G 37
MK18: Pad 6A 38
MK18: Wins 5H 39
MK19: Cast 7C 8
OX27: M Gib 5C 42
SL1: Slou 4G 123
SL3: Lang 1A 130
SL6: Tapl 4B 122
SL7: Marl 1J 115
SL8: Bou E 6G 107
SL9: G Cro 3J 111
UB7: W Dra 7K 127
UB8: Cowl 2J 127
Station Sq. *HP6: Amer 5A 86*
(off Station App.)
MK9: C Key 5C 22
Station Ter. MK14: G Lin 3E 16
MK18: Buck 5G 37
Station Way HP20: Ayle 6J 61
Staunton Rd. SL2: Slou 3B 124
Staveley Cl. HP21: Ayle 1E 66
Stavordale MK10: Monk 5C 24
Stayning La. MK14: N Hill 1F 23
STEEPLE CLAYDON 3B 42 (1A 134)
Steeple Cl. MK4: Tatt 7A 28
Steinbeck Cres. MK4: S Wes 2A 32
Stephenson Cl. HP13: Down 6K 89
HP19: Ayle 6G 61
Stephenson Ct. *SL1: Slou 7D 124*
(off Osborne St.)
Stephenson Dr. SL4: Wind 5K 129
Stepnells HP23: M'rth 7C 50
STEPPINGLEY 3D 133
Stevens Cl. HP15: H Grn 7H 83
HP16: Pres 1D 82
Stevens Fld. MK7: W Gat 1F 31
Stevens Ho. HP7: Amer 7K 85
Stevenson Rd. SL2: Hedg 7B 110
STEVINGTON 1D 133
Stewart Av. SL1: Slou 3D 124
STEWARTBY 2D 133
Stewarts Ct. UB9: Den 4F 113
Stewart's Dr. SL2: Farn C 2K 117
Stewarts Way SL7: Marl 1H 105
STEWKLEY 3C 46 (1C 135)
STEWKLEY DEAN 1C 135
Stewkley La. LU7: Wing 2A 48
MK17: Mur 3D 40
Stewkley Rd. LU7: Cubl 2H 47
LU7: Soul 7F 41
LU7: Wing 3C 48
Stilebrook Rd. MK46: Oln 1G 7
Stile Mdw. HP9: Bea 5G 101
Stirling Av. HP20: Ayle 5K 61
Stirling Cl. MK15: Penny 7G 17
SL4: Wind 7F 129
UB8: Cowl 1J 127
Stirling Ho. HP13: H Wyc 1F 99
MK3: Blet 1D 32
(off Chester Clo.)
Stirling Rd. HP12: H Wyc 3H 97
SL1: Slou 3J 123
Stockdale MK13: Hee 1C 22
Stockdales Rd. SL4: E Wick 2H 129
Stocken Cl. MK46: Oln 3G 7
Stock Fld. Cl. HP15: Haz 4H 91
Stockfields Pl. HP14: Stoke 5B 72
Stockhall Cres. LU7: Stew 2B 46
Stock Ho. Pas. *HP20: Ayle 6J 61*
(off Market St.)

Stocking Grn. Cl. MK19: H'ope ... 1E 8
Stocking La. HP14: Nap ... 7H 81
Stocklake HP20: Ayle ... 5A 62
Stocklake Ind. Est. HP20: Ayle ... 5A 62
Stocklake Pk. Ind. Est. HP20: Ayle ... 5B 62
Stocklands Way HP16: Pres ... 1D 82
Stock La. MK17: Whad ... 6F 27
Stockleys La. MK18: Ting ... 2C 36
Stocks, The MK19: Cosg ... 3C 14
Stocks Cl. MK18: Wins ... 6H 39
Stockway HP22: W'don ... 7J 45
Stockwell HP17: Hadd ... 6C 58
Stockwell Furlong HP17: Hadd ... 6C 58
Stockwell La. HP17: Mead ... 1G 71
MK17: Wave ... 6F 25
OX33: Water ... 7B 54
Stockwells SL6: Tapl ... 2A 122
STOKE BRUERNE ... 2B 132
STOKE COMMON ... 2E 118
Stoke Comn. Rd. SL3: Fulm ... 2E 118
Stoke Ct. Dr. SL2: S Pog ... 6C 118
Stoke Farm La. HP21: Ayle ... 4K 65
Stoke Gdns. SL1: Slou ... 6C 124
STOKE GOLDINGTON ... 6C 6 (2C 133)
STOKE GREEN ... 2F 125
Stoke Grn. SL2: S Pog ... 2E 124
STOKE HAMMOND ... 2H 41 (1C 135)
Stoke La. MK17: G Bri ... 7E 34
Stoke Leys Cl. HP21: Ayle ... 4K 65
STOKE LYNE ... 1A 134
STOKE MANDEVILLE ... 5C 66 (2C 135)
Stoke Mandeville Sports Stadium ... 3A 66
Stoke Mandeville Station (Rail) ... 5C 66
STOKENCHURCH ... 5C 72 (1A 136)
Stokenchurch Pl. MK13: B Com ... 2C 22
Stoke Pk. ... 5D 118
Stoke Pk. Av. SL2: Farn R ... 1A 124
STOKE POGES ... 5E 118 (2C 137)
Stoke Poges La. SL1: Slou ... 6C 124
SL2: Slou, S Pog ... 4C 124
Stoke Rd. HP21: Ayle ... 1K 65
MK2: Blet ... 2K 33
MK17: New L ... 5D 32
SL2: Slou, S Pog ... 6D 124
STOKE ROW ... 2A 136
Stokesay SL2: Slou ... 5D 124
Stokesay Ct. MK4: K'ead ... 5J 27
Stokes Cft. HP17: Hadd ... 6C 58
(not continuous)
Stokes End HP17: Hadd ... 5C 58
Stokes La. HP17: Hadd ... 5C 58
Stokesly Ri. HP10: Woob G ... 1A 108
STOKE TALMAGE ... 3A 134
Stoke Vw. SL1: Slou ... 6D 124
Stoke Wood SL2: S Pog ... 2D 118
Stolford Ri. MK4: Tatt ... 6B 28
Stomp Rd. SL1: Burn ... 3D 122
STONE ... 2B 64 (2B 134)
STONEBRIDGE ... 6K 15
STONEBRIDGE ... 5J 15
Stonebridge Fld. SL4: Eto ... 3K 129
Stonebridge Rd. HP19: Ayle ... 3G 61
Stonechat HP19: Ayle ... 3K 61
Stone Ct. MK46: Emb ... 7G 7
Stone Cft. HP17: Sto ... 2C 64
Stonecroft HP6: H Hea ... 2E 84
Stonecroft Av. SL0: Ive ... 4E 126
Stonecrop Pl. MK14: Conn ... 2E 22
Stonefield Rd. HP14: Nap ... 6G 81
Stonegate MK13: Ban ... 1A 22
Stonehaven Rd. HP19: Ayle ... 4G 61
Stone Hill MK8: T Ash ... 5H 21
Stone Ho. La. SL6: Cook ... 7C 106
Stoneleigh Ct. MK4: West ... 5J 27
Stone Pit Cl. MK46: Oln ... 4G 7
Stonepitts Pk. HP18: Chil ... 1B 56
Stone Pl. MK4: E Val ... 4C 28
Stones Courtyard *HP5: Ches ... 5A 78*
(off High St.)
Stones Way MK17: Dray P ... 6C 40
Stone Vw. HP22: Ovi ... 5D 44
Stoneyfield SL9: G Cro ... 6G 111
Stoney Gro. HP5: Ches ... 4B 78
Stoney La. SL2: Farn R ... 6J 117
Stoney Meade SL1: Slou ... 6K 123
Stoney Ware SL7: Marl ... 2J 115
Stoney Ware Cl. SL7: Marl ... 2H 115
STONOR ... 2A 136
Stonor Ct. MK8: G Hol ... 6K 21
STONY GREEN ... 2A 82
Stony La. HP6: L Chal ... 5J 87
HP16: L Kin ... 3J 83
STONY STRATFORD ... 1A 20 (2B 132)
STONY STRATFORD ... 7C 14
Stony Stratford Nature Reserve ... 6A 14
Stookslade HP22: W'rave ... 6B 48
Stopps Orchard HP27: Mon R ... 3H 71
Stork Cl. HP19: Ayle ... 3A 62
Stornaway Rd. SL3: Lang ... 2C 130
Stotfold Ct. MK11: S Strat ... 2C 20
Stour Cl. HP21: Ayle ... 3H 65
MK3: Blet ... 7E 28
MK16: New P ... 2A 18
SL1: Slou ... 1K 129
Stourhead Ga. MK4: West ... 5J 27
Stovell Rd. SL4: Wind ... 5K 129
Stowe Av. MK18: Buck, Chac ... 1F 37
Stowe Cl. MK18: Buck ... 3G 37
Stowe Ct. MK14: Stan ... 5C 16
Stowe Ri. MK18: Buck ... 3G 37
Stowe Rd. SL1: Slou ... 5G 123
Stowe Vw. MK18: Ting ... 1B 36
Straight Bit HP10: F Hea ... 1G 107
Strand, The HP22: Q'ton ... 5J 43
Strangers La. MK18: Ting ... 2B 36
Strangford Dr. MK2: Blet ... 4J 33
Stranraer Gdns. SL1: Slou ... 6C 124
Stratfield Ct. MK8: G Hol ... 5K 21
Stratfield Rd. SL1: Slou ... 7E 124
Stratford Arc. MK11: S Strat ... 7B 14
Stratford Cl. SL2: Slou ... 2F 123
Stratford Dr. HP10: Woob G ... 5J 107
HP21: Ayle ... 1G 65
Stratford Ho. MK11: S Strat ... 1B 20
Stratford Office Village MK12: W Mil ... 7E 14
Stratford Rd. MK12: W Mil ... 7D 14
MK17: Nas ... 6A 26
MK17: Whad ... 4E 26
MK18: Buck, M M'ton ... 3J 37
MK19: Cosg ... 5A 14
Strattords Way HP17: Hadd ... 6C 58
Strathcona Cl. HP10: F Hea ... 2J 107
Strathcona Way HP10: F Hea ... 2J 107
Strathnaver Pl. MK12: H Lea ... 2H 21
STRATTON AUDLEY ... 1A 134
Stratton Chase Dr. HP8: D Gil ... 6E 94
Stratton Grn. HP21: Ayle ... 1C 66
Stratton Path HP21: Ayle ... 1D 66
Stratton Pl. HP7: Amer ... 6D 86
Stratton Rd. HP9: Bea ... 6D 100
HP27: Prin R ... 5F 71
Strauss Gro. MK7: Brow ... 3E 30
Strawberry Cl. HP16: Pres ... 1D 82
Streamside SL1: Slou ... 6H 123
Streamside Wlk. HP21: Ayle ... 1H 65
Streatham Pl. MK13: B Com ... 4C 22
Streeton Pl. HP6: Amer ... 5D 86
Stretton Cl. HP10: T Grn ... 7H 91
Stringers Cotts. *SL9: C Pet ... 6H 103*
(off The Vale)
STRIXTON ... 1D 133
Stroma Ct. SL1: Slou ... 5F 123
Strudwick Dr. MK6: Old ... 6F 23
Stuart Cl. MK2: F Str ... 6K 29
SL4: Wind ... 7H 129
Stuart Ct. *HP6: Amer ... 5B 86*
(off King George V Rd.)
Stuart Rd. HP13: H Wyc ... 2C 98
Stuart Way SL4: Wind ... 7G 129
Stubble Hill HP19: Ayle ... 6F 61
Stubbs End Cl. HP6: Amer ... 3C 86
Stubbs Fld. MK5: S Broo ... 4A 28
Stubbs Wood HP6: Amer ... 3C 86
Stuchbury Cl. HP19: Ayle ... 6F 61
Studdridge Ct. HP14: Stoke ... 6A 72
STUDHAM ... 2D 135
Studham La. HP4: Dag ... 6J 49
Studio Ct. MK2: Blet ... 7K 29
Studland Cl. HP21: Ayle ... 2C 66
Studley Knapp MK7: Waln ... 1D 30
Studridge La. HP27: Spee ... 1F 81
Stumpwell La. HP10: Pen ... 1K 99
Sturges Cl. MK7: Walt P ... 2C 30
Stylecroft Rd. HP8: D Gil ... 7H 95
Styles Cl. OX27: M Gib ... 6B 42
Sudgrove Ho. MK15: D Park ... 7G 17
Suffield Rd. HP11: H Wyc ... 1K 97
Suffolk Cl. MK3: Blet ... 6F 29
SL1: Slou ... 4G 123
Suffolk Ct. OX27: M Gib ... 5C 42
Sulby Cl. HP21: Ayle ... 2H 65
SULGRAVE ... 2A 132
Sulgrave Ct. MK8: G Hol ... 6K 21
Sullivan Cres. MK7: Brow ... 2E 30
Sultan Cft. MK5: S Broo ... 3A 28
Sumburgh Way SL1: Slou ... 3C 124
Summergill Ct. MK13: Hee ... 1C 22
Summerhayes MK14: G Lin ... 6F 17
(not continuous)
Summerhouse La. UB7: Harm ... 4K 131
Summerlea SL1: Slou ... 6K 123
Summerleys LU6: E Bra ... 2J 49
Summerleys Rd. HP27: Prin R ... 3D 70
Summerson Rd. MK6: Blea ... 2F 29
Summers Rd. SL1: Burn ... 1E 122
SUMMERSTOWN ... 6D 42
Sumner Ct. MK5: Lough ... 6A 22
SUNBURY ... 3D 137
Sunbury Cl. MK13: B'lle ... 7A 16
Sun Cres. HP18: Oak ... 5H 53
Sunderland Ct. MK4: Tatt ... 6K 27
SUNNINGDALE ... 3C 137
Sunningdale Cl. HP12: Book ... 3F 97
Sunningdale Ho. MK7: Cald ... 5C 30
Sunningdale Way MK3: Blet ... 7C 28
SUNNINGHILL ... 3C 137
Sunny Bank HP15: W End ... 1F 91
LU7: Ched ... 2B 50
Sunnybank SL7: Marl ... 5H 105
Sunny Brook Cl. HP22: Ast C ... 1A 68
Sunnycroft HP13: Down ... 5G 89
Sunnymede Av. HP5: Ches ... 2C 78
Sunnyside Rd. HP5: Ches ... 4K 77
Sunray Av. UB7: W Dra ... 7K 127
Sunridge Cl. MK16: New P ... 2J 17
Sunrise Parkway MK14: L Woo ... 7E 16
Sunset Cl. MK2: Blet ... 1J 33
Sunset Wlk. *MK9: C Key ... 4E 22*
(off Silbury Boulevd.)
Sunters Wood Cl. HP12: Book ... 3F 97
Surly Hall Wlk. SL4: Wind ... 6H 129
Surrey Av. SL2: Slou ... 3A 124
Surrey Pl. MK3: Blet ... 5F 29
Surrey Rd. MK3: Blet ... 5F 29
Susan Edwards Ho. *SL9: C Pet ... 2J 103*
(off Chesham La.)
Sussex Cl. HP8: D Gil ... 7F 95
HP13: H Wyc ... 6D 90
HP19: Ayle ... 3F 61
SL1: Slou ... 7F 125
Sussex Ho. SL2: Farn C ... 4A 118
Sussex Keep SL1: Slou ... 7F 125
Sussex Pl. SL1: Slou ... 7E 124
(not continuous)
SL9: C Pet ... 4J 103
(off Gravel Hill)
Sussex Rd. MK3: Blet ... 6F 29
Sussex Way UB9: Den ... 3F 113
Sutcliffe Av. MK6: Old ... 5E 22
Sutherland Grange SL4: Wind ... 5F 129
Sutherland Gro. MK3: Blet ... 5F 29
Sutherland Wlk. *HP21: Ayle ... 2A 66*
(off Mellstock Rd.)
Sutleye Ct. MK5: S Chur ... 2A 28
Sutmers Ct. HP8: D Gil ... 2D 102
SUTTON ... 3C 130 (3D 137)
Sutton Av. SL3: Lang ... 7G 125
Sutton Ct. MK4: E Val ... 6C 28
Sutton La. SL3: Lang ... 4B 130
Sutton Pl. SL3: Lang ... 4B 130
Swabey Rd. SL3: Lang ... 2A 130
Swains Ct. *MK46: Oln ... 3H 7*
(off High St.)
Swains La. HP10: F Hea ... 7G 99
Swakeleys Rd. UB10: I'ham ... 2K 121
SWAKELEYS RDBT. ... 2K 121
Swale Rd. HP21: Ayle ... 2H 65
Swallow Cl. MK18: Buck ... 5J 37
Swallowdale SL0: I Hea ... 1D 126
Swallow Dr. HP15: Haz ... 2H 91
Swallowfield MK8: G Hol ... 5J 21
Swallow La. HP22: Sto M ... 5B 66
Swallows La. HP19: Ayle ... 6E 60
Swallow St. SL0: Ive, I Hea ... 1D 126
SWANBOURNE ... 1C 135
Swanbourne Rd. MK17: Mur ... 4C 40
Swan Cl. HP5: Ches ... 1K 77
HP19: Ayle ... 3A 62
HP22: W'urch ... 3H 45
MK18: Buck ... 5J 37
Swan Ct. MK46: Oln ... 3J 7
Swan Hill HP18: Cudd ... 1B 58
Swan La. OX27: M Gib ... 5D 42
Swan M. HP22: Wend ... 3H 69
Swann Ct. SL1: Slou ... 7C 124
Swann Rd. HP22: Halt ... 7K 67
Swan Pool Leisure Cen. ... 5H 37
Swan Rd. SL0: Ive ... 4F 127
UB7: W Dra ... 7K 127
Swansons LU6: Edle ... 3K 49
Swan Ter. MK11: S Strat ... 1B 20
SL4: Wind ... 5K 129
Swan Wharf Bus. Cen. UB8: Uxb ... 7H 121
Swanwick La. MK10: Bro ... 3D 24
Swanwick Wlk. MK10: Bro ... 3D 24
Swayne Ri. MK10: Midd ... 4C 24
Sweetlands Cnr. MK7: K Hil ... 6D 24
Swift Cl. HP19: Ayle ... 3A 62
MK16: New P ... 7G 11
Swimbridge La. MK4: Fur ... 3D 28
Swinden Ct. MK13: Hee ... 2B 22
Swinfens Yd. MK11: S Strat ... 1B 20
Sycamore Av. MK2: Blet ... 7A 30
Sycamore Cl. HP6: Amer ... 4B 86
HP8: D Gil ... 1E 102
HP18: Long C ... 6C 56
LU7: Stew ... 2B 46
MK18: Buck ... 5K 37
SL8: Bou E ... 6H 107
Sycamore Cnr. *HP6: Amer ... 4B 86*
(off Sycamore Rd.)
Sycamore Ct. HP12: Book ... 4G 97
HP19: Ayle ... 5J 61
(off Willow Rd.)
SL4: Wind ... 7K 129
Sycamore Dene HP5: Ches ... 2B 78
Sycamore Dr. SL7: Marl ... 4H 105
Sycamore Ho. *HP6: Amer ... 4B 86*
(off Woodside Rd.)
Sycamore Leys MK18: S Clay ... 2C 42
Sycamore Pl. *HP6: Amer ... 5A 86*
(off Station Rd.)
Sycamore Ri. HP8: D Gil ... 1E 102
Sycamore Rd. HP6: Amer ... 4A 86
HP8: D Gil ... 1E 102
HP12: Book ... 4G 97
Sycamore Wlk. SL3: G Grn ... 4J 125
Sycamore Way HP15: Haz ... 4G 91
SYDENHAM ... 3B 134
Sydney Gro. SL1: Slou ... 4A 124
Syke Cluan SL0: R Pk ... 7E 126
Syke Ings SL0: R Pk ... 1E 130
Sykes Cft. MK4: E Val ... 6C 28
Sykes Rd. SL1: Slou ... 4K 123
Sylvia Cl. HP16: G Mis ... 2H 83
Symington Ct.
MK5: S Lod ... 2B 28
Syon Gdns. MK16: New P ... 3J 17
SYRESHAM ... 2A 132

T

Tabard Gdns. MK16: New P ... 3J 17
Tachbrook Rd. UB7: W Dra ... 6K 127
UB8: Uxb ... 7J 121
Tack La. HP17: Hadd ... 6B 58
Tacknell Dr. MK5: S Broo ... 3K 27
Tadmarton MK15: D Park ... 7G 17
Tadmere MK8: T Ash ... 5H 21
Tadros Ct. HP13: H Wyc ... 2D 98
Talbot Av. HP13: Down ... 5G 89
SL3: Lang ... 7K 125
Talbot Ct. MK15: Wool ... 5J 23
Talbot Rd. HP22: Ast C ... 2B 68
Talbots Hyde MK46: Oln ... 3G 7
Talland Av. MK6: Fish ... 5F 23
Tallis La. MK7: Brow ... 2E 30
Tall Oaks HP6: Amer ... 4B 86
Tall Trees SL3: Coln ... 6D 130
Tamar Cl. HP13: H Wyc ... 4H 99
HP21: Ayle ... 3H 65
Tamar Ho. MK3: Blet ... 6E 28
Tamarisk Ct. MK7: Waln ... 2D 30
Tamarisk Way SL1: Slou ... 7J 123
Tamar Way SL3: Lang ... 3B 130
Tamworth Stubb MK7: Waln ... 2C 30
Tancred Rd. HP13: Down ... 6A 90
Tandra MK6: Bean ... 2H 29
(not continuous)
Tanfield La. MK10: Midd ... 3C 24
MK16: Bro ... 3C 24
Tank Ho. Rd. MK18: Wins ... 5K 39
Tanners Dr. MK14: Blak ... 3G 17
Tannery Ind. Est. HP13: H Wyc ... 4G 99
Tannery Rd. HP13: H Wyc ... 4G 99
Tansman La. MK7: Old P ... 2F 31
Tapling Trad. Est. UB7: Yiew ... 5K 127
Taplin Way HP10: T Grn ... 7H 91
TAPLOW ... 2A 122 (2C 137)
Taplow Comn. Rd. SL1: Burn ... 4B 116
Taplow Rd. SL6: Tapl ... 4C 122
Taplow Station (Rail) ... 4B 122
Tapping Rd. HP14: L End ... 4A 96
Tap Yd. MK16: S Gold ... 6C 6
Taranis Cl. MK7: W Gat ... 7E 24
Tarbay La. SL4: Oak G ... 7D 128
Tarbert Cl. MK2: Blet ... 3J 33
Tarmac Way UB7: Harm ... 5H 131
Tarnbrook Cl. MK4: E Val ... 5B 28
Tarragon Cl. MK7: Waln ... 1C 30
Task, The MK46: Oln ... 3J 7
Taskers Row LU6: Edle ... 2K 49
Tate Ho. SL9: C Pet ... 2K 103
Tate Rd. SL9: C Pet ... 3K 103
TATHALL END ... 2H 9 (2C 133)
TATLING END ... 6B 112 (2D 137)
Tatling Gro. MK7: Waln ... 1C 30
Tattam Cl. MK15: Wool ... 4J 23
TATTENHOE ... 7A 28
TATTENHOE ... 1A 32
Tattenhoe La. MK3: Blet ... 7D 28
(not continuous)
TATTENHOE PARK ... 7K 27
Tattenhoe St. (V2) MK8: Mil K ... 2H 27
Tattershall Cl. MK5: S Chur ... 1A 28
Tattlers Hill HP22: W'rave ... 6C 48
Taunton Deane MK4: E Val ... 6D 28
Taurus Cl. MK18: S Clay ... 3B 42
Tavelhurst MK8: T Ash ... 5J 21
Taverner Cl. MK7: Old P ... 2F 31
Tavistock Cl. MK17: W San ... 1J 31
Tavistock M. HP12: H Wyc ... 1J 97
Tavistock Rd. UB7: Yiew ... 6K 127
Tavistock St. MK2: Blet ... 6J 29
Tavistock Wlk. *HP20: Ayle ... 4K 61*
(off Elmhurst Rd.)
Taylor Rd. HP21: Ayle ... 2J 65
Taylor's Cl. SL7: Marl ... 7K 105
Taylors La. HP7: L Miss ... 3C 84
LU7: Stew ... 5C 46
Taylors M. MK14: N Hill ... 7F 17
Taylors Rd. HP5: Ches ... 3B 78
Taylors Turn HP13: Down ... 4H 89
Taymouth Pl. MK9: Camp ... 3H 23
Tay Rd. MK3: Blet ... 6E 28
Teasel Av. MK14: Conn ... 1E 22
TEBWORTH ... 1D 135
Tedder Rd. HP22: Halt ... 3K 69
Teesdale Rd. SL2: Slou ... 3H 123
Tees Rd. HP21: Ayle ... 2H 65
Tees Way MK3: Blet ... 6D 28
Teign Cl. MK16: New P ... 1K 17
Telford Cl. HP19: Ayle ... 5E 60
Telford Dr. SL1: Slou ... 7J 123
Telford Way HP13: Down ... 6K 89
MK14: Blak ... 4H 17

Telston Cl. SL8: Bou E 4G 107
Temperance Ter. MK11: S Strat 7A 14
Templars Pl. SL7: Marl 1J 115
TEMPLE 5G 115
Temple MK14: Stan 6C 16
Temple Cl. MK3: Blet 1D 32
MK18: Buck 2J 37
Templecroft Ter. HP17: Upt 1J 59
Temple End HP13: H Wyc 1A 98
Temple La. SL7: Marl 5G 115
Temple Mill Island SL7: Marl 5F 115
Temple Orchard HP13: H Wyc 7B 90
Temple Pk. SL6: Hur 7D 114
Temple Sq. HP20: Ayle 6J 61
Temple St. HP11: H Wyc 1A 98
HP18: Bril 2J 53
HP20: Ayle 6J 61
Temple Way SL2: Farn C 3A 118
Templewood HP14: Walt A 6F 81
Templewood Ga. SL2: Farn C 3A 118
Templewood La.
SL2: Farn C, S Pog 3A 118
Tenby Gro. MK4: K'ead 6H 27
Tene Acres MK5: S Chur 1K 27
Tennant Cl. MK8: G Far 1H 27
Tennis La. MK18: Wins 7J 39
Tennyson Dr. MK16: New P 1G 17
Tennyson Gro. MK3: Blet 1F 33
Tennyson Rd. HP11: H Wyc 3A 98
HP21: Ayle 1A 66
Tennyson Way SL2: Slou 2G 123
Tenterden Cres. MK7: K Hil 7D 24
Tenzing Dr. HP13: H Wyc 2E 98
Terrent Ct. SL4: Wind 6J 129
TERRICK 3C 135
TERRIERS 5D 90
Terrington Hill SL7: Marl 7F 105
Terry Dr. HP19: Ayle 3H 61
Terry Orchard HP13: H Wyc 7C 90
Terry Pl. UB8: Cowl 3J 127
Terry Rd. HP13: H Wyc 7C 90
Terry's La. SL6: Cook 7E 106
Testwood Rd. SL4: Wind 6F 129
Tetherdown HP16: Pres 1C 82
(off Lodge La.)
TETSWORTH 3A 134
Tewkesbury La. MK10: Monk 5B 24
Thackeray End HP19: Ayle 4E 60
THAME 3B 134
Thame Rd. HP17: Hadd 7K 57
HP18: Bril 3J 53
HP18: Chil 1B 56
HP18: Long C 6C 56
HP18: Oak, Bril 5J 53
HP21: Ayle 7H 61
HP27: Long 1B 70
OX9: Tha 7H 57
Thame Rd. Sth. HP19: Ayle 1G 65
Thamesbourne M. SL8: Bou E 6G 107
(off Station Rd.)
Thames Cl. MK3: Blet 7E 28
SL8: Bou E 5G 107
THAMES DITTON 3D 137
Thames Dr. MK16: New P 2A 18
Thamesfield Gdns. SL7: Marl 1J 115
Thames Ind. Est. SL7: Marl 7K 105
Thames Mead SL4: Wind 6G 129
Thames Reach SL7: Medm 4B 114
Thames Rd. SL3: Lang 2A 130
SL4: Wind 5E 128
Thames Valley University
Slough Campus 6C 124
Thane Ct. MK14: Stan 6C 16
Thanestead Copse HP10: Loud 6J 99
Thanestead Ct. HP10: Loud 6J 99
Theatre Wlk. MK9: C Key 3F 23
Theydon Av. MK17: W San 3K 31
Thicket, The HP10: T Grn 6G 91
Third Av. MK1: Blet 5H 29
SL7: Marl 7A 106
Third Cres. SL1: Slou 3A 124
Third St. HP11: H Wyc 4B 98
Thirkleby Cl. SL1: Slou 6A 124
Thirlby La. MK5: S Chur 1A 28
Thirlmere Av. MK2: Blet 2K 33
SL1: Slou 3E 122
Thirsk Gdns. MK3: Blet 2C 32
Thomas Dr. MK16: New P 6G 11
Thomas Rd. HP10: Woob G 5K 107
Thompkins La. SL2: Farn R 5H 117
Thompson Cl. HP21: Ayle 1G 65
SL3: Lang 2A 130
Thompson Rd. UB10: Uxb 6K 121
Thompson St. MK13: New B 5A 16
Thompson Wlk. HP21: Ayle 1G 65
(off Primrose Dr.)
Thornaby Pl. HP10: Woob G 1A 108
THORNBOROUGH 2C 38 (3B 132)
Thornborough Rd. MK17: Nas 7A 26
Thornbridge Rd. SL0: I Hea 6C 120
Thorncliffe MK8: T Ash 5H 21
Thorndike SL2: Slou 3J 123
Thorn Dr. SL3: G Grn 4J 125
Thorne Rd. HP14: L End 4A 96
Thorne Way HP20: Ayle 4A 62
HP22: B'land 3D 68
THORNEY 1H 131
Thorney Country Pk. 1H 131
Thorneycroft La. MK15: D Park 7H 17
Thorney La. Nth. SL0: Ive 4F 127
Thorney La. Sth. SL0: R Pk 7F 127
Thorney Mill Rd. SL0: Thor 1G 131
(not continuous)
UB7: W Dra 1J 131
Thornhill MK18: T'ough 2D 38
Thornhill Cl. HP7: Amer 7K 85
Thornlea MK46: Oln 4H 7
Thornley Cft. MK4: E Val 5C 28
Thorns Cl. HP27: Whit 3K 71
Thorns La. HP27: Whit 2K 71
THORNTON 3B 132
Thornton Cres. HP22: Wend 3G 69
Thornton Rd. MK17: Nas 6A 26
THORPE 3D 137
Thorpe Cl. HP21: Ayle 3B 66
Thorpeness Cft. MK4: Tatt 7K 27
Thorwold Pl. MK5: Lough 1B 28
Thrasher Rd. HP21: Ayle 1J 65
Three Gables HP9: Bea 6G 101
THREE HOUSEHOLDS 2D 102
Three Households HP8: D Gil 2D 102
THREE LOCKS 4J 41
THREE MILE CROSS 3A 136
Three Shires Way MK19: H'ope 2J 9
MK46: Lave 3A 6
Thresher Gro. MK12: Gree 1E 20
Thrupp Cl. MK19: Cast 6E 8
Thrupp Wharf MK19: Cosg 1B 14
(off Station Rd.)
Thrush Cl. HP12: Book 4G 97
HP19: Ayle 3A 62
THURLEIGH 1D 133
Thurne Cl. MK16: New P 2A 18
Thursby Cl. MK15: Will 6K 17
Thurston Rd. SL1: Slou 4C 124
Thyme Cl. MK16: New P 7F 11
Tibbys La. HP18: Cudd 1B 58
Ticehurst Cl. MK7: K Hil 7D 24
TICKFORD 3B 18
Tickford Arc. MK16: New P 1K 17
TICKFORD END 1A 18
Tickford St. MK16: New P 1K 17
Tidbury Cl. MK17: W San 3J 31
TIDDINGTON 3A 134
Tierney Ct. SL7: Marl 1J 115
Tiffany Cl. MK2: Blet 2K 33
TIFFIELD 1A 132
TILBROOK 3D 30
TILBROOK 5D 30
Tilbrook Ind. Est. MK7: Tilb 4D 30
Tilbury Wlk. SL3: Lang 1B 130
Tilburywood Cl. HP13: Down 5G 89
Tilecotes Cl. SL7: Marl 7H 105
Tilehouse La. UB9: Den 1E 112
WD3: W Hyd 1E 112
Tilehouse Way UB9: Den 5F 113
TILEHURST 3A 136
Tilers Rd. MK11: Kiln 4F 21
Tilling Cres. HP13: H Wyc 1G 99
Tillman Cl. MK12: Gree 1G 21
Tilstone Av. SL4: E Wick 3G 129
Tilstone Cl. SL4: E Wick 3G 129
TILSWORTH 1D 135
Tilsworth Rd. HP9: Bea 7E 100
Timberscombe MK4: Fur 4D 28
Timberwood SL2: Farn C 1B 118
Timbold Dr. MK7: K Par 7B 24
Timor Ct. MK11: S Strat 7B 14
Timpson La. MK46: C Rey 4K 7
Timpsons Row MK46: Oln 4J 7
Tindal Rd. HP20: Ayle 4K 61
TINGEWICK 2C 36 (3A 132)
Tingewick Rd. MK18: Buck 4F 37
Tingewick Rd. Ind. Pk. MK18: Buck 4F 37
TINGRITH 3D 133
TINKERS BRIDGE 1K 29
Tinkers Dr. MK18: Wins 7H 39
TINKERS END 7H 39
Tinkers La. SL4: Wind 7F 129
Tinkers Wood Rd. HP13: Down 6J 89
Tintagel Ct. MK6: Fish 6G 23
Tintern Cl. SL1: Slou 7A 124
Tinterne Cl. HP21: Ayle 1D 66
Tippett Cl. MK7: Brow 3F 31
Tiree Ho. SL2: Slou 2K 123
Titchmarsh Ct. MK6: Old 6E 22
Tithe Barn Dr. SL6: Bra 3A 128
(not continuous)
Tithe Ct. SL3: Lang 2A 130
Titmus Rd. HP22: Halt 1K 69
Tiverton Cres. HP19: Ayle 3H 61
MK4: K'ead 6J 27
Toby's La. HP7: Bea E, L Miss 7B 84
(not continuous)
Tockley Rd. SL1: Burn 1D 122
Todd Cl. HP15: H Grn 1H 91
HP21: Ayle 1G 65
TODDINGTON 1D 135
TOKERS GREEN 3A 136
Tolcarne Av. MK6: Fish 5G 23
Toll Bar Cnr. HP27: Long 1C 70
Tolman Ct. HP21: Ayle 1G 65
Tom Evans Ct. HP13: H Wyc 7B 90
Tomkins Cl. HP22: Ast C 3C 68
Tomlin Rd. SL2: Slou 2G 123
Tomo Ind. Est. UB8: Cowl 4J 127
Tompion Rd. HP19: Ayle 5E 60
Tompkins Cl. MK5: S Broo 4B 28
Tompkins La. OX27: M Gib 6B 42
Tom Scott Ho. HP5: Ches 3K 77
(off Pearce Rd.)
Toms Turn HP15: Haz 2F 91
TONGWELL 5K 17
TONGWELL 5K 17
Tongwell La. MK16: New P 3J 17
Tongwell St. (V11) MK7: Mil K 2E 30
MK10: Mil K 2B 24
MK15: Mil K 5K 17
TOOT BALDON 3A 134
Toot Hill Cl. MK5: S Chur 2K 27
Top Angel MK18: Buck 7H 37
Topaz Cl. SL1: Slou 6K 123
Top Farm Cl. HP9: Bea 7C 100
Topland Rd. SL9: C Pet 5H 103
Top Mdw. MK7: Cald 4D 30
Topnotch Health Cen.
Chesham 7K 77
Top Pk. SL9: G Cro 4G 111
Topping La. UB8: Cowl 1K 127
Torbay HP22: Q'ton 6J 43
Torquay Spur SL2: Slou 1K 123
Torre Cl. MK3: Blet 5G 29
(not continuous)
Torridge Rd. HP21: Ayle 3J 65
SL3: Lang 4B 130
Torridon Ct. MK2: Blet 4K 33
Tottenhoe La. HP13: H Wyc 6E 90
TOTTERIDGE 7E 90
Totteridge Av. HP13: H Wyc 1D 98
Totteridge Dr. HP13: H Wyc 6D 90
Totteridge La. HP13: H Wyc 5E 90
Totteridge Pde. HP13: H Wyc 7C 90
Totteridge Rd. HP13: H Wyc 1B 98
TOTTERNHOE 1D 135
TOUCHEN-END 3B 136
Tourist Info. Cen.
Amersham Old Town 7K 85
Aylesbury 6J 61
Marlow 1H 115
Princes Risborough 5G 71
Uxbridge 5K 121
Wendover 4H 69
Towan Av. MK6: Fish 6G 23
TOWCESTER 2A 132
Towcester Rd. MK18: M M'ton 1J 37
MK19: O Stra 6A 14
Tower Cl. HP10: F Hea 2J 107
Tower Cres. MK14: N Hill 7F 17
Tower Dr. MK14: N Hill 7E 16
Towergate Cl. UB8: Uxb 3K 121
Tower Ho. HP20: Ayle 6K 61
(off High St.)
SL0: Ive 4E 126
SL1: Slou 7C 124
Toweridge La. HP12: H Wyc 7G 89
HP14: W Wyc 6D 88
Tower Rd. HP7: Cole 3J 93
TOWERSEY 3B 134
Towersey Way HP21: Ayle 7G 61
(not continuous)
Towers Lea HP13: H Wyc 1C 98
Town Bri. Ct. HP5: Ches 6K 77
TOWN END 3A 72
Town End Ct. HP16: G Mis 6G 75
Town End Cres. MK16: S Gold 7C 6
Town End Rd. HP14: Rad 3A 72
Town Farm LU7: Ched 2C 50
Town Farm Barn HP27: Prin R 5G 71
Townfield HP5: Ches 6A 78
Townfield La. HP8: D Gil 1G 103
Townfield Rd. HP13: H Wyc 1C 98
Town La. HP10: Woob G 5K 107
TOWN'S END 6B 42
TOWNSEND 5C 58
Townsend OX27: M Gib 6B 42
Townsend Cotts. MK17: G Hor 2K 39
Townsend Gro. MK13: New B 5B 16
Townsend La. OX27: M Gib 6B 42
Townsend Piece HP19: Ayle 5H 61
Townsend Rd. HP5: Ches 4K 77
Townside HP17: Hadd 6B 58
LU6: Edle 3K 49
Town Sq. SL1: Slou 7D 124
Tozer Wlk. SL4: Wind 7F 129
Trafalgar Av. MK3: Blet 5E 28
Trafford Cl. HP16: G Mis 7G 75
Trafford Rd. HP16: G Mis 6G 75
Tramhill HP18: Bril 1J 53
Tranlands Brigg MK13: Hee 2B 22
Trapp's Ct. HP5: Ches 7A 78
Trapp's La. HP5: Ches 6B 78
(Rose Dr.)
HP5: Ches 7A 78
(Waterside)
TRASH GREEN 3A 136
Travell Ct. MK13: B'ell 3B 22
Travic Rd. SL2: Slou 1H 123
Travis Ct. SL2: Farn R 1K 123
Travis Gro. MK3: Blet 7G 29
Treacher's Cl. HP5: Ches 5K 77
Treadaway Bus. Cen. HP10: Loud 7J 99
Treadaway Hill HP10: F Hea, Loud 7H 99
Treadaway Rd. HP10: F Hea 1H 107
Trebah Sq. HP19: Ayle 6E 60
Treborough MK4: Fur 5D 28
Tredington Gro. MK7: Cald 3D 30
Treefields MK18: Buck 4H 37
Trees Av. HP14: H Vall 1A 90
Treeside Cl. UB7: W Dra 2K 131
Trees Rd. HP14: H Vall 1K 89
SL8: Bou E 6H 107
Tree Tops SL9: C Pet 3J 103
Trelawney Av. SL3: Lang 2A 130
Tremayne Ct. MK6: Fish 6G 23
Trenchard Av. HP22: Halt 2K 69
Trenchard St. HP19: Ayle 6F 61
Trenches La. SL3: Lang 5A 126
Trent Dr. MK16: New P 2K 17
Trentishoe Cres. MK4: Fur 4D 28
Trent Rd. MK3: Blet 7E 28
SL3: Lang 4B 130
Tresham Ct. MK5: Lough 7A 22
Trevelyan Ct. SL4: Wind 7K 129
Treves Grn. HP21: Ayle 2K 65
Trevithick La. MK5: S Lod 2B 28
Trevone Ct. MK6: Fish 6G 23
Trevose Ho. SL2: Slou 2K 123
(off Franklin Av.)
Trewarden Av. SL0: I Hea 7D 120
Triangle Bus. Pk. HP22: Sto M 7E 66
Trident Ind. Est. SL3: Poy 7E 130
TRING 2D 135
Tring Hill HP22: Ast C, B'land 4E 68
HP23: Tring 4E 68
Tring Rd. HP20: Ayle 6A 62
HP22: Halt, Wend 4J 69
HP22: W'rave 7D 48
LU7: I'hoe, I Ast 4J 51
Trinity Av. SL7: Marl 6H 105
Trinity Cen. MK6: Fish 5G 23
Trinity Cl. MK19: O Stra 6A 14
Trinity Ct. HP5: Ches 6A 78
(off Punch Bowl La.)
HP19: Ayle 5J 61
Trinity Rd. HP15: Haz 4F 91
MK12: O Wol 6F 15
SL7: Marl 7H 105
Tripps Hill Cl. HP8: D Gil 1E 102
Trispen Ct. MK6: Fish 5G 23
Troutbeck MK6: P Bri 6J 23
Troutbeck Cl. SL2: Slou 5E 124
Trout Cl. SL7: Marl 2G 115
Trout Hollow HP27: Saun 7E 70
Trout La. UB7: Yiew 5J 127
Trout Rd. UB7: Yiew 6K 127
Trubys Gdn. MK6: Coff 7G 23
Trueman Pl. MK6: Old 6F 23
Truesdale Dr. UB9: Hare 2J 113
Trumper Way SL1: Slou 6H 123
UB8: Uxb 5J 121
TRUMPS GREEN 3C 137
Trumpton La. MK7: W Gat 7E 24
Trustees Cl. UB9: Den 4F 113
Trustees Way UB9: Den 3F 113
Tubwell Rd. SL2: S Pog 6F 119
Tucker Cl. HP13: H Wyc 7C 90
Tuckers Dr. HP15: H Grn 7J 83
Tudeley Hale MK7: K Hil 6D 24
Tudor Ct. HP6: Amer 5B 86
(off King George V Rd.)
HP14: Pidd 6A 88
(off King St.)
HP20: Ayle 6B 62
Tudor Dr. HP10: Woob G 1K 107
Tudor Gdns. MK11: S Strat 2C 20
MK18: S Clay 2B 42
SL1: Slou 4E 122
Tudor Mill HP10: Woob G 3A 108
Tudor Pk. HP6: Amer 4B 86
Tudor Rd. HP15: Haz 4J 91
Tudor Way SL4: Wind 6G 129
Tuffnell Cl. MK15: Will 6A 18
Tulip Way UB7: W Dra 2K 131
Tulkers Cl. HP16: Pres 1D 82
Tulla Ct. MK2: Blet 4J 33
Tummel Way MK2: Blet 3J 33
Tunbridge Gro. MK7: K Hil 6C 24
Tunmere Ct. SL9: C Pet 6G 103
(off Narcot La.)
Tunmere Ho. SL9: C Pet 6G 103
(off Narcot La.)
Tunmers End SL9: C Pet 6G 103
Tunnel Way LU7: Pits 7E 50
Tuns La. SL1: Slou 7A 124
Turnberry Cl. MK3: Blet 1C 32
Turnberry Ho. MK7: Cald 5C 30
Turner Cl. HP20: Ayle 3A 62
Turner Rd. SL3: Lang 7G 125
Turners Dr. HP13: H Wyc 7E 90
Turners Fld. HP13: Down 4J 89
Turner's Mdw. HP22: Ast C 1J 67
Turners M. MK14: N Hill 7F 17
Turners Pl. HP15: H Grn 1J 91
Turners Way HP5: Ches 4A 78
Turners Wood Dr. HP8: D Gil 1H 103
Turner Wlk. HP20: Ayle 3A 62
(off Turner Cl.)
Turneys Dr. MK12: W Mil 7E 14

Turnfields HP18: Ick 5E 54
Turnfurlong HP21: Ayle 7A 62
Turnfurlong La. HP21: Ayle 7A 62
(not continuous)
Turnfurlong Row *HP21: Ayle* *1B 66*
(off Turnfurlong La.)
Turnham Way HP19: Ayle 7G 61
Turnip Cl. HP18: Che 2H 57
Turnmill Av. MK6: Sprin 4H 23
Turnmill Ct. MK6: Sprin 4H 23
Turnpike, The HP18: Oak 5H 53
Turnpike Ct. MK17: W San 2J 31
Turnpike End HP21: Ayle 1A 66
Turnpike La. UB10: Uxb 1K 127
Turnpike Rd. HP12: H Wyc 4G 97
Turnpike Way HP12: H Wyc 4G 97
Turnstone Way HP19: Ayle 3K 61
Turpyn Ct. MK6: W Grn. 6K 23
TURVEY 1D 133
Turvey Cl. HP22: Ast C 2B 68
TURVILLE 1A 136
TURVILLE HEATH 1A 136
Turvill End MK5: Lough 6B 22
Turville Rd. HP21: Ayle 1E 66
TURWESTON 3A 132
Tweedale Cl. MK17: Mur 1B 40
Tweed Dr. MK3: Blet 6D 28
Tweed Rd. SL3: Lang 4B 130
Tweenways HP5: Ches 4B 78
Twelve Leys HP22: W'rave 6B 48
Twinches La. SL1: Slou 6K 123
Twinflower MK7: Waln 1D 30
Twitchell La. HP22: Ast C 2B 68
Twitchell Rd. HP16: G Mis 6G 75
Twitchell's La. HP9: Jord 3D 102
Twitchen La. MK4: Fur 4D 28
Two Dells La. HP5: A Grn, O L'gh 1E 78
TWO MILE ASH 4J 21
Two Mile Dr. SL1: Slou 7G 123
TWYFORD
Buckingham 1A 134
Reading 3A 136
Twyford La. MK7: Waln 2E 30
Tyburn Av. MK6: Sprin 4H 23
Tylers Cres. HP15: Haz 5H 91
TYLERS GREEN 6H 91 (1B 136)
Tylers Grn. MK13: B Com 3D 22
TYLER'S HILL 5E 78
Tylers Hill Rd. HP5: Ches 4D 78
Tylers Rd. HP15: Haz 5H 91
Tylsworth Cl. HP6: Amer 5B 86
Tyneham Cl. HP21: Ayle 3C 66
Tynemouth Ri.
MK10: Monk 5C 24
Tyne Rd. HP21: Ayle 3J 65
Tyne Sq. MK3: Blet 6D 28
Tyrell Cl. MK18: Buck 5G 37
Tyrell Gdns. SL4: Wind 7H 129
Tyrells Gdns. MK17: S Ham 1H 41
Tyrells Rd. MK17: S Ham 1H 41
Tyrill MK14: Stan 6C 16
TYRINGHAM 2G 11 (2C 133)
Tyson Pl. MK6: Old 6E 22
Tythe Cl. LU7: Stew 4C 46
Tythe Gdns. LU7: Stew 4C 46
Tythe M. LU6: Edle 3J 49
Tyzack Rd. HP13: H Wyc 6F 91

U

Ufton Ct. Yd. SL8: Bou E 5H 107
Ullswater Cl. SL1: Slou 3E 122
Ulverscroft MK10: Monk 4C 24
Ulyett Pl. MK6: Old 6E 22
Umberville Way SL2: Slou 1H 123
Underwood Pl. MK6: Old 6E 22
Underwood Rd. HP13: H Wyc 1D 98
Union Bus. Pk. UB8: Uxb 5H 121
Union St. HP11: H Wyc 1A 98
MK16: New P 1K 17
Union Wharf *UB7: Yiew* *6K 127*
(off Bentinck Rd.)
UNIVERSITY 7C 24
Up Corner HP8: D Gil 7F 95
Up Corner Cl. HP8: D Gil 7F 95
Upcroft SL4: Wind 7K 129
UP END 3J 13
Upland Av. HP5: Ches 2K 77
Uplands SL7: Marl 3H 105
Uplands, The SL9: G Cro 6J 111
Uplands Cl. HP13: H Wyc 7E 90
SL9: G Cro 6J 111
Uplands Ct. HP5: Ches 4A 78
Upminster Cl.
MK10: Monk P 5A 24
Up. Abbotts Hill HP19: Ayle 7F 61
UPPER ARNCOTT 2A 134
Up. Belmont Rd. HP5: Ches 2K 77
Up. Church St. HP18: Cudd 1B 58
Upper Dr. HP9: Bea 3F 101
UPPER DUNSLEY 2D 135
Up. Fifth St. MK9: C Key 4D 22
Up. Fourth St. MK9: C Key 4D 22
Up. George St. HP5: Ches 4A 78
Up. Gladstone Rd. HP5: Ches 4A 78
Upper Grn. St. HP11: H Wyc 1J 97
UPPER HALLIFORD 3D 137
UPPER HARTWELL 2C 64
UPPER HEYFORD 1A 132
Up. Hollis HP16: G Mis 6E 74
Up. Hundreds Way HP20: Ayle 6K 61
Up. Icknield Way
HP22: Ast C, Halt 2J 69
HP23: Buld 7G 51
HP27: Bled, Prin R 7F 71
HP27: Prin R, Whit 6G 71
(not continuous)
LU7: I'hoe, Pits 7G 51
Up. Lees Rd. SL2: Slou 1K 123
Up. Lodge La. HP15: Haz 1F 91
Upper Mdw. HP5: Ches 4K 77
UPPER NORTH DEAN 4H 81 (1B 136)
Up. Riding HP9: Bea 7D 100
Upper Rd. UB9: Den 5D 112
Up. Second St. MK9: C Key 5C 22
UPPER SHELTON 2D 133
Up. Stonehayes MK14: G Lin 5F 17
UPPER STOWE 1A 132
Upper St. HP22: Q'ton 5H 43
MK18: Ting 2B 36
UPPER SUNDON 1D 135
Up. Third St. MK9: C Key 5D 22
Upper Way MK17: G Bri 6E 34
UPPER WEALD 6E 20 (3C 133)
UPPER WEEDON 1A 132
UPPER WINCHENDON 2B 134
Up. Wingbury Courtyard Bus. Cen.
HP22: W'rave 5E 48
Up. Wood Cl. MK5: S Broo 4K 27
Upside Ho. HP7: Amer 5D 86
UPTON
Aylesbury 1J 59 (2B 134)
Northampton 1B 132
Slough 7E 124 (3C 137)
Upton Cl. SL1: Slou 7D 124
Upton Gro. MK5: S Lod 3C 28
Upton Lea Pde. SL2: Slou 5F 125
UPTON PARK 7D 124
Upton Pk. SL1: Slou 7C 124
Upton Rd. HP17: Dint, Upt 2G 59
SL1: Slou 7E 124
Upton Ter. HP17: Upt 1J 59
Upway SL9: C Pet 6K 103
UXBRIDGE 5K 121 (2D 137)
Uxbridge Ind. Est. UB8: Uxb 7H 121
UXBRIDGE MOOR 7H 121
Uxbridge Rd. SL0: I Hea 1A 126
SL1: Slou 7E 124
SL2: Slou 7F 125
SL3: G Grn, Wex 3J 125
Uxbridge Station (Tube) 5K 121

V

V1 (Snelshall St.) MK4: Mil K 5J 27
V2 (Tattenhoe St.) MK8: Mil K 2H 27
V3 (Fulmer St.) MK5: Mil K 3B 28
MK8: Mil K 7H 21
V4 (Watling St.) MK1: Blet 5J 29
MK2: F Str 5K 29
MK5: Mil K 3F 29
MK8: Mil K 4G 21
MK11: Mil K 2D 20
MK17: Mil K 5K 29
V5 (Gt. Monks St.) MK12: Mil K 7E 14
V6 (Grafton Ga.) MK9: Mil K 4C 22
V6 (Grafton St.) MK6: Mil K 6D 22
MK13: Mil k 5J 15
V7 (Saxon Ga.) MK9: Mil K 3D 22
V7 (Saxon St.) MK1: Mil K 6J 29
MK2: Mil K 7J 29
MK6: Mil K 3J 29
MK6: Mil K 5F 23
MK14: Mil K 5C 16
V8 (Marlborough St.) MK6: Mil K 1J 29
MK9: Mil K 2F 23
(not continuous)
MK14: Mil K 5C 16
V9 (Overstreet) MK14: Mil K 6F 17
V10 (Brickhill St.) MK7: Mil K 6B 24
MK10: Mil K 3K 23
MK14: Mil K 3F 17
MK15: Mil K 1J 23
V11 (Tongwell St.) MK7: Mil K 2E 30
MK10: Mil K 2B 24
MK15: Mil K 5K 17
Vache La. HP8: D Gil 7G 95
MK5: S Chur 1K 27
Vache M. HP8: D Gil 6H 95
Vale, The HP5: Ches 1A 78
SL9: C Pet 6H 103
Vale Cl. SL9: C Pet 6H 103
Vale Ho. HP19: Ayle 6H 61
Vale Ind. Cen., The
HP19: Ayle 5H 61
Valens Cl. MK8: C'ill 7J 21
Valentine Ct. MK8: C'ill 7J 21
Valentine Way HP8: D Gil 1H 103
Vale Pk. Dr. HP20: Ayle 6K 61
Vale Retail Pk. HP20: Ayle 6K 61
Valerian Pl. MK16: New P 1F 17
Vale Ri. HP5: Ches 2A 78
Vale Rd. HP5: Ches 2A 78
HP20: Ayle 5K 61
SL4: Wind 5H 129
Valley Cen., The HP13: H Wyc 2C 98
Valley Cl. LU6: Whip 4K 49
Valley End SL3: Wex 2G 125
Valley Rd. HP14: H Vall 7A 82
MK18: Buck 4K 37
Valley Vw. HP5: Ches 3J 77
Valley Way SL9: G Cro 4G 111
Van Der Bilt Ct. MK13: Blue B 7K 15
Vandyke Cl. MK17: W San 1K 31
Vanguard Cl. HP12: H Wyc 1H 97
Vansittart Est. SL4: Wind 6K 129
Vansittart Rd. SL4: Wind 6K 129
SL7: Marl 3J 115
Vantage Ct. MK16: New P 2B 18
Vantage Rd. SL1: Slou 6K 123
Vaughan Gdns. SL4: E Wick 2H 129
Vaughan Way SL2: Slou 2G 123
Vauxhall MK13: B'lle 7B 16
Vellan Av. MK6: Fish 5G 23
Venables La. MK15: Bolb 6G 17
Venetian Ct. MK7: W Gat 7E 24
Venus Hill HP3: Bov 5K 79
Verbena Cl. UB7: W Dra 3K 131
Verdi Cl. MK7: Old P 2F 31
Verdon Ct. SL2: Farn R 1K 123
SL2: Slou 1K 123
Verdon Dr. MK15: W Par 6H 17
Verity Pl. MK6: Old 5F 23
Verley Cl. MK6: W Grn. 6J 23
Vermont Pl. MK15: Tong 4J 17
Vermont Rd. SL2: Slou 2H 123
Verney Av. HP12: H Wyc 4H 97
Verney Cl. MK18: Buck 3H 37
SL7: Marl 7H 105
Verney Rd. MK18: Wins 6G 39
SL3: Lang 2A 130
Verney Wlk. HP21: Ayle 1J 65
Vernier Cres. MK5: Medb 3J 27
Verona Cl. UB8: Cowl 4J 127
Verwood Rd. HP20: Ayle 4K 61
Veryan Pl. MK6: Fish 5G 23
Vicarage Cl. HP9: S Grn 5A 102
HP22: Wend 3G 69
MK18: S Clay 3B 42
Vicarage Ct. MK18: S Clay 2B 42
MK19: H'ope 2F 9
Vicarage Gdns. HP23: M'rth 7C 50
MK13: B'ell 2A 22
Vicarage La. LU7: I'hoe 4H 51
LU7: Wing 3C 48
MK18: S Clay 3B 42
Vicarage Rd. HP21: Ayle 2J 65
HP23: M'rth 7B 50
LU7: Pits 5F 51
MK2: Blet 7K 29
MK11: S Strat 7B 14
MK13: B'ell 2A 22
MK17: Whad 7F 27
MK18: Wins 6H 39
Vicarage St. MK17: W San 3K 31
Vicarage Wlk. MK11: S Strat 7B 14
Vicarage Way SL3: Coln 5C 130
SL9: G Cro 4K 111
Vickery Cl. HP21: Ayle 2K 65
Vickery Way *HP21: Ayle* *2K 65*
(off Vickery Cl.)
Victoria Ct. HP11: H Wyc 7K 89
SL1: Slou *6C 124*
(off Blair Rd.)
Victoria Cres. SL0: Ive 5F 127
Victoria Dr. SL1: Burn, Farn C 4G 117
SL2: Farn C 4G 117
Victoria Gdns. HP11: H Wyc 4K 97
SL7: Marl 7J 105
Victoria Ho. *SL9: C Pet* *2J 103*
(off Micholls Av.)
VICTORIA PARK 6B 62
Victoria Rd. HP5: Ches 5A 78
MK2: F Str 7K 29
SL2: Farn C 4A 118
SL2: Slou 6F 125
SL4: E Wick 2G 129
SL7: Marl 7J 105
UB8: Uxb 5J 121
Victoria St. HP11: H Wyc 1K 97
HP20: Ayle 6A 62
MK12: Wolv 7H 15
SL1: Slou 7D 124
Victor Lay Pl. HP11: W Mar 4F 99
Victory Ct. MK1: Blet 5H 29
Victory Rd. HP22: Wend 3H 69
MK18: S Clay 2B 42
Vienna Gro. MK13: Blue B 1J 21
Village Cl. MK16: Sher 2B 12
Village La. SL2: Hedg 6B 110
Village Rd. HP7: Cole 5H 93
SL4: Dorn 1D 128
UB9: Den 7F 113
Village Shop. Cen. *SL1: Slou* *7D 124*
(off Buckingham Gdns.)
Village Way HP7: L Chal 7H 87
Villiers Bldgs. *HP20: Ayle* *6J 61*
(off Buckingham St.)
Villiers Cl. MK18: Buck 2J 37
Villiers Ct. SL4: Wind 5J 129
Villiers Rd. SL2: Slou 3B 124
Villier St. UB8: Uxb 1K 127
Vincent Av. MK8: C'ill 6J 21
Vincent Rd. HP19: Ayle 3F 61
Vincents Way HP14: Nap 1H 89
Vine, The HP18: Shab 5H 55
Vine Cl. HP15: Haz 4G 91
Vine Cotts. *SL9: C Pet* *4J 103*
(off Gravel Hill)
Vine Rd. SL2: S Pog 4D 118
Vine St. UB8: Uxb 6K 121
Vinetrees HP22: Wend 4H 69
Vineyard Dr. SL8: Bou E 4G 107
Vineyards, The HP27: Bled 6A 70
Viney La. HP19: Ayle 6E 60
Vintners M. MK14: N Hill 7F 17
Violet Cl. HP27: Loos 1B 80
Violets Cl. MK16: N Craw 6J 13
Virginia MK6: Coff 7G 23
Virginia Gdns. HP14: Bled R 3C 72
VIRGINIA WATER 3C 137
Viscount Cl. HP20: Ayle 4A 62
Viscount Ct. SL4: Wind 6K 129
Viscount Ind. Est. SL3: Poy 7E 130
Viscount Way MK2: Blet 6J 29
Vivaldi Ct. MK7: Brow 2F 31
Volta Ri. MK5: S Lod 3C 28
Vyne Cres. MK8: G Hol 5K 21

W

Waborne Rd. SL8: Bou E 5H 107
WADDESDON 6C 52 (2B 134)
Waddesdon Cl. MK8: G Hol 6K 21
Waddesdon Grn. *HP21: Ayle* *4K 65*
(off Winterton Dr.)
Waddesdon Manor 6A 52
Wade Dr. SL1: Slou 6J 123
Wadesmill La. MK7: Cald 3C 30
(not continuous)
Wadhurst La. MK10: Monk 5C 24
Wadworth Holme MK10: Midd 3A 24
Wagner Cl. MK7: Brow 3E 30
Wainers Cft. MK12: Gree 2F 21
Wainwrights HP18: Long C 6D 56
Waivers Way HP21: Ayle 3B 66
Wakefield Cl. MK14: N Hill 6F 17
Wakefield Cres. SL2: S Pog 4D 118
Wakeman Rd. SL8: Bou E 6G 107
Walbank Gro. MK5: S Broo 4K 27
Walbrook Av. MK6: Sprin 3H 23
Waldens Cl. SL8: Bou E 6G 107
Walducks Cl. LU7: Stew 4C 46
Walford Rd. UB8: Uxb 7J 121
Walgrave Dr. MK13: B'ell 3A 22
Walk, The MK18: Wins 7H 39
SL4: E Wick 3J 129
Walker Av. MK12: W Mil 7E 14
Walker Cres. SL3: Lang 3A 130
Walkers Rd. HP27: Long 1C 70
Walkham Cl. HP13: H Wyc 4H 99
Walkhampton Av. MK13: B Com 3B 22
Walkwood End HP9: Bea 7E 100
Walkwood Ri. HP9: Bea 1E 108
Wallace Cl. SL7: Marl 5K 105
UB10: Uxb 7K 121
Wallace Dr. LU6: E Bra 1J 49
Wallace End HP21: Ayle 1B 66
Wallace St. MK13: New B 6J 15
Wallbridge Cl. HP19: Ayle 7G 61
Waller Rd. HP9: Bea 6H 101
Wallinger Dr. MK5: S Broo 4A 28
Wallingford MK13: B'lle 1B 22
Wallingford Gdns. HP11: H Wyc 4B 98
Wallingford Rd. UB8: Uxb 7H 121
Wallington Rd. HP5: Ches 4K 77
Wallis Ct. SL1: Slou 7E 124
Wallmead Gdns. MK5: Lough 7B 22
Walney Pl. MK4: Tatt 6K 27
Walnut Cl. HP16: G Mis 6G 75
HP18: Long C 5C 56
HP22: Sto M 5D 66
MK16: New P 2G 17
Walnut Cres. HP27: Long 1C 70
Walnut Dr. HP22: Wend 2H 69
MK2: F Str 7A 30
MK18: M M'ton 1J 37
Walnut Gro. HP10: Woob G 3A 108
Walnut Lodge SL1: Slou 7B 124
WALNUT TREE 2D 30
WALNUT TREE 7E 24
Walnut Tree Cl.
HP12: H Wyc 7F 89
Walnut Tree Ct. HP22: Sto M 4D 66
SL8: Bou E 7H 107
Walnut Tree La. HP27: Long 2C 70
Walnut Way HP6: H Hea 2E 84
SL8: Bou E 7H 107
Walpole Rd. SL1: Slou 4F 123
Walsh's Mnr. MK14: Stan 6D 16
Walsingham Ga.
HP11: H Wyc 4A 98
WALTER'S ASH 5G 81 (1B 136)
Waltham Dr. MK10: Monk 5C 24
WALTHAM ST LAWRENCE 3B 136

WALTON
Aylesbury 7K 61
Milton Keynes 2C 30 (3C 133)
WALTON 1C 30
Walton Cl. HP13: H Wyc 6E 90
WALTON COURT 2H 65
Walton Ct. Cen. HP21: Ayle 2H 65
Walton Dene HP21: Ayle 7A 62
Walton Dr. HP13: H Wyc 6D 90
MK7: Walt H 1B 30
Walton End MK7: W Gat 1E 30
Walton Grn. HP21: Ayle 7K 61
Walton Gro. HP21: Ayle 7K 61
WALTON HALL 1B 30
Walton Heath MK3: Blet 7D 28
Walton La. SL2: Farn R 7H 117
WALTON PARK 3C 30
WALTON PARK 3D 30
Walton Pl. HP22: West T 4G 67
Walton Rd. MK7: Cald 4D 30
MK7: W Gat 1F 31
MK7: Waln 1C 30
MK10: M Vill 4B 24
MK17: Wave 7G 25
Walton St. HP20: Ayle 6J 61
HP21: Ayle 7K 61
Walton Way HP21: Ayle 7B 62
Wandlebury MK14: G Par 5G 17
Wandsworth Pl. MK13: B Com 3D 22
Wannions Cl. HP5: Ches 4E 78
Wantage Cl. LU7: Wing 2C 48
Wantage Cres. LU7: Wing 2C 48
WAPPENHAM 2A 132
Wapping HP18: Long C 6D 56
Wapseys La. SL2: Hedg 4C 110
Wapseys Wood Cvn. Site
SL9: Bea 2C 110
Warbler Cl. HP19: Ayle 6E 60
Ward Cl. SL0: Ive 5F 127
Wardes Cl. HP16: Pres 1C 82
Ward Gdns. SL1: Slou 5G 123
Wardle Pl. MK6: Old 6D 22
Ward Pl. HP7: Amer 7K 85
Ward Rd. MK1: Blet 4A 30
Wardrobes La. HP27: Loos 7K 71
Wardstone End MK4: E Val 5B 28
Ware Leys Cl. OX27: M Gib 5B 42
WARFIELD 3B 136
WARGRAVE 3A 136
Warmington Gdns. MK15: D Park 1H 23
Warmstone Cl. HP18: Wadd 6D 52
Warmstone La. HP18: Wadd 6D 52
Warneford Av. HP22: Halt 3K 69
Warner Cl. SL1: Slou 6G 123
Warners Cl. MK17: G Bri 7E 34
WARNERS END 3D 135
Warners Rd. MK17: New L 5D 32
Warren, The HP5: Ches 2G 77
HP15: Haz 2G 91
SL9: C Pet 5K 103
Warren Bank MK6: Simp 2A 30
Warren Cl. HP17: Sto 2A 64
MK18: Buck 5J 37
Warren Ct. SL2: Farn C 3A 118
Warrendene Rd. HP14: H Vall 6A 82
Warrender Rd. HP5: Ches 3C 78
Warren Fld. SL0: I Hea 7C 120
Warren Pde. SL2: Slou 6G 125
WARREN ROW 2B 136
Warren Wood Dr. HP11: H Wyc 3C 98
Warren Yd. MK12: W Mil 7E 14
WARRINGTON 1C 133
Warrington Av. SL1: Slou 4A 124
Warrington Rd. MK46: Oln 2H 7
Warwick Av. HP12: Book 2F 97
SL2: Slou 2A 124
Warwick Cl. HP22: Ast C 2B 68
Warwick Ct. HP9: Bea 5F 101
SL4: Wind 7K 129
(off Alma Rd.)
Warwick Dr. LU7: Wing 3C 48
Warwick Ho. *HP13: H Wyc 1F 99*
(off Gayhurst Rd.)
Warwick Pl. MK3: Blet 1E 32
UB8: Uxb 5J 121
Warwick Rd. HP9: Bea 5F 101
LU7: Pits 7F 51
MK3: Blet 7F 29
MK19: H'ope 1E 8
UB7: W Dra 7K 127
Warwick Row HP20: Ayle 5B 62
Washfield MK4: Fur 4D 28
Wash Hill HP10: Woob G 5A 108
Wash Hill Lea HP10: Woob G 5K 107
Washington Ct. SL7: Marl 6A 106
Washington Dr. SL1: Slou 5F 123
SL4: Wind 7G 129
Washington Row HP7: Amer 7A 86
Wastel MK6: Bean 2H 29
(not continuous)
Watchcroft Dr. MK18: Buck 2J 37
Watchet Ct. MK4: Fur 4D 28
Watchet La. HP15: H Grn 1H 91
HP16: L Kin 4J 83
Waterbeach Cl. SL1: Slou 4B 124
Waterbeach Rd. SL1: Slou 4B 124
Water Cl. MK19: O Stra 6A 14
WATER EATON 1K 33
Water Eaton Ind. Pk. MK2: Blet 2J 33
Water Eaton Rd. MK3: Blet 1H 33
WATER END 2D 135
Waterford Cl. MK3: Blet 6E 28
Waterford Ho. UB7: W Dra 1J 131
Water Gdns., The HP15: Haz 5E 90
Waterglades, The HP9: Bea 2E 100
Waterhouse Cl. MK16: New P 1K 17
Water La. HP17: Ford 5K 59
HP27: Spee 2G 81
MK16: Sher 3K 11
Waterlilly HP19: Ayle 2K 61
Waterloo Ct. MK3: Blet 5E 28
Waterloo Rd. UB8: Uxb 6J 121
Waterlow Cl. MK16: New P 3J 17
Waterman Ct. SL1: Slou 6G 123
WATERMEAD 2K 61
Watermead HP19: Ayle 3J 61
Water Mdw. HP5: Ches 6K 77
Watermeadow HP19: Ayle 3A 62
Water Mdw. Way HP22: Wend 2H 69
Watermead Ski & Water Sports Cen.
. . . . .2J 61
WATER MILL 5C 30
Watermil La. MK12: W Mil 6D 14
Watermill Way HP22: West T 5G 67
WATER OAKLEY 4B 128
WATERPERRY 6A 54 (3A 134)
Waterperry House (Horticultural Cen.)
. . . . .7A 54
Waterperry M. HP19: Ayle 6E 60
Waterperry Rd. HP18: Worm 3B 54
WATERSIDE 6A 78 (3D 135)
Water Side UB8: Cowl 3J 127
Waterside HP5: Ches 6A 78
HP10: Woob G 2A 108
LU6: E Bra 2K 49
MK6: P Bri 6J 23
UB7: Harm 5J 131
Waterside Ct. *HP5: Ches 6A 78*
(off Waterside)
Waterside Dr. SL3: Lang 7K 125
Waterslade Pens HP17: Hadd 6A 58
Watersmeet Cl. MK4: Fur 3D 28
WATERSTOCK 7B 54 (3A 134)
WATER STRATFORD 3A 132
Water Stratford Rd. MK18: Ting 1B 36
Water Twr. Cl. UB8: Uxb 3K 121
Water World 7A 22
Watery La. HP10: Woob G 7A 100
HP23: M'rth 7B 50
WATFORD 1D 137
Watling St. (V4) MK1: Blet 5J 29
MK2: F Str 5K 29
MK5: Mil K 3F 29
MK8: Mil K 4G 21
MK11: Mil K 2D 20
MK17: Mil K 5K 29
Watling Ter. MK2: F Str 6A 30
WATLINGTON 1A 136
Watlington Ct. HP16: G Mis 5G 75
Watling Way Cen. 2D 20
Watlow Gdns. MK18: Buck 2J 37
Watson Cl. MK8: G Far 1H 27
Watten Ct. MK2: Blet 4A 34
Wattleton Rd. HP9: Bea 1E 108
Watts Cl. MK19: H'ope 1E 8
Watts Grn. HP18: Che 2H 57
Wavell Ct. MK15: Bolb 6H 17
Wavell Gdns. SL2: Slou 1H 123
Wavell Rd. HP9: Bea 7K 101
WAVENDON 7G 25 (3D 133)
Wavendon Flds. MK17: Wave 1H 31
WAVENDON GATE 1E 30
Wavendon Ho. Dr. MK17: Wave 6K 25
Wavendon Rd. MK17: Salf 4K 25
Waveney Cl. MK16: New P 2A 18
Waverley Cft. MK10: Monk 5B 24
Waverley Rd. SL1: Slou 3A 124
Waverley Wlk. HP20: Ayle 4J 61
Waxwing Cl. HP19: Ayle 3K 61
Wayside HP13: H Wyc 1D 98
HP27: Spee 2G 81
Wayside Ct. *HP6: Amer 5A 86*
(off Chesham Rd.)
Wayside Gdns. SL9: G Cro 5H 111
Wealdstone Pl. MK6: Sprin 4G 23
Weasel La. MK17: New L 3A 32
Weathercock Cl. MK17: W San 2K 31
Weathercock Gdns. HP15: H Grn 7J 83
Weathercock La. MK17: W San 2K 31
Weavers End MK19: H'ope 2F 9
Weavers Hill MK11: F Sla 3E 20
Webb Cl. HP5: Ches 4K 77
Webber Heath MK7: Old P 3F 31
Webbs Home Cl. MK10: Midd 4C 24
Webbs Mdw. HP19: Ayle 6F 61
Webster Rd. HP21: Ayle 1B 66
Websters Mdw. MK4: E Val 6C 28
Wedgwood Av. MK14: Blak 4G 17
(not continuous)
Wedgwood Dr. HP14: H Vall 1A 90
WEEDON 7J 45 (2C 135)
WEEDON BEC 1A 132
Weedon Cl. SL9: C Pet 6F 103
Weedon Ct. HP19: Ayle 4J 61
WEEDON HILL 1H 61
Weedon Hill HP6: H Hea 1E 84
Weedon La. HP6: Amer 3J 85
WEEDON LOIS 2A 132
Weedon Rd. HP19: Ayle 4H 61
Weekes Dr. SL1: Slou 6K 123
Weill Rd. HP21: Ayle 3B 66
Weint, The SL3: Coln 5C 130
Weir La. HP22: W'urch 3F 45
Weirside Gdns. UB7: W Dra 6K 127
Welbeck Av. HP21: Ayle 1D 66
Welbeck Cl. MK10: Monk 5B 24
Welburn Gro. MK4: E Val 5B 28
Welden SL2: Slou 4G 125
Welders La. HP9: Jord 5D 102
SL9: C Pet 5D 102
Weldon Ri. MK5: Lough 6B 22
Welford Way HP18: Cudd 1B 58
Welland Cl. HP21: Ayle 3H 65
SL3: Lang 4B 130
Welland Dr. MK16: New P 2A 18
Welland Ho. MK3: Blet 7E 28
Welland Rd. HP21: Ayle 2H 65
Wellbank SL6: Tapl 2A 122
Wellcroft LU7: I'hoe 4H 51
Wellcroft Rd. SL1: Slou 6K 123
WELL END 4G 107
Weller Cl. HP6: Amer 4C 86
Weller Rd. HP6: Amer 4C 86
Wellesbourne Grn. HP13: H Wyc 5D 90
Wellesley Av. SL0: R Pk 1F 131
Wellesley Ct. SL0: R Pk 7F 127
Wellesley Ho. *SL4: Wind 6K 129*
(off Vansittart Rd.)
Wellesley Path *SL1: Slou 7E 124*
(off Wellesley Rd.)
Wellesley Rd. SL1: Slou 6E 124
Wellfield HP15: Haz 4H 91
Wellfield Ct. MK15: Will 5K 17
Wellfield Rd. HP14: Pidd 7A 88
Wellhayes MK14: G Lin 5F 17
Wellhouse Way HP14: Nap 1J 89
Wellingborough Rd. MK46: Oln 2H 7
Wellington Av. HP27: Prin R 4G 71
Wellington Pl. HP21: Ayle 3K 65
MK3: Blet 1H 33
Wellington Rd. HP12: H Wyc 4J 97
HP21: Ayle 3K 65
UB8: Uxb 6J 121
Wellington St. SL1: Slou 6C 124
Well La. LU7: Wing 3D 48
Wellmore MK18: M M'ton 1K 37
Wells Cl. SL4: Wind 6J 129
Well St. MK18: Buck 4H 37
Welsummer Gro. MK5: S Broo 4A 28
Welton Rd. HP21: Ayle 7C 62
WENDLEBURY 2A 134
WENDOVER 4H 69 (3C 135)
Wendover By-Pass HP22: Wend 3F 69
Wendover Hgts. HP22: Halt 2K 69
Wendover Rd. HP21: Ayle 7K 61
HP22: Sto M, Wend, West T 5D 66
HP22: Wend 5F 69
SL1: Burn 3D 122
SL8: Bou E 5G 107
Wendover Station (Rail) 4H 69
Wendover St. HP11: H Wyc 1K 97
Wendover Way HP11: H Wyc 2B 98
HP21: Ayle 1A 66
Wenlack Cl. UB9: Den 1H 121
Wenning La. MK4: E Val 5A 28
Wentworth Av. SL2: Slou 7J 117
Wentworth Cl. HP13: H Wyc 7C 90
Wentworth Ind. Ct. SL2: Slou 1H 123
Wentworth Pl. *HP5: Ches 7A 78*
(off Waterside)
Wentworth Way MK3: Blet 1C 32
Wenwell Cl. HP22: Ast C 3D 68
Werner Ct. HP21: Ayle 3K 65
Werth Dr. MK17: A H'th 5K 31
Wescott Way UB8: Uxb 7J 121
Wesley Cl. HP20: Ayle 4B 62
Wesley Dene HP13: H Wyc 1B 98
Wesley Hill HP5: Ches 4K 77
Wessex Rd. SL8: Bou E 7H 107
Wessex Rd. Ind. Est. SL8: Bou E 7H 107
West Acres HP7: Amer 7B 86
Westanley Av. HP7: Amer 6B 86
WEST ASHLAND 3H 29
West Av. HP10: T Grn 6J 91
WEST BLETCHLEY 7F 29
Westbourne Ct. MK13: B'lle 7A 16
Westbourne St. HP11: H Wyc 1K 97
Westbrook SL6: Bra 3A 128
Westbrook End MK17: New L 5C 32
WESTBURY 3A 132
Westbury Cl. MK16: New P 1H 17
Westbury La. MK16: New P 7G 11
Westbury Ter. OX27: M Gib 6B 42
Westcliffe MK8: T Ash 4G 21
West Cl. SL7: Medm 3B 114
West Comn. SL9: G Cro 3H 111
(not continuous)
West Comn. Cl. SL9: G Cro 3J 111
West Comn. Rd. UB8: Uxb 3K 121
WESTCOTT 2B 134
West Ct. HP13: Down 4H 89
West Cres. SL4: Wind 6H 129
WESTCROFT 5K 27
WESTCROFT 5A 28
Westcroft SL2: Slou 2K 123
West Dales MK13: Hee 1C 22
Westdean La. HP5: Char 2E 76
WEST DRAYTON 7K 127 (3D 137)
West Drayton Station (Rail) 6K 127
West Dr. HP13: H Wyc 7D 90
West Edge OX27: M Gib 6B 42
WEST END
Aylesbury 5F 67
Bedford 1D 133
Reading 3B 136
West End HP22: West T 5F 67
West End Cl. MK18: S Clay 3A 42
West End Ct. SL2: S Pog 6D 118
West End La. SL2: S Pog 6C 118
West End Pl. HP22: West T 5F 67
West End Rd. HP11: H Wyc 1K 97
LU7: Ched 2B 50
West End St. HP11: H Wyc 1K 97
Western Av. MK18: Buck 3G 37
UB9: Den, Uxb 2J 121
UB10: Hill 2J 121
Western Dene HP15: Haz 1G 91
Western Dr. HP10: Woob G 4A 108
MK19: H'ope 1E 8
Western La. MK18: Wins 7G 39
Western Perimeter Rd.
TW6: L Hea 7H 131
TW6: L Hea, Long 7H 131
UB7: Long 7H 131
Western Rd. MK2: Blet 6J 29
MK12: Wolv 7G 15
MK17: G Hor 2J 39
W. Farm Way MK46: Emb 7G 7
Westfield HP6: H Hea 2E 84
HP21: Ayle 4K 65
Westfield La. SL3: G Grn 4H 125
Westfield Rd. HP9: Bea 7E 100
LU7: Pits 6E 50
MK2: Blet 7J 29
SL2: Slou 2K 123
Westfields HP27: Whit 4J 71
MK18: Buck 4F 37
Westfield Wlk. HP12: H Wyc 2H 97
West Furlong MK18: Pad 6A 38
Westgate Ct. HP13: H Wyc 4G 99
Westgate Cres. SL1: Slou 5H 123
Westgate Retail Pk. SL1: Slou 5J 123
Westhill MK14: Stan 5D 16
Westhorpe Rd. SL7: Marl 6K 105
WEST HYDE 1D 137
W. Hyde La. SL9: C Pet 5K 103
Westlands Av. SL1: Slou 4E 122
Westlands Cl. SL1: Slou 4E 122
Westlands Rd. HP27: L Grn 1C 80
West La. HP27: Bled 6A 70
MK46: Emb 7G 7
WEST LEITH 2D 135
WESTLINGTON 3G 59 (2B 134)
Westlington La. HP17: Dint 3G 59
Westlington Lea HP17: Dint 2G 59
Westmead HP27: Prin R 3G 71
SL4: Wind 7K 129
Westminster Cl. HP11: H Wyc 4B 98
Westminster Dr. HP21: Ayle 1A 66
MK3: Blet 6F 29
WEST MOLESEY 3D 137
Westmorland Av. HP21: Ayle 1C 66
Westmount Av. HP7: Amer 6A 86
WESTON .2A 132
Weston Ct. HP22: Ast C 2K 67
WESTON FAVELL 1B 132
WESTONING 3D 133
Weston La. OX9: N West 7K 55
Weston Rd. HP22: Ast C 3J 67
MK46: Oln 4F 7
SL1: Slou 3H 123
WESTON TURVILLE 5G 67 (2C 135)
Weston Turville Golf & Squash Club . . .3F 67
Weston Turville Reservoir 7H 67
WESTON UNDERWOOD 1C 133
Weston Way HP22: Sto M 5B 66
Weston Way Ind. Est. HP22: Sto M 5B 66
Westover Ct. HP13: Down 6H 89
Westover Rd. HP13: Down 6H 89
Westpits MK46: Emb 7G 7
West Point SL1: Slou 6F 123
W. Richardson St. HP11: H Wyc 1K 97
Westrick Wlk. *HP16: Pres 1D 82*
(off Lodge La.)
West Ridge SL8: Bou E 5H 107
West Rd. MK17: W San 2K 31
Westside La. MK16: S Gold 6C 6
West Side Ri. MK46: Oln 3G 7
W. Spur Rd. UB8: Cowl 1K 127
West Sq. SL0: Ive 4F 127
West St. HP19: Ayle 5J 61
MK18: Ads 6E 38
MK18: Buck 3G 37
MK18: S Clay 3A 42
MK46: Oln 4H 7
SL7: Marl 1G 115
West Vw. HP5: Ches 3B 78
HP22: H'ick 5H 45

West Wlk. MK9: C Key 4E 22
West Way HP9: Bea 7B 100
West Waye HP13: H Wyc 5C 90
West Well Cl. MK18: Ting 2B 36
West Well La. MK18: Ting 2B 36
Westwood HP12: Book 5F 97
Westwood Cl. HP6: L Chal 6H 87
MK8: G Hol 6J 21
Westwood Dr. HP6: L Chal 6H 87
Westwood Rd. SL7: Marl 1G 115
Westwood Wlk. HP20: Ayle 4A 62
WEST WYCOMBE 5D 88 (1B 136)
W. Wycombe Hill Rd. HP14: W Wyc 5D 88
West Wycombe House 6D 88
W. Wycombe Rd. HP11: H Wyc 5F 89
HP12: H Wyc 5F 89
West Yd. Ind. Est.
HP14: Saun 6A 80
Wetherby Gdns. MK3: Blet 2D 32
Wethered Dr. SL1: Burn 3D 122
Wethered Pk. SL7: Marl 1H 115
Wethered Rd. SL7: Marl 7H 105
WEXHAM 2G 125
WEXHAM COURT 4G 125
Wexham Pk. La. SL3: Wex 2G 125
Wexham Pk. Stadium 4E 124
Wexham Pl. SL2: Wex 4H 119
Wexham Rd. SL1: Slou 7E 124
SL2: Slou, Wex 4F 125
Wexham Springs SL3: Wex 5H 119
WEXHAM STREET 7G 119 (2C 137)
Wexham St. SL2: Wex 2F 125
SL3: S Pog 2F 125
Wexham Woods SL3: Wex 3G 125
Weybourne Rd. MK10: Bro 2C 24
Wey La. HP5: Ches 6K 77
WHADDON 6F 27 (3C 133)
Whaddon Chase HP19: Ayle 4H 61
Whaddon Pk. MK17: Whad 5F 27
Whaddon Rd. MK4: K'ead 7J 27
MK5: S Broo 4A 28
MK16: New P 2H 17
MK17: Mur 1C 40
MK17: Nas 6A 26
MK17: New L 3A 32
Whaddon Way MK3: Blet 1D 32
Whales La. OX27: M Gib 6B 42
Whalley Dr. MK3: Blet 4G 29
Wharf, The MK2: Blet 2A 34
MK14: G Lin 3E 16
Wharf Cl. HP22: Wend 3H 69
MK19: O Stra 6A 14
Wharf La. MK19: O Stra 6A 14
SL8: Bou E 6G 107
Wharf Rd. HP22: Wend 3H 69
Wharf Row HP22: B'land 3E 68
Wharfside MK2: F Str 7A 30
Wharfside Pl. MK18: Buck 3J 37
Wharf Vw. MK18: Buck 3J 37
WHARLEY END 2D 133
Wharton Ho. *HP20: Ayle* *5J 61*
(off Silverdale Cl.)
Wheatbutts, The SL4: E Wick 2H 129
Wheat Cl. HP21: Ayle 4K 65
Wheatcroft Cl. MK6: Bean 2G 29
Wheathouse Copse MK17: G Hor 2J 39
WHEATLEY 3A 134
Wheatley Cl. MK4: E Val 5C 28
Wheatley Way SL9: C Pet 4J 103
Wheeler Av. HP10: T Grn 7J 91
Wheeler Cl. HP20: Ayle 7C 62
WHEELER END 1J 73
WHEELER END COMMON 1K 73
Wheelers Flats *HP10: T Grn* *7K 91*
(off Church Rd.)
Wheelers La. MK13: B'lle 7A 16
Wheelers Orchard SL9: C Pet 4J 103
Wheelers Pk. HP13: H Wyc 1D 98
Wheelers Yd. *HP16: G Mis* *6H 75*
(off Church St.)
Wheelwright Rd. HP27: Long 1C 70
Wheelwrights HP22: West T 4G 67
Wheelwrights M. MK14: N Hill 7F 17
Wheelwrights Pl. SL3: Coln 5C 130
Wheelwrights Way MK19: O Stra 6A 14
Wheelwrights Yd. HP22: Q'ton 5H 43
WHELPLEY HILL 1H 79 (3D 135)
Whetstone Cl. MK13: Hee 2B 22
Whichcote Gdns. HP5: Ches 7B 78
Whichert Cl. HP9: Bea 3E 100
Whichford MK14: G Par 4G 17
Whielden Cl. HP7: Amer 7K 85
Whielden Ga. HP7: Winc 3G 93
Whielden Grn. HP7: Amer 7K 85
Whielden Hgts. HP7: Amer 7J 85
Whielden La. HP7: Amer, Winc 3F 93
HP7: Winc, Amer 4E 92
Whielden St. HP7: Amer 1K 93
Whinchat HP19: Ayle 3K 61
Whincup Cl. HP11: H Wyc 4K 97
Whinneys Rd. HP10: Loud 5J 99
WHIPSNADE 2D 135
WHISTLEY GREEN 3A 136
WHISTON 1C 133
Whitby Cl. MK3: Blet 5F 29
Whitby Rd. SL1: Slou 5A 124
Whitby Rd. Bus. Cen. SL1: Slou 5A 124
WHITCHURCH 2G 45 (1C 135)
Whitchurch La. HP22: Ovi 4D 44
Whitchurch Rd. LU7: Cubl 3G 47
White Alder MK12: S Bus 1J 21
Whitebaker Ct. MK14: N Hill 7F 17
White Cl. HP13: Down 6H 89
SL1: Slou 6B 124
White Cres. HP22: Halt 1K 69
White Cross Rd. HP17: Hadd 7B 58
Whitefield La. HP16: G Mis 7G 75
Whiteford Rd. SL2: Slou 3C 124
Whitegate Cross MK6: E Wes 1H 29
Whitehall MK46: Oln 2G 7
Whitehall Av. MK10: K'ton 5F 25
Whitehall Cl. UB8: Uxb 6J 121
Whitehall Rd. UB8: Uxb 6K 121
Whitehall St. HP20: Ayle 6J 61
White Hart Cl. HP8: D Gil 1E 102
HP18: Ludg 3B 52
White Hart Fld. HP22: Q'ton 6J 43
White Hart La. HP17: Hadd 7C 58
White Hart Mdw. HP9: Bea 7G 101
White Hart Rd. SL1: Slou 7B 124
White Hart St. HP11: H Wyc 1A 98
Whitehaven SL1: Slou 5D 124
Whitehead Way HP21: Ayle 1K 65
White Hill HP5: Ches 5A 78
HP10: Woob G 7A 100
HP14: H Vall 5B 90
Whitehill Cl. SL7: Marl 3G 105
White Hill La. LU7: Pits 7F 51
White Horse Dr. MK4: E Val 5C 28
White Horse La. HP22: W'urch 2G 45
White Horse Rd. SL4: Wind 7F 129
Whitehorse Yd. *MK11: S Strat* *1B 20*
(off High St.)
White Ho., The MK16: Tyr 1F 11
White Ho. Cl. SL9: C Pet 5J 103
Whitehouse Cl. HP10: Woob G 7A 100
Whitehouse La. HP10: Woob G 7A 100
Whitehouse Way SL0: I Hea 1D 126
SL3: Lang 7H 125
Whitelands Rd. HP12: H Wyc 2H 97
Whitelead Hill Nature Reserve 3K 71
WHITELEAF 3J 71
Whiteleaf Way HP27: Whit 3J 71
Whiteley SL4: Wind 5G 129
Whiteley Cres. MK3: Blet 2E 32
(not continuous)
White Lillies Island SL4: Wind 5J 129
White Lion Cl. HP7: Amer 6E 86
White Lion Rd. HP7: Amer, L Chal 6D 86
White Lodge Cl. SL7: Marl 3G 105
Whitepit La. HP10: F Hea 2J 107
Whites Cl. MK18: S Clay 3B 42
Whitethorn Cl. HP22: Sto M 7B 66
Whitethorns MK16: New P 2H 17
White Vw. HP20: Ayle 4A 62
WHITE WALTHAM 3B 136
WHITFIELD 3A 132
Whitfield Rd. HP14: H Vall 1A 90
Whitington Chase MK4: K'ead 7J 27
Whitle Hill Cl. HP5: Ches 4A 78
Whitley Ct. HP21: Ayle 3K 65
Whitmees Cl. MK46: Oln 3G 7
WHITNEY 5J 27
Whitsun Pasture MK15: W Par 6H 17
Whittaker Rd. SL2: Slou 2F 123
Whittenham Cl. SL2: Slou 6E 124
WHITTLEBURY 2A 132
Whittle Parkway SL1: Slou 4F 123
Whitton Way MK16: New P 2J 17
Whitworth La. MK5: Lough 6B 22
WICKEN 3B 132
Wickstead Av. MK8: G Far 1H 27
Widdenton Vw. HP14: L End 3A 96
Widecroft Rd. SL0: Ive 4E 126
Widewater Pl. UB9: Hare 3J 113
Widmere Fld. HP16: Pres 1C 82
Widmere La. SL7: Marl 3E 104
WIDMER END 1E 90 (1B 136)
WIDMOOR 6A 108
Wigan's La. HP27: Bled R 1A 72
WIGGINTON 2D 135
Wigmore Ct. HP19: Ayle 4F 61
Wigmore Rd. HP19: Ayle 4F 61
Wigwell Gdns. MK17: G Hor 3J 39
Wildacre Rd. MK5: S Woo 2K 27
Wildgreen Nth. SL3: Lang 2A 130
Wildgreen Sth. SL3: Lang 2A 130
Wiles Cft. MK5: S Chur 7K 21
Wilford Cl. MK15: Wool 4J 23
Wilfridswood Cl. HP10: F Hea 3H 107
WILLEN 6K 17 (2C 133)
WILLEN 6H 17
WILLEN LAKE 1J 23
Willen Lakeside Pk. 2K 23
Willen Lake Water Sports Cen. 2K 23
Willen La. MK14: G Lin 5F 17
WILLEN PARK 7H 17
Willen Pk. Av. MK15: W Par 6H 17
Willen Rd. MK10: M Vill 3B 24
MK15: Will 7K 17
MK16: New P 2K 17
Willets Ri. MK5: S Chur 2A 28
Willetts La. UB9: Den 3F 121
Willey Ct. MK11: S Strat 2D 20
William Bandy Cl. LU7: Wing 2D 48
William Burt Cl. HP22: West T 6G 67
William Harding Cl. HP21: Ayle 7K 61
William Hartley Yd. SL3: Wex 2F 125
William Hill Dr. HP22: Bier 2D 62
William Moulder Ct. HP5: Ches 2K 77
Williams Circ. MK7: Walt P 3C 30
Williams Cl. HP19: Ayle 5J 61
MK19: H'ope 1D 8
William Shakman Ho. *HP8: D Gil* *7F 95*
(off School La.)
William Smith Cl. MK15: Wool 3J 23
William St. SL1: Slou 7D 124
William Sutton Ho.
MK5: S Chur 1A 28
Williams Way HP27: Long 2C 70
Willington Ct. HP9: Bea 7G 101
Willis Rd. HP17: Hadd 7C 58
Willoners SL2: Slou 3J 123
Willoughby Rd. SL3: Lang 1A 130
Willoughby's Wlk. HP13: Down 5H 89
Willow Av. UB9: Den 4J 121
WILLOWBANK 3J 121
Willow Bank SL7: Marl 4H 105
Willowbank Ter. HP21: Ayle 6K 61
Willowbrook HP22: Wend 1H 69
Willow Chase HP5: Ches 4K 77
HP15: Haz 4E 90
Willow Cl. HP10: F Hea 3J 107
MK16: Moul 5G 19
SL3: Coln 5C 130
SL9: C Pet 7J 103
Willow Ct. HP11: H Wyc 4E 98
HP14: Nap 6G 81
HP19: Ayle 4F 61
HP21: Ayle 1H 65
Willow Cres. E. UB9: Den 3J 121
Willow Cres. W. UB9: Den 3J 121
Willow Dr. MK18: Buck 5K 37
Willow End HP22: West T 5G 67
Willowford MK13: B Pk 1J 21
Willow Ga. HP18: Che 2H 57
Willow Gro. MK19: O Stra 7A 14
Willow Herb HP19: Ayle 2K 61
Willow La. HP7: Amer 1D 94
MK11: S Strat 1A 20
Willowmead HP17: Hart 2E 64
Willowmead Cl. SL7: Marl 6K 105
Willowmead Gdns. SL7: Marl 6K 105
Willowmead Rd. SL7: Marl 6K 105
Willowmead Sq. SL7: Marl 6K 105
Willow Pde. SL3: Lang 1A 130
Willow Pk. SL2: S Pog 5E 118
Willow Pl. SL4: Eto 4K 129
Willow Ri. HP17: Hadd 5C 58
Willow Rd. HP19: Ayle 5J 61
MK17: G Hor 2J 39
SL3: Poy 7E 130
Willows, The HP6: Amer 2K 85
HP27: Long 2D 70
LU6: Edle 3K 49
SL4: Wind 5F 129
Willows Lodge SL4: Wind 5F 129
Willows Path SL4: Wind 6E 128
Willows Riverside Pk.
SL4: Wind 5E 128
Willows Rd. SL8: Bou E 6H 107
Willow Wlk. HP15: Haz 4G 91
Willow Way HP11: W Mar 6H 99
HP27: Prin R 5F 71
LU7: Wing 2C 48
MK2: Blet 1J 33
Willow Wern MK14: G Lin 3E 16
Willow Wood Cl. SL1: Burn 7D 116
Wilmar Cl. UB8: Uxb 5K 121
Wilmin Gro. MK5: Lough 7B 22
Wilmot Rd. SL1: Burn 1D 122
Wilsley Pound MK7: K Hil 6D 24
Wilson Ct. MK8: C'ill 7J 21
WILSTONE 2D 135
Wilton Av. MK3: Blet 7G 29
Wilton Cl. UB7: Harm 4K 131
Wilton Cres. HP9: Bea 5G 101
Wilton La. HP9: Jord 5B 102
WILTON PARK 7K 101
Wilton Rd. HP9: Bea 4G 101
Wiltshire Av. SL2: Slou 2A 124
Wiltshire Rd. SL7: Marl 4K 105
Wiltshire Way MK3: Blet 6E 28
Wimbledon Pl. MK13: B Com 3C 22
Wimblington Dr. MK6: Red 3G 29
Wimborne Cres. MK4: West 5K 27
Wimpole Rd. UB7: Yiew 6K 127
Wincanton Hill MK3: Blet 2C 32
Winchbottom La.
HP10: H Wyc 6J 97
SL7: L Mar 2B 106
Winchester Circ. MK10: K'ton 5D 24
Winchester Cl. HP7: Amer 6D 86
SL3: Poy 6E 130
Winchester Ct. HP11: W Mar 5H 99
Winchester Ho. *HP21: Ayle* *1A 66*
(off Bishops Wlk.)
WINCHMORE HILL 5E 92 (1C 137)
Windermere Cl. HP21: Ayle 1C 66
Windermere Dr. MK2: Blet 3K 33
Windermere Way SL1: Slou 3E 122
Windmill Cl. HP19: Ayle 6G 61
LU7: I'hoe 4H 51
MK18: Buck 3K 37
SL4: Wind 7K 129
Windmill Dr. HP15: W End 1F 91
WINDMILL HILL 6C 28
Windmill Hill HP7: Cole 5H 93
HP27: Prin R 6G 71
Windmill Hill Dr. MK3: Blet 1C 32
Windmill La. HP15: W End 1E 90
Windmill Rd. HP17: Hadd 6B 58
SL1: Slou 6B 124
SL3: Fulm 3H 119
SL9: C Pet 5H 103
Windmill St. HP18: Bril 2H 53
Windmill Wood HP6: Amer 4J 85
Windrush Av. SL3: Lang 1B 130
Windrush Cl. MK15: D Park 7G 17
Windrush Ct. HP13: H Wyc 2F 99
HP21: Ayle 3J 65
Windrush Dr. HP13: H Wyc 2F 99
Windrush Ho. SL8: Bou E 5G 107
WINDSOR 6K 129 (3C 137)
Windsor & Eton Relief Rd.
SL4: Eto, Wind 6K 129
Windsor Av. MK16: New P 1J 17
Windsor Boys School Sports Cen. 6K 129
Windsor Bus. Cen. SL4: Wind 5K 129
Windsor Cl. HP3: Bov 2K 79
SL1: Burn 2E 122
Windsor Ct. *HP6: Amer* *5B 86*
(off King George V Rd.)
HP11: W Mar 5H 99
Windsor Cres. HP10: Loud 6J 99
Windsor Dr. HP13: H Wyc 6D 90
Windsor End HP9: Bea 7H 101
Windsor Fitness and Rackets Club, The
.....6K 129
Windsor Hill HP10: Woob G 4A 108
HP27: Prin R 3H 71
Windsor La. HP16: L Kin 4G 83
SL1: Burn 2E 122
Windsor Leisure Cen. 5K 129
Windsor Rd. HP5: Ches 2K 77
HP9: Bea 2J 109
HP21: Ayle 7B 62
LU7: Pits 6E 50
SL1: Slou 7C 124
SL2: G Cro, S Pog 2E 118
SL4: W Oak, Wind 3A 128
SL4: Wind 5D 128
SL6: Bra 3A 128
SL9: G Cro 6F 111
Windsor St. MK2: Blet 1J 33
MK12: Wolv 6G 15
UB8: Uxb 6J 121
Winemar Cl. MK19: H'ope 1E 8
Winfold La. MK4: Tatt 6B 28
WING 2C 48 (1C 135)
Wingate Av. HP13: H Wyc 1E 98
Wingate Circ. MK7: Walt P 3C 30
Wingate Ct. HP13: H Wyc 1E 98
Wingate Wlk. HP20: Ayle 5B 62
Wing Cl. SL7: Marl 1G 115
WINGFIELD 1D 135
Wingfield Gro. MK10: Midd 4C 24
WINGRAVE 6C 48 (2C 135)
Wingrave Rd. HP22: A Abb 7J 47
HP23: Gubb 7A 50
Wing Rd. LU7: Cubl 2H 47
LU7: Stew 5C 46
Winkers Cl. SL9: C Pet 6K 103
Winkers La. SL9: C Pet 6K 103
WINKFIELD 3C 137
WINKFIELD ROW 3B 136
WINNERSH 3A 136
Winnock Rd. UB7: Yiew 6K 127
Winsford Hill MK4: Fur 4E 28
WINSLOW 6H 39 (1B 134)
Winslow Fld. HP16: G Mis 5F 75
Winslow Gdns. HP13: H Wyc 1G 99
Winslow Rd. HP22: W'rave 6A 48
MK17: G Hor 4H 39
MK17: Nas 7A 26
Winstanley La. MK5: S Lod 3B 28
Winstone Cl. HP6: Amer 1K 85
Winston Ho. HP11: W Mar 4G 99
Winterburn MK13: Hee 1B 22
WINTER HILL 7C 106
WINTERHILL 7E 22
Winter Hill SL6: Cook 7C 106
Winterhill Retail Pk. MK6: Wint 7D 22
Winter Hill Rd. SL6: Cook, Maid 4K 115
Winters Way HP15: H Grn 7K 83
Winterton Dr. HP21: Ayle 4K 65
Wintoun Path SL2: Slou 2G 123
Winwood SL2: Slou 4G 125
SL4: Wind 6H 129
Winwood Dr. HP22: Q'ton 5H 43
Wise La. UB7: W Dra 1K 131
Wisewood Rd. MK4: Wood 3H 27
Wishart Grn. MK7: Old P 2G 31
Wisley Av. MK13: B Com 3D
Wistmans MK4: Fur 3D
Witan Ga. MK9: C Key 4D
Witan Gate W. MK9: C Key 4D
Witchell HP22: Wend 4H

Witham Ct. MK3: Blet 6D 28
Witham Way HP21: Ayle 3H 65
WITHERIDGE HILL 2A 136
Witheridge La. HP9: Bea 1B 100
HP10: Pen 1B 100
Withey Cl. SL4: Wind 6G 129
Withington MK13: B'lle 1A 22
Withycombe MK4: Fur 4E 28
Withycroft SL3: G Grn 4J 125
Wittmills Oak MK18: Buck 3J 37
Wivelsfield LU6: E Bra 1J 49
Wixon Path HP19: Ayle 6F 61
Woad La. MK14: G Lin 5E 16
WOBURN 3D 133
Woburn Av. MK12: Wolv 7G 15
Woburn Rd. MK17: A H'th, Wob 4K 31
MK17: L Bric 2G 35
WOBURN SANDS 1K 31 (3D 133)
Woburn Sands Rd. MK17: Bow B 5F 31
Woburn Sands Station (Rail) 2J 31
Wodehouse Wlk. MK16: New P 7G 11
WOKINGHAM 3B 136
Wolf La. SL4: Wind 7F 129
Wolfscote La. MK4: E Val 4B 28
WOLLASTON 1D 133
Wolsey Gdns. MK13: B'ell 2A 22
Wolstan Cl. UB9: Den 1G 121
Wolston Mdw. MK10: Midd 3B 24
WOLVERTON 7H 15 (2C 133)
WOLVERTON MILL 6D 14
WOLVERTON MILL EAST 7E 14
WOLVERTON MILL SOUTH 7D 14
Wolverton Rd. MK11: S Strat 1B 20
MK14: G Lin 5C 16
MK19: Cast 7E 8
Wolverton Sports Club 7H 15
Wolverton Station (Rail) 6J 15
WOOBURN 5K 107 (2C 137)
WOOBURN COMMON 6D 108
Wooburn Comn. Rd.
HP10: Woob G 5C 108
SL1: Burn 7D 108
Wooburn Grange HP10: Woob G 6K 107
WOOBURN GREEN 2B 108 (2C 137)
Wooburn Grn. La. HP9: Bea 2C 108
Wooburn Mnr. Pk. HP10: Woob G 4A 108
Wooburn Mead HP10: Woob G 3A 108
Wooburn M. HP10: Woob G 4A 108
WOOBURN MOOR 7A 100
Woodall Cl. MK10: Midd 3K 23
Woodbank HP27: Loos 1A 80
Woodbank Av. SL9: G Cro 4H 111
Woodbank Dr. HP8: D Gil 1H 103
Woodbine Cl. HP27: Long 3D 70
WOOD BURCOTE 2A 132
Woodbury Cl. SL8: Bou E 6J 107
Woodchester Pk. HP9: Bea 2E 100
WOODCOCK 6G 81
Woodcock Av. HP14: Walt A 6F 81
Woodcote Grn. HP13: Down 5H 89
Woodcote Lawns HP5: Ches 1J 77
Woodcroft Rd. HP5: Ches 2B 78
WOODEND 2A 132
Wood End MK17: Nas 7A 26
Wood End Cl. SL2: Farn C 1B 118
Wood End La. MK16: Moul 4G 19
WOODFIELD 1A 134
Woodfield HP27: L Grn 1B 80
Woodfield Pk. HP6: Amer 4J 85
Woodfield Rd. HP27: Prin R 5H 71
Woodfield Ter. UB9: Hare 1H 113
Woodford Cl. HP19: Ayle 7F 61
WOODFORD HALSE 1A 132
Woodford Way SL2: Slou 1J 123
Woodhall Cl. UB8: Uxb 3K 121
WOODHILL 3J 27
Woodhill Av. SL9: G Cro 4A 112
Woodhill Ct. *HP6: Amer* *4B 86*
(off Shortway)
SL9: G Cro 5J 111
Woodhouse Ct. MK14: Stan 7C 16
Woodhurst Dr. UB9: Den 3F 113
Woodland Av. SL1: Slou 5B 124
Woodland Cl. HP12: Book 2G 97
SL7: Marl 5J 105
Woodland Ct. HP6: Amer 2B 86
Woodland Glade SL2: Farn C 1B 118
Woodland Grange SL0: R Pk 1E 130
Woodlands HP17: Hadd 6C 58
SL9: G Cro 4K 111
Woodlands, The HP6: Amer 2A 86
HP10: T Grn 4F 91
Woodlands Cl. HP15: H Grn 1J 91
MK18: Buck 2H 37
SL9: G Cro 4A 112
Woodlands Cres.
MK18: Buck 2H 37
Woodlands Dr. HP9: Bea 4E 100
HP14: Nap 6G 81
Woodlands Glade HP9: Bea 4E 100
Woodlands Hill HP9: Bea 5G 109
WOODLANDS PARK 3B 136
Woodlands Vw. HP13: H Wyc 1G 99
Woodland Vw. HP5: Ches 6B 78
MK12: Wolv 1H 21
Woodland Way MK17: W San 4J 31
SL7: Marl 5J 105
Wood La. HP16: S Hea 5A 76
MK14: L Woo 7D 16
(not continuous)
MK18: Ting 2C 36
SL0: Ive, I Hea 1C 126
SL1: Slou 1H 129
SL2: Hedg 7C 110
Wood La. Cl. HP10: F Hea 7F 99
SL0: I Hea 1B 126
Woodlane Gdns. HP10: F Hea 7G 99
WOODLEY 3A 136
Woodley Ct. HP7: Amer 6B 86
Woodley Headland MK6: P Bri 7J 23
Woodley Hill HP5: Ches 1B 86
Woodman Cl. LU7: Wing 2D 48
Woodmans Cft. HP19: Ayle 6F 61
Woodpeckers HP9: Bea 7D 100
Wood Pond Cl. HP9: S Grn 4A 102
WOODROW 2E 92
Woodrow High House 1E 92
Woodruff Av. MK14: Conn 2D 22
Woodrush Cl. MK6: Bean 3H 29
Woods Dr. SL2: Farn C 3H 117
WOODSIDE 3C 137
Woodside HP10: F Hea 3J 107
MK11: S Strat 7C 14
Woodside Av. HP6: Amer 3B 86
HP9: Bea 5E 100
HP10: F Hea 3J 107
Woodside Cl. HP6: Amer 4A 86
HP9: Bea 5E 100
HP11: W Mar 6H 99
SL9: C Pet 7J 103
Woodside Hill SL9: C Pet 7J 103
Woodside Rd. HP6: Amer 4B 86
HP9: Bea 5E 100
HP13: H Wyc 7F 91
Woodside Way HP10: T Grn 7J 91
Woodspring Ct. MK10: Monk 5B 24
Woodstock Cl. HP21: Ayle 1C 66
Woodstock Ct. MK13: B'lle 6B 16
Wood St. HP18: Wadd 5C 52
MK13: New B 6K 15
MK17: W San 3K 31
Woodview Cl. HP12: H Wyc 5F 89
Woodview Dr. HP27: Spee 1G 81
Woodward Pl. MK8: L Lodg 5A 22
Wood Way HP9: Bea 7B 100
Woodway
HP27: Loos, Prin R 7G 71 & 1B 80
(not continuous)
Woodways HP17: Hadd 6C 58
Woollerton Ct. HP27: Prin R 4G 71
Woollerton Cres. HP22: Wend 3J 69
Woolmans MK11: F Sla 2E 20
Woolrich Gdns.
MK11: S Strat 1C 20
WOOLSTONE 3J 23
WOOLSTONE 2K 23
Wooster Rd. HP9: Bea 4E 100
Wooton Ct. MK13: New B 5K 15
Wooton Dr. HP10: Woob G 1A 108
Wooton La. HP17: Dint 2G 59
WOOTTON
Bedford 2D 133
Northampton 1B 132
Worcester Cl. MK16: New P 1G 17
Worcester Gdns. SL1: Slou 7B 124
Worcester Rd. UB8: Cowl 3J 127
Wordsworth Av. MK16: New P 7F 11
Wordsworth Dr. MK3: Blet 1G 33
Wordsworth Rd. HP11: H Wyc 3K 97
SL2: Slou 2F 123
Wordsworth Wlk. *HP21: Ayle* *1A 66*
(off Byron Rd.)
WORLD'S END 1F 69
World's End La. HP22: West T 5F 67
WORMINGHALL 3C 54 (3A 134)
Worminghall Rd. HP18: Ick 5D 54
HP18: Oak 5H 53
Wormsley Cres. HP14: Stoke 6A 72
Worrelle Av. MK10: Midd 3C 24
Worth Ct. MK10: Monk 5D 24
Worthies, The *HP7: Amer* *7K 85*
(off High St.)
Wotton End HP18: Ludg 3C 52
Wotton Path *HP21: Ayle* *4K 65*
(off Winterton Dr.)
WOTTON UNDERWOOD 2A 134
WOUGHTON ON THE GREEN 6K 23
WOUGHTON PARK 1K 29
Wray Ct. MK4: E Val 5A 28
WRAYSBURY 3D 137
Wren Cl. MK18: Buck 5K 37
Wren Ct. SL3: Lang 1A 130
Wren Dr. UB7: W Dra 1K 131
Wren Path *HP19: Ayle* *6E 60*
(off Spruce Rd.)
Wrensfield SL7: Marl 7G 105
Wrens Pk. MK10: Midd 4C 24
Wren Va. HP13: Down 7A 90
Wren Wlk. LU6: Edle 2J 49
Wright SL4: Wind 7E 128
Wright's Cl. HP14: L End 3K 73
Wright's Cotts. *SL9: C Pet* *6H 103*
(off Church La.)
Wright's La. HP16: Pres 1C 82
Wright Sq. SL4: Wind 7F 129
Wrights Yd. HP16: G Mis 6G 75
Wright Way SL4: Wind 7E 128
Wroxton Ct. MK4: West 5J 27
Wyatt Cl. HP13: Down 7K 89
Wyatt Rd. SL4: Wind 7F 129
Wyatt's Covert UB9: Den 2F 113
Wychwood HP16: L Kin 2H 83
Wychwood Gdns. HP12: Book 3G 97
Wychwood Ri. HP16: G Mis 2G 83
Wycombe Air Pk. 6C 96
Wycombe Badminton Cen. 5H 97
Wycombe Cl. HP21: Ayle 3C 66
Wycombe End HP9: Bea 1F 109
Wycombe Ind. Mall HP11: H Wyc 1K 97
Wycombe La. HP10: Woob G 2A 108
WYCOMBE MARSH 4D 98 (1B 136)
Wycombe Mus. 1B 98
Wycombe Retail Pk. HP11: W Mar 4F 99
Wycombe Rd. HP10: H Wyc 6J 97
HP14: Saun 2A 80
HP14: Stoke 5C 72
HP15: H Grn 1H 91
HP16: Pres 7B 74
HP27: Prin R, Saun 6F 71 & 2A 80
SL7: Marl 6J 105
Wycombe Sports Cen. 5K 97
Wycombe Summit 5D 98
Wycombe Swan Theatre 2B 98
Wycombe Vw. HP10: F Hea 6F 99
Wycombe Wanderers FC & Wasps RUFC
1D 96
Wye Cl. HP21: Ayle 2H 65
MK3: Blet 6E 28
Wye Gdns. HP12: H Wyc 7H 89
Wye Ind. Est. HP11: H Wyc 3F 99
Wye Rd. HP10: Woob G 1K 107
WYFOLD GRANGE 2A 136
Wykeham Ga. HP17: Hadd 7B 58
Wykeham Way HP17: Hadd 6B 58
Wykeridge Cl. HP5: Ches 1K 77
Wylands Rd. SL3: Lang 2A 130
Wylie End MK13: B'lle 6A 16
WYMBUSH 4K 21
Wymering Rd. HP21: Ayle 1D 66
Wymers Cl. SL1: Burn 7D 116
Wymer's Wood Rd. SL1: Burn 6C 116
Wymondham MK10: Monk 5D 24
Wynbury Dr. HP13: H Wyc 6E 90
Wyndham Av. HP13: Down 6K 89
Wyndham Cres. SL1: Burn 7D 116
Wyness Av. MK17: L Bric 3G 35
Wynford Grn. HP21: Ayle 1A 66
Wyngrave Pl. HP9: Bea 3E 100
Wynne Jones Cen. HP21: Ayle 6A 62
Wynn Gro. HP15: Haz 4H 91
Wynnstay Gdns. SL7: Marl 4J 105
Wynnswick Rd. HP9: S Grn 3A 102
Wynyard Ct. MK6: Old 7E 22
Wyre Cl. HP17: Hadd 7C 58
Wyvern Way UB8: Uxb 5H 121

X

Xscape Ski, Leisure & Entertainment Cen.
4F 23

Y

Yalts Brow MK4: E Val 5B 28
Yardley Av. LU7: Pits 5E 50
YARDLEY GOBION 2B 132
Yardley Grn. *HP20: Ayle* *4K 61*
(off Balfour Way)
YARDLEY HASTINGS 1C 133
Yardley Ind. Est. MK46: Oln 1H 7
Yardley Rd. MK19: Cosg 2A 14
MK46: Oln 1G 7
Yarmouth Rd. SL1: Slou 5A 124
Yarrow Pl. MK14: Conn 2E 22
Yarrowside HP7: L Chal 7F 87
YEADING 2D 137
Yeates Cl. MK18: Wins 6H 39
Yeats Cl. MK16: New P 7F 11
Ye Meads SL6: Tapl 6A 122
YEOMANS 5G 17
Yeomans Dr. MK14: Blak 5G 17
(not continuous)
Yeovil Ent. Cen. SL2: Slou 3H 123
Yeovil Rd. SL1: Slou 3G 123
Yew Tree Cl. HP5: Ches 4E 78
HP9: Bea 7H 101
HP22: Sto M 6B 66
LU6: E Bra 1K 49
LU7: I'hoe 4G 51
MK17: New L 5C 32
Yew Tree Dr. HP15: W End 1F 91
Yew Tree Rd. SL1: Slou 7E 124
Yew Wlk. HP15: Haz 4G 91
YIEWSLEY 6K 127 (2D 137)
Yiewsley Swimming Pool 5K 127
Yolsum Cl. HP17: Hadd 6A 58
Yonder Slade MK18: Buck 6H 37
York Av. SL1: Slou 4A 124
SL4: Wind 7K 129
York Cl. HP7: Amer 6D 86
Yorke Cl. HP22: Ast C 2B 68
York Ho. MK3: Blet 1E 32
York Pl. HP21: Ayle 7J 61
York Rd. MK11: S Strat 1B 20
SL4: Wind 7K 129
SL7: Marl 7H 105
UB8: Uxb 5K 121
York Way HP12: H Wyc 4J 97
Youens Rd. HP12: Book 3G 97
Young Cl. HP21: Ayle 1B 66

Z

Zealand Av. UB7: Harm 5K 131
Zodiac Bus. Pk. UB8: Cowl 4K 127

HOSPITALS and HOSPICES covered by this atlas.

N.B. Where Hospitals and Hospices are not named on the map, the reference given is for the road in which they are situated.

CHILTERN BMI HOSPITAL, THE . . . 2J **83**
London Road
GREAT MISSENDEN
HP6 0EN
Tel: 01494 890890

AMERSHAM HOSPITAL . . . 1J **93**
Whielden Street
AMERSHAM
HP7 0JD
Tel: 01494 526161

BLETCHLEY COMMUNITY HOSPITAL . . . 6G **29**
Whalley Drive
Bletchley
MILTON KEYNES
MK3 6EN
Tel: 01908 376415

BUCKINGHAM COMMUNITY HOSPITAL . . . 3H **37**
High Street
BUCKINGHAM
MK18 1NU
Tel: 01280 813243

CHADWICK LODGE . . . 7H **23**
Chadwick Drive
Saxon Street
Eaglestone
MILTON KEYNES
MK6 5LS
Tel: 01908 593000

CHALFONTS & GERRARDS CROSS HOSPITAL, THE . . . 6H **103**
Hampden Road,
Chalfont St Peter
GERRARDS CROSS
SL9 9DR
Tel: 01753 883821

CHESHAM HOSPITAL . . . 6A **78**
Hospital Hill
CHESHAM
HP5 1PJ
Tel: 01494 783961

DEBENHAM HOUSE . . . 2J **103**
Chesham Lane,
Chalfont St Peter
GERRARDS CROSS
SL9 0RJ
Tel: 01494 871588

FLORENCE NIGHTINGALE HOUSE (HOSPICE) . . . 3A **66**
Stoke Mandeville Hospital
Mandeville Road
AYLESBURY
HP21 8AL
Tel: 01296 394710

HARLOW HOUSE . . . 2C **98**
Harlow Road
HIGH WYCOMBE
HP13 6AA
Tel: 01494 436393

MAIDENHEAD HUNTERCOMBE HOSPITAL . . . 5E **122**
Huntercombe Lane South
Taplow
MAIDENHEAD
SL6 0PQ
Tel: 01628 667881

MANOR HOUSE . . . 5A **62**
Bierton Road
AYLESBURY
HP20 1EG
Tel: 01296 393363

MARLOW COTTAGE HOSPITAL . . . 7J **105**
Glade Road
MARLOW
SL7 1DJ
Tel: 01628 482292

MILTON KEYNES GENERAL HOSPITAL . . . 7H **23**
Standing Way
Eaglestone
MILTON KEYNES
MK6 5LD
Tel: 01908 660033

NATIONAL SOCIETY FOR EPILEPSY, THE . . . 2K **103**
Chesham Lane
Chalfont St Peter
GERRARDS CROSS
SL9 0RJ
Tel: 01494 601300

NHS WALK-IN CENTRE (SLOUGH) . . . 7D **124**
Upton Hospital
Albert Street
SLOUGH
SL1 2BJ
Tel: 01753 635505

PADDOCKS BMI HOSPITAL, THE . . . 4H **71**
Aylesbury Road
Monks Risborough
PRINCES RISBOROUGH
HO27 0JS
Tel: 01844 346951

ROYAL BUCKINGHAMSHIRE HOSPITAL, THE . . . 5J **61**
Bicester Road
AYLESBURY
HP19 9AB
Tel: 01296 330575

RUSHYMEAD DAY HOSPICE . . . 3K **93**
Tower Road
Coleshill
AMERSHAM
HP7 0LA
Tel: 01494 434110

SAXON BMI CLINIC . . . 7H
Chadwick Drive
MILTON KEYNES
MK6 5LR
Tel: 01908 665533

SHELBURNE BMI HOSPITAL, THE 2A **98**
Wycombe Hospital
Queen Alexandra Road
HIGH WYCOMBE
HP11 12P
Tel: 01494 888700

SHRUBLANDS DAY HOSPITAL 2C **98**
Queens Road
HIGH WYCOMBE
HP13 6PT
Tel: 01494 426597

SOUTH BUCKS HOSPICE 7C **90**
9A Amersham Road
HIGH WYCOMBE
HP13 6PN
Tel: 01494 537775

STOKE MANDEVILLE HOSPITAL 3A **66**
Mandeville Road
AYLESBURY
HP21 8AL
Tel: 01296 315000

THAMES VALLEY HOSPICE 7J **129**
Pine Lodge
Hatch Lane
WINDSOR
SL4 3RW
Tel: 01753 842121

THAMES VALLEY NUFFIELD HOSPITAL 6G **119**
Wexham Street, Wexham
SLOUGH
SL3 6NH
Tel: 01753 662241

UPTON HOSPITAL 7D **124**
Albert Street
SLOUGH
SL1 2BJ
Tel: 01753 821441

WEXHAM PARK HOSPITAL 2G **125**
Wexham Street, Wexham
SLOUGH
SL2 4HL
Tel: 01753 633000

WILLEN HOSPICE 6K **17**
Manor Farm, Milton Road
Willen
MILTON KEYNES
MK15 9AB
Tel: 01908 663780 / 663636

WYCOMBE HOSPITAL 2A **98**
Queen Alexandra Road
HIGH WYCOMBE
HP11 2TT
Tel: 01494 526161

The representation on the maps of a road, track or footpath is no evidence of the existence of a right of way.